ENTREPRENEURSHIP: A PLANNING APPROACH

ENTREPRENEURSHIP: A PLANNING APPROACH

Fred L. Fry

Bradley University

WEST PUBLISHING COMPANY
Minneapolis/St. Paul New York Los Angeles San Francisco

WEST'S COMMITMENT TO THE ENVIRONMENT

In 1906, West Publishing Company began recycling materials left over from the production of books. This began a tradition of efficient and responsible use of resources. Today, up to 95 percent of our legal books and 70 percent of our college texts are printed on recycled, acid-free stock. West also recycles nearly 22 million pounds of scrap paper annually—the equivalent of 181,717 trees. Since the 1960s, West has devised ways to capture and recycle waste inks, solvents, oils, and vapors created in the printing process. We also recycle plastics of all kinds, wood, glass, corrugated cardboard, and batteries, and have eliminated the use of styrofoam book packaging. We at West are proud of the longevity and the scope of our commitment to our environment.

Copyediting: Faren Bachelis
Text design: Tara Bazata
Composition: The Clarinda Company
Cover image: © 1992 Connie Helgeson-Moen
Production, prepress, printing, and binding: West Publishing Company

Library of Congress Cataloging-in-Publication Data

Fry, Fred L.
    Entrepreneurship : a planning approach / Fred L. Fry.
        p.   cm.
    Includes index.
    ISBN 0-314-00948-5 (alk. paper)
    1. New business enterprises—Planning.   2. Entrepreneurship—
Planning.   I. Title.
    HD62.5.F79   1993
    658.4'21—dc20   92-26326

CIP

•

To my wife, Lois, and our two children, Jana and David

•

. . . .

. . . .

. . . .

. . . .

THE SCOPE OF ENTREPRENEURSHIP

. . . .

PLANNING FOR ENTREPRENEURIAL MANAGEMENT

12 Structuring the Venture   318

13 Managing Growth   346

14 Intrapreneurship   370

PART V

PLANNING THE ENTREPRENEURIAL FINALE

15   Valuing the Venture   **400**

16   Harvesting the Venture   **428**

PART VI

BUSINESS PLANS

. . . .

CASES

Entrepreneurship is one of the fastest-growing disciplines in colleges and universities throughout the United States. The number of schools with a major, minor, or concentration in entrepreneurship or small business management has increased substantially within the past decade. Entrepreneurship is also of increasing interest as a career field for college graduates. Some will start a venture immediately after completing their academic work. Others will work for large corporations or for smaller businesses until they have accumulated sufficient capital and experience to start their own ventures. Still others will work with emerging businesses either as consultants or as members of the financial community.

The percentage of small ventures that fail is significant, though not easily measurable. What is important is not the number of ventures that fail but the reason that so many do fail: most failures are attributed to poor management in general and inadequate planning in particular. This textbook addresses both of these issues. It has as its basic premise that planning is essential to good management and is particularly critical to successful entrepreneurship. Thus, each aspect of entrepreneurship is considered from the viewpoint of planning. This planning approach permeates the analysis of opportunities, the launch of the venture, the acquisition of financing, the development of strategies, and ultimately the harvesting of the venture.

Entrepreneurship: A Planning Approach was developed after a number of years of working with small businesses and teaching small business management and entrepreneurship classes. The book is based on extensive research, yet is written in a manner that should be appealing to instructors and students alike. Many of the examples come from the experience of working with hundreds of small ventures while directing the Small Business Institute and Small Business Development Center at Bradley University.

The Plan of the Book

Entrepreneurship: A Planning Approach has several characteristics that differentiate it from competing textbooks. First is the chronological order of the presentation. Part I contains three chapters of conceptual material on entrepreneurship and entrepreneurs.

Part II begins the planning process for the potential venture. A chapter on business plans establishes the importance of planning the entrepreneurial venture. The planning process is discussed, and frameworks for strategic and financial plans are presented. This chapter sets the stage for the host of analyses and decisions that must be made in order to launch and grow a venture effectively. Discussion then turns to analyzing opportunities, making decisions associated with the actual launch of the venture, and financing the potential venture.

Part III considers strategies for entrepreneurial ventures. Chapter 8 discusses strategies for the overall venture. Chapter 9 follows with a focus on the supporting strategies that aid in achieving overall objectives. Chapters 10 and 11 consider two specific but important types of strategies—franchising strategies and international strategies.

Part IV turns to the management of the venture once it has been fully launched. Chapter 12 focuses on the organizational structure of the venture both for the original venture and for any acquisitions that might be added as part of the growth of the firm. Chapter 13 considers the issues surrounding planning for growth. Finally, Chapter 14 looks at providing entrepreneurial management to existing stable firms to ensure that innovation continues.

The last step in the entrepreneurial process is ending the venture. Part V consists of two chapters that drive home the importance of planning for the end of the venture. Chapter 15 discusses the valuation of the venture. Although ventures may be valued at any time for a number of reasons, most are valued prior to transferring the business to others. Valuing the venture is an important step in planning the finale of the process. The final step is developing plans for harvesting the venture. Planning the harvest of the venture is almost as important as planning its launch.

Pedagogical Features

A second differentiating aspect of *Entrepreneurship: A Planning Approach* is its pedagogical features. Each chapter begins with **Learning Objectives** that can be achieved by studying the chapter. **Key Terms** lists the new or unique words or phrases that will be encountered in the chapter. This is followed by **Consider This!**, a group of thought-provoking statements or questions that relate to the chapter. These are designed to pique the reader's interest in the forthcoming chapter. An **Entrepreneurial Profile** focuses on a successful entrepreneur who was notable in a way that enhances the chapter. For example, Fred Deluca of Subway Sandwiches is featured in the chapter on franchising, and Michael Dell is featured in the chapter on managing growth. **Venture Perspectives** appear periodically throughout each chapter to further illustrate or amplify topics discussed in the text.

Each chapter includes **Discussion Questions** that relate to and extend the material of the chapter. Some of these make good test questions and most are good for generating class discussion. **Exercises** are included for each chapter. These may include self-analysis exercises, group discussion assignments, or the analysis of an entrepreneurial situation.

Finally, each chapter ends with a segment of **Conveniesse, Inc.** Conveniesse, Inc., is a continuous case that runs through the entire text. Installments of the case appear at the end of each chapter. They detail the challenges, frustrations, and achievements of three individuals who decide to start an upscale convenience store chain. The problems the three entrepreneurs encounter in each segment relate to the chapter material preceding it. The reader is given the analysis or resolution of those problems as an assignment. These range from deciding whether or not to start the venture to developing strategic and financial plans, considering whether to franchise, expanding into Canada, dealing with declining growth, and ultimately deciding whether or not to sell the chain.

Part VI of the text includes two business plans. The first is the Conveniesse, Inc., plan that the three entrepreneurs write in order to launch their convenience store chain. The second is for a bio-tech venture, Kryos, Inc., written in an attempt to gain major funding for the development of vitrification technology for storage of transplant organs. The plan is an excellent example of business plans written for high growth ventures.

Part VII consists of eighteen cases dealing with entrepreneurial issues. These cases are purposely placed at the end of the text rather than after particular chapters, because several of them are applicable to more than one chapter. Some examine writing or analyzing business plans. Some cover financing. Some address managing growth. And others deal with valuing an existing organization. The cases vary in length, difficulty, and in the issues they treat.

Ancillaries

A variety of ancillary materials is provided to adopters of *Entrepreneurship: A Planning Approach*. An instructor's manual/test bank is provided. The instructor's manual focuses on methods of teaching an entrepreneurship class, suggestions for class discussion, and analyses of case material. The test bank is available on Westest—a computerized test generator—as well as in hard copy form, and provides true/false, multiple choice, and essay questions that may be useful for examinations.

Financial analysis software is included with *Entrepreneurship: A Planning Approach*. The software is entitled fisCAL and is written by the Halcyon Group. It can do financial statement analysis, ratio analysis, comparisons with industry norms, valuation, and proforma income and balance sheets. A master disk is provided to each adopting school. Instructions for using fisCAL appear in the appendix to this book. A key disk is bound in the book. It provides access to the fisCAL programs and the financial information for Conveniesse, Inc., and many of the cases found in Part VII of the text. The fisCAL financial analysis software is excellent for use in analyzing venture financial information, developing business plans, and doing valuations of companies. Instructors can receive a demonstration disk on request.

Videotapes of successful entrepreneurs are also provided to instructors. These tapes, from the Blue Chip Enterprise Institute, will supplement lectures on various subjects throughout the term and are cross-referenced in the Instructor's Manual.

Acknowledgments

Many people had input regarding the content and tone of this book. Thanks go to the reviewers who spent many hours considering each chapter. Most suggestions were taken, and much of the quality of *Entrepreneur-ship: A Planning Approach* is attributable to their thoughtful suggestions. The reviewers include

C. William Roe
University of Southwest Louisiana

William Palmer Sineath
Appalachian State University

Barry L. Van Hook
Arizona State University

Bradley R. Johnson
University of Nebraska-Omaha

John Todd
University of Arkansas

James F. Molloy, Jr.
Northeastern University

David R. Decker
Youngstown State University

Judy A. Barille
Miami University of Ohio

Newell Gough
Boise State University

John R. Miller
Johns Hopkins University

Harold K. Wilson
Southern Illinois University-
 Carbondale

William R. Soukup
University of San Diego

Joseph Singer
University of Missouri-
 Kansas City

Charlotte D. Sutton
Auburn University

I also wish to thank my friend Richard Judd of Sangamon State University, his coauthor Robert Justis, and South-Western Publishing Company for permission to adapt their material on franchising. Dr. Clyde Goodheart provided the Kryos, Inc., business plan, which is included in abbreviated form in this book.

Appreciation is also expressed to the authors of the cases. Cases add significantly to the value of any textbook as they bring a sense of realism into the classroom. Case authors include John Dunkelberg and Robert Anderson (Doorstep Video, Inc.); Timothy Singleton, Robert McGlashan, and Mike Harris (Southern Cabinet Company); Herbert Brown, Paula Saunders, and Rich Gulling (Mail Order Pharmacy); James Carland, JoAnn Carland, and Kirk Stephens (Movies R Us and Campground for Sale); Jon Ozmun (Martin Enterprises); Neil Snyder (Artisan's Haven); Jeff Totten and Jeff Cornwall (Wisconsin Sealcoating); John McCray and Juan Gonzalez (Gal-Tech and Melanin); Jerry Katz (TeleSell); Thomas Wheelen, Moustafa Abdelsamad, Jeff Curry, Dean Salpini, Art Scibelli, and Gordon Shanks (Christian's); Phil Carpenter (The Fab Lab); David Tipton and Janet Gillespie (The Creative Mind); Carol Jessup (Comic Relief); Alexis Downs (Environmental Systems); and Catherine Ward and Marilyn Taylor (International Learning Corporation).

My colleagues at Bradley University also contributed in significant ways. Philip Horvath was instrumental in portions of the valuation chapter and provided the case example. John Ruble and Charles Stoner made suggestions throughout the writing process. Barbara Keim, Yvonne Beechler, Mike Rellihan, and Chris Valin assisted with the Instructor's Manual. Three students in my entrepreneurship class, Dennis McClain, William Welch, and David Hoover, prepared a business plan as a class assignment that was the basis for the Conveniesse, Inc., continuous case. Mary Lu Reither spent many hours printing out the various versions of chapters as the book progressed, made numerous copies, helped secure permissions, and provided moral support. Gale Sullenberger, Dean of the College of Business Administration, deserves thanks for setting a tone that encouraged the writing effort. The members of the Business Management and Administration Department are appreciated for their forbearance during the project.

The West Educational Publishing staff provided immeasurable assistance. Arnis Burvikovs and Susan Smart were especially helpful throughout the development of the book. Laura Evans's excellent work in the production of the book is greatly appreciated.

Finally, I want to thank my wife, Lois, for her help in proofreading and her moral support. Without it, this project could never have been completed.

Fred L. Fry
Professor and Chair
Business Management and Administration Department
Bradley University
October, 1992

ENTREPRENEURSHIP:
A PLANNING APPROACH

I

THE SCOPE OF ENTREPRENEURSHIP

Introduction to Entrepreneurship
•
The Nature of Entrepreneurship
•
The Entrepreneur

1

Introduction to Entrepreneurship

LEARNING OBJECTIVES

After reading this chapter, you should know:

1. What needs entrepreneurship can meet for individuals
2. Why America is turning to entrepreneurship
3. The significance of entrepreneurship
4. The nature of the challenges of entrepreneurship
5. Some examples of America's entrepreneurs
6. The need for vision in entrepreneurship
7. The need for ethics in entrepreneurial ventures

KEY TERMS

Entrepreneurship
New venture
Entrepreneurial society

CONSIDER THIS!

- Why are some of the classic entrepreneurs the equivalent of American folk heroes? What is so inspirational about being a successful entrepreneur?
- Is there as much room for successful entrepreneurs today as there was fifty or seventy-five years ago?
- Are there new frontiers of entrepreneurship still to be exploited?
- What differentiates ethical entrepreneurs from unethical ones?
- Who are your favorite entrepreneurs? Why are people like Steve Jobs of Apple Computer, Donald Burr of People Express, or Donald Trump still seen as entrepreneurial heroes even though their companies either forced them out, no longer exist, or have decreased in stature?

Entrepreneurship is the dream of millions of individuals in America and around the world. Owning a business, investing one's personal capital, making executive-level decisions, and maneuvering past the competition all have the thrill of risk and challenge. Taking an idea from concept into reality is one of the most gratifying acts possible.

Starting one's own venture fulfills several psychological needs. It may fulfill **status** needs, in that running a successful business surely appeals to

ENTREPRENEURIAL PROFILE

JOHN J. STOLLENWERK
Allen-Edmonds Shoe Corporation

John Stollenwerk and two partners bought a struggling shoe company in 1980 that was losing $40,000 a month. Under Stollenwerk's entrepreneurial leadership, the firm's equipment was modernized, the manufacturing process was streamlined, a quality control program and an aggressive marketing program were started, and employee training was broadened. The firm turned a profit within a year. Today, Allen-Edmonds is a recognized leader in the men's quality shoe market, with sales in the United States and in thirty-three overseas markets. The shoes are handcrafted and come in 164 sizes and widths. Sales for 1991 were estimated at $45 million and the firm employs about four hundred workers.

John Stollenwerk, president and owner of the Allen-Edmonds Shoe Corporation of Port Washington, Wisconsin, doesn't look or act the part of a company president. His manner is low-key; every one of the four hundred employees calls him John. John Stollenwerk does, however, epitomize an entrepreneur. When he and two partners bought the sixty-nine-year-old men's shoe manufacturing company in 1980, it was operating at 65 percent capacity and was losing more than $400,000 a year. Since the purchase, sales have increased from $9 million to an estimated $45 million in 1991. Stollenwerk is modest and attempts to give

the credit to everyone else. Yet some of his employees consider him "a magician" because of his decisive management decisions.

Stollenwerk knew nothing about making shoes when he took over the company, but he did know the international market and he knows how to deal with people. He speaks at least three languages, and Allen-Edmonds advertises in fifteen languages.

Stollenwerk's expertise in entrepreneurial management is exemplified by two incidents. The first occurred in January 1984, when a fire ravaged Allen-Edmonds' prime production facility, destroying most of its equipment and fifty thousand pairs of shoes. The temperature was a cool twenty-five below zero. Within seventy hours, the company had resumed some production, and within two weeks, it was turning out one thousand pairs of shoes per week, one-sixth of its normal output. The company's

staff also called on many of their distributors personally to assure them that they were not out of business. Dealers were encouraged to return any excess inventory they had so the shoes could be reshipped to dealers who were low on inventory.

In the second incident, Stollenwerk was told in Washington that it was impossible to break into the closed Japanese market. Undaunted, he "crashed" a Japanese trade show for shoe manufacturers, where he was told foreigners were not permitted to exhibit. He conducted what amounted to a sit-in at the trade show, and eventually was allowed to display his merchandise. His high-quality shoes sell in the United States for about $220 a pair, but because of import tariffs, they sell in Japan for $400 a pair. Today, Allen-Edmonds shoes are sold in elite department stores throughout Japan.

More than eight hundred footwear companies have closed their doors due to the import crisis in the United States. Allen-Edmonds continues to grow because the firm's products continue to be handcrafted in the same 212 steps that were used when the firm was founded in 1922 and because John Stollenwerk provided the entrepreneurial management necessary to turn around the failing company.

SOURCE: Allen-Edmonds documents. Used with permission.

the ego. This satisfaction of ego needs may come either from the respect given to an entrepreneur by others or from the amount of wealth that can be generated by a successful venture. **Social** needs may be satisfied in that many ventures require a large amount of interaction with employees, customers, investors, and suppliers, as well as associations with people in the community and the government.

Perhaps most important, becoming an entrepreneur is **self-satisfying.** While an entrepreneur may acquire personal wealth in the process, that is not the most significant factor. There may be no other occupation in which self-actualization is better achieved. For in no other job can one person be completely in charge. Nowhere else can the successes and the failures of a venture be traced to a single individual. The entrepreneur is responsible for every action in the venture. It is one person's vision that takes an idea from concept to reality, from a startup venture to a successful, growing business. The satisfaction lies in knowing that one's own actions beat the competition, that the venture survived, and that the idea actually worked in the real world. And it feels good to know that the venture also contributed something to others in the form of jobs or a new product or service.

Entrepreneurship can also meet **financial** needs for entrepreneurs and their families. Even though many new ventures fail, many others provide a more than adequate standard of living for their owners, and some entrepreneurs become quite wealthy. Owning one's own venture is, for many business owners, an alternative to working for someone else for a fixed salary. Entrepreneurs may pay themselves a salary, but they also receive a return in the form of profits or free cash flow.

Entrepreneurship is indeed a satisfying process even though it can be risky and may lead to loss of wealth. A survey of business owners whose businesses had survived at least three years found few had regrets over their decision to form a business. Eighty-two percent said they would still form their business if they knew then what they know now. Even though some were disappointed with the results, only about 14 percent said that they would not start their particular business again, and only three percent said that they would never start another business of any kind.[1]

THE TREND TOWARD AN ENTREPRENEURIAL SOCIETY

There is evidence that America is moving toward an **entrepreneurial society.** Ours is an entrepreneurial society because ever-increasing numbers of individuals are accepting the challenge of entrepreneurship, and new and growing ventures make up an increasing percentage of the 14 million businesses in the United States. Robert Ronstadt suggested in 1985 that there are a number of fundamental changes occurring in the United States that encourage entrepreneurship. These include:

- The institutionalization of the two-income family.
- The growing recognition that larger organizations do not fulfill basic needs for autonomy and security.
- The shift in women's roles in economic life along with a parallel shift in the belief that women can be entrepreneurs—to the point

that the current growth rate of new ventures created by women is considerably higher than the rate of new ventures created by men.

- A desire by local government officials to avoid falling hostage to large corporations that become a city or town's dominant employer.

- A growing appreciation that the risks of venture failure have been grossly overstated and that entrepreneurship is not just the province of a few superstars or celebrity entrepreneurs.

- An understanding that owning one's own business still represents one of the few pathways left for the middle and lower classes to build wealth in an ever increasing tax-conscious society that all too often penalizes the achiever who works for someone else.

- A computer and information revolution that is presenting new venture opportunities while often lowering entry costs and other startup barriers in many industries.

- The development of programs to study, teach, promote, and accelerate entrepreneurship in many nations around the world, giving credence to the belief that entrepreneurship is an international phenomenon, not just a national one.[2]

The trends suggested by Ronstadt are likely to continue over the next several years, if not decades. The increase in diversity within the corporate work force has been and will continue to be followed by an increasingly diverse ownership base. Women are continuing to form new businesses at a rate much higher than men. The number of ventures started by blacks, Hispanics, Asian Americans, and others is also increasing. Increased education of the general population should lead to even more objective analysis of opportunities that could decrease the failure rate of new ventures. Further, the 1980s trend among large corporations toward mergers, acquisitions, and leveraged buyouts has been countered in the 1990s by downsizing, spin-offs, and corporate-sponsored venture capital. State and local interest in entrepreneurship rises and falls with changes in administrations and success of past efforts at economic development. But over the years, the fostering of entrepreneurship through increased public funding, increased education, changes in tax structures, and other incentives is likely to have a continuing positive effect on the number of new ventures started.

THE SIGNIFICANCE OF ENTREPRENEURSHIP

Entrepreneurship has had a substantial impact on society throughout history. This impact has historically been because of inventions. To get a feel for the significance of early entrepreneurs, consider the McCormick reaper, the John Deere plow, the products of Benjamin Franklin and Thomas Edison, and the development of the steam engine. Former president Ronald Reagan once recalled an earlier entrepreneurial age by noting the "routine miracles" of the late 1800s and early 1900s. These routine miracles included such things as fans, stoves, refrigerators, phonographs, and the further development of photography. These were followed by automobiles, tractors, and airplanes.[3] More modern "routine miracles" in the past few decades have included computers, medical diagnostic equipment, and synthetic sweeteners and fats.

New businesses are significant simply by virtue of their sheer numbers. An estimated 1.3 million new businesses were started in 1991, which was considered a recessionary year.[4] In fact, many workers who lost their jobs during the recession used their severance pay to start a business. Some managers of stores that were closed by a financially strapped parent corporation found financing to reopen the store as an independent business.

In recent years, the significance of entrepreneurship has been in job creation. The net increase in jobs during the 1970s and 1980s was almost exclusively in small or medium-sized firms. While Fortune 500 firms and other mega-corporations actually lost jobs, new ventures and small companies created millions of new jobs. The increase in jobs created by smaller firms more than offset the decrease in jobs among large corporations.

The media give primary attention to the large businesses in the nation. But the number of large businesses is very small compared to the vast majority of new and small businesses. The precise definition of a small business depends upon the industry.[5] In general, a small business is one with less than one hundred employees. Using tax returns, the Bureau of the Census found that 99.8 percent of U.S. businesses have less than one hundred employees. Nearly 90 percent of these have less than twenty employees and sales of under a million dollars per year. Even more dramatic is the fact that almost 75 percent of these businesses have no employees other than the owner (Table 1-1). Less than 0.3 percent of all sole proprietorships filing income tax returns in 1986 had over $1,000,000 in sales.[6]

The vast majority of businesses are actually quite small, yet there are more than thirteen million entrepreneurs in the United States, with 1.3 million new ones each year. Most new ventures will stay quite small; some will be modest, but growing. And some will become high-growth ventures reaping the rewards of entrepreneurship to the fullest.

Number of Employees	Number of Firms	Percentage
0	10,208,026	74.5
0*	967,944	7.0
1–4	1,711,787	12.5
5–9	447,382	3.3
10–19	204,901	1.5
20–49	103,742	0.8
50–99	31,095	0.2
Total less than 100	13,674,877	99.8
100 or more	20,603	0.2
Total number of businesses	13,695,480	

TABLE 1-1

Percentage of Small Businesses by Size

Source: U.S. Department of Commerce, Bureau of the Census, *1987 Economic Census: Women-Owned Businesses*, page 149.

*Firms that reported annual payroll but had no one listed during the reporting period.

VENTURE PERSPECTIVE 1-1

. . . .

THE AMPLIPHONE

Adam Anderson was feeling somewhat smug as he walked into his friendly banker's office with his product and some scribbled notes in hand. He had a prototype of what he called an "ampliphone," which he had put together in his basement. The ampliphone was a sort of combination Walkman-type headset and hands-free microphone that switchboard operators use. The product had a connector jack that would connect into the handset cord of a telephone. Each earpiece had its own volume dial, and the entire unit was held together with a tension spring mechanism that allowed it to be slipped on and off easily with one hand.

Anderson's father was hearing impaired and especially had trouble hearing over the telephone with his normal hearing aids. He had tried a number of amplifiers, but most of them

were unsatisfactory. One reason that many of the products were unsatisfactory was that room noise bothered the ear opposite the telephone. Others amplified both the outgoing voice and the incoming message. Further, since Anderson's father's hearing was impaired in both ears, Anderson reasoned that by using the Walkman-type headsets that covered both ears, it would not only block out room noise, but it would amplify the sound in both ears rather than in one. The nice thing about using the hands-free version was that the user's hands could then be used to adjust the volume up or down for each ear.

The prototype wasn't really difficult to put together. In fact, Anderson used parts from existing radios and telephone headsets. He gave the prototype to his father who was immediately impressed by the

ease of use and the improvement of his ability to hear telephone calls.

Anderson calculated what the individual pieces should cost, added labor costs, and determined a price for the product. Then, with his product and his cost figures in hand, he met with the commercial loan officer of his bank to request $10,000 to start production.

A very dejected Adam Anderson left the bank a few minutes later, devastated by a polite, but pessimistic, banker who explained to Anderson that his cost figures were no good, he had no business plan, he had no idea how to market his product, and the price he quoted was (in the banker's view) about what the product should sell for at retail, not what a manufacturer should get.

Three months laer, a confident Adam Anderson strolled

THE CHALLENGE OF ENTREPRENEURSHIP

Entrepreneurship can be an exciting challenge. Virtually all aspects of entrepreneurship are exhilarating. Certainly, conceptualizing an idea that has potential is challenging. Simply thinking about whether an idea makes sense, whether it could be put into action, how much capital it would require, how many people would have to be employed, and how the venture would be operated is food for the best of daydreams. Yet, if simply thinking about entrepreneurship is exciting, how exciting must the actual doing be? Consider the highs and lows that Adam Anderson felt in Venture Perspective 1-1.

Once a venture is launched, entrepreneurship is still a challenge. Keeping the operation afloat and working with suppliers, customers, and investors is a hectic, but satisfying, set of tasks—if things go well. If things don't go well, the scrambling to save the venture or to find additional funding or to find a buyer for the business can be a high stress time. If the into the commercial loan officer's office, armed with a refined product, a new cost estimate, sources of supply for the components, letters from several people who had tried the product, and a five-page business plan that showed how he would sell the product.

Again, a dejected Anderson exited the bank. This time, he had convinced the loan officer of the viability of his product even though the cost estimates were still somewhat high. But the banker was not willing to underwrite the startup costs necessary to put the product into mass production. The banker was also not impressed with Anderson's selling method, which was to sell the product through specialty mail order catalogs. He felt that potential users would want to try them on to make sure they would work. Anderson also had no conception of how large

the market would be, and had suggested only that the senior citizen market is the fastest growing segment of the population. The loan officer did, however, offer to continue to work with him to develop a better business plan and to look into the possibilities of some additional funding if Anderson could solve some of the remaining problems.

A cautiously optimistic Adam Anderson walked into the office of a local venture capital company that was a subsidiary of a large corporation headquartered in the city where Anderson lived. By this time Anderson had begun the patent process for his product, had letters of support from a manufacturer's representative that called on stores that sold hearing aids, and had an agreement from a local electronics firm to provide space and assistance in assembling the product

in exchange for an undetermined percentage of the business.

An elated Adam Anderson answered the telephone two weeks later to hear the venture capital company propose a second meeting to include Anderson, the venture capitalist, the electronics assembler, and attorneys for all parties. There would be no guarantee that anything could be worked out, but perhaps a team could be put together to produce and market the product—if, of course, Anderson was willing to give up thirty percent of the equity and accept additional management of the venture capitalist's choosing.

venture goes quite well and achieves rapid growth as planned by the entrepreneurial team, then the challenge becomes how to maximize growth without losing control of the company. All of these scenarios include the pride of ownership. The entrepreneur can either grow a venture that can provide a comfortable life-style with the possibility of becoming independently wealthy, or lose the entire venture and face financial and sometimes physical ruin.

ANYONE CAN BE AN ENTREPRENEUR

One of the great things about entrepreneurship is that anyone can be an entrepreneur. In general, there are no laws against starting one's own venture. The kinds of ventures created are subject only to the entrepreneur's vision. Some ventures require virtually no capital, while others may require millions of dollars to launch. Locations of ventures are subject to the entrepreneur's personal choice and/or market demands. Ventures may be started on a part-time basis with little intent of making the business a full-time career. Others may be started in such a way that a person's entire mind, body, spirit, and finances are on the line. In the first case, failure is of no particular consequence; in the latter case, failure is everything.

In his classic book *Animal Farm*, George Orwell said that, "All animals are equal, but some animals are more equal than others."[7] Such is the case with entrepreneurship. Anyone can start a venture, but some have a higher probability of succeeding than others. This probability is a function of how much previous experience and management skills one has, how much capital can be obtained, how well the opportunity was researched before the launch, and how effective the strategy is. Somewhat like a card game, entrepreneurship is part the luck of the draw and part how well the cards are played. The "cards" in entrepreneurship are those things outside the realm of the entrepreneur's control. They include the economy, the dynamics of the industry, the availability of capital, and a plethora of unknown but possible events that may or may not be predictable. Little can be done about how the cards are dealt. This book is all about how to play the cards better.

NEW VENTURES AND SURVIVAL

The survival rate of new businesses is an elusive statistic and one that has been distorted by the media and others. Quotes are heard often that 50 percent of all new businesses fail within the first year and that 90 percent fail within five years. These figures may or may not be true depending on who is asked and how the economy is at the time. Jeffry Timmons combined a number of studies and concluded that 40 percent of new businesses fail in the first year, 60 percent fail by the end of the second year, and 90 percent fail by the end of the tenth year.[8] On the other hand, another study of almost three thousand new ventures found that 77 percent of them survived at least through the third year.[9] The studies found that the failure rate depends on the industry, whether or not the venture is a franchise, the education of the entrepreneur, and the size of the venture.

Regardless of which statistics are correct, a significant portion of new ventures do fail within the first few years. This suggests that new entrepreneurs must be as well prepared as possible before launching the venture. As will be seen throughout this book, successful entrepreneurship is more than just finding an idea today and opening the doors tomorrow. In order to be one of the survivors rather than one of the failures, the entrepreneur must have a vision, but must also carefully plan each step in order to best capture the opportunity.

AMERICA'S ENTREPRENEURS

America has been blessed with thousands of entrepreneurs over the years who have made significant contributions to society's well-being. It is impossible to enumerate all of them, although there are a number of books available that tell the story of many classic entrepreneurs. This section will focus on a few memorable entrepreneurs. Some of these are laureates of the American National Business Hall of Fame, an organization whose primary purpose is to collect and share the stories of significant entrepreneurs who may be role models for entrepreneurship.[10] All are prime examples of the risk-assuming, creative nature of entrepreneurs, and they illustrate the challenge and rewards of entrepreneurship.

Gustavus Swift

Born on June 24, 1839, Gustavus Swift was one of twelve children. At the age of fourteen, Gus went to work for his brother, a local butcher. Over a period of years, Swift ran his own retail butcher shop, a wholesale meat business, and then became a cattle buyer for two other companies. In his role as a cattle buyer, Swift began to focus on the inefficiencies of buying cattle in small lots that would then be sold to other small purchasers. He found that by moving to Chicago where the rail lines converged from the farmland, he could purchase large numbers of cattle directly and then ship them to the east coast for sale.

Unfortunately, cattle are bulky to ship. Gus Swift realized that it would be far more efficient to slaughter the cattle in Chicago and then ship only the edible parts to the east. This would result in a freight savings of 60 percent. In addition, he could eliminate the cost of feeding the cattle during shipment and the lost weight and bruises that usually occurred during transit.

Swift had to overcome four obstacles. First and foremost, there was the technological problem of developing a refrigerated rail car that would work. Next was the problem of assembling the capital needed to build the cars and setting up cold storage facilities at delivery points. Third, there was the problem of high rail rates for shipments of dressed beef. And finally, there was the problem of opposition by eastern butchers and others who felt that cattle should be shipped live and then slaughtered.

Railroads were not interested in building the cars for Swift, but he finally found a producer of the cars. He also had to set up "icing" stations along the route and cold storage facilities at each end of the route. Railroads also refused to ship the cars over their tracks because of the potential reduced demand for existing cattle cars, so Swift found a railroad in Canada that would ship the meat. He also overcame eastern resistance to the western dressed meat, but only after a substantial amount of work and personal involvement.

With his idea a success, Swift entered into a period of extremely rapid growth. His formula was to lower costs of production through larger scale production, greater specialization, and increasing mechanization and efficiency of the production line. He also searched for ways to turn waste into profitable by-products. These ranged from edible products to soap, fertilizers, pharmaceuticals, and animal and poultry feeds.

Gustavus Swift's success can be traced to a number of factors typical of 19th century entrepreneurs. He had an almost fanatical drive to continue to find ways to cut unit costs of operations. He was never satisfied with the business. He maintained close personal control of the operations, with little sympathy for those who made mistakes. He encouraged employees to buy stock in the company, thereby increasing the capital base while gaining loyal employees.

Many changes have been made in Swift & Company and it no longer remains an independent company. However, the innovation and growth in Swift & Company and in the meat packing industry was clearly the result of the early entrepreneurial work done by Gustavus Swift.

Richard Sears

There was hardly a farmer in the Middle West around the turn of the century who did not have a copy of the latest Sears and Roebuck catalog. The catalog was, after all, directed toward rural families, who found its offerings of farm equipment, tools, plain clothing, and simple but reliable household goods an endless source of fascination—and temptation. But the great mail-order book worked its spell on small-town families, too, and on busy men and women in suburban and urban centers. They gazed just as longingly at its pictures of the latest stereopticans, crank-powered "talking machines," and pneumatic-tubed bicycles, as the farmers did at its "walking plows," hay rakes, and delivery wagons.[11]

Richard Sears began to support himself and most of his family at age sixteen. He worked as a laborer, then as a telegraph operator, and finally as a freight agent for the Minneapolis and St. Louis Railroad. While working as a freight agent, Sears also began selling merchandise that could be shipped on the railroad. His most notable sales of the day were watches that he sold for fourteen dollars each to other agents up and down the railroad line. He then began selling the watches and other jewelry through the mail. Later Sears started advertising his merchandise in the newspaper in order to reach a larger market. He began the Sears Watch Company, but needed a technician to handle repairs and some assembly. Alvah Roebuck was that person.

Within a year the office was flooded with orders for watches by mail. Sears and Roebuck began putting out a small catalog that advertised their watches and other jewelry. By 1888 they had enough business to establish an office in Canada, and by 1889 they ordered watches sixty thousand at a time.

Sears briefly left the company in 1889 to try his hand at banking, but found that his true love was in the field of mass merchandising. He eventually rejoined what was to become Sears, Roebuck and Company. Sears' expertise was in the area of advertising. Sometimes his advertising was somewhat exaggerated, but nobody complained. He thrived by selling products at low prices, often at half the purchase price elsewhere. For example, in 1895 he advertised men's suits that normally sold for $10 for $4.95. In 1897 a $16.55 sewing machine was sold for $13.50 and in 1901 he sold cream separators through the mail to farmers for half the normal dealer price.

Few companies have seen the growth that Richard Sears developed with his watches in the 1880s. Ironically, approximately one hundred years later, the Sears empire was surpassed by another entrepreneur—Sam Walton.

Paul Galvin

Paul Galvin was born on June 29, 1895. After attending two years of college, serving in World War I, and two failed attempts to run a battery manufacturing business, in 1928 Galvin started building and selling a device that would allow radios to be run on house electrical current. He then began building the radios themselves. Although sales initially were acceptable, the beginning of the depression forced Galvin to the brink of bankruptcy again.

About this time, however, Galvin heard of a new innovation—custom installations of radios in cars. After weeks of work on developing an auto radio, a working model was installed in his car in time for the Radio Manufacturers' Association Convention in Atlantic City in June 1930. The world's first practical and affordable auto radio was not an immediate success; in 1930 the company lost $3,745 on sales of $287,000. Galvin decided that marketing was one key to success. He finally came up with a name that to him suggested both motion and radio. The name was Motorola.

In 1933 Galvin came out with a new model, but it had so many defects that the company had to recall thousands of them. Paul Galvin was so angry that the sets were smashed with a sledgehammer. He then set about developing models that worked well. Galvin re-entered the home radio business in 1937, but shortly afterward the economy turned downward and he almost lost the business again. Fortunately for Motorola, a contract to produce radios for a competitor was secured.

Paul Galvin was an innovator. In addition to his car radio and home radio, he began developing police communications radios in 1936. Anticipating war in Europe, he asked his engineers to develop a field radio, despite the lack of a government contract. The "Handie-Talkie" portable two-way radio was in production as World War II broke out. In the postwar period, Galvin decided to diversify further. He expanded home radio sales, produced phonographs, became a leader in the emerging television industry, and entered the semiconductor business. Typical of Galvin's entrepreneurial style is Motorola's entry into the television market. RCA had pioneered in the industry and had brought out a fine ten-inch set retailing for over $300 (1946 dollars). Galvin realized that in order to break into the market he would have to beat RCA in both quality and price. He assigned two competing engineering teams to develop a television that could be sold retail for $179.95. Motorola enjoyed a tremendous volume of sales and quickly moved up in the industry rankings.

Paul Galvin died of leukemia in 1959. But the little company that he finally founded after a number of failures had grown to the point where it was, and still is, a major competitive force in the electronics industry.

John Johnson

Ebony Magazine celebrated its fortieth anniversary in 1985. Much of its success is attributable to the work of its founder, John Johnson. Johnson began his life in Arkansas as the son of poor parents. He and his mother moved to Chicago after his father was killed in a sawmill mishap.

Johnson developed an interest in journalism while attending college and working for an insurance company editing its employee publication. While still at the insurance company, Johnson conceived the idea for a black-styled *Reader's Digest*. He felt that most of the white-edited publications did not paint a fair picture of the typical black person.

Johnson was convinced that his idea was a good one, but found that financing for the project was impossible to get. He was finally forced to put his mother's furniture in hock to obtain $500. With that money, he was able to launch *Negro Digest* in 1942. He was twenty-four at the time. By using an insurance company list to secure subscriptions, he managed to turn a profit on the first issue.

Johnson's entrepreneurial spirit and creativeness was evidenced by his strategy for getting distributors to handle *Negro Digest*. He and his friends went around to the magazine stands in the area asking for that new magazine, *Negro Digest*. After enough requests, the magazine stand operators went back to their distributors and demanded that they carry the magazine. On another occasion, after being refused advertisements from white advertisers, he did research on Chicago retailer Marshall Field's hobbies and reading interests. He then made an appointment with Mr. Field, discussed Field's interests, and then convinced him to buy ads and influence others to buy ads.

On the success of *Negro Digest*, Johnson began *Ebony* in 1945. It was patterned after *Life* and was filled with success stories. "We have always been a magazine of success and achievement, which we've redefined over the years," explained Johnson. "When we started, success might have meant big cars, mink coats, and fancy houses—material evidences. Now it might be raising a family, overcoming a racial handicap, or sending your kids to college. We want to give great emphasis on the positive side of things."[12]

Today, *Ebony* has a circulation of over a million and is the cornerstone of Johnson Publishing, which also includes *Jet*, *Black Stars*, *Ebony, Jr.*, and a black radio station in Chicago. Johnson has also branched out into other areas. One of the most profitable is a cosmetics line for people of color called Fashion Fair, which competes against the major mainline cosmetics firms that have attempted to move in on Johnson's market upon seeing his success.

Sam Walton

Sam Walton was born in 1918 in Kingfisher, Oklahoma. His father was a natural salesperson, and Sam adopted his father's aptitude for selling. He also developed the characteristic of a "penny-pincher," a trait that he maintained into adulthood. Even when he retired, Walton still drove to work in a beat-up 1978 pickup. While completing his B.A. degree from the University of Missouri, he was dubbed "Hustler Walton" by his fraternity brothers for his active role in the fraternity, in athletic endeavors, and for paying for his college education with a paper route.

Walton started his retail experience working for JC Penney and learned the basic techniques of retailing and the value system that was characteristic of Penney. In 1945 he started a Ben Franklin franchise, his first retail venture. By 1962 he had opened fourteen more stores, primarily in rural areas. Walton tried to convince the Ben Franklin company to move into discount retailing. When they refused, he opened his first Wal-Mart Discount City in Rogers, Arkansas.

Throughout the growing Wal-Mart empire, Sam Walton maintained his two overriding objectives. The first was to cut costs, and the second was customer relations. Other aspects of the Wal-Mart culture included employee participation in decision making, reliance on seat-of-the-pants judgments, solicitation and use of employee suggestions, frequent store visits by top executives, and performance based on recognition of employees. In addition to Walton's characteristic entrepreneurial drive to cut costs and provide customer service, he also was intensely patriotic. As such, his policy was to "Buy American" if he could find suitable U.S.-made products for his stores.

By 1983, the Wal-Mart model had grown to the point that Sam Walton was ready to try something new. In that year, he opened the first Sam's Wholesale Club, a membership-based retail outlet focusing on the discount philosophy.[13]

Sam Walton died in April 1992. But he lived long enough to see Wal-Mart overtake both Sears and K mart and become the number one retailer in the nation. He had also been listed among the richest individuals in the United States. His entrepreneurial vision included attention to detail, attention to costs, and attention to the customer.

J. W. Marriott

The Marriott Corporation is known today primarily for its high-quality hotels. Few people know, however, that the business began as an A & W Root Beer stand in Washington, D.C.[14] J. W. Marriott and a partner started a nine-seat A & W Root Beer stand in suburban Washington, D.C., in 1927 after Marriott could not find a cold drink while visiting Washington one summer. Within a year, Marriott opened another stand and bought out his partner. Marriott's A & W franchises were the first of the franchises to be allowed to sell hot food, and they took on the name "Hot Shoppe." A third Hot Shoppe opened as a drive-in to service the increasing number of automobiles in the area. At the time Marriott opened his drive-in, there was no competition that catered to in-the-car eating with food being delivered to the car by runners.

By 1931, there were six Hot Shoppes in the area. Marriott expanded by carefully evaluating locations for traffic volume. He and his wife would literally stand on a street corner counting cars as they passed. He kept very close control of his restaurants, visiting each site at least once a day to monitor operations.

The eighth Hot Shoppe was established near an airport, and Marriott was surprised at the number of customers who would grab a meal to carry onto an airplane. With this in mind, he approached Eastern Air Transport to see if it would be interested in a meal service. His first meals were box lunches, and soon all the airlines at the airport were using Marriott's meals.

During World War II, Marriott learned that the government agencies and defense plants around Washington did not have cafeterias. As a typical entrepreneur might do, he took advantage of the opportunity to provide on-site meals to employees for a small fee in space that the companies provided to him.

Marriott did not build his first hotel until 1955. At that time sales were approximately $40 million. With the move into hotels, growth was rapid. Additional diversification began in the late 1960s with the acquisition of Roy Rogers (fast food), Big Boy (coffee shops), Casa Maria (Mexican food), theme parks, and cruise ships. Sales rose from approximately $100 million in the mid-1960s to $7.6 billion in 1990. That's not too bad for someone who was thirsty in 1927.

Mary Kay Ash

In a trivia quiz, if someone asks what business the name Sam is associated with, nearly everyone guesses Wal-Mart. Likewise, if someone asked what business the name Mary Kay represents, most would easily guess Mary Kay Cosmetics.

Mary Kay (Wagner) Ash was born in Hot Wells, Texas. Like many entrepreneurs, Mary Kay was raised by parents who were also business owners; they ran a hotel and restaurant near Houston. When Mary Kay was seven, her father became ill, and she assumed many of the household duties while her mother ran the restaurant.

One of Mary Kay's first jobs was selling for Stanley Home Products, which were sold via "home shows" at customers' residences. In her second year, she became the top salesperson for Stanley. She later left Stanley, started her own venture in St. Louis, which failed, and returned to Houston to work for the World Gift Company, which was another direct sales organization. She had accumulated a total of twenty-five years of direct sales experience at Stanley and World Gift Company when a disagreement led to her resignation.

At age forty-nine, she and her son founded Mary Kay Cosmetics. Feeling that she had been treated poorly at both Stanley Home Products and World Gift Company, she vowed to treat her employees as she would like to have been treated. Using essentially the same "home party" techniques that she was accustomed to, she made some changes that would be significant for the growth of Mary Kay Cosmetics. First, Mary Kay limited the product line so each "beauty consultant" (salesperson) could be thoroughly knowledgeable. She emphasized teaching rather than selling. She insisted that the beauty consultants keep an inventory so the product could be delivered immediately. Mary Kay offered superior compensation, including an array of bonuses for excellent performance and the use of a now classic pink Cadillac for two years.

But the most entrepreneurial part of her venture was simply the culture of the company. The culture included the following:

1. Pride in the organization
2. The need to constantly improve
3. A willingness to take risks

4. Belief in the dignity of the selling profession
5. Belief that life's priorities should be God first, family second, and career third
6. Belief that work should be fun
7. Belief that the Golden Rule is a practical guide to conducting one's business affairs.

The culture also includes the "Seminar," an annual convention that includes everything from parties to workshops to the "Awards Night," when thousands of awards—including the pink Cadillacs—are presented. The annual convention attracts more than twenty-six thousand beauty consultants who pay their own way to Dallas to be part of the enthusiasm.

Mary Kay's principles worked. In 1964, the first year of operation, total sales were $198,514. She took the company public in 1967, and averaged 28 percent growth over the next several years. In 1986, the company returned to private ownership through a successful leveraged buyout. It had sold more than $280 million of wholesale products.

Roy Speer

There may be no better example of the inveterate, compulsive entrepreneur who thrives on launching and growing businesses than Roy Speer. Roy Speer likely makes—or loses—more money in a week than most people do in a lifetime. He owns seventeen businesses, two Mercedes, two airplanes, and a mansion on forty acres of land that he bought for "a couple of million" in 1973.[15]

Speer grew up tough, having a difficult childhood that included spending three years in a military school. He earned a business degree from Southern Methodist University and later received a law degree from Stetson University in Florida. He practiced law for twenty-five years, but was always more intrigued by business dealings. Speer moved into real estate development in Florida, which made him very wealthy. When real estate values dropped, he avoided losing money by astutely selling his assets or returning property to his creditors. He did suffer a large loss in the oil industry in 1981, but that did not deter the invincible Speer.

In 1982 Speer and a partner launched the "Home Shopping Channel," through which shoppers could order merchandise by telephone after viewing it on TV. Within three months, the Florida venture was making a profit. After seeing the success in the communities in which it was launched, the partners decided to expand nationwide. Speer made sure the groundwork was laid well, however, since he knew that a venture of this type would not live long if it were not done well. A computer system and trained operators were required so that someone ordering from Washington or Maine or California would be assured that their product would be delivered on time and billed correctly.

An initial public offering of Home Shopping Network, Inc., stock in 1986 saw the stock price jump from the opening $18 to over $40 by the close of the first day. The stock has been up and down a number of times, but this does not worry the unflappable Roy Speer. Revenues were $3.6 million in 1983, over $1 billion in 1991.

Bob Levine

Bob Levine is distinguished as a contemporary example of entrepreneurship, having been named *Inc.*'s entrepreneur of the year in December 1990.[16] He is the founder of Cabeltron, a provider of computer cable and other computer related equipment.

Levine exemplifies the often independent nature of entrepreneurs by his unorthodox life-style. He lifts weights daily, wears ostrich-skin boots, drives a Harley-Davidson, and owns a tank. He has great disdain for authority, excessive hierarchy, and large meetings. Levine once told an eighteen-person meeting that if all those people had time for meetings there must be too many people employed. Somewhat like Sam Walton, he insists on excellent customer service—calls must be returned within one hour—and pays tremendous attention to costs. Headquarters furnishings are spartan at best and manufacturing plants are located in depressed communities where rent is cheap and people are willing to work.

Bob Levine began his first successful venture in 1983 (he had three earlier ventures that failed miserably). He was a sales rep for his father's cable company and found that many customers needed cable immediately and were unable to wait the typical six months lead time. Levine formed Cabeltron with $100,000 of his own money, some help from his father, and loans from a helpful banker. The company now installs cable and has diversified into the manufacture of network-testing devices, transceivers, and other specialty computer products. Its uniqueness is in the quickness with which customer needs can be researched and their problems solved with new or existing products.

Levine and his partner Craig Benson took Cabeltron public in 1989 and now employ 1,300 workers. Cabeltron has sales of over $100 million, after-tax profits of over 20 percent, and earns 25 percent of its sales from abroad.

ENTREPRENEURIAL VISION

The entrepreneurs featured here were visionaries—entrepreneurs in the truest sense of the word. In addition to possessing drive and a commitment to hard work, perhaps the one characteristic that epitomized the individuals is the ability to find a need and to fill it. They all had the ability to focus on the market for their product or service and marshall the resources necessary to successfully launch and grow the venture. There is little evidence that the entrepreneurs, especially in the early years, had formal, written business plans. They had vision and dedication, and that was sufficient to carry them through.

Vision and dedication are still necessary ingredients of entrepreneurship. But as industries become more complex, as technology changes more rapidly, and as financial decisions are made with increasing objectivity, the need for planning becomes evident. It may still be possible to succeed today in business with Walton's seat-of-the-pants judgment. Increasingly, however, the odds are against the intuitive manager and in favor of the entrepreneur who consciously lays out a path to follow. In this way, the environment is objectively analyzed, the resources are logically gathered, and a strategy is carefully developed to maximize the odds in favor of success. Today's entrepreneurial vision is to study carefully the market and the potential venture's strengths and weaknesses as it faces the competitive marketplace. Thus, entrepreneurial vision is still important, but there is more to that vision than there was in the past.

ETHICS AND ENTREPRENEURSHIP

It is important to note at the outset of a book on entrepreneurship the role and importance of ethics. Ethics plays a particularly crucial role in entrepreneurial ventures. There are two reasons for this. First, smaller ventures are not in the public eye to the extent that large businesses are. Since most entrepreneurial ventures are small, fewer outsiders are aware of their actions unless something extraordinary occurs. The Securities and Exchange Commission monitors publicly traded firms but has little interest in the firm that is not publicly traded. Government agencies regulating businesses are stretched far too thin to be interested in small companies unless severe problems develop. Further, if the ventures are small enough, they are exempt from some laws that affect larger firms. Thus, the owners of small and emerging ventures have more freedom to act as they choose regardless of whether the acts are ethical or not, since the likelihood of their being caught or exposed is much smaller.

At the same time, a second factor makes ethics even more important for the smaller firm. This is the major impact that the exposure of an unethical act can have on the financial health of the firm. A large company can withstand negative publicity up to a point. A smaller firm often can be terminally damaged by the exposure of a questionable practice. As an example, some restaurant patrons contracted food poisoning from food that had been improperly stored. Whether this was unethical or simply bad management is debatable. The more important fact, however, is that this single incident that affected no more than a handful of people caused the restaurant to go bankrupt. As another example, a roofing contractor has the image of bidding low to get work and then making a profit by cutting corners. The company is still in operation, but much of the community refuses to have them do work.

These two factors—that entrepreneurial firms have more freedom of movement and are more vulnerable if exposed—put a heavy responsibility on the entrepreneur. They can choose how ethical they want their venture to be and may never be caught or exposed. But if they should be exposed, the penalty is great.

The founder of a new venture has a significant influence on the tone or philosophy that permeates the launch and operation of the venture. Whereas a large organization takes on an ambience of its own that is hard to change, new and emerging organizations are typically an extension of the entrepreneur's value system. Given this influence, the level of ethics that the entrepreneur possesses will determine the level of ethics that the venture's operations will exhibit. This tone or climate of ethics affects day-to-day decisions and relations with each of the stakeholder groups.

Few entrepreneurs will have a written ethical code before launching a venture. They will, however, have a mental picture of what they consider to be ethical or unethical. This mental picture, such as the creed in Table 1-2

· · · · · · ·

TABLE 1-2
The Walgreen Creed
Source: Herman Kogan and
Rick Kogan, *Pharmacist to
the Nation,* The Walgreen
Company, Chicago, 1989,
p. 65.

- We believe in the goods we merchandise, in ourselves and our ability to render satisfaction.
- We believe that honest goods can be sold to honest people by honest methods.
- We believe in working, not waiting; in laughing, not weeping; in boosting, not knocking; and in the pleasure of selling our products.
- We believe that we can get what we go after and that we are not down and out until we have lost faith in ourselves.
- We believe in today and the work we are doing, in tomorrow and the work we hope to do, and in the sure reward the future holds.
- We believe in courtesy, in kindness, in generosity, in cheer, in friendliness and in honest competition.

espoused by Charles Walgreen as he developed the Walgreens drug store chain, permeates the action of the venture.

As this book is studied, it is important to remember the role of ethics throughout the entrepreneurial process. Since ethics is so crucial to new and emerging ventures, and since the entrepreneur plays such a heavy role in shaping the ethical tone for the venture, it is imperative that readers consider each aspect of the entrepreneurial process in light of the ethical impact of each act.

THE PLAN FOR THIS BOOK

Entrepreneurship: A Planning Approach is presented in a logical order for those who are studying the theory of entrepreneurship as well as those who are contemplating launching their own venture. Part I lays the groundwork for the rest of the book. Chapter 2 focuses on the nature of entrepreneurship. It discusses the uniqueness of entrepreneurship as compared with management in general. It also discusses different levels of entrepreneurship and the nature of entrepreneurial behavior. Chapter 3 discusses the entrepreneur as a person. It answers the question, "What, if anything, makes the entrepreneur different from any other person?" It looks at different characteristics that might be useful in identifying an entrepreneur and then focuses on different types of entrepreneurs.

Part II, Planning the New Venture, covers the tasks necessary to launch a new venture. Chapter 4 focuses on business plans, which is one of the key elements of this book. Carefully written business plans can help the enterprise succeed in the way that was envisioned by the entrepreneur. This chapter is placed early in the text so that all other aspects of the entrepreneurial process can be considered in terms of the business plan. Chapter 5 discusses the analysis of entrepreneurial opportunities. In particular it looks at how to identify significant opportunities and how to separate them from pseudo-opportunities. It also considers developing a match between those opportunities and the capabilities of the proposed venture. Chapter 6 then discusses the different methods of starting a venture. It addresses the question of whether a venture should be "started from scratch" or if an existing business should be purchased. It discusses the variety of legal forms such as sole proprietorship, partnership, and corporation. It also discusses two unique types of businesses: the family business and the incubator start-up. Chapter 7 then concludes Part II with a discussion of obtaining capital for the venture, which is often the most difficult part of entrepreneurship.

Planning Venture Strategies, Part III, consists of four strategy-related chapters. The first, Chapter 8, is a more general chapter on developing entrepreneurial strategies. Chapter 9 discusses support strategies necessary to implement the venture strategy. Chapters 10 and 11 then address two specific types of entrepreneurial strategies: franchising and international venturing.

Three chapters in Part IV, Planning for Entrepreneurial Management, treat the management of the ongoing venture. Chapter 12 discusses how to structure an existing venture and includes a discussion of how to assimilate an acquisition into an existing venture. Managing the growth venture is discussed in Chapter 13. Discussion centers on topics that are especially important to new and growing ventures rather than management in general. The final chapter in this part, entitled Intrapreneurship, discusses entrepreneurial management in large corporations.

Part V, Planning the Entrepreneurial Finale, discusses "harvesting" the venture. Harvesting is the selling or closing of a venture, passing it on to the next generation, or taking it public. Chapter 15 presents the methods available to value the venture before harvesting it. Even though a venture may need to be valued at different times, the most critical time for an accurate valuation is before harvesting it. The final chapter focuses on developing a harvest strategy. For some, harvesting the venture is a critical part of the entire entrepreneurial process. In some cases, ending the venture is an unplanned process that may be followed by bankruptcy. In other cases, harvesting one venture is the prelude to beginning another or reaping wealth from a successful venture.

Part VI provides two examples of business plans. One is for Conveniesse, Inc., and the other is for Kryos, Inc. Conveniesse, Inc. is the firm featured in the continuous case found at the end of each chapter. Kryos, Inc., is a company that was seeking external funding when the plan was written. Part VII offers the opportunity to analyze a number of entrepreneurial situations and pose solutions to the problems presented. These provide the opportunity to study actual situations and determine what is the best strategy or response for that situation.

. . . .

This chapter has set the stage for the study of entrepreneurship. It has set forth the proposition that entrepreneurship is a challenge, is significant to the American business scene, and is part of a growing trend in America. Several examples of classic and successful entrepreneurs were presented. It was shown how entrepreneurs of the past overcame adversity and competition to make their ventures real growth companies. There are still entrepreneurial frontiers to be conquered and many opportunities for individuals to become classic entrepreneurs of the 21st century. The need for

SUMMARY

vision in entrepreneurship was also noted. As contemporary society becomes more complex, it is important that the entrepreneurial vision be objective and leave room for analysis. Equally important as vision is ethics. An entrepreneur plays a pivotal role in establishing an ethical tone for the venture that can affect actions throughout the entrepreneurial process.

DISCUSSION QUESTIONS

1. Why is entrepreneurship both challenging and rewarding? Is it more rewarding than other occupations? Why?
2. Becoming an entrepreneur can result in substantial wealth. What psychological needs does that satisfy?
3. What evidence is there that America is really turning to entrepreneurship? What is there about industry today that could support your answer?
4. Explain why, in the late 1980s, there were more new jobs created by small firms than there were by large firms.
5. Consider the entrepreneurs profiled in this chapter. Are they unique? Did they have specific skills that made them successful, or were they lucky?
6. Are entrepreneurs born or made? Did the entrepreneurs profiled seemed to have entrepreneurial characteristics that would give them a tendency to start their own venture?
7. Sam Walton and Mary Kay Ash both started their famous businesses because of disagreements with previous employers. What are the similarities in their management style and corporate cultures?
8. Do opportunities "just happen"? Consider the case of J. W. Marriott. Explain how he took advantage of separate but related opportunities.
9. What is meant by "entrepreneurial vision"? Is the vision the same for all entrepreneurs? Are there common threads?
10. Why is ethics so important for entrepreneurial ventures? To what extent can a single person affect the ethics of a venture?

EXERCISES

EXERCISE 1-1

For each name below, indicate the product, service, or company that the person made famous.

Fred Smith	John Styth
Cyrus McCormick	W. T. Coleman
George Eastman	William Proctor
Charles Walgreen	David Sarnoff
Ole Evinrude	Frank Perdue
William Carrier	Steven Jobs
F. W. Maytag	Michael Dell
William Wrigley	Cyrus Curtis
Michael Owens	

EXERCISE 1-2

Select a notable entrepreneur either from those in Exercise 1-1 or from ones supplied by your instructor or found in books in the library. Study them by using history books or current periodicals. Then interview a business owner that you know. Write a three- to five-page report comparing the backgrounds, vision, and management styles of both.

· ·

1. Arnold C. Cooper et al., *New Business in America: The Firms and Their Owners* (Washington, D.C.: The NFIB Foundation, 1990), 11.

2. Robert Ronstadt, "The Educated Entrepreneurs: A New Era of Entrepreneurial Education is Beginning," *American Journal of Small Business* 10, no. 1 (Summer 1985): 7–23.

3. Ronald Reagan, "Why This Is an Entrepreneurial Age," *Journal of Business Venturing* 1, no. 1 (Winter 1985): 1–4.

4. Thomas McCarroll, "Starting Over," *Time*, January 6, 1992, 62.

5. The U.S. Small Business Administration, *The State of Small Business: A Report of the President* (Washington, D.C.: U.S. Government Printing Office, 1990), 10–11.

6. U.S. Department of Commerce, Department of the Census, *1987 Economic Census: Women-Owned Businesses* (Washington, D.C.: U.S. Government Printing Office, 1987), 149.

7. George Orwell, *Animal Farm* (New York: Harcourt, Brace, Jovanovich, 1982), 148.

8. Jeffry A. Timmons, *New Venture Creation: Entrepreneurship in the 1990s* (Homewood, IL: Richard D. Irwin, 1990), 9.

9. Cooper, *New Business in America*, 1.

10. Unless otherwise noted, all of the entrepreneurial profiles are based on information published by the American National Business Hall of Fame housed at Western Illinois University, Macomb, Illinois. Used with permission.

11. Brian McGinty, "Mr. Sears & Mr. Roebuck," *American History Illustrated* 21 (July 1986): 34–37, 48–49. For additional reading on Sears, Roebuck, and Julius Rosenwald, who gave additional leadership after 1895, see publications of the American National Business Hall of Fame.

12. David Gelman and Janet Huck, "Success Story," *Newsweek*, November 10, 1975, 54.

13. Y. T. Abraham, Yunus Kathawala, and Jane Heron, "Sam Walton," *The Journal of Business Leadership* 1, no. 1 (Spring 1988): 95–102.

14. "Marriott Corporation," in *Strategic Management: Concepts, Decisions, Cases,* Lester Digman, (Plano, TX: Business Publications, Inc., 1986), 914–946.

15. Ellen James, "So What's a Billion to Roy Speer," *Venture*, May 1987, 40–48.

16. Joshua Hyatt, "Born to Run," *Inc.*, January 1991, 36–50.

ENDNOTES

. . . . . .

The following case is called a continuous case. It appears at the end of each chapter of the text. In each of the cases, there will be information to read and absorb that relates to the chapter just finished. Each case then ends with an assignment. You will follow Conveniesse, Inc., throughout the book and will consider the problems and opportunities that Conveniesse's owners face. A unique aspect of the continuous case is that time both moves and stands still. The three major participants in the case age over a fifteen-year period. Yet the problems and situations they face are always contemporary. The complete business plan for the company is found in Part VI.

. . . . . .

◆ Conveniesse, Inc. ◆

Introduction

Conveniesse, Inc., is an upscale convenience store chain whose stores are located in street-level locations of major office buildings that are near hotels in medium to large cities. It caters to two distinct target markets. The first is office workers in the downtown area. Customers within this target market typically buy medicine and drugs, cosmetics, hosiery, and food from the high-quality deli. Limited groceries will be sold to those who prefer to pick up needed items on their way to their cars at the end of the day. The second target market is those people who stay at the hotels in the area. These people often find that there are no easily available places to buy deli sandwiches, medicine, magazines, soft drinks, and alcohol.

Convenience stores generally sell limited merchandise at a price somewhat higher than that of grocery or drug stores. Conveniesse's prices are even higher because of the somewhat captive market in the downtown area and because they target the more upscale customers with higher quality products. Conveniesse's product mix and services are somewhat different from those of a typical convenience store. For example, most convenience stores carry large quantities of milk, eggs, and bread. Conveniesse carries smaller amounts of these because its customers typically are not stopping on the way home to pick up food for dinner. On the other hand, it carries a larger selection of hosiery products because of the number of women working in the area. And it carries more expensive brands of soft drinks and alcoholic beverages to serve the hotel convention market. Conveniesse also has a fax machine, a copier, an automated teller machine, and a referral service for flower delivery.

The uniqueness of a store such as Conveniesse is that service is more important than price. Products are not particularly price sensitive. It is important, however, that the upscale image be enhanced wherever possible. The decor must exude an ambience of class. The personnel must be impeccably dressed and be knowledgeable not only about products in the store but also about happenings in the city. They must be able to give directions to any downtown location.

The chain was started in Buffalo, New York, by three individuals: Jason Stone, Yolanda Williams, and Sarah Tondeur. The three owners met in a nearby hotel while attending a week-long executive management seminar. During one of the breaks, the three were lamenting the absence of a place except for the hotel's gift shop to get needed items. As the days passed, the three became more familiar with each other. They found that they each had an interest in someday running their own venture. Even though they worked in different cities at different companies and in different areas of management, they found some commonality of backgrounds and interests. At the end of the seminar, they agreed to keep in touch.

Led by Sarah Tondeur's increasing interest in entrepreneurship and disillusionment with her future in her own company, the three continued to research the concept of an upscale convenience store. Eighteen months later, Stone and Tondeur quit their jobs and opened the first store in Buffalo. Ten months later, Williams joined them.

Assignment

Discuss Conveniesse. Does this seem like a good idea? What information do we need to determine its potential? Have you seen similar opportunities or unfulfilled needs?

2

The Nature of Entrepreneurship

LEARNING OBJECTIVES

After reading this chapter, you will be able to:

1. Define entrepreneurship and the important elements that make up entrepreneurship
2. Understand that entrepreneurship is a process
3. Explain how entrepreneurship differs from corporate management
4. Explain the five components of an entrepreneurial venture
5. Work with the entrepreneurship equation
6. Recognize that different amounts of entrepreneurship exist in various ventures
7. Recognize differences in the amount of entrepreneurial activity as venture growth increases

KEY TERMS

Creativity

Entrepreneurship

Innovation

Elements of entrepreneurship

Antecedent factors

Triggering factors

Entrepreneurship equation

Enabling factors

CONSIDER THIS!

- Are all new businesses "entrepreneurships"?
- Many people would like to start a business; few do.
- Innovation and entrepreneurship are closely related.
- Some ventures are more "entrepreneurial" than others. That may be because the founder was more entrepreneurial or because the venture itself had more potential.
- If any of your acquaintances operate a business, think about how entrepreneurial it is. Does it have growth potential, or will it remain stable? Is it likely to be the only venture that person will ever have, or is it only a step to larger opportunities?
- All ventures will vary, but each will have five basic components.

This chapter begins with a discussion of the meaning of the word *entrepreneurship*. It looks at entrepreneurship as contrasted with management in general. It also examines the necessary components for an entrepreneurial venture and the factors likely to be present when a venture is started.

DEFINITION OF ENTREPRENEURSHIP

Entrepreneurship is the launch and/or growth of ventures through the use of innovative, risk-assuming management. Dictionaries typically list the

ENTREPRENEURIAL PROFILE

LARRY RISLEY
Mesa Airlines, Inc.

Mesa Airlines, Inc., is a commuter airline with operations in fifteen states. Formed in 1980 in Farmington, New Mexico, it initially served small cities in New Mexico with airports that were too small for conventional carriers. Mesa and its subsidiaries now fly into Denver, Kansas City, Milwaukee, Detroit, Phoenix, and Baltimore, although the company still specializes in small city airports.

Mesa began as the charter division of Mesa Aviation Services in October 1980 with flights from Farmington to Albuquerque. Larry Risley was a mechanic who managed the division. When the oil bust occurred, the company was on the verge of failure and the charter business was put up for sale. In 1982, Larry and his wife, Janie, mortgaged their house and everything else they owned to come up with a $140,000 loan to buy a Piper Chieftain, some tools, and parts. This began what is now Mesa Airlines, Inc. Larry Risley is the president and chief executive officer of Mesa. Janie is executive vice-president. But in the beginning, both did everything from taking reservations to loading baggage onto the planes.

The growth at Mesa Airlines has been phenomenal. Starting with a one-plane operation in 1982, the company now flies under the banners of Mesa Airlines, Air Midwest, United Express, and Skyway. It operates fifty-six aircraft in eighty cities in the Southwest, Midwest, and Rocky Mountain states. Revenues reached almost $10 million in 1986, $46 million in 1990, and were forecast to be $129 million in 1992.

The growth in Mesa's assets is as phenomenal as the growth in revenues. Total company assets in 1985 were slightly over a million dollars. At the end of fiscal year 1991, total company assets were over $76 million. It now has hubs in Albuquerque and Phoenix, as well as a hub in Milwaukee.

The Risleys' success in the growth of Mesa Airlines is due to their ability to control costs while operating in a unique market niche. Their ASM (average seat-mile) cost of approximately fifteen cents allows them to keep their fares low while still producing an excellent RPM (revenue passenger-mile). The low cost is a function of high employee productivity, the right airplanes, and a lean corporate structure. The Risleys began by buying primarily new planes that were simple to operate and did not have many of the frills that more luxurious planes have. Buying new planes kept maintenance to a minimum, and buying simple planes left fewer things that could go wrong. In 1989, they began using leased planes to present a less asset-heavy balance sheet. The Risleys have no intention of moving up to larger planes. Instead, they intend to stay with the thirteen-to eighteen-seat planes, allowing them to service the lean routes that have become their competitive advantage.

The Risleys decided to take the company public in 1987 in order to provide funding for additional growth. In 1991, their stock price was as high as 13¼, compared with a high of 4¼ in 1988. In its first month of operation, Mesa Airlines carried 800 passengers. In a typical month now, Mesa carries 105,000 passengers. Mesa has the lowest cost structures of any publically held commuter airline in the nation. In August 1991 it owned fifty-eight aircraft, served eighty-four cities, and employed 1,039 workers. By May of 1992, Mesa had purchased two additional commuter airlines to become the largest commuter airline in the nation.

SOURCE: Mesa Airlines documents. Used with permission.

word "entrepreneurship" as a noun. This may suggest to some that one can launch "an entrepreneurship." More astute readers, however, will realize that entrepreneurship is a process rather than a result. Entrepreneurship is not something one forms. It is something one does. Entrepreneurship means the act of creating or growing a business through innovative and risk-assuming management.

Entrepreneurship connotes action rather than a static event. It involves taking the action necessary to analyze opportunities, to launch and/or grow a business, to finance the venture, and possibly even to harvest the venture.

ELEMENTS OF ENTREPRENEURSHIP

Entrepreneurship may include one or more of the following elements:

- Starting a business
- Being creative and innovative in developing new products or services
- Managing an existing venture in such a way that it grows rapidly and consistently
- Seeking significant financing and other resources for a potentially high-growth venture
- Accepting risk in the development of a new or growing venture

These elements are important aspects of the entrepreneurial process. It is not necessary, however, to have all elements present in every entrepreneurial situation.

Starting a Business

Starting a business is considered by many to be the sine qua non of entrepreneurship. Some instructors and writers insist that entrepreneurship can occur only with the launch of a venture. And this is perhaps the most visible sign of the entrepreneurial process. But there is more to entrepreneurship than simply starting a business. Some entrepreneurial ventures are not started from scratch, but are developed from existing businesses. Venture Perspective 2-1 is an example of a business that was anything but entrepreneurial for years and became an entrepreneurial venture only in the second generation.

Further, just because a new business is started does not mean that it is entrepreneurial. If, for example, you have a hobby of making wedding cakes for friends' weddings and then decide to start doing the same thing for others as a business, some would suggest that this is not entrepreneurship at all. At best it could be called a small business, and at worst it could be called a profitable hobby. This example does involve an element of entrepreneurship—planning the launch of the venture. But the amount of planning, risk-taking, or personal capital needed for the cake business is minimal in comparison with most entrepreneurial ventures.

• • • • • • • • • • • •

RECYCLED AUTO PARTS, INC.

Harold Gorman grew up in the auto salvage and parts business. His father and uncle had started the business before Harold was born. The business had been mildly successful for many years, giving the two families an adequate but modest living. It had always been assumed that Harold would formally join the business and eventually take it over since he had worked there throughout his teenage years.

Unfortunately, Harold's chance came earlier than anticipated when his father suffered a severe stroke and died only a few days later. His uncle, who was nearing retirement, asked Harold to buy him out and assume all operational control. Uncle Jim would continue to serve as a consultant for a year and then retire completely. This left Harold, who was now in his late twenties, co-owner (with his mother) and sole manager of Gorman Auto Parts.

Harold continued the business at approximately the same level for a few more years, with increasing profits due to improvements in marketing and cost control. After a while, it appeared that sales had reached their peak and would not likely increase significantly. Harold reasoned that if increases in profits were to be obtained, additional sources of revenue would have to be found. He began to wonder if auto salvage yards could be franchised just as fast-food restaurants or, in the auto field, the various franchised muffler, rustproofing, and tune-up shops have been. If possible, this would provide several benefits. By franchising, one could obtain better control of the site aesthetics, better tracking of inventory, better marketing and name recognition, and better accessibility of parts. In essence, significant economies of scale were possible in the auto salvage business even with each site being relatively small.

After researching the franchising industry, Harold founded Recycled Auto Parts, Inc. He brought in two partners. One had been a regional manager for an auto painting franchiser. The other had experience with computer applications, a necessity to achieve economies of scale and expedient inter-franchisee sales and inventory control. With each of the partners contributing capital, and with additional financing available from banks, Recycled Auto Parts, Inc., grew from the original unit in the beginning to nearly twenty units in four states three years later. Harold figured that an increase of ten units per year could be maintained almost indefinitely, since existing small salvage yards seemed quite willing to pay the modest franchise fee and clean up their exterior surroundings in order to get better control and name recognition for their facilities.

Creativity and Innovation

Being creative and innovative is also one of the key elements of entrepreneurship. **Innovation** is the development and introduction of a new product, a new process, or a new service to a market. Examples of new products may range from the simple Post-it Note by 3M Corporation to a highly complex piece of medical diagnostic equipment. An innovative process is one that replaces an old way of doing something with a more efficient, effective, or less costly method. An innovative service is illustrated by the rapid package delivery service introduced by Federal Express.

Creativity is the force behind innovation. Creativity is the link between pure imagination and the introduction of an innovative product, process, or service. Both creativity and innovation are necessary ingredients for entrepreneurship. In fact, Peter Drucker believes that innovation is so critical that entrepreneurship cannot exist without it.[1]

Creativity, by itself, does not define entrepreneurship. Creativity without innovation does not produce results. And innovation, without effective management, does not produce marketable products, processes, or services. Creativity also characterizes inventors, artists, musicians, and writers. Yet these individuals do not epitomize the entrepreneur. Thus, although creativity and innovation are necessary ingredients, they are not sufficient by themselves to establish entrepreneurship.

In order for innovations to be fruitfully introduced into the marketplace, some amount of administrative structure is needed. **Administrative structure** is that combination of direction, policies, controls, and managerial supervision that ties an organization and its people to its overall mission. Entrepreneurs need some administrative structure in order to be able to function. Otherwise, they are akin to the mad scientist jumping from one idea to the next.

Managing for Growth

Creating, managing, and maintaining growth in a new venture are key aspects of entrepreneurship. Growth separates entrepreneurial ventures from non-entrepreneurial ventures. The amount of entrepreneurial activity required to maintain growth may be as great as that required to launch the venture in the first place. Thus, in a broad sense, managing growth is indeed synonymous with entrepreneurship. And that growth can be started or maintained long after a company has ceased being a "new venture." Only those purists who insist that only startup situations meet the strict definition of entrepreneurship would disagree.

Seeking Financing

Seeking financing for fast-growth ventures is also evidence of entrepreneurship. This financing can be either debt financing or equity financing and may be either traditional or venture capital. **Venture capital** is high-risk equity funding provided for high-potential ventures in exchange for a significant share of ownership. This and other forms of capital may be required in order to achieve major growth. Creative financing is a basic tenet of entrepreneurship. In fact, a significant characteristic of growth-oriented ventures is the use of *multiple sources* of financing. However, many ventures are successful without infusions of venture capital. Internally generated funds may, in some cases, be sufficient to achieve the growth desired by the entrepreneur.

Assuming Risk

One of the most popular views of entrepreneurs is that of risk-takers who invest all they have to start new ventures in uncharted waters. The material presented in Chapter 3 will dispel that myth to some extent. Still, substantial risks are inherent in any new venture. And some believe that a willingness to take risks is the primary difference between entrepreneurs and corporate managers.

The Essential Ingredients?

Each of the items discussed—starting a venture, new product innovation, managing for growth, seeking financing, and assuming risk—is a key element of entrepreneurship. Of those, which are essential? The above discussion has pointed out exceptions to most of the items. Yet the greater the number or magnitude of the items that exist, the greater the degree of entrepreneurship. Entrepreneurship is not something that either exists or does not exist. All ventures contain some amount of entrepreneurship. The amount may be miniscule in most small businesses and may be significant in high-growth ventures.[2]

ENTREPRENEURSHIP VERSUS CORPORATE MANAGEMENT

All entrepreneurs are managers in that they must manage their venture, but all managers are not entrepreneurs. To a great extent, this is because most large corporations have become highly structured with restrictive rules necessary to control an entity of that size. Small ventures do not have these problems. Entrepreneurship includes a healthy dose of management. But entrepreneurship and management are not synonymous. Entrepreneurship involves a unique brand of management, with its own philosophies, goals, and methods. It differs from corporate management in a number of ways.

Risk Management versus Risk Minimization

Corporate management deals in risk minimization; entrepreneurship deals in risk management. Corporate management tends to be risk-averse. Its goal is to reduce risk to a minimum while being as productive and as profitable as possible. Corporate management, for example, is heavily budget oriented. Capital budgets, production budgets, marketing budgets, and personnel budgets are all aimed at constraining activities to predetermined limits, thereby minimizing the risk of loss. Unfortunately, the budgets add excessive structure to operations.

Entrepreneurship is not necessarily risk-seeking, but it is risk-assuming. Entrepreneurship realizes that startup or high-growth ventures, by nature, entail amounts of risk. Risk, in many cases, cannot be reduced significantly in entrepreneurial situations. But it can be subjectively measured, and actions can be taken to offset risk. **Risk management** involves the acknowledgment that risk exists and the actions that are taken to shift as much risk as possible to others and control the remainder. Risk management does not attempt to eliminate or even minimize risk because risk is a necessary part of entrepreneurial growth.

Table 2-1 lists some of the ways that assumed risk may be managed. For example, to reduce the impact of a risky venture, an entrepreneur may obtain multiple sources of financing rather than a single source. And to the extent possible, those sources will come from outside the venture rather than from internal equity. An entrepreneur will keep fixed assets to a minimum, preferring to rent facilities and subcontract production rather than maximize internal investment. An entrepreneur will hedge bets and

1. Renting, rather than owning, equipment and facilities
2. Using multiple sources of financing
3. Building an entrepreneurial team whose members have different but compatible skills
4. Undertaking multiple ventures simultaneously with varied degrees of risk
5. Committing only a portion of the total resources to any one project
6. Assigning a team member the responsibility of monitoring short-term performance with the anticipation of cutting losses if early performance indicates unfavorable returns

TABLE 2-1
Risk Management
Methods

keep avenues of disinvestment open in case the venture does not go as planned. These activities do not eliminate risk. But they do aid in managing or working with the risk that is inherent in the venture.

Opportunity Driven versus Resource Driven

Corporate management tends to be resource driven; entrepreneurship tends to be opportunity driven. Corporate management first asks the question, "How much capital do we have to invest?" It then looks for opportunities that fit within the limits of the available capital. For example, management often considers new investments yearly, after the previous year's performance is known. This is resource-driven investment. It determines the amount available to invest first and then determines where that investment should be made. Even if a number of opportunities have crossed management's desk, the issues are often put on hold until available resources are determined.

Entrepreneurship, on the other hand, is opportunity driven. It first asks the question, "What are the commanding opportunities?" Once these are identified, then efforts are made to find the resources necessary to capture those opportunities. Opportunities are studied from the viewpoint of what the eventual payoff might be. If the payoff is great enough, capital can be found to underwrite it. If the payoff is not great, then the entrepreneur must decide whether the venture should be funded at some lower level, spun off to a subsidiary venture, or scrapped completely.

Action versus Analysis

Corporate management moves methodically, studying each move carefully; entrepreneurship involves a sense of urgency, realizing that many opportunities have a short window. Management in large corporations is characterized by multiple layers of hierarchy and a large staff. Thus, whenever an opportunity arises, the study of that opportunity will often be delegated to lower levels or to staff workers. Large corporations function by committees. Committees take time, even though they may produce well-studied, well-written decisions. Unfortunately, many opportunities have a short window—that is, a short period in which resources must be committed and action taken before the opportunity runs its course or competitors move in. Entrepreneurs realize that action often must be taken quickly, sometimes without full knowledge and without an unequivocal answer.

Lean Management Team versus Personnel Heavy

Corporate management tends to become personnel heavy over time; entrepreneurship tends to stay lean with overworked team members. Corporations tend to grow over time due, generally, to increases in volume. However, in many cases the growth in staff does not result in increased volume or profit. In the early 1980s, many large corporations found themselves to be very top heavy, especially in middle management and staff positions. These positions became very expensive as the recession reduced revenues. Entrepreneurial firms, on the other hand, have lean management teams and few layers of management, most of which are directly related to providing the product or service. These team members are willing to work long hours, often at low pay, in order to reap the payoff at a later time.

INTRAPRENEURSHIP: THE CORPORATE COMPROMISE

The preceding discussion suggests that corporate management tends to be more traditional, more cautious, and perhaps less exciting than entrepreneurship. However, some corporations are taking steps to gain the benefits of entrepreneurship within the corporate framework. These steps may take the form of instilling an entrepreneurial spirit throughout the entire organization. They may take a more formal approach by creating venture groups within the corporation, spinning off subsidiaries that invest in high-risk ventures, or contributing capital to selected ventures outside the corporation. This corporate entrepreneurship, or **intrapreneurship,** has substantial potential if done correctly because of the amount of ready capital, the industry experience, and the knowledge of the production and marketing processes. This will be discussed in more depth in Chapter 14.

The significance of intrapreneurship here is that intrapreneurship, like its independent cousin, entrepreneurship, is a process. It is something that is done rather than an event or a structure. Inside the major corporation, it is a process that must be encouraged, cajoled, supported, and rewarded if it is to survive.

THE COMPONENTS OF ENTREPRENEURIAL VENTURES

The previous sections have discussed what entrepreneurship is and how it differs from corporate management. In order to complete the picture of the entrepreneurship process, it is necessary to consider the components of an entrepreneurial venture. These components are the necessary parts that must be present in order for a venture to be launched. There may be many specific parts existing in a given start-up. Yet, there are five parts that are

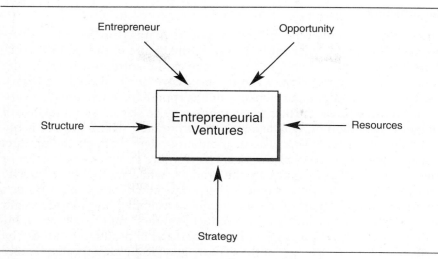

FIGURE 2-1
The Five Components of
Entrepreneurial Ventures

common to any venture launch. These five components are the entrepreneur, the opportunity, the structure, the resources, and the strategy (Figure 2-1).

The Entrepreneur

The managerial and entrepreneurial skill of the entrepreneur is perhaps the most significant key to success. Financing specialists consistently assert that they would rather have a good management team with a lower quality idea than a great opportunity with less skillful entrepreneurs. The lead entrepreneur plays such a crucial role in the launch and development of a venture that a weakness in this area is almost certain to ensure either failure or limited growth potential.

The Opportunity

There are thousands of "opportunities" available to would-be entrepreneurs. Unfortunately, many of these opportunities are not real entrepreneurial opportunities with high potential. There may be a great difference between the opportunity in the mind of an individual and the same opportunity in the minds of financiers or customers. Any consultant who has worked with potential small business owners can tell stories of the wild ideas that some individuals bring to the table. Many are not well thought out, many are simply schemes, many are ideas for products that have extremely limited market potential, and some may be excellent ideas but would require far more funding than would be available to the individual. Some opportunities could have potential, but government constraints impede a successful attempt to exploit the opportunity. Fortunately, some are high-potential opportunities for which continued growth prospects are likely. This is a real entrepreneurial opportunity that is worthy of outside financing.

The Structure

Structure refers to the type or kind of venture that is launched. The structure will include the legal entity as well as the nature of the venture itself. There are a number of choices to be made as the entrepreneur plans the launch of the venture. First, a venture may have one of three legal forms: a sole proprietorship, a partnership, or a corporation. There are also variations on these three. Further, the venture may be started as a franchise of a larger corporation or, conversely, as a corporation whose growth is obtained by selling franchises. The distribution system that gets the product or service to the customer also varies. One venture may use wholesalers or other intermediaries to distribute the product, while another goes directly from the venture to the customer. The production process in a product-oriented firm is also part of the structure. For example, one venture might do complete manufacturing of a product, another might only assemble components, and a third might only be a marketer of products produced by someone else. The structure of the venture is typically an important choice for the entrepreneur since it can be critical to the long-run growth and success of the venture.

The Resources

Most new ventures are undercapitalized when launched. This is one of the major causes of new venture failure. Typically, the entrepreneur can marshal the resources to launch the venture but often does not have sufficient capital to give the secondary boost to the venture. Just as a space launch requires a second-stage booster rocket, a business venture requires second-stage financing to boost it from the launch phase to the growth phase. Many ventures are aborted within eighteen months after launch because there is either insufficient capital to carry the venture safely through the launch or too little to boost it beyond the initial level.

In addition to financial resources, human resources must be assembled. The number of managerial staff will depend heavily on the nature of the venture and the amount of growth desired by the entrepreneur. Like financial resources, new ventures are typically understaffed. Material resources in the form of the plant and equipment, inventory, and supplies must also be assembled. Likewise, information resources must be gathered so that rational decisions can be made.

The Strategy

The competitive strategy that the entrepreneur chooses will significantly affect the potential for success. Competitive strategy refers to those plans or activities the firm uses to achieve growth in sales, increase market share, or maximize profits. K mart's competitive strategy is to sell products at the lowest possible prices and derive profits from the volume of sales. A small appliance manufacturer might have as its competitive strategy to produce only house brand products for retailers such as J.C. Penney or Sears.

It is not uncommon for a business owner to have the basis for an excellent venture and then develop an inappropriate strategy for the venture given the changing competitive environment. Thus, the venture may succeed or fail not because of specific shortcomings but because of the long-run competitive strategy selected. There are a number of different strategies that may be appropriate for given situations. Some are more appropriate for slow-growth intentions, others may be appropriate for pioneering work in new areas, and still others might be appropriate in situations where the new venture faces substantial challenges from major corporations. The entrepreneur must choose an initial strategy and then adapt it as necessary over time.

THE ENTREPRENEURIAL PROCESS

Figure 2-2 lists the five components of the entrepreneurial process, with particular emphasis on the required action. The process begins with the entrepreneur, who makes a conscious decision to launch a venture. The opportunity is then analyzed to determine the magnitude of expected returns. A structure must then be determined, such as the form of ownership and the relationship to franchisers or other companies. The all-important resources must then be obtained. Once the launch appears viable, then a specific strategy must be developed.

The Entrepreneurial Process Illustrated

The entrepreneurial profile at the beginning of this chapter illustrates the five components of entrepreneurship. Recall from the profile that Mesa Airlines is a commuter airline operating out of Farmington, New Mexico. It now flies into a number of Midwestern and Southwestern cities under four different names. The company went public after achieving substantial growth in the number of planes and the number of passenger-revenue miles.

The Entrepreneur

Larry and Janie Risley founded the airline in 1982 with a single aircraft. Larry Risley had previously served as the manager of Mesa Aviation Services. He had previous training and experience as a mechanic and also had an associate's degree in business management. Risley's experience in the operations end of the business gave him the skills necessary to manage the growth-oriented airline. By the time Mesa Airlines was launched, he had substantial experience in all facets of the operation.

The Opportunity

The commuter airline industry has taken on new forms in recent years because of changes in the structure of traditional trunk line carriers. Opportunities for small regional commuter lines have arisen as a means of bringing passengers from small cities into the airports of larger cities where they can board traditional airlines for flights to distant cities. The Risleys determined that there were opportunities to fly small, thirteen-seat commuter planes between small cities and larger hubs and, in addition, to fly the same type of planes among the small cities of the region.

FIGURE 2-2
The Entrepreneurial
Process

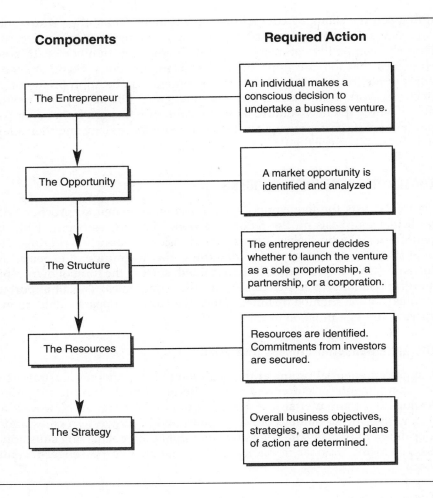

The Structure

Many small commuter lines are established either as a subsidiary of a major airline or as an independent company that contracts exclusively with a major airline. The Risleys determined that, in the area in which they wanted to operate, tying in with a major airline would be more restrictive than it would be helpful. As a result, they originally determined to set up a totally separate entity with its own reservation codes. They later contracted with United Airlines to operate its United Express route in their area. The ownership structure the Risleys used was the Sub-chapter S corporation, which was later changed to a regular corporation.

The Resources

Initially, the Risleys mortgaged everything they owned in order to underwrite the purchase of their first plane. Later they were able to obtain loans to purchase additional aircraft. After the company grew substantially and required still more planes, the Risleys decided to take the company public.

The Strategy

The basic strategy that the Risleys adopted was to enter into those markets that were not profitable enough for two airlines and then defend that territory aggressively. They realized that the market for a commuter airline in small communities was not highly price elastic. There appeared to be a more or less fixed number of passengers regardless of the price as long as it was not completely out of line. They were able to enter a market with low fares to attract customers who otherwise would drive to their destinations and then raise the fares somewhat after the market was established. The Risleys entered other markets as opportunities developed and adapted strategies as expansion plans and new territories dictated.

THE ENTREPRENEURSHIP DECISION

There are three sets of variables that contribute to an entrepreneur's motivation to launch a venture.[3] These three groups of variables are the antecedent, or background, variables, the triggering, or precipitating, variables, and the enabling variables. All three groups are typically present as motivating forces in the entrepreneurship decision.

The Antecedent Factor

The **antecedent factor** involves "stage-setting" variables. These are situations or characteristics that cause the individual to begin considering the possibilities of entrepreneurship either consciously or unconsciously. Some of these variables are historical or environmental in nature. For example, many entrepreneurs grew up in entrepreneurial families. Many entrepreneurs were identified early in their lives as having something resembling an entrepreneurial personality. Both of these will be discussed in more depth in the next chapter.

Other situations develop over time that lead to the entrepreneurial decision. An individual's education may be a factor. Some educational paths tend to lead more naturally to entrepreneurship than others, and these paths may or may not be business related. A college student majoring in chemistry may be excited by a professor's discovery and agree to assist in marketing the discovery after graduation. An art student may find a career path into entrepreneurship by beginning a small graphics firm while still in college.

Current jobs are often antecedents to venture creation. Jobs may be antecedent variables in two ways. One is that jobs often create opportunities for ventures. In fact, many ventures were started as a result of either the skills or the ideas that the entrepreneur developed while working in an existing job. The second reason that the job may be an antecedent to entrepreneurship is that the job may be seen as increasingly dissatisfying. Thus, the seed of "going out on my own" is planted and increasingly nurtured, although this may be an unconscious development for some time before the individual ever realizes that the entrepreneurial desire is sprouting.

The Triggering Factor

Whereas the antecedent factor tends to set the stage for venture creation over time, the **triggering factor** is that event or situation that specifically triggers the entrepreneurial act. These have been referred to as "salient life events" and are personal, professional, or financial changes in an entrepreneur's life that are perceived as important to the entrepreneurial decision.[4] For example, being laid off or fired from a job can be a triggering factor. Being approached by another entrepreneur who is seeking a partner could cause one to leave an existing job and begin a venture. Sometimes, if the situation is ripe already, nothing more than a caustic remark by a supervisor, an insufficient raise, or a missed promotion may be enough to spark the entrepreneurial flame. In some cases, an impending change in life-style or a desire to broaden one's horizons becomes the impetus. Many ventures have been launched by women who have chosen to stay at home with young children but who want a new challenge once those children begin school. Some ventures are launched by retirees who see the venture as an avenue to continue being active, to meet new challenges, and to increase their level of income.

Neither the antecedent variables nor the triggering variables by themselves are enough to cause a new venture creation. Without the seeds planted by a number of antecedent variables in earlier time periods, the appearance of a triggering variable will not be sufficient to cause one to start a venture. Likewise, the antecedent variables by themselves may "prime the pump," but will not cause the entrepreneurial water to flow without the final push by a precipitating variable. Thus, both antecedent variables and triggering variables must be present in order for the individual to be motivated to launch a venture.

The willingness or motivation to start a venture is illustrated in equation form and schematically in Table 2-2. Note that this theoretical model is multiplicative rather than additive. This means that if either factor is zero, the motivation to launch a venture will be zero. Although we can only subjectively "measure" variables in the two factors, we know that as the number or strength of the variables increases, so will the motivation to launch a venture.

TABLE 2-2
Entrepreneurship
Motivation Equation

The entrepreneurial motivation, $M = \Sigma A_i \times \Sigma T_j$, where

A_i = antecedent variables, and

T_j = triggering variables.

Antecedent Factor	×	Triggering Factor	=	Motivation to Start a Venture
Creativity		Loss of job		
Background		Invention or idea		
Personality		Offer from partner		
Past experience				
Education				

The motivation to launch a venture increases as either the number or the strength of variables in either set increases. Thus, the more antecedent variables that are present, the more likely the individual will want to launch a new venture. Similarly, if one or more triggering variables occur, the motivation to launch increases. If either factor results in too low a "score" as the variables within the factor are summed, then the probability of a venture launch will be low.

The entrepreneurship motivation equation explains how some individuals stay in a dissatisfying job for years rather than breaking loose. The triggering variable—job dissatisfaction—is clearly present. But if the individual does not have the experience or personality indicated by the antecedent variables, the individual will not consciously look for entrepreneurial opportunities. Conversely, an individual may be a latent entrepreneur with a significant entrepreneurial background. Yet, if the current job is fulfilling and no opportunities have developed, the individual will not be enticed into launching a venture.

The Enabling Factor

The antecedent variables and triggering variables together comprise the potential entrepreneur's motivation to launch a venture. However, this does not mean a venture actually will be launched. Being motivated to start a business does not mean that starting one is either wise or possible. The entrepreneur is only one of the five components of entrepreneurial ventures discussed earlier in this chapter. Two more of the components—the opportunity and resources—are critical to the decision to launch a venture.

The entrepreneurial equation now can be expanded to include these two critical variables.[5] In Table 2-3, we have the antecedent and triggering factors plus the added **enabling factor,** which is comprised of

• • • • • •
TABLE 2-3
Expanded
Entrepreneurship Equation

Venture Launch Likelihood, $L = \Sigma A_i \times \Sigma T_j \times \Sigma E_k$, where
A_i = antecedent variables,
T_j = triggering variables, and
E_k = enabling variables.

Antecedent Factor	×	Triggering Factor	×	Enabling Factor	=	Likelihood of Venture Launch
Creativity		Loss of job		Opportunity		
Background		Invention or idea		Resources		
Personality		Offer from partner				
Personal experience						
Education						

FIGURE 2-3
The Entrepreneurial
Decision

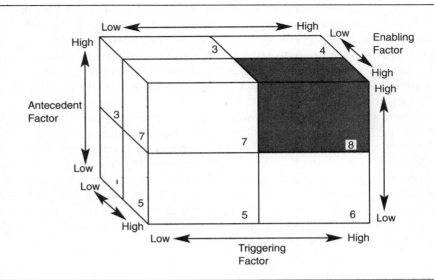

opportunities and resources. Once we add these, the entire equation becomes a schematic of the entrepreneurship process. Again, the model is
multiplicative in that a zero score on any of the three factors will reduce to
zero the likelihood of a venture launch. Conversely, the greater the number or strength of variables in any of the three factors, the greater will be
the likelihood that a venture will be started.

Figure 2-3 graphically illustrates the entrepreneurship process. In block
1, neither triggering variables nor antecedent variables are high. The motivation to start a venture should therefore be low. In blocks 2 and 3, one
set of variables is high but the other is low. Thus, the motivation to start a
venture is still probably low, although it is higher than in block 1. In block
4, both antecedent and triggering variables are high. Hence, the motivation
to start a venture is likely to be high. However, in all four cases, the
enabling factor—consisting primarily of opportunities and resources—is
still low. This means that although the individual wants to start a business, either insufficient resources are available or no viable opportunity
exists.

In all four of the remaining blocks, the resources and opportunities are
assumed to be present. Still, in block 5 the motivation is quite low, and in
blocks 6 and 7, low to moderate motivation exists. Thus, only in block 8 is
a venture launch highly probable. Only in block 8 are all three sets of
variables favorable to the launch of a venture. It is, of course, unrealistic to
assume that each factor *must* receive a "high" score in order for a venture
launch to be either expected or successful. Yet, as more variables are
present in any of the three factors or as existing variables become stronger,
it *is* logical to expect that a potential entrepreneur will more seriously
consider beginning the pre-launch planning.

ENTREPRENEURSHIP AND VENTURE GROWTH

Earlier in this chapter, the definition of entrepreneurship included the launch and/or growth of ventures using innovative, risk-assuming management. All new business ventures require at least some amount of entrepreneurial behavior. The analysis of a potential venture, the creative launch of even the smallest venture, the efforts to obtain financing, and the development of a management team and structure are all part of the entrepreneurial process. Yet some ventures are far more entrepreneurial than others. Some ventures are launched and grow quickly into profitable and/or harvestable enterprises. Others start small and stay small.

Given the differences in rates of growth, what is it that makes some ventures grow and other ventures not grow? Sometimes the answer lies simply in the nature of the product or opportunity. More often, however, the difference is a function of the "amount" or magnitude of entrepreneurship or entrepreneurial behavior in the venture. The amount of entrepreneurship means the degree to which actions taken by the owner over time are risk oriented, aggressive, innovative, take advantage of opportunities, maximize use of all funding sources, and are constantly aimed at increasing the growth of the venture. The amount of entrepreneurship required in a high-growth venture is, of course, much greater than that required for a low-growth or no-growth business.

The Key Role of the Entrepreneur

The amount of entrepreneurship evident in ventures varies considerably from the smallest part-time venture to the rapid-growth venture such as Mesa Airlines, which was profiled at the beginning of this chapter. It is important to realize, however, that the amount of entrepreneurship in a venture is primarily a function of the desires and skills of the founder. If the entrepreneur desires rapid growth and has the skills and capabilities necessary, then actions will be taken to achieve that growth. Conversely, if the owner does not want a high-growth venture or does not have entrepreneurial capabilities, the venture will stay small. Most ventures start small and stay relatively small. Although an argument could be made that the market is limited or the competition is too fierce, the skilled entrepreneur can often overcome those limitations. Growth-oriented ventures are often started by entrepreneurs who have high-growth goals in mind at the time the venture was launched.

The following sections will discuss two types of ventures and the amount of entrepreneurship necessary to sustain each. The first is the low-growth venture, and the second is the growth-oriented venture.

The Low-Growth Venture

The significance of low-growth ventures is that they are typically started with the intention of remaining relatively small. These are normally referred to as "small businesses."[6]

Any community has its share of small businesses. Most service businesses—plumbing and heating firms, auto mechanic shops, small income tax or bookkeeping services, insurance agents, and others—fit the definition of a small business. In spite of the number of national chains, the number of small retail stores that are low-growth ventures far outnumbers the large companies.

The factor that differentiates the low-growth venture from others is not that they start small, since virtually all ventures start small. The differentiating factor is that they are not intended to grow beyond some small limits consciously or unconsciously set by the owner. Thus, they start small and they purposely stay small.

Several characteristics typify the low-growth venture. The venture is usually a sole proprietorship or a small partnership. The low-growth venture will usually, but not always, be the only significant venture owned by the entrepreneur. Seldom will a single entrepreneur have more than one distinct venture at a time even though different parts of the venture may be formed as separate entities. The ventures typically are limited to one location or, at most, two or three locations within a single geographical area. This allows the entrepreneur to maintain constant contact with the operations of the business. The ventures generally serve only a single market or sell a single line of products. Virtually all will have fewer than fifty employees, most will have under twenty employees, and many will have no employees besides the owner.

A final characteristic that typifies the low-growth venture is the most significant. A lack of strategic innovation most clearly separates low-growth ventures from more entrepreneurial ventures. This is not to say that there is no innovation of any kind. Indeed, a cake decorator may be extremely innovative in cake design. An auto repair shop owner might be innovative in repair methods and in diagnostics. But the owners of low-growth ventures are not innovative in a strategic sense. That is, their innovation is limited to operational issues rather than strategic issues. Thus, they use little or no innovative combinations of financing for the firm. They will use relatively small amounts of market research that could lead to strategic adaptations or avenues of capturing market share or growth. And they do not, in general, have a long-range outlook on either the growth or harvest of the venture.

The Growth Venture

The growth-oriented venture is significantly different from the small business venture. The most obvious difference is the amount of growth desired by the venture's owners. The growth venture is typically better capitalized than is the low-growth venture. Financing for the venture will typically include a higher degree of debt financing and will be far more likely to use significant outside equity financing. It is common to have a number of investors, and some growth firms will use multiple sources of financing. Growth ventures will often have stock sold on the open market.

Growth ventures will tend to have an entrepreneur with at least some college experience. The entrepreneur will often have had managerial experience in another firm that may have been a growth firm. The firm's strategy will be based on significant strategic planning. As such it often is started based on some objectively determined opportunity. Strategic planning implies that the focus of the venture is on the future. The planning horizon may be five or more years rather than the typical one-year focus of the small business venture.

The growth venture may expand to a regional or national market, whereas the low-growth venture almost always serves either a local market or a small region. The growth venture may be started within a local market but with the intention to expand to a larger region or customer set as soon as the startup pains have subsided. The growth firm may or may not use acquisitions as a method of growth, but will constantly be studying avenues to achieve growth.

The Very High Growth Venture

A small subset of growth ventures is the high-growth venture. Although companies regularly featured in *Inc.* and other business magazines are typical of the very high growth companies in the United States, the number of these ventures is quite small as a percentage of the total number of ventures launched. Perhaps no more than 1 percent or 2 percent of all new ventures fit this category. Yet this is the epitome of entrepreneurship.

High-growth ventures differ from the more normal growth ventures primarily in the magnitude of the growth, the strength of the management team, and the sources of financing used to achieve the very rapid growth desired by the entrepreneurs. The high-growth venture often has a complete managerial team in place before the venture is launched. The managerial team will typically have a lead entrepreneur whose task is to oversee the entire operation of the venture. An idea person, often the developer of the product or service to be marketed, will be on the team, but this person may or may not be the lead entrepreneur. A third person on the team is often a financial expert. This person is in charge of securing adequate financing for the rapid growth envisioned for the venture.

The high-growth venture will make extensive use of outside funding. Although the entrepreneurial team will have significant funds invested, the majority of funding will come from outside the firm. In many cases, venture capitalists will be involved. Multiple sources of funding are the norm. These may include personal funding, bank funding, venture capital, private investors, state economic development funds, and public stock offerings.

The Distribution of Ventures

Figure 2-4 shows the distribution of businesses by size and growth rates. A very small proportion of the total number of businesses is made up of large corporations. The Small Business Administration (SBA) estimates that no more than 3 percent to 5 percent fall into that category. More than 95 percent of all businesses fall into the SBA's category of "small business," which includes all businesses with fewer than five hundred employees. The vast majority of these—perhaps 85 percent—are low-growth ventures, and most have fewer than twenty employees. Approximately 12 percent to 15 percent of businesses fall into the growth category, and a minute portion—1 percent or 2 percent—are high-growth ventures.

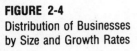

FIGURE 2-4
Distribution of Businesses
by Size and Growth Rates

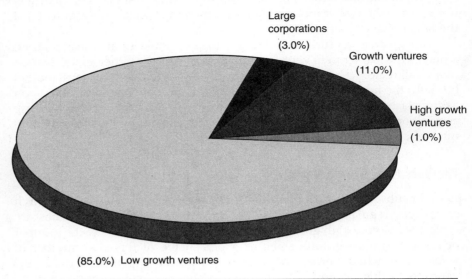

Large
corporations
(3.0%)

Growth ventures
(11.0%)

High growth
ventures
(1.0%)

(85.0%) Low growth ventures

The size of the venture should not be confused with growth rates. Large corporations may have thousands of employees and not be growing at all. Most large corporations have quite small *internal* growth rates, and the trend in recent years is toward downsizing. The growth among large corporations is predominantly via acquisitions. Similarly, small firms may be emerging growth ventures or they may be simply low-growth ventures that will never grow appreciably. Likewise, midsized firms may reflect past rapid growth, but they also may be very stable firms that have grown slowly over several decades.

Entrepreneurial Activity in the Ventures

Although it is difficult to measure entrepreneurial activity, new ventures require more than others. The amount of entrepreneurial activity varies over time and across the different levels of ventures. Even the smallest venture requires more entrepreneurship at the outset than it does later in the venture's operation. The planning, financing, and other activities associated with launching a venture require higher amounts of entrepreneurship during the critical launch period than after the business stabilizes. Spurts of activity occur any time the entrepreneur makes significant strategic changes.

The low-growth firm requires a modest amount of entrepreneurial activity at the time of launch and little after that. The only real entrepreneurial activity beyond the launch period occurs when the entrepreneur makes a significant change in the strategy for the venture. Since the venture is planned as a "small business," there will be little competitive jockeying or planning of new strategies. Little additional financing will be required other than seasonal or working capital loans from banks. Due to this low level of entrepreneurial activity, some writers do not include the small business within the purview of entrepreneurship.[7]

Growth ventures will require significant entrepreneurial activity at the time of launch with increases in the amount of entrepreneurship over time as the management team develops new ways to compete and new sources of financing to underwrite the desired growth. This increasing level of entrepreneurship reflects the need to continually increase the level of innovation in order to meet competitive needs. The increases may occur in somewhat stepwise fashion rather than continuously. This is due to both the random competitive changes in the environment and the tendency of the entrepreneur to make occasional changes in the firm's operation rather than keep the firm on an ever-increasing growth pattern. The high-growth ventures will require even more entrepreneurial activity because of the magnitude of the growth rate.

Figure 2-5 illustrates the amounts of entrepreneurial activity for the two types of ventures. In the diagram, assume that each of the ventures was conceived at the same time. Note that the launch dates differ because of the time required to assemble the necessary resources. The amount of entrepreneurial activity required to launch the venture is higher for growth ventures than for the intentionally small businesses. But more important is the amount of entrepreneurship that remains after the launch. In low-growth ventures, the amount of entrepreneurship declines shortly after the launch and stays low except for occasional changes in the business operations. In growth-oriented ventures, the amount of innovation declines somewhat after launch to absorb the venture's startup pains, but then rises more or less steadily.

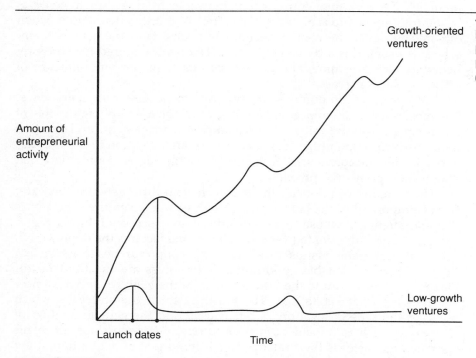

FIGURE 2-5
Entrepreneurial Activity in Low-Growth and Growth-Oriented Ventures

There are other significant characteristics shown in Figure 2-5. First, in each level there are bursts of entrepreneurial activity followed by "absorption periods." Absorption periods refer to temporary declines in innovative activity while the results of previous activity are assimilated into the venture's daily operations. Even for high-growth ventures, the amount of entrepreneurship varies over time. There are periods of intense entrepreneurial activity as the owners launch their ventures, make competitive changes, and prepare their ventures for even more growth. After each burst of activity, an absorption period follows. During this time the managerial team assimilates new activities into the venture, ensures control of operations, and assesses the potential of the implemented strategies.

The length of the absorption period is a function of both the growth level and the number of prior entrepreneurial thrusts. For example, the small business owner requires a long absorption period because of both limited managerial capabilities and limited desired growth. The growth-oriented entrepreneur may require a significant absorption period after the initial launch. Successive bursts of entrepreneurial activity will require a shorter absorption period because of prior learning.

SUMMARY

Entrepreneurship is the act of starting or growing a business through innovative, risk-assuming management. There are several key elements that are part of entrepreneurship, although they are present in varying degrees in different entrepreneurial situations. These elements include starting a business, being creative, managing growth, financing a venture, and assuming risks. Although all new ventures contain at least some entrepreneurship, the amount of entrepreneurship varies from venture to venture.

Entrepreneurship is a process, not a result. Entrepreneurship is action oriented. It is not the result of actions but consists of the actions themselves. As such it is a dynamic process. The tasks required for entrepreneurship vary over time, and no one set of actions nor one sequence of actions ensures success.

Entrepreneurship differs from corporate management in many ways. The most notable differences are the degree of risk assumption, the role of resources and opportunities, the makeup of management, and the tendency toward action rather than analysis. A rare exception to these differences is the intrapreneurial firm, which is the larger corporation that adopts entrepreneurial principles.

There are five components in the launch of an entrepreneurial venture. Each is important in the launch and growth of a new venture. The first is the entrepreneur, whose skills are critical for successful funding and launch of a growth-oriented venture. The second factor is the opportunity. Potential entrepreneurs must carefully analyze opportunities to assure that they are real, exploitable opportunities. Resources are the third factor. Financing is important to the future growth of the venture, and most new ventures are undercapitalized. The fourth factor is the structure, which refers to the type of legal organization used and the general method of competing, such as franchises, manufacturers, distributorships, or retailers. The final factor is the strategy. This is important in determining how the venture will compete.

Three sets of variables help determine whether or not a venture is likely to be launched. The antecedent factor consists of variables in a person's background or current job that make entrepreneurship appealing. The triggering or precipitating factor consists of variables that encourage the individual to take the steps necessary to actually launch the venture. These include being laid off from a job, moving to a new location, discovering or developing a new product, or a change in life-style. The enabling factor consists of those variables that allow a venture to be launched. These include an opportunity and necessary resources. The greater the number or strength of variables present in any of the three factors, the greater will be the likelihood that the venture will be launched.

Two broad types of ventures exist. The first is the typical small business venture that is started small with the intention of remaining small. The second type is the growth-oriented venture that is started with the intention of achieving sustained growth. The growth venture will be better capitalized and will typically have a developed competitive strategy. A small number of ventures are very high-growth ventures. These require major financing, a strong management team, and actions necessary to increase and maintain growth.

The amount of entrepreneurial activity a venture exhibits will be a function of the entrepreneur's desires and skills. This amount of activity will increase over time for growth ventures and will be much lower for low-growth ventures.

· ·

DISCUSSION QUESTIONS

1. Define entrepreneurship. Check definitions found in other sources. Are they similar?

2. What are the elements of entrepreneurship? Which is most important, if any? Why?

3. What is the significance of considering entrepreneurship as a process rather than as a result?

4. The five components of a venture launch are the entrepreneur, the opportunity, the structure, the resources, and the strategy. In what order should the entrepreneur determine the details of the remaining four elements?

5. Why is the "antecedent" factor called antecedent? Are variables in this category absolutely necessary?

6. Consider the triggering factor. Which triggering variables are likely to occur in your experience in the near future? Within five years?

7. Differentiate between a low-growth venture and a growth-oriented venture in terms of:

   • The size of the management team
   • The experience of the management team
   • The amount of analysis required to determine the feasibility of success
   • The amount of additional financing necessary
   • The likelihood that the venture will still be in operation five years from now and then ten years from now

8. Which is easiest to start, a low-growth venture or a growth-oriented venture? Why?

9. Consider some of the businesses in your hometown. Are they low growth or growth oriented? Are any of them high-growth oriented? What facts lead you to your conclusion?

10. Is it easy to differentiate between a growth venture and a high-growth venture? Why or why not?

EXERCISE   **EXERCISE 2-1**   Determining Your Entrepreneurial Likelihood

The following exercise will give you an idea of the likelihood that you will start a venture in the reasonably near future. It will not, of course, tell you that you *will* start a venture, or if you do, whether or not it will succeed. You can, however, compare yourself with another person to get a feel for the relative likelihood that you will someday become an entrepreneur.

Select two friends to complete the form with you. In order for the exercise to be most instructive, pick one other person from your class and a friend who is in a nonbusiness curriculum. Use a sheet of paper to record your responses. Then calculate a final score for each.

Let 0 = not important, 2 = minimal impact, 5 = somewhat important, 8 = significantly important, and 10 = a dramatic impact on your way of thinking.

Antecedent Factor

For each item below, indicate the extent to which the variable was or is important to you.

Variables	You	Classmate	Nonbusiness friend
Close relative was entrepreneur	_____	_____	_____
Friend grew up in family venture	_____	_____	_____
Worked for a small company	_____	_____	_____
Had a paper route or other part-time job for year or more	_____	_____	_____
Enjoy "doing" more than "studying"	_____	_____	_____
Enjoy creating things or ideas	_____	_____	_____
Have had managerial experience	_____	_____	_____
Others (list on separate sheet of paper)	_____	_____	_____
Total score for antecedent factor (A)	_____	_____	_____

Triggering Factor

Indicate the triggering variables that have occurred or are likely to occur in the relatively near future, using the same scale as above.

Laid off or fired from job	_____	_____	_____
Invented a new product	_____	_____	_____
Have a significant idea for a business	_____	_____	_____
Others	_____	_____	_____
Total score for triggering factor (T)	_____	_____	_____

Enabling Factor

Indicate your *ability* to launch a venture in the foreseeable future, using the same scale as above.

Have ready access to substantial capital	_____	_____	_____
Have significant knowledge of how to operate a business	_____	_____	_____
Have identified a specific need or target market for product/ service	_____	_____	_____
Have or can easily acquire facilities	_____	_____	_____
Others	_____	_____	_____
Total score for enabling factor (E)	_____	_____	_____

Now multiply your total scores for each factor.

$$A \times T \times E \underline{\hspace{1cm}} \times \underline{\hspace{1cm}} \times \underline{\hspace{1cm}} = \underline{\hspace{1cm}}.$$

Compare your score with your classmate's score and your nonbusiness friend's score. Are there significant differences? Can you explain the differences or lack of differences?

· ·

ENDNOTES

1. Peter F. Drucker, *Innovation and Entrepreneurship: Practice and Principles* (New York: Harper & Row, 1985).

2. Wayne Long, "The Meaning of Entrepreneurship," *American Journal of Small Business* (Fall 1983): 47–56.

3. This discussion is based loosely on Albert Shapero and Lisa Sokol, "The Social Dimensions of Entrepreneurship" in *Encyclopedia of Entrepreneurship*,

Calvin A. Kent, Donald L. Sexton, and Karl H. Vesper, eds. (Englewood Cliffs, N.J.: Prentice-Hall, 1988), 83.

4. Val Miskin and Jerman Rose, "New Venture Initiation: Factors Influencing Success," *The Journal of Small Business Strategy* 1, no. 2 (October 1990): 2.

5. Adapted from William D. Bygrave, "The Entrepreneurship Paradigm (II): Chaos and Catastrophes among Quantum Jumps?," *Entrepreneurship Theory and Practice* 14, no. 2 (Winter 1989): 8.

6. James W. Carland et al., "Differentiating Entrepreneurs from Small Business Owners: A Conceptualization," *Academy of Management Review* 9, no. 2 (April 1984): 354–59.

7. Ibid.

◆ Conveniesse, Inc. ◆

The Entrepreneurial Equation

Jason Stone, Yolanda Williams, and Sarah Tondeur met at an executive management seminar. The seminar was put on by a consortium of training, economic development, and educational organizations. The seminar, whose topic was "Managing the Future," was an in-depth, week-long program with dynamic lecturers and intensive breakout sessions. The program had gained some notoriety in the region and attracted more than three hundred participants from eight states and three Canadian provinces.

Because of the $800 per person fee plus hotel costs, virtually all who were there had been sent by their companies. Typically, the companies represented were medium-sized to large firms that had identified individuals who either had great potential or needed executive training to round them out and make them more productive. In any case, all the participants were ambitious and dedicated to getting all they could from the convention. During breaks, most seating areas were full of participants either discussing the seminar or networking with participants from other companies.

During many of the breaks and in the evenings, participants would stroll around the hotel area and shop in the hotel shops. It was not unusual that groups of participants would adjourn to one of the hotel bars or restaurants in the evening to relax and either continue discussions or simply meet for friendly conversation. It was in such a situation the first evening that Jason Stone, Yolanda Williams, and Sarah Tondeur met for the first time. Their discussion initially centered on the conference and what they were likely to realize from it. Other topics were then discussed, ranging from war and religion to politics, the economy, and their own goals in life.

The three sensed a camaraderie and stayed until the late hours of the evening after others had departed. Someone mentioned the dearth of shopping in the immediate area and, in particular, the need for a place to pick up something to eat late at night. One of them laughingly mentioned that at the end of this management seminar they would probably all be qualified to start their own business. Perhaps they should just start a convenience store that catered to hotel guests. Lighthearted discussion continued about their hypothetical dream store for travelers. Thinking that it would need to be a very upscale store, they even came up with a name for it—Conveniesse.

The next evening, Stone, Williams, and Tondeur continued their discussions about the world and its problems. The topic of the convenience store arose again, and the three realized that they had a mutual interest in someday opening a business. As discussion increasingly focused on starting a business, and particularly a retail business, they began to wonder if they might work together some day. After it became apparent that the three had some shared goals, they decided to take turns providing information about their backgrounds and current situation. In particular, the three were interested in assessing each other's true motivation and ability to start a venture. Each shared relevant information with the others.

Yolanda Williams: I'll go first. I was born right here in Buffalo. I attended an inner-city grade school, but my parents enrolled me in a parochial high school. It was quite an experience being one of three blacks in the entire school and also not being Catholic. But I survived and graduated in the top 25 percent of my class while being active in the debate team, music, and the French club. I attended SUNY (the State University of New York at Buffalo) on a minority scholarship majoring in marketing with a minor in French. In order to supplement my income, I worked as a waitress in one of the nicer restaurants here in Buffalo and eventually was made crew chief.

After graduation, I moved to New York City with my current employer, a major pharmaceutical company. I have been with them for eight years and received three promotions. The last promotion was to my current position of product manager within the over-the-counter drug lines. I like my work, but I don't particularly like New York City. Coming to this conference for a week is like a breath of fresh air. I haven't given much thought to starting a business, but I might consider it if the situation were right. I am pretty well tied to my present company and am happy to work there. The pay is good and the benefits are unbeatable. So it would take something really good to pull me away.

Jason Stone: My story is a little different. My parents owned a small business selling automotive parts. They assumed that I would join them in the business; I did not. I hated automotive parts. Upon graduation from high school in Dallas, I attended the University of Texas at Arlington with a major in English and a minor in business. I had no intention of going back into the auto parts business, and wanted to make a clean break, so I moved to Chicago. I got a job with a public relations firm and, after two years, moved to Detroit with a larger company. The company apparently has plans for me since they sent me to this seminar. But growing up in my parents' business must have had some effect. I keep having the urge to do something on my own—but not auto parts!

Sarah Tondeur: Well, as you can probably tell by my accent, I am a native of Montreal and have lived there virtually all my life. You can also see that I am several years older than either of you. My formal education beyond high school consists of secretarial training and a number of continuing education courses on accounting and tax preparation. I have run my own accounting and tax service for the past ten years. My children are grown, and I am divorced. My accounting service has been relatively profitable, but it has its ups and downs. This is a down period because tax season is over, and that is why I sent myself to this seminar. I recently merged the company with one across town that does similar work. We thought we could cut down on overhead and do more marketing. I'm not convinced that was a good idea, and if she would offer to buy me out, I would take her up on it.

Assignment

Analyze the three entrepreneurs' motivation and ability to launch a new venture using the entrepreneurship equation discussed in this chapter.

3 The Entrepreneur

LEARNING OBJECTIVES

After reading this chapter, you will be able to:

1. Define the term *entrepreneur*
2. Recognize typical characteristics of entrepreneurs
3. Identify entrepreneurial personality traits
4. Understand similarities between male and female entrepreneurs, minority and nonminority entrepreneurs, and successful and unsuccessful entrepreneurs
5. Describe the unique problems facing women entrepreneurs, minority entrepreneurs, and family business entrepreneurs
6. Differentiate between entrepreneurs who own low-growth ventures and those who own higher-growth firms
7. Understand the need for carefully developing an entrepreneurial team and advisory team

KEY TERMS

Entrepreneur

Entrepreneurial role model

Push/pull hypothesis

Entrepreneurial personality

Internal locus of control

Tolerance for ambiguity

Small business entrepreneur

Growth entrepreneur

Co-entrepreneur

CONSIDER THIS!

- What is "the right stuff" needed to be an entrepreneur?
- Think about some entrepreneurs or small business owners that you know. Describe their personalities. Are they just like anyone else except that they happen to run a business, or do they seem to have unique personalities?
- Can entrepreneurial characteristics be developed or are they innate?
- Entrepreneurs quite often have entrepreneurial role models.
- Many entrepreneurs would rather fail by themselves than work for someone else.
- Even though entrepreneurs share many characteristics, there is a great variety among entrepreneurs.

Entrepreneurs come in all shapes, sizes, colors, and backgrounds. They have different value systems, launch different types of ventures, operate them differently, and even end them differently. In fact, the differences among entrepreneurs may be as great as the differences between entrepreneurs and nonentrepreneurs.[1] At the same time, entrepreneurs do tend to share some common characteristics. This chapter will focus on many of the characteristics, motivations, and broad types of ventures launched by entrepreneurs. In addition to discussing characteristics attributable to most entrepreneurs, the chapter will examine the differences between

ENTREPRENEURIAL PROFILE

DAVID RANSBURG
L. R. Nelson Corporation

David Ransburg, chairman and chief executive officer of L. R. Nelson Corporation, typifies the growth-oriented entrepreneur. With a family background in business, Ransburg received his undergraduate degree in the engineering sciences from Purdue University. After college, he worked for IBM as a systems engineer and then went to Harvard, where he received an M.B.A. After Harvard, Ransburg joined Keene Corporation, an acquisition-oriented conglomerate, and later moved to Skyway Engineering, an aircraft research and development company.

Ransburg had been involved in several ventures and he wanted to buy a company that he could grow according to his own vision. L. R. Nelson, which was founded in 1911 and, made lawn sprinkling equipment, was the company David Ransburg identified. He purchased the company from Nelson's heirs in 1972. Since

then, Ransburg has added sixty new products to the L. R. Nelson line, and those products now account for 90 percent of current Nelson sales. Products range from the original product, The "Perfect Clinching Hose Mender," to electronic water timers and controllers.

New high-impact strength and corrosion-resistant plastics have replaced most of the original cast iron, zinc, and brass components, resulting in supe-

rior products at a significantly lower production cost. By applying new technology to the manufacturing process, the company also has been able to remain cost competitive with overseas manufacturers noted for their cheap but lower-quality products.

David Ransburg has no intention of selling the company. Rather, his goal is to continue to grow L. R. Nelson much as its customers might grow a carefully tended lawn. According to Ransburg, "Our aim is to enable the L. R. Nelson Corporation to complete the next twenty-five years and celebrate its centennial as the dynamic leader of the lawn care industry. We have the people and the technology to reach this goal and to create the necessary brand awareness and preference for our products."

SOURCE: L. R. Nelson Corporation. Used with permission

low-growth and higher-growth oriented entrepreneurs. Attention will then be given to some of the unique challenges facing women and minority entrepreneurs. Finally, the chapter will consider the need for a carefully developed entrepreneurial team.

DEFINITIONS OF THE ENTREPRENEUR

Experts tend to disagree on the meaning of the term *entrepreneur*. Some authors define an entrepreneur as the individual who is primarily responsible for gathering together the necessary resources to start a business.[2] The key to this definition is the start-up of the business. Whether the business later succeeds or fails is irrelevant.

Others define an entrepreneur as an individual who marshals the resources necessary to launch and/or grow a business that focuses on innovation and development of new products or services.[3] The importance of this definition is the tie between innovation and entrepreneurship. Individuals are not entrepreneurs simply because they have started a business; innovation must be present. This definition also recognizes that there may be entrepreneurs within a large organization or in the public sector. The definition that will be used throughout this text is: An **entrepreneur** is an individual who launches a venture and/or significantly improves it through innovative means. This parallels the definition of entrepreneurship in Chapter Two and leaves open the possibilities of both innovation and launch activities.

CHARACTERISTICS OF ENTREPRENEURS

As a group, entrepreneurs are both unique and diverse. Their similarities tend to separate them from nonentrepreneurs, regardless of race or sex. Yet entrepreneurs are a diverse group, with many differences among them.

Entrepreneurs have been studied a great deal with limited success. One reason for the limited success is that researchers have studied various aspects of entrepreneurial characteristics in a multitude of different settings. It is difficult, therefore, to reach absolutely defensible conclusions regarding "the right stuff" for entrepreneurs. An additional reason for the lack of unanimity regarding the nature of entrepreneurs is simply that entrepreneurs are like any other group of people. There are so many differences within the group that it is difficult to reach any firm conclusions about their similarities.

While realizing that entrepreneurs cannot be identified conclusively, it is still useful to study them in order to develop a clearer picture of the typical entrepreneur. As will be shown throughout this chapter, entrepreneurs tend to exhibit characteristics that set them apart from other managers and from the population in general. Thus, in the following sections the focus is on entrepreneurial tendencies rather than absolutes.

Entrepreneurs as a group also may *not* exhibit some characteristics that we assume they do. This is because we may be aware of a particular person who overemphasizes a given characteristic. Or it may be because entrepreneurs have found a place in the legend of American business just as cowboys did in the legend of the frontier. That legend is part fact and part fiction. But legends persist in the face of reality.

Entrepreneurial Backgrounds

Popular writing about entrepreneurs suggests that entrepreneurs were destined to start their own firms because of their upbringing. Entrepreneurship is not hereditary, of course, but many future entrepreneurs do have **entrepreneurial role models,** either family members or acquaintances who have influenced them during their developmental years. At least 40 percent of all entrepreneurs do come from families with entrepreneurial experiences.[4] An entrepreneur's children often hear the day's business discussed at the dinner table, may go to the business site while young, and

VENTURE PERSPECTIVE 3-1

JERRY ABRAHAMS

Jerry Abrahams did not grow up in an entrepreneurial family. In fact, his father was a traveling salesperson and was gone much of the time Jerry was growing up. His mother received her college degree before Jerry was born and stayed out of the workforce until he was about ten. She then returned to school, received her master's degree in biology, and began teaching at a community college.

But Jerry lived in an "entrepreneurial neighborhood." His best friend's father ran an auto repair shop, and Jerry spent hours watching cars being repaired. The next-door neighbor ran her own interior design business, and often hired Jerry as a gofer. The husband and wife across the street were both CPAs. Although Jerry was aware of the long hours they put in at their own accounting firm, he was also impressed with their resulting life-style. They had many of the amenities that his own family could not afford, and they also were able to set their own hours and take vacations when they wanted except, of course, during tax season. Jerry had spent many evenings during his high school and college years visiting with them about career opportunities.

Considering Jerry's influences, no one was surprised when he graduated from college with a degree in computer science, joined a major computer software firm for a year or so, became dissatisfied with it, and returned "home" to begin his own venture—a firm selling personal computers and packaged software to individuals and small businesses.

may work at the business during afternoons, weekends, or summers. The daughter or son of an entrepreneur cannot help but be influenced by the parent. If the entrepreneur's family was not the prime influence, then some other role model was often present as in Venture Perspective 3-1.

Entrepreneurs often had early experience as "budding entrepreneurs." A high proportion of entrepreneurs had a paper route as a teenager, and may have had a sidewalk lemonade stand as a child. They seemed, at an early age, to know the value of money.

Age

There is no ideal age at which to launch a venture. Figure 3-1 includes the results of a survey of almost three thousand entrepreneurs. Note that 88 percent of entrepreneurs launched their ventures between the ages of twenty and fifty. Almost 65 percent launched during their twenties or thirties. This time period is referred to as an entrepreneurial window. This is because before that time, most do not have sufficient experience or capital to launch a successful venture. Once individuals reach their forties, many are locked into a career with "golden handcuffs," a term referring to a salary/bonus/benefits package that is so good that a person will not leave even though the job may not be highly satisfying. Others, as they age, become more risk averse and do not want to risk savings on a venture that might fail. Still others are highly involved with children or community affairs and do not want to invest the time needed to begin a venture.

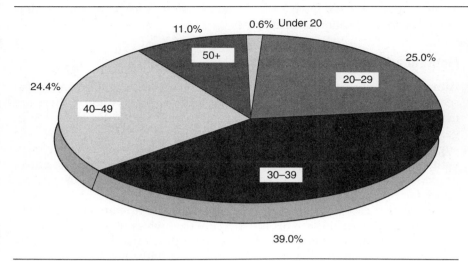

FIGURE 3-1
Age of Entrepreneur at
Time of Launch
Source: Arnold C. Cooper et
al., *New Business in America:
The Firms and Their Owners*
(Washington D.C.: The NFIB
Foundation, 1990), 19.

Using different data, Barbara Bird concluded that there are three groups of ages that yield large numbers of entrepreneurs.[5] The first group is made up of those in their early twenties who start a business soon after graduation from high school or college. A second group consists of those in their late twenties to early thirties who work for someone else for a while, but have the intention of starting a venture as soon as they have amassed the necessary capital and experience. A third group consists of those who had no intention of starting a venture but who encounter a compelling reason to do so later in life.

A significant subgroup in this latter category is those who start a venture after retiring. The data in Figure 3-1 showed that more than 10 percent of entrepreneurs started their ventures after age fifty. Some who retire early may launch a venture in their mid-fifties. A few will be sixty or more. To find examples of these, we need only to look at Ray Kroc who founded McDonald's, Sam Walton, founder of Wal-Mart, or Harland Sanders, founder of Kentucky Fried Chicken, who were all in their fifties or sixties when they began their most famous ventures.

Educational Level

The educational backgrounds of entrepreneurs are as varied as their ages. Some entrepreneurs are high school dropouts who either had to leave school to help out with family finances or who found school to be less exciting than the "real world." As a whole, however, entrepreneurs increasingly have a college education and many have graduate degrees. This, of course, parallels society in general. As society as a whole has become better educated, so have its entrepreneurs. Shortly after World War II, the median education for entrepreneurs was a high school degree. By the 1980s the median level of education was a college degree. In the high-tech field, the education level is even higher, with a substantial number of entrepreneurs having a master's degree in business or in one of the sciences. A small proportion even have a Ph.D., which is often in either a computer-related field or a scientific field.[6]

Motivation for Starting the Venture

Although we normally think of the entrepreneur as an opportunist who searches the environment for the best opportunity for a venture, there are many reasons why people become entrepreneurs. Robert Brockhaus suggested a **push/pull hypothesis** regarding entrepreneurial motivation.[7] He suggested that entrepreneurs are either pushed by necessity into starting a venture or pulled into it by opportunity and desire. In terms of the entrepreneurship equation introduced in Chapter 2, the triggering or precipitating factor can be either positive or negative.

In the first case, individuals are attracted to a venture and are "pulled" into starting the business. This is especially true when they start ventures in a field similar to that in which they have previously worked.[8] These entrepreneurs were not particularly dissatisfied with their previous jobs. And they were not forced out of them. They simply saw an opportunity or challenge to begin a similar venture on their own. For example, a person who works for a software firm for a few years and then leaves to start a new firm would fit the pull motivation. In fact, many Silicon Valley high-tech firms were started in exactly that way. These individuals were pulled into starting new ventures because they felt that they could do it better on their own than they could in their old firm.

Some industries are more conducive to attracting or pulling opportunistic entrepreneurs than others. The restaurant industry is an example. In spite of the high failure rate among restaurants, most facilities are not vacant for long. There always seems to be another individual who is lured into taking over the location by the possibilities of becoming rich in the food business.

The challenging opportunity, or pull, thesis also explains the motivation of the software entrepreneurs cited earlier. A large majority had college degrees with several having a master's or Ph.D. But more interesting is the fact that more than 40 percent had previous experience in software or software-related firms. More than half had worked in large firms, and nearly two-thirds of those even had equity participation in existing firms. Yet the attractiveness of high-tech entrepreneurship lured them away.[9]

Potential entrepreneurs are "pushed" into beginning their own venture when some negative event triggers the launch. Individuals may have had no initial interest in starting ventures, but something pushed them into it. That push may have been the result of being fired or laid off from a job. The person may have been in a dead-end job with no promise of either challenge or recognition. Sometimes the push was geographical in that the individual was forced to relocate. Many entrepreneurs were immigrants who came to the United States or to Canada to escape either a tyrannical government or a particular life-style. There are, for example, more than five thousand businesses in the United States owned by Vietnamese refugees.

Albert Shapero contended that, "Most entrepreneurs are D.P.s, displaced persons, who have been dislodged from some nice familiar niche, and are tilted off course."[10] In one of his studies, nearly two-thirds of the entrepreneurs noted that the primary impetus for starting their own business was negative. His D.P.s were either displaced from a job, displaced from a family, or displaced from a country or geographical region.

In the case of the D.P.s, there is no particular relationship between the type of business started and the business in which the entrepreneur previously worked. Some may have started a firm similar to their previous work experience not because of their assessment of the opportunity, but because it was the only field they knew. Others rejected the field altogether and began a venture in an unrelated field.

In summary, some individuals are pushed into starting a venture because of the lack of a long-term challenging job elsewhere. They see venture creation as an escape from an undesirable situation. Others are pulled into a venture by the opportunity that the venture provides. It is possible that both forces may be at work in a given situation. A person may be existing in a less-than-favorable situation, but not have an impetus to leave. If an opportunity arises, regardless of how desirable it is, it may be the springboard to entrepreneurship. Skeeter's Skateboards in Venture Perspective 3-2 is an example of both the push forces and the pull forces working together.

THE ENTREPRENEURIAL PERSONALITY

Probably no other aspect of entrepreneurship has been studied more than the traits and characteristics that make up the **entrepreneurial personality.** Factors such as a propensity to take risks, a need for achievement, a need for autonomy, willingness to work long hours, and willingness to delegate to others have been studied by scores of researchers. The paragraphs that follow review the findings of the studies of the entrepreneurial personality. It must be kept in mind, however, that entrepreneurs vary greatly in many ways. It is simplistic to assert that one particular personality type must be present in order to launch a successful venture. The characteristics discussed below, however, are the most salient and appear to be common to most entrepreneurs. They are: a tendency to take risks, a need for autonomy, a need to achieve, and tolerance for ambiguity.

Risk-Taking Tendency

Popular thought describes the entrepreneur as a lover of risk—a gambler who plays with high stakes. Research suggests that this is not typical.[11] Entrepreneurs, whether they are male or female, are only moderate or calculated risk-takers. Rather than being risk seekers, entrepreneurs are better characterized as *risk assumers*. They do not necessarily seek out high-risk ventures, but they are willing to assume a moderate amount of risk that would be normal for a venture launch.

When discussing risk, we also must qualify the discussion by noting the difference between *absolute* risk and *relative* risk. Most venture launches are risky. However, if the potential entrepreneur has just been fired or is in a dead-end job, the *relative* risk may be much smaller. This involves the concept of opportunity cost or opportunity risk. That is, what is the cost or

VENTURE PERSPECTIVE 3-2

. . . .

SKEETER'S SKATEBOARDS

Shirley McDonald grew up as a traditional 1950s child with traditional values. For women of that era, a job outside the home usually meant nursing, secretarial work, or teaching. McDonald chose teaching. She went to a southern university and began teaching in a suburban Dallas high school. But after eight years, she felt that she was becoming burned out in the classroom. In her view, the teaching profession had become nothing more than a legitimized, state-supported babysitting job. Her students had not grown up with the traditional work ethic that she had and many lacked a real desire to learn. She increasingly resented having to force students to do even minimal work.

At the same time, McDonald's nine-year-old son discovered skateboarding. He started out on a neighbor's board, talked her into buying him a

"cheap" $40 board, and became a reasonably accomplished boarder. With the obvious help from her son, McDonald noticed that many of the other kids had higher-quality boards, with specially ordered parts. The total price of the outfit (each part selected with the same care that a long-distance trucker uses to select the components of the semitrailer rig) could easily be $150 to $200. Accessories such as helmets, kneepads, gloves, and other equipment added to the price.

McDonald realized that some of the people buying these boards were the same unmotivated but affluent students who were not interested in learning in her class. And there were many of them. In checking out the source of these boards, she found that no one had opened a store strictly for skateboard enthusiasts. Feeling sure that a market was there,

and with her ever-increasing disdain for teaching, she decided to give it a try. McDonald resigned her teaching job after sufficiently researching the industry.

Using primarily her own savings and a bank loan, Shirley McDonald opened her first store that spring. The immediate, overwhelming success of Skeeter's Skateboards showed McDonald that she had struck gold at least for a while. With additional bank financing, she opened two more Skeeter's Skateboards in other affluent Dallas suburbs the following year.

Although the skateboard craze tapered off somewhat a few years later, business was still acceptable due to hard-core skateboard enthusiasts. As the skateboard market matured, McDonald prepared her stores for the next craze—in-line skates.

risk of continuing on the present course? If someone has just been fired or laid off, the risk of becoming an entrepreneur may be small compared to other choices. In the case of the dead-end job, staying in a boring, unchallenging job with no future may have a very high opportunity cost as compared with the financial and psychological rewards possible in one's own business.

Autonomy and Locus of Control

Like the popular conception of the entrepreneur as a high risk taker, popular thought characterizes the entrepreneur as a tough, independent breed with a compelling need to be in control. In this case, however, popular thought and research results are similar. Entrepreneurs do tend to have a great need for independence and they do tend to desire autonomy. They want to make their own decisions. In a study funded by the NFIB Foundation, 39 percent of entrepreneurs listed, "To avoid working for others," as either the most important or the second most important reason they started their own business.[12] This was equal to the number who reported that they wanted to start their venture to make more money than they could otherwise.

Entrepreneurs have a need to be leaders rather than followers. For example, if entrepreneurs serve on church committees or civic groups, they quite frequently will chair the committee rather than simply serve behind the scenes. They may prefer to be the driver rather than the passenger in a car. They feel that they can do most things better than others around them. This isn't so much a quest for outright power as it is a desire to be in control of situations in which they are involved.

Related to the need for autonomy is what psychologists call an internal locus of control. **Internal locus of control** is the feeling that individuals are personally in control of their own fate. On psychological tests, entrepreneurs typically score high on internal locus of control.[13] They believe that their success or failure is a result of their own actions rather than fate. They believe that they are personally involved in the success or failure of their ventures rather than being lucky.

Putting the need for autonomy and the internal locus of control together gives a picture of entrepreneurs who not only want to be in control, but who also feel that they will succeed or fail on their own. The autonomy and internal locus of control typify the entrepreneur perhaps more than any other characteristic.

Need for Achievement

David McClelland, in his classic book, *The Achieving Society*,[14] suggested that the achievement motivation is the underlying trait for economic development within nations. More important, it is one of the underlying dimensions of the entrepreneurial personality. In fact, this is one of the overriding motives behind the decision to become an entrepreneur. This, along with the need for autonomy, explains the decision to leave the safe confines of a corporation and risk personal capital in a venture. The entrepreneur is goal oriented and is motivated by the challenge to achieve objectives. The basic objective to be achieved may be profit or wealth, but it may also be to grow an organization, to market a new product, or to successfully establish a service.[15]

The need for achievement is also sometimes mistaken for a need for power. Entrepreneurs are not power-hungry, Machiavellian people who will do whatever is necessary to get what they want. In research studies, entrepreneurs have not been shown to have a high need for power.[16] However, their very high need for achievement may sometimes be confused with a need for power since the individuals seem to be totally involved with achieving some goal.

Tolerance for Ambiguity

Tolerance for ambiguity is the acceptance of uncertainty as a normal part of one's life. It is the ability to live with less than total knowledge about the environment. It is the willingness to begin a venture without knowing

whether it will succeed, how competitors will react, or exactly what resources might be needed.

Even though some entrepreneurs may give the impression of being
overly structured, as a rule they tend to be relatively tolerant of uncertain
situations and willing to work with a less-than-complete knowledge of
facts. Entrepreneurs tend to have much more tolerance for ambiguity than
do managers in corporations.[17] Managers tend to want a more structured
environment with sufficient information-gathering activities available to
make well-informed decisions. Entrepreneurs do not need that level of
certainty. Further, they typically do not have that luxury, even if they do
feel a need for it, because a startup situation is necessarily without all the
answers. Hence, the tolerance for ambiguity is both useful and necessary
for entrepreneurs.

As an example, consider the case of John Roberts. Roberts began a
venture making accessories for small fishing and pleasure boats. Through
personal contacts, magazines, visits with dealers, and actually looking at
boats in marinas, he identified a small number of manufacturers of similar
products. But there was no way to determine market share or even sales for
each company because most were small privately held firms just as his
was. The "fishing accessories" subcode in the Standard Industrial Classification (SIC) listings includes everything from lures to boat lights. Not
knowing how large the market was or how competitors would react to his
entry, Roberts was left with the decision of whether or not to go ahead and
produce what he thought were higher quality products. Undaunted by the
uncertainty, Roberts decided to press onward.

SUCCESSFUL VERSUS UNSUCCESSFUL ENTREPRENEURS

Differentiating between successful and unsuccessful entrepreneurs is a
difficult, if not impossible, task. Part of the problem is simply that there are
many differences among entrepreneurs as a group. For example, some
entrepreneurs are more outgoing than others, some are better educated
than others, some are more risk averse than others. Some prefer high tech,
some prefer low tech, some prefer manufacturing, while others prefer
retail or service. Since there are so many complicating variables, it is difficult to pinpoint a single set of characteristics that determines whether
success will be achieved in a given situation. An entrepreneur with a
particular set of educational, personality, and background characteristics
might be quite successful in one type of venture but would be unsuccessful
in another venture. Conversely, two quite different individuals might be
equally successful in similar ventures. Thus, there is no single set of characteristics that defines a *successful* entrepreneur.

An additional problem centers around the definition of success. As will
be seen in a later section, entrepreneurs differ markedly in regard to the
amount of growth desired. Entrepreneurs with different orientations toward growth have different views of success. One views success as a
pleasant, comfortable life-style, one views success as a growing business,
and another views success as a profitably harvested venture. Hence, if we
were to seriously study successful versus unsuccessful entrepreneurs, we

would first have to determine which *type* of entrepreneur we were considering. Thus, though there may, indeed, be differences in the personalities or backgrounds of successful and unsuccessful entrepreneurs, these differences are not pervasive enough to be meaningful.

LOW-GROWTH VERSUS HIGH-GROWTH ENTREPRENEURS

Chapter Two discussed low-growth ventures and high-growth ventures. The low-growth venture was started with the intention of staying small. The growth-oriented firm was begun with the intention of achieving substantial growth. Research has shown that different types of entrepreneurs may be attracted to the two kinds of ventures. These two types will be referred to as the small business entrepreneur or low-growth entrepreneur and the growth entrepreneur.

The Small Business Entrepreneur

The person who launches a low-growth venture is referred to in research studies variously as a craftsman-entrepreneur, a life-style entrepreneur, or simply as a small business owner.[18] Recognizing that anyone who starts a business is, in fact, an entrepreneur and that the business started may or may not be craft oriented, a better designation for this individual is a **small business entrepreneur.** However, the terms small business owner, small business entrepreneur, and low-growth entrepreneur may be used interchangeably.

Small business entrepreneurs often come from a blue-collar background with the father possibly working in the trades. They are exposed to work early in life, and their educations are technical in nature. The major personal goal for small business entrepreneurs is technical proficiency. Small business entrepreneurs tend to be very individualistic, identifying neither with top management nor with unions in previous work experience. Usually a specific event triggered the entrepreneurial launch. Funding for the business came from personal funds, family, or a partner. Due to their individualistic nature, small business entrepreneurs share a dislike for banks and other impersonal funding institutions. Small business entrepreneurs are not growth oriented, and they prefer personal selling based on their own expertise. Barbara Bird refers to the small business entrepreneur as "means-oriented." That is, the venture is a means to practicing a craft and to a comfortable living.[19] Although research is not conclusive, it appears that up to 85 percent of ventures may fall into this group.[20]

This type of entrepreneur epitomizes independent small business owners. They have their own ideas about how the business should be run, they often do not take advice well, and they are not interested in achieving corporate growth if it infringes on their life-style. They may, however, be very hard working, quite the expert in their fields, interact well with customers, and have a very firm grasp of where they want the business to go. Examples of the small business entrepreneur include a plumber, the founder of a dry cleaning establishment, some (but not all) franchises, an auto mechanic shop owner, or the owner of a small accounting/bookkeep-

VENTURE PERSPECTIVE 3-3

LARSON HEATING & AIR CONDITIONING

Ray Larson was about fifty years old when he started his first and only company. He had worked for twenty years as an installer for a local heating, ventilating, and air conditioning company. Larson was an excellent worker—highly skilled, extremely hard working, and dedicated to quality. But because of his dedication and his desire for quality, he finally tired of working with colleagues who were not nearly as dedicated as he was. He also tired of being told to shortcut operations by a boss who was more interested in short-run profits than in doing the best possible job. Starting his own business seemed to be a solution to all these problems.

When Larson Heating & Air Conditioning was launched, the company policy was to do a quality job with the highest of ethics. Larson's wife, Donna, was the office person while he was the technician. He spent long hours each day getting to each of his customers as quickly as possible. He sometimes refused projects if he did not believe in them. For example, Larson refused to install the newer heat pumps that many companies sold because he believed that they were neither as durable nor as effective in their colder climate as the conventional furnace and air conditioner combinations.

Although Larson taught his son the intricacies of heating and air conditioning, he never hired any permanent workers because he could not assure the customer of top-quality installation and repairs unless he did them himself. As a result, Larson Heating & Air Conditioning could not grow beyond the number of projects that Ray Larson could handle in his sixty- to eighty-hour weekly schedule. This was acceptable, however, because it provided his family with a comfortable life-style and allowed him to be proud of his work.

ing firm. Small business entrepreneurs are seldom found in the high-tech area, but occasionally may be found among computer hardware dealers and small software firms. Venture Perspective 3-3 profiles a small business entrepreneur.

The Growth Entrepreneur

Growth entrepreneurs are often referred to as "opportunistic entrepreneurs" or simply as entrepreneurs.[21] This entrepreneur not only launches a business, but also has a desire to see the business grow and develop. Rather than being means oriented, the growth entrepreneur is goal directed.[22] Growth entrepreneurs differ significantly from small business entrepreneurs in many ways. Growth entrepreneurs often come from white-collar families. Sometimes the family owned a business. Growth entrepreneurs usually received a well-rounded education and were involved in social and athletic activities. They had a variety of work experience rather than the narrow technical background of the small business entrepreneur. They had a number of role models, and they tended to identify with management rather than with a union. Growth entrepreneurs may have planned to start a business for some time and were willing to use any available capital sources that did not involve their giving up control of the company. They actively market their business rather than using the small business entrepreneur's personal selling methods. They desire growth and possibly diversification as long as it does not take them too far away from their original business. They tend to be more forward thinking than low-growth owners and may be less concerned with structure and control.

Charles Ginn and Donald Sexton found that growth entrepreneurs differ markedly from low-growth entrepreneurs regarding their personality types. They found that the growth entrepreneurs tended much more to be intuitive thinkers and were more disposed to a future orientation than were their slow-growth counterparts.[23] Growth entrepreneurs, like small business entrepreneurs, work long hours for the benefit of the company. But the nature of the work may be different. Small business entrepreneurs work, to a large extent, in the operations end of the business. Growth entrepreneurs delegate much of the operations duties and usually have staff managers in most areas. They may be involved with the operations of the business, but that involvement is of a policy nature rather than actual hands-on efforts. They stay close enough to the operations to maintain control, but seldom are involved in the actual process except to keep on top of things. Thus, growth entrepreneurs have more time to spend in ensuring that the desired growth is attained.

As before, there are not unequivocal figures regarding the percentage of growth entrepreneurs, but one author estimates that 12 percent to 15 percent fall into this category.[24] Examples of growth entrepreneurs are frequently found among franchised food outlets where a single person may own several stores or an entire territory. They may also be found in growing manufacturing firms, retail stores, or service companies. Table 3-1 summarizes the differences between the two types of entrepreneurs.

Characteristic	Small Business	Growth	
Family background	Blue collar	White collar	**TABLE 3-1**
Education	Technical	Broad	Differences among Entrepreneurial Types
View of risk	Risk-avoider	Moderate or calculated risk-taker	
View of planning	Does little long-range planning	Plans for the future	
View of growth	Not desired	Moderate to rapid growth desired	
View of harvest	None until near retirement	May or may not have harvesting as a goal	
View of delegation	Does not delegate well	Delegates operational control but monitors closely until the firm is larger	
View of funding	Distrusts outside sources but may use bank financing	Uses multiple sources depending on rate of growth desired	
View of success	Comfortable living	Profitable, competitive force or profitable harvest	

The High-Growth Entrepreneur

A small subset of the growth entrepreneur category is the high-growth entrepreneur. One textbook referred to the high-growth entrepreneur as a "promoter."[25] These entrepreneurs use all means possible to grow the venture as fast as possible. High-growth entrepreneurs share many of the background characteristics of the growth entrepreneur. They tend to be highly educated, often with an MBA degree from a good school. They are risk-takers, but not uncalculated risk-takers. They willingly use multiple sources of financing for ventures. They see as their primary goal the creation of value, the bringing of innovation to the marketplace, and the maximization of return to the investors. They may have a number of ventures on-line simultaneously.

Earlier thought suggested that the high-growth entrepreneur was interested in growing one venture as fast as possible, harvesting it, and using the funds to start another venture. This launch, grow, and harvest cycle would be kept going as long as possible. According to an article in *Inc.* magazine, this may no longer be true.[26] Curtis Hartman tracked down the members of the 1983 *Inc.* 100, the one hundred fastest growing privately held companies in 1983. He found that in 1990, seven years later, more than half of the companies were still run by the same people who started them.

WOMEN, MINORITY, AND FAMILY BUSINESS ENTREPRENEURS

Entrepreneurs face a number of problems associated with launching a business such as lack of financing, inadequate planning, and lack of managerial experience. Some groups of entrepreneurs, however, face additional problems. In particular, women and minority entrepreneurs have historically endured the problems of discrimination and the inability to be taken seriously by financiers, suppliers, and customers. Family business entrepreneurs, whether male or female, have the additional constraint that the needs of a family must be considered along with the needs of the business.

Women Entrepreneurs

The number of women-owned businesses grew from 2,612,621 in 1982 to 4,114,787 in 1987, a 57.5 percent increase. Sales and receipts grew from $98.3 billion in 1982 to $278.1 billion in 1987, a 184 percent increase.[27]

The primary reason for growth in the number of women-owned ventures can be traced ultimately to the 1970s. During this decade, an unprecedented number of women moved out of the traditional roles of housewife, teacher, nurse, and secretary. The dramatic change in values coupled with the large increases of entrepreneurial-aged women from the earlier baby boom led to a major increase in the number of women who were potential entrepreneurs. Some became entrepreneurs immediately after high school or college. Some went the corporate route and then moved into entrepreneurship. Some raised families and then started their own ventures. Some took over ventures left by husbands or fathers. Others started their own from scratch.

Similarities among Male and Female Entrepreneurs

Research studies have found that there are more differences between *entrepreneurial* women and *nonentrepreneurial* women than there are between men and women who are entrepreneurs. For example, entrepreneurial women are more risk-taking and more assertive than nonentrepreneurial women. Female entrepreneurs have a more internal locus of control than women in general. Robert Masters and Robert Meier found no difference in risk-taking propensity of male and female entrepreneurs.[28] Ellen Fagenson and Lyn Coleman, in a study of entrepreneurial values, found only three significant differences between male and female entrepreneurs out of twenty-nine items tested.[29] Donald Sexton and Nancy Bowman-Upton found that women scored higher than men in willingness to accept change and the need for autonomy and lower than men in energy level and risk-taking. There were no significant differences in the other psychological scales tested.[30]

The very slight differences in the research results tend to refute any sexual stereotyping that would indicate that women are psychologically less effective than men in managing and growing business ventures. The significance of this is that entrepreneurial tendencies are pervasive. Even though there are certainly many differences among entrepreneurs, as a group they are much more similar than we might think.

Problems Encountered by Women Entrepreneurs

The previous section suggested that there are few differences between the personalities of male and female entrepreneurs. Similarly, there are few differences today in the education that women and men receive. Yet women face a number of problems that men do not typically face.

Banks and other financing institutions historically resisted working with women entrepreneurs and either subtly or overtly discriminated in lending practices.[31] For example, in a survey of bank loan officers, Holly Buttner and Benson Rosen found that characteristics normally attributed to successful entrepreneurs were more commonly ascribed to men than to women. A second problem with financing is that most women launch service or retail ventures, and these businesses typically have more trouble obtaining financing than manufacturing firms do. Fortunately, some of these concerns are waning. Younger women are better educated now and often have both more relevant education and more job experience. Anti-discrimination laws have reduced the overt discrimination against women among lending agencies. Further, some lenders now have female loan officers, signalling their commitment to women-owned ventures both internally and to potential clients. Venture Perspective 3-4 discusses Kim Howard, a bank loan officer. She simply does her job and really has no idea of the extent to which her presence affects entrepreneurship among women in the community. But the fact that she is available may encourage some women to seek her out.

VENTURE PERSPECTIVE 3-4

• • • • • • • • • • • • •

KIM HOWARD
Community Bank of Greater Peoria

Kim Howard received a B.S. degree from the University of Iowa in the early 1980s, played team handball in the 1984 Olympics, and received her M.B.A. from Bradley University in 1986. While working on her M.B.A. degree, she was first a graduate assistant in Bradley's Small Business Institute program and then assistant director of its Small Business Development Center. Upon finishing the degree, Howard was named director of the center. In these positions, she developed an awareness of small business owners and their typical problems. She could determine relatively easily whether an entre-

preneur had a good idea and the management skills to bring the idea to market. In 1987, Howard was hired as a loan officer for Community Bank of Greater Peoria, the newest bank group in Peoria. She was the first female loan officer of that bank and one of few in the city.

In her role as loan officer and now as assistant vice president, Kim Howard does not go out of her way to seek out women-owned ventures, regardless of the quality of their loan package. She also does not give special consideration to women who may feel that they deserve favorable treatment

simply because they are women. On the other hand, Howard does attempt to stay visible in the community. She served a term as a chamber of commerce ambassador, meeting individually with members to keep them informed of chamber activities and to keep the chamber current on business needs. She is serving her second term on the private industry council, which works with businesses in the area. She also willingly speaks about bank lending to university entrepreneurship classes and to small business seminars.

SOURCE: Personal interview. Used with permission.

An additional problem that women entrepreneurs face is work/family stress. The popular press has allocated considerable space to the problems of working women and their impact on families. Some scholarly research is now being done to address the relationships between business ownership and family stress. Stoner, Hartman, and Arora found that there is considerable overlap between the demands of the business and the demands of the family. Two significant findings are of particular interest. First, the amount of family stress is *not* a strong function of the number of hours spent with the business. A stronger relationship exists between the satisfaction with the business and the happiness within the family. Those entrepreneurs whose businesses were performing well and equal to or greater than their expectations experienced less home stress than those whose ventures were not doing well. In addition, they found that women business owners experienced more life satisfaction and less stress than did women managers in corporations.[32] The reason is that business owners can control their lives more than corporate managers. They have more flexibility to schedule their hours as desired. Small children can sometimes even be taken to the business, and this would not be possible in a normal management situation. Some women entrepreneurs can also work totally or partially out of their home. Again, this can relieve some of the family stress.

Minority Entrepreneurs

Minority-owned ventures also grew between 1982 and 1987 at a rate higher than the national average. Minority-owned enterprises totaled 1,213,750 in 1987, a 63.7 percent increase over 1982. Sales and receipts were $77.8 billion, a 126 percent increase from 1982. Minority enterprises tend to be in the transportation, services, retail, and agricultural industries with less concentration in manufacturing, mining, construction, or financial sectors. Like most ventures, minority-owned ventures are small, with 80 percent having no employees besides the owner. However, those with employees increased by 87 percent from 1982 to 1987.[33]

Table 3-2 and Figure 3-2 illustrate statistics for the different categories of minority-owned ventures. Table 3-2 shows the numbers of minority firms by race and gender, and the percentage change since 1982. Figure 3-2 shows minority-owned firms by industry division in 1987.

As with male and female entrepreneurs, there are more similarities than differences among minority and nonminority entrepreneurs.[34] And like female entrepreneurs, minority entrepreneurs—especially black and Hispanic entrepreneurs—have faced discrimination and other problems in launching their ventures. The success of changes made to correct these problems has varied somewhat with differing political situations. With government pressure to use more minority suppliers, and with training workshops designed to overcome the lack of entrepreneurial expertise, the number of minority suppliers increased significantly during the 1980s. Many of those gains were threatened in the late 1980s and early 1990s by recessionary times, the decline in defense spending, and decreased pressure from the government to include minority suppliers.[35]

Family Business Entrepreneurs

A vast majority of new and small ventures are considered family businesses. More than 90 percent of all businesses are classified as small businesses, and most of these would also be considered family businesses. Thus, the category of family business entrepreneur is a large one, indeed.

TABLE 3-2 Minority Enterprises by Race and Gender

Source: *Survey of Minority-Owned Business Enterprises* (Washington, D.C.: Bureau of the Census, U.S. Department of Commerce, 1987), 2.

Minority	Male	Female	Total	Percent change since 1982
Black	265,889	158,278	424,165	37.6
Hispanic	307,348	115,025	422,373	80.5
American Indian & Alaska Native	15,072	6,308	21,380	57.5
Asian & Pacific Islander	243,442	111,889	355,331	89.3
Total (all)	825,443	388,309	1,213,750	63.7

Note: Detail in this table does not add to total because of duplication of some firms. Firms that were owned equally by two or more minorities are included in the data for each minority group but counted only once at total levels.

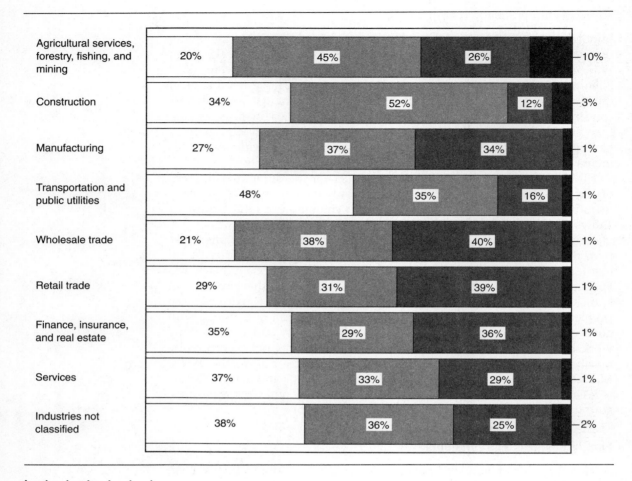

FIGURE 3-2

Minority-Owned Firms by
Industry Division: 1987

Source: *Survey of Minority-
Owned Business Enterprises*
(Washington, D.C.: Bureau of
the Census, U.S. Department
of Commerce, 1987), 8.

The significance of the family business entrepreneurs is that they face
a set of constraints that the nonfamily venture does not. Family businesses
reflect the overlap between the demands of the family and the demands of
the venture. The success or failure of the family business directly affects the
livelihood of the family. Spouses and children of the entrepreneur become
entwined in the problems of the venture. If the business is launched by
more than one person, and each has family responsibilities, then the busi-
ness/family relationships become even more complicated.

Family ventures will be discussed throughout this text. In this discussion of entrepreneurs, it should be noted that there are no personal differences between family business entrepreneurs and nonfamily entrepreneurs other than family involvement. Yet, the problems and stressors faced
by the family business entrepreneur create concerns for both the individual
and the family. The individual's role as an entrepreneur often conflicts
with the role as a parent or a spouse or other family member. Decisions
made by family business entrepreneurs must consider the interrelationship
between the family system and the business system. This is especially true
when the venture involves both spouses as discussed below.

Co-entrepreneurs

The term **co-entrepreneur** refers to ventures run by a husband/wife team. Businesses with both spouses involved have existed for years. Jointly owned ventures, however, have increased 63 percent between 1980 and 1986. In addition to the number of jointly owned businesses increasing more rapidly than before, the role that each spouse plays has changed. In earlier years, the husband ran the venture and the wife played a lesser role of being either the company's bookkeeper or perhaps being on the sales floor of a retail firm. Increasingly, however, there are examples of ventures that are truly jointly run by both spouses as partners.

In a co-entrepreneur situation, both spouses have typically had previous managerial or professional experience before joining forces to launch the venture. The two spouses may work together on all tasks or, more likely, they will each have particular skills to offer the partnership. *Inc.* magazine recently featured one such couple.[36] Karl Friberg was a Harvard Business School graduate and an "up-and-comer" in Citibank's international banking division. Lyn Peterson was an interior designer. They now own Motif Designs, a $10 million designer and manufacturer of upscale wallpaper and home fabrics. They run the business out of their home and a large warehouse. Karl's expertise is in the financial and growth aspects of the venture while Lyn's is in designing the products. Their house is often the target of new products, with some rooms being redecorated almost daily to accommodate photographing. In spite of the close proximity of their business, they attempt to separate the business part of their life from the family part by agreeing not to discuss business after 5 P.M. or on weekends.

Three caveats exist for being successful co-entrepreneurs. First, just as in any partnership, there should be a *clear sense of direction* for the venture with a well-written business plan and partnership agreement. Second, the two spouses should have a *clear understanding of the role each will play.* They should decide which types of decisions will require a joint decision compared to those that will be made by one or the other. They should establish if and when each has veto power over the other's ideas. They should also agree about the time each will spend with the venture. The third caveat is that the spouses should agree, as the co-entrepreneurs in Motif Designs did, that they *will not take work home with them.* In this way, the family and business concerns will not overlap to the detriment of either. This will also allow them to spend personal time with each other as individual people rather than as partners. This agreement also formally allows time for children and other activities rather than having to squeeze in time between business discussions. Establishing family time reduces the day-to-day stress in the family and thereby allows for better absorption of stress caused by the business venture.

ASSEMBLING THE ENTREPRENEURIAL TEAM

The actual makeup of the entrepreneurial team assembled for a venture is partially a function of the nature of the venture and partially a function of the amount of growth desired. The structure of the entrepreneurial team should be determined before the venture is begun. Indeed, the strength of a venture may depend heavily on the type of team assembled.

If a low-growth venture is planned, the founding entrepreneur will usually be the only person on the "team." Since growth is not desired, the complexity of the venture does not require additional team members other than those that may be hired by the founding entrepreneur. The additional members are not required by the demands of a small business venture, and the small business entrepreneur often will not want to share power or profits with another person. Interestingly, many small business ventures start out as partnerships. But within a few months, one partner often leaves the firm. This is because the small business venture neither required two partners nor provided enough financial return for two.

The growth venture requires a more formalized venture team. Typically, there will be a lead entrepreneur. This person, however, may either associate with a partner or immediately hire additional high-level staff to help manage the growth. In a growth venture, one of the team members will typically be the planner for the group. Some refer to this person as a visionary who has in mind the long-range potential for the firm. Additional team members will come from either the financial, marketing, or operational areas in order to complement the strengths of the lead entrepreneur.

ASSEMBLING AN ADVISORY BOARD

Seldom does a single entrepreneur have sufficient knowledge and skills without the help of others. Even those ventures with an entrepreneurial team can have members who still sometimes suffer from myopia. This is because they are so intent on the operation of the business that they fail to see the larger picture.

It is important, then, that entrepreneurs solicit the wisdom of outsiders to help guide the overall strategy of the firm. Most successful entrepreneurs establish an advisory board of some type to provide support and guidance. The particular composition and formality of the advisory board is not important. Some ventures, especially growth-oriented corporations, will have a duly constituted board of directors whose members may also own stock in the company. Smaller companies may have an informal board that meets periodically. Individual board members may be selected from key internal managers, friends who own their own ventures, community leaders, and other acquaintances. The compensation of board members, if any, is determined by the entrepreneur. In smaller firms, board members may serve gratis. Other firms may pay expenses or a small honorarium. Still others may put board members on retainer.

The more important issue is the role the advisory board plays. Advisory boards should serve as a sounding board for the entrepreneur's ideas. Board members can be objective since they are outsiders. Depending on the structure, they may or may not have the power to override the entrepreneur's decision. However, the value of the advisory board comes not from a veto power but from the advice given to the entrepreneur. The advisory board also often assists with business contacts. Sometimes board members can generate sales leads, find suppliers, and direct the entrepreneur toward sources of funding. These contacts, by themselves, are worth the effort of the entrepreneur to establish the advisory board.

. . . .

This chapter has presented the entrepreneur as a relatively independent, achievement-motivated individual who is a moderate or calculated risk taker. Entrepreneurs often begin their first venture while they are in their twenties or thirties, although a number begin later in life. Most entrepreneurs are inner directed; that is, they believe they are in command of their fate. They are achievement motivated, have a high need for autonomy, and have high tolerance for ambiguity or uncertainty. They are increasingly higher educated, especially if they start high-tech related firms.

Some entrepreneurs are "pushed" into starting a venture because they were fired or laid off from their jobs, because of a geographic move, or for other reasons that form a negative encouragement to start a venture. Dissatisfaction with jobs or the role of homemaker causes many women to launch their first venture. Other entrepreneurs are "pulled" into starting a venture by a potential opportunity. Many high-tech entrepreneurs were attracted to their venture by the opportunities of the fast-growth computer-related industry.

Differentiating successful entrepreneurs from unsuccessful entrepreneurs is difficult because of the inability to unequivocally define the term *successful*. However, there are salient differences between high-growth entrepreneurs and low-growth entrepreneurs.

Small business entrepreneurs typically start ventures that remain relatively small. The business is seen as a means of earning a comfortable living, and growth of the business is neither planned nor desired. Growth entrepreneurs are far more growth oriented and take the necessary planning steps to achieve that growth. Low-growth entrepreneurs have different philosophies regarding delegation of authority, financing, risk, and their definition of success.

Women and minority entrepreneurs tend to be more like their white male entrepreneurial counterparts than they are like other women or minorities, and they tend to start ventures for the same reasons. They sometimes have trouble gaining financing and other assistance because of discrimination, inadequate training, or the type of venture they start.

Family business entrepreneurs, though little different from nonfamily entrepreneurs, face added challenges because of the relationship between the family and the business. Co-entrepreneurs—husband/wife combinations—are increasing in numbers. These combinations offer substantial advantages if the work/home responsibilities can be kept separate.

Entrepreneurs must consider the makeup of their venture team as part of the pre-launch planning. Growth ventures require experienced team members who can make significant contributions to the success of the venture. The lead entrepreneur must determine exactly which managerial positions are necessary and what skills are needed to balance the strengths and weaknesses of other team members. Finally, every venture should have an advisory board of some type to give objective advice to the owner and to provide contacts with others.

. . . .

DISCUSSION QUESTIONS

1. Why are entrepreneurs similar in their basic personality characteristics?

2. An entrepreneurial role model has been shown to be evident in many entrepreneurs' backgrounds. Does this relationship exist more for entrepreneurs than for other careers?

3. Discuss the "entrepreneurial window." Why is it important? What would you say to someone who wants to start a venture but whose age is outside the time frame suggested by the window?

4. It has been suggested that *successful* is a relative term. What does this mean? Why is it important?

5. The "push" and "pull" hypotheses explain most first-time venture launches. Will there likely be only a push or only a pull rather than a combination of the two?

6. Speculate whether women have a harder time starting a business in your area than men do. Is the environment changing?

7. Interview your classmates. Do they want to become entrepreneurs? Who in your group seems closest to having an entrepreneurial personality as discussed in this chapter?

8. Would an entrepreneur make a good manager in a large corporation? Why or why not?

9. Low-growth entrepreneurs and growth-oriented entrepreneurs were discussed. What are the differences in education between small business entrepreneurs and growth entrepreneurs? Why are small business entrepreneurs more risk averse than are growth-oriented entrepreneurs?

10. Would a growth entrepreneur be content in a small business venture? What would you expect to happen if this occurred?

11. The chapter discussed the fact that the motivation to start ventures differs between low-growth entrepreneurs and high-growth entrepreneurs. Do the motivational differences account for the differences in growth?

12. What factors are most important for a lead entrepreneur to consider in selecting the rest of the entrepreneurial team?

13. Why is it important for entrepreneurs to solicit the help of an advisory team? Should all team members be from outside the venture?

. . . .

EXERCISES

EXERCISE 3-1   Personality Assessment

Most campuses have a testing or diagnostics center where personality and interest tests are given. Arrange to take one or more of the assessment tests that provide personality or value profiles. Then discuss the results with the administrator of the tests. How do your results compare with those characteristics suggested in the chapter for small business entrepreneurs, growth entrepreneurs, or managers?

EXERCISE 3-2   Association of Collegiate Entrepreneurs

The Association of Collegiate Entrepreneurs (ACE) is a national organization headquartered at Wichita State University that is designed for college students who either have a business or have an interest in someday starting a business. If your school does not have one, see your instructor, department chair, or dean to investigate starting one. If there is an ACE chapter on your campus, interview ACE members to learn about their backgrounds and career aspirations.

EXERCISE 3-3   Business-Family Stressors

Divide the class into two groups. The first group should be those who grew up around family businesses. The other group should be those who did not have early experiences in family ventures. Using brainstorming or other idea generation techniques, make a list of examples of business/family stress. Discuss within each group the impact of each. Then bring the two groups back together to discuss the differences in the results.

ENDNOTES

1. William B. Gartner, "A Conceptual Framework for Describing the Phenomenon of New Venture Creation," *Academy of Management Review* 10, no. 4 (October 1985): 696–706.

2. Arthur H. Cole, *Business Enterprise in the Social Setting* (Cambridge, MA: Harvard University Press, 1959); Norman R. Smith, *The Entrepreneur and His Firm: The Relationship Between Type of Man and Type of Company* (East Lansing, MI: Bureau of Business and Economic Research, Michigan State University, 1967).

3. J.A. Schumpeter, *The Theory of Economic Development* (New York: Oxford University Press, 1961).

4. John R. Thorne and John G. Bell, "Entrepreneurs and Their Companies: Smaller Industrial Firms in the Pittsburgh Metropolitan Area," in *Frontiers of Entrepreneurship Research 1981*, edited by Karl Vesper (Wellesly, MA: Babson College, 1981), 65–83; Robert D. Hisrich and Marie O'Brien, "The Woman Entrepreneur from a Business and Sociological Perspective," ibid., 21–39; Donald R. Sexton and Calvin A. Kent, "Female Executives and Entrepreneurs: A Preliminary Comparison," ibid., 40–55.

5. Barbara J. Bird, *Entrepreneurial Behavior* (Glenview, IL: Scott, Foresman, 1989), 69, 70.

6. Richard D. Teach, Fred A. Tarpley, Jr., and Robert G. Schwartz, "Who are the Microcomputer Software Entrepreneurs?" in *Frontiers of Entrepreneurship Research 1985*, edited by J. H. Hornaday et al. (Wellesly, MA: Babson College, 1985), 435–51; Orvis F. Collins, David G. Moore, and Darab B. Unwalla, *The Enterprising Man* (East Lansing, MI: Bureau of Business and Economic Research, Michigan State University, 1964); Thomas M. Begley and David P. Boyd, "Company and Chief Executive Officer Characteristics Related to Financial Performance in Smaller Business," in *Frontiers of Entrepreneurship Research 1985*, edited by J. H. Hornaday et al. (Wellesly, MA: Babson College, 1985), 452–67.

7. Robert H. Brockhaus, "The Effect of Job Dissatisfaction on the Decision to Start a Business," *The Journal of Small Business Management* 18, no. 1 (January 1980): 37–43.

8. Charles R. Stoner and Fred L. Fry, "The Entrepreneurial Decision: Dissatisfaction or Opportunity," *The Journal of Small Business Management* 20, no. 2 (April 1982): 39–44.

9. Teach, "Who are the Microcomputer Software Entrepreneurs?" 435–51.

10. Albert Shapero, "The Displaced, Uncomfortable Entrepreneur," *Psychology Today*, November 1975, 84.

11. John A. Hornaday and John Aboud, "Characteristics of Successful Entrepreneurs, *Personnel Psychology* 24 (1971): 141–53; Donald R. Sexton and Calvin A. Kent, "Female Executives and Entrepreneurs: A Preliminary Comparison," Vesper, 40–55; Robert H. Brockhaus, "The Psychological and Environmental Factors Which Distinguish the Successful from the Unsuccessful Entrepreneur: A Longitudinal Study," *Academy of Management Proceedings* (1980), 368–72; Bruce Kemelgor, "A Longitudinal Analysis of the Transition from 'Organization Man' to 'Entrepreneur,' " *Academy of Management Proceedings* J.A. Pearce II and R. B. Robinson, Jr., eds., (1985), 67–70.

12. Arnold C. Cooper et al., *New Business in America: The Firms and Their Owners* (Washington, D.C.: NFIB Foundation, 1990), 18.

13. Robert H. Brockhaus, "The Psychology of the Entrepreneur," in Calvin A. Kent, Donald R. Sexton, and Karl H. Vesper, eds., *Encyclopedia of Entrepreneurship* (Englewood Cliffs, N.J.: Prentice-Hall, 1988), 43.

14. David C. McClelland, *The Achieving Society* (New York: D. Van Nostrand Company, 1961).

15. Cooper et al., *New Business in America*, 18.

16. Brockhaus, "The Psychology of the Entrepreneur," 42.

17. Jean Schere, "Tolerance for Ambiguity as a Discriminating Variable Between Entrepreneurs and Managers," *Academy of Management Proceedings*, Kae Chung, ed., 1982.

18. Smith, *The Entrepreneur and His Firm*; Norman R. Smith, Gary McCain, and Audrey Warren, "Women Entrepreneurs Really Are Different: A Comparison of Constructed Ideal Types of Male and Female Entrepreneurs," Vesper, 68–77; Norman R. Smith and John B. Miner, "Motivational Considerations in the Success of Technologically Innovative Entrepreneurs: Extended Sample Findings," Hornaday, 482–88.

19. Barbara J. Bird, *Entrepreneurial Behavior*, 18.

20. Ibid., 337.

21. Smith, McCain, and Warren.

22. Bird, *Entrepreneurial Behavior*.

23. Charles W. Ginn and Donald L. Sexton, "A Comparison of the Personality Type Dimensions of the 1987 *Inc.* 500 Company Founders/CEOs With Those of Slower-Growth Firms," *Journal of Business Venturing* 5 (1990): 313–26.

24. David Birch, "Matters of Fact," *Inc.*, April 1985, 31–42.

25. Howard H. Stevenson, Michael J. Roberts, and H. Irving Grousbeck, *New Business Ventures and the Entrepreneur*, 2d ed. (Homewood, IL: R. D. Irwin, Inc., 1985).

26. Curtis Hartman, "Whatever Happened to the Class of '83," *Inc.*, December 1990, 122–35.

27. *1987 Survey of Women-Owned Businesses* (Washington, D.C.: Bureau of the Census, U.S. Department of Commerce, 1987): 7.

28. Robert Masters and Robert Meier, "Sex Differences and Risk-Taking Propensity of Entrepreneurs," *Journal of Small Business Management* 26, no. 1 (January 1988): 31–35.

29. Ellen A. Fagenson and Lyn L. Coleman, "What Makes Entrepreneurs Tick: An Investigation of Entrepreneurs' Values," paper given at the 1987 Frontiers of Entrepreneurship Research Conference and summarized in *Frontiers of Entrepreneurship Research 1987*, edited by Neil Churchill et al. (Wellesly, MA: Babson College, 1987), 202–203.

30. Donald L. Sexton and Nancy Bowman-Upton, "Sexual Stereotyping of Female Entrepreneurs: A Comparative Psychological Trait Analysis of Female and Male Entrepreneurs," paper given at the 1988 Frontiers of Entrepreneurship Research Conference and summarized in *Frontiers of Entrepreneurship Research 1988*, edited by Bruce Kirchhoff et al. (Wellesley, MA: Babson College, 1988), 654–55.

31. E. Holly Buttner and Benson Rosen, "Bank Loan Officers' Perceptions of the Characteristics of Men, Women, and Successful Entrepreneurs," *Journal of Business Venturing* 3, no. 3, Summer 1988, 249–58.

32. Charles R. Stoner, Richard I. Hartman, and Raj Arora, "Differences Between Female Entrepreneurs and Female Professional Managers," *Proceedings of the 1991 Midwest Business Administration Association*, Chicago, April 4, 1991.

33. Eugene Carlson, "Black-Owned Firms in U.S. Are Increasing at Rapid Pace," *Wall Street Journal*, September 12, 1990, B2.

34. James F. DeCarlo and Paul R. Lyons, "A Comparison of Personal Characteristics of Minority and Non-Minority Female Entrepreneurs," *Journal of Small Business Management* 17, no. 4 (October 1979): 22–29.

35. Brent Bowers, "Black Owners Fight Obstacles to Get Orders," *Wall Street Journal*, November 16, 1990, B1; Dorothy Gates, "Minority-Owned Business's Surge of the '80s is Threatened," *Wall Street Journal*, March 13, 1991, B1.

36. Jill Andresky Fraser, "The New American Dream," *Inc.*, April 1990, 42–51.

◆ Conveniesse, Inc. ◆

The Entrepreneurs

Jason Stone answered the phone in his Detroit apartment.

"Hi, this is Sarah Tondeur in Montreal. I've just talked with Yolanda in New York. We are interested in getting together again. Are you?"

"I guess so," Jason said with anticipation. "When did you have in mind?"

"How about this weekend in Buffalo? The same hotel."

"That soon, huh? Sure, why not?"

When the three arrived Friday evening, they checked into the hotel, ordered dinner, and continued their conversation.

"So you must be serious about this idea, Sarah," Jason said. "Why the sudden interest?"

"Well, I just sold out to my partner, and I can't think of a better opportunity than opening a store or chain like we discussed," Sarah said. "I decided to call you two and see if you were at all interested in pursuing either the Conveniesse idea or some other venture together. I don't have to have a partner but it might be more fun and it would provide more capital. Since we had discussed the idea during the conference, I decided we might as well try this idea first. Then, if we decide we don't want to do anything together, I'll move along to whatever opportunity arises."

"I'm not opposed to continuing the discussion," Yolanda responded. "As I told you earlier, I am perfectly happy with my job, so the opportunity would have to be compelling for me to leave. On the other hand, I have a few dollars saved up and wouldn't mind investing in something. And I am always up for a challenge."

"I guess I agree," said Jason. "I am relatively happy in my public relations work. I'm not sure how good I am at it nor how long my boss will put up with me. He thinks I am disorganized and a little prone to try something outside the normal tradition. I guess I am a maverick of sorts."

The three decided that they should first spend more time considering the degree of compatibility they had. Ironically, they had each taken a series of personality and interest tests at the seminar a few months earlier and they could pretty well remember their scores. As might be expected for someone in public relations, Jason scored high in creativeness and extraversion, and low in organization and mathematical interests. He was a medium to high risk-taker. Yolanda was also somewhat extraverted, had good organization skills, and had especially good communications skills. She was middle of the road regarding risk-taking. She had scored the highest of the three on internal locus of control and self confidence. Sarah scored far and away the highest on risk-taking even though she leaned more toward an external locus of control. As a self-taught accountant, Sarah was good with numbers and analysis. She also leaned toward introversion.

Each acknowledged weaknesses. Jason acknowledged sometimes being too quick to endorse a new idea or concept. He mentioned that his manager periodically has to slow him down to "get my act together" so clients aren't left hanging on a project. Yolanda's primary weakness was that she was somewhat of a plodder. "If Jason is the hare," she said, "I am the tortoise." Sarah admitted that she had been accused of "mother henning" those around her, but that her biggest fault might be her willingness to go for broke. If it had not been for her children whom she raised as a single parent, she would have started a number of different ventures— and probably be either really rich or really in debt.

The three talked long into the night and again the next day about the venture, themselves, finances, and operational details. They realized that starting a convenience store or any retail store would require long hours. One problem would be finding a location that would meet the needs the three had identified. By the end of the weekend, however, they had decided to at least pursue the idea some more.

Assignment

Do you think the three are compatible enough to begin an entrepreneurial venture? Discuss the strengths each brings to the team. What problems do you foresee?

II

PLANNING THE NEW VENTURE

Business Plans and Planning
•
Analyzing Entrepreneurial Opportunities
•
Planning the Launch of the Venture
•
Financing the Venture

4 Business Plans and Planning

LEARNING OBJECTIVES

After reading this chapter, you should know:

1. The strategic planning process
2. The use of business plans
3. The difference between a strategic plan and a financial plan
4. The benefits derived from developing business plans
5. Important considerations in developing plans
6. Formats of strategic plans and financial plans
7. How to do a rough estimate of sales for new and existing firms

KEY TERMS

Business plan

Financial plan

Strategic plan

The planning process

Support strategies

CONSIDER THIS!

- Some successful growth ventures did not have business plans.
- The benefits of doing a business plan may come more from the process of doing it rather than from the resulting document.
- Can a generic business plan be used, or must a distinct plan be developed for each funding source for the venture?
- Some venture capitalists want a plan to be "no more than forty pages long or one-half inch thick."
- Business plans for startup ventures are quite difficult to do well. However, carefully written plans are critically important as the venture is being launched.

This chapter serves as the bridge between Part I and the rest of the text. Part I discussed the nature of entrepreneurship and the nature of entrepreneurs. The chapters beyond this one treat the many issues associated with the launch and growth of ventures. This chapter discusses how to do planning and how to develop business plans. The plans can then be used to obtain funding for the venture and to guide the venture's strategy.

The business plan is the most important document relating to a venture. It is the instrument that must be presented to potential lenders or investors who may stand between the rapid growth of a venture and

GAIL AND ALAN HERING
Atmosphere Processing, Inc.

. . . the company became profitable and found itself doubling in size every three years. But the growth was unplanned; too few people, insufficient plan—a painful experience . . . we had heard about something called strategic planning and decided there had to be a better way . . . We started talking to some consultants about strategic planning. It made sense . . . I hope today that we're in a position to take a more disciplined approach . . . We need it so everyone knows where we are going and how we're going to get there.[1]

Alan Hering's background almost fits the classic entrepreneurial background that might be expected of someone launching an automotive industry venture. Both of his parents worked in the automotive industry, and his father was a plant supervisor. Alan did well in high school, but he found the academic environment to be highly repressive and unrelated to the demands of the real world. Ford Motor Company provided an apprenticeship in industrial instrumentation after high school, and Alan found this to be exciting and challenging training. It became a prelude to the launch of Atmosphere Processing, Inc. (API), a venture that provides heat treating of heavy metal parts of cars to add strength and hardness to the high-stress components of engines and transmissions.

Gail Hering did not share her husband's background. She studied English literature and improvisational theater at the undergraduate and graduate levels and taught theater classes in the public schools. Alan asked her to help run API, so she learned to load blast furnaces, to Brinell test, and to

stagnation or failure. It is the result of major study of both the opportunities to be exploited and the venture's ability to exploit them. It reflects the entrepreneurial team members' vision and their plan to lead the venture toward that vision.

This chapter will first discuss the nature of two types of plans—the strategic plan and the financial plan. It then examines the benefits of business plans. It will look at a number of factors that should be considered in developing the plans. A format for each type of business plan will be presented. The chapter concludes with a discussion of methods of developing a sales forecast that is the key to a successful plan.

THE NATURE OF BUSINESS PLANS

A **business plan** may be defined as a document developed by the venture team to guide the strategy of the firm and/or to attract investors to the firm. Stanley Rich and David Gumpert stated in a *Harvard Business Review* article that, "A comprehensive, carefully thought-out business plan is essential to the success of entrepreneurs and corporate managers. Whether you're starting up a new business, seeking additional capital for existing product drive a semi and a hi-lo. Gail is now the "people and money" person of the team and holds the position of chief executive officer of API. She claims she learned management from American Management Association seminars and Peter Drucker books.

Atmosphere Processing, Inc., was started with a $150,000 bank loan and is located in Holland, Michigan. Its location is ideal because it is near its customers including Ford, Dana Corporation, General Motors, Columbus Foundries, and Brillion Iron Works. API is a high-volume operation specializing in heavy manufacturing procedures. The com-

pany won Ford's prestigious Q-1 award for supplying Ford with more than a million pounds of heat-treated parts per week with no defects for more than a year. That award has been given to fewer than .2 percent of Ford's vendors. Gail asserts that their quality and quantity of output is because they "heat treat right and treat people right." They have a strong emphasis on the "people" side of the business, an almost religious devotion to communicating with customers, a fine appreciation of marketing, and a determinedly disciplined approach to planning.

The Herings have to be good at their operation, for it is one

that could be done by large manufacturers themselves. API is part of the trend toward "outsourcing" by major manufacturers. Outsourcing refers to the contracting of services to companies such as API rather than doing the job in-house. Outsourcing reduces the manufacturer's fixed costs, and the job can often be done substantially cheaper by the outside firm. This is the case with API, whose dedication to volume, quality, attention to the customer, and on-time delivery all account for its success.

SOURCE: Atmosphere Processing, Inc., company documents. Used with permission.

lines, or proposing a new activity in a corporate division, you will never face a more challenging writing assignment than the preparation of a business plan."[2]

Some confusion exists about business plans. When some people discuss business plans, especially with regard to new ventures, the discussion will almost invariably be about financial plans. On the other hand, when managers of existing companies talk of their business plan, they may be discussing their strategic plan. The two types of plans are related but separate types of documents (Table 4-1).

The **financial plan** is required by bankers, venture capitalists, and others who may invest in the company. The financial plan is heavily numbers oriented, with those numbers being aimed at convincing investors of the future potential of the company. A **strategic plan** focuses much more on the strategic direction of the firm rather than on just the financial aspects of the venture.

Strategic Plans

The major difference between a strategic plan and a financial plan is the focus of the plan itself. The strategic plan is designed to be an internal

. . . .

	Strategic Plans	Financial Plans
TABLE 4-1	Prepared by top management and key operating managers	Prepared by top management with help from CPA firms and/or the firm's financial staff
Differences between Strategic Plans and Financial Plans	Read by management and key employees	Read by investors outside the firm
SOURCE: Fred L. Fry and Charles R. Stoner, "Business Plans: Two Major Types." Reprinted from *Journal of Small Business Management* (January 1985): 1–6. Used with permission.	Focus on strategy and operations	Focus on sources and uses of funds
	Require information about the economy, industry, and competitors	Require projections of sales, expenses, profits, and losses
	Revised at least annually	Revised whenever additional funding is needed
	Document length is as needed to discuss strategy	Document length is 20–40 pages and no more than 50

guide of actions necessary to achieve the firm's goals. It is not intended to be read by outsiders and, in fact, is often protected from outside viewing for competitive reasons. It is developed by top management and key operative personnel in order that a broad spectrum of ideas can be considered in developing the plan. It focuses heavily on an analysis of the environment in which the firm operates. As such, items such as the economy, trends in the industry, and a thorough competitive analysis are key parts of the document.

Although this objective information is not considered part of the company's specific strategy, the information is needed as a baseline that can then be compared with later information in the firm's environment. It should be revised or at least reconsidered at least annually. Many firms make a five-year plan and a one-year plan at the beginning of each year. In successive years, the process will add the next year to the five-year plan and update the one-year plan. In this way, the venture's managers can keep on top of both the current situation and a projection of the future.

Financial Plans

The financial plan is a document that is prepared with one overriding goal in mind. That goal is to obtain some kind of funding for the firm. Funding may be in the form of debt capital from a local bank. It may come from private investors who may have either an active or a passive interest in the firm. It may be venture capital that usually takes the form of equity or a combination of equity and debt. The funding may be public money from an initial public offering (IPO) of stock. Or it may be funds from the bond market if the firm is large enough to warrant that kind of funding. Any of these types of funding will require an extensive financial plan or, as it is more commonly known, a business plan.

The financial plan has a different nature and approach than the strategic plan. The primary readers of the business plan are outsiders. The bankers, venture capitalists, underwriters, brokers, and others who may have an interest in the venture want to see what the business is all about, what its financial projections are, and how investors can expect to recoup their investment.

Investors are not particularly interested in the operational details of the business. But they are very interested in two general aspects of the plan: the *marketing considerations* and the *investor considerations*. They want to know the scope of the opportunities presented. This may include how solid the market is, what rate of growth may be expected, and the amount of time before sales will be sufficient to make a profit. In addition, they want to know when to expect a return on their investment, how much that return is likely to be, what the probability of continued return is, and how long the profits are likely to continue.

The financial plan requires extensive financial analysis and projections. Because of this, it is strongly advised that experienced accountants or financial managers assist in the preparation of the plan. If the venture's management team does not include these people, then consideration should be given to getting assistance from a CPA firm. The strategic plan should be reviewed and revised periodically. The financial plan, because of its nature, is only prepared when funding is needed. It should be kept in mind, however, that the financial projections should be included in both plans. In this way, the projections can be compared with later performance.

BENEFITS OF PLANS AND PLANNING

Business plans, whether strategic or financial, provide clearly identifiable benefits for the new or small venture. These benefits result from the planning *process* as well as from the *plan* itself (Table 4-2).

First, the planning process forces the entrepreneur to determine some relevant *planning horizon*. A planning horizon is the distance into the future for which it is logical to plan. Low-growth ventures may have a very short planning horizon of a year or less. Other ventures such as a manufacturing firm will necessarily look three to five years into the future. Larger firms and high-growth firms may need to look five to ten years out. The distance to the planning horizon is not as important as the fact that some planning horizon exists. The actual horizon will be unique for any given venture, but the orientation toward the future is key to the planning process.

- Establishes a planning horizon
- Requires analysis of external environment
- Requires analysis of the venture's internal strengths and weaknesses
- Gives an identifiable direction for the venture
- Allows the focusing of resources on specific objectives
- Provides communication and motivation channel for employees and information to outsiders
- Provides the bases for comparison with later plans

TABLE 4-2
Benefits of Developing
Business Plans

The planning process encourages the entrepreneur to look externally at the competitive nature of the venture. If a plan is to be developed well, the owner must carefully study the economy, the competition, the community, the customers, and other factors that can impact the venture. These factors must be considered not just in a general way, but very specifically in regard to how they can affect the venture. For example, competitors must be considered in relation to *how* they compete. Are they price competitive? Do they have major strengths that our firm doesn't? Are they doing well or just struggling to survive?

The planning process requires the entrepreneur to assess the internal strengths and weaknesses of the venture. By doing the analysis specifically for the business plan, the entrepreneur has the opportunity to look objectively at the venture. In particular the venture must be analyzed as it relates to the external environment. Its own strengths and weaknesses must be compared to those of competitors. Its ability to compete must be compared with the demand for the product or service.

An important benefit of planning is that the process gives a *direction* for the venture. The plan helps determine where the business is headed and, perhaps more important, where it is not headed. It helps managers focus on specific objectives rather than flounder from one idea to the next. In Venture Perspective 4-1, for example, the planning process forced Barnwald to clearly choose whether she wanted to become a high-volume producer or stay with low volume.

By having clear direction and focus, the entrepreneur can operate in a *planning mode* rather than in a *crisis management mode*. With a plan, the venture team knows how to react to new information or new developments outside the firm. Without a plan, every new piece of information is a potential crisis. The crisis must be dealt with, often to the detriment of the rest of the venture's operations.

A resource allocation benefit derives from the direction-setting process. By having clear objectives for the venture, the entrepreneur can then focus resources on the accomplishment of those objectives. Once Barnwald decided to go the high-volume route, her resources and time could then be directed toward obtaining the necessary equipment, raw plastic, and storage, and developing distribution methods rather than using effort and money in producing the low-volume product.

Another benefit of plans, and especially strategic plans, is their *communication* benefit. As the entrepreneur works with employees to obtain input on the plan and then later shares that plan with them, the employees receive valuable information regarding the direction of the venture. This has both an efficiency value and a motivation value. The efficiency value results from the knowledge of the venture's direction and the cohesion of worker efforts toward a single set of objectives. The motivation value derives from the feeling of inclusion into the decision-making process. Employees will be more dedicated and will work harder if they know what is happening and if they have some part in establishing the direction of the firm.

In addition to internal communication, the plan can be used for communicating with key individuals outside the venture. These individuals will include those interested in financing the venture, key customers or suppliers, and outside members of the board of directors if applicable.

JULIE BARNWALD

Julie Barnwald developed an accessory for kite flying that assisted in reeling the string in and out. The market was obviously seasonal, and she thought the product should sell for approximately $10. She treated the making and selling of the product as a hobby, but soon found that there was a ready market among the independent retailers she contacted. Barnwald could produce them by hand and make perhaps fifteen to twenty per day. But as sales seemed to take hold, she began to wonder if the toy could be sold on a larger basis.

In researching methods of selling the product, Barnwald contacted major toy store chains such as Toys "R" Us and Kay-Bee Toy & Hobby, and discount stores such as K mart. She learned two things. One, if the large companies bought the product, they would buy in lots of ten thousand and twenty-five thousand. Second, each of the major sellers wanted to see a finished product before they would commit to placing an order. Unfortunately, Barnwald made her low-volume product by hand out of wood. The high-volume version would be made out of molded plastic using a mold that cost approximately $20,000.

Barnwald faced a problem that many first-time entrepreneurs face. Low volume did not produce enough profit to be worth the effort, but there was insufficient capital available to invest in a $20,000 piece of equipment without knowing whether the high-volume demand existed or not. The analysis that Barnwald had done as part of her planning process gave her critical information that she did not have before. It was simply that one has to have money to make money. She then spent considerable time deciding whether to find $20,000 or to give up the high-volume idea completely and continue to make enough products to furnish local independent retailers.

After a year of selling locally while taking no money out of the venture, she finally saved enough money to approach a bank for a small loan. In order to convince the banker to make even a relatively small loan and also to convince the chain store buyers of her competence to manufacture sufficient quantities, Barnwald developed a business plan that explained the product, how it could be used in kite flying, and the number of products that could be manufactured with the new machine. Barnwald knew that the new product was risky, but felt confident that the business plan gave her the direction needed for her venture.

Another benefit of producing a strategic or financial plan is that the data become baseline data for future comparisons. If, for example, the strategic plan notes weaknesses or vulnerabilities of the venture, those weaknesses will be considered whenever the plan is reviewed or redone. Similarly, a key part of the financial plan is specific financial projections. The financial projections are then available for review in later months or quarters to see how the venture has performed compared with forecasts in the plan.

THE STRATEGIC PLANNING PROCESS

The previous section discussed the nature of business plans. These plans cannot be written, however, without first developing the firm's strategy. Once the strategy is developed, then the plan can be written on paper. Similarly, a financial plan will not be accurate or well documented unless the planning process is completed and a sales forecast is developed.

VENTURE PERSPECTIVE 4-2
· · · · · · · · · · · · ·

WHITE SPACE DESIGN, INC.

"**O**ur first formal business plan was just a fluff piece that we had to do for the bank," says Sara White, owner of White Space Design, Inc., a Midwest design firm. "When my partner and I bought this firm, we had to do a business plan, but it really did not help us. We said whatever we thought the banker wanted to hear."

Three years later, when Sara bought out her partner's share of the business, she had to put together a formal plan again. This time, she took a course in planning, and had an entirely different experience.

"I learned how to do a market analysis. As part of that, I made a grid of the characteristics of an ideal client, so that I would know who I should be targeting and who I should be turning down. I analyzed traits (like budget-consciousness and the number of decision makers) of fifty or sixty of my current clients, and came up with some very interesting information.

"My financial projections turned out to be pretty accurate too—within a couple of hundred dollars. Before I took the course, I didn't think I'd be able to do the financial part. I had planned to give that assignment to the bookkeeper. But I figured it out. Knowing how to do all of that has really helped me manage my business better."

SOURCE: Catherine Stover, "Planning in Existing Businesses: Four Vignettes," *Small Business Forum* (Winter 1991/1992): 66. Used with permission.

The strategic planning process is perhaps the most important task for the entrepreneur. All other activities—financing, marketing, hiring personnel, production, distribution, and more—draw upon the overall venture strategy selected. Considerable time must be given to developing the venture strategy and the supporting strategies that go with it. The process is time consuming, but it is a valuable process and one that pays for itself over and over.

The strategic planning **process** for entrepreneurial ventures is not significantly different than it is for large businesses. There are some differences in the names of the steps of the process, and the strategies developed for a large multi-business corporation will differ from those of a single venture. The strategic planning process itself remains essentially the same. The planning process is also relevant for both new ventures and existing ventures. With existing ventures, the planning process may be somewhat easier because a history or track record exists that can be used as the basis for the process. New ventures do not have a history. Thus, forecasting is more difficult and the accuracy of the forecasts is questionable. Still, the process is similar.

The strategic planning process consists of four stages or phases (Figure 4-1). The first is the premise stage in which the basic nature of the venture is considered. The second is the analysis stage in which the venture's capabilities are compared with the environment the firm will face, and distinctive competencies are identified. The third is the strategy development stage in which the venture's primary strategy and supporting strategies are developed. The final stage, the implementation stage, consists of the actions necessary to actually put the strategy into action.

VENTURE PERSPECTIVE 4-3

· · · · · · · · · · · · ·

ELECTRIC MOTOR SERVICE, INC.

When Electric Motor Service, Inc., a fifty-six-year-old family business, entered a transition period, Peter Sutherland and Bill Hinnendael decided it would be a good idea for the four top managers to spend a week writing a business plan. "It was strictly an internal document," Sutherland said. "We weren't seeking financing, so we weren't in a situation where a bank was telling us to put a plan together.

"We just all realized that we had to be focused. The process enabled us to be more focused, and to get our minds together on where we were going.

"It forced us to deal with important issues, which are sometimes easy to neglect when operating a business. We took a good look at the entire picture and set goals.

"The chief benefit was that it was a good communication tool. We all knew what we were going to try to do. During transition times, especially, that is critical."

SOURCE: Catherine Stover, "Planning in Existing Businesses: Four Vignettes," *Small Business Forum* (Winter 1991/1992): 66. Used with permission.

Determining the Nature of the Venture

Before any logical analysis of a venture's capabilities or its environment can take place, the basic premise or context for the analysis must be determined. This means that the entrepreneur must define the basic nature of the business—how it will operate, how much growth is intended, and what kind of structure it will have. Once this is determined, this becomes the premise that underlies the rest of the planning process. The nature of the venture is a broad picture of the business and its product or service. The rest of the planning process is, to an extent, just filling in the details of the broad picture.

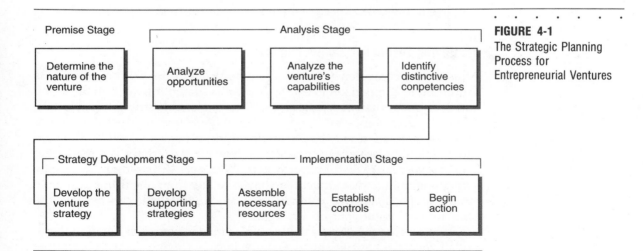

FIGURE 4-1

The Strategic Planning Process for Entrepreneurial Ventures

Assessing Entrepreneurial Opportunities

The opportunity assessment is critical to the strategic planning process. Analysis of opportunities is necessary to differentiate between real opportunities that may be exploited and those ideas or fads that have either a very short opportunity window or have a very small market. This analysis should determine the nature and size of the opportunity, and its viability for a significant investment return. It should consider both current opportunities and future developments. It should take into account those trends that appear to be pervasive over time.

Analyzing the Venture's Capabilities

Opportunities may exist that offer exceptional potential for returns on the investment. But if the entrepreneur cannot take advantage of these opportunities, then the investment will be lost. Human, financial, and physical resources must be in place or readily available to capture opportunities in a timely fashion. The internal analysis must be objective, and it must keep the opportunities in mind.

It is not enough to simply say that the company is a strong or weak company. The analysis must report what strengths the venture has in regard to the potential opportunities being considered. For example, an analysis of an existing venture may suggest that the company has had substantial experience in marketing products to the consumer market. If, however, the opportunity consists of marketing a product or service to the industrial market, then the retail marketing experience may not be transferable to the industrial market.

It is difficult to analyze a venture's internal capabilities objectively. This is because the entrepreneur is too close to the venture and cannot take an arm's-length view of the venture. In order to get an objective analysis of the venture, the entrepreneur may need to turn to an outside consultant or to organizations such as the Service Corps of Retired Executives, small business development centers, or small business institutes. Members of these organizations, while not necessarily professionally trained analysts, can give a low-cost, objective analysis of the venture.

Identifying Distinctive Competencies

A distinctive competency is a competitive strength the venture has that is significant in comparison to competitors. It is something the firm does well and does better than everyone else. It is an exploitable strength (Table 4-3). The distinctive competency may be a highly desired product that is protected by patents. It may be a manufacturing process that allows the venture to manufacture quality products at lower cost. Perhaps it is marketing skill or a successful distribution system. Whatever the strength, it must be something unique that attracts customers to buy from one firm rather than another. The distinctive competencies, once identified, can become the basis for successful venture strategies.

Two caveats concerning distinctive competencies merit mention. First, not all ventures have distinctive competencies. Having distinctive compe-

- Unique product, preferably protected by patents
- Unique distribution system such as delivery direct to the customer
- Unique customer service
- Specialized repair service
- Unique communications network with customers
- Warranties that are above the norm
- Friendly service representatives
- Employee programs that promote intense loyalty
- Unusually knowledgeable sales force

TABLE 4-3
Distinctive Competencies
for Entrepreneurial Firms

tencies helps ensure success for the business. Not having distinctive competencies does not, however, guarantee failure. Many businesses exist that are not substantially different from others, and they may be quite successful over time. If the market is large enough to support a number of similar competitors, all may exist without any of them having any significant competitive advantage over the others. The distinctive competency helps the entrepreneur achieve rapid growth and become a market leader.

The second caveat is that seldom are distinctive competencies sustainable over an extended period of time. If one business has a competitive advantage that allows it to be highly profitable over time, eventually other competitors will mimic the strategy or improve upon the technology. Strategies enhanced by protective patents will delay the deterioration of the distinctive competency assuming that similar products cannot be made without violating patents. Yet, sooner or later the advantage will be overcome. The task for the entrepreneur is to maximize the return from the distinctive competency and then monitor inroads by competitors and adjust the strategy appropriately.

Developing Venture Strategies

Once the analysis of the venture's opportunities and capabilities is complete, the task is then to use that information to develop the overall venture strategy and its supporting strategies. The strategies that are developed during this phase of the process guide the actions of the firm.

The development of venture strategies may be a very straightforward process or it may be a complicated, time-consuming task. If the venture has distinctive competencies that may be exploited, or if the opportunity/capability match is so compelling as to virtually dictate the strategy, then the task of determining the venture strategy is relatively simple. If the opportunity/capability match is not so evident, then effort must be expended to determine the best strategy for the venture. Chapter 8 will discuss a variety of strategies available for entrepreneurial firms.

Developing Supporting Strategies

Some readers may think that once the overall venture strategy is developed, all that remains is to push a magic button and the strategy is automatically implemented. Unfortunately, it is not that easy. **Supporting strategies** must be developed for each functional area such as marketing, production, finance, and personnel. It is also advantageous for the entrepreneur to consider what community involvement should be undertaken in order to make a true contribution to the community. Table 4-4 lists supporting strategies for a car wash featuring both self-service and automatic wash bays.

Marketing Strategies

When developing marketing strategies, the entrepreneur must consider whether to market directly to the consumer or through one or more intermediaries. The advertising and promotion strategy must be delineated. The image that will be conveyed to customers must be established before the venture is begun. Each of the marketing support strategies must be consistent with both the other marketing strategies and the overall strategy. For example, a venture whose strategy is to sell high-quality children's furniture at retail must ensure that all of the marketing efforts support the image of high quality and concern for children. The design of the store must be plush and well done. The advertising should have a quality theme. The owners may desire to offer warranties above and beyond those of the manufacturers. The sales force must be knowledgeable about their competitors' products and be able to demonstrate their own products to the customers and explain the quality aspects of the construction. This sets the image of the store apart from a discount store whose products are crowded together on tile floors and sold using a self-service customer policy. Whatever the product or service provided, consistency is the key to the marketing strategy.

TABLE 4-4
Supporting Strategies for a Car Wash

Marketing		
	Advertising	Advertise in local newspaper
		Advertise on TV one week after snowstorms
	Promotion	Give tokens for discount on next wash
Operations		Provide eight self-service and four automatic bays at each location
		Provide soft water rinses at all bays
		Provide coin-operated vacuum machines
Financing		Use only personal equity, supplemented by seasonal bank loans
Human resources		Hire two managers for each location. Part-time help will be high school or college students. All training will be brief orientation plus on-the-job training.
Community involvement		Donate to schools that employees attend
		Sponsor Little League baseball or soccer
		Underwrite printing of high school athletic game programs

Operations Strategies

An entrepreneur beginning or growing a venture makes many decisions in operations management or production management. Plans in this area are necessary regardless of whether the venture is a manufacturing, retail, or service entity. Anything dealing with getting the actual product or service to the customer is part of the production function, and many of these items are strategic in nature. That is, the production decisions that are made affect the overall strategy of the venture.

Three aspects of operations are especially important to the entrepreneur. One is the *purchase* versus *lease* of facilities. Some entrepreneurs, in an attempt to be totally in control, may buy facilities even though they could better manage risk by leasing. They may lock up scarce capital that could be better used as working capital to underwrite marketing, inventory, or personnel.

A second area of strategic significance consists of *make* or *buy* decisions in product manufacturing. These decisions address the trade-offs between control of product manufacture and limiting the investment in plant and equipment. Entrepreneurs have the option of manufacturing the product completely in-house, making only part of it by using components made by others, or making none of it and only packaging or marketing the product. Thus, it is strategically important to decide how much investment in plant, equipment, and personnel should be made. In some cases, outside contractors can produce products cheaper because of already established equipment and expertise.

The third major production-related issue that must be planned for is the *quality* of the product or service. This is a strategic issue because it affects marketing, overall costs, image, product return costs, and profit. The entrepreneur must plan for the level of quality in the product or service, how to ensure that the desired level is reached, and how to best exploit that quality through marketing.

Financial Strategies

Financing is, of course, one of the most critical parts of entrepreneurship. Chapter 7 will deal with financing considerations in depth. The issue here is that there must be a financial *strategy*. Financing is too important to leave to chance or to a "when needed" decision. Whether the strategy is to use primarily equity financing, primarily debt financing, or a combination of both is not as important as the need for a definitive strategy regarding which methods will be used.

Human Resources Strategies

Like financing, the venture should have a definitive personnel strategy. The human resources or personnel strategy tells the entrepreneur what kind of employees to hire, how to hire them, what kind of promotion system to use, and how to pay them. The personnel strategy relates to decisions that affect the long-range strategy of the venture. Hiring only trained workers rather than untrained workers is a strategic decision. Promoting exclusively from within is a strategic decision and is worth considering because of its motivational impact. The strategy of using employment agencies and executive search firms eases the hiring process but increases the direct cost of hiring. Again, the critical issue is not which type of personnel strategy is developed, but that some definitive strategy exists to guide the firm and that it is consistent with the overall venture strategy.

Community Involvement Strategies

This area can be important from both a conceptual viewpoint and a pragmatic one. Conceptually, all businesses have a responsibility to the community in which they are located, as well as responsibilities to their customers, their suppliers, and their investors. Businesspersons have a general responsibility to act in the most ethical manner possible given their situation. In fact, the need for ethical conduct is critical in the new or emerging firm for the simple reason that there is less policing of smaller ventures than there is of large corporations. In order that the venture be viewed as an ethical business by all who have a stake in it, it is important that the entrepreneur have a keen sense of ethics from the beginning. Thus, ethics and community responsibility must be part of the strategic planning process.

From the pragmatic view, the venture is a part of the community. As such, there will be many opportunities to get involved with community projects. Virtually all of the projects will be valuable, and all will be time consuming. Most will have some benefit to the community, but the benefit to the company will usually be difficult if not impossible to measure. Other projects may have some positive but intangible returns. A retail business sponsoring a Little League team might fit this category if some customers would be encouraged to buy from the store since it sponsors the team. Other projects may have a closer tie to the venture. In these cases, both the venture and the community benefit from the involvement. The entrepreneur may then choose projects based on the amount of "return" desired.

The significance of this to the strategic planning process is that the entrepreneurial team should plan for these activities. In this way, all will know which activities the venture supports and which ones it does not. They will know how to respond when the telephone rings or when the solicitor knocks on the door. The result is that the community involvement will be as effective as possible and have the tie to operations that is desired by the entrepreneur.

Implementation of Strategies

The implementation stage of the planning process consists of three steps. The first step is to assemble the necessary resources to underwrite the strategy. This involves primarily the arranging of financing, although other resources are also included. These include human resources, plant and equipment, and necessary inventory and/or supplies.

Establishing controls is the second aspect of the implementation process. This consists of actions taken to ensure that the venture's strategies work as planned. Budgets, quotas, quality assurance programs, and monthly reporting procedures all fall into this category. The issue facing entrepreneurs is to establish enough control to ensure proper functioning of the business without having so much control that the entrepreneurial spirit is stifled.

Finally, the last step is to start the action. This is the actual launch of a new venture or the launch of relevant new strategies for an existing venture. The launch activities consist of the acquisition of facilities, obtaining necessary licenses, developing grand opening strategies for retail operations, securing supplier contracts, signing financial agreements, drawing up partnership agreements if applicable, registering the names of the venture and/or products as required, hiring staff, printing stationery and other materials, and a host of other actions.

WRITING THE STRATEGIC PLAN

Since the strategic plan is an internal document, the format for it is not as critical as for the financial plan. Still, it must be adequately organized, thoroughly researched, and effectively written in order to be useful in the future and understood by all who may read it. The following guidelines apply to the development of the plan (Table 4-5).

The plan must reflect the objectives set by the venture team members. The strategic plan includes a mission statement, which is a statement of the venture's basic nature and the philosophy of the entrepreneurial team. It will also include specific goals that the owners believe are achievable in the coming year and five years in the future. They will necessarily be a reflection of the personal goals of the team members. The mission statement and goals serve as a focusing mechanism for all who are involved in the venture.

The plan must be based on an extensive analysis of the opportunity. The opportunity must be studied carefully to determine if it is truly an opportunity that can be exploited over time. Key aspects of the analysis should be included in the document so that comparisons may be made at a later date. Chapter 5 will discuss the opportunity analysis in greater depth.

A thorough assessment of venture capabilities should be made before determining the strategy. Some entrepreneurs assume they know everything about their capabilities. This is seldom true. Even if it were true, the assessment should be made for baseline purposes. The internal assessment should include a financial analysis, an assessment of personnel or human strengths, a study of marketing capabilities, and an examination of the operations aspect of the venture. Both strengths and weaknesses should be studied.

A detailed strategy, resulting from the above analyses, should be described. The strategy may be clear in the minds of the venture team members, but it needs to be written down in order to be communicated with others. The strategy should be sufficiently detailed as to be meaningful to readers. If the strategy is broad, then substrategies should be delineated.

The strategic plan should end with extensive financial statements. These statements are the primary vehicles for measuring the firm's performance.

I.   Mission
     A. Nature of the venture and its products or services
     B. Venture philosophy

II. Analysis of the venture's external environment
     A. Analysis of the economy, social trends, and government regulation
     B. Analysis of competitors, customers, key suppliers, and other factors
        directly affecting the venture

III. Analysis of venture strengths and weaknesses
     A. Marketing
     B. Personnel
     C. The product or service
     D. Production processes
     E. Financial condition
        1. Cash flow
        2. Income and expenses
        3. Borrowing capability
        4. Need for equity capital

IV. Venture strategy
     A. Overall strategy
     B. Marketing strategy
     C. Production strategy
     D. Financing strategy
     E. Human resource strategy
     F. Community involvement strategy

V.   Specific goals and objectives
     A. Goals for the next year
     B. Goals for five years from now

VI. Financial projections
     A. Cash flow projections
     B. Pro forma income statements
     C. Projected balance sheet

WRITING THE FINANCIAL PLAN

The financial plan must be done with great care. Typically, the entrepreneur has only one chance with each potential funding source. Generally, investors will not tell venture managers that their idea is good but the plan is poorly written. They simply return it to the entrepreneur with a ''Thanks, but no thanks'' response.

Investors assume that part of an entrepreneur's skill in managing a venture is evident in the preparation of a plan. If an idea is good but the plan is not well written, then the investor will likely assume that the entrepreneur's management skills are weak.

In addition, venture capitalists often receive more than three hundred business plans a year. This is an extremely large number of plans to consider, and venture capitalists may underwrite less than 5 percent of what they see. Thus, a first-cut decision may be made after studying a plan for less than an hour. The serious entrepreneur must make the plan so objective and so attractive to the investor that it is worthy of additional study. The following are some considerations to use in developing the plan.

The plan should be kept short and crisp, but thorough. The plan must be sufficiently thorough to let potential investors know what the company is and why it is worthy of their capital. But a rambling, wordy monograph that drones on and on extolling the virtues of the firm and its product is not likely to be funded. Some entrepreneurs, enamored by computer print-outs, include page after page of detailed analysis from a computerized spreadsheet program. This will turn investors off rather than excite them to the possibilities of the venture. One rule of thumb is that the plan should be no more than one-half inch thick—about fifty pages.

The plan should look professional, but not gaudy. With the advent of desktop publishing, it is possible to make a plan look professionally done with little difficulty. On the other hand, care should be taken not to overdo the cover, the graphics, and other parts of the plan so that the plan has more fluff than substance. A simple cover with the company name and logo will suffice.

The executive summary is the most important part of the plan. The executive summary is a two- or three-page summary of the rest of the plan. It includes a brief description of the venture, the amount and type of capital desired, a summary of the compelling reasons why the investor should underwrite the venture, and the nature of the payback to the investor. The executive summary is the *first thing* the reader sees after the table of con-tents. It is the part that investors will read before they decide whether to read the rest of the plan. In some cases, it is the *only* part they read. Thus, the executive summary must be done extremely well. It must lay out the opportunities, the amount of funds requested, the uniqueness of the ven-ture, how investors will benefit, the skills of the management team, and any other pertinent information—all within two or three pages.

The plan should have a market orientation. The developer of a busi-ness plan should not labor over the technical aspects of the product or give an in-depth discussion of the product itself. Instead, the plan should focus on the market served. Who are the customers? How will they benefit? How will the product or service meet customer needs better than existing prod-ucts?

Projections must be documented. One of the most frequent problems with business plans is that the entrepreneur makes sales projections that are unfounded at best and, at worst, are based on either incorrect infor-mation or the entrepreneur's dreams. If the plan projects sales of $300,000 in year one and $1.2 million in year five, there must be some basis for the projections. Getting accurate forecasts of sales in a startup situation is, admittedly, a very difficult task. Sometimes the data are simply not avail-able or are not available in the form necessary. Consider the following example.

An entrepreneur hoped to produce and sell a unique trailer for alumi-num flat-bottomed fishing boats known as johnboats. In order to assess the market, he needed to know the number of those boats currently sold each year. Substantial information was available about boats and trailers. But analyzing the data in order to get the specific information was difficult. Information was available on the number of trailers currently sold, but that information was not broken down by type of boat. Information was available on outboard motor boats, but it included both aluminum and fiberglass. Even if information on aluminum boats were available, it would not be specifically available for the type of boats desired. It also did not give good information about market share, geographical distribution of sales, demographics of customers, or profit margins that could be expected. Thus, the forecast that was eventually made was extremely tenuous.

Expenses should match sales projections. In any venture, there will be some fixed expenses and some variable expenses. These must be considered in light of sales projections. Further, the fixed expenses may be fixed only over a particular range. Capital equipment falls in this category. A given piece of equipment might be able to produce anywhere from 10,000 to 100,000 units, but if demand is projected at 120,000 units, then an additional investment in equipment will be necessary.

Assistance in determining expenses can be gained by consulting industry averages. Industry averages are available for most SIC codes. These averages can be used to develop spreadsheets for sales and cash flow projections. Since the data are only averages, a margin of error exists. But in the absence of better data, industry ratios and averages may be the best possible estimation.

The plan should be tailored to specific types of investors. Many startup ventures have a number of options for funding, but may not be able to obtain the type of financing initially desired. A fatal mistake is to give to an equity investor a business plan that was initially developed for debt financing. Although much of the plan will be the same, there are unique aspects of the plan that will vary depending on whether banks, individual investors, or venture capitalists are the readers. For example, if debt financing is used heavily, then the financial projections must account for the debt servicing and should reflect different levels of profit with and without the desired debt. If equity capital is desired, then the focus must be on the nature of the return to the investor.

The plan must address risk. Financial plans are, by nature, optimistic. But at the same time, they cannot be Pollyannaish. They must state objectively what risks are likely to be incurred. Without some indication of possible downside risks, investors will perceive that the venture managers have not fully considered the proposed venture and its environment.

The amount of capital needed must be determined carefully. From a long-term perspective, this may be the most critical part. Undercapitalization is one of the primary causes of venture failure. Far too many entrepreneurs start ventures "on a shoestring," only to find later that the amount of capital was woefully inadequate. On the other hand, if the amount of capital requested is excessive and cannot be justified, then investors are unlikely to put their capital in something they view as a "pie in the sky" business plan.

THE FINANCIAL PLAN FORMAT

The outline for a financial plan is somewhat more restrictive than that for the strategic plan because of the items that must be included in the plan. Still, considerable variation exists. For example, the Kryos, Inc., plan in

Part VI is somewhat different than the format suggested in Table 4-6. Some of the ventures in Part VII use a still different form. The outline presented in Table 4-6 is typical and will be used throughout this text. Some venture capitalists and lenders will insist upon a particular format for their institution. The outline in Table 4-6 can be adapted to fit the needs of specific investors or software.

Computer software such as fisCAL (included with this text) can be used to develop necessary financial statements and proformas. Some publicly available software provides templates for the narrative portion of the business plan. The advantage of using fisCAL is that it can compare the financial condition with industry norms, calculate financial ratios, create projections, and do a valuation of the firm.

TABLE 4-6
Financial Plan Outline

I.   Executive summary
II. Nature of the venture
     A. Background
     B. The product/service
     C. Location of venture
III. Description of the market
     A. Market trends
     B. Demographic trends
     C. Current competitors
     D. Comparison of proposed venture to competitors
IV. Description of the product/service
     A. Uniqueness of product/service
     B. Advantage over competing products
     C. Alternative uses of product/service
V.   The management team
     A. Description of role each team member will play
     B. Resumes of each team member
VI. Objectives and goals
     A. Long-term objectives
     B. Short-term goals
VII. Venture strategies
     A. Marketing strategy
     B. Product strategy
     C. Human resource strategy
     D. Financial strategy
     E. Overall strategy for growth
VIII. Financial data
     A. Historical data (if any)
        1. Balance sheet
        2. Income statement
        3. Cash flow statement
     B. Financial projection
        1. One year by month
        2. Five years by quarter
     C. Break-even analyses

DEVELOPING THE SALES FORECAST

A key ingredient in both the strategic and financial plans is the sales forecast. Preparing an accurate sales forecast, however, is perhaps the most difficult task for any entrepreneur. It is particularly difficult, if not impossible, for a startup situation. Yet, investors and lenders insist on a sales projection by month for the first year or two and quarterly or annually for the next three to five years. This section will discuss methods of forecasting sales for existing firms and for startup firms.

Forecasting for Existing Firms

Existing firms with adequate records have an advantage over startup firms because of the historical data available. If three to five years of data are available, an extrapolation of the data into the future is the primary method of forecasting sales. It can also be quite wrong. For example, steadily increasing sales may be relatively accurately projected simply by assuming that the future will be the same as the present and sales will continue to increase at the same rate. If historical sales are *not* uniformly increasing, then projecting sales into the future is more problematic. Thus, existing data must be carefully examined to identify trends, aberrations, significant changes in data that are due to explainable forces, and other patterns that may affect projections. Several steps are necessary in order to develop an accurate forecast of sales (Table 4-7).

Statistical analysis of sales data is recommended. This gives a more accurate projection than simply looking at graphic plots. If a statistical analysis is not possible, then greater margins for error must be allowed.

Forecasting for Startup Ventures

Forecasting for startup ventures is far more difficult than forecasting for existing firms. The reason is obvious. There is no statistical basis for the forecast. Thus, other measures will be necessary to develop an estimate of

---

TABLE 4-7
Forecasting with Existing Data

1. Plot monthly data on a graph for at least the last three years.
2. Determine seasonality by looking at peaks and valleys in the data.
3. Determine trends either by looking at the graphs or by statistically analyzing the data.
4. Explain aberrations (hot summer, new competitor, strike, etc.)
5. Extend monthly data for two more years.
6. Determine total *annual* sales for each of the past three to five years.
7. Determine trends and extrapolate three to five years out.
8. Consider events or occurrences that could influence projection.
9. Adjust projected sales based on qualitative information from step 8.
10. Using firm's historical ratios and industry ratios, complete remainder of financial statements.

1. Determine total population of city (city census).
2. Determine usage of health foods by various age and income brackets (industry information).
3. Determine percentage of population in each customer age and income bracket (city census).
4. Determine percentage of population living within logical geographical distance from proposed store.
5. Determine average sales per customer visit (industry information or noncompeting store).
6. Determine number of times per month typical person shops in health food store (personal knowledge or industry data).
7. Determine number of direct and indirect competitors. Divide total market sales among competitors in an appropriate percentage.
8. Considering all of the above, calculate estimate of sales per month.

TABLE 4-8
Forecasting Health Food Sales through Target Market Refinement

sales. Two sources of information exist that can be incorporated into a forecast.

Since most new ventures are not totally original, one method of data collection is interviewing other entrepreneurs in the industry. This is particularly useful in retail businesses where similar firms exist in other cities. Care must be taken to assure that only noncompeting entrepreneurs are interviewed since it would be unwise both ethically and pragmatically to surreptitiously solicit information from current or potential competitors. If a noncompeting entrepreneur in a similar firm can be located, significant qualitative and quantitative information can be gained through frank discussions. This information can then be tailored to fit the startup venture's situation.

A second source is secondary data such as that available from government and industry. The United States Government provides Census Bureau information that is specific to individual census tracts. This information can be used to determine demographic information for the forecast. Trade associations exist for virtually every industry and subindustry in the nation. Most trade associations have statistics that can be helpful in preparing a forecast.

Once sufficient data are collected, the material can be manipulated to provide at least a rough forecast based on the successive refinement of the target market. Table 4-8 illustrates the process, using a health food store as an example.

Using this method, the target market for health foods is successively refined at each step in order to determine an estimate of the total market. Once the first six steps are done to indicate an estimate of the total market, then that figure is divided among the relevant competitors. Obviously, a number of assumptions have to be made such as the distance a customer will drive to get to a health food store, what percentage of the market share can be logically expected, and the effect that the proposed venture will have on competitors and customers. The resulting estimate will certainly be rough, but at least it will be an estimate. The results can then be compared with others in the industry or with secondary data to confirm or adjust the projection.

A CONCLUDING NOTE

Throughout this chapter, the focus has been on planning. In particular, discussion has centered on the strategic planning process. The rest of the text will continue to emphasize planning. For example, the next chapter's discussion of analyzing venture opportunities will consider the steps necessary to analyze the opportunities and plan methods of exploiting them. The launch of the venture requires substantial amounts of planning to assure that the best launch method is used. The three chapters in Part III address the development of entrepreneurial strategies. Even the final chapter on harvesting the venture will note the importance of planning the harvest well in advance.

It should also be noted that the planning process, if done well, will provide information for both the strategic plan and the financial plan. Market and competitor analysis is important for each, strategies are a key part of each, and financial projections are necessary for each. Even though the two types of plans are different and are used for different purposes, there is much overlap between them. Because of the similarity between the two and because most interest is in the financial plan, reference to a "business plan" throughout the rest of the text will generally refer to the financial plan. Specific references to strategic plans will be so noted. Part VI of the book shows excerpts from an actual business plan that was done to obtain financing for a biotech venture.

SUMMARY

This chapter has discussed the value and nature of business plans. The benefits of developing a plan come both from the future use of the plan itself and from the planning process that leads to the actual written plan.

The strategic planning process is a critically important prelude to writing either a strategic plan or a financial plan. The planning process includes determining the basic nature of the firm, analyzing opportunities and capabilities, identifying distinctive competencies, developing the venture strategy and supporting strategies, acquiring resources for the venture, and implementing the strategy.

Strategic plans are guides to the operation of the venture over the next year or years. They are internal documents designed to present the strengths and weaknesses of the venture compared with the opportunities facing the venture team. This plan should be developed with the help of key people in the organization and should be communicated to others within the venture.

The format of a strategic plan is not critical. However, several elements are important. It should include the venture mission statement, which states the nature of the venture and its philosophy. It should include a significant assessment of the venture's environment. This should be followed by an analysis of the firm's strengths and weaknesses. The major part of the plan should be the venture strategies. The plan should include both one-year and five-year goals, and it should end with carefully determined financial projections.

Financial plans are generally written to obtain funding for the venture. They must be done carefully and in such a way as to convince lenders or investors to underwrite the venture. The plan must be succinct, yet thorough. It must be objective and include substantial financial analyses and projections. The parts of the plan include the all-important executive summary, the nature of the venture, a description of the market, an explanation of the product or service being proposed, resumes of the management team, objectives and strategies for the venture, and financial statements and projections.

1. If business plans are so valuable, as suggested in this chapter, why do so many entrepreneurs fail to prepare them?

2. Compare a financial plan with a strategic plan in terms of its uses, readers, and preparers. What are their similarities and differences?

3. How do the two types of plans differ in their tone or the way they are written?

4. Why should many employees be consulted when preparing the strategic plan? Why is it not sufficient for the venture team members to use their judgment and vision in preparing the plan?

5. Why should a separate financial plan be prepared for each type of funding source? Suppose multiple sources of financing are used at the same time. Should a single plan or multiple plans be prepared?

6. Visit a local entrepreneur. Does the venture have a strategic plan? A financial plan? If so, is it used regularly?

7. Should an entrepreneur develop a financial plan in-house or seek help from a CPA firm or other venture assistance group?

8. How often should a strategic plan be prepared and reviewed?

9. Do low-growth ventures need a strategic plan?

10. Why do the formats of strategic plans and financial plans differ?

11. Read the Kryos, Inc., business plan in Part VI. How does it compare with the material in this chapter?

DISCUSSION QUESTIONS

EXERCISE 4-1

EXERCISES

Read the excerpts from Kryos, Inc., business plan in Part VI. Divide the class into two groups. One group will represent the entrepreneurs and the second group will represent a venture capital firm.

For the entrepreneurial team:

Develop a presentation for the venture capital firm that will capture the essence of your plan. From the plan, determine what facts are critical, how to present the data, and how to make a conclusion.

For the venture capital firm:

> Determine from the plan what salient information you need. Is there information you want that is not present or clear in the plan? What will you look for in the presentation beyond the information itself? What will you use as deciding criteria in determining whether you would underwrite their venture?

EXERCISE 4-2

Using the fisCAL software provided with your textbook, other business plan software, or spreadsheet software, develop projected cash flow statements for three years into the future for either the Wisconsin Sealcoating or The Artisan's Haven case in Part VII of the text.

. . . .

ENDNOTES

1. Gail Hering, quoted in Karen Boiko, "Atmosphere Processing, Inc.: Highly professional heat treaters," reprinted from *Heat Treating* (April 1986).
2. Stanley R. Rich and David E. Gumpert, "How To Write a Winning Business Plan," *Harvard Business Review* 63, no. 3 (May-June, 1985): 156–166.

◆ Conveniesse, Inc. ◆

Beginning the Planning

It has now been six months since the executive management seminar in Buffalo that sparked the idea for Conveniesse, an upscale convenience store to be owned by Jason Stone, Sarah Tondeur, and Yolanda Williams. The three have decided to continue their planning. Over the new few weeks, they made heavy use of conference calls, faxes, and an occasional meeting back in Buffalo. Buffalo had been picked as the site of the first Conveniesse because it was more or less centrally located between their three home cities and because that's just where they decided to do it.

The trio decided that they should start with a roughed out strategic plan even before collecting data for a financial plan. Since this was a startup situation, they knew that information would be transferred back and forth.

Starting with the nature of the venture, they concluded that they wanted it to be a very upscale convenience store. Everything, from the decor to the food and liquor items to the fax and ATM machines, would give the connotation of quality. With prices that were admittedly higher than other convenience stores, it was hoped that Conveniesse would attract a higher class of customer. Even the name, Conveniesse, combined part of the word convenience with a more exotic-sounding European ending.

The philosophy of the group was to provide a product/service mix in a store that would be impeccably laid out and operated in a highly professional and ethical manner such that anyone coming in the door could immediately identify both the nature of the business and its target market.

The three realized that more had to be done, but they began to put together their thoughts on the environment they would face. They thought the business would be relatively recession proof up to a point—when companies reduced corporate travel to convention center hotels. The office worker portion of the market should be relatively stable because of the number of professional people working in the downtown area. That part might be more seasonal, however, as cold weather months might keep employees inside. The ATM machine would counter that to some extent. They realized that everyone would have to learn government regulations, since no one was familiar either with Buffalo laws or with food and liquor laws in general.

A walking tour of the area of Buffalo that Stone, Tondeur, and Williams were interested in showed two things. First it showed no direct competition other than hotel gift shops. The closest other competition was an old drug store a block or so in one direction, and a liquor store two blocks in the other direction that obviously sold cheap liquor. The tour also showed something else that they had not considered. There were no available sites!

Assignment 1: What would you do now?

Continuing their discussion, they compared their own strengths and weaknesses for the venture. Marketing and advertising should be no problem because both Jason and Yolanda had several years' experience in different areas of marketing. Sarah assured them that she knew accounting. Each of them had supervised workers before although their management styles were not known. Knowledge of the food and liquor business would have to be developed, as would the intricacies of a convenience store. They decided to each join whatever organization seemed most helpful in their home cities. The cost of that could be significant, but the knowledge gained over the next few months would more than offset the cost. Sarah said she might even consider getting a part-time job at a convenience store just to see how one operates. In addition, they agreed to spend time in their business libraries learning about the convenience food business and entrepreneurship in general.

Assignment 2

In an outline form, write a strategic plan for Sarah, Jason, and Yolanda. In particular, write a mission statement for Conveniesse and a description of the venture as it is envisioned.

5 Analyzing Entrepreneurial Opportunities

LEARNING OBJECTIVES

After reading this chapter, you should know:

1. How to find or develop opportunities
2. How to evaluate opportunities, both informally and formally
3. Common sources of opportunities
4. Characteristics of opportunity windows
5. Components of marketing, financial, and technological feasibility analyses
6. How to match opportunities with capabilities

KEY TERMS

Opportunity	Informal analysis
Sources of opportunities	Feasibility analysis
Window of opportunity	Opportunity/capability match

CONSIDER THIS!

- Are opportunities something that exist outside the venture, or are they something that the entrepreneur creates?
- How does an entrepreneur determine if an opportunity has potential?
- Is it possible to have too many opportunities?
- Consider any significant product that has been developed within the last five years. Could that same product have been developed fifteen years ago? Thirty years ago?
- Some opportunities tend to develop over time while others tend to be sudden developments. What causes the difference?
- Again, consider some product that was developed in the last five years. Would you still consider that product a good opportunity today? Why do some products have a very rapid growth cycle while others progress very slowly?

Entrepreneurship has been called the last American frontier. The term *frontier* conjures images of pioneers in early America moving West, surviving perils, and hewing out new homes and new lives in uncharted territories. These pioneers searched for new freedoms, new challenges, and new life-styles. Entrepreneurship is not unlike that early American search

RUTH OWADES
Calyx & Corolla

Taking advantage of an opportunity is one thing. Creating the opportunity is quite another. Creating an opportunity and then building the company to exploit it is precisely what Ruth Owades did with her latest venture, Calyx & Corolla.

"Until Calyx and Corolla came along," writes Ellie Winninghoff in *Working Woman*, "the hugely lucrative $8.4 billion American flower industry had encountered few innovations. There had been flowers by wire, but not garden-fresh, exotic flowers displayed in a beautiful catalog (you actually get to *see* what you're ordering), with a money-back guarantee."[1]

Ruth Owades is a Harvard M.B.A. who had previously owned a mail-order business, Gardener's Eden, which she had grown into a $15 million business. After leaving Gardener's Eden, she began researching the possibility of delivering fresh flowers direct from the grower to the customer. This eliminates both the wholesaler and the retailer intermediaries. Using Federal Express allows the delivery to be overnight from the grower to the customer rather than the ten days or so required to transport flowers by truck from growers to traditional retail florists.

Thus, fresh flowers from Calyx and Corolla actually are *fresh* flowers.

Owades had three problems when launching her new venture. First, she had to convince growers to accept this method of distribution and to pack flowers for delivery to individual customers. In order to convince them to support her concept, she took her business plan directly to the independent growers and asked for their input. The growers were impressed with her honesty and innovation. They were convinced that Calyx and Corolla could enlarge the total market for fresh flowers.

The second hurdle Owades had to overcome was to get investors. Although investors knew of Owades from her ear-

lier venture, getting them to buy into her mail-order flowers concept was not easy. A normal business—if liquidation should be necessary—has inventory and equipment that could be sold. But in the case of Calyx and Corolla, there is no inventory. What impressed the investors, however, was the quality of her business plan and presentation. She had done her homework, had researched the industry, and had addressed the possible risks.

The third problem to solve was delivery. In order to get Federal Express to handle her business, she had to convince them to (1) add computer links at the locations of the numerous growers that were her suppliers, (2) make deliveries on Saturdays, and (3) leave the flowers at the door if no one was home rather than take them back to some distant warehouse.

In starting her venture, Owades rented more than fifty mailing lists for a one-time use giving her 500,000 addresses. She now has her own mailing list of 400,000 addresses, and she mails six catalogs a year. Sales for her second year were $5 million and she projects sales of $25 million by 1995.

for new freedoms, challenges, and life-styles. And entrepreneurs of today share some of the characteristics of those early day pioneers.

Pioneers moved westward without clear information regarding the opportunities that they sought. One can only speculate that if more had been known, two things would have happened. First, it is likely that fewer people would have ventured forth. Second, those who did venture forth might have been better prepared for the trials that lay ahead of them. Again, similarities exist between the pioneers of yesterday and the entrepreneurs of today. If more were known about the opportunities and risks that lay ahead, fewer entrepreneurs would start a venture and those that did would be better equipped for survival.

This chapter will focus on analyzing entrepreneurial opportunities and assessing the feasibility of beginning a venture to capitalize on the opportunity. We will look at sources of opportunities, a process for opportunity analysis, and techniques that may make that analysis more objective. We begin, however, by discussing several opportunities for ventures.

VENTURE OPPORTUNITIES

A number of books and magazine articles espouse **opportunities** for ventures that allegedly will make the entrepreneur rich overnight. Headlines or titles such as "How to Get Rich in Real Estate," "You, Too, Can Make a Million Dollars Before You Are Thirty," "Turn Your Hobby into a Multi-million-Dollar Venture," or "Starting a Profitable Business With No Money Down," all suggest that money is "out there" for the taking. It may be that the primary person getting rich from a "get-rich-quick" book is the author of the book. It is better to search out genuine opportunities or develop one's own opportunity than to trust the entrepreneurship equivalence of television evangelists.

In 1987, *Venture* magazine listed its one hundred best ideas for new start-ups.[2] (Unfortunately, *Venture* magazine itself failed after ten years of publishing.) Several items of interest can be gleaned from a study of this sample of ventures (Table 5-1). First, they are not all high tech. In fact, of the entire list of one hundred ideas, more are low tech than are high tech. Second, note the capital required to launch the venture. There is a substantial difference in amounts required, ranging from a low of $10,000 to $1.5 million. Third, the ventures represent a wide variety of different industries and products or services. Some products offer a significant improvement in the medical diagnostics field while others are in the luxury service field that caters to the whims of affluent individuals.

The variety of venture types and sizes, the amounts of capital needed to start them, and industry niches they fill illustrates that the opportunities available to the prospective entrepreneur are limited only by one's imagination and the ability to fully develop and fund the idea. This suggests that the key to successfully pursuing an entrepreneurial opportunity is not in coming up with the right idea, but analyzing the opportunity well in order to maximize the probability for success.

SOURCES OF VENTURE OPPORTUNITIES

Opportunities for new ventures come from sources that are as varied as the ventures themselves may be. These include inventions, spin-offs, purchase of existing ventures, and capitalizing on a number of trends that occur in society. This section will examine **sources of venture opportunities.** The next section will focus on criteria for evaluating these opportunities.

TABLE 5-1
Samples from *Venture's* 100 New Ideas for Business

Company Name	Product/Service	Start-up Cost
Edmonds Medical Systems	Underwater treadmill	$ 400,000
Professional Dental Technologies	Rotating toothbrush	500,000
Infantest Corp.	Test for infant retardation	320,000
National Equipment Network, Inc.	Used equipment locator	75,000
Saba Technologies, Inc.	Hand-held text scanner	700,000
Beta Medical Products	Under-bed X-ray	350,000
Nutronics Corp.	Alternator interrupter	500,000
Waddles Sportswear	Executive boxer shorts	10,000
Radair, Inc.	Weather tracker	500,000
Arnox Corp.	Fire retardant	1,500,000
Games Gang, Ltd.	Pictionary (game)	35,000
Cease Fire Corp.	Aerosol fire extinguisher	1,350,000
Sealed With a Kiss	Gift-sending service	10,000

Identifying Trends

Opportunities often develop from demographic, social, technological, or business trends. The past thirty years have witnessed dramatic changes in all four areas. These trends are often the source of significant venture opportunities. Successful entrepreneurs watch developing trends to see if the trends create needs that have not existed in the past.

Demographic Trends

Demographics is the study of population characteristics. Of particular interest is the study of population segments or "cohorts of population" as they age over the years. Two cohorts that are significant from the perspective of venture opportunities are baby boomers and senior citizens. The baby boom refers to those people born in the fifteen-year period following World War II. This cohort is approximately 40 percent larger than the 15-year cohorts before and after it. As the baby boom generation ages, the age group they are in at a given time swells for over a decade and then falls to pre-baby boom levels. Due to the very large relative size of the baby boom cohort, the needs of that age group create significant venture opportunities. As the cohort moves slowly to the next age group, different opportunities are created. This phenomenon will continue for at least the next forty years (Table 5-2).

Decade	Baby Boom Age Range	Products/Concerns
1950s	Preschool, grade school	Children's clothes, toys, grade school buildings
1960s	Grade school, high school	Records, clothes, used cars, high schools
1970s	College, early family	Apartments, houses, cars, entry-level jobs, baby furniture, fast food, insurance, college buildings
1980s	Early/mid-family	Cars, entertainment, IRAs, college funds, teenage clothes, larger houses
1990s	Mid-family	College tuition, home remodeling
2000s	Empty nest	Vacations, investments
2010 and beyond	Retirement	Travel, health care, retirement facilities

TABLE 5-2
Effects of the Baby Boom Generation
SOURCE: Adapted from U.S. Bureau of the Census data.

Another significant aspect of the baby boom generation is that in addition to their large numbers, baby boomers tend to be relatively more affluent than their predecessors. Thus, the total increase in buying power is doubly significant.

Fewer people are as familiar with the baby "bust" that followed the baby boom. The years following the baby boom decade saw a significant *decline* in the number of babies born. One impact of the baby bust was being felt in the late 1980s in the entry-level job market where fewer numbers of high school and college graduates entered the labor force. Typical of this was the move toward hiring older workers in fast-food restaurants because fewer teenagers were available.

Approximately twenty-five years after the baby boom era, there was another pronounced, though smaller, bulge in population. This time period has been referred to as the baby boomlet or echo boom. These were the children of the baby boomers. Even though the birth rate declined during the sixties and seventies, the large number of baby boom families yielded a large increase in the number of births. Perhaps more important for product manufacturers of service providers is that there were more, but smaller, families. Thus, each family had more money to spend per child. Tracing both the baby boom and echo boom can create tremendous venture opportunities.

An additional demographic group to be considered is the senior citizens. Because people are living longer, this category of people is increasing dramatically. Many members of this generation are relatively affluent and do not mind spending their money. At the same time, the older generation will require additional health care, services, and the like.

Along with age-related trends are a number of other trends that may affect venture opportunities. These include geographic shifts in population, increases in levels of education, changes in spending patterns, changes in racial percentages within the population, and the changes in earnings of those groups.

VENTURE PERSPECTIVE 5-1

THE BABY BOOM TURNS 45

The baby boom's 45th birthday may prove to be as momentous as its first. It will begin a population explosion among affluent, maturing householders. And it will turn the 1990s into peak years for consumer spending. Consider the following.

- Consumer demand for bifocal eyeglasses will grow rapidly in the 1990s, for example, and low-fat food will fly off the shelves.
- People aged 45 to 64 are four times more likely to suffer from arthritis than are younger adults. They are six times more likely than younger adults to have diabetes.
- . . . are eating more poultry and fish, fresh fruits and vegetables, low-fat milk, and whole-grain breads and cereals. But they are also eating more desserts.

- While 44 babies a year are born to every 10,000 women aged 40 to 44, only 2 are born to women aged 45 to 49. . . .
- After the age of 45, single people are less likely to marry, and married people are less likely to get divorced.
- Baby boomers aged 25 to 34 had a 1989 median family income of $31,000 . . . The median family income for older boomers (aged 35 to 44) was over $40,000. . . .
- In 1986, the net worth of householders under the age of 35 averaged only $40,000 . . . the average net worth of householders aged 35 to 44 was over $100,000, those aged 45 to 54 averaged nearly $175,000.
- Baby boom women are far more likely than their

predecessors to have gone to college.
- By their sheer numbers, they will overwhelm the corporate structure with qualified applicants for top jobs. Compared with previous generations, a larger share of baby boomers will never realize their career goals. Some will go into business for themselves, thereby increasing competition in many markets.
- Today, 25.6 million people are in their peak income years, aged 45 to 54. When all of the baby boomers pass their 45th birthday, in 2010, that number will increase by 47 percent, to 37.7 million.

SOURCE: Judith Waldrop, "The Baby Boom Turns 45," *American Demographics* (January 1991): 22–27. Used with permission. © American Demographics, January 1991.

Social Trends

Numerous opportunities arise from social trends that have occurred in the past twenty years and are likely to continue to occur. Examples of social trends that can affect opportunities include a decline in the number of smokers, increased interest in exercise and other health-related issues, increased interest in environmental issues, shifts in political persuasion, shifts in dating and cohabitation patterns caused by AIDS, the number of dual career families, the number of single-parent families, changes in church and religious affiliations, and attitudes toward such issues as abortion, war, and the homeless.

There is perhaps no single trend that has been more pervasive in society over the past twenty years than the phenomenon of women entering the labor force. Not only are women entering the workforce in unprecedented numbers, but they are increasingly entering managerial and professional occupations. This, coupled with changes in marriage and divorce rates, changes in education, and delayed child bearing, has led to dramatic changes in the number of products and services available.

Technological Trends

Computer-related trends are among the most notable trends evident today. Laptop computers have more computing power than room-size computers did thirty years ago. Scanners, fax machines, electronic mail, and desktop publishing were not commonly known in the mid-1980s. Other technological trends are also evident. Development of diagnostic equipment has completely changed the health care industry. Automobiles are more technologically complex than they were ten to fifteen years ago. Microwave ovens have changed the way families cook. Music recording and listening has changed twice in the past twenty years. It would be nearly impossible to buy an eight-track tape now, and it is getting more difficult to find record albums. Record stores now carry more compact discs than cassettes. Videocassette players and tapes have significantly changed the movie industry.

Business Trends

A number of trends have developed in the way businesses operate. *Outsourcing* refers to the trend among large corporations to contract with other, often small, firms to produce components for them or to provide services. In either case, these products or services are often ones that were previously managed within the corporation. Unionized firms, for example, have realized that products can be outsourced cheaper from small nonunion plants that work to the corporation's specifications. In some cases the outsourcing is for services such as medical claims processing, technical manual preparation, and cafeteria operations.

Another business trend is the *management development seminar*. Increasingly, corporations either send managers to seminars or bring seminars to the corporation as part of their corporate development program. Company training departments may prefer to have an outside vendor provide these seminars rather than use their own staff.

Technology consultants illustrate another trend in business. As technology becomes more complex and more rapidly obsolete, opportunities exist both for the technology itself and for consultants who can demonstrate the technology. Few firms have the expertise in-house to make optimal decisions regarding computers, telephone systems, plant layout and equipment, or office systems. Potential entrepreneurs who do have expertise in the field may find consulting to be a most lucrative business.

The business trend that will dramatically affect both large and small businesses throughout the 1990s is *total quality management* (TQM). Total quality management is a new philosophy of management based primarily on the work of W. Edwards Deming and Joseph M. Juran shortly after World War II. Largely ignored in the United States for forty years, Deming and Juran taught the Japanese how to make quality the number one goal in their companies. U.S.-based companies are now beginning to see the benefits of the total quality management philosophy.

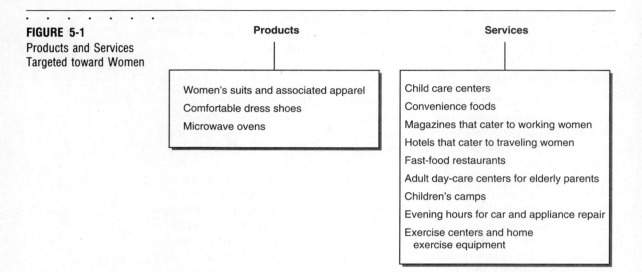

FIGURE 5-1
Products and Services
Targeted toward Women

Products	Services
Women's suits and associated apparel	Child care centers
Comfortable dress shoes	Convenience foods
Microwave ovens	Magazines that cater to working women
	Hotels that cater to traveling women
	Fast-food restaurants
	Adult day-care centers for elderly parents
	Children's camps
	Evening hours for car and appliance repair
	Exercise centers and home exercise equipment

The focus of TQM is on customer satisfaction and employee involvement. Bertrand Schwartz of the Modernization Association calls TQM "market-driven quality" that is based on the combination of the needs and wants of customers and excellence in everything a company does across the whole business.[3]

New and emerging businesses can find opportunities in TQM in two ways. First, there will be many opportunities for entrepreneurs to provide training and consulting to existing businesses. Second and more important, entrepreneurs who can incorporate TQM into their own ventures may find that the enhanced quality that results gives them a competitive advantage over those businesses that have not embraced the total quality management philosophy.

Information Sources

Awareness of trends is useful, but specific information regarding trends is far more useful. Without specific information, entrepreneurs are only guessing as to the magnitude of a particular trend. Fortunately, an entire industry has developed that can assist in translating data into useful information. American Demographics, Inc., publishes a directory of marketing information companies as an annual supplement to its *American Demographics* magazine. Table 5-3 shows its "Best of the Best" listing of information sources in various categories. This list is, however, a small portion of the total number of information sources.

Other Sources of Opportunities

The previous section noted a number of trends that can be the source of new venture ideas. These opportunities build on changes in population segments, social trends, or business trends, and the concomitant demands

Geodemographic Sources

CACI Marketing Systems
Claritas
Donnelley Marketing Information Services
Equifax Marketing Decision Systems, Inc.
National Planning Data Corporation

Consumer Purchasing Information

Information Resources, Inc.
Mediamark Research, Inc.
NPD/Nielsen
NPD Group
Simmons Market Research Bureau

Attitude/Life-style Information

Cambridge Reports
National Opinion Research Center
The Roper Center for Public Opinion Research
Yankelovich Clancy Shulman

Public Sources

U.S. Bureau of Labor Statistics
U.S. Bureau of the Census
National Center for Education Statistics
National Center for Health Statistics
State data centers

TABLE 5-3
American Demographics, Inc., Information Sources
SOURCE: *1991 Directory of Marketing Information Companies* (Ithaca, NY: American Demographics, Inc., 1990), 7–10.

for new products or services. Trends are not the only source of new ventures, however. The sections that follow point out other sources of ideas that may be equally valuable.

Launchpad Jobs

Chapter 3 noted that many entrepreneurs are "pulled" into starting their own ventures. Those individuals who started ventures similar to their previous jobs were often attracted to a new venture because of some experience or discovery in a prior job or company. These previous jobs or companies are referred to as "launchpad" jobs because they are the base from which the new venture is launched. A National Federation of Independent Business (NFIB) study found that almost half of entrepreneurs got the idea for their current venture from either a prior job or a family business.[4]

A variety of scenarios exist. In some cases the launchpad job is one that is held only until capital can be raised to underwrite some new venture. In some cases, a new discovery is made in the old job. The old company is not interested in pursuing the new idea, so the individual leaves and launches a new venture. Sometimes the old company serves as a formal launchpad by providing not only an environment that encourages the new development, but also possibly provides initial funding for a spin-off. In other cases, the original company is completely unaware of the entrepreneur's development. In this situation, the entrepreneur develops an idea for a

TABLE 5-4

Launchpads to Launches

SOURCE: Phil Lemmons "Ferment in Silicon Valley," *Byte* (May 1983): 266–70. Cheryll Aimee Barron "Silicon Valley Phoenixes," *Fortune* (Nov. 23, 1987): 128–37. Dirk Hanson, *The New Alchemists* (Boston: Little, Brown & Co., 1982), 115.

These Individuals	Left These Firms	And Formed These
Steve Wozniak	Hewlett-Packard	Apple Computer
James Treybig and Michael Green	Hewlett-Packard	Tandem Computers
Roger Vass	Altos Computer Systems	Victory Computer Systems
Larry Boucher	IBM	Adaptec
George Brennen	Memorex, Honeywell	Evotek
T. J. Rodgers	Advance Micro Devices	Cypress Semiconductor
Allen Michels	Convergent Technologies	Dana Computer
Gorden Campbell	Intel	Chips & Technologies
Gene Amdahl	IBM	Amdahl Corp.
Robert Noyce, Gordon Moore, and Andrew Grove	Fairchild Semiconductor	Intel
Steve Jobs	Apple Computer	NeXT, Inc.

new venture while holding the launchpad job and retains the old job until the new venture is ready to launch. A final situation is one in which the founder or manager of one venture quits or is fired and then uses the experience gained there to launch another company. This is precisely what Steve Jobs did. He co-founded Apple Computer and was part of the growing company until he was pushed out by John Sculley. A short period later, Jobs founded NeXT Computers.

The launchpad concept is especially prevalent in the high-tech area where individuals conceptualize a new venture while working for another company. Once the new venture idea is sufficiently developed, the entrepreneur and possible associates quit their existing jobs and immediately launch the new venture. Many ventures have been begun by executives who left their companies either voluntarily or involuntarily and then formed their own new ventures (Table 5-4).

Moonlighting

Many new ventures have been started as hobbies or sideline jobs. In these situations, the entrepreneur may have had a full-time job that is totally unrelated to any hobby or moonlighting venture. The entrepreneur knows that the new venture is not sufficient to risk giving up the security of the full-time job. Sometimes the person's spouse manages the business until it grows sufficiently to provide enough profits for both spouses to live comfortably without the second income. The moonlighting venture is often run out of the home or in a storefront location. This kind of venture typically will be a low-growth venture but some moonlighting ventures tap into a new market that eventually exhibits substantial growth.

> ### VENTURE PERSPECTIVE 5-2
> • • • • • • • • • • • • •
>
> ## BUSINESS SERVICES, INC.
>
> Business Services, Inc., began as an idea of Pamela and Jerry Goodson. Pam Goodson had been an executive secretary for a marketing company and Jerry was employed by a major manufacturer in the community. From her dealings with the public through the marketing firm, Pam became aware that many small companies and independent sales representatives had need for only occasional use of typewriters, copiers, computers, and office space. The need was not consistent nor was it enough to warrant having a full-time office. With her experience in the secretarial field, Pam felt that she could start a venture that provided temporary services to this particular target market. She did a substantial amount of research on the necessary equipment, staff, marketing, and total financing necessary to launch the venture. With her plan developed, equipment purchased, and a location secured, Pam quit her job and launched Business Services, Inc. Pam's role was to do all day-to-day management of the company with the help of two or three employees. Jerry decided to keep his job with the manufacturing company, at least for the short run. However, because of his job in the accounting department of that company, he believed that he could do the necessary bookkeeping and billing for BSI at night.
>
> Business Services, Inc., turned out to be just as Jerry and Pam had envisioned it. Business was slow in the beginning and generally consisted of copying, typing resumes, and doing some mass mailings. After a while, however, business began to grow. They added two more staff workers and took over the adjoining building, which was converted into short-term rentable office space and conference room facilities. Pam and Jerry eventually added an accounting service and a temporary worker agency to their list of services. Jerry decided then that the business was secure enough and demanding enough that he should quit his secure job with the manufacturer and concentrate his efforts on Business Services, Inc.

Invention-Related Opportunities

Venture opportunities related to inventions may arise in one of two ways. In the first situation, the entrepreneur is also the inventor. In the second case, an entrepreneur searches for existing inventions that could be marketed.

Some inventions are born out of perceived needs. Some are the result of the creative genius of the inventor. And some are accidental discoveries. Whatever the source of the invention, the opportunities for marketing the new product or service may be great. However, they also may not be great. The product must be analyzed objectively to determine the extent of the opportunity.

A person who attempts to produce and market a newly invented product is sometimes called an "inventrepreneur." Two problems exist with inventrepreneurs. First, an inventor creates what *appears to be* a significant product, but that product may be either of more limited use than was thought or already on the market. The second problem is that inventrepreneurs may embody the characteristics of inventors far more than they do the characteristics of good entrepreneurs. In some instances, a new product is developed by someone who has little sense for business, little knowledge of good management practices, and little ability to either raise funds or control operations. In these cases, an opportunity may exist but the inventrepreneur is not the best person to take advantage of the opportunity. Selling a patent, contracting for the production of the product, or taking in one or more partners might be a far more advantageous method of bringing the product to market. In other words, the inventor may be most benefitted by finding an entrepreneur to produce and market the product.

The entrepreneur searching for an invention to market faces the problem of finding a suitable product. Some companies regularly advertise themselves as invention marketers. These companies attempt to find an inventor who has developed a product. They then contract to take whatever action is necessary to bring the product to market. Another method besides advertising for products is to check the publications of the United States Patent Office. Thousands of products have been patented that have not been brought to the market. Admittedly, many of them have little market potential. On the other hand, some may have substantial opportunity if an entrepreneur with the capability to develop them is available. Universities and government agencies sometimes develop marketable products, and these products may be licensed to individuals or firms for production and marketing.

RECOGNIZING OPPORTUNITIES

Some entrepreneurs create opportunities by creating a product that hopefully meets some need. Others identify an obvious need and attempt to fill it by creating a product or service. Other opportunities are not so obvious. The key to exploiting those not-so-obvious opportunities is to recognize them, see the possibilities, and then marshall the resources to exploit them. The first step, however, is to recognize the possibilities.

How does one recognize a not-so-obvious opportunity? One way involves speculation based on existing products. That is, start with an existing product or service and then look beyond it to see if that product or service can meet other needs. A producer of military equipment might look beyond the military applications to civilian applications. A company producing general accounting software might look to see what *specific* applications could be used and then tailor it to those uses. Perhaps a computerized billing and appointment system for a doctor's office could be adapted to use in dentists' offices and then adapted again for orthodontists.

A second way to recognize opportunities is to look at a particular target market and study that market carefully to identify latent wants or needs. An example of this is the recently introduced single-serving packages of frozen vegetables. Producers realized that the number of single people is increasing dramatically. Traditional packages of frozen vegetables, bread, ice cream, and other foods are designed for families. When singles are identified as a separate target market, producing foods in smaller containers becomes an opportunity worth considering.

A third possibility is to examine trends and see if producers have either missed aspects of a trend or have lost part of the potential market in the effort to better serve another part of the market. For example, televisions and VCRs have become more and more high tech. Remote control units for them have masses of buttons that, if pushed accidentally, can create a number of unwanted responses. This can be especially difficult for elderly people, who may only want to change channels and the volume of the sets. But even the universal remotes are far more complicated than needed for basic usage. To meet the needs of a segment of the market, Mitsubishi Electric brought out a revolutionary product: a pen-shaped remote control with only three buttons! One turns the TV on or off, one changes the channel, and one adjusts the volume.[5]

A number of methods can be used to recognize or generate ideas for opportunities. Many readers are already familiar with *brainstorming*, where members of a group throw out ideas about the topic in rapid succession with no time spent measuring their worth. A variation, called *brainwriting*, has individuals in a group write their ideas and then pass them to the next person who must amplify the idea and pass it on. *Judgment panels* are groups of experts in an area who openly discuss the topic in question. Market researchers often use *focus groups* of product or service users who discuss aspects of the product or service. The *Delphi approach* is a nonverbal, sequential forecasting technique where individuals write down their assessments and give them to a coordinator who then returns summarized answers to the participants for refinements.

THE NEED FOR OPPORTUNITY ANALYSIS

The previous section discussed sources of venture opportunities. Once opportunities are identified, however, it is critical that they be objectively evaluated. This objective evaluation is necessary for at least two reasons. First, the objective assessment reduces the probability that a decision to pursue a venture will be based on intuition, or "seat-of-the-pants" management. It is true, of course, that successful entrepreneurs often do have a knack for intuitively assessing the future. But this ability is not a universal trait among entrepreneurs. Sometimes potential entrepreneurs have a fixation on their product or service that results in tunnel vision. Thus, they can see only the goal and not the impediments to achieving the goal. In one case, an individual wanted to build a $7 million facility to train auto mechanics. Once objective analysis of the venture was made, it became clear that: (1) there was little demand by students for a private school for auto mechanics, (2) most dealers and many independent garages would not use the graduates, and (3) the individual had virtually no personal capital to invest and had little business experience.

The second reason for an objective assessment is that investors typically are very astute and they will not consider a venture at all unless there is some documentation of analysis showing the venture's probability of success. Most investors have read hundreds of plans. Only a small percentage are funded. But they have vast experience at considering ventures, and they also have a "feel" for what makes a good venture. The entrepreneur must build a case that confirms an investor's positive feelings for a venture and overcomes any negative feelings the investor might have.

CRITERIA FOR ANALYSIS

Potential opportunities should meet several criteria in order to be worthy of pursuing. These include a sufficiently large window of opportunity, a market that has either breadth or depth and is acceptably large, some protection from competition, the ability to spread risk, and a reasonable investment that provides an acceptable return. Seldom will an opportunity meet all these criteria. Yet, those that do not come close should be scrutinized carefully.

The Window of Opportunity

No opportunity lasts forever. The key to this criterion is to determine how long an entrepreneur has to take advantage of the opportunity. The **window of opportunity** is the period of time during which an investment has maximum potential for success.[6]

Imagine that you are playing a game in which you are to throw balls through a window that randomly opens and closes. You are rewarded for each ball that you throw through the open window and penalized for each ball that hits a closed window. In order to score as many points as possible, you would start throwing just as the window begins to open and stop just before it closes.

Entrepreneurship is much the same. A venture that is launched before the window opens may fail because it was launched prematurely. An example of this might be software that was written for a new computer system coming on the market. If the software is written too soon, it might have to sit on the shelves too long if the hardware happens to be delayed, or it might not incorporate late changes in the hardware.

Some ventures are launched so late into the opportunity window that the window begins to close shortly after the launch. In this case, the entrepreneur loses because insufficient time is allowed to recoup the investment and harvest the venture. The software example above can illustrate this problem, too. Suppose the software was developed for the machine too late instead of too early. By the time the software hits the market, the hardware was being phased out and/or competing versions of the software had already been accepted by customers. The entrepreneur's capital might never be recovered before the demand for the software ended.

Determining when the entrepreneurial window will close is difficult in most cases. It is somewhat akin to selling stock just before the price drops. This is especially true if the product is in an industry where products are superceded by new models frequently. On the other hand, if growth in sales of similar products is beginning to decline, it may be a sign that the window is beginning to close.

Depth and Breadth of the Market

Depth of the market for a product refers to how intensively a product is purchased by its customers. A product with a high volume of sales to loyal customers can be considered to have a substantial depth. Conversely, a product with a number of different uses would be considered to have a broad market. In either case, the greater the depth or breadth of a proposed product the greater the probability that the product will succeed.

Size of Total Market

The size of the total market is important for two reasons. First, the market for the product must be sufficiently large to be attractive. Second, the size of the market may affect the amount of investment required to exploit it. In most cases, the larger the market the better. Occasionally a small market may be desirable if a larger market would invite competition or if the large market would require too much investment. That is the situation that Mesa Airlines exploited in the entrepreneurial profile in Chapter 2. The Risleys entered the commuter airline market because it was more affordable and because the major airlines were not interested in it at the time.

The economies of scale issue may or may not be relevant to the actual launch of the product and may become relevant only much later. Yet, the need for future investment must be considered at the outset. For example, the manufacture of some products is labor intensive up to some point where automation is necessary. The cost of automating the production, however, may be quite high. A decision must then be made about whether the entrepreneur wants a small-volume production with low capital investment or high-volume production with major capital investment.

Protection from Competitors

The key to the protection issue is to have some aspect of the product or service that is not easily duplicated by others. Patents and trademarks sometimes give protection, and trade secrets occasionally do. G. D. Searle produces a product called aspartame and marketed under the trade name Nutra-Sweet. It is the only producer of aspartame since it holds a patent on the product. IBM, tiring of the number of clones of its personal computer, produced the PS/2 personal computer, which allegedly was more difficult to clone.

In most cases, it is difficult to maintain protection from competition during the life of the product. Electronics firms have great difficulty recouping investments in research and development because of the rapidity with which competing products appear on the market. The lag time is often no more than a few months from the time a new product is introduced until competitors have similar products on the market.

Investment Requirements

Some investors believe that if an opportunity is good enough, capital can be found somewhere. On the other hand, investors often have several choices of ventures. If there are two roughly similar plans being considered with similar returns expected, the one with the lower front-end investment will normally get the nod. Sometimes an opportunity is indeed desirable but the amount of cash needed up front is simply prohibitive. This is particularly true when the entrepreneur or entrepreneurial team does not have sufficient capital of their own to invest. Many potential ventures are never launched because the entrepreneur cannot raise even 5 percent of the funds from personal capital. Most investors want more financial involvement from lead entrepreneurs than many entrepreneurs can provide.

Return on Investment

Various investors have different definitions of an acceptable return on invested capital. Low-growth entrepreneurs may be willing to accept low returns if the cash flow is sufficient to provide a satisfactory living. Venture capitalists, at the opposite extreme, may require ten times their investment within five years.

Ability to Spread Risks

The risk of a venture will be higher if:

- The amount of capital required is high.
- The payback period is long.
- The product is totally new.
- The product is the only product produced by the venture.
- There are no alternative uses of the product.
- The product can be easily copied.
- The investment in fixed assets is high.

An entrepreneur may not be able to spread the risk sufficiently if this is the only venture being considered. Investors, on the other hand, may have a number of different projects funded simultaneously, thereby spreading the risks among several projects.

THE OPPORTUNITY EVALUATION PROCESS

Once a venture possibility is determined, actions should then be taken to determine the feasibility of the venture. This should be done first from the perspective of the entrepreneur and then repeated, as applicable, from the perspective of an investor. If a favorable conclusion is reached in both analyses, then the venture should be pursued. If a negative finding is determined from the entrepreneur's perspective but a positive result is found from the investor's perspective, then the venture should be altered or a change in the entrepreneurial team should be made. If the entrepreneurial perspective is favorable, but the investor perspective is unfavorable, then the venture might have to be re-evaluated to determine if there are other ways to launch the same venture with less funding. Perhaps the venture can be scaled down to a level where funding is available either from personal sources or from low-level investors. If the venture receives an unfavorable rating from both the entrepreneur's perspective and the investor's perspective, then serious consideration should be given to dropping the venture idea completely and considering other ideas (Figure 5-2).

The analysis process for any new venture should consist of two stages. The first is an informal analysis to determine whether the venture idea in

	Entrepreneur's Perspective	
	Favorable	Unfavorable
Investor's Perspective — Favorable	Launch venture	Reformulate management team
Investor's Perspective — Unfavorable	Downscale or locate other types of investors	Look for other opportunities

general is sound. The second stage is a more sophisticated, objective analysis of the venture that determines its possibilities for growth and the likelihood of a successful harvest if desired. Specific parts of the analysis may not be relevant for some new ventures. For example, a service business will not be concerned about product-related costs. Retail businesses may have to spend more time considering suppliers and suggested markups than the cost of the product itself.

Stage I—The Informal Analysis

The **informal analysis** should in no way be considered the final analysis of the venture. It is simply a first pass through the consideration of a venture opportunity to see if it merits additional formal analysis. As such it serves as a screening device to determine quickly if an opportunity is worth the effort of further analysis.

A number of questions or checklists are available in popular magazines or from the Small Business Administration.[7] The items below are typical and are a useful place to start in the analysis process.

1. *The aha! factor.* If the new product or service is shown to a dozen friends, do they all say "Aha! I must have one of those!" (or something similar)? If they do not say "Aha!", the likelihood of strangers doing so is slim. If friends are impressed, then find twenty strangers. Are they excited? If so, then they should be asked if they would definitely buy the product, might buy the product, or would not likely buy the product. Further, how much would they be willing to pay for the product?

2. *The 10:1 ratio.* To get a product from the manufacturer to the customer, the product may go through a manufacturer's representative, a wholesaler, a retailer, and then to the customer. Each of these will either raise the price or charge a commission. In addition, there must be some marketing, packaging, shipping,

financing, and allowance for defects or returns. Each of these also takes money. A rule of thumb is the 10:1 ratio. A customer must be willing to pay ten times the manufacturer's cost in order for everyone in the chain to have some profit. Will the friends still be excited at that price? At what price will they be excited, and will 10 percent of that be sufficient to cover costs and allow some profit?

A service business, of course, will not be as concerned about the cost of products. However, the cost of the service must be considered. Included in the cost of the service is labor, equipment costs, cost of supplies, and other advertising costs. So even though there is not a product per se to evaluate, the cost of providing the service must be considered fully.

3. *The look-alike test.* One inventrepreneur developed a product to be sold through hardware stores. This was a unique product that served a small but viable market. Unfortunately, while checking out the 10:1 ratio at a local hardware store, an almost identical product was discovered. The market was simply too small for two similar products. If a product's market is sufficiently large, then there may be room for two similar products. Certainly the computer industry is an example of this with the many clones of the personal computer available. On the other hand, the size of the market must be carefully considered if the product is developed allegedly as a new and unique product when existing products are already on the market.

4. *The "If it's so great, why hasn't it been done?" test.* This is the flip side of the look-alike test. If there is nothing like it on earth, the reason may be that no one was creative enough to invent it. The reason might also be, however, that it is an idea whose time has not come.

5. *The friendly banker test.* Many potential entrepreneurs come away from their first meeting with a banker very depressed at the cool reception they receive for an idea they thought was excellent. A better way to address this issue is to go to the banker with the idea as part of market research rather than to get money. Bankers and other financing specialists have often had years of experience and may have a good "feel" for whether a product is good or not. These bankers are usually quite willing to discuss an idea frankly with a potential entrepreneur without the threat of having to make a yes/no decision on financing. Later, if the idea passes more objective tests on its feasibility, the banker may have the opportunity to look at the plan again. If, on the other hand, the bank representative gives honest negative feedback, this gives the entrepreneur the opportunity to refine the proposal without the stigma of a "turn-down" from the earlier meeting.

6. *The prototype pre-test.* Developing a prototype of a product may be extremely expensive. But it won't be nearly as expensive as the cost of failure if the product fails after mass production and marketing have occurred. A marketable prototype should be developed and, if possible, marketed locally through an appropriate retail store at a price that might be expected once actual mass production begins.

This price will likely be far below what the prototype cost. But the point is to determine whether customers will actually spend their money on the product at some logical price.

Stage II—The Formal Analysis

Once the opportunity has passed an informal analysis, a formal **feasibility analysis** can then be made. The feasibility analysis should include three parts: the marketing feasibility, the financial feasibility, and the technical feasibility.[8] A final category, called "fatal flaws," completes the analysis.

Marketing Feasibility

The marketing feasibility looks outside the opportunity to determine if there is a fit between the venture and the environment it will be facing. Depending on the nature of the proposed venture, the amount of research may be extensive and require some high-cost market research, or it may be such that a moderate amount of market research can give a ballpark answer that is sufficient for the needs of the entrepreneur. Answers to the following questions should be determined.

1. How large is the total market? That is, approximately how many total customers are there that might purchase the product or service? Does the market seem to be growing significantly (more than 25 percent a year) or is growth slow?
2. Are the customers identifiable or known only in general terms?
3. How many competitors are there currently for this or similar products?
4. Are there other products available that, although not the same as the proposed product, are close enough to take sales away from the proposed venture?
5. What demographic or social trends are relevant? Will the trends increase or decrease sales over time? Are the trends pervasive or are they somewhat faddish?
6. Is the product one in which the government will have a role? Will that role be one of regulation or encouragement?
7. What are the competitive dynamics in the industry? Are some competitors dominating the industry or are most competitors of equal size? Does competition appear to be aggressive or more passive?
8. How long will the window of opportunity stay open? Is there sufficient time to get the venture launched, achieve desired growth, and perhaps harvest the venture before the demand declines?
9. How easy will it be for new competitors to enter the market?

Financial Feasibility

Determining the financial feasibility of the opportunity must necessarily follow initial determination of the marketing portion of the study since a good estimate of total sales is the basis for most of the financial analyses.

Once that is determined, then a number of questions regarding the financial feasibility can be answered.

1. What fixed costs must be incurred either before or during the first three years of the venture? Can any of these fixed costs be either shifted or reduced through leasing or subcontracting?
2. How long will it be before profit is achieved? What is the break-even point for the venture and when is it likely to occur?
3. How long will it be before a positive cash flow occurs? In some cases the positive cash flow is more important than profit.
4. What gross margins can be expected? How much administrative costs will be incurred?
5. How much total financing will be needed? What kinds of financing will be necessary? Will debt financing or equity financing or some combination of these be most beneficial? How much control will have to be given up?
6. What overall return on investment can be expected?

Technical Feasibility

If it appears by now that the opportunity is viable, there is still the issue of the feasibility from a production process perspective. These questions may not determine for sure *whether* the venture should be launched, but they may determine *how* the venture will be launched. In some cases, however, the viability of the venture itself may be determined by whether the operations portion of the venture can be put into action.

1. What equipment will be needed to produce the product? Is the equipment specialized so it must be designed specifically for the venture or is it "off the shelf" equipment? Will it be salable in the event that the venture does not succeed? Can used equipment be purchased?
2. Are plant sites available that will meet the needs of the venture?
3. If equipment has already been identified, is it obsolete? Is new equipment available that will be more efficient? If so, what is the cost of the new equipment?
4. How much lead time will be necessary to launch the venture in order to install equipment, train employees, or locate suppliers?
5. Can any of the production process be subcontracted? If so, what kind of contract will be needed?
6. Does the product meet requirements for design, durability, reliability, product safety, and standardization?
7. Will a prototype of the product be necessary? If so, what will be the cost?

Fatal Flaws

Once the categories of marketing, financial, and technical feasibility have been studied and determined to be favorable, one remaining aspect of the overall feasibility remains. That is the concept of fatal flaws.[9] These are situations in which a single event or condition overrides all other favorable results. If this condition is encountered, then serious consideration *must* be given to abandoning the venture or at least revising it significantly. If two or more fatal flaws are uncovered, then even more thought should be given to dropping the idea. These fatal flaws should be very carefully considered. An entrepreneur should be careful about attempting to rationalize away negative results in these categories, because of the overwhelming importance of the issues.

1. *Very small market for the product.* Occasionally an entrepreneur will contend that there is an opportunity because "no one else has done this before." This may be an indication of an emerging trend, but it may also be an indication that the market is so small that no one can survive in it. This is an area where outside objective advice is far superior to that of friends and acquaintances.

2. *Overpowering competition and a high cost of entry.* Once in a great while a newcomer with a new vision can encroach on the territory of established players. People Express Airline was created as an attempt to enter the low-cost, no-frills segment of the airline industry. It succeeded for a period of time and might still be in business had it stuck with the initial plan. Significant reaction by major carriers coupled with inappropriate strategic moves by People Express CEO Donald Burr led to the eventual failure of the venture. Federal Express, on the other hand, appears to have made it in the package delivery side of air transport. As a general rule, unless the entrepreneur has a significant new idea and access to substantial funding, entering a market against the deep pockets of established competitors must be considered quite carefully.

3. *Inability to produce a product at a competitive price.* The ability to produce a product or service at a profit must be a serious consideration. This is especially true if existing competitors have already moved down the experience curve to the point that prices must be kept extremely competitive in order to gain market share.

4. *Lack of influence and control over product development and component prices.* The entrepreneur has little control if a major portion of the product, or perhaps a single key part, is produced by someone else. This may be especially true if the venture uses a relatively small number of the parts compared to other manufacturers. Component producers can be expected to give preference to established customers over a new customer with small demand. This lack of control may extend both to the availability and to the price of the components.

5. *Inability to expand beyond a one-product company.* One risk of being an inventrepreneur is that the venture usually hinges on a single product. If so, marketing the product competitively may be difficult because of lack of economies of scale in production, distribution, and advertising. More important, the risk of having a single product is significant. If the market should decline for that product or if large competitors move into the market, there may be no place for a one-product company to turn.

6. *Overwhelming financial requirements.* It has been said that if the project is good enough, capital for it *will be* available. This of course brings up the definition of "good enough" and also of "available." In many cases, the up-front investment is so great that the venture is unfundable even if the return does appear to be adequate. The contention that one has to have money to make money is at least partially true, for many entrepreneurs with excellent ideas fail to reach the market because they have little of their own funds to invest in the business and others will not invest without the entrepreneur's personal financial commitment.

7. *Inability to achieve rapid growth within two years.* This factor may not be important for the low-growth entrepreneur who sees the venture as a small business career rather than as a growth or harvestable venture. But entrepreneurship is more than the corner grocery store. If an opportunity is a true opportunity, it must offer significant returns to investors and it should offer the possibility of harvesting the venture at some time in the future.

ANALYSIS OF ENTREPRENEURIAL CAPABILITIES

The preceding sections dealt with the feasibility of an opportunity from the perspective of the opportunity itself. The analysis is not complete, however, unless the nature or capabilities of the entrepreneur is considered. An opportunity may make an excellent venture for one entrepreneur but a poor venture for another. Similarly, a venture might be a good idea in one time period but not as good in another time period because of changes in the entrepreneur's current status. It is necessary then to suggest key areas of analysis of the entrepreneur's capabilities in order to complete the determination of a venture's feasibility.

Individual Attributes

Chapter 3 discussed the entrepreneur as an individual. Entrepreneurial strengths and weaknesses should be related specifically to the opportunity being analyzed. Investors almost unanimously agree that the strength of the entrepreneurial team is the prime determinant in the decision to provide external capital to a venture. It is not critical that all members of the entrepreneurial team have previous experience in the specific area of the new venture. Indeed, having a variety of viewpoints lends stability to the venture. But it is necessary that at least some experience be related to the new venture in order to reduce the number of unnecessary mistakes by ill-informed team members.

Managerial experience in some venture is important. This is at least as important as the area-specific experience just discussed. We may all have met a person who has given thought to starting a venture but who has little business sense. This business sense can only come through experience. It is not an ingrained biological trait. The ability to make sound business decisions may often be the difference between success and failure or between funding and no funding.

Financial Resources

Financial resources comprise the second major factor that must be considered before launching a venture. Undercapitalization is the most striking characteristic of entrepreneurial ventures. Most are undercapitalized and some are severely undercapitalized. Chapter 7 will discuss financing the venture. It should be noted here that financing must be adequate for both the initial launch and second-stage growth of the venture.

Many investors require substantial hard cash from the entrepreneurial team. This is not to be confused with the ability to acquire the cash. It must be in hand, in the bank, immediately accessible for the launch of the venture. Other investors are not concerned about the source of the available personal funding as long as the entrepreneur can tap into it. Whichever the case may be, the entrepreneurial team must be able to personally contribute anywhere from 10 percent to half the capital depending on the nature of the venture.

Other Resources

The entrepreneurial team often brings substantial capabilities to a proposed venture. These include the individual team members' characteristics and experience as well as the financial resources mentioned above. Other resources may enter the equation, however. In some cases, plant and equipment currently owned or operated by the management team in an existing venture can be used in the proposed venture. Earlier experiences may lead to a distribution channel or other contacts that would assist in marketing the product or service. Ruth Owades of Calyx & Corolla exemplified this. Because of her previous mail-order venture, she had both a significant amount of cash and a knowledge of the mail-order industry.

Personal contacts of team members can be extremely useful in an entrepreneurial venture. These may be in the areas of financing, government contracting, industry sales, insurance, research and development, or a number of other areas important to the venture. Contacts can pave the way for entering a market, gaining financing, or developing suppliers or customers. In fact, some individuals join chambers of commerce or other local business organizations solely for the contacts they may develop. A word of caution, however, is that the contacts must indeed be firm contacts. If the contacts are to be used as trump cards to be played in gaining financing, it is critical that the contacts be viable and not a casual acquaintance. It is often helpful to have an "intent to buy" letter or some other support letter from the contact person before using the person's name.

MATCHING CAPABILITIES AND OPPORTUNITIES

The entrepreneurial team brings to the table a number of resources and capabilities. Some of the capabilities are general in nature, such as past managerial experience and some minimum level of financial resources. Other resources are unique and are of value only to specific venture opportunities. Regardless of whether the venture is being considered by an individual entrepreneur, a team, or an investor, these unique capabilities must be studied to determine if there will be a good **match between the capabilities and the opportunity.**

Consider again the example of Ruth Owades in the entrepreneurial profile leading off this chapter. In spite of her entrepreneurial skills and financial resources, Owades would have had a far more difficult time in interesting investors in a proposal to launch a major food processing firm. Her experience in mail order was a major factor in gaining investor acceptance of her business plan.

. . . .

SUMMARY

Opportunities for entrepreneurial ventures must be carefully considered in order to prevent unnecessary failures and inefficient use of resources. Some opportunities are either developed by the entrepreneur or are presented to an entrepreneur for analysis. In other situations, the entrepreneur must search for an opportunity. In either case, the opportunity must be studied for its feasibility.

Societal trends are the source of many opportunities for new ventures. Demographic and social trends are particularly ripe sources of entrepreneurial opportunities. Business and technological trends are also frequent sources of ideas. Opportunities may also be found through current experiences on the job. Some jobs lend themselves naturally to the launch of new opportunities. Other opportunities may be found through casual contacts, inventions, hobbies, or part-time jobs.

Some opportunities are not obvious. Entrepreneurs may have to be innovative in analyzing markets, products, trends, and target populations to uncover opportunities that could become the basis for real entrepreneurial ventures.

Once an opportunity is identified, then the entrepreneur must evaluate the opportunity. A suggested format is first to do an informal analysis followed by a formal, objective analysis. The objective analysis should include a determination of the marketing feasibility, the financial feasibility, and the technical feasibility. The marketing feasibility study considers whether the opportunity is trend based, the size of the total market, the number and type of competitors, and the timing of the window of opportunity. The financial feasibility must consider the startup costs, the breakeven point in both quantity and time, the overall return on investment predicted, and the projected cash flows. Finally, the technical feasibility should address concerns of necessary equipment, lead times, the possibility of subcontracting, and design requirements.

A final step in the analysis of opportunities is the consideration of fatal flaws. These are conditions that may kill the project regardless of the other aspects of the feasibility analyses. These fatal flaws may include extremely high startup costs relative to projected returns, a quite small market, significant competition, and the inability to successfully grow or harvest the venture.

Finally, the feasibility of the venture must be matched with the capabilities of the entrepreneurial team. The entrepreneurial capabilities must not only be acceptable in general, they must also be acceptable for the specific venture being considered.

1. Anyone who has worked with entrepreneurs knows that some ideas are good, but many potential ventures are ill-conceived, "off the wall" creations. How can you tell the difference between an obviously good venture idea and an obviously bad venture idea?

2. What are the advantages and disadvantages of going with an opportunity that developed naturally (some trend or invention) as opposed to consciously seeking out an opportunity in which to invest?

3. What sources of opportunities would be most relevant for someone who is about to graduate from college?

4. Why is it important to do the informal analysis before the formal analysis?

5. Would the analysis techniques you use for a low-growth venture be the same as for a growth venture? Why or why not?

6. Consider a small venture in your home town. If it were for sale, would you buy it? Explain your reasons in terms of the factors included in an opportunity analysis.

7. What is meant by an "opportunity/capability match"?

8. How does the opportunity analysis fit into the business plans discussed in Chapter 4?

9. Is it important for an entrepreneur considering a significant venture to get outside help in making a formal feasibility analysis?

10. How would opportunity analysis differ for service ventures compared with manufacturing ventures?

DISCUSSION QUESTIONS

EXERCISE 5-1 Opportunity Identification Exercises

EXERCISES

Using brainstorming techniques—group members throwing out ideas as fast as possible without considering their worth—identify as many uses as possible that *are not the primary use* for the following existing products. Assign one member as the recorder. Time the process so that no more than two minutes is spent on each item. When finished, count the total number of uses identified.

1. Tennis balls
2. Defective 5 ¼ inch floppy disks
3. Orange juice
4. Pictures of the White House
5. This textbook
6. Used printer ribbon
7. A new Nissan Sentra
8. An apartment house near campus
9. A cement truck

EXERCISE 5-2 Opportunity Analysis

For an identified product or service opportunity, make an estimate of its possibilities using the checklist below.

Estimation of Sales and Net Income

1. Total population of market area   _____
2. Percentage of total population in target market   _____
3. Number of times product/service will be purchased   _____
4. Total sales of product ($1 \times 2 \times 3$)   _____
5. Number of competitors   _____
6. Market share of each existing competitor   _____
7. Expected market share for this venture   _____
8. Forecast unit sales (4×7)   _____
9. Total revenue (price per unit times unit sales)   _____
10. Cost of goods sold   _____
11. Gross profit   _____
12. Administrative & marketing expenses   _____
13. Estimated net income   _____

Other Factors to Consider

14. Nature of trends_____
15. Protection from competitors_____
16. Initial investment required_____
17. Equity funds currently available_____
18. Estimated time to payback_____
19. Equipment needed_____
20. Special considerations_____
21. Fatal flaws_____
22. Additional information needed_____

ENDNOTES

1. Ellie Winninghoff, "Growing a New Market Niche," *Working Woman*, February 1991: 42–46.
2. David M. Roth, et al., "100 Ideas for New Businesses," *Venture*, December 1987, 35–70.
3. Lloyd Dobyns and Clare Crawford-Mason, *Quality or Else: The Revolution in World Business* (Boston: Houghton Mifflin Company, 1991), 187.
4. Arnold C. Cooper et al., *New Business in America: The Firms and Their Owners* (Washington, D.C.: NFIB Foundation, 1990), 19.
5. "The Best of 1990," *Business Week*, January 14, 1991, 123–128.
6. Jeffry A. Timmons, *New Venture Creation: Entrepreneurship in the 1990s*, 3d ed. (Homewood, IL: Richard D. Irwin, 1990), 73.
7. Wilson Harrell, "But Will It Fly?," *Inc.*, January 1987: 85–89.

8. Hans Schollhammer and Arthur H. Kuriloff, *Entrepreneurship and Small Business Management* (New York: John Wiley & Sons, 1979); Timmons, *New Venture Creation,* chapters 3 and 4.
9. Timmons, *New Venture Creation,* 81.

◆ Conveniesse, Inc. ◆

Collecting Information

Before leaving, the three agreed to more or less divide up the tasks they had identified. Since Sarah had driven to Buffalo this time, she agreed to stop by the convention and tourism center to find all the information she could about hotels and office buildings in the downtown area. She also knew that the 1990 Census data were available and could provide a variety of information including changes in the size and demographics of Buffalo.

Although Yolanda's product marketing expertise was in pharmaceuticals instead of food, she said she knew someone who could give her all the information they would need to know about product selection and costs. Jason knew demographics from his PR work and offered to track down market studies that had been done on the convenience industry in general. In so doing he might be able to adjust the data as much as possible to the particular concept they had in mind.

A week later, Yolanda answered her office phone to hear a very excited Jason Stone calling from Detroit.

"Sorry to call you at the office, Yolanda, but this couldn't wait! Guess where I've just been." And without waiting for her to guess, Jason continued, "Well, in the first place, we weren't the first ones with this idea. I just came from one of the big convention center hotel complexes here in Detroit. See, I cut through there occasionally when I decide to have lunch at this neat Chinese restaurant. Do you like Chinese food? Anyway, right there on the concourse level was a place—I don't even remember its name—that's very close to what we have in mind—very close. The only difference is that all the stores on the concourse are either owned or contracted by the hotel and serve almost exclusively conventioneers, which they have a ton of.

"Anyway," Jason continued, "I ambled around the store for a while and then found the manager. Using my best PR training, I struck up a conversation with him. I told him in general what we had in mind. I guess it must have been a quiet day as he was willing to sit and visit. I kind of let time slip by and ended up having to sprint back for my 1:30 appointment. (They don't really like us to go into meetings twenty minutes late, all sweaty, and with no clue what it is we are supposed to be doing.) Anyway, this guy said—Yolanda are you still there?"

"Yes, Jason, I'm still here. What did he say?"

"What did who say? Oh, you mean the guy. I thought you meant my boss, and that's not repeatable. Anyway, the guy said that these places are primarily in the super hotel class like his is. He's not sure he has seen one where it is located in an *office* building and caters to two markets. He thought trying to do it in a "one beltway town" that has a single downtown office area combined with relatively small hotels might work. Anyway, he went on to say—how many beltways does Buffalo have?—he went on to say, and this is the best part, that if we all wanted to meet with him he would be willing to share what he knew. Could you spring loose for a quick trip up here Friday afternoon?"

"Well," said an interested but much calmer Yolanda, "I had blocked off Friday afternoon, but the client canceled. Sure, I can make it. Call me this evening with the details. I'll give Sarah a call. And, Jason?"

"Yes, Sarah. No, I mean Yolanda? Well, anyway."

"Do you get this excited very often?"

Yolanda called Sarah to begin the arrangements for their meeting that weekend in Detroit. She really was somewhat interested in starting a business although she couldn't decide why. She also wasn't sure that she wanted a somewhat excitable PR person and a small accounting service owner as partners, but they might be acceptable in the right situation. She began thinking about what questions to ask Jason's contact person in Detroit. She also quickly made a phone call to her friend to get product and pricing information.

Assignment

What questions do they need to take with them to the meeting? What other information do they need? How can it be found, if at all?

6 Planning the Launch of the Venture

LEARNING OBJECTIVES

After studying this chapter, you should have a feel for the following:

1. The advantages of a start-up as compared with a buyout
2. The nature of leveraged buyouts
3. The significance of franchises
4. The nature of incubators
5. The uniqueness of a family venture
6. The differences between a sole proprietorship, a partnership, and a corporation

KEY TERMS

Start-up	Incubator
Buyout	Family business
Leveraged buyout	Sole proprietorship, partnership,
Franchise	and corporation

CONSIDER THIS!

- Would you like to start a venture with your best friend? With your parents? With a co-worker?
- Speculate about why most business failures are among low-growth ventures and occur between eighteen months and three years after the launch.
- Why are start-ups more risky than buyouts?
- Is the type of launch used a critical issue in the growth of the venture or is it a matter of personal preference of the entrepreneur?
- How should the survival and growth of a family venture differ from that of a nonfamily venture?
- Do incubators foster entrepreneurship?

The arduous task of analyzing entrepreneurial opportunities, discussed in Chapter 5, leads to the equally arduous task of planning the launch of the venture. Unlike the opportunity analysis, which is, in essence, a yes-no process, planning the venture's launch is a how-to process. All activities in the launch planning process have the goal of determining the best method for entering the market and the optimal structure for the venture. As such, they are choice-oriented activities with a variety of factors involved in the decision process.

LINDA AND FRANK SHANNON
Finishes, Ltd.

Linda Shannon was a moderately successful real estate salesperson in San Francisco, California. She had recently been asked to join the management of the firm. The real estate industry, however, requires long hours that are primarily in the evenings and on weekends, and this had become increasingly unacceptable to Linda. She had an opportunity to leave the real estate business when her husband, Frank, took early retirement from AT&T at age forty-seven. Together they set out to achieve their lifelong goal of owning their own business.

The Shannons had read that 85 percent of all start-ups fail and 85 percent of all buyouts succeed. Thus, they decided to buy a business rather than start one from scratch. They set some very restrictive criteria and began looking for a venture to buy. Their criteria of no retail, no real estate, and no weekends, coupled with Linda's background in her parents' tool and die business, led them to look for a manufacturing business. They engaged a business broker in Colorado Springs, Colorado, a city they both felt would be a good place to live.

The business broker provided them with a list of more than thirty possibilities. Most were ruled out quickly, but they looked carefully at three or four. One of these was a turn-around situation that looked challenging. It was eventually rejected as being too risky. Linda decided on Finishes, Ltd., a metal plating business whose customers included computer firms, oil drillers, and manufacturers of lasers and medical equipment such as pacemakers.

Linda and Frank Shannon studied Finishes, Ltd., over a period of three months. They established rapport with the previous owner who was an excellent technician but had little interest in expanding the firm's business. The Shannons were impressed with the owner, the employees, the quality workmanship, and the expansion possibilities in the Colorado Springs area. The firm was eventually purchased for $180,000. The Shannons used part of Frank's retirement package to put 25 percent down on the business with the remainder being carried by the previous owner, who continues to work for the firm.

Linda serves as president and Frank as operations manager. Their assessment of expansion possibilities was correct; within twelve months, the sales and number of employees doubled. More important, they estimate that they should be able to double sales again within the near future by expanding their customer base throughout Colorado. And, except for occasional computer work at home, they do not work on weekends.

SOURCE: Jay Finegan, "The Insider's Guide," *Inc.*, October 1991, 26–34, and personal interview with the Shannons. Used with permission.

This chapter is divided into two distinct but related parts. The first part discusses methods of starting a venture. These methods include the two primary options of the start-up and buyout. Four special situations include the leveraged buyout, the franchise, the family business, and an incubator start-up. The second half of the chapter will discuss legal forms of business including the sole proprietorship, partnership, and corporation.

THE START-UP

The **start-up** is often the best method for launching the venture and sometimes the only method available. Ventures that capitalize on developing opportunities can sometimes be launched only via start-ups since the opportunities are developmental. If the venture is built around a new product or service, there may be no alternative to the start-up. If the product is completely new, there would be no existing firm to purchase. If the product or service is not new but is in a growth market, there may be a few other firms in the market, but these are seldom for sale. The fact that none are for sale in a given market signals that there are still untapped opportunities.

One entrepreneur exemplifies this situation well. She analyzed an opportunity and concluded tentatively that a market did exist for the proposed product, although she was not sure how large the market was. She decided that the preferred way to enter the market was to buy an existing firm. She visited several firms that were competing in the product market and discovered two things. First, none of the firms were available for sale. Second, each of the firm's facilities seemed quite plush. Both of these facts convinced the entrepreneur that the market was sufficiently large for her to enter even though she was forced to start the venture from scratch.

Another reason for the start-up that is independent of the size of opportunity is that the start-up may simply be the only available method to launch any kind of venture. Consider the case of John Yeh in Venture Perspective 6-1. Yeh did not set out to start his own firm. In fact, he did not intend to own his own business at all. But because he was deaf, he could not get a job. Thus, he and his brothers started their own firm, which today is quite profitable.

Advantages of Start-ups

Launching a venture via a start-up provides benefits that buyouts and other methods do not. These advantages include flexibility, image, staffing, and cost.

Flexibility

One of the most important benefits of launching a venture via start-up is flexibility. If the venture is launched this way, it can be structured in any form the entrepreneur desires. If an opportunity seems somewhat limited, the venture can be launched on a part-time basis. If the opportunity is in the developmental stage, the venture can be launched with leased facilities and equipment in order to hedge on the investment. If the opportunity is so great that success is assured, then the startup entrepreneur can

. . . .

INTEGRATED MICROCOMPUTER SYSTEMS, INC.

Watching two executives who are able to speak and hear communicate in sign language may seem strange to outsiders visiting Integrated Microcomputer Systems, Inc. (IMS). But signing is not unusual at IMS and is necessary for one very important reason—it is the way employees communicate with their boss, John Yeh.

John Yeh was born deaf in Taiwan in 1947. Seeking the opportunity for a high-quality education, rarely available in Taiwan for the hearing impaired, John and his family moved to the United States when he was fifteen. Although John did not know a single word of English when he arrived, he rapidly achieved fluent understanding of English by memorizing a Chinese/English dictionary. After graduating from the Kendall School for the Deaf in Washington, D.C., he entered Gallaudet College (now University), the internationally known college for the deaf. He earned a bachelor of arts degree in mathematics.

Knowing that job opportunities for the deaf were limited, John pursued higher educational goals by enrolling in the University of Maryland's Computer Science Department. With the support of classroom interpreters, a classmate who shared classroom notes, dedicated professors, and study sessions with three brothers who already held computer science degrees, he earned a master's degree in computer science in 1973.

Despite the fact that his educational credentials were identical to those that landed his brothers excellent jobs in the computer industry, Yeh discovered that employers were unwilling to hire a deaf individual for a responsible and challenging technical or management position. He refused to accept the barriers to his professional advancement and in 1979 created his own opportunity. Yeh founded Integrated Microcomputer Systems, Inc. He began with two employees and later persuaded his brothers to join the company. Together they built the company's sound financial structure, stable customer base, and excellent technical reputation. Today IMS employs 375 persons.

IMS is a high-technology company providing full-service scientific, engineering, management, and other contract support to government and industry. The company specializes in computer science research, system engineering, telecommunications, network design and implementation, software development, system integration, logistics, security, system training, and program management support.

IMS's advanced development and integration techniques are building the "software factory" of the future. Its 44,000 square-foot headquarters facility in Rockville, Maryland, is the nerve center of IMS's national and international operations. It offers clients the benefits of an in-house digital design and test laboratory, PC assembly and test facilities, extensive research and program libraries, secure space for secret and top secret storage, and very cost-effective facilities for labor-intensive tasks such as software conversion and system integration.

John Yeh's accomplishment—founding a high-tech company and turning it into a multimillion-dollar enterprise—would be admirable in itself. But there's another dimension to his story that makes it even more impressive. More than 12 percent of the 375 employees of IMS are either deaf or hearing impaired, and half of those with normal hearing use sign language.

SOURCE: Integrated Microcomputer Systems documents.

structure the venture in a way that maximizes returns on investment. This might include launching in a way that the venture can be replicated in franchises, or it could mean launching with few investors but structuring the stock in such a way as to take the firm public within a short time. It could mean structuring in either a partnership or a small corporation with the intent of buying out other investors at a later date.

Image

Another advantage of the start-up is the ability to create a market image or competitive strategy unfettered by actions of past owners. A start-up has no image and no reputation before the launch. Thus, any desired image may be created. It is much easier to develop an image and competitive strategy from the beginning than it is to alter that of an existing firm. Having the desired public image is one of the most critical aspects of entrepreneurial strategy.

Staffing

A third advantage is the ability to staff the firm any way the entrepreneur wants. Buying an existing operation often requires keeping many of the employees, at least in the short run. In addition to starting with one's own people, starting the venture from scratch allows the entrepreneur to structure the employee *positions* in a way that is both efficient and effective for the venture.

Cost

A final advantage of launching via a start-up is that it may be cheaper. Buying an existing venture means buying a going operation. This is almost certain to cost more, since all the pieces of the venture are already in place. Although the start-up may take longer to enter a market, it may be less costly, particularly if the market is growing.

Disadvantages of Start-ups

The disadvantages of start-ups must be considered carefully. Most of the disadvantages of start-ups are, not surprisingly, advantages of buyouts.

Time to Launch

The lack of a track record means that everything will have to be started from the ground up. Suppliers, financing, and a location must be found, facilities must be built, equipment must be purchased, and employees must be hired. Each of these is a somewhat difficult task in any situation. Doing these as part of the start-up process is doubly difficult. Each of these tasks takes time. Thus, the amount of time between the point when a decision to launch is made and when it actually occurs may be substantial. If a short opportunity window exists or if the market is such that competitors are easily attracted, the lost time may be critical. Additional time is, of course, necessary before the business becomes stabilized.

Credibility

A new venture must establish its own credibility. This is particularly true in the case of retail establishments and is especially true in the case of restaurants. Growth may be slow until the credibility is established enough that repeat business is gained.

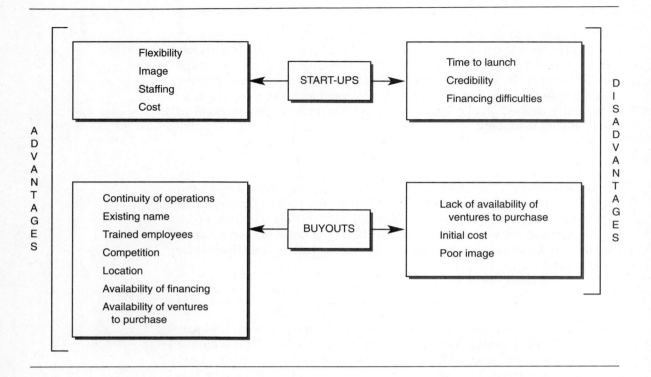

FIGURE 6-1
Advantages and
Disadvantages of Start-
ups and Buyouts

Difficulty in Financing

Because of the above, start-ups are relatively more difficult to finance than
buyouts. The lack of a track record gives lenders or equity investors little to
look at and little prediction of success. Some of this difficulty can be offset
if the entrepreneurs have had previous successful ventures.

THE BUYOUT

The preceding section discussed launching a venture via a start-up. But the
start-up is certainly not the only method that may be used. The **buyout** is
another viable method, although the nature of the process differs.

Linda and Frank Shannon, in the entrepreneurial profile leading off
this chapter, concluded that they would rather buy a company than start
their own from scratch. They believed that the risk of a buyout was considerably less than the risk of a start-up. Buyouts are often preferred by
growth-oriented entrepreneurs who prefer to take an existing venture and
introduce entrepreneurial management to help it reach its potential for
rapid growth. They think that starting with an existing company is better
than going through the stress and uncertainty of starting a new venture. In
an *Inc.* article, John Case suggested that the boom in start-ups in the 1980s
would lead to a boom in buyouts in the 1990s.[1] These 1980 start-ups would
be put on the market either by disillusioned entrepreneurs or by owners

who see growth via mergers. Further, investors are seeing the benefits of purchasing going concerns rather than funding start-ups.

There are several advantages and some disadvantages to launching via the buyout rather than the start-up.

Advantages of Buyouts

The advantages of buyouts include the continuity of operations, the value of an existing name, trained employees, the impact on competition, location advantages, and the ease of financing.

Continuity

Most of the advantages of launching ventures via buyouts revolve around the fact that the venture is an *ongoing business*. Hence, a primary advantage of the buyout is that there is a continuity of operations from the viewpoint of customers and suppliers. This is particularly true among retail and service firms. Continuity of service means that the customers may never even know that the firm has been purchased. If the name and location remain the same, customers may only think that some personnel changes have been made. Customers often don't know who actually owns a business anyway and may not care as long as the products or services are available. Likewise, suppliers have established relationships with the venture, which may already have an established credit rating with the supplier.

Name

A major portion of the benefit of continuity of service is the continuance of the existing name. Company names become imbedded in a customer's mind along with a perception of what that name represents. If a firm has been associated with high quality, then it is quite logical to continue that name. In fact, the entrepreneur may include the purchase of the name as part of the buyout agreement for precisely the reason that it masks the fact that the business changed owners. At the time of the buyout, the new owner must make a decision regarding the purchase of the name of the existing firm. If the operation is to be continued approximately as it was, and if the existing firm has had a good reputation and a stable customer base for a number of years, then careful consideration must be given to purchasing the name. On the other hand, if only the assets or operations portion of the business are being purchased and either the name will be changed or the nature of the firm will be significantly changed, then purchase of the name is not as critical.

Employees

Purchasing a going concern also assures a ready pool of trained employees. Like the value of a firm's name, the value of its employees must be carefully studied. Employees are often the firm's greatest asset, especially immediately after the purchase. Having employees who are adept at running specialized or temperamental equipment, dealing with customers, completing payroll forms, handling billing, understanding the product line, knowing competitors, having rapport with suppliers, and working with advertisers means that an existing firm is more efficient than one started from scratch. This advantage, alone, is enough to convince many entrepreneurs that purchasing an existing venture is ultimately the most cost-effective method for entering a market, even though the initial cost may be greater.

Competition

Launching a venture via the buyout solves a problem that many potential entrepreneurs overlook. This is that buying an existing firm effectively eliminates part of the competition. Suppose, for example, that there are five competitors in a given market area. If a new business is started in the area, six competitors split up the same target market. The start-up is handicapped anyway because it faces the normal problems of a start-up situation. But additionally, it is facing five existing, experienced competitors. Many competitors are more than willing to aggressively compete when a new firm enters the market in hopes that it can be eliminated before gaining a viable share of the market. If an existing business is purchased, however, there are only four competitors. And the personnel in the purchased firm should know the four competitors well. The choice is between being a new competitor with five experienced competitors or being a veteran competitor with four other firms in the market. Thus, the buyout offers significantly greater competitive possibilities than does the start-up.

Having too many competitors in a given market may preclude any of them from making an acceptable profit. In one medium-sized city, for example, two independently owned children's clothing stores failed within one month of each other. Given that there is always competition from department stores, one can only speculate that if either of the stores had left the market six months earlier, the other could have survived. The Census Bureau has estimated that there are approximately one thousand inhabitants, for each small grocery store. A bakery typically services ten thousand residents in the area. Bookstores serve twenty-five thousand inhabitants, and there are forty thousand residents per camera store.[2] In deciding whether to buy or start a firm, the size of the total market should be compared with the number of existing competitors operating in the market.

Location

Location can also be a factor in going with the buyout instead of the start-up. Marketing experts are fond of the cliche that there are only three important factors in the success of a retail venture: location, location, and location. This may be somewhat overstated, but the point is well made that location of the firm is critically important. Retail firms live or die based on their location. If the best locations are already taken in a market area, then the buyout may be well-advised.

GENERAL TECHNOLOGY CORPORATION

Growth, staying power, innovation in products and services, response to adversity—all of these are characteristics of ongoing entrepreneurship. And all are true of Ralph Anderson and General Technology Corporation.

Ralph Anderson was a senior vice president of Missouri Research Labs (MRL) in Albuquerque, New Mexico, in 1981. Due to a restructuring of MRL, Anderson was provided the opportunity to purchase the Special Products Division of MRL. The division contained the Mechanical Design Services, which provided mechanical design work on classified government projects. It also provided chemical engineering work to a variety of customers. Anderson purchased the assets of the Special Products Division and renamed it the General Tech-

nology Corporation (GTC). Identifying a market for high-quality printed circuit boards, he sold the chemical portion of the venture and expanded the existing services to include the manufacture of double-sided and multilayer boards. The industries served include high-technology, aerospace, and military markets. GTC was established with nineteen hundred square feet of space and seventeen employees.

Since its beginning, GTC has expanded to the extent that it now serves industry in three distinct areas:

1. High reliability electronic fabrication and assembly including satellite subsystems and other space-related areas
2. Printed circuit boards

including double-sided, multilayer, and flex circuits
3. Contract employment services at customer locations or at GTC facilities including technical personnel such as engineers, project management, CAD professionals, designers, technical writers, and others

Customers include the military, Honeywell, Sandia National Laboratories, Litton, Bendix, Eagle-Picher, Motorola, McDonnell-Douglas, Bell Helicopter, and others. GTC now resides in thirty-five thousand square feet and employs a staff of 160.

SOURCE: General Technology Corporation documents. Used with permission.

Financing

A final advantage of the buyout compared with the start-up is that financing may be more readily available for the buyout even though the initial amount needed will often be greater. Financiers are generally more willing to go with existing firms than they are with a start-up. This is because the firm has established a track record. The fact that the entrepreneur does not have to go through the launch pains that a start-up requires reduces the risk of failure. In addition to the availability of bank or venture capital financing, often the previous owner will underwrite some of the purchase price. Thus, the entrepreneur may not have to go outside for financing. This is especially true when the previous owner is retiring.

Availability

Occasionally, a firm or a spin-off of a firm becomes available for a manager or a group of managers to purchase. This has been occurring increasingly as large corporations have begun downsizing. This is especially desirable because the employee already has experience in the firm and can simply move from being a manager to being an owner.

The above discussion makes a convincing case for the buyout rather than the start-up. If a buyout target is available, serious thought should be given to going with that option. It has a much higher probability of success if the purchase can be made for an acceptable price and without undue restrictions.

Disadvantages of Buyouts

Although buyouts tend to be more desirable than start-ups, there are some disadvantages of buyouts. These disadvantages may be such that a potential entrepreneur would be well-advised to use the start-up method.

Lack of Availability

Potential entrepreneurs may have to launch their venture via the start-up simply because there are no appropriate ventures to purchase. Locating ventures that are for sale may be difficult, and locating a highly desirable venture in a desirable geographical location may be even more difficult. David Ransberg, featured in the entrepreneurial profile in Chapter 3, searched for two years before he located L. R. Nelson Corporation. Further, many ventures that are for sale have limited potential. Thus, the potential entrepreneur may have only three choices: buying an undesirable venture, starting a venture from scratch, or waiting until an appropriate venture is found.

Initial Cost

Buyouts typically have more potential than start-ups. And they may be more cost effective over the long run even if they are not high-growth ventures. On the other hand, the purchase price may simply be prohibitive to a given buyer. Thus, the entrepreneur may be forced into launching via the start-up since it is the only affordable method of launch.

Poor Image

One of the advantages of the buyout is having the continuity of an existing business, including its image. If, however, that image is not good in the eyes of the customer, then image becomes a disadvantage. Some businesses seem to be perennially changing owners or managers. One restaurant went through four changes in ownership in six years, with each new owner trying something slightly different in hopes that success could be achieved. But the restaurant became a joke in the community as people took bets on how long the next owner would last. The image of the business had become one of predicted failure.

THE BUYOUT SEARCH PROCESS

Locating firms to purchase depends a great deal on the kind of opportunity the entrepreneur wants to pursue and the decision-making process used. Two methods for selecting a firm are available.

The first method entails setting some specific criteria regarding what would be an acceptable firm. This is the approach that Linda and Frank Shannon used before purchasing Finishes, Ltd. They wanted a firm in the Colorado Springs area, and their criteria limited their search to manufacturing firms.

Once the criteria analysis process is completed, the remaining task is simply to search for a company that fits the specific predetermined criteria. The problem, of course, is the frustration of searching for the "perfect" firm. The more restrictive the requirements are for an acceptable firm to purchase, the more difficult will be the search for an available venture.

The second method is to set only the broadest predetermined criteria. Since the criteria are broad, a number of ventures may fit those criteria. Once a company or companies are identified, then careful studies are made before a final purchase decision. Using this method gives a much larger pool of prospective firms. It does require more individual analysis and has a greater probability that an identified company will be eventually rejected.

Industry Searches

Regardless of whether the entrepreneur uses a broad-based search with a later in-depth selection process or an in-depth criteria analysis process before the actual search, the nature of the industry selected may require using different search processes. Evolving or fragmented industries may require substantial effort in order to locate an acceptable firm because the industry is not easily trackable. The pool of possible firms may be quite large and geographically dispersed. There could be hundreds of small firms across the United States and Canada, most of which are privately held and perhaps serve a quite small segment of the total market. Thus, the task of locating target companies is an arduous process itself, aside from the process of analyzing the firms that may have only sketchy financial data available.

Established industries have more readily available information on possible target firms through trade associations and other sources of information. Firms in this case frequently will be publicly held, making the task of identifying firms easier. In addition, it will be easier to compare the health of the firm with industry standards to determine if the identified firm is desirable from a competitive standpoint. Industry analysts who work for investment bankers or brokerage firms maintain information on selected industries and thus may be the source of information regarding both the availability of firms in a developed industry and the comparative health of those firms.

Contacting trade associations in selected industries may yield names of companies that might be ripe for purchasing even though they have not made a formal move to sell. Direct contact with firms in a given industry may be fruitful. In this case, names of all industry participants may be obtained from either a trade association or an encyclopedia listing of firms by industry such as the Thomas Register of Manufacturers.[3]

Location-based Searches

Searching for buyout targets also depends upon the flexibility the entrepreneur has regarding relocating. Virtually all start-ups and perhaps most small buyouts are launched within the general area of the entrepreneur's home neighborhood or city. In a study for the National Federation of Independent Business Foundation, Arnold C. Cooper and his associates found that almost 80 percent of entrepreneurs did not move their residence at all when starting their current business.[4] If a potential entrepreneur wants to buy a venture in a particular local area, the search will naturally be one that focuses on that area. Searching for a local area buyout may entail reading the local newspaper classified advertisements for "business opportunities," contacting the chamber of commerce, visiting with local bankers and brokerage houses, and simply putting out the word that there is an interest in purchasing a going concern.

The search for a growth-oriented venture typically will not be restricted to a local community, although this certainly is possible in larger cities. Sometimes a growth-oriented business may be discovered in one's own backyard even in smaller communities, but generally the growth entrepreneur will not restrict the search to the local area.

Third Party Searches

Using third parties for the search process is a fruitful method of locating buyouts, and it provides additional benefits. For a fee, third party business brokers or investment bankers will search for potential target companies. In addition they will screen clients according to the buyer's criteria. As a result, the entrepreneur need not be bothered with a plethora of firms that may be for sale but do not meet the criteria. The third party can complete the search without disclosing the buyer's name, thus not tipping the buyer's hand in case more than one firm is considered simultaneously. Both those firms that are known to be for sale and those that have not indicated a desire to sell may be contacted. In this way, one can find exactly which firms are available and, in addition, gain substantial information about the competitive nature of the industry and relative position of each firm. This is particularly important in a close-knit industry. In this case it may not be competitively wise to let the word out that a firm is being considered for purchase. Thus, all discussions with potential sellers, as well as those with businesses that are determined not to be for sale, can be handled in strict confidence.

Using a business broker is also useful when the entrepreneur wants to change locations. Linda and Frank Shannon decided to move to Colorado Springs from San Francisco. Because of the distance, they enlisted the aid of a business broker to search for and screen possible firms.

Advertised Intentions

A final search method that is sometimes fruitful is for the entrepreneur to put an advertisement in either a local or a national paper indicating an interest in purchasing a firm. This may result in a number of offers to sell that are not of interest to the buyer, but it could also provide a range of possibilities from which to choose.

SPECIAL LAUNCH SITUATIONS

The start-up and buyout are the standard methods used to launch a venture. Other situations exist, however, that are variations of the start-up and buyout but are unique in one or more aspects. These are the leveraged buyout, the franchise, the incubator start-up, and the family business.

The Leveraged Buyout

The **leveraged buyout** will be discussed in more depth in Chapter 7 when financing the venture is discussed. Here, the leveraged buyout is seen as a means of creating a new venture. It is a buyout and, as such, is similar to other buyouts. The difference between the leveraged buyout and other buyouts is primarily in the financing of the buyout and the impact of the buyout on the new venture's ability to compete. A firm purchased via a leveraged buyout is purchased with a high percentage of debt. That debt is then transferred to the firm being purchased rather than held in the name of the owners.

The leveraged buyout is a complicated process and is not designed for the novice entrepreneur. Indeed, due to the risk involved, only experienced entrepreneurs or managers are able to successfully complete a leveraged buyout. Further, the purchased firm is typically an established firm with a substantial track record instead of a newly created firm. The purchase price may reach into the hundred million dollar range.

The Leveraged Buyout Process

The leveraged buyout centers around the purchase of an existing firm, using a substantial amount of debt that is then transferred to the balance sheet of the purchased firm. In some leveraged buyouts the management of the existing firm becomes the new owners. This often happens when the subsidiary of a larger firm is to be closed or sold. The managers of the subsidiary then scramble to arrange leveraged buyout funding in order to save the firm as an independent entity. In other cases, the firm exists as a free-standing, publicly held company that may have become the target of a takeover attempt or whose managers simply decide to take the firm private to avoid some of the problems unique to publicly held firms.

The new owners of the leveraged buyout have a significant entrepreneurial task in arranging funding for the venture. Typically they put up a small portion of the purchase price from their own capital or from funds they personally raise. They then go to an investment firm that specializes in leveraged buyouts. The investment firm may provide a combination of equity and debt financing to the firm. However, the key to the leveraged buyout is that it is the *firm* that assumes the debt rather than the individual owners. This does two things. First, it allows the transaction to take place since the owners likely will not have sufficient funding or borrowing capacity to purchase the firm outright. Second, it lays a significant amount of debt on the balance sheet of the firm. Even though the firm now has new owners, it may have some difficulty operating in the future because of the high debt it is carrying. The leveraged buyout is consequently a viable method of entrepreneurship, but it is not without its downside risks.

The Franchise

The franchise will be discussed in more detail in Chapter 10 when strategies are discussed. In this chapter, the primary focus is whether the franchise is a good method to use in launching the venture.

The great advantage of franchises is that they are ongoing operations and the franchisor provides management training, advertising help, store layout, operations structure and control, and financing of the venture. On the other hand, the great disadvantage of the franchise is the cost. Some franchises in the fast-food industry cost more than $500,000. Even among small, relatively unknown franchises, the franchise fee may be anywhere from $20,000 to $100,000.

The issue for the entrepreneur in deciding whether to launch via a franchise is simply whether the venture will be better off as part of a franchise or as a totally independent venture. Many franchises are simply not worth the cost. Either the venture is one that is not really conducive to franchising, or the franchise is so unknown that the name provides no value. In addition, the franchise agreement may be so skewed in favor of the franchisor that the franchisee gains little net benefit from the franchise.

The Incubator Start-up

The **business incubator** is a new concept in entrepreneurship that shows promise in successful new venture creation and management.[5] It has its roots in economic development and is often seen as a means of helping out state or local economies. An incubator is a large building—often an old warehouse, an abandoned school, or a vacant university dormitory. The building is refurbished if necessary in order to house a number of new ventures. In addition to simply sharing space in a building, however, incubators typically offer shared administrative support such as copiers, receptionists, mail processing, computers, employee lunchrooms, and shipping facilities. Beyond that, since the new ventures are all located together, an informal network often develops in which the entrepreneurs share problems and solutions. In many cases, one venture may use the services of another in the incubator. Incubators also typically offer on-site management assistance. This assistance, often offered by a university's small business assistance program or a state or local business support center, gives the advantage of immediately available help to new entrepreneurs at the time they need it most. Having assistance available at the time of start-up and in the months immediately following may be one of the strongest calling cards for incubators.

New venture tenants may stay in the incubator for either a predetermined time period or until they are sufficiently established to go out on their own. Some incubators have the policy that tenants may only stay for two or three years. They must then find other space regardless of the health of the venture. Others will have the policy of allowing tenants to remain in the incubator as long as the space is not needed for others. Thus, if the incubator is not crowded, a tenant could stay there indefinitely. That arrangement has value in that the tenant would be contributing to the funding of the incubator by paying rent.

Types of Incubators

Incubators take one of three forms based on the nature of their sponsoring group. Some incubators are *privately held, for-profit corporations*. The owners of private incubators see the incubator as a way to screen new ventures for possible venture capital infusions at later dates in addition to the rent that is received from the tenants. Other incubators are *state- or community-sponsored* facilities that are seen primarily as an economic development medium. For local governments this has an added benefit in that it provides an avenue to rehabilitate old buildings—often in poorer parts of the city— into usable, productive structures. The third category of incubator is the *university-sponsored* incubator. These incubators are often in vacant dormitories and sometimes also house the small business assistance program and a technology development center. In addition to providing a community service, the university incubator also serves as an outlet for university professors who either provide consulting to the tenants or have their own sideline business on campus. Tenants especially benefit from locating in a university-sponsored incubator because of the nearby location of faculty who are willing to lend their experience to help solve problems.

Although private, state/local, and university-sponsored incubators exist, most will use at least some government funding for the refurbishing of the incubator itself. The funding, which may be federal, state, or local, may also be used for operation of the incubator or its affiliated management and technical assistance programs. The incubator profiled in Venture Perspective 6-3 illustrates how private, local, and state funding can work together to launch and underwrite an incubator complex.

The Impact of Incubators

Interestingly, incubators have not been as much of a significant boon to economic development as many first thought. This is simply because most entrepreneurs who decide to locate in the incubator would have started their business anyway. It is still not known whether businesses started in incubators ultimately perform better than their non-incubator colleagues. The incubator concept is relatively new and, as a result, insufficient time has passed to determine conclusively if the success rate is better than for new ventures in general. Early reports appear to support the incubator concept. The reasons for the success vary, but they seem to include the value of the on-site administrative and management help. An additional benefit that was not intended comes from the requirements for entry and tenure in the building. Most incubators require the new entrepreneur to prepare a full-scale business plan before entry into the incubator. Some also require periodic updates to the plan in order to stay in the incubator. This forced planning may be one of the primary causes of the success of businesses in incubators.[6]

VENTURE PERSPECTIVE 6-3
. . . .

MAPLE CITY TECHNOLOGY, INC.

An abandoned plow factory sat for years in Monmouth, Illinois. It had seen a few other uses over the years, but its most outstanding characteristic was that it was an eyesore in this small rural community. The building could have been torn down years before but no one wanted to pay the cost of demolition. On the other hand, the building was in good structural condition, but it was too large for any particular use in the community.

A group of individuals who were interested in rehabilitating the building contacted Control Data Corporation (CDC) to ascertain its interest in the venture. In exchange for a fee, CDC provided management and technical help to the group. The state of Illinois provided substantial capital for the refurbishing of the building, while the city of Monmouth provided the building and additional funding. The building was converted to a number of different types of facilities within the primary structure and some outlying buildings in the complex. The business technology center housed its offices there. A small business development center, which was funded by state and federal dollars, was housed there to provide assistance to tenants and other community businesses. The town's chamber of commerce moved its offices there. The building's space was flexible enough to house different kinds of service and/or light manufacturing businesses. As new tenants expressed an interest in the incubator, space was customized to the needs of the entrepreneur.

As a result of the combination of local, state, federal, and private funding, the town of Monmouth now has a thriving incubator, a number of new ventures, and a building that is being well used instead of deteriorating.

SOURCE: Personal visit.

The Family Business

At the outset of this chapter, the statement was made that there are only two ways to launch a venture. One is to start it from scratch and the other is to buy an ongoing venture. The **family business,** if passed on from one generation to the next, is an exception to that rule. If a daughter or son takes over the venture from a parent, then money may not change hands. In fact, many family businesses are slowly passed from one generation to the next. The children of the owner often have worked in the business for years. Even younger children may have worked in the business after school or during summers. By the time the parents are ready to retire, one or more children may have already worked in the business for twenty-five years. If the parent chooses to turn the reins over to the next generation, it may be done so slowly that customers are unaware that the process even occurs. Thus, it appears that no new venture has even been created. Still, the transfer of the venture from parent to child does constitute a new venture in a legal sense, and it may constitute a new venture in a psychological sense as ownership is formally transferred from one to the other.

Two situations exist that merit discussion under the heading of family business creation. In the first case, the family venture is being created for the first time by the entrepreneur. In the second case, the entrepreneur is assuming operational control of a second- or third-generation business. Starting a new family business has different constraints than taking over an old family business. The two situations will be discussed in turn.

The New Family Venture

The establishment of a family venture for the first time has most of the characteristics of a typical start-up. In addition, however, the entrepreneur must make additional decisions regarding how the venture will be structured in order to make optimal use of family members. The family members need not all be co-owners or co-managers. Indeed, some family members may be employed full time with the business, others may be part time in the business, and still others may not have a role in the business at all. Nancy Bowman-Upton suggests four categories of relationships of family members to the business.[7] Family members may be:

1. Neither an employee nor an owner
2. An employee but not an owner
3. An employee and an owner
4. An owner but not an employee

Children and in-laws often fall into category 1. They are not active in the business, but they may have claims on the entrepreneur's time and may exert considerable pressure within the family for a redirection of priorities. For those in the second category, potential conflict exists between the family member and the entrepreneur and between the family member and other employees. Concerns with favoritism top the list of problems that must be addressed. Family members in the third group have the hardest job. A person may be a spouse, a sibling of the entrepreneur, a parent, or an older child. Whatever the family relationship, being an owner and an employee and a family member means that they have some responsibility for the day-to-day operations, they have a vested interest in the long-run profitability of the firm, and they must deal with family relationships. The last group, the owner but not employee, usually consists of siblings and may include other relatives. They often have concerns about continued income and security. Thus, they may resist moves by the entrepreneur to invest in long-range or somewhat risky investments that could take away from more short-run proceeds of the company.

Sometimes the family venture grows because of the need to accommodate members of the family. This may occur in low-growth ventures when younger family members decide to stay with the venture rather than move on to other careers. The original entrepreneur may take the initiative to expand the venture into new geographical areas or new product areas in order for the new member of the management team to have opportunities and responsibilities. In some cases the reverse is true. That is, the venture has a need, or an opportunity to expand occurs. An additional family member is then recruited to join the venture to manage the new portion of the venture.

The task before the entrepreneur at the time of launch is to structure the new venture in such a way as to consider all possible conflicts among the players in each of the above roles. This is a Herculean task at best and impossible at worst. It must be kept in mind that, regardless of the entrepreneur's desires, family versus business conflicts *will* arise. Actions that can be taken at the outset to minimize future problems are well advised.

VENTURE PERSPECTIVE 6-4

ESCARGOT SPORTSWEAR

Many family ventures consist of a parent who brings in children and their spouses as well as the entrepreneur's own siblings. Brenda Widdows did the opposite. When she identified her market, she realized that she needed additional team members to take advantage of it, so she brought in her mother, a sister, a sister-in-law, and an aunt. Each had a particular skill that was needed to make the venture work efficiently.

Escargot Sportswear was launched to exploit a rather narrow niche in the apparel market. Brenda Widdows, who was a French major in college, was visiting friends who were also fluent in French. One of the friends was wearing a sweatshirt with a French saying on it. The product was intriguing to Widdows, who determined that there might be a market for them in foreign language classes in high schools. Launching a venture to capitalize on the excitement that many

foreign language club members have was a natural extension of her own interest in foreign languages. Getting the venture launched successfully required some effort, however. Widdows determined that using a mail-order brochure sent to high schools across the country was the appropriate way to enter the market. In order to do that, she purchased a mailing list from a direct marketing company specializing in school lists. She enlisted the help of her mother and sister to do the shipping. Her aunt had secretarial skills. Brenda had the business skills and did the ordering, had the brochures printed, and did other activities in "the business end" of the venture. The screen printing on the shirts was contracted out.

Within a year, Widdows realized that contracting out the screen printing was costing her one dollar per shirt. By that time she had sold approximately ten thousand of them.

Thus, she was spending $10,000 just to get the wording on the apparel. In order to gain control of the screen printing plus reduce her costs, she brought in her sister-in-law, who learned screen printing. She purchased equipment in order to do the screen printing in-house.

The market is seasonal for T-shirts and sweatshirts that are sold through foreign language clubs or classes. The screen printing became the medium to offset the seasonality of the foreign language apparel. Thus, Escargot Sportswear began to branch out into other markets for screen printed apparel. One such market was bike and foot racing custom T-shirts. Another was shirts for summer youth baseball leagues. A line of Irish shirts was produced and is now being sold in Irish boutiques.

SOURCE: Escargot Sportswear documents. Used with permission.

The Old Family Business

Assuming control of a second- or third-generation business poses a different set of problems that must be addressed. Fortunately in this case, most of the issues surrounding start-ups no longer exist. But issues of control, and of ownership itself, do arise in a transitional period. Management succession will be discussed in later chapters from the viewpoint of the previous owner planning the succession strategy. The view in this chapter is from the successor's vantage point. The issues in the transition fall into two groups. First, how will the new entrepreneur deal with the previous owner who is likely to be a parent? Second, how will the new owner deal with employees now that she or he is in control of the business? This is particularly troublesome if some of those employees are also family members. And it may be even more troublesome if the previous owner did not make good succession plans and slowly work the new entrepreneur into the power base of the company.

The new entrepreneur must continue the rapport held previously with employees, suppliers, and financial investors. At the same time it must be realized that the two individuals may not be alike and the successor entrepreneur may have new and different agendas for the company. In some cases, the new owner may have substantially different views of growth. Sometimes the parent is satisfied with a low-growth type of business and does not desire high rates of growth. A daughter or son, on the other hand, may see substantial opportunities for the firm if an entrepreneurial strategy can be adopted. The new ideas, however, may be difficult to sell to the parent and to the employees.

The problems of the new entrepreneur in taking over the family business also depend on the time period over which the changeover occurs. If the new entrepreneur has worked in the firm for a number of years, then the changeover may be evolutionary. If, on the other hand, the previous owner dies or decides to retire or sell the business suddenly, then the change in control must be almost immediate. This, of course, happens sometimes with any business, but the prospects for problems are much greater if the venture is a family business.

The management of the family ventures will be discussed a number of times throughout the rest of the text. In particular, Chapter 16 (Harvesting the Venture) will discuss issues in succession policy and its effect on both an entrepreneur who is retiring and other members of the family.

DETERMINING THE LEGAL FORM OF THE VENTURE

Most students taking an entrepreneurship class have encountered the topic of the legal forms of businesses at least once and perhaps a number of times in their academic career. This section of the chapter will discuss the forms a business may take, but it will do so from the viewpoint of the new venture entrepreneur. Thus, this section should be read from the perspective of someone currently planning the launch of a venture.

Three general forms of business exist, and there are some variations within each category. The three primary forms are the sole proprietorship, the partnership, and the corporation. Variations of the partnership and the corporation exist.

The Sole Proprietorship

More than two-thirds of all ventures are **sole proprietorships.**[8] These range from the smallest one-person business to relatively large businesses with several levels of management. Most sole proprietorships are quite small and consist of either a single individual such as an independent insurance broker or a plumber, or a small single-product manufacturer.

Advantages of Sole Proprietorships

From a *new venture perspective*, the sole proprietorship has a number of advantages. The biggest advantage is that it is simple to launch. There are no required forms other than those that might be required by a local or state government for a specific type of venture. The venture is considered to be an extension of the entrepreneur. Thus, any profits realized from the venture are taxed on the entrepreneur's personal IRS 1040 form. There are no particular requirements for starting and stopping the business. As a result the owner has considerable flexibility in how the venture is launched, operated, and terminated.

The ease of launch is the reason why many low-growth entrepreneurs start a venture using the sole proprietorship. The low-growth venture typically is not complex, and there is no need to use extensive controls that would be required by a corporation.

Disadvantages of Sole Proprietorships

There are, however, a number of weaknesses of the sole proprietorship form that should be of concern even to the low-growth entrepreneur. The first is that it is much more difficult for a sole proprietor to raise capital than it is for either a partnership or a corporation. This may or may not be of concern, particularly if the venture is planned to stay small. However, if the market for the venture does grow, the entrepreneur may find that sufficient capital cannot be raised to take advantage of the opportunity. In other words, if a favorable market would permit a venture to take on more rapid growth, the entrepreneur's decision to remain as a sole proprietorship may restrict growth needlessly.

The second major drawback of the sole proprietorship is that it is owned by a single person, and that person is also often the only manager of the firm. Having only a one-person management limits the ability to plan effectively or to take advantage of changing opportunities. In addition, the single manager may have skills that are limited to one or a few functional areas. Thus, the venture may suffer because the owner/manager simply cannot attend to all the problems that may arise.

A final drawback of the sole proprietorship is the unlimited liability of the owner. If the business is sued for some accident or if the business fails financially, the entrepreneur is personally liable. This liability extends to the entrepreneur's personal assets in addition to those of the company.

Ultimately, the new venture entrepreneur must make a judgment call. The decision is simply whether the ease of launch and operation offsets the increased risk associated with the sole proprietorship. In fact, more bankruptcies occur among proprietorships than any of the other forms. Since many proprietorships are low-growth ventures, it is understandable that they will be neither large nor well financed. Hence, they are more vulnerable than the other forms of ventures to changes in the economy, competition, interest rates, and so on. But the high failure rate is due to the fact that they tend to be small and underfinanced and not because they are sole proprietorships.

The Partnership

Approximately 10 percent of the business ventures in the United States are partnerships. The **partnership** shares many of the characteristics of the sole proprietorship. It is easy to form and its owners have unlimited liability. Its

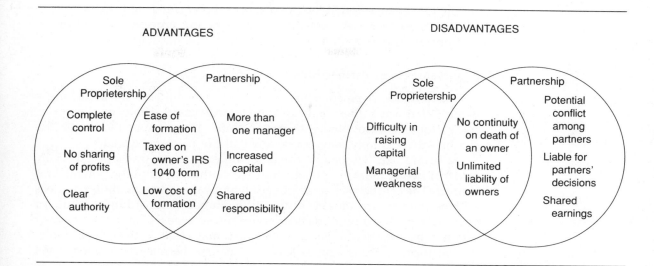

ADVANTAGES

DISADVANTAGES

Sole Proprietership
- Complete control
- No sharing of profits
- Clear authority

(overlap)
- Ease of formation
- Taxed on owner's IRS 1040 form
- Low cost of formation

Partnership
- More than one manager
- Increased capital
- Shared responsibility

Sole Proprietership
- Difficulty in raising capital
- Managerial weakness

(overlap)
- No continuity on death of an owner
- Unlimited liability of owners

Partnership
- Potential conflict among partners
- Liable for partners' decisions
- Shared earnings

FIGURE 6-2
Advantages and Disadvantages of Sole Proprietorships and Partnerships

profits are taxed on the owners' IRS 1040s. There is no stock since it is not a corporation. The partnership has some advantages over the proprietorship as well as some disadvantages (Figure 6-2).

Advantages of Partnerships

The partnership has several advantages over the sole proprietorship. The degree to which a partnership is better than the proprietorship depends on the particular type and size of the venture, the stage in the venture life cycle, and the individuals involved.

When a business is first being launched, having two or more owners involved can help significantly. Seldom is one person well-versed in all facets of venture creation. Thus, partners often complement each other's strengths and weaknesses. One partner may be strong in marketing while another is strong in accounting or finance. One may be outgoing and prefer to mingle with customers and the other one may be more comfortable "behind the scenes." Even without the complementary characteristics, simply having someone to discuss problems with on a peer basis rather than a manager/subordinate basis is important. Partners also tend to balance each other's thinking process. If one partner, for example, tends to be overly cautious or overly liberal with the venture resources, the other partner can sometimes bring them back to an equilibrium position.

In addition to the management needs that can be better met with two individuals than with one, simply having two or more partners is important. Lenders and other investors look more favorably upon partnerships than they do upon sole proprietorships (assuming similar ventures) because they perceive the risk to be lower. Having more than one partner adds control to the business. If one partner is on vacation, another can watch the operation. If one partner spends time outside the business soliciting customers, dealing with suppliers, or acquiring additional funding, then the other can maintain operational control of the venture. If there is simply too much action in the internal operations of the venture, having an additional partner may ease the decision-making process and add to the efficiency of the operation.

Disadvantages of Partnerships

The advantages of partnerships make a convincing case for launching a venture that way rather than as a sole proprietorship. There are, however, some problems associated with partnerships. These are in addition to the fact that there simply may not be any suitable partners available.

It is rare that two people can agree on everything, and it is especially rare that two or more people can launch a venture without the potential for conflict. The conflict may arise from different value systems, different ideas on how the venture should be run, different beliefs regarding funding, or even from personality conflicts or nonbusiness issues. Conflict can be devastating to a new venture and, at its worst, may result in the dissolution of the business. Partners often leave a business because they cannot get along. Even if they do not leave, the efficiency of the venture may fall substantially. If the conflict arises during the launch phase, the venture may fail before it ever gets off the ground.

It was noted earlier that in the partnership all owners have unlimited liability. The critical issue for partnerships is that all partners are liable regardless of who is at fault. Thus, if one partner creates a liability for the firm, all partners are at risk. If one partner makes an error in the venture's business strategy that causes losses to the business, all partners lose. If a customer is injured because of the fault of one partner (or an employee), all partners lose.

A final disadvantage is that the business may not generate sufficient earnings to satisfy all partners' needs. Many partnerships break up, not because of conflict, but because the venture simply does not make enough profits for more than one owner.

The Limited Partnership

The limited partnership resolves some of the unlimited liability problem of regular partnerships. The limited partnership has at least one general partner and one or more limited partners. The limited partners are liable only for the amount they have invested in the venture. Typically, limited partners may not participate in the active management of the firm. Laws on limited partnerships vary from state to state.

The Need for a Partnership Agreement

The discussion on partnerships has indicated that partnerships are an important possible launch method. Many of the problems facing partnerships can be prevented by a partnership agreement. The Uniform Partnership Act, passed by most states, spells out general obligations of team members in a partnership. These are not specific enough, however, to cover all situations. A specific partnership agreement should be prepared by the partners with the assistance of a knowledgeable attorney.

1. Names and addresses of partners
2. Name and address of the venture
3. General purpose of the venture
4. Contributions of each partner
5. Duties and responsibilities of each partner
6. Salary or draw provisions
7. Distribution of profits or losses
8. Buy/sell agreements if a partner decides to leave the venture
9. Provisions for additional partners or assets
10. Dissolution of assets if the venture is terminated
11. Provision for continuing the venture upon the death or disablement of a partner
12. Provisions unique to the venture

TABLE 6-1
Components of a
Partnership Agreement

Many potential entrepreneurial partners resist preparing a partnership agreement, contending that they are friends or colleagues and really do not need an agreement. This feeling changes as soon as the first conflict arises. It is extremely important that the agreement be written and signed *before* the venture is launched. In this way, all team members know the relationships and agreements before committing to the venture. The agreement should, at a minimum, contain the items shown in Table 6-1.

Among the most important components of a partnership agreement are the duties and responsibilities, the distribution of profits or losses, and the buy/sell agreements. These three items are the source of most of the conflicts that arise among partners. The buy/sell agreement should be carefully worded to account for differences in the future value of the venture. A highly successful venture might command far different prices and different percentages to each partner than one that is only moderately or marginally successful. A second major problem that arises in many partnership ventures is the need for additional partners or capital. Will additional needed capital be required at the same percentages as before? Suppose one partner initially invested little capital but substantial technical skill. In this case, who invests the next infusion of capital? If a new partner joins the firm, will the required investment be the same as the original partners or should it be more since the venture is underway? These and other concerns must be addressed before the venture is officially launched.

The Corporation

The **corporation** is the preferred form of launch for many potential entrepreneurs and for most investors. About 15 percent of all businesses are corporations, and most medium to large businesses are incorporated. There are advantages to the corporate form of ownership, but there are also some disadvantages.

Advantages of Corporations

The two primary advantages of corporations are that raising capital is much easier in the corporation and all owners have limited liability. The corporation is launched with shares of stock distributed among initial stockholders or held within the corporation. Then, if additional equity capital is needed, additional shares of stock may be sold. In addition, shareholders who want to leave the corporation can easily sell their ownership in the venture. Under the corporate form, investors are liable only to the extent that they have invested. Thus, investors may be more willing to invest because they know that their liability is limited to the amount they have invested and that they can more easily sell their shares in a corporation than in a partnership.

A qualification on the limited liability advantage must be made. Entrepreneurs may opt for the corporate form in order to have limited liability from creditors. However, lenders frequently require the owner of the firm to pledge personal assets regardless of the form of business ownership. Thus, if the business fails, the creditor can attach personal assets even though the business was a corporation.

Disadvantages of Corporations

The corporation has two disadvantages that are of concern primarily to low-growth entrepreneurs. These are, first, the cost and administrative requirements to launch the venture and report its progress each year, and second, the double taxation of profits. In the corporation profits are taxed as corporate profits. Then those profits are taxed again as dividends if the owners withdraw them from the business. This compares with the simple reporting of proprietorship or partnership profits on the owners' IRS 1040 forms. Double taxation can be minimized to some extent through paying reasonable salaries and fringe benefits and by establishing pension fund contributions for the owners.

The Sub-chapter S Corporation

The Sub-chapter S corporation (also known as a Sub S corporation or simply as an "S corp") is a variation on the regular corporation that assists in reducing taxes among small corporations. The Sub S corporation has all the characteristics of a corporation except that it is taxed as a partnership. The owners are taxed on their normal IRS 1040s. Thus, they have all the advantages of the corporation—most notably, the limited liability and ease of exchanging ownership—but still have a key advantage of the partnership. The Sub S corporation may have up to thirty-five stockholders.

Tax status will not be of concern for rapid-growth ventures. The reason for this is that, with rapid growth, stock will likely be sold widely if not publicly. Thus, the Sub-chapter S corporation will be of no value.

Low-growth entrepreneurs must make a decision at launch time whether to launch their venture as a proprietorship, a partnership, a corporation, or a Sub S corporation. There are advantages to each. Tax accountants or attorneys should be consulted regarding which form is best for a particular launch. Entrepreneurs may also change the form of the venture periodically if situations warrant. Again, tax accountants are important here because the IRS has specific guidelines concerning the frequency of change.

. . . .

Launching a venture requires several major decisions about the type and form of the venture. Each of these major decisions then leads to numerous smaller, administrative decisions that must be made in order to achieve a successful launch. This chapter has illustrated some of the key planning issues that are included in the decision process.

The startup venture has advantages with regard to the flexibility it affords the entrepreneur. Issues to consider include the ability to create the desired image, the ability to choose employees, the possibly lower initial cost, and the ability to locate the venture in a desired location. The start-up may be the only method available to launch some ventures.

The buyout has many advantages, and it is a more desirable method if a firm is available and certain conditions are met. Nevertheless, there are some disadvantages to buying a venture. These may include the existing poor image, resistant employees, and the condition of the firm.

Specialized situations also exist. The leveraged buyout is a form of buyout with the extensive debt necessary to purchase the firm being applied to the purchased firm's balance sheet. Franchises offer extensive management training, structured operations, and a known name but at a substantial cost and with restricted flexibility. Incubators are a new method of starting ventures in a sheltered environment. Incubators offer substantial services to fledgling ventures when they are most at risk. The family firm is often passed from generation to generation. It presents both opportunities and concerns that should be considered.

A final decision to be made is to determine the legal structure of the firm. The sole proprietorship, the partnership, and the corporation all have advantages that make them worthy of consideration during the launch phase. The sole proprietorship is easy to start and operate. Its problems are that it is difficult to raise capital and that the owner has unlimited liability. Partnerships are also easy to form, but share some of the disadvantages of sole proprietorships. They have the advantage of additional owners. A partnership agreement is strongly recommended. The corporation is more difficult to launch but has the advantages of ease of raising capital, the limited liability, and ease of transferring ownership.

SUMMARY

. . . .

1. For each of the following examples discuss the advantages and disadvantages of buying a venture versus starting one. Make sure your answers are specific to the example rather than general answers.
   a. A motorcycle shop
   b. A venture that manufactures high-tech equipment

DISCUSSION QUESTIONS

   c. A consulting business specializing in buying and selling
       businesses for clients
   d. A specialty grocery store that sells primarily ethnic foods for the
       community residents of that ethnic group

2. How would you advise someone who wants to start a venture and
   has substantial capital but little management expertise? Suppose
   someone had substantial management expertise but little capital?

3. The leveraged buyout is seldom used to purchase small ventures.
   Why? Why can't the use of substantial debt that will be assumed by
   the venture work just as well for small ventures as for large
   businesses?

4. Among the many topics of entrepreneurship, one of the most
   frequently discussed is the management of the family venture. Some
   universities even have a unit called a "Family Business Center" that
   specializes in consulting with family operated businesses. Why is
   there so much interest in family businesses?

5. Business incubators provide many services to their clients, and the
   sheltered environment surely helps many new firms survive. Yet,
   research has shown that incubators have not increased the number
   of new ventures in their communities. If that is true, why is it true?
   What is the real value of incubators, considering that many states
   are pumping substantial tax dollars into underwriting them?

6. What are the most important questions you should ask a franchisor
   before you invest in the franchise?

7. What circumstances would dictate to you that a venture should be
   launched as a corporation rather than as a partnership?

8. The Sub-chapter S corporation is popular with low- to
   moderate-growth ventures. What will determine when a venture
   should be changed from a Sub S corporation to a regular
   corporation?

9. Partnerships can operate quite well if the partners are compatible.
   What can you do to assess the compatibility between you and
   potential partners before you launch the venture?

10. Is there necessarily a relationship between the growth of a venture
    and the organizational form of the venture?

EXERCISES   **EXERCISE 6-1** The Decision to Buy

You have just been made aware of a venture for sale. It currently manufactures components for defense equipment, and was one of the component manufacturers for the equipment used in the Persian Gulf War in
1991. Given the company's ability to produce high quality products, the
firm may be a desirable purchase. Aside from financial figures, what information do you need to know in order to determine whether purchasing
it would be wise for you? If you do buy it, what legal form should you use
for it?

ENDNOTES

1. John Case, "Buy Now—Avoid the Rush," *Inc.,* February 1991, 36–45.
2. *1982 Census of Retail Trade,* Department of Commerce, U.S. Bureau of the Census (Washington, D.C.: U.S. Government Printing Office, 1984), Table 3.
3. *Thomas Register of Manufacturers,* Thomas Publishing Company, New York, 1992.
4. Arnold C. Cooper, et al. *New Business in America: The Firms and Their Owners* (Washington, D.C.: The NFIB Foundation, 1990), 19.
5. David N. Allen and Syedur Rahman, "Small Business Incubators: A Positive Environment for Entrepreneurship," *Journal of Small Business Management* 23, no. 3 (July 1985): 12–22; U.S. Small Business Administration, *Small Business Incubator Handbook: A Guide for Start-up and Management* (Washington D.C.: U.S. Government Printing Office, March 1986); For an up-to-date bibliography on incubators, contact the National Business Incubation Association, 153 South Hanover Street, Carlisle, PA 17013.
6. Fred L. Fry, "The Role of Incubators in Small Business Planning," *American Journal of Small Business* 12, no. 1 (Summer 1987): 51–61.
7. Nancy Bowman-Upton, "Family-Owned Businesses: Challenge and Survival," in *The New Adventurers: Entrepreneurs Surviving and Growing,* edited by Alan Carsrud, (Los Angeles: The University of Southern California, 1987).
8. *The State of Small Business, 1990* (Washington, D.C.: U.S. Government Printing Office, 1990), 13.

◆ Conveniesse, Inc. ◆

The Launch

Jason Stone, Yolanda Williams, and Sarah Tondeur had just left a meeting with the manager of a hotel complex in Detroit. He had been gracious and had shared information with them about the launch of an upscale convenience store in or near a convention hotel. The three had also collected information regarding the proposed store during the previous week.

They discussed the hotel manager's information as well as the information that each of them had uncovered the week before. They concluded that the information was supportive enough to at least form the company and begin looking for sources of capital. Jason, who was more excitable than the others, seemed more exuberant with each new piece of information.

Then Sarah, who had been quiet during the latter part of the conversation, spoke. "Jason, I don't want to send you into orbit again, but I have some news. Remember, I stayed behind last weekend to gather some information. Actually, I stayed a couple of days. I spent a fair amount of time walking around the downtown area and talking to realtors. Are you ready? I may have found a location. One of the realtors I visited was in a ground-floor location in a fairly large office building. The agency is a subsidiary of a development company which owns the building. She said they are moving the realty agency upstairs, are taking over the entire sixth floor of the building, and so will be moving out of the ground floor area."

"When?" yelled an excited Jason and a now excited Yolanda.

"Six months."

When the two had settled down, Sarah continued. The location is in an office building approximately two blocks north of the Buffalo Convention Center. She drew the location on the back of a napkin. Yolanda recognized the location immediately and gave her glowing approval. Sarah then showed them the current floor plan that the realtor had given her. This, too, met with Yolanda and Jason's approval, even though none of them had given any specific thought to the size or layout of the store. It appeared to be about the size they thought a store of this nature should be.

"Now you do realize, don't you," cautioned Sarah, "that the rent will be quite high?"

"How high?"

"The space is approximately five thousand square feet at a cost of approximately $20 per square foot. So the rent alone would cost us in the neighborhood of $100,000 for the year." Jason almost fainted.

Assignment

What legal form would you recommend for the three? Will relatively high startup costs affect your answer? Cite advantages and disadvantages of each possible form as it applies to *this* situation.

7 Financing the Venture

LEARNING OBJECTIVES

After reading this chapter, you should be familiar with:

1. The need to finance a venture adequately
2. The need to analyze carefully the amounts and kinds of financing that are best for a particular venture
3. The nature of equity financing
4. The different kinds of debt financing
5. The nature and use of venture capital and initial public stock offerings
6. Considerations in developing a financial package

KEY TERMS

Equity financing   Initial public offerings
Debt financing   SBA loans
Venture capital   Stages of financing
Investment bankers

CONSIDER THIS!

- Virtually all new and/or small ventures are undercapitalized.
- It may be easier to get a $100,000 loan than a $10,000 loan.
- It takes money to make money.
- Financing may be readily available for some ventures while being virtually unavailable for others.
- There is a direct relationship between the amount of outside equity financing required and the amount of ownership or control that must be given up in order to get that financing.
- Venture capital is a key way to finance high-growth ventures, but less than 1 percent of all businesses receive venture capital funding.
- Public stock offerings should be made only for several million dollars since the cost of the offering is so great.

Financing the venture can be one of the most challenging and frustrating tasks facing the entrepreneur. Virtually all new ventures and most small ventures are undercapitalized. Seldom is sufficient capital available to launch a venture in the optimal way, and most ventures are continually limited in their strategies by scarce capital resources. Yet, surmounting the challenge of obtaining capital for the venture can be one of the most financially and psychologically rewarding aspects of entrepreneurship. Making

RAY LARKIN
Nellcor, Inc.

Seldom does an entrepreneurial firm's product develop an entire industry. Nellcor, Inc., did just that with a product called the N-100 pulse oximeter, which monitors oxygen saturation in a patient's arterial blood during surgery. It created a multimillion-dollar industry, of which Nellcor owns about 70 percent.

Jack Lloyd, William New, and James E. Coreman developed the product and launched Nellcor along with partner Robert S. Smith. The founders pooled $75,000 of their own money and raised $1 million from friends and acquaintances. In 1982, a group of venture capital investors led by Technology Venture Investors of Menlo Park, California, put up more than $3 million, for which Nellcor gave up 35 percent of its equity. The N-100 hit the market in 1983, selling for $5,800. By 1986, the American Society of Anesthesiologists set standards for care in operating rooms that encouraged use of pulse oximeters. Today the pulse oximeter is standard equipment in hospital operating rooms.

The introduction of the N-100 revolutionized patient monitoring practices by providing a dependable way of monitoring blood oxygen levels. The device has improved operating room safety dramatically. Before its introduction, anesthesiologists relied on visual observation to monitor whether anesthetized patients were re-

ceiving enough oxygen.

Although none of the original entrepreneurs are now with the firm, Nellcor has continued to grow. The current CEO, Ray Larkin, was Nellcor's ninth employee. The company now has 1,350 employees and 1991 sales of almost $160 million. The company went public in 1987.

Building on the success of the pulse oximeter, Nellcor has introduced the OXINET pulse oximetry network, a device that allows remote monitoring of oxygen saturation for up to eight patients from one location. The N-1000 multi-function monitor tracks carbon dioxide and nitrous oxide levels in addition to oxygen levels. The N-2500 anesthesia safety monitor combines the functions of the N-1000 with the N-1500 anesthetic agent module that automatically identifies and measures three common anesthetic gases.

Recent acquisitions have begun to contribute to Nellcor's growth even more. Radiant

Systems, a software and systems development company, was acquired in the first quarter of 1990 to accelerate the development of new network-based products. EdenTec, acquired in 1991, specializes in infant and adult breathing monitors and recording systems for the home health care market. Fenem, Inc., another acquisition, produces a disposable carbon dioxide detector for the pre-hospital and emergency department environments. Nellcor's latest introduction is N-CAT, a continuous noninvasive blood pressure monitor that has the potential to revolutionize blood pressure monitoring in much the same way as the N-100 revolutionized pulse oximetry. Nellcor has exclusive rights to market the Japanese-made N-CAT in North and South America, major European countries, Australia, and New Zealand.

A product currently under development is a fetal oximeter which, if brought to market, may be one of the most significant advancements in obstretrics in twenty years.

Sales in 1991 were essentially double those of 1987, as was net income. The company has no debt and had an average return on equity of 14.8 percent.

SOURCE: Ann Handley, "Pulsing the Market," *Venture*, 11, May 1989: 36; "Research: Ideas for Today's Investors," *Research* 15, No. 1 (January 1992) 51; and telephone interview with Susan Freschi, Manager, Investor Relations, Nellcor, Inc. Used with permission.

a company grow with new infusions of cash that fuel necessary expansion is one of the real thrills of being an entrepreneur.

Obtaining capital for a *new* venture is even more difficult than obtaining cash for an existing venture. It is difficult because the venture has no track record and the entrepreneur may also have only a modest history of managing a venture. Most lenders tend to be conservative in lending to new ventures, and it is appropriate that they should be. Most business failures occur in the first few years of existence. Thus, lenders and venture capitalists tend to favor those firms that have survived the startup phase.

This chapter will first consider the need for financing. It will then discuss the various types of financing for a venture. Discussion then moves to matching the types of financing to the specific needs and stages of a venture. The chapter concludes with the requirements for a financial package.

THE NEED FOR FINANCING

New and growing ventures require financing for a variety of needs as they develop over time (Table 7-1). These needs are a function of the type of venture, the rate of growth, and the stage of the venture's development. Low-growth firms, for example, require smaller amounts of funding than do higher-growth firms. Service ventures require less than manufacturing firms. Ventures poised to enter their rapid growth stage will require more funds than one which has just been launched.

Pre-startup capital is the investment required long before the venture is launched. If a new product is involved, prototype development must come before the venture is launched. Significant research and development and market research may be necessary. Funds for strategic plan development and initial site acquisition may also be necessary at this time.

Startup expenses are those costs incurred shortly before, during, and immediately after the actual launch of the venture. Expenditures at the time of start-up include facilities and equipment, inventory, grand opening

Stage of Development	Financing Needs
Pre-start-up	Prototype development, site acquisition, business plan preparation, research and development, market research
Start-up	Inventory, plant and equipment, grand opening advertising, professional fees, prepaid expenses
Post-start-up	Advertising, sales expenses, wage and salaries, rent, utilities, additional inventories, seasonal/cyclical cash flow needs
Growth	Facility expansion, additional distribution methods, geographical expansion, acquisitions, cost of underwriting more financing

TABLE 7-1
Financing Needs for Various Stages of Development

advertising, prepaid expenses such as deposits and insurance, licenses, and professional fees for accountants and attorneys.

Additional funding will be necessary once the venture is begun. Typical operating expenses such as advertising, additional inventory, salaries, and sales expenses are included here. Of particular interest is the need to balance seasonal or cyclical cash flow deficits. Virtually all businesses will have uneven cash flows. The purchase of inventory is an example of this since inventory must be purchased weeks or months before it can be sold. Thus, inventory financing becomes the major financing need for most retail businesses as well as for many manufacturing ventures.

Low-growth small businesses typically do not need substantial funding once the initial launch and stabilization occur. Moderate- or high-growth ventures, on the other hand, will require major additional inflows of capital to underwrite expansion. Additional plant and equipment may be required, additions or changes in distribution systems may be costly, geographical expansion can absorb significant funding, acquisition of other firms can be quite expensive, and substantial funding may be required before going public.

Some of the financing needs will be short term. Other needs can be met only by using longer-term financing methods. Short-term capital may be that which is necessary to launch the venture or to finance development costs before the venture is formally launched. Long-run capital is typically used to finance fixed equipment and facilities or major research and development efforts.

There are two basic sources of financing: equity and debt. **Equity financing** is capital provided in exchange for ownership. **Debt financing** is provided to the venture in exchange for interest payments and does not include the ownership provision. Each of these types of financing will be discussed in depth before considering their appropriateness for specific situations.

EQUITY FINANCING

All ventures will have some equity funding since all ventures are ultimately owned by someone. The venture need not be managed by the owner, but an owner who has contributed capital to the venture must exist somewhere. The amount of equity funding required for a given venture will depend upon the nature of the venture. Small ventures may be funded entirely by equity capital provided by the owner. Larger ventures will use more debt financing, and some ventures will have only a small amount of equity capital invested. There are many different sources of equity capital. These range from the personal funds of the entrepreneur to publicly traded stock.

Personal Funds

Virtually all ventures will have personal funds of the entrepreneur invested in the venture. Most entrepreneurs prefer to use at least some personal funds in a venture to assure that they have a true investment in the venture. Similarly, most lenders will insist that the entrepreneurs invest personally in the venture even if most of the funding is via debt financing. Lenders feel that entrepreneurs without a substantial personal financial stake in the venture may not be sufficiently committed to remain with the venture if problems develop.

Personal funds may be the only viable source of funds for some ventures. Ventures that appear to be high risk for one reason or another may not be able to attract either other owners or lenders. The riskiness may be either because the venture concept is new and untested or because the entrepreneur has some personal characteristics that discourage investors. These characteristics may include a lack of experience or some personality quirk that investors think would detract from the viability of the venture.

Friends and Family

Friends and family are a common source of equity capital for new ventures. Friends and family can be relatively accessible sources of funding for new ventures, and they are sometimes quite willing to invest. This is because they know the entrepreneur. Thus, that portion of the uncertainty that must be overcome by impersonal investors is eliminated. Further, they may have implicit trust in the entrepreneur and not question the efficacy of the venture concept.

Friends and family typically provide relatively small amounts of equity funding for ventures. Part of this is because many small business ventures need relatively small amounts of total funding. There are exceptions to this, of course. The Nellcor example in the entrepreneurial profile leading off this chapter is such a case. John Lloyd was able to raise $1 million from friends and acquaintances. This is not typical. More typical amounts would be in the $5,000 to $50,000 range, with some investing up to $100,000.

Obtaining equity funds from friends and family has both pluses and minuses. The investment of equity funds means financial ownership. Friends and family who provide equity capital to the venture become part owners with the entrepreneur. The ownership percentage may be small, but it is still part ownership. Thus, the investors may feel that they have a say in the operation of the venture. Sometimes, minor owners suddenly come into the business and demand action from the entrepreneur or attempt to direct employees or redesign the facilities. This can be disastrous to the operations of a small or new venture. On the other hand, friends and family are often patient, and do not mind waiting for any return that might be realized from the operations of the venture.

Informal Investors

Family and friends are, of course, informal investors. There are other categories of informal investors, however, that merit discussion. An informal investor is any noninstitutional investor who may, as an individual, invest in a given venture. An informal investor may be any person who has capital to invest in a venture. Many of these investors are wealthy, and images come to mind of doctors, lawyers, and retired individuals who have accumulated wealth, or successful entrepreneurs who invest in other ventures. Informal investors may invest in a wide range of ventures from industrial manufacturing to wholesale, retail, or service operations. They may invest in only a few deals per year; the size of the deal may be from $10,000 to $500,000 with the average being $175,000. If larger deals are desirable, some informal investors will join in underwriting ventures in the $1 million range.[1] Informal investors deal directly with the entrepreneur and typically buy stock in the company. Some investors prefer Sub S corporations or limited partnerships in which the investors are liable only to the extent of their investments.

Informal investors provide risk capital to growth ventures. That is, they provide capital to ventures that have a high probability of loss, but also have a reasonable probability of substantial gain. The difficulty with informal investors is connecting the investors with the entrepreneurs needing capital. Many investors have capital to invest, and many entrepreneurs need that capital, but there is usually no organized method of getting the two groups together. Accountants, attorneys, and local brokerage houses often have knowledge of informal investors. Sometimes these groups themselves are interested in investing in promising ventures. Still, there is not a commonly accepted system for bringing together entrepreneurs and investors.

Fortunately for entrepreneurs in some areas, a system has been developed to assist in linking entrepreneurs and informal investors. Variously called venture capital networks, exchanges, or clearinghouses, these organizations play the role of a facilitator in bringing the two groups together. There are increasing numbers of venture capital clearinghouses around the country. Some require memberships of individuals of one or both groups in order to be part of the service. The clearinghouse plays only the role of facilitator. Entrepreneurs fill out detailed questionnaires about their venture concept. The data are then matched with the interests of potential investors. The investor member is then provided a list of venture concepts that are available for funding. The investor picks projects that are of interest and then requests more information. After seeing more information, the investor then selects one or more ventures that look especially appealing and is put in contact with the entrepreneurs. The Securities and Exchange Commission regulations prevent the clearinghouse from playing an advisory role. Thus, the actual exchange of funds and/or ownership is totally on a one-on-one basis just as it would be without the clearinghouse.

Venture Capital Firms

Venture capital firms deal only with ventures with high-growth potential. They deal with high-risk deals and are rewarded commensurately. In fact, the essence of **venture capital** is the raising of money for high-potential firms in order for them to reach their potential as quickly as possible while providing substantial returns to their investors.

Venture capitalists know that many of their investments will not achieve the growth rates or return on investment that the entrepreneurs had hoped for. Thus, they screen venture concepts carefully and invest only in those that they think have an exceptional chance of success. They realize also that a few of the ventures will do exceptionally well. The ones

VENTURE PERSPECTIVE 7-1

• • • • • • • • • • • • • •

VENTURE CAPITAL EXCHANGE

Venture Capital Exchange (VCE) is a not-for-profit corporation located at the Enterprise Development Center at the University of Tulsa with funding provided by the Grace and Franklin Bernsen Foundation. The main purpose of VCE is to introduce entrepreneurs to active, informal investors commonly referred to in the industry as business angels.

Venture Capital Exchange was organized to provide equity financing options in the $20,000 to $500,000 range, the type of financing most difficult for new and emerging firms. Informal risk capital investors represent a major source of risk capital with the ability to underwrite perhaps five times as many ventures as public equity and professional venture capitalists combined. But contact among informal investors and entrepreneurs is usually quite haphazard and difficult to arrange. VCE seeks to make this process more productive for both parties.

Venture Capital Exchange maintains a computerized data base of entrepreneurs and investors. This information is accessible only to VCE and its designees. The data base contains entrepreneur opportunity profiles, which describe basic information about investment opportunities, and investment interest profiles, which describe potential investors. VCE maintains an ongoing comparison between the two data bases in an effort to match opportunities and interests. When matches occur, information regarding a venture and a copy of the executive summary portion of the venture's business plan (referenced by a file number) is sent to the investor. Up to this point, both parties are anonymous. After this information has been reviewed by the investor and if further information is desired, the name and address of the entrepreneur is provided to the investor and, concurrently, the entrepreneur

is advised of the name and address of the investor. At this point, VCE's involvement ceases, and either party may pursue the opportunity through direct contact.

There is a $100 fee for each entrepreneur opportunity application. This payment covers the cost of VCE's service for twelve months. Investors may also register for one year of VCE activity with a $100 application fee. VCE receives no fees or commissions related to the eventual outcome of the information it exchanges.

VCE is neither an investment advisor nor a broker-dealer of securities. It purposefully avoids these functions and makes specific disclaimers regarding the viability of enterprises or the success potential for any matches that might occur.

SOURCE: R.D. Hisrich, Venture Capital Exchange, Enterprise Development Center, The University of Tulsa, Tulsa, Oklahoma. Used with permission

that return more than the projected rate then offset those that either fail or produce at a lower level than expected. Figure 7-1 illustrates the number of ventures that are funded (along with the results) compared with the number of plans submitted. Of every one thousand plans submitted for review, nine hundred of them are rejected immediately. Of the remaining one hundred, half will be rejected after further study. Of the fifty remaining, forty will be rejected after due diligence analysis—an in-depth study of the proposal's potential. This leaves ten that actually receive funding of the original one thousand. The concern over the risk of the projects is evident from the results of the funding. Even though only ten out of one thousand are funded, only two of those will meet the expectations of the venture capitalists. Six will be moderately successful, and two will go broke.

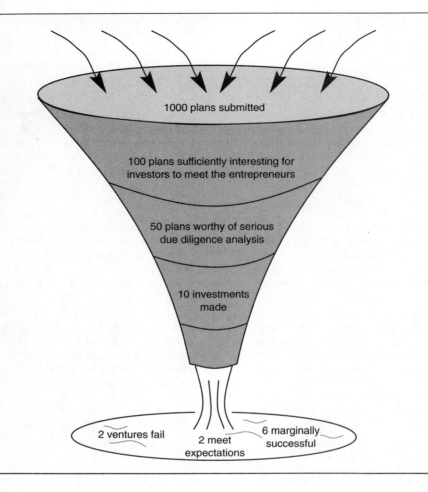

FIGURE 7-1

Disposition of Business
Plans Submitted to
Venture Capitalists
SOURCE: Adapted from A.
David Silver, *Venture Capital:
The Complete Guide for
Investors* (New York: John
Wiley & Sons, 1985), 51.

1000 plans submitted

100 plans sufficiently interesting for
investors to meet the entrepreneurs

50 plans worthy of serious
due diligence analysis

10 investments
made

2 ventures fail   2 meet   6 marginally
                       expectations   successful

Venture capitalists generally have three characteristics in common:

1. They usually have equity participation in the venture either through
   direct purchase of stock or through warrants, options, or convertible
   securities.

2. They usually invest for a five- to ten-year period before receiving
   their returns.

3. They usually actively monitor the performance of the companies in
   which they invest.

Venture Capital Financing and Stages of Development

As growth oriented ventures move through each development stage, they
use several rounds or **stages of financing.** Seed capital is pre-launch financing for entrepreneurs to develop new products or prototypes. This
capital is extremely high risk. Start-up capital is that cash needed to launch
and stabilize the venture. Once the venture is launched, it will move
through up to three additional stages or rounds of financing before going

public. The first two are typically referred to as Stage 1 and Stage 2 financing. These stages are reached when the firm is purchasing a plant and equipment and developing marketing campaigns for the product to compete in increasingly large markets. Stage 3 is usually referred to as mezzanine financing. It is the additional financing necessary to gear the firm up for an initial public offering (IPO).

Separate from the stages of financing are two special situations. One is the financing of Employee Stock Option Plans (ESOPs). This is financing that allows employees to buy the company from the current owner. A leveraged buyout (LBO) is financing to purchase a company with debt financing, which is then transferred to the company itself rather than the owners. In either the ESOP or the LBO cases, venture capitalists or investment bankers may provide funding for the transition of the firm from one owner to the other.

Private Venture Capital Firms

There are different kinds of venture capital firms just as there are different kinds of firms in any other industry. Some tend to invest solely in a specific industry, while others invest only in certain types of ventures. Some primarily invest in particular stages of financing such as seed capital, startup financing, or second-stage financing (Table 7-2).

Private venture capital firms themselves may be funded by accumulated wealth, investment by pension funds or insurance companies, or limited partnerships. The venture capital firm managers then invest in high-potential ventures.

Venture capital firms tend to be located in major metropolitan areas. Further, the venture capital market tends to be located in areas that support high-technology start-ups. One study suggested eight geographical regions in the United States that are prime areas for the match between venture capital and entrepreneurial firms.[2] These areas are:

1. San Francisco Bay Area complex (San Jose/Palo Alto/San Francisco) and the L.A. complex
2. Boston, Massachusetts (the Route 128 complex)
3. Florida
4. Houston, Texas
5. Kansas City, Missouri
6. Phoenix, Arizona
7. Portland, Oregon, and Bellevue/Seattle, Washington
8. The Research Triangle (Durham, North Carolina, area)

Private venture capital firms have played an increasingly important role in underwriting high-growth ventures. In 1984 alone, $4.8 billion of new capital was committed to the industry, more than six times as great as in 1980. The size of venture capital firms varies from a low of $600,000 to a high of $600 million in assets. The size of the investment in a specific venture will range from $100,000 to $3.5 million, with the average being in the $650,000 to $1 million range. The firms invest in an average of about fifty ventures, and they will be the lead investor in about half of those.

This, too, varies among firms. Some venture capitalists will invest in only a few new ventures, but they will be the lead investor and play a major role in most of the ventures in which they invest. Others will tend to be "late-stage investors," coming in only after another firm has committed the major part of the funds necessary. Some will invest primarily in early stage firms, that is start-ups, pre-start-ups, or early development stages. Others will come in only in later stages of a venture's development, perhaps in second- or third-round financing. In many cases the venture capital representative will serve on the board of the funded venture.[3]

Venture capitalists have the primary role of providing funds for new and growing ventures. In addition, however, they often will play significant roles in the management or planning of the venture. For example,

· · · · · · · ·
TABLE 7-2
Selected Venture Capital Firms
Source: Jane K. Morris, Susan Isenstein, and Anne Knowles, eds., *Pratt's Guide to Venture Capital Sources,* 1990 Edition (Needham, MA: Venture Economics, Inc., 1990).

Name/Location	Type of Firm	Stage of Venture	Preferred Location	Preferred Investment (in millions)
Norwest Venture Capital Management Minneapolis, MN	Subsidiary of bank holding company	Seed, startup 1, 2, Mezzanine, LBO	National	$2–4
Alpha Partners Menlo Park, CA	Private	Seed	San Francisco area	1–1.5
Benefit Capital Los Angeles, CA	Investment banker	Mezzanine, LBO, ESOP	National	0.5–2.5
Venture Associates Denver, CO	Private	Startup, 1, 2	None	0.5–6
Frontenac Venture Company Chicago, IL	Private, Small Business Investment Company (SBIC)	Startup, 1, 2, LBO	Midwest	1 plus
Humana Louisville, KY	Corporate	1, 2, Mezzanine, LBO	None	1 plus
Oxford Venture Corp. Stamford, CT	Private	Startup, 1, 2, Mezzanine, LBO	None	0.5–2
MESBIC Financial Corp. Dallas, TX	Minority Enterprise Small Business Investment Company (MESBIC)	2, Mezzanine, LBO	Southwest	0.1–0.25
Johnson & Johnson New Brunswick, NJ	Corporate	Seed, startup, 1	None	No preference
AQVIR Montreal, Quebec	Quebec government	Seed, R & D	Quebec	0.1–1
Vengrowth Capital Funds Toronto, Ontario	Private	1, 2, Mezzanine, LBO	Northeast U.S. & Canada	0.5–1

These venture capital firms are typical of the eight hundred venture capital firms listed in *Pratt's Guide to Venture Capital Sources.*

most will assist in obtaining additional financing. Most will help in strategic and operational planning. Some will assist in finding additional managers for the firm, and some will fire existing managers if the firm is not doing well. In general, venture capitalists perform three critical tasks: (1) building the investor group and getting financing, (2) reviewing and helping formulate the business strategy, and (3) filling in the management team.[4]

Small Business Investment Companies

A hybrid of private funding and government funding for new and small ventures is the Small Business Investment Company (SBIC), along with its minority counterpart, the Minority Enterprise Small Business Investment Company (MESBIC). The advantage of the SBIC and MESBIC is that government funds are added to private funds to form a sizeable venture capital pool for the firm. These funds can then be invested in new or growth ventures.

The major benefit of the Small Business Investment Company or Minority Enterprise Investment Company is simply the total amount of funds that can be offered. The SBIC can leverage private funds through the addition of loaned funds from the government. Thus, an SBIC or MESBIC can invest in far more deals than a similar sized totally private venture capital firm.

Corporate Sponsored Venture Capital Firms

Entrepreneurship has entered big business in recent years. A number of large companies have attempted to foster entrepreneurship within their own walls. They have found, however, that the bureaucracy of the large corporation stifles creativity and risk-taking among their employees. They later discovered that a better way to foster entrepreneurship was simply to provide venture capital to new or growing firms to increase their rate of growth and development. Some of the corporations have started venture capital divisions within their own firms, some have started a separate venture capital firm with limited ties to the parent company, and some have simply made significant investments into already established venture capital companies.

Some of the corporate venture capital firms have restricted their funds to new ventures that are suppliers for their own companies. Others spin off service activities that previously were in-house. Still others are less restrictive and make investments in any type of venture, regardless of how similar it is to the parent company. A study of corporate venture capital firms found that the most important factor for them in deciding to underwrite a venture was the degree of corporate fit with the parent company.[5] Other important factors were similar to what might be expected from other venture capital firms—low total investment, high rates of returns, quality entrepreneurial team, and new technology.

An advantage for a large corporation in having a corporate venture capital firm is that the health of sponsored ventures does not affect the

VENTURE PERSPECTIVE 7-2

CRAY RESEARCH, INC.

Seymour Cray of Cray Research, Inc., had orders for only fifty-three computers during the entire year of 1987. But Mr. Cray is not terribly concerned; he sells supercomputers, which cost between $4 million and $16 million each. The supercomputers are used by meteorologists to track massive amounts of weather data, by oil explorers to handle seismic data processing, and by cancer researchers to study genetic sequences and molecular structures to find the cause of cancer. The weather computer, for example, must digest eighty million bits of information collected from nine thousand manned ground stations, 750 weather balloons, thousands of

marine buoys, two thousand ships, and some six hundred aircraft.

Seymour Cray began his modest computer business in 1972. The following year, Cray secured $300,000 in equity capital from the Northwest Growth Fund, Inc., an SBA-backed Small Business Investment Company. It was a long shot bid on a small firm with only

twelve employees that had grossed only $58,308 in its first year and made barely $3,000 in profits. Northwest Growth invested another $250,000 in 1975, and another SBIC invested $150,000. Fifteen years after being launched, Cray Research, Inc., had more than four thousand employees and sales of $687 million. Nearly 40 percent of Cray's customers in 1987 were foreign. Cray continues to be the undisputed leader in supercomputers and holds approximately two-thirds of the market.

SOURCE: "SBICs Gave Birth to Supercomputer Giant—Cray," *Network* (Small Business Administration) 4, no. 1 (Jan–Feb 1989): 2.

health of the parent firm. Thus, the venture capital arm can invest in a number of risky projects, knowing that some of them will not meet expectations. Even if a particular venture fails, however, the impact will not be felt directly by the parent company. Hence, the parent firm need not hold the reins so tightly on a new or growing venture. In this way the new venture can grow without being stifled by the controls of the parent firm.

Investment Bankers

Venture capital firms typically provide equity capital in the $100,000 to $3.5 million range. Entrepreneurs seeking funds in excess of $1 million may find investment bankers to be a more viable source of funds. **Investment bankers** deal in major financing for high-potential ventures but typically are short of public offerings, at least initially. They do, however, work to provide substantial funds for a venture and often will be involved in more than one round of financing.

Investment bankers are often involved in combination deals in which a private placement of a venture's stock is made to interested investors. Investment bankers come in at least three categories, based roughly on size of firm, geographical spread, and number and breadth of clients.[6]

The first category of investment banker is made up of what are referred to as boutiques. Boutiques are small firms that specialize in private placements for small companies. They will do perhaps less than a dozen placements a year; most will be local firms wanting funds in the $1 million to $30 million range. The boutique firms raise the cash from insurance companies, banks, finance companies, and individuals. They generally charge 4 percent to 8 percent on equity deals and 1 percent to 5 percent on debt capital. Because they are small, boutiques can give personal attention to the entrepreneur both during and after the deal.

The second category of investment banker is the regional banker. Regional bankers are larger and may invest in firms over a fairly large geographical area. They may have hundreds of brokers, analysts, and deal-makers, who may orchestrate ten to fifty private placements a year, with the placements ranging from $5 million to $100 million. Some prefer companies that will eventually go public while others will work with firms that want to remain private.

Major Wall Street investment firms are a third category. Although traditionally interested in more established or major corporations, the Wall Street firms are moving more into the entrepreneurial territory. These firms are typically interested in ventures that will be going public within a relatively short time, but may occasionally work with private placements that do not plan to enter the public market.

Public Offerings

Entrepreneurial firms with high potential often want to get into the public market as soon as possible. Few ventures are launched with public funding, and virtually no "first launches" are done with public offerings. The first attempt at public funding by a firm is referred to as an **initial public offering** or IPO. Going public is akin to moving from a closet to a goldfish bowl, with all the attending pressures, problems, and benefits.[7] The disadvantages of going public include increased regulatory requirements, an obligation to release considerably more corporate information, and possible future loss of control. The benefit of going public, however, is simply that substantially more funding is available for the operations of the firm as well as for the entrepreneur's personal wealth. To go public, a firm must hire legal counsel and investment banking services. Financial and other information must be assembled, audited, filed with the SEC, and presented in a prospectus. The investment bankers then market the issue to potential investors.

The amount of funds raised through an initial public offering is limited only to the perceived value of the firm and the ability of the investment banking firm to market it well to investors. IPOs will be for several million dollars and those in excess of $100 million are not uncommon. Entrepreneurs must consider carefully whether going public is in their best interest. It is true that substantially more funding can be generated through an IPO than through a private placement or a venture capitalist. But it is also true that the expenses, time, and attention required are substantial. Fees for the investment banker, accountants, and attorneys together can exceed $1 million.

DEBT FINANCING

The previous section discussed the options available to the entrepreneur in the realm of equity financing. Debt financing can be equally desirable, depending on the conditions. The advantage of debt financing for the entrepreneur is that full ownership remains with the entrepreneur. The owner does not have to share profits (or losses) with other investors. More important, the entrepreneur maintains full operational control of the venture without the undue influence of outsiders. Interest on debt is a deductible expense, thereby reducing the tax liability for the firm.

The disadvantage of using debt financing is the cost of interest. Servicing debt can become an unbearable task for some ventures and may, in fact, be one of the most direct causes of business failures. This is especially true among smaller ventures that have become excessively leveraged or for companies that have been purchased via the leveraged buyout.

Virtually all firms use a combination of debt and equity to finance the venture's growth and operations. A strategic decision that all entrepreneurs must make is to decide what percentage of debt to use. Certainly, using no or little debt is unwise because of the limitations this strategy places on the firm. Conversely, using too much debt makes the firm extremely vulnerable in case of a downturn in sales. Although there are general rules of thumb in determining the relative amounts of debt and equity to use, the optimal percentage as well as the average percentage will vary from firm to firm, industry to industry, and development stage to development stage (Table 7-3).

This section will discuss the various sources of debt financing, which include traditional sources such as friends, relatives, and banks. The following section will then discuss other sources such as suppliers or customers, economic development agencies, and other companies.

TABLE 7-3

Debt / Net Worth of Selected Venture Types

Source: Financial Research Associates, *Financial Studies of the Small Business*, 11th ed. (Winter Haven, FL, 1988), S-1–S-60.

Type of Venture	Size (sales in thousands)	Total Debt / Net Worth (%)
Computer stores	$250–500	63.4%
Video sales/rentals	10–250	52.9
Furniture/appliances	500–1,000	15.0
Plastics manufacturing	1,000-plus	146.1
Electronic component manufacturing	500–1,000	21.7
Realtor	500–1,000	82.9
Engineering firm	250–500	45.6
Fast food restaurant	250–500	30.3
Printing	1,000-plus	83.4
Motels	500–1,000	38.2

Borrowing from Friends and Family

The section on equity financing discussed having friends or relatives invest in the venture. In that case, acquaintances *invested* in the ventures and became part owners. In the case of debt financing, the friends or relatives simply *lend* money to the entrepreneur for use in the venture. In this case they do not have an ownership role. These loans, however, are limited— often to no more than a few hundred dollars. The interest rate charged, if any, is irrelevant except for determining repayment. The aspect that is more relevant is the *expectation* by the lending individuals. Relatives may lend money for the venture with no real expectations regarding when, if, or how the funds will be repaid. Some, however, feel that the loan gives them part ownership just as an investment in the firm would. While on the one hand, individuals may be totally unconcerned about the use or return of the loan, others may be quite restrictive and feel that they have the right to special treatment or even the right to be involved in management decisions because of the loan. Since the loans are seldom formal, or "arm's length," transactions, insufficient formality may create problems at a later date.

Larger amounts may also be obtained from friends or relatives, but somewhat more formal arrangements for repayment and interest may be expected. In these cases, formal notes or agreements will be made regarding interest rates, payment schedules, and use of funds. Thus, even though the amount loaned is greater, the relationship between the lender and the entrepreneur may be more sound.

Banks

Bank loans are the most commonly known source of debt funds besides friends and family, and they are the primary source of outside financing for small businesses and many growth ventures. Bankers tend to be conservative and are somewhat reluctant to loan money to an entrepreneur for a new venture concept. They prefer to lend in areas where there is some track record. That is, they prefer to lend to entrepreneurs whose ideas are not foreign to their existing loan portfolio.

The conservatism of bankers in dealing with small business borrowers underscores the need for careful planning of avenues for financing the venture. Although a business plan need not be as detailed for a smaller bank loan as it would be for a venture capital request, the entrepreneur still must ensure that sufficient homework is done before going in with the request.

Bank loans may be obtained for a variety of uses. These include startup expenses such as remodeling facilities, initial inventory purchases, marketing expenses, and any other expenses that could be classified as overhead. It is assumed, of course, that the entrepreneur has invested personal funds into the venture. The bank loan then supplements the personal funds until revenues provide sufficient operating capital.

General criteria for bank loans center around the quality of the entrepreneurial team, the quality of the venture concept, the amount of capital needed, and the expected ability to repay the loan. The loan package must be able to communicate these ideas to the lending officer. Bank loans will typically require collateral to back up the loan in case of default.

Central to the loan package is the business plan, which was discussed in Chapter 4. The plan must set forth the nature of the venture and its product, the competition, the entrepreneurial team, the strategies planned for the venture, and financial projections. In addition, the loan package may include specific forms required by the bank, a statement of personal history, and an indication of how and when the loan will be repaid.

Bank lending officers will also have specialized criteria, unique to their particular bank, that they use in assessing loan packages. These criteria will vary substantially from bank to bank. Some banks, for example, are quite conservative and tend not to loan to a small start-up. Other banks aggressively seek small business loans. Small-town banks may have looser criteria than their city cousins because of the visible role they play in the community. Some banks willingly handle Small Business Administration loans while others do not.

In addition to variation among banks, the criteria may vary over time. An entrepreneur requesting a loan in 1983 near the bottom of the recession would have faced a different reaction than the same entrepreneur would have in 1990 after several years of economic expansion. Variation in a bank's loan portfolio may also influence the willingness to grant a loan request at one time more than another. A bank will keep track of how many loans it has that are considered safe as opposed to risky. They may also have internal policies regarding how many retail loans, manufacturing loans, and service industry loans they have. A loan package that might be accepted in one situation might be rejected out of hand at another because of the bank's portfolio at a given time.

Venture plans in some industries will automatically receive a better reception than others. During the oil boom of the early 1980s in the Oklahoma/Texas area, virtually any entrepreneur with a proposal for a venture in the oil industry could get a loan. Even ill-conceived ventures were lent money because it was assumed that the booming economy would carry the day and make the venture profitable. Unfortunately, the oil boom did not continue, thousands of ventures failed, and banks that had lent substantial amounts in the oil business also failed. Even a decade later, some areas in the oil-producing states are still feeling the impact. Needless to say, the banks remaining in those areas are now far more conservative in their loan policies.

The entrepreneur seeking a loan should shop for financing just as carefully as for other resources or materials. In the case of a first startup situation, the shopping should begin with the entrepreneur's personal bank. In this case, the bank's staff may know the individual and be somewhat more amenable to granting the loan request. But the entrepreneur's personal bank may not have the lowest rates or best terms, regardless of prior association with the bank. Applying to only one bank is akin to buying a car from the nearest dealer and choosing the car that is closest to the window of the showroom. The first car may not be the best nor have the equipment desired. Similarly, the first bank may not have the best rates nor allow the terms desired.

Small Business Administration

Many entrepreneurs are rejected by banks. An avenue for debt capital that is available to some of these entrepreneurs is a **Small Business Administration loan**. The U.S. Small Business Administration (SBA) was established in 1955 to provide funding and assistance to small businesses. Later, it expanded to provide focused support to ventures owned by women, minorities, and veterans.

Today, the SBA primarily makes guaranteed loans through commercial banks. The SBA guarantees 80 percent of the loan, so a bank risks only 20 percent. For this reason, some banks are willing to work with an entrepreneur to obtain an SBA loan when they would not underwrite the same loan by themselves. SBA loans can be used for the same purposes as a bank loan.

Small Business Administration loans have become administratively easier to obtain in recent years. In the past, all potential borrowers were referred to an SBA office after being turned down by a bank (or two banks). The SBA would then process the loan, and this processing would take up to six months. In more recent years, the SBA has streamlined the process by having the banks do much of the paperwork. The time required to fully process an SBA loan has been reduced from a few months to a few days.

OTHER CAPITAL SOURCES

The preceding sections have discussed the more common sources of debt and equity capital for new and growing ventures. There are, however, other sources of capital that are overlooked by many. These include supplier or customer funding, economic development agencies, and relationships with other companies. In addition, internal policies can free up capital if necessary.

Supplier Capital

One of the most frequently used sources of small amounts of capital is credit terms from suppliers. Most suppliers will provide their products on credit to qualified buyers. This may or may not be available for the first order a startup firm makes from a supplier, but most will be willing to extend limited credit after the first purchase. Credit terms of 2/10, net 30 are common. This means that the entrepreneur can take a 2 percent discount if the bill is paid within ten days. This can be a substantial savings if cash flow allows. On the other hand, it is also a ready source of short-term, but expensive, capital if cash flow is tight. In essence, the supplier is furnishing a loan for the amount of the inventory for a twenty-day period. In the above example, the effective interest rate is approximately 36 percent per year. Yet, if the inventory or product is purchased infrequently, or the dollar amount is low, then the entrepreneur may still be well advised to use the credit terms. In any case, the bill should be paid on the tenth or thirtieth day to maximize the use of creditor's money.

Additional use of supplier capital can come from knowledge of supplier billing procedures. Some suppliers routinely send out all invoices at the end of the month. They also often include credit terms such as the 2/10, net 30 discussed above. With this in mind, the astute entrepreneur can purchase a product on the first of the month knowing that the invoice will not be mailed until the last of the month. Thus, instead of ten days of free use of capital, the entrepreneur actually has approximately forty days use of supplier capital without any interest charge.

Customer Capital

Entrepreneurs who sell major products or services to either industrial or retail customers can make use of customer capital. In this case, the entrepreneur requires a deposit of, say, 20 percent at the time an order is placed, 50 percent of the remaining balance within forty-five days, and the remainder before the product is shipped. The logic of this is clear. Without the payment terms suggested, the producer's cash flow would be negative while the product is being produced. Only when the product is finally delivered is the cash received. However, if a deposit is required at the time of order and is coupled with a major percentage of the remaining balance due a few weeks later, then the producer can use that cash to order the raw materials necessary to produce the product and pay at least part of other expenses such as labor and overhead. The following example illustrates this.

The University Avenue Church decided to order an electronic pipe organ for the sanctuary at a cost of approximately $200,000. The organ manufacturer required a $50,000 deposit at the time of the order. An additional $100,000 was required no more than sixty days later. The final $50,000 was required six months later. The organ manufacturer made the smaller pipes domestically, but the large center pipes were handcrafted in Germany. With the initial payment, the manufacturer had the church's commitment to purchase, had $50,000 to begin assembly of the small pipes, and had documentation to use as collateral for a loan to begin work on the large pipes. Sixty days later, $100,000 more arrived to cover the full cost of assembly of the large pipes, the cost of installing the small pipes, and the balance of the short-term loan used to acquire material for construction of the large pipes. The final $50,000 arrived at approximately the time the large pipes were completed and shipped to the church for installation. Thus, the manufacturer used virtually none of its own capital invested in the production of the product and used only a short-term loan to purchase raw material inventory. Further, it used the church's commitment documentation as collateral for a conventional forty-five-day bank loan, which was a cheaper rate than the raw material supplier's terms.

Economic Development Funding

The decade of the 1980s saw major advances in federal, state, and local funding of new ventures as part of an economic development program. This was especially true in the Midwest, which was hit hard by the recession beginning in 1981, and the oil-producing states, which saw record

VENTURE PERSPECTIVE 7-3

• • • • • • • • • • • •

SPORTS TECHNOLOGY, INC.

Indianapolis, Indiana, is becoming increasingly known for its interest in sports competition, particularly as it relates to amateur athletes and teams training for the Olympics. Consider the following hypothetical situation. Suppose entrepreneur Gerald Abel formed Sports Technology, Inc. (STI), as a means of cashing in on the national trend toward fitness in general and the local emphasis on team training for the Olympics. Sports Technology, Inc., would create a major data base for tracking all aspects of training. This would include everything from recording blood tests for athletes, drug testing, and performance records, to costs and performance reports of equipment and uniforms. In addition, STI would do statistical research on performance results as tied to diet, training programs, and the uniform gear.

In order to accomplish these tasks, Abel might calculate that Sports Technology, Inc., needed approximately $2 million in capital to purchase necessary computer equipment and hire approximately twenty individuals to do the data collection and analysis.

Abel could approach a local bank for the capital with the idea of investing no more than $100,000 of his own funds. The bank would likely be unwilling to underwrite the entire amount, but might be willing to participate if substantial funding could be garnered elsewhere. Thus, Abel might then approach the city of Indianapolis, which in turn could contact the state of Indiana. At the same time, local investors could be courted. The final deal could be as follows:

Funding Source	Amount	Terms
Gerald Abel	$100,000	Personal funds
Bank	200,000	Loan at 12 percent interest payable in three years
Private investors	700,000	Equity investment with 40 percent ownership
Indianapolis	500,000	Loan from tax increment financing and a commitment to purchase services of STI for two years
State of Indiana	400,000	Loan at 3 percent interest
Computer manufacturer	100,000	Loan for $75,000 plus $25,000 donation in exchange for advertising

bankruptcies in the mid-1980s. State and local governments were quite interested in attracting new or growing businesses to their communities. They made combinations of grants, loans, and tax abatement commitments to industries willing to locate in the community and provide jobs for local residents. In some cases, the amount of dollars committed was specifically tied to the number of jobs provided. In some cases, the funding took the form of outright grants to the company for locating in the community. Sometimes the city purchased vacant facilities from the private sector and then deeded them to the new venture in exchange for a commitment to stay in the community for five years and employ a given number of workers. Low-interest loans were also used. The ventures did not have to be in high-technology industries, and the key was often how many workers would be hired rather than how profitable or how much growth the venture could expect. In a majority of cases, the government funding was coupled with private funding, thereby making a larger amount of total financing available.

Relationships with Other Companies

Many entrepreneurs pride themselves on being heroically independent. Astute entrepreneurs, however, realize that cooperation with others can often be useful to both. This can be in the form of formal joint ventures between the companies or less formal agreements to share costs. For example, two variety stores that are far enough apart that they are not considered competitors may decide to do joint advertising. The cost is little more for two than it is for one. The cost can be shared between the two retailers, and this conserves cash for both. If they decide to also share inventory ordering, even more savings can be achieved.

Internal Cash Management

The methods of financing discussed so far have dealt almost exclusively with generating outside funding for the venture. In addition, it is important to realize that many of an entrepreneur's decisions can affect the amount of financing required. For example, leasing equipment rather than buying it may be more expensive in the long run but may conserve cash in the short run. In addition, harvesting the venture is easier if assets are leased instead of purchased. Leasing equipment may also positively affect the balance sheet and thereby make the acquisition of outside funding easier.

Developing a sound accounts receivable policy may also impact financing needs. Establishing credit terms that encourage customers to pay in cash may reduce the need for outside financing. Ensuring that customers pay their accounts promptly can sometimes mean the difference between a surviving venture and a bankrupt one.

Figure 7-2 lists the major sources of financing for the new or growing venture. Note that some of the sources are debt financing, some are equity financing, some are combinations, and some fall more into the working capital management area.

MATCHING FINANCING TO VENTURE DEVELOPMENT

This chapter has presented a number of different funding sources for new and existing ventures. However, the capital sources are not all relevant for all ventures or ventures in all stages of development. For example, low-growth ventures will never use venture capital because they do not need it and because venture capitalists do not have an interest in intentionally small ventures. Conversely, rapid-growth ventures will not normally use friends and family because they need far more capital than typical friends and family can provide (Table 7-4).

The type of funding required is a function of the type or nature of the venture itself, which includes the industry in which it competes and the

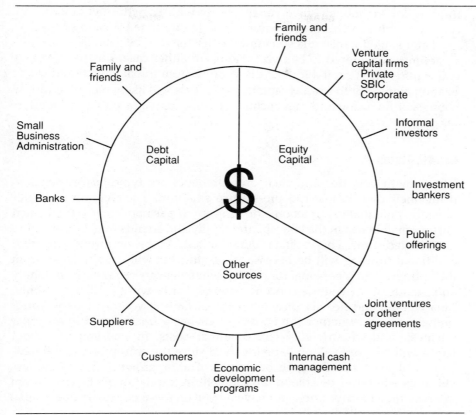

FIGURE 7-2
Types of Financing for
New and Growing
Ventures

product or service provided. It is also a function of two major variables: the stage of the venture's development and the amount of growth desired.

Stage of Development

The type of financing used is dependent to a large extent on the stage of development of the venture. As discussed earlier, ventures go through at least three stages. The first is the pre-launch stage. In this stage, the entrepreneur or entrepreneurial team plans the venture and determines what the venture concept will be, the level of growth desired, the amount of funding needed, and a general idea of the strategies it will use. In some cases, such as a new product development venture, the team members must do a substantial amount of work to develop and/or test the product and its acceptance before the venture can be begun. Hence, significant funding may be required before the venture can even be launched. Other ventures, particularly low-growth ventures, do not require significant pre-launch funding.

Startup funding refers to the capital needed to get the venture into operation and stabilized. This includes final product development, manufacturing facilities, marketing expenses associated with the launch, setting up distribution networks, and hiring personnel. Although the amount of funding for the launch stage varies greatly with growth orientations and types of ventures, this stage requires a large one-time infusion of capital.

Later stage financing is sometimes considered to be a single stage and sometimes considered to be two or more. In either case, this funding is a major infusion of capital to take the venture from initial launch and stabilization along a path toward rapid growth. This will likely require multiple sources of financing and may include venture capital or public stock offering.

Growth Rates

Low-growth ventures and their entrepreneurs are typically restricted to using their own funds in a pre-startup situation. Their ventures do not have the potential to attract outside funding. If partners are involved, each partner may invest in the concept and family and friends may be enticed to loan limited sums. This capital is quite limited. As the venture is launched, additional funding will be necessary. Again, this will usually come from the entrepreneur's personal funds plus whatever can be raised from family and friends. If the venture concept is sound, banks will usually loan funds. This will depend heavily on whether it is the first venture for the entrepreneur or not, whether the entrepreneur has a track record in a similar business, and whether sufficient collateral exists. In later stage funding, banks will be more willing to be involved since the entrepreneur will have shown at least some degree of stability and/or growth. Small business ventures will never be able to tap the venture capital market, will seldom interest informal investors, and have no reason for or capability of an initial public offering (IPO).

Initial funding for moderate-growth firms will come largely from personal sources and banks. These firms will often be corporations, but the number of stockholders will often be small or the stock will be family held. Banks will typically be willing to lend to these entrepreneurs because they have either an established venture or at least a venture plan that clearly appears to be sound. The Small Business Administration is also a prime source of funding for the moderate-growth ventures. Depending upon the growth rate desired, personal, bank, SBA, and internally generated funding may be sufficient. If higher rates of growth are desired than these sources can underwrite, then selling additional stock to acquaintances or to informal investors may be useful. Venture capitalists will generally not be involved although there may be exceptions to this rule. If the venture grows sufficiently that it needs major funding, then the entrepreneur may eventually take the company public.

The high-growth or rapid-growth venture uses different combinations of funding. The entrepreneurial team will often have substantial funds to invest in the venture although their personal funds may still be a small part of the total package. When Steven Jobs founded NeXT, Inc., he used some of his personal wealth to help launch the venture. He later contributed $7 million more. Most entrepreneurs do not have that flexibility, although many rapid-growth entrepreneurs do have substantial personal funds from earlier successful ventures. Large banks, venture capitalists, and informal investors may enter the picture early in the fast-growth venture. If the

venture goes as planned, however, the need for major infusion of funds
will come within a few years. Thus, the IPO is common. Later stock offerings will further propel the venture toward its competitive goal.

DEVELOPING THE FINANCIAL PACKAGE

In cases where small amounts of capital are needed, developing a financial
package is relatively simple. It involves putting together a loan request to
a bank, asking friends to contribute either debt or equity capital, or perhaps
applying for a Small Business Administration loan. The documentation
required may be only a brief business plan and whatever papers the lending institution requires. Most of this can be done by the entrepreneur,
perhaps an accountant, and the lending institution staff.

As the amount of capital needed increases, the complexity of the packaging process increases dramatically. Amounts in excess of $100,000 will
usually involve some combination of debt and equity funding. Amounts
beyond perhaps $250,000 will require valuing the venture, at least in the
case of equity capital. Obtaining major infusions of capital by involving
venture capitalists will require extensive planning and assistance from accountants, attorneys, and a variety of financial representatives. In the case
of initial public offerings, brokers or investment bankers will certainly be
involved. The decision to grow via an IPO must be made only with great
care due to the cost, time, and effort involved.

Any financing other than the most simple forms will require a well-
written business plan with each of the items discussed in Chapter 4 carefully researched and written. Venture capital firms fund an average of one

Stage of Development	Low Growth	Moderate Growth	High Growth	
Pre-start-up	Personal funds,* friends+	Personal funds, friends, banks	Personal funds, informal investors, existing ventures	**TABLE 7-4** Most Common Sources of Financing for Venture Stages and Growth Rates
Start-up	Same as above, plus banks	Same as above, plus informal investors	Same as above, plus venture capital	
Post-Start-up	Same as above	Same as above, plus IPOs	Same as above, plus IPOs, additional stock offerings	

*Personal funding refers to equity dollars from sole owner or partners regardless of whether the venture is
a sole proprietorship, partnership, or corporation.
+Friends refers to contributions from families and friends, regardless of whether it is debt or equity.

percent of the plans received. This underscores the need to write a thorough but concise plan that clearly lays out the strategies of the venture, the amount and type of funding desired, and the nature of the return to the investor. All of this information must be condensed in the executive summary portion of the plan and must be written in a way to capture the attention of the investor and describe the true status and plans of the venture.

SUMMARY

Capital is the lifeblood of any business venture. Few ventures, and virtually no new ventures, have enough capital to begin life and grow without an infusion from external sources. This chapter has discussed the various needs for capital, the sources of equity and debt capital, and the relationships between growth rates of ventures, stages in venture development, and the types of capital that are most appropriate.

Equity capital provides ownership to the investors. Some amount of equity capital will be required regardless of the type or level of the venture. Equity capital includes personal funds of the entrepreneurs, partners, private stockholders, informal investors, venture capitalists, or public stockholders. Debt capital does not provide ownership, but provides a return to the investor in the form of interest on capital supplied. The most common form of debt capital is loans from banks. The U.S. Small Business Administration also provides money to those whom banks will not lend unassisted. In addition to traditional debt and equity capital, entrepreneurs can also obtain the use of capital from suppliers, customers, and efficient use of their own internal policies.

Some forms of financing are more viable for some types and levels of ventures than others. Small business ventures are, by their nature, restricted to their own personal funds for pre-launch financing. They may use banks and the SBA for later-stage financing. Moderate-growth ventures will make extensive use of bank financing, and some of these may go public after several years of sustained growth. Venture capital and initial public offerings are more applicable for rapid-growth ventures, and they will more likely be used for later-stage financing than for start-ups and pre-launch financing.

Regardless of the type of financing used, substantial planning must be done to ensure that funding can be generated. A business plan is necessary for virtually all types of funding, and a carefully written plan is a must for anything other than the most simple financing sources.

DISCUSSION QUESTIONS

1. Why must personal funds be invested in a venture regardless of the nature, level, or stage of the venture?
2. Why are banks reluctant to lend to pre-launch situations? What, if anything, can an entrepreneur do to increase the willingness of bankers to lend in these cases?
3. How would you advise a potential entrepreneur who came to you seeking information on financing sources? What questions would you need to ask in order to give a good response?

4. Why do interest rates vary for different kinds of ventures?

5. Discuss the venture capital process. In what situations is it most appropriate?

6. Why do venture capitalists invest in so few deals? Should they be less restrictive?

7. Why are investment bankers necessary for initial public offerings? Is it possible to have a public offering without this kind of assistance? Why?

8. Interview several entrepreneurs. Into which growth category do they fall? Which kinds of financing have they used in the past five years? Would a different type of financing be better, given their situation?

9. Interview at least two bank lending officers. One should be from a small bank and one should be from a large bank. Are their criteria for granting loans the same? Why or why not?

10. Why does the amount of work necessary to put together a loan package for a small business differ from the work necessary for venture capital financing or informal investors?

EXERCISE 7-1

EXERCISES

For the hypothetical Sports Technologies, Inc., venture in Venture Perspective 7-3, write a possible executive summary of their business plan (realizing, of course, that the executive summary is usually written last rather than first).

EXERCISE 7-2

For each of the following ventures and development stages, indicate the type of financing that is most appropriate. Justify your reasoning.

Venture	Stage of Development
A Baskin-Robbins franchise	Start-up
A biotech company researching uses of synthetic fats	Pre-start-up
An independent retail store selling professional women's clothing	Later stage (seasonal financing)
A small auto repair business	Pre-start-up
A generic producer of laptop computers	Early growth

ENDNOTES

1. Robert D. Hisrich and Michael P. Peters, *Entrepreneurship: Starting, Developing, and Managing a New Enterprise,* 2nd Edition (Homewood, IL: Irwin, 1992), 275–77.

2. L. N. Goslin and B. Barge, "Entrepreneurial Qualities Considered in Venture Capital Support," in *Frontiers of Entrepreneurship Research 1986*, edited by Robert Ronstadt et al. (Wellesley, MA: Babson College, 1986), 367.

3. Michael Gorman and William Sahlman, "What Do Venture Capitalists Do?" in *Frontiers of Entrepreneurship Research 1986*, edited by Robert Ronstadt et al. (Wellesley, MA: Babson College, 1986) 418–436; John B. Miner II and David

A. Walker, "The Role of Venture Capital in Financing Small Business," *Journal of Business Venturing* 2, No. 3 (Summer 1987): 207–14.

4. Gorman and Sahlman, "What Do Venture Capitalists Do?", 426.

5. Wayne DeSarbo, Ian MacMillan, and Diana Day, "Criteria for Corporate Venturing: Importance Assigned by Managers," *Journal of Business Venturing* 2 (1987): 329–50.

6. Sallie Hofmeister, "Of Bankers, Boutiques, and Middlemen," *Venture*, September, 1987, 38–42.

7. Robert A. Schwartz, *Equity Markets: Structure, Trading, and Performance* (New York: Harper and Row Publishers, 1988), 89.

◆ Conveniesse, Inc. ◆

Gaining Financing

Yolanda Williams, Jason Stone, and Sarah Tondeur studied the information they had received. The figures that the hotel manager in Detroit and the real estate agent in Buffalo had put together suggested a total investment of between $400,000 and $450,000. This caused the three friends concern, especially when they considered their own capital sources. Jason thought he could probably come up with $30,000 if it included borrowing $20,000 from his parents in Texas. Yolanda, who had come out of college debt-free because of her scholarships, had put some away each month. She could access $40,000 easily and another $20,000 if necessary. Sarah was in the best shape. Although her divorce settlement provided no cash, she did keep a house that she later sold and had recently sold her business for $35,000. If she combined those funds with all of her retirement money, she could come up with $90,000 to $100,000. Being a risk-taker, she was willing to do this immediately.

Both Jason and Yolanda rejected that idea because it was too risky and because it would give Sarah at least double the equity investment that they would have. Jason suggested that he might take a 20 percent share for $30,000 and the others could each have a 40 percent share for $60,000 each. That would give them a total of $150,000 equity.

A loan from a bank might be possible, although none of the three had a rapport with any banks in Buffalo. Further, none of the three had any collateral to pledge against a loan. Thus, the only collateral would be the inventory and equipment of the business itself. They discussed getting money from family in the form of either debt or equity capital. Jason's parents would be willing to loan him $20,000, but he wasn't really interested in them taking an equity position. He had worked with them in the auto parts business, and the one thing he was sure of was that he did not want them owning any business that he would operate. They were nice enough, but they wouldn't be able to resist telling him what to do. Sarah said she had no source of capital other than her own. Her parents had just retired, and they would have trouble meeting their own needs. Although she knew several business people in Montreal, her clients and contacts tended to be small operators rather than wealthy investors. Yolanda noted that her parents were fairly conservative and probably would be unwilling to invest in a new venture start-up. She also could not ask colleagues to invest without the risk of losing her own job if the word got out.

Selling stock to outsiders would be an option, but that would mean dilution of their own investment. If they did sell to outside investors, the three agreed that there needed to be enough of them that the investment each made would be relatively small. That way no one of them would have controlling interest. Currently, they did not know of any investors who fit the qualifications they had in mind. Since they were not located in Buffalo, it was impossible to know people in the financial community.

One other option would be to work through the developer who owned the office building in which the store would be located. Since the space would be vacant in six months, the developer might have a vested interest in getting it leased immediately. Further, having an upscale convenience store right on the ground level might be appealing both to current and to future tenants. Perhaps he would either give them a break on the lease or might even loan them some money.

They wondered if there might be other sources available.

Assignment

In groups of three to five, develop a financial package for Conveniesse. Once each group is finished, report to the instructor, who will record the amount from each source. Once these are listed, discuss the differences among the teams' responses.

PLANNING VENTURE STRATEGIES

Developing Entrepreneurial Strategies
•
Developing Supporting Strategies
•
Franchising
•
International Entrepreneurship

8

Developing Entrepreneurial Strategies

LEARNING OBJECTIVES

After reading this chapter, you should be familiar with:

1. The strategic planning process
2. Generic strategies for entrepreneurial ventures
3. Entry wedges for new ventures
4. How new products are introduced
5. The advantages and disadvantages of niche strategies
6. Ways to exploit competency based strategies
7. Captive supplier strategies
8. Key factors in retail strategies
9. Considerations in developing service venture strategies

KEY TERMS

Generic strategies
Entry wedges
Derivative product strategy

Support product strategies
Niche strategy
Captive supplier

CONSIDER THIS!

- Most entrepreneurial strategies evolve rather than being major shifts from previous strategies.
- Venture strategies must have supporting strategies in order to be effective.
- There is no such thing as the best strategy for a venture nor the best strategy for a given situation.
- Being "high-tech" still allows a wide variety of competitive strategies.
- Sometimes being the number two or number three firm is as good as being number one.
- A niche strategy is a double-edged sword that is very sharp on both sides.
- A captive supplier strategy can be one of the most desirable of all entrepreneurial strategies, yet many entrepreneurs will not consider it.
- The largest failure rate among new ventures is in the retail sector.

Developing the strategy for the new or emerging venture is perhaps the most important task for the entrepreneur. All other activities—financing, marketing, hiring personnel, production, distribution, and more—draw upon the overall venture strategy selected. Considerable time must be

SUZANNE RIDENOUR
Ridenour & Associates

One of the strategies to be discussed in this chapter is the niche strategy. In the niche strategy, the entrepreneur competes in a relatively narrow market, providing a specialized service to a small target market. Suzanne Swenson Ridenour typifies the entrepreneur with a successful niche strategy.

Executive search firms are those businesses whose mission it is to locate management-level personnel for their clients, who may be corporations, government, or other not-for-profit organizations. The executive search business is one subindustry of a larger industry made up of public and private employment agencies, temporary agencies, and executive search firms. Ridenour and Associates occupies an even smaller segment of the executive search firm subindustry in

that it specializes in finding executives who are specialists in the direct marketing business community. Thus, although Ridenour and Associates is an international firm, it occupies a very small niche in the recruitment field.

The staff of an executive search firm provides very important services for its clients. First, staff members develop specifications for the position to be filled. They then search the field to identify potential candidates whose qualifications closely match the specifications. They conduct review meetings with the clients and determine which candidates may be most qualified and desirable. The search firm consultant interviews the most qualified candidates, checks references, and assesses the personality of the candidates to determine the fit with the client. The firm's owners then recommend the top two or three candidates to the client for final selection.

Suzanne Ridenour had extensive background in the recruiting field before launching

given to developing the venture strategy and the functional strategies that support it. The process is time consuming, but it is a valuable process and it pays for itself.

Entrepreneurial strategies may be either evolutionary or distinctly divergent. Evolutionary strategies tend to evolve over time and are only incrementally different from earlier strategies or from competitor strategies. Divergent strategies are those that are distinctly different from others in existence. These strategies may be the result of rapid decisions to exploit new opportunities. They may be developed when a new product is invented or when major changes in the industry or market are predicted.

This chapter begins with a brief review of the strategic planning process. Chapter 4 discussed the planning process and the strategic or financial plans that derive from the process. This chapter focuses on the variety of entrepreneurial strategies that may be developed as a result of the planning process. The following three chapters will continue the discussion of strategies as they consider functional support strategies and the important strategies of franchising and international entrepreneurship.

Ridenour and Associates in 1982. She worked in management positions with Quaker Oats and American Express and with firms in the temporary-worker industry. She also had been the placement director for a business college and taught courses on professional development. Her previous venture was a partnership that specialized in locating and testing legal secretaries. She admits that it was just "dumb luck" when someone called and asked if her company could find an account executive for a direct marketing advertising agency. Not knowing the definition of either "account executive" or "direct marketing," she immediately set out to study the industry. She soon began redirecting her company's efforts toward the executive search business while keeping the secretarial search business as a base. Later, the secretarial employment agency business was phased out as the firm became more involved with the executive search area.

By focusing primarily on the direct marketing business community, Ridenour and Associates not only develops a specialized database of potential candidates, but also knows the needs of its clients and has an expert knowledge of the industry. In the executive search industry the importance of "who you know" is critical. Thus, public visibility within the industry is necessary for survival. As a result, Ridenour is an active member of the Chicago Association of Direct Marketing, the Direct Marketing Association, the National Association of Women Business Owners, the British Direct Marketing Association, the European Direct Marketing Association, the Swedish-American Chamber of Commerce, the Japan-America Society, and a number of public service organizations.

The future looks promising for Ridenour and Associates. Growth in 1988 was 35 percent, and even in the recessionary 1991 it experienced a 20 percent growth rate. It has affiliates (other search firms that cooperate with Ridenour and Associates) throughout the world. In a recent year, 25 percent of its revenues came from Japanese firms searching for executives with U.S. expertise to work for their businesses.

SOURCE: Company documents. Used with permission.

THE STRATEGIC PLANNING PROCESS

Figure 8-1 has been reproduced from Chapter 4 to provide a review of the strategic planning process. Most important for this chapter are the blocks in the illustration under the heading "Strategy development stage." It is assumed, for now, that the entrepreneur has determined the general nature of the venture and analyzed the opportunities to be exploited and the ability of the firm to capitalize on those opportunities.

Once the analysis of the venture's opportunities and capabilities is complete, the task is then to use that information and analysis to develop the overall venture strategy and its supporting strategies. The strategies that are developed during this phase of the process guide the actions of the firm. They are also written into the strategic plan and the financial plans as discussed in Chapter 4.

Just as the strategies selected may be either evolutionary or distinctly divergent, the *development* of the strategies may be either very straightforward or quite involved. If the venture has distinctive competencies that

FIGURE 8-1
The Strategic Planning
Process for
Entrepreneurial Ventures

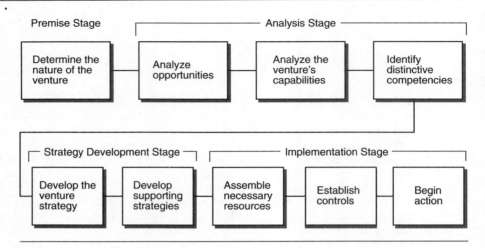

may be exploited, or if the opportunity/capability match is so compelling as to virtually dictate the strategy, then the task of determining the venture strategy is relatively simple. On the other hand, if a variety of alternatives is possible, then effort must be expended to determine the best strategy for the venture.

One all-important caveat must be made at the outset of the discussion on venture strategies. *There is no single best strategy for a venture or for a given situation.* One strategic management textbook lists strategies for dominant firms, runner-up companies, and weak companies; vertical integration strategies, diversification strategies, and turnaround strategies; strategies appropriate for emerging industries, transitional industries, declining industries, fragmented industries, and international markets; and offensive strategies, defensive strategies, and harvest strategies, among others.[1] In the sections that follow, discussion will first focus on generic strategies. Attention will then turn to competitive entry wedges. Finally, strategies for specific types of ventures or market situations will be addressed. Yet even these strategies are discussed only as possible strategies and not as *the best* strategies. Again, there are no absolutely best strategies for either particular ventures or particular situations.

GENERIC STRATEGY TYPES

A **generic strategy** is a broad-based strategy that is generally appropriate as an overall guide. Three generic strategies have been suggested for ventures.[2] These are:

1. Differentiation
2. Low-cost leadership
3. Focus

These strategies are as applicable to new and emerging ventures as they are to existing companies or large corporations.

Differentiation Strategies

Differentiation strategies are those strategies that create value for the customer beyond that available from competing products. Lawrence Finley suggested that the new firm pursuing a differentiation strategy must produce products or services that do more, or look prettier, or work faster, or run longer, or come in more flavors, colors, shapes, and sizes; or that make the buyer feel younger or sexier; or that withstand greater pressure, or that can be delivered on shorter notice, or can be sold on easier credit terms, or can be installed better, or can be more durable, or can be repaired with less hassle than competing products.[3] An appliance repair firm that is open twenty-four hours a day is differentiated from others. The early laptop computer makers were differentiated for a while until traditional computer manufacturers finally entered the market. Software firms that produce spreadsheet or data base software that does more than the standard products are using a differentiation strategy.

Differentiation strategies are useful in that the entrepreneur can charge a premium price for the product. Customers are willing to pay the premium because the product provides more benefit to them. If successful, the differentiation provides some protection against brand switching and price pressure by customers. The profit margins available from differentiated products can then be used to continue to exploit or refine the products.

Low-Cost Leadership

Low-cost leadership may or may not be difficult for a new venture to establish. Typically, low-cost leadership requires high relative market share, and this would not be available to the startup firm competing with established producers.[4] On the other hand, low-cost production can come from lower overhead, new or more efficient processes, or simply more attention to costs. The low-cost leadership strategy does not imply the lowest possible quality. In fact, the quality must be near that of competitors in order to attract their customers away.

Low-cost leadership strategies often work best when the product is a commodity product or an otherwise undifferentiated product. Products such as milk, nuts and bolts, soap, notebook paper, and computer diskettes are examples where cost leadership can be viable. In these situations, the customer has little concern for the relative quality of the products because the quality is similar for all and most competitors' versions will meet at least minimal quality standards. Thus, the decision to purchase logically becomes one of paying the least for indistinguishable products. This strategy can be maintained amidst competition as long as the firm's management is constantly vigilant about cost savings. The goal for the low-cost leadership venture is to continually reduce the cost of the product without concomitant reduction in quality.

Focus Strategies

The focus strategy may combine parts of both the differentiation and the low-cost leadership strategies. However, the key to the focus strategy is the target market. The focus strategy is not market share oriented. Rather, it is oriented toward serving the small target market in the best way possible. Customers within the narrow target market willingly pay a premium to the producer because of the specialized attention given to the customer. Barnes and Noble, a book retailer specializing in university bookstores, uses a focus strategy. The plethora of small companies that do work for a particular government agency use a focus strategy. Airplane manufacturers that produce only private jets for corporate use have a focus strategy.

The focus strategy is protectable to the extent that the business can continue to provide the specialized attention desired by the customer. The customer prefers the attention of the venture to that given by larger industry-wide firms. If, however, the venture fails to provide value to the customer, that customer will look for another small supplier or will use the more generic services provided by larger firms.

ENTRY WEDGES

Karl Vesper has suggested fourteen entry wedges for new ventures.[5] The term **entry wedge** refers to a strategy or method of entering a market for the first time in the midst of existing competitors.

The *new product or service* wedge refers to the development of a product or service never before offered. Vesper suggests that this wedge is rarely used. Most new ventures are *not* associated with totally new products or services. *Parallel competition* is more frequent. In this situation, the entrepreneur begins a venture that is similar to one already existing. The product or service may be marginally different or may be virtually identical to existing competitors. The *franchise* is a frequent entry wedge either as a franchisee or franchisor. This strategy will be discussed in depth in Chapter 10.

TABLE 8-1
New Venture Entry Wedges
Source: Karl H. Vesper, *New Venture Strategies*, rev. ed. (Englewood Cliffs, NJ: Prentice Hall, 1990), 193–194, 226.

1. New product or service
2. Parallel competition
3. Franchise
4. Geographical transfer
5. Supply shortage
6. Tapping unused resources
7. Customer contract
8. Becoming an additional supplier
9. Joint ventures
10. Licensing
11. Market relinquishment
12. Selloff of a division
13. Favored purchasing
14. Rule changes

Vesper believes that these three strategies are the main competitive wedges for new ventures. Eleven other strategies exist, however. The first of these is the *geographical transfer*. Frequently a potential entrepreneur will spot a venture while traveling. Upon returning home, the entrepreneur then attempts to copy the venture as closely as possible. This is particularly true among individuals who travel from their homes in the central United States to the two coasts. Many new venture ideas originate on the coasts and then make their way to the interior by geographical transfer.

The *short supply* entry wedge occurs simply when demand for a product or service exceeds supply. Thus, a vacuum is created until a new venture fills it. The demand attracts entrepreneurs who can move quickly to eliminate the vacuum. Sometimes the opposite occurs. Here an entrepreneur discovers or controls a resource and starts a venture to supply that resource to a waiting market. Here, the *untapped resource* is the impetus behind the venture rather than unmet demand.

Two wedges are customer based. In the first, the entrepreneur contacts a major customer to negotiate a deal before launching the company. In *contracting with a customer*, the new venture owner is assured of a significant customer before launching the venture. An example of this could be a company that processes insurance claims. The potential owner of a claims processing firm contacts a major insurer to become that firm's claim processor within a region. If accepted, the entrepreneur then sets up the necessary equipment to provide the service. The second wedge is similar, except that a competing supplier already exists. Here the entrepreneur negotiates with the customer to become an *additional supplier*. Many companies are willing to have more than one supplier in order to ensure an uninterrupted supply of the product or service.

The next five wedges result from support from a parent company. In a *joint venture*, an existing company forms a new venture that is partially owned by the parent company and partially owned by an entrepreneur. The joint venture either makes products for the parent company or produces products in which the parent company has only a modest interest. Sometimes these are funded by the parent company and are operated by the entrepreneur (Venture Perspective 8-1).

A *licensing agreement* is negotiated with an existing company to produce the product using the name and trademark of the existing company. A company in California, for example, might license the production of a toy from a firm that produces it in Chicago but does not wish to expand to the West Coast. The licensing agreement is also a method of producing a product domestically that is currently produced abroad. The domestic firm licenses the manufacture and/or distribution of the product from the foreign firm for sale in the United States.

Rather than expand into markets, a large company may decide to get out of a market. In *market relinquishment*, the large company may negotiate with existing managers or other interested entrepreneurs to take over the production of the product. This often happens when the market is not sufficient to hold the interest of the original producer or when labor problems make the production of the product uneconomical. The new venture, being smaller, can produce the product with lower overhead or with nonunion labor and make a profit when the parent company could not. Instead

---

VENTURE PERSPECTIVE 8-1

. . . .

EXABYTE CORPORATION

Exabyte Corporation produces an innovative product that stores large amounts of computer data using 8-millimeter videotape. Harry Hinz developed the idea while working at Storage Technology Corporation, which was not interested in the product. So Hinz and two colleagues quit their jobs and formed Exabyte. A venture capital firm eventually invested $2 million in the venture. But Exabyte got a real boost by forming strategic alliances with Sony Corporation and Kubota.

Sony was interested in finding new outlets for its videotape. Buying components from Sony gave Exabyte a substantial cost savings. Just as helpful was an agreement with Kubota, which makes almost 60 percent of what Exabyte sells. Kubota finances the entire cost of manufacturing and inventory for these products.

Exabyte began by bypassing big computer makers and selling first to value-added resellers. These small companies customize computers and sell them to special markets. Today, nearly 50 percent of Exabyte's sales come from large computer companies, including IBM, Sun Microsystems, and Germany's Siemens. In four years, sales went from zero to $160 million and profits increased fivefold from 1988, reaching $13.9 million.

Source: Udayan Gupta, "Strategic Alliances Play Big Role in Start-Up's Success," *Wall Street Journal*, December 12, 1990, B2.

---

of just phasing out the product, leaving a vacuum for a new venture, a parent company may actually *sell an entire division* to new owners who may be employees within the division.

The last two entry wedges reflect government sponsorship rather than corporate sponsorship. The first of these is *favored purchasing*. Government agencies often use discriminatory purchasing in order to give preference to small ventures. Others give preference to minority- and women-owned ventures. In either case, this gives the new or small venture opportunity to make a wedge into the government contracting business that might otherwise be extremely difficult. The second government-influenced opportunity is the *rule change* wedge. In this case the entrepreneur takes advantage of a change in government regulations that creates an opportunity. A new regulation within an industry requiring safety devices for equipment could create the possibility of producing those devices. For example, the law mandating airbags for cars created opportunities for new ventures to produce the airbags or their components for auto makers.

STRATEGIES FOR UNIQUE SITUATIONS

The previous two sections discussed Porter's generic strategies for ventures and Vesper's fourteen entry wedges. The sections that follow address entrepreneurial strategies for specific types of situations. These include strategies for firms in high-tech industries and for firms in decidedly low-tech industries, as well as niche strategies, competency based strategies, captive supplier strategies, retail strategies, and service venture strategies. Because of their significant impact, franchising strategies and international strategies will each be discussed in separate chapters.

Strategies for High-Tech Manufacturers

Despite the glamour associated with high-tech ventures, the percentage of new ventures that can be categorized as high-technology ventures is quite small. Strategies for high-tech ventures virtually always revolve around a new product or process. The entrepreneur or entrepreneurial team develop a new product or process that is then produced and marketed to others.

In some cases the high-tech products will be totally new products for new or existing markets. In more cases, the product is a spin-off of existing products. Each of these will be discussed in turn.

New Product Innovation Strategy

The new product strategy is often referred to as a pioneering strategy. This is an apt description since new trails are being cut in the product market. Just as pioneering in early America was risky, the introduction of a totally new product—one that is not directly related to any existing product—is quite a risky entrepreneurial strategy. It should be kept in mind, of course, that high risk often has high rewards. The introduction of compact discs and video cassette recorders is indicative of the rewards for introduction of new products. But many new products do not experience the growth that the CD and VCR industry did. The risks and costs of introducing a new product are so great that most inventions—even those with patent protection—are not introduced to major markets. Most languish in the garage of the inventor, never to reach a viable market.

The risk of introducing totally new products is increased greatly if the product is also for a new *market*; that is, a market in which the entrepreneur does not have extensive past experience. In this case, the entrepreneur has neither a tested product nor a known market. Either is risky, but both together are extremely risky.

Producing a new product in a high-technology field requires extensive research and development followed by extensive market research. Feasibility studies must be made for both the technological feasibility and the marketing feasibility. In some cases, a product is easily produced but difficult to market. Conversely, a product may be easily marketable but difficult to produce.

Market research on a totally new product poses an additional risk. That is the issue of how to gather sufficient information to ascertain the demand for the product without giving away any competitive information about the product. Collecting information about the potential demand for a product is difficult without fully describing the product. However, if knowledge of the product gets out, competitors may be able to duplicate the product and, in some cases, get the product to the market first.

Derivative Product Strategy

The **derivative product strategy** emphasizes developing a product that is either developed from or is similar to an existing product. The product is then developed either for an existing market or for a new and different market. An example of this is Biosyn, whose product was initially tested as a mouthwash (Venture Perspective 8-2). The tests, however, showed that the product "worked against everything they put in the test tube."

BIOSYN, INC.

Ann-Marie Corner and her mentor, Dr. Daniel Malamud, chair of the Biochemistry Department of the University of Pennsylvania, spent hours testing an antibacterial agent concocted by an inventor and licensed to a firm for possible sale as a mouthwash. To their surprise, it worked against everything they put in the test tube. A few years later, as Corner was just finishing her M.B.A. at the Wharton School, Malamud informed her that the product might have potential as a killer of the AIDS virus.

By this time, the company that had the licensing rights had folded. Malamud and Corner formed Biosyn, with Corner as president and Malamud as research director. Corner then spent the next several months trying to find cash to complete the research and market the product. She got a seed grant of $25,000 from the state of Pennsylvania, and later received an $80,000 state loan. Venture capitalists refused to take a chance on her ambitions, but a private placement raised $100,000, and the state came up with a second loan, for $90,000.

With a quarter of a million dollars in the bank and a location in a state-sponsored incubator, Corner hired an office assistant and a lab technician. She claims that her product is far less toxic than many alternatives, and does not irritate the skin, eyes, nasal passages, or have other unpleasant side effects. Because Biosyn is small, Corner plans to license the marketing rights to pharmaceutical companies, which will give her needed cash flow and allow Biosyn to concentrate on additional products.

SOURCE: Brent Bowers, "A Biotech Worker Pursues the Formula for Success," *The Wall Street Journal*, January 30, 1991, B2.

The task in the derivative product strategy is to find the problems that the solution fits. In the Biosyn case, the antibacterial agent may have a number of different uses, including use as a wash for hands and instruments and perhaps as part of the fight against AIDS and other sexually transmitted diseases.

Product Variation Strategy

The product variation strategy is perhaps the most often used entrepreneurial strategy regardless of whether the industry is a high-tech or low-tech product or a service industry. This is essentially the parallel strategy suggested by Vesper. It is a lower risk strategy from a customer acceptance viewpoint, because the product or service variant is similar to those already on the market.

The product variation may be somewhat different than the original, but often the difference is minimal. Customers buy the product not because it is different but because it is similar. Computer clones are prime examples of the derivative product strategy. The IBM clones try as much as possible to duplicate the structure, look, and operation of IBM machines. The value of a clone is how compatible it is with IBM. To the customer, the only desired differences are price and speed.

The advantage of the product variation strategy is that it is both a lower cost and a lower risk strategy. Lower research and development costs, both in terms of facilities and personnel, make the production of the derivative product much cheaper. Marketing the product may not require as much advertising expenditure since the customer already knows of the existing product. The only task is to explain the similarities between the existing and new product. Since there will be lower research and development costs as well as lower advertising costs, significant price breaks can be given to the customer.

High-Tech Differentiation Strategy

In high-tech industries, product development can take the form of making entirely new products, making similar products cheaper, or making variations of products that are somehow better than existing products. This is the essence of Porter's differentiation strategy discussed earlier. Depending on the nature of the industry, producing a better product can yield high returns as customers realize that "new" is quite often "better." Thus, instead of trying to capitalize on cost savings, the product differentiator focuses on making products better.

The differentiation strategy takes on a new urgency in high-tech industries because of the rapidity of obsolescence. High-tech differentiation can be considered a leapfrogging strategy as competing firms jockey to make the latest version of their product better than the previous version of their own product and the current version of competing products. Although Porter contends that the differentiation strategy is defensible over time, this is seldom the case in high-tech areas.

The high-tech differentiation strategy points out a problem that is inherent in most high-tech industries. Because of the rapid changes in high-tech industries, the life cycle for individual products is often quite short. The life cycle is becoming shorter and shorter over time, as companies learn how to copy or adapt products quickly and get them to the market. Sony Corporation has found that it often has no more than a few months between the time a product hits the market and when the first competing product arrives.[6]

A high-tech venture's management must be aware that any product they introduce will, if prospects for success are good, soon be copied or improved upon by competitors. Thus, they must invest significant funds into product development while realizing that their products will have a short life before still better products must be produced.

Support Product Strategies

In *Business Week's* 1989 listing of the hottest small businesses (ranked by sales growth, earnings growth, and return on invested capital), twenty of the top fifty firms produced computer-related products.[7] Not one of them made computers. Software Toolworks publishes software, American Power Conversion makes surge protectors and power systems, Aldus sells desktop publishing software, Rainbow Technologies sells protection systems to ward off software pirating, and Sigma Designs sells graphics enhancers. All of these companies sell support products. That is, they produce products that enhance or support computers. Without computers, they would have no product. Thus, the ventures are dependent upon the computer industry although they do not make computers.

The **support product strategy** is interesting in that the product itself may not be high tech at all, even though it keys on a high-tech industry. A manufacturer of computer tables or a swivel stand for a monitor would not be considered high tech, even though its sales are totally dependent upon the computer industry. Similarly, a producer of cases for video recorders is not a high-tech venture, but is dependent on the video recorder industry.

Support product strategies tend to have varying risks depending upon the specific nature of the product or service. Since the basic product—computers in the above case—exists and is well accepted, the risk tends to be less. And since the computer industry has grown consistently over the years, this would indicate a lower risk. On the other hand, if the product is strictly a luxury product or one that has a low incremental value, or if it faces stiff competition from original equipment manufacturers, then the risk of entering with that product may be high.

Strategies for Low-Tech Manufacturers

In the previous section, mention was made of the twenty high-tech ventures among *Business Week*'s fastest growing companies. Not mentioned, however, were Critical Industries, which makes asbestos removal equipment, Catalina Lighting, which makes light fixtures, Pentech International, which makes crayons, TCBY, which sells frozen yogurt, or Crown Crafts, which produces bedspreads and blankets. In Chapter 2, the point was made that a critical aspect of entrepreneurship was innovation. The critical aspect was not that the venture be high tech.

Low tech does not infer low quality. A furniture manufacturer may have a low-tech product and actually use extensive handcrafting in producing the product. But it is the handcrafting that assures the quality of the furniture, and advertising the attention to detail may be a key to the company's sales strategy. There is actually little relationship between the quality of the product and the amount of technology used in its production. Some products may use high technology to produce relatively inferior merchandise. Similarly, low-technology companies may make either high-quality or low-quality products. Vater Percussion makes high quality drumsticks (Venture Perspective 8-3). The high quality is the key to their increasing sales. Yet in the beginning of their venture, the production of drumsticks was decidedly low tech and the company is still not what most people would call a high-tech venture.

Virtually all high-tech strategies and many low-tech ones are product related. Many of the strategies for introducing the products are similar. Like high-tech products, many low-tech products can be easily copied or mimicked. Also like high tech, the low-tech venture can create totally new products, derivative products, or support products. One difference for some low-tech products, however, is that the low-tech products face a much different life cycle. In many cases, the low-tech products have a longer and more stable life cycle as compared with that of the high-tech products. Even this difference is debatable since we can point to products like the hula hoop, the pet rock, and others that had a rapid rise and fall.

Key considerations in launching a low-tech manufacturing venture relate to the ability to produce the product cost effectively and sell to a

VENTURE PERSPECTIVE 8-3

· · · · · · · · · · · · · · ·

VATER PERCUSSION, INC.

Hand-sanding drumsticks, using a vacuum cleaner hose with one end capped as a lacquer container, and hanging the sticks to dry with bent coat hangers wasn't exactly high technology, but it worked.

Vater Percussion, Inc. (VPI) was formed by the owners of a music store whose drumstick supplier went on strike. Unable to obtain drumsticks for his customers, Clarence Vater began shaping his own drumsticks out of white hickory in the basement of his music store. His wife and sons also worked in the company. The production method was slow, but the Vaters produced quality drumsticks to meet the demand. By the time the suppli-

er's strike was over, the Vaters had enough customers to make the drumstick production worth the effort. Eventually, the demand grew enough that they sold their music store and began making drumsticks full time.

Today, Vater Percussion has more than five hundred wholesale and retail accounts throughout the United States, Canada, Japan, Australia, and Europe. VPI has become the third largest manufacturer of drumsticks in the United States, producing more than 750,000 pairs of drumsticks a year.

Vater Percussion is a family operation, initially founded in Norwood, Massachusetts, by

Clarence Vater. Because of Vater's failing health, his wife, Joan, and their sons began running the business. Now Joan is president, Ronald is the quality control expert, and Alan is in charge of marketing. VPI is careful to ensure that each drumstick is made precisely the same way, weighs the same as all others, and is perfectly straight. Automated equipment has replaced the hand-sanding and vacuum cleaner hose, but quality is still the key characteristic of the drumsticks, and this is what keeps customers coming back.

SOURCE: Materials provided by Vater Percussion, Inc. Used with permission.

sufficiently large market that can be protected. These concerns will vary based upon the nature of the product and the nature of the competition.

When launching a venture producing a new product, *product protection* is one of the most critical keys to success. Patents are, of course, invaluable aspects of the process. However, patents are valuable only to the extent that the product cannot be easily duplicated, and many low-tech products are quite easy to copy. This does not mean that a competitor will steal a patent, but that they produce a product that is essentially the same. The product may look similar and perform the same function and still not violate patents. Other methods of protecting products include secret ingredients, specialized manufacturing processes, or knowledge of applications.

A second strategic issue that is important for new product introduction is *cost control*. Because low-tech products are often easy to copy, it is imperative that the entrepreneur focus on cost. Whether the differentiation, low-cost leadership, or focus strategies are used, attention to cost must receive high-priority attention. For example, suppose a focus strategy is used to provide products to a small target market of industrial end users. If the price charged to the customer is allowed to slide upward, the customer may decide to build the product in-house instead of purchasing it. In the consumer product area, if an easily producible product is seen as being quite profitable, competitors can be expected to enter the market.

A third consideration for the new venture producing a low-tech product is the *size of the market* compared with the number and size of competitors. New or small ventures typically cannot compete successfully against a very few large competitors. Competing against a number of smaller competitors may be easier. Thus, the competitive dynamics of the market or industry will suggest different strategies. For example, a new venture that produces ice cream would be considered a low-tech venture. The strategy it would use depends on whether it produces an exclusive, high-quality ice cream (differentiation) or a lower-quality, generic ice cream (low-cost leadership). In the latter case, producing the generic ice cream could be successful if the entrepreneur could produce it more cheaply than competitors or if deals could be worked out to produce a house brand for grocery stores. In the case of high-quality ice cream, the competition should be based primarily on the quality of the product rather than the cost. But the entrepreneur must carefully consider the probability of success given existing brands like Häagen Dazs, Edy's, Fruzen Gladjen, and others. The venture may have to start small and expand slowly from region to region to prevent a counterstrategy by the major brands. Ben and Jerry's Ice Cream in the entrepreneurial profile of Chapter 9 illustrates how this strategy can be successful.

Niche Strategies

Entrepreneurial firms breaking into a market for the first time face a unique situation if they attempt a niche strategy. A **niche strategy** is the provision of a product or service to a small segment of customers that is not well served by major companies. The strategy, like Porter's focus strategy, can be profitable for new or small ventures because it allows the entrepreneur to focus on a specific set of customers with a specific set of needs that are not being met by larger competitors in the industry. The customers, realizing that the venture caters specifically to them, are willing to pay premium prices in exchange for the specialized product or service. The market is small enough that larger companies have little interest in moving into it.

The niche strategy can be very profitable if done well. With a small but well defined market, the entrepreneur can focus marketing as well as production or service on the identifiable customers. The marketing efforts are specifically tailored to the unique needs of the particular group of customers in the niche. Ridenour and Associates in the entrepreneurial profile at the beginning of this chapter exemplifies this well. It does not attempt to find executives for firms not specifically in the direct marketing business. But the account representatives are experts in that particular segment, and they know the needs of their customers. They know how to make the necessary contacts that are required to meet the needs of both their clients and the executives they place.

The niche strategy is a double-edged sword, however. It is a relatively high-risk strategy depending on the size of the niche and the nature of the competitors that surround the niche. The reason for the double-edged nature of the risk is that the company may suffer either from too little success or from too much success. If the venture does not cultivate the niche well enough, the niche may dry up. A niche is, by definition, a small segment of a market. Sometimes that segment is simply too small to be viable over time. The number of customers in a given geographical area may be so small that an excessively wide area is required to provide necessary revenues. Further, the loss of a few customers who become dissatisfied can be lethal. In either case, the niche is not sufficiently large to allow the entrepreneur to make necessary profits to stay solvent.

The other side of the sword is that the venture may be *too* successful. Competitors continually monitor their markets. If they find that a new venture is becoming highly profitable in a niche, they may move into the niche themselves. In most cases, the smaller company then has difficulty surviving because of the greater financial capabilities of the larger company. Small companies seldom win head-on battles with larger aggressive firms. An example of the inability to compete is the diminishing number of corner grocery stores in large cities. Their niche is the small, neighborhood grocery store with friendly service and front door parking. But as large supermarkets and shopping centers encroach more and more into their territory, smaller stores find it harder and harder to survive. Specialized retail shops of all kinds face the same fate as mega-stores and malls change the retail landscape.

Competency Based Strategies

All entrepreneurial ventures should have management skills and competitive strengths to increase the odds of success. Indeed, the greater the level of skills and strengths, the greater the probability of success. Yet some ventures are designed specifically around unique competencies of the entrepreneurial team or resources associated with the venture. The competency becomes a competitive advantage for the firm. Among low-growth ventures, entrepreneurs with specific technical skills such as plumbing, carpentry, cooking, engine repair, or bookkeeping often launch firms using those skills. Among the professional ranks, professors, therapists, counselors, and the like often launch their own consulting ventures based upon their professional expertise. Many of these are also low-growth ventures, sometimes operated in addition to the professional's primary job.

Growth entrepreneurs can also exploit a competency based strategy over time, providing competitors do not overcome their competitive advantage. Seldom, however, do competency based strategies continue successfully for more than a few years. Just as in the niche strategy, a successful competency based strategy will attract competitors.

One concern with a competency based strategy arises when the competency is closely tied to a single person. If the competency is that of the founding entrepreneur and the entrepreneur leaves the venture, the competency also leaves. Thus, it is imperative that the competency be developed within other team members in the venture in order to continue the success of the venture in case of the departure of the entrepreneur. This sharing or teaching of the competency to other team members has its own downside, however. That is the risk of a trained team member deserting the venture to start a similar one using the technology or skills learned in the previous venture.

The key to the competency based strategy is to exploit that competency through effective marketing and defend it against encroachment by others. In small ventures, advertising must be used to spread the word as effectively as possible. Such mundane tactics as well-written yellow pages advertising in the local telephone book can assist small ventures in maintaining growth in their area. Larger growth ventures may need to develop regional or national advertising campaigns and develop networks of offices or distributors to extend the product or service delivery geographically. All marketing efforts must focus specifically on the competency base rather than address general themes. Customers are drawn to the venture because of the strength of the competency rather than the value of the overall venture.

An example of a competency based business is a growing architectural firm in the Midwest. It designs the typical office buildings, university residence halls, and medical clinics just as other architectural firms do. Its special competency, however, is the design of prisons and correctional facilities. Since most communities do not have a prison, the special competency must be marketed nationwide. Thus, they have offices in three different locations in the United States and are in frequent contact with state and federal correction agencies to assure that they will be included in any bid proposals throughout the country.

Captive Supplier Strategies

A strategy that has many merits for entrepreneurs willing to assume a low profile is that of the **captive supplier.** A captive supplier is a producer of either a product or a component of a larger product who sells the product to only one customer. The supplier makes the product to the precise specifications, quality, and quantity demanded by the single customer. The captive supplier strategy has become more popular in recent years as many large companies have moved to reduce corporate assets and outsource more of their products. Entrepreneurial companies have shown that they can produce products or components for larger companies cheaper than the large firms can produce them themselves.

The captive supplier strategy offers several advantages to the new or small firm. Once the agreement is in place, the firm has a solid customer that will provide a continuous outlet for products over the next several years. Thus, part of the normal risk associated with new or small ventures is underwritten by the stability of the larger firm. The captive supplier has no need for marketing, thus reducing a major portion of a new firm's expense. Distribution costs are lower since the entire production run is delivered to a single location. In some cases, the customer even picks up the goods in its own trucks, thereby further reducing costs to the entrepreneur.

The captive supplier strategy is one of the lowest risk strategies of all of those discussed in this chapter. The stability provided by the larger firm gives the entrepreneur assurance of a ready market for the products. The strategy is not without its downside, however. Some entrepreneurs refuse to become captive suppliers. The primary reason for this is that the small venture is tied too closely to the larger one and is at its mercy for survival. It can grow no faster than the larger firm grows. If the larger firm has a downturn, the supplier will also. Further, while most large corporations have resources to survive a recession, many small ventures do not.

A partial captive supplier strategy gives the best of both worlds if satisfactory arrangements can be made. In this situation, the entrepreneurial firm provides the majority of its output to the single buyer. Sometimes the percentage is as high as 90 percent. But the entrepreneur also produces some products for sale to other customers. The product may or may not be similar to that produced for the major customer. The advantage to this is that the venture has the stability offered by the large customer, but still has products being sold to others in case of problems with the larger firm. This gives flexibility along with stability.

Strategies for Retailers

New retail ventures face severe competitive environments because of the competition from major retailers which are often chains or franchises. This, plus the fact that retailing is appealing to many would-be entrepreneurs who do not have sufficient management skills, accounts for the fact that a greater percentage of retail ventures fail than any other category of ventures. Entrepreneurs contemplating retail ventures absolutely must consider the competitive dynamics of the industry and the community. It is critical that a thorough analysis be made of competitors, locations, inventory required, necessary advertising, mark-ups, and innumerable other factors before launching a retail venture.

There are only two ways in which a new retail venture can make sales. Either it provides products for which customers are willing to spend more money than they have in the past, or it takes sales away from existing retailers. Some growth will occur from the natural growth in population and from tapping into an increasing standard of living and changing trends. The larger share of the growth, however, comes from shifting customer dollars from existing products into new products or from existing stores to new stores. Thus, the retailer must provide products to customers in such a way as to lure them away from existing competition and then maintain their loyalty in order to keep them.

Owners of new retail ventures must consider their own objectives in developing a strategy, but they must also consider the current situation of their major competitors. There are six aspects of the retailing strategy that must be considered (Figure 8-2). Each of the items must be considered as part of the strategy formulation process for retailers. For each of the factors, the proposed venture should be compared carefully to others in order to assess the competitive edge or vulnerabilities the new venture has.

Facilities and their location are critical in retail strategies. Some franchises, for example, have as their sole location policy to locate a store in every enclosed mall that has major anchor tenants.[8] Depending on the

FIGURE 8-2
Key Strategic Issues for
Retailers

SOURCE: Adapted from
William R. Davidson,
Daniel J. Sweeney, and
Ronald W. Stampfl, *Retailing
Management*, 6th ed. (New
York: John Wiley & Sons,
1988), 149.

| | | Competitors | | |
Aspects to Consider	Our Venture	A	B	C
Facilities				
Merchandise				
Pricing				
Promotion				
Service				
Personnel				

product, the location may be *the* most important factor in retail success. The importance of the location, however, is a function of the nature of the venture. Shoe stores, apparel stores, and toy stores, for example, are well advised to follow the model set by the chains and locate only in enclosed malls or large shopping centers. Auto parts stores, on the other hand, have no need to be located in malls and may benefit from being free standing or in small shopping centers. This is because customers needing auto parts are willing to drive wherever necessary to get the parts. The importance of location may also be a function of the entrepreneur's desire for growth. If low growth is desired, then location may not be as important as if rapid growth is desired.

The second critical need in the retail strategy is the *merchandise* strategy. The breadth versus depth issue must be addressed as well as decisions relating to the quality of merchandise, the total amount of inventory stocked, the number of competing brands to carry, the amount of backroom stock to maintain, and whether to use private brands versus major brands of merchandise.

Pricing is often used as one of the key aspects of marketing. The 50-Off Stores is a chain of discount clothing and housewares stores that sells all the items in the store for half the regular price. This rather unique use of the pricing strategy accounts for its ranking in *Business Week*'s listing of rapid-growth companies.[9] Other products—often those whose price relative to competition is difficult to compare—do not require the keen attention to price. In the automotive parts industry, for example, motor oil may be very price sensitive while automotive paint is not at all sensitive to price.

All of the retailing factors must combine and be consistent with each other. The item for which consistency is most important is the *promotional strategy*. The promotional strategy that is appropriate for a used furniture venture would not be appropriate for a jewelry store. The strategy used for an independent ice cream store would likely differ greatly from that used by TCBY or Häagen Dazs. Thus, the product offered, its quality, its cost, and its frequency of purchase all affect the promotional strategy used. The advertising strategy, in particular, must match the product quality, the type of store image created, and the type of service offered.

The *service* offered by retailers is a key determinant in differentiating retailers. Many customers buy from one retailer rather than another because of the service they provide either in the actual purchase of the product, the after-sale service, or items such as warranties and return policies. The number of services provided by the retailer can affect the amount of sales on the one hand and the costs to the venture on the other.

The final item, *personnel*, is also important in retail, and must mesh with the rest of the strategy. Discount stores use relatively few clerks given the amount of floor space in the store. Specialty apparel stores use many more employees for the equivalent amount of floor space, because they emphasize personal attention to the customer.

Strategies for Service Ventures

Most of the caveats from the previous section on retailing are also relevant for service ventures. For example, starting a service business may be difficult if formidable competitors are already in the area. Small accounting firms face that kind of competition from the Big 6 accounting firms. In earlier years, the major firms generally avoided the small business sector, preferring to focus their energies on larger corporations. In recent years, however, those firms have moved into the small business arena by setting up specialized divisions that focus on consulting with new and small ventures. This puts pressure on a new or small accounting firm whose primary market is other small businesses.

Many of the keys to a successful service venture strategy are similar to those of retail businesses. The most important is to provide a cost-effective service that is of sufficient quality to attract and maintain a customer base. If the service is new, then the task is one of convincing potential customers that they really need the service. If providing the service puts the company in competition with existing vendors, then the task is to convince customers that the new venture can provide a better-quality service for the same or lower price.

Service strategies have a unique aspect not experienced by retail firms. The nature of a service firm dictates that its efforts will be in a one-on-one relationship with its customers. Regardless of whether the venture is a barber shop, an architectural firm, or a custom software design company, the contact with the customer is on a person-to-person basis. This underscores the need for employees and managers who can interact well with customers. Since word of mouth is one of the forms of advertising for service ventures, a few bad experiences with customers can be devastating to the future of the venture.

The venture's location, which is so important for retail firms, is of little concern for most service firms. Some service ventures are such that employees go to the client rather than have the client come to the business. Thus, location is of no concern to the customer. In other situations, the customer will go to the venture's location as long as it is within some logical range. In most cases, it is not the location that determines the customer base as much as the quality of the services rendered.

Strategies for Direct Marketing Ventures

Direct marketing is one of the growth industries in business today.[10] Demographic analysis tells us that more families either have both spouses working or are headed by single heads of households. As such, the convenience of shopping via mail or electronic media is becoming more and more desirable. Even personal computers are being purchased by mail order in record numbers. A *Business Week* article predicted that 30 percent of all PCs will be purchased by mail in 1995.[11]

Direct marketing has the advantage of focusing marketing on specific target markets. In addition, direct marketers do not have to maintain retail facilities. The disadvantage of direct marketing is the low response rate caused partially by the inability of the customer to see or test the product before ordering it.

Entrepreneurs considering direct marketing have a number of choices of strategies to use in getting product information to the consumer and to accept orders for the merchandise. These include mass media advertising in newspapers, magazines, radio, or television, direct mail advertisements, electronic advertising, or participating in a catalog mailing.

Mass Media Advertising

Producers of products or services can reach large numbers of customers via advertising in one or more mass media. These include placing classified ads in newspapers, half-page ads in targeted magazines, and advertising on television. Regardless of the medium used, the customer is encouraged to either send a check and order form for the merchandise or call a toll-free number and order with a credit card. Targeting advertisements to specific target markets can be done via advertisements in magazines likely to be read by individuals in the target market.

Entrepreneurs launching their first ventures may find that advertising is far more expensive than anticipated. For example, the Accuset advertising in one woodworking magazine cost $4,000 for a one-time half-page insertion (Venture Perspective 8-4). Advertising costs can be hedged somewhat by advertising in regional or local media first and then later expanding into national markets. But regardless of the cost, the advertising must be considered an investment instead of an expense. It must be done "on the front end" in order to generate sales.

Direct Mail

Rather than advertise in trade magazines, entrepreneurs may opt to advertise their products via direct mail. This has the advantage of reaching very specific target markets. Accuset bought mailing labels from a direct mail broker to use in sending advertisements for the Paragauge directly to consumers who should be interested in woodworking tools. The problem with direct mail, of course, is that much direct mail is considered junk mail by consumers who never bother to open it. Response rates for direct mail pieces are expected to be quite low. A response rate of 1 percent or 2 percent may be good in some cases. Assuming a 1 percent response rate for direct mail gives the entrepreneur an idea of how many pieces must be

VENTURE PERSPECTIVE 8-4

. . . .

ACCUSET TOOL CO., INC.

Robert Riesberg and a friend developed the Paragauge, a high-precision measuring device used to perfectly align table saws, radial arm saws, and other woodworking tools. A prototype was developed and a limited market test was done. In spite of an only moderately favorable response, Riesberg and his friend continued to develop the Paragauge. They changed the design somewhat and changed materials to make the Paragauge even more accurate and more durable than it had previously been. Riesberg enlisted his son, Jim, who had worked in the automotive component manufacturing business, to help market the product.

Bob and Jim Riesberg formed Accuset Tool Co., Inc., in Troy, Michigan. They found contractors who could produce the Paragauge to their exact specifications. They then turned to the task of marketing

the product. Because the Paragauge was a specialty product, the Riesbergs determined that direct marketing was the preferred method of advertising the product. They used three methods. First, they advertised the Paragauge in three woodworking magazines. Second, they bought labels

from a direct mail broker. And third, they had the product listed in a woodworking catalog. They experimented with advertisement size in the woodworking magazines and found that a half-page, full-color advertisement was necessary to convey the message. The cost of the ad was $4,000 for a one-time insertion. Results for the three methods of advertising were mixed, and sales continued to grow at a moderate rate. Desiring even more growth, the Riesbergs determined that getting the product into retail stores was a necessary approach. This would allow customers to see and touch the product and see how it works. They therefore developed a video of the Paragauge and set up a booth at a major hardware trade show in order to entice retail chains to purchase the product.

SOURCE: Accuset Tool Co., Inc. Used with permission.

mailed in order to get a desired number of favorable responses. Sending a one million–piece mailing, for example, could be expected to generate ten thousand responses. If the target market consists of only fifty thousand individuals, that mailing might return only five hundred responses. The entrepreneur must determine whether that number of responses is worth the expense of buying the labels, developing and printing the mailer, purchasing the outgoing and return envelopes, and paying the postage both ways.

The Electronic Marketplace

A subset of mass media advertising is electronic shopping, which may take one of two forms. One is the Home Shopping Network (HSN) or competing firms that continuously advertise goods on cable TV. These networks advertise products that are likely to sell well over television. Operators

· · · · · · ·

TABLE 8-2
Products Available from
the Electronic Mall
Source: Cindy Morgan and
Pam Busch, "Go Mall,"
CompuServe Magazine (April
1991): 47–55.

1. Autographed baseballs (Mickey Mantle, $99.95)
2. BMA stepper
3. In-line skates
4. Ultrasonic pest control
5. *The Mensa Genius Quiz Book*
6. Mercedes coffee cup
7. Paul Fredrick shirts
8. Pet car seat travel bed
9. Valencia oranges
10. Blueberry treats

stand by phones with "800" numbers to receive orders from customers who buy the products essentially on impulse. Orders are then immediately processed via computer to be shipped within a few hours.

The second method is the computer shopping done from one's home computer via a modem. Software such as Prodigy or CompuServe allows individuals to view products on their computer screen, find more information about the product or service by pressing appropriate keys on the keyboard, and then confirming an order by entering a credit card number. Products or services available include cruises, automobiles, and other high-priced items as well as a plethora of lower-priced items. Table 8-2 lists a sample of products found in "The Electronic Mall" in a recent issue of *CompuServe Magazine*. The advantage of the computer shopping method over television sales is that customers can browse through the offerings at their leisure, twenty-four hours a day, collecting comparative information, and then purchasing the product with a touch of a few keys.

Catalog Sales

An alternative to mass media, direct mail, or electronic advertising is to list products in a catalog. Typically the catalog is published by someone who lists a variety of products produced by several different suppliers. The catalog is mailed in a large mailing either to a targeted audience or to a wide general audience. The catalog company receives part of the price of the products as the fee for listing the product. The major advantage of advertising in a catalog is the wide exposure of the product. A disadvantage is that the product is one of many in the catalog and the fee represents a substantial reduction in profit margins.

SUMMARY

Key to the success of a new or emerging venture is the development of a definitive entrepreneurial strategy. The strategic planning process, discussed in Chapter 4, consists of analyzing the new venture and its environment in order to develop a viable strategy. With the strategy and its support strategies in mind, attention then turns to obtaining necessary resources and implementing the strategy.

Strategies tend to fall into one of three broad categories. Firms with differentiation strategies create value in products beyond what competing products have. Low-cost leadership strategies concentrate on providing competing products at the lowest possible cost. Focus strategies may be either differentiation or low-cost, but they target a specific set of customers.

Karl Vesper suggested fourteen "entry wedges" for new ventures. These include new products or services, parallel competition, franchising, geographical transfer, supply shortage, tapping unused resources, customer contract, becoming an additional supplier, joint ventures, licensing, market relinquishment, sell off of a division, favored purchasing, or rule changes.

There are numerous specific entrepreneurial strategies available to ventures, and no one strategy will necessarily be successful in a given situation. High-tech strategies typically revolve around a product. That product can be either a brand-new product, a derivative product, or a variation of an existing product. It can also be a support product that is related to the existing product. In high-tech industries, new products have a relatively short window before competitors bring similar or superior products to the market. Ironically, low-tech products face many of the same problems as high-tech products except for the fact that they are not produced by or for high-technology industries. They still face the problems of obsolescence or competing with other newer or superior products.

Niche strategies are those where the entrepreneur attempts to serve a small segment of a larger market. The advantage of a niche strategy is that the entrepreneur can become an expert within the narrow scope of the market. The problems with niche strategies are that the niche may be too small or that large companies may move into the niche and squeeze out the entrepreneurial firm.

Rather than focusing on a particular market, competency based strategies build upon special skills, products, or processes unique to the venture. The entrepreneur then exploits the strength through effective marketing and continued development of the competency. In the captive supplier strategy, the entrepreneur provides a product or service to one customer only. Once the arrangement is complete, the small venture has to do no marketing and simply produces the product in the amounts and specifications demanded by the larger customer.

Most new and small ventures are retail or service. In either case, launching the venture may be risky because of the intense competition from other small ventures and from larger chains and franchises. Keys to success revolve around the effective design and location of facilities, effective merchandising, promotion, and pricing strategies, and the provision of appropriate services to the customer. In both cases, the need is to provide a product or service with a sufficient price/value ratio to attract customers away from competitors.

Direct marketing is a broad category that includes advertising in mass media for direct response, direct mail, electronic shopping, and advertising through catalogs. Direct marketing has the advantage of targeting specific markets and not requiring retail showrooms. The disadvantage is that customers cannot see or test the product without ordering it first.

The next three chapters continue the development of issues surrounding strategies and planning. Chapter 9 will discuss support strategies that are developed after the overall strategy is identified. Chapters 10 and 11 then discuss two specific strategies that are applicable to entrepreneurial firms. Chapter 10 discusses franchising from the perspective of both the potential franchisee and the potential franchisor. Chapter 11 follows with a discussion of international strategies for growing firms.

DISCUSSION QUESTIONS

1. This chapter suggests that there are no "right" strategies for a venture. If this is true, then why is the discussion of various strategies necessary? If there are no "right" strategies, does this mean there are also no "wrong" strategies?

2. Discuss the three generic strategies suggested by Porter. Why are these strategies just as appropriate for new ventures as they are for large corporations?

3. Compare Porter's generic strategies to Vesper's competitive entry wedges. Do they mesh well with each other? Which of Vesper's entry wedges fit with each of Porter's generic strategies? Are there some that do not fit any of Porter's strategies?

4. What is meant by parent company sponsored entry wedges? What is significant about them?

5. If there is a government procurement office in your city, interview its manager. Is the government-sponsored entry wedge a viable wedge for a new business?

6. How does the derivative product strategy differ from the product variation strategy for high-tech ventures? Which is more risky?

7. Does "low tech" have a derogatory connotation? Should it? Do you know of companies that are clearly low tech but that are quite successful?

8. What is the difference between a niche strategy and a competency based strategy? Is one inherently more risky than the other?

9. Why does the captive supplier strategy seem boring? Would you recommend it to your friends? To someone with limited capital? (Be careful on that one.) To someone who is a high risk-taker?

10. Which of the factors mentioned in the discussion of retail strategies is most important for the following retail ventures? Why do they vary?
    a. A car dealership
    b. An auto parts store
    c. An exclusive dress and furs store
    d. A large supermarket
    e. A small corner grocery store
    f. A Wal-Mart or another discount store

11. Consider the discussion of the Paragauge in Venture Perspective 8-4. Would you have started that venture using direct marketing? Why or why not?

12. Interview an entrepreneur who has recently started a venture. Does the strategy used fit well with the discussion of this chapter?

EXERCISE 8-1

Suppose you and a friend have each decided to launch a new venture. Your venture is based on your invention of a monitor that straps onto the wrist with Velcro and measures pulse and blood pressure as a runner runs. You don't know whether others are already on the market. Your friend has invented a large print equivalent of a television remote control for those who have poor vision or poor coordination. Evaluate the two products and determine what kind of a strategy each should use. In addition, should you create a single venture to market both products?

EXERCISE 8-2

Make a list of all the companies you know of that are using a niche strategy. What are the similarities and differences among the companies? What are the most likely risks for each?

EXERCISE 8-3

Working in small groups, list the strategies covered in this chapter. Discuss the list and rank them from most risky to least risky. Then, compare your list with that of other groups. Are the rankings very similar or quite different? Explain the differences.

1. Arthur A. Thompson and A. J. Strickland, *Strategic Management: Concepts and Cases*, 5th ed. (Homewood, IL: Richard D. Irwin, Inc., 1990).

2. Michael Porter, *Competitive Strategies* (New York: The Free Press, 1980), Chap. 2.

3. Lawrence Finley, *Entrepreneurial Strategies: Text and Cases* (Boston: PWS-Kent Publishing Co., 1990), 70–71.

4. Porter, *Competitive Strategies*, 36.

5. Karl H. Vesper, *New Venture Strategies*, rev. ed. (Englewood Cliffs, NJ: Prentice Hall, 1990), Chaps. 7 and 8.

6. Larry Armstrong, "Sony's Challenge," *Business Week*, June 1987, 64.

7. "The Best Small Companies," *Business Week*, May 22, 1989, 101–106.

8. William R. Davidson, Daniel J. Sweeney, and Ronald W. Stampfl, *Retailing Management*, 6th ed. (New York: John Wiley & Sons, 1988), 149.

9. "The Best Small Companies," *Business Week*, May 25, 1992, 97–102.

10. John G. Burch, *Entrepreneurship*, (New York: John Wiley & Sons, 1986), Chap. 8.

11. Sunita Wadecker Bhargava, "Computers By Mail: A Megabyte Business Boom," *Business Week*, May 11, 1992, 93–96.

◆ Conveniesse, Inc. ◆

Update and Strategy

Jason Stone, Sarah Tondeur, and Yolanda Williams worked feverishly to prepare their convenience store for opening. The six months lead time before the site was available proved to be barely enough, and the three entrepreneurs frequently told each other that it was fortunate that the space wasn't available before that. Like many entrepreneurs, they underestimated the length of time to do everything. They still had to do massive research of the convenience industry, particularly as it applied to upscale stores. They had to order equipment, determine the store layout, solicit suppliers, work with the city regarding permits, work with the developer and contractors to remodel the space, and attend to a host of other details.

It now appeared that the financing arrangements would fall into place, although neither the debt terms nor the additional equity they had to solicit were particularly desirable. The lease arrangements were worked out pretty much as expected except for being more restrictive than they would have desired. The cost of the lease did turn out to be in the $100,000 range, but was mitigated somewhat by the fact that the developer provided an $80,000 loan to them, identified three informal investors who each provided $20,000 in equity, and helped work with banks to get the rest of the money.

There was also the task of getting the three participants moved to Buffalo. Sarah, who had sold her business and her house several months earlier, immediately moved to an apartment in Buffalo. The entrepreneurs decided that she should start out as president of Conveniesse, Inc., primarily because she would be dealing with the suppliers, contractors, and others. Jason decided he would move to Buffalo about three months later, after he finished two public relations campaigns he was working on. This was assuming that he did not get fired for inattention to the work in Detroit. This would allow him to be on site for three months before the store opened. Yolanda, on the other hand, had not decided when to join the other two. As a product manager at her current job, she not only had a position of high responsibility that paid very well, but she also had just begun a major new product introduction. It was definitely going to take six months to work through. Yolanda felt both morally and economically tied to her job for the time being but agreed to commute on weekends and be available for phone calls most evenings. This was acceptable to both Sarah and Jason since there wasn't a need for all three of them to be on site constantly before the store opened and Yolanda would not be paid a salary except for her weekend work.

The financial plan the entrepreneurs had put together for financing (reproduced in Part VI) had been done relatively quickly with the help of a consultant in Buffalo. The consultant, who had good rapport both with the developer and with other debt and equity providers, had taken the lead in developing the plan. Sarah, Jason, and Yolanda had input, of course, but the consultant designed the format and "ran the numbers." Thus, the entrepreneurs were pleased with the speed and thoroughness of the plan development but were somewhat disappointed that they did not have the time or expertise to put it together themselves. As is typical of business plans, the final financing was somewhat different than the plan proposed.

Work at the location went well. The contractors had worked on the building when it was first built five years ago, so they were familiar with the building and the developer. Equipment included freezers, refrigerators, shelving, counters, food preparation equipment, cash registers, and other miscellaneous equipment. Signs with the distinctive Conveniesse logo were ordered and would arrive a few days before the opening. In general, the food suppliers were cooperative. As might be expected, sales representatives tried to sell them more inventory than they really needed. Distinctive uniforms that enhanced the image of the store were ordered for workers.

During one of their meetings a few weeks before opening, Sarah suggested that they needed to put together a working plan of some sort that would delineate for the three of them the direction they were headed, identify up front what their weaknesses as well as their strengths would be, and lay out an overall strategy for the firm. This would give them a document both to refer to and to use as a baseline for future reference. Fortunately, they had the financial plan available as a starting point.

Assignment

Using the financial plan in Part VI, a format similar to that discussed in Chapter 4, and information gleaned from the Conveniesse case so far, develop the beginnings of a strategic plan. Include in item 3–E your assessment of the opening day financial condition. Stop after item 4–A.

9

Developing Supporting Strategies

LEARNING OBJECTIVES

After studying this chapter, you should be aware of:

1. The importance of developing functional strategies to support the overall venture strategy
2. The need to do analysis and research before developing functional strategies
3. The need to ensure that functional strategies mesh with the overall venture strategy
4. The ingredients in a marketing plan
5. The financial planning process
6. The most important financial ratios for emerging ventures
7. The different possible human resource strategies
8. The importance of an ethics strategy

KEY TERMS

Supporting strategies
Marketing strategy
Financial strategy

Human resource strategy
Ethics strategy

CONSIDER THIS!

- Some entrepreneurs have a good overall strategy but can't implement it well because they can't see the small picture.
- Functional strategies may require more time to develop than does the overall strategy.
- Some new ventures mistakenly spend their entire advertising budget on the grand opening.
- An emerging venture's financial strategy will change as the firm develops.
- Human resource strategies are especially important for small ventures because of the key role that all employees play.
- Hiring highly trained workers may or may not be a good strategy for new ventures.
- Being ethical does not mean giving away the firm's profits.

Chapter 8 discussed in detail the need to develop a well-planned venture strategy. It reviewed the strategic planning model and then focused on how to translate the planning process into a venture strategy. It discussed a number of different venture strategies that were appropriate for various competitive situations. Simply developing an overall strategy does not

BEN COHEN AND JERRY GREENFIELD
Ben and Jerry's Homemade, Inc.

Can a startup company in Vermont be featured in *USA Today*, *The New Yorker*, *Esquire*, *Family Circle*, *Dairy Foods*, *The San Francisco Examiner*, and *The Boston Globe*? Can two crazy guys in T-shirts with pictures of cows on them consider expanding to Russia? Can someone start a business in a renovated gas station and compete head-on with corporate names like Pillsbury and Kraft? Can a small business "go public" within a single state and have one of every one hundred state residents buy stock in the company? And can a company be known almost as much for its interest in social causes as it is for its prime product? The answer is, of course, yes, if the two entrepreneurs involved are Ben Cohen and Jerry Greenfield of Ben and Jerry's Homemade, Inc.

Ben Cohen's childhood memories include mushing up cookies and candies in a bowl

of ice cream to develop his own concoctions and watching his father eat an entire half gallon of ice cream at one sitting. In high school, Ben became an "ice cream man," selling ice cream to kids out of a truck he drove through the neighborhood. He dropped out of at least three universities, made pottery, worked as a night mopper at restaurants, was a

security guard at a racetrack, taught crafts to emotionally disturbed adolescents, and built his own house.

Jerry Greenfield met Ben Cohen in high school. Jerry graduated as a National Merit Scholar and attended Oberlin College in Ohio. He was rejected for medical school twice and worked for a period as a lab technician. He eventually rejoined Ben as they decided whether to open a bagel store or an ice cream store. After splitting the cost of a $5 correspondence course on ice cream making and experimenting with different taste combinations, they opened their first shop in a renovated gasoline station with a $12,000 investment.

Ben and Jerry's has been featured in numerous magazines and papers, was rated in *Inc.'s* top one hundred fastest growing businesses in 1986 and

finish the planning task. In order for the venture strategy to have a chance of succeeding, it must be supported by functional area strategies that guide the firm in more detail in the achievement of its goals. Functional area strategies—or **supporting strategies**—are those plans that address a single portion of the overall venture strategy. These supporting strategies consist of the marketing, financial, and human resource strategies for the emerging venture. In addition to the supporting strategies in each functional area, the venture must have an ethics strategy to guide the decision making within the firm. A prelude to each area is the analysis necessary to make logical decisions regarding the strategies.

DEVELOPING THE MARKETING STRATEGY

The **marketing strategy** is the most visible functional strategy and the one that can have the most impact on the short-run success of the venture. The

1987, and has become the number two producer of super-premium ice cream in America. The company's 1991 sales were $97 million with sales in forty-six states. Their store in Russia opened in 1992 and they have written a book on how to make homemade ice cream.

Although some refer to Cohen and Greenfield as "Vermont hippies" with a social conscience and a sense of humor, others call them capitalist folkheroes.[1] They believe firmly in returning part of their earnings to those around them. Employees participate in a profit-sharing plan and the company contributes 7.5 percent of pre-tax earnings—far more than the typical 1 percent or 2 percent for most firms—to various charities.

Ben and Jerry's was an instant hit in the Vermont town where they started. But it also created demand in surrounding towns in upper New England. They expanded their manufacturing plant into a former truck repair building. Expanding into lower New England and beyond required overcoming two major hurdles. One was capital. To solve this, the duo and their general manager went from town to town in Vermont offering samples and selling stock. They raised $750,000, which was then combined with an urban development grant and industrial revenue bonds. The second hurdle was overcoming practices by the manufacturers of Häagen-Dazs, who were requiring their distributors not to carry Ben and Jerry's if they wanted to remain Häagen-Dazs distributors. Ben and Jerry's filed a lawsuit against Pillsbury (the parent company of Häagen-Dazs), but doubted whether a suit would be successful against the food giant. In addition, relying on legal ac-

tion would not be Ben and Jerry's style. They instead mounted a marketing campaign centering on the theme, "What's the Doughboy afraid of?" Thousands of letters rolled into Pillsbury headquarters admonishing them for taking on the entrepreneurial team. Eventually, the public relations approach, coupled with an excellent attorney, prevailed, and Pillsbury dropped the practice.

What will happen in the future for Ben and Jerry's is anyone's guess. The manufacturing facility and retail store in Petrozavodsk may be the beginning of a truly significant market in republics that formerly made up the Soviet Union because of the Soviets' desire for good quality ice cream.

SOURCE: Ben and Jerry's Homemade. Used with permission.

venture whose owners develop an aggressive marketing strategy will typically reap rewards far greater than the venture whose owners are very cautious and conservative. Similarly, the entrepreneur who carefully performs market research as a prelude to developing the strategy will have a better strategy than one who does not. It is important that the plan be done well and that the entrepreneur then stay close to the plan's prescribed actions.

Figure 9-1 illustrates the steps in developing a marketing strategy. Note that it *starts* with market research and is then followed by the development of an overall marketing strategy, a product and service strategy, a promotion strategy, a pricing strategy, and a distribution strategy.

Conducting Market Research

Retailers are fond of saying that the three most important aspects of a business are location, location, and location. A broader marketing focus

FIGURE 9-1
Steps in Developing a
Marketing Strategy

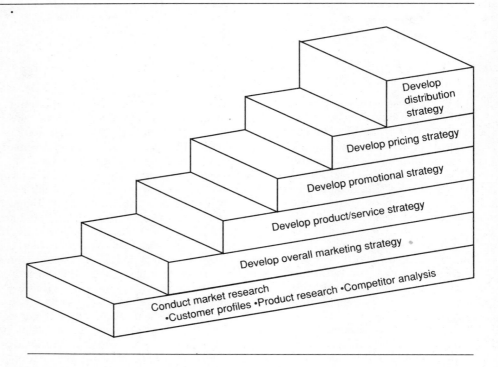

might say that the three most important aspects are research, research, and research. In particular, it is important to research the customer, research the product, and research the competitors.

Customer profiles can be developed through formal or informal surveys of the customers. Analyzing customer profiles is important for two reasons. The first is to discover the size and characteristics of the market. This is important in developing the venture's financial plan or strategic plan. Only with a good estimate of sales can the financial projections of business plans be logical. The second reason for studying the customer is that a marketing strategy can be developed around the customer profile. Virtually everything in the marketing plan hinges on a careful analysis of the target market. For example, knowing the makeup of the target market allows the development of an advertising campaign that focuses specifically on the target market. Knowing the target market tells the entrepreneur how price sensitive the customers may be. It can even suggest packaging ideas. Thus, this first step is critical to the rest.

Product research is done to determine if the product being sold provides the best value per dollar in the market. The product should be researched regarding possible uses by target market customers, the value that the product has for the customer, and the psychological reasons why customers choose this particular product. This will include analyzing packaging, labeling, and methods of displaying the product. The marketing strategy should also have a section dedicated to product/service improvement. Key to the product-related improvement is analysis of the firm's products as compared with those offered by others.

The final aspect of market research is *competitor analysis*. Competitors' products should be analyzed, their marketing strategies and campaigns should be studied, and their financial condition should be analyzed if possible. If competitors are public companies, their annual reports should be obtained routinely in order to learn as much as possible about them.

It should be noted that when doing competitor analysis, the entrepreneur should use only ethical means of gathering information. Competitor products can be purchased, annual reports can be obtained if available to the public, and information readily available through trade associations or other public sources can be gathered. It is even acceptable to call and check prices on products and services if that is something any customer might do. It is *not* ethical, however, to surreptitiously gain information by talking with employees, gaining unauthorized access to data or property, or posing as someone other than an interested consumer to gain information. The ethical rule of thumb is that anything that is readily available to the general public is fair game. Anything that requires deception is unethical.

Developing the Overall Marketing Strategy

Once information has been gathered about consumers, the product, and competitors, the marketing plan can be developed. The marketing strategy is an integral part of the overall strategy for the venture and therefore must be based on the venture strategy. The marketing strategy should delineate how the entrepreneur proposes to get the product successfully to the customer. It should identify which market segments will be targeted and how each segment will be approached. The segments may be based on the age of customers, their incomes, their occupations, or other demographic variables. Or they may be based on different uses of the product. For each market segment, the marketing plan will include how to best reach the market with the desired product or service. The various parts of the marketing strategy are then broken down as shown in the top four steps of Figure 9-1.

The Product/Service Strategy

The product plan should detail which products will be produced and sold, which among them will be emphasized, and what new products are envisioned. Included in the product plan is the depth and breadth of the product lines being offered, the quality of the product, how it will be positioned among competitor products, and the unique characteristics of the product that will encourage customers to buy it. Similarly, service firms should delineate exactly what services are going to be provided and how they will be marketed. Like products, services can be positioned among competitor's services based on the desired perception of the service. The product/service strategy should be sufficiently detailed so that appropriate personnel can clearly understand what is planned.

The Promotion Strategy

Promotion strategies deal with getting information to the consumer. Two major decisions and a host of smaller decisions must be made in developing the promotion strategy. The two major decisions are what the promotion mix should be and how many dollars should be allocated to each part of it.

Promotion includes advertising, personal selling, use of coupons, in-store displays, specialty premiums, and free publicity. The entrepreneur must determine which combination of promotional methods is most effective for the type of product or service being offered. Department stores typically use large amounts of newspaper advertising. Consumer services may require relatively less total advertising depending on the nature of the venture, and may rely heavily on yellow pages advertising. Industrial goods marketing may emphasize personal selling. For example, a printing company that deals primarily with other businesses may emphasize both personal selling and well-done novelty advertising to keep its name in front of customers. Consumer goods producers, such as potato chip manufacturers, will use a combination of advertising, couponing, and in-store promotion to encourage customers to select their brands.

Of particular importance in the promotion plan is the advertising strategy. For new and emerging ventures, advertising is critical, and timing of advertising is especially critical. At the same time, owners of new ventures are usually strapped for funds at the very time when advertising needs to be at its highest. Thus, effective use of scarce resources is imperative. A frequent cause of failure among new entrepreneurs is that they use inappropriate advertising media, schedule the advertising at the wrong time, and do not budget sufficient funds for an acceptable campaign. Making this even more critical is the fact that many emerging companies compete against larger, established, and better financed companies.

The advertising strategy typically should include use of more than one medium, and will use differing amounts of advertising throughout the year. The media mix and timing schedule go together to make up the advertising strategy for the venture.

Given the scarce resources available, entrepreneurs must carefully consider which media combination is likely to give the best return per dollar for the target market identified (Table 9-1). And they must plan ahead in order to ensure that the advertising reaches the public at the appropriate

TABLE 9-1 Advertising Media	Medium	Advantages	Disadvantages
	Newspapers	Wide circulation	Little target marketing
	Yellow pages	Serious buyers	Few casual readers
	Radio	Targeted market	Easily forgotten
	Television	Impact, coverage	High cost
	Cable TV	Targeted impact	Fewer viewers
	Direct mail	Specifically targeted customer list	High cost per customer

time. For example, service businesses such as plumbers, pest control specialists, and contractors live or die by the yellow pages. An entrepreneur considering one of these businesses must realize that the yellow pages order must go in three months or more before the phone book is delivered. Thus, a carpenter wishing to launch a business in February may find that the telephone directory is delivered in March but that the order is due in December. If the deadline is missed, the business will operate for more than a year with no yellow pages advertisement.

It is generally accepted that using multiple media while concentrating advertising in relatively short time periods is better than using only a single medium and spreading the advertising dollars across a broader time frame. The reason is that the different media tend to reinforce each other. In addition, focusing advertising in a relatively short time period such as the beginning of a season may be sufficient for the small firm and will save total marketing dollars.

Once the medium has been selected, still more study should go into designing the advertisement. Advertisement sellers will, of course, attempt to convince buyers that more is better. This is not always true, especially regarding yellow pages advertising. A study by Kelly and Hoel on yellow pages advertising found, for example, that two-color ads did *not* generate more sales than single-color ads. Further, large ads did not generate more sales than moderately sized ads. Relative size seems more important than absolute size. Conventional wisdom suggests limited copy in advertisements, but Kelly and Hoel found that increasing the amount of information in a yellow pages ad can be useful. This is because yellow pages readers are searching for specific information. Thus, they are not necessarily attracted to color or size as much as they are to the information they are seeking.[2]

The remaining promotion items—personal selling, displays, sampling, couponing, premiums, and publicity—are also important to the overall marketing strategy. They must be coordinated with the advertising plan in order that each aspect complements the other and there is consistency throughout the entire plan.

The Pricing Strategy

The third important marketing function is the development of a pricing strategy. Pricing is not independent of other marketing, strategy, or operations issues. Nor should it be done arbitrarily. The new entrepreneur must be extremely careful in pricing the firm's products in order for them to be competitive but profitable. Several general pricing strategies can be used to establish prices for products (Table 9-2). Typically, combinations of strategies must be used in order for the venture to be both profitable and competitive.

Cost based pricing considers the concept of markup. The seller determines the total cost of the products and divides the cost by the expected number to be sold to determine a cost per product. The price is then increased by some percentage to cover administrative costs and provide a profit. Manufacturers must determine the markup percentage on their own. Retailers often have suggested markups provided to them by the

. . . .

DARLING'S SKI AND TENNIS SHOP

Tom Darling took one last trip down the slope before packing in for his last night at Estes Park, Colorado. It was, indeed, his last trip, for he missed a curve, went over an embankment, and became the final casualty of the season at the ski lodge. He now has a plastic knee, and the pins in his leg often set off metal detectors at airports.

While recuperating and realizing that he would never ski or play tennis again, Darling gave some thought to sports. If he could not enjoy sports himself, he wondered if there was a way that he could enjoy them vicariously and perhaps help others enjoy their favorite sports. He also realized the difficulty he had had in getting professional help in purchasing sports equipment. Thus, he started doing some research on

the possibility of starting a ski and tennis shop in his home town of St. Louis that would be staffed with knowledgeable people, carry quality merchandise, and provide up-to-date information on ski slopes, tennis tournaments, and other aspects of the two sports.

Tom's research showed that there was, indeed, a market for the shop. Although there was a ski club in St. Louis, and a number of country clubs had tennis courts, there was no store that catered specifically to the more affluent, serious participants. He found a location in a shopping center being constructed in a growing part of the city. Through the ski club, he met a married couple who were avid outdoor enthusiasts and had just moved to St. Louis from Breckenridge, Colorado. They agreed to become part-

ners. They would handle the sales and public contact while Darling handled ordering and other business-related affairs.

The three figured that their marketing strategy should have three parts. The first part was the constant advertising in the telephone yellow pages. This would give them exposure throughout the year for those customers who were specifically in the market for tennis or ski gear. The second part was a grand opening campaign that was timed for the beginning of the tennis season. The third part was periodic advertising throughout the year. This advertising, keyed to the beginning months of each season and a clearance week near the end of the season, would be sufficient to keep customers coming in.

. . . .

TABLE 9-2	**Strategy**	**Significance**
Pricing Strategies for New Ventures	Cost based	Takes cost of product into account, but may not consider competition.
	Demand based	Assumes downward sloping demand curve. Not specific without experimentation.
	Competitor based	Takes competition into account. Encourages discounting, which may result in losses.
	Skimming	Charges highest possible prices when product is first introduced. Helps recover development cost if there is little competition.
	Prestige pricing	High prices imply high quality. May attract upscale customers if product differentiation is possible.
	Penetration pricing	Low prices designed to capture market share. Can be effective, but costly.

The telephone directory in their area was to be delivered on April 15 with an ad deadline of February 1. This was perfect for them because they would have their lease signed by then and would have a telephone number to list in the directory. They decided that the grand opening would be the heaviest use of their remaining advertising budget because of the need to inform people of the new store. The remainder of the budget would be used for advertising at the beginning of each season and at the end.

The grand opening would use television, radio, and newspaper. This would expose potential customers to three versions of the advertisement. The seasonal advertisement would be primarily on rock and oldies radio stations to reach those between the ages of twenty-five and forty. Some advertising would be done in newspapers and on local cable TV at the beginning of the season and at the beginning of their clearance sales. The time line of their first year of advertising is as shown below.

They then concluded from studying advertising rates what the total cost of the campaign would be.

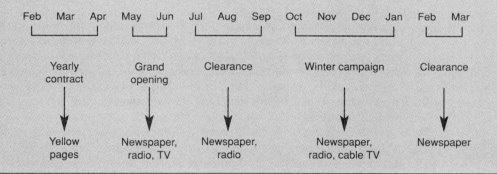

manufacturers. The advantage of the cost based system is, of course, that costs are considered in the pricing strategy. It is important that all costs are considered. Failure to include overhead or desired profit may result in too low a price for a product. Another problem with cost based pricing is that it fails to consider competition. Thus, using markup alone may cover costs but may price the product so high that sales are limited or so low that costs are not fully covered.

Demand based pricing recognizes the inverse relationship between price and quantity demanded. The precise slope of the demand curve varies with different products. Some products, such as soft drinks, may be quite sensitive to changes in price. Other products, such as medicines, may not be price sensitive at all. Thus, experimentation may have to occur in order to determine what the relationship is.

Competitor based pricing bases the price on those charged by the competition for similar products. Gasoline stations use this method in addition to cost based pricing. Grocery store managers routinely "shop" other stores to determine prices of products. Competitor based pricing does not automatically mean that competitors try to undercut each other. Doing that would ensure permanent price wars as well as the demise of many businesses. It does mean that a strategy is adopted that considers the price of competitors' products. Often it means that most competitors charge virtually the same price. It may mean that the relationship among competing businesses' prices remains stable with some firms consistently being the highest priced and some typically being the lowest priced.

Skimming refers to charging the highest possible prices for a new product while it has little or no competition. This allows the quick recovery of development costs. It works only as long as competitors do not undercut the prices. Texas Instruments used this strategy years ago when pocket calculators first appeared on the market and again when digital watches first came out. A plain, four-function calculator cost $50 to $80 until competition forced it to lower the price. Now the same calculator can be purchased for under $5 and is often a giveaway product. Digital watches that now sell for under $10 were likewise initially priced well over $50. The skimming strategy is not envisioned as a long-run pricing strategy because of the potential for competitors to enter the market. It can yield good short-run returns however. Careful consideration should be given to the possibility of competitors, substitute products, and the protection the product has against copying.

Prestige pricing is pricing higher than most competitors to give an aura of quality to the product. In most cases, the product is indeed better quality than that of competitors. But the percentage difference in quality may or may not be equivalent to the difference in price. Sellers using prestige pricing must be prepared to sell a lower quantity of the product. Yet, if the quality image can be maintained, the prestige pricing strategy can be a profitable strategy.

Penetration pricing is a market share-oriented strategy. Prices are pegged at or near the lower end of the competitive spectrum in order to maximize gains in the market. This is often done when new products are introduced into an already crowded field. The penetration strategy may be continued until the brand is established in the market. The price is then slowly raised to match competition if desired. The risk of penetration pricing is that competitors may match the low price and thus prevent the raising of the price to recover costs at a later date.

Other issues will affect the pricing strategy. Most retail stores will have end-of-season sales to clear old merchandise in order to make room for the new season's goods. Loss leaders—selected products priced below cost—are used to attract customers into a store in the hopes that they will buy other goods while there. Quantity discounts are often offered in order to encourage volume buying.

The importance of this discussion is that the entrepreneur should consciously adopt a pricing strategy. This strategy will then remain constant except for purposive changes or exceptions. The pricing strategy also affects other parts of the venture such as purchasing, production, and other parts of marketing.

The Distribution Strategy

Having the best promotion plan in the world is of little value if there is not an adequate distribution system. Retailers need only worry about goods getting *to* their store. Manufacturers, however, must be concerned with getting goods *from* the plant into the hands of the customer. A number of distribution systems can be used. The venture can use its own sales people. It can use manufacturer's representatives, who are self-employed or are independent businesses that represent a number of manufacturers and sell to wholesalers or retailers. The venture can sell directly to wholesalers who may purchase large amounts of the product and then break them down into amounts that individual retailers desire. Or it can sell via direct mail and ship using the mail or other delivery services.

Distribution and shipping are not the same. Distribution refers to the distribution channels used in transferring ownership from the producer to the customer. Shipping refers to the methods of transporting the goods to the ultimate customer. A number of different combinations of distribution and shipping are available to entrepreneurs and may be more or less appropriate in different situations.

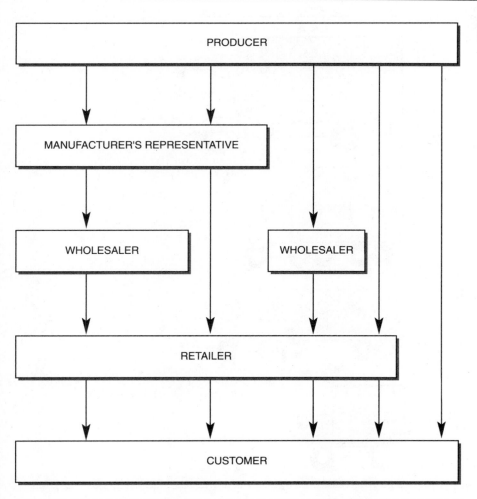

FIGURE 9-2
Distribution Systems

The difference among distribution systems is typically one of cost versus the ability to control how the product gets to the customer. Another way of saying this is the choice between efficiency and effectiveness. Using the firm's own sales force may be very effective. But it may be extremely inefficient if the products sell over a wide geographical area. Using manufacturer's reps, on the other hand, is much more efficient but may not be as effective as would be desired. The nature of the product may also determine the distribution channel used. Heavy equipment may be sold directly from the producer to the customer. Consumer goods such as hardware products are often sold via manufacturer's reps to wholesalers who then sell to retailers.

Similarly, the entrepreneur has a choice of shipping methods that are determined primarily by cost and type of product. Established manufacturers may use their own fleet of trucks. Franchisors also have their own shipping system. And retailers such as Wal-Mart have their own distribution system. Many emerging ventures, however, cannot afford their own distribution system and use either contract carriers or mail or package

FIGURE 9-3
Shipping Methods

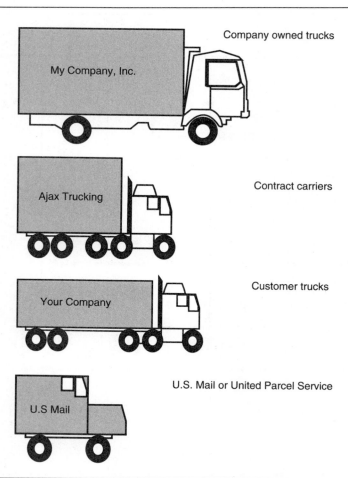

Company owned trucks

Contract carriers

Customer trucks

U.S. Mail or United Parcel Service

delivery services. In somewhat rare cases, primarily where a small producer sells to a large company, the customer sends its own trucks to the producer's plant to pick up goods. This is prevalent among large manufacturers that use a host of entrepreneurial firms as suppliers.

The Need for Consistency

A concluding note on the development of the marketing strategy is the need for consistency. The discussion of strategies in Chapter 8 alluded to this concern. A venture's image is determined by its products, its prices, and its promotion. It is important that everything in the overall strategy and the supporting strategies be consistent. Without consistency, customers become confused and may resist buying because they are unclear as to the real image of the product. For example, furniture stores that sell high-quality furniture but use methods more appropriate to discounters may find that they lose their upscale customers and can't make sales to other customers. Entrepreneurs must study each aspect of their marketing strategy to assure that they mesh with each other and that they give the image desired. If inconsistencies appear, the entire strategic planning process must be studied again to determine what is inconsistent, what image and strategy is desired, and how to implement the strategy correctly.

DEVELOPING THE FINANCIAL STRATEGY

Just as entrepreneurs should develop a specific marketing strategy for their firms, they should also develop a carefully analyzed financial strategy. Similarly, just as the marketing strategy is a function of the overall strategy of the venture, the financial strategy must be both a function of and mesh with the venture strategy.

The Financial Strategy Process

The **financial strategy** process has six steps and is somewhat analogous to the strategic planning process discussed in Chapter 4 (Figure 9-4).

The first step of the process is to review the overall venture strategy. This should include not only how the firm will compete, but also how much growth is desired and how that growth will be achieved. Only after the overall strategy is formulated can the entrepreneur or team members begin to determine which financial strategy will best support the venture strategy.

Step two of the financial strategic process is to analyze the financial condition of the firm. Included here is the traditional ratio analysis and break-even analysis. The purpose of the analysis is to determine the current condition and therefore determine the necessary changes in the financial mix in order to achieve the venture's overall goals. These will be discussed below.

The third step is to analyze the venture's environment as it relates to the financial strategy. For example, early 1992 saw the lowest interest rates in two decades. Many firms found that the declining interest rates made

FIGURE 9-4
The Financial Planning
Process

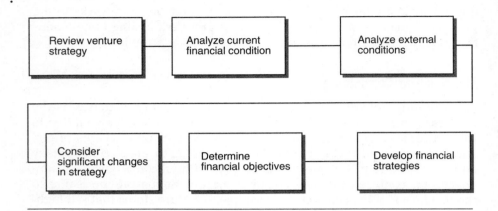

borrowing a much more appealing strategy than it had been some years earlier. Likewise, the willingness of banks to loan money, the nature of the economy, the inflation rate, and other economic variables may have an impact on the financial strategy selected. Growth-oriented entrepreneurs may also consider trends in the venture capital market and stock market to determine if either of these funding sources are advisable.

A very important fourth item is to consider any potential changes in the venture's strategy or needs within the next two years. Consider the possibility that the firm may add an entire new product line sometime in the future, or it may expand from a local market into a regional market. Perhaps an acquisition will be made in the near future. Any of these changes will have a dramatic impact on the amount and kind of financial needs in the future.

Once these different analyses are completed, then the financial goals and objectives of the venture must be considered. For example, if the entrepreneur is very conservative, a low-debt position may be desirable. If the entrepreneur wants to maintain complete ownership and control of the venture, outside equity funding would not be part of the strategy. Perhaps the entrepreneur sets as a goal to keep the debt/equity ratio within some percentage of the industry norm. Another goal might be to keep the current ratio as high as possible. This could affect the amount of long-term versus short-term debt used to purchase inventory.

The final step, then, is to develop the financial strategy. In particular, the strategy should address the total amount of capital used, the various sources of funds, the debt/equity mix, the distribution or retention of profits, credit policies, and cash and receivables policies.[3]

Analyzing the Current Financial Condition

The most important step of the financial planning process is the analysis of the current financial condition of the firm. Other steps in the process are important, but they are primarily subjective in nature. Analyzing the current financial condition, however, requires a substantial amount of analysis. Two major parts of the financial analysis are the budget analysis and the ratio analysis.

Item	Budgeted	Actual	Deviation	Percentage	Comments
Cash Inflow					
Sales	$540,000	$600,000	$60,000	11%	Good for 2d quarter
Cash Outflow					
Cost of goods sold	324,000	380,000	56,000	17.2	Far too high
Salaries					
Management	30,000	30,000	0	0	
Employees	80,000	85,000	5,000	6	Added two employees
Benefits	33,000	34,500	1,500	4.5	New employees
Advertising	10,000	8,000	−2,000	−20	Low on cash
Facilities	10,000	10,000	0	0	
Utilities	4,000	3,000	−1,000	−25	Warm spring
Insurance	2,000	2,000	0	0	
Other administrative expenses	3,000	5,000	2,000	66	Need to analyze in more depth
Taxes	1,500	1,750	250	16.6	First quarter profits
Net cash flow	42,500	40,750	−1,750	−4.1	Net is O.K.

TABLE 9-3
Budget Analysis for Second Quarter ULUVIT Foods, Inc.

Budget Analysis

Budgets, in their simplest form, are charts that lay out expected revenue and expenses that are then compared with actual revenue or expenses. Well-managed firms will have capital budgets, cash budgets, manufacturing budgets, travel budgets, and a host of other budgets. Table 9-3 shows a typical budget for a hypothetical food manufacturing company called ULUVIT Foods, Inc. Note that this budget is shown after the end of the quarter in order to illustrate all aspects of it. The first column shows the budgeted amount for each item. The second column shows the actual amount. Column 3 shows the deviation and Column 4 shows the percentage deviation. Budgets similar to this should be constructed at the beginning of *each* quarter (or more frequently) and then analyzed at the end of the quarter before preparing the next quarter's budget.

The analysis of Table 9-3 illustrates well the need for budgets. The net cash flow was only $1,750 less than budgeted. This was only 4 percent off budget and could be considered to be within the acceptable range. But the budget entries show a completely different picture. First, sales were up 11 percent for the quarter, generating $60,000 additional cash inflow. But cost of goods sold was up 17 percent compared to only 11 percent in sales. The increased cost of goods sold ate up all but $4,000 of the increased sales. If the cost of goods sold percentage had stayed at 60 percent as budgeted, this figure would have been only $36,000 instead of $56,000. Something is wrong here.

The additional employee expense is probably justifiable given the increase in sales. The reduction in advertising expense did save $2,000, but one must ask what effect that might have on the next quarter sales. The greatest concern is with "other administrative expenses." What is happening here? Granted, $2,000 isn't much, considering sales of $600,000, but it is a 66 percent increase. Why is that? In fact, if it had not been for the warm spring and the decision to reduce advertising expenses, there would have been a net cash flow of $4,750 less than was budgeted, or 11 percent less than budgeted. Thus, sales went up by 11 percent while cash flow could have declined by 11 percent.

This example demonstrates the need to project cash flows carefully and then to analyze variances from the budget. But in evaluating performance, the use of budgets tells the entrepreneur that there *is* a problem. It does not say *what* the problem is nor *how* to solve the problem. In the example, "cost of goods sold" and "other administrative expenses" are excessive. But it doesn't show why. A budget analysis points the direction to the problem so that the entrepreneur can then take steps to identify specifically what the problem is and solve it.

Ratio Analysis

Financial statement figures are important in themselves as indicators of a venture's health. They become even more useful when compared with similar companies or with other measures within the balance sheet or income statement. There are several sources of industry ratios that can be used for comparative purposes.[4] Some of the common ratios are discussed below.[5] The discussion includes, where appropriate, expected differences in the ratios for the growth ventures as compared with low-growth ventures. No attempt is made to assert the appropriate figure or rule of thumb for the ratios since these vary by industry. Instead, the impacts of high or low ratios are noted.

Current Ratio: Total Current Assets/Total Current Liabilities   This ratio indicates how able a business is to pay current debts using only its current assets. A ratio that is too low suggests that a firm may have difficulty paying creditors. Too high a ratio, however, suggests that the firm is not using its current assets to its best advantage. Growth-oriented ventures will often be low because of frequent short-term borrowing to underwrite growth. This would be especially true in growth-oriented manufacturing firms because of the need to purchase raw material inventory. A consistently low current ratio may indicate the need to add more long-term debt or equity to increase the level of cash.

Quick Ratio: Quick Assets/Current Liabilities   Quick assets are those assets that could be quickly turned into cash. They include cash, accounts receivables, marketable securities, and any other liquid assets. Inventory is not included. This indicates the extent to which the firm could pay current debt without relying on future sales. For service businesses, the quick ratio would be essentially the same as the current ratio. Again, growth ventures will often have low values because of the need for short-term borrowing to finance growth.

Debt to Equity: Total Debt/Total Equity   Dividing total liabilities by total net worth gives the percentage of total funding that is provided by credi-

CHAPTER 9 • Developing Supporting Strategies

245

tors compared with that invested by owners. A low-growth venture, characterized by conservative entrepreneurs who do not desire growth, will have a quite low debt to equity ratio—certainly less than 20 percent and sometimes zero. Some low-growth entrepreneurs simply will not take on debt, preferring to limit growth to internally generated funds. Moderate growth ventures can be characterized by slowly rising debt to equity ratios over time, punctuated by drops as more equity is periodically infused from personal capital or additional sales of stock. Rapid-growth ventures will be characterized by a high debt to equity ratio, possibly 5 to 1 or more, again punctuated by infusions of equity.

Net Income to Equity: Net Income/Total Equity   This ratio measures the owner's, partners', or shareholders' rate of return on investment. This is, of course, one of the major ratios from the perspective of venture capitalists. Naturally, the higher the ratio, the better the position of the company will be. In newly developing growth firms this ratio will initially be quite low or negative with the hope that it will be quite high within a short time. In some biotech research and development firms, several infusions of capital may be required before the return on investment is realized.

Net Income to Net Sales: Net Income/Net Sales   This ratio is a measure of profitability that shows how much profit is derived from every dollar of sales. It measures the operating efficiency of the venture. This figure will vary widely from industry to industry. For example, grocery stores will have only a 1 percent to 2 percent ratio where manufacturing firms may have much higher ratios. It should be kept in mind that the net income to net sales ratio is not the same as net income to total equity. One measures return on sales while the other measures return on investment.

Inventory Turnover: Cost of Goods Sold/Average Inventory   This ratio measures the number of times inventory turns over in one accounting period. Dividing this result into the number of days in the period gives the number of days of inventory in stock. This ratio is valuable for spotting understocking, overstocking, and product obsolescence. This ratio is important for retail firms and especially important for low-growth ventures that may, over time, build up excessive obsolete inventory. This ratio will not be meaningful for service firms or for high-tech firms in their research and development stages.

Accounts Receivable Turnover: Net Credit Sales/Average Accounts Receivable   This ratio measures the time it takes for management to collect for products and services purchased from the venture on credit. The higher the turnover rate, the faster the business is collecting from its customers. Dividing this ratio into 365 days gives the average number of days required to collect receivables. If receivables can be collected faster, the firm will be in better financial health and can pay its own bills faster. The credit management strategy, however, can affect cash flow. A low accounts receivables turnover ratio indicates poor credit management and can put the venture at financial risk. At the same time, being too restrictive in a credit policy can drive away potential customers.

Operating Expense Ratios: Any Operating Expense/Net Sales   The numerator of this set of ratios will be any measurable expense category such as selling, advertising, wages, or depreciation. The value of looking at these is to develop a feel for how efficient the individual aspects of the venture are. This can be especially valuable when trends are analyzed. The ratio in any particular time period may be compared to that of other firms, but the real benefit is to examine how the firm is doing compared with its own past. These ratios can be critical for growth-oriented firms as they can be indicators of control problems as the firm grows. If sales in a growing venture are increasing rapidly but expenses are increasing more rapidly, these ratios will show an increase and an indication of the need for control. In a stable venture deterioration in these ratios can indicate the adding of staff, advertising, or employee benefits with no accompanying increase in sales.

Analyzing the Entire Firm

When considering the ratios discussed above, it is important to consider all the relevant ratios rather than just one or two. These should be tracked over time in order to develop trends for the business. Analyzing the entire venture is especially important for the growth business because of the great demands growth ventures have on cash. Growth ventures are typically net cash users, that is, they tend to use excessive amounts of cash in early years until sales and market share are stabilized. Thus, because of the tenuous nature of the growth firm's financial position and the rapidity of changes, it is very important that the entrepreneur be continuously aware of the firm's financial condition.

Determining the Financial Strategy

The final step in the financial planning process is to determine the financial strategy for the venture. This strategy is, of course, dependent on the entrepreneur's goals and personality as well as the assessment of the firm's condition and the environment surrounding the venture. The strategy should include decisions regarding the amount of financing to be used, the relative amounts of debt and equity, the sources of the funds, and the uses of the funds. The debt/equity mix is perhaps the most important financial strategy decision because of the effect of the decision on the financial condition of the firm. Heavy use of debt allows the entrepreneur to maintain control, but the firm may suffer because of the amount of interest incurred. Restricting funding to equity capital, however, may limit growth and may require sharing profits with others. Internal cash management policies should also be included. For example, the entrepreneur must decide what credit policies will be, the percentage of profits to be retained in the venture rather than passed to the owners, and where short term cash will be invested.

THE HUMAN RESOURCE STRATEGY

One of the areas that is often poorly managed in emerging ventures is the human resource or personnel area. Part of the reason for this is that en-

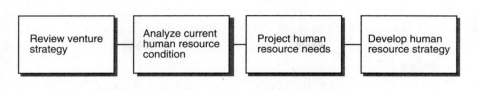

FIGURE 9-5
Human Resource Strategy
Process

trepreneurs often do not develop a **human resource strategy** for their venture. Just as the marketing and financial areas benefit from a carefully delineated strategy, the human resource function should have an objectively analyzed and carefully crafted strategy. It is necessary to develop a strategy and set of policies that can guide the venture's human resource actions over time. The benefit from this is that once human resource guidelines are set for the firm, decisions will be consistent throughout the firm and over time.

Again like the marketing strategy, the human resource strategy must be consistent within the human resource function and between the human resource function and the rest of the venture. For example, the training function must be consistent with the recruiting function. The human resource plans must also be consistent with the venture's overall plans for expansion or new product introductions.

As shown in Figure 9-5, the human resource strategy process begins with a review of the overall strategy. It then moves to an analysis of the current condition of human resources. The third step then is to project needs into the future. Finally, a strategy must be developed to match the needs with capable employees.

Analyzing the Current Condition

The task of analyzing the current human resources condition will depend on the stage of development for the venture as well as other factors. For example, a pre-startup situation will be easily analyzed. A venture that has been in existence for several months will have a much different set of variables to consider. Other things to consider in this analysis include the number of hours each employee works, the problems in communication either internally or with outsiders, errors or defects, the ability of managers to effectively deal with employees, the rate of growth of the company, the skill levels of employees and their ability to accept additional responsibility, the opportunities for personal growth for management and nonmanagement personnel, and satisfaction with wage and salary policies.

It is sometimes more difficult to analyze the human resource area than it is the financial area. The reason is that instead of dealing with dollars, which can be objectively quantified, one is dealing with individual people who have various skills, attitudes, and desires. Analyzing job satisfaction, for example, is difficult because individual employees have vastly different psychological needs and reap different outcomes from the same job. That which satisfies and encourages one employee may cause another employee to be highly dissatisfied. Further, morale is a function of many different factors—the actual dollars received, the amount received compared with others, working conditions, benefit packages, supervisory capabilities, and the general tenor of the venture's culture. These are difficult to quantify, but are critically important for the emerging venture.

Projecting Needs

Once the current condition of the human resources is analyzed, the next step is to forecast the needs for the future. The total number of individuals and types of skills needed must be based on a relationship between projected sales and necessary human resources plus an estimate of those who may leave the firm for one reason or another. A crude estimate is simply to assume that human resource needs in each job category will increase in direct proportion to increases in sales. A more acceptable method would be to study carefully the productivity of personnel and relate that productivity to the projected sales levels. Turnover can be roughly estimated based on industry figures. Promotions should also be considered since a promotion opens up a lower-level position. The following questions can help in the analysis phase if initial evidence suggests the need for additional employees.

Is the New Position Really Needed?

In most growing enterprises, the answer is likely to be yes, but this is not always the case. In some cases, rearranging tasks may solve the management crisis. This could be true if some managers are greatly overworked while others are only slightly overworked. Another situation could be when two or more managers' duties are overlapping. Rearranging duties and responsibilities may spread the work in a better fashion and may also reduce duplication in dealing with customers.

Can Some Tasks Be Contracted Out to Other Firms?

Secretarial help, computer services, accounting, and even personnel record keeping and reporting are all examples of tasks that can be contracted out to others. This is especially true in the new or emerging firm which may have little expertise in some administrative areas. Contracting out the personnel record keeping and reporting is a recent development that is particularly valuable to the small firm. Personnel administration is relatively complex compared to other aspects of the firm, and most entrepreneurs are not trained in that area. Outside firms can do all the records posting, insurance claims, employee taxes, fringe benefit calculation, equal employment opportunity and affirmative action reporting, and payroll deductions and check writing. By contracting out some of the routine tasks, nonmanagement employee costs are saved in addition to possibly negating the need for additional management level staff.

Can Current Employees Be Promoted to Higher Level Positions?

Promoting from within has many advantages. First, current employees may be more knowledgeable than outsiders and, hence, need less training. Second, promoting from within has a powerful motivating force. It not only gives the person being promoted more responsibility and recognition, but it opens up that person's position for someone lower in the organization. Third, promoting from within may well be cheaper than hiring a trained person from outside. Bringing in an outsider may entail a premium salary as an enticement away from the person's current job plus possible relocation expenses. Since the promotion itself is a motivating force for the internal candidate, a premium salary may not be necessary.

There are two disadvantages of the promote-from-within philosophy. First, promoting an internal candidate requires that someone be hired or promoted into the vacant position. Second, bringing someone from outside into the venture brings new ideas to the company. The venture benefits from the different perspectives and knowledge that the outsider brings. The entrepreneur—or staff if the venture is large enough—must carefully calculate both the needs from expansion and the needs from turnover. The total needs of the venture in each job category can then be determined. Once these needs are estimated, the final step of developing an overall human resources strategy is appropriate.

Developing the Human Resource Strategy

The human resource strategy is similar to what some might call human resource *policies*. The difference is that a strategy deals with how the venture competes and operates to achieve its overall objectives, whereas a policy deals more with day-to-day action. Thus, Figure 9-6 illustrates those *strategies* the entrepreneur should consider in order to develop and maintain a dynamic venture team.

The term *venture team* is used here to signify the total employment of personnel for the venture. Entrepreneurial ventures, more so than large businesses, thrive and grow because of the team concept. The employees, whether a half dozen or several hundred, have a sense of identity and camaraderie in the venture. This is the essence of the team concept, and it is as applicable to an entrepreneurial venture as it is to a college football team. The hiring strategy for entrepreneurial firms necessarily considers the team concept.

The strategy for hiring managers deals with determining precisely what managerial team players are necessary and then beginning the process to find them. This is important because entrepreneurial firms will have only a few managers, and those managers must work at full capacity, often sixty to eighty hours a week. Thus, the hiring decision must be made carefully and accurately.

Job descriptions are rare among management personnel, especially in emerging firms. Thought must be given to concerns such as which responsibilities the person will have, how these responsibilities may be shifted from existing managers, what ownership if any will be accorded the new person and at what price, what salary and fringe benefit package will be offered, and what education or experience levels are desired or required.

The strategy must also consider the specifics of the recruiting and hiring process. Advertising the position must be done carefully in order to attract the correct applicant pool. An inappropriately written advertisement may attract a large number of applicants who are clearly not what is desired while other applicants who would be qualified do not apply. The

FIGURE 9-6
Components of a Human
Resource Strategy

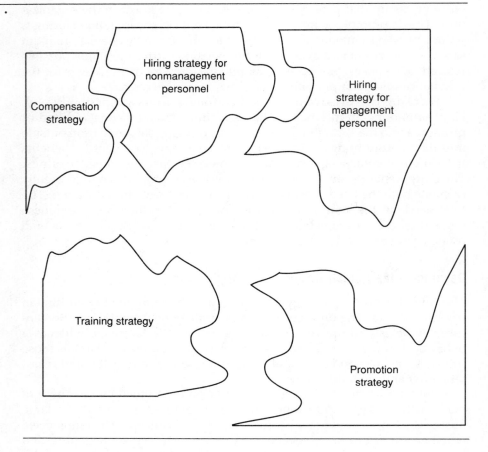

entrepreneur must be concerned that resumes are read carefully, references are checked, and interviews are done thoroughly and within equal employment opportunity guidelines. Particular concern should be given to why the applicant wants the new position and why the old job is not satisfactory. Any doubts that occur should be double-checked through references or other means.

In some industries, firms require their managerial employees to sign noncompete agreements promising not to work for direct competitors if they terminate their employment. These agreements have generally held up in court. Thus, if the strategy focuses on hiring managers away from a competitor, extreme care should be given toward uncovering any such agreement.

The strategy for hiring nonmanagement personnel must consider decisions such as where and how to advertise, the area from which to draw, the experience and education levels required, and the actual hiring process. For example, the strategy should include whether to use public or private employment agencies rather than hiring directly. It should include whether to hire only fully trained and experienced persons or to hire unskilled, entry-level workers who can be paid less but will require more supervision.

The compensation strategy should consider the impact of the wage, salary, and benefit packages on the ease of attracting and maintaining a venture team. For example, paying higher than normal wages may cost more in labor, but should result in lower turnover. Consideration of benefit packages should be done carefully to determine if it does, in fact, have an impact on either recruiting or keeping workers.

Training strategy decisions revolve around who should do the training, how it should be done, and to what extent it should be done. In the majority of smaller ventures, the training consists of on-the-job training. In these cases, someone must be designated as trainer in order for the new employee to receive adequate and consistent training. This task is eased somewhat if the hiring strategy includes hiring previously trained workers.

The promotion strategy should consider whether a promote-from-within strategy will be used, whether promotions require specific skills, education, or experience, and whether promotions in rank or title are independent of position. The important factor here is to remember the relationship between promotion strategies and job satisfaction, morale, and turnover.

The human resource strategy is, of course, critical in any venture. It is especially important in high-growth and high-technology ventures. Chapter 12 will return to the human resource issue as it discusses problems unique to high-growth firms.

DEVELOPING AN ETHICS STRATEGY

Chapter 1 discussed the need for ethics among entrepreneurial ventures. It noted that ethics is especially critical for emerging ventures because of the lack of government interference and the vulnerability of new and small firms if unethical acts are discovered. Attention turns now to the development of an **ethics strategy** that not only guides the other aspects of the strategy, but also serves as an aid to day-to-day decision making.

Areas of Ethical Concerns

Any area of a venture can be the subject of ethical decision making. It is helpful, however, to delineate areas in particular that should be monitored by the entrepreneur to assure that the highest standards of ethics are maintained. Each of the groups listed in Table 9-4 should be viewed as stakeholders of the company. This means that each has some direct or indirect claim on the business. Consumers should be treated honestly, with products, labeling, and advertising being of high quality and value per dollar spent. Employees should be treated as individuals with respect for their individual rights freely given. Suppliers should be dealt with on a peer basis with dealings above board and open. Most highly ethical firms are also good community citizens and recognize the firm's responsibility to contribute to the community's welfare. Ethical or socially responsible firms must keep their investors' best interest in mind regardless of whether they are primary owners, debt lenders, or other investors. Even competitors deserve respect. The venture's owners must not compete unfairly to the detriment of the firm's competitors. Finally, a responsibility to social needs

TABLE 9-4
Areas of Ethical Concerns
SOURCE: Adapted from
"Guidelines for Laureates,"
Illinois Business Hall of Fame,
Western Illinois University,
Macomb, Illinois.

- Responsibility to consumers
- Responsibility to employees
- Responsibility to suppliers
- Responsibility to the community
- Responsibility to investors
- Responsibility to competitors
- Responsibility to society

should be evident. Social needs will be viewed differently by different people. Yet, the ethical entrepreneur should address social needs to the extent possible.

Developing Ethical Philosophies

It is important that overall venture strategies as well as the venture's day-to-day operations exhibit a consistent ethical tone. Thus, there is a need to develop an ethical philosophy that undergirds all other actions. The ethical philosophy will vary from venture to venture. Some entrepreneurs will adopt a philosophy of maintaining only the highest level of ethics possible even if it means forgoing some opportunities for profits. Others will accept a somewhat less strict view that treats customers and other stakeholders well but takes advantage of all opportunities for revenues. Still another may adopt a belief that whatever is legal is acceptable regardless of the consequences.

Developing ethical philosophies and strategies can have both conceptual and pragmatic benefits. Conceptually, the venture benefits by having a tone or culture in which ethics permeates all the decisions made in the venture. Pragmatically, being aware of the need for ethics and social responsibility can pay dividends in the form of venture opportunities.

The Ethical Decision Process

The ethics philosophy and strategy set the ethics tone for the venture much as Walgreen's creed in Chapter 1 set the tone for Walgreens in its developmental phase. The philosophy does not, however, cover every situation. Hence, there is a need for a decision process through which specific situations may be considered. This is equivalent to marketing policies that help in the implementation of the marketing strategies. A seven-step process can be used as a more specific guide to ethical decision making by entrepreneurs (Figure 9-7).

As in making any entrepreneurial decision, facts must be collected first. It is likely that some of the facts will be very objective, some will be subject to interpretation, and some will be missing completely. Seldom are all the facts available and seldom are those facts as objective as desired. Nevertheless, an attempt must be made to gather as many facts as possible.

VENTURE PERSPECTIVE 9-2

. . . .

VENTURE CAPITALISTS AND THE ENVIRONMENT

Environmentally related start-ups are attracting the attention of venture capitalists who are moving away from some of the high-tech ventures of the past. Venture capital firms have invested more than $100 million in such companies recently. Some venture capitalists believe that environment-related ventures will face a higher growth market than electronics in the next few years, buttressed partly by increased government regulation and community awareness.

An example of investment in environmental firms is that of Galson Remediation Corporation of Syracuse, New York.

Two venture capital firms invested a total of $3.5 million in Galson because it has a patented chemical treatment technology to clean up dioxins and PCBs. In another case, a venture capital firm invested $600,000 in Groundwater Technology, Inc., of Norwood, Massachusetts, a pollution-control concern. Its investment had grown to more than $16 million six years later. And $1 million invested in Tetra Technologies, Inc., of Woodlands, Texas, a recycling and waste-treatment concern, is now valued at $6.5 million.

BioTrol, Inc., has developed a microbe that degrades certain

kinds of toxic waste. Bio-Care, Inc., uses benign bacteria to clean drain pipes and grease traps. Mycogen Corporation uses genetic engineering techniques to produce biologically safe pesticides. Each received substantial funding from venture capitalists.

These and other ventures show that meeting the public's needs for a cleaner environment can, in the process, create significant opportunities for new and growing ventures.

SOURCE: Udayan Gupta, "Venture Capitalists Invest In Environmental Concerns," *Wall Street Journal*, April 20, 1990, B2.

Once the facts are in hand and have been analyzed, then the ethical issues involved can be determined. This may take some time and should involve more than one person in order to get a variety of views on the possible ethical impacts. Discussion may begin by asking if this indeed appears to have ethical ramifications. If any person in the group feels even slightly uncomfortable with the situation, then it is safe to say that there may be ethical issues involved. To determine if ethical issues are involved, the decision might be weighed against an established code or creed developed for the venture.

Identification of relevant stakeholders should be in two steps. First, those stakeholders should be identified who are directly involved or affected. These are the primary players in the decision. The second step, however, is to determine if there are any indirectly affected stakeholders. This step is important. Some actions may appear at first to have a very small scope of effects. Only after studying it do the indirect impacts develop. Thus, care should be taken to identify *all* relevant stakeholders.

Notice that step 4 uses the plural form of alternatives. This means that seldom will there be only one alternative. In fact, if there is only one possible alternative, then there is no decision to be made. Even with the straightforward and legal issue of paying taxes, there could still be the decision of paying all taxes now or delaying a portion until later and paying penalties associated with the delay. Thus, as many alternatives as possible should be developed regarding the decision.

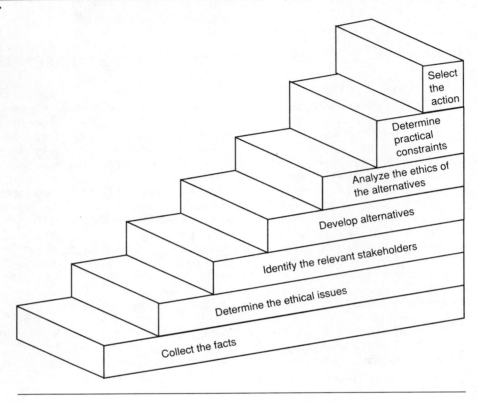

FIGURE 9-7
Steps In An Ethical
Decision-Making Process
SOURCE: Manuel Velasquez
and Norman Bowie, lecture
materials for Arthur Andersen
seminars on teaching
business ethics, Chicago:
Arthur Andersen Corporation.
Used with permission.

The ethics of the alternatives should be carefully determined. This means that each alternative should be weighed against the venture's code or creed and that the stakeholder impacts should be determined for each. This would appear to be a lengthy process although the effort should be reduced with practice.

Step 6 is to determine any practical constraints regarding the proposed alternatives. If a particular action cannot be taken without bankrupting the company, then it probably should be eliminated. Similarly, if an action is desirable, but it could not be implemented in time to solve the problem, then that solution also should be eliminated. Care should be given, however, that alternatives are not eliminated for convenience purposes under the guise of necessity. Thus, resources or time or lack of trained staff or lack of experience could all be practical constraints on a given alternative, but caution must be used to assure that these are truly constraints rather than excuses for elimination of the alternative.

The last step, of course, is to implement the best of the alternatives. In some cases, more than one alternative may be desirable for different reasons. Here, the entrepreneur must simply make a judgment call as to which is the best decision overall. Once the decision is made, then the effects of the decision should be monitored to see if any latent or undiscovered relationships occur.

Adopting an ethical strategy to set the overall tone of the venture and using an ethical decision criteria model helps the entrepreneurial firm in two ways. First, since the tone is set at the outset by the entrepreneur, the ethical stance taken will be reflected in the strategies adopted by the venture. In fact, even the analysis of opportunities will include an ethical dimension if desired. Equally important, the ethical climate of the venture will affect how the strategy is implemented. Thus, both the strategy development and the day-to-day implementation of the strategy are affected by the ethical philosophy developed by the entrepreneur.

. . . .

This chapter has considered the development of supporting strategies for the entrepreneurial venture. In particular, the functional strategies of marketing, finance, and human resources were discussed. Then attention turned to the important topic of the role of ethics in the venture's strategies.

SUMMARY

The marketing strategy delineates the actions necessary to get the venture's products or services to the customer. Included in the strategy should be a product/service strategy, a promotion strategy, a pricing strategy, and a distribution strategy. Important within the promotion strategy is the advertising plan. Throughout the marketing strategy development process, the entrepreneur should consider the need for consistency among the components.

The financial strategy process begins with an analysis of the venture strategy, the firm's current condition, the external situation, and the overall goals of the entrepreneur. The entrepreneur should analyze the venture's condition through budget analysis and ratio analysis. The financial strategy should include the total amount of capital needed, the mix between equity and debt, and the sources of both debt and equity.

Entrepreneurs should develop a human resource strategy that will guide them over time. Like the other functional areas, the human resource strategy process should begin with an analysis of the current venture team along with the plans for the future. The human resource strategy should include a hiring strategy for both management and nonmanagement personnel, a compensation strategy, a training strategy, and a promotion strategy.

Ethics is critically important to the entrepreneur because of the relatively greater freedom a small business has and because of the deleterious effects that an unethical act could have on the venture. The need for an ethics strategy as well as an ethical decision-making process were discussed. It is important that the entrepreneur set an ethical tone or philosophy for the venture.

. . . .

1. Do the product, promotion, pricing, and distribution strategies need to be developed in a particular order?

DISCUSSION QUESTIONS

2. How can an entrepreneur ensure consistency within the four marketing strategies?

3. Why is an advertising budget important?

4. Why are clusters of advertisements more effective than the same amount of advertisements spread out over time?

5. Will the amount of advertising required vary with the type of pricing strategy? If so, how?

6. Suppose you have just launched a firm that makes silk plants. You have the capability to produce large amounts of the plants, and they are well accepted in the marketplace. What is the best way to distribute them (a) within a two-state region and (b) throughout the northeastern and Atlantic Coast states?

7. How do stores such as Kmart and Wal-Mart sell high-quality products at discount prices? Could a small firm do the same? If not, how can the small firm compete?

8. Define consistency in marketing as it relates to a newly launched accounting firm.

9. Consider the financial strategy process. How is it similar to and different from the overall strategic planning process?

10. Discuss the various financial ratios that were discussed in this chapter. Which, if any, are more important for a newly started venture? Is your answer the same for a more established venture?

11. What are the advantages and disadvantages of a high-equity strategy versus a high-debt strategy for a growth venture?

12. Why is it important to consider significant future uses of cash in developing a current financial strategy?

13. What is the difference between a human resource strategy and a human resource policy?

14. What are the ramifications of a hiring strategy to hire only highly trained and experienced workers?

15. Discuss "promote from within." Is it good as a general rule? When would it not be the best strategy?

16. Why do new and emerging firms have more flexibility with regard to their ethical behavior than larger firms?

17. Why is the entrepreneur's ethical influence both so great and so important in the newer venture?

18. This chapter discussed both the need for an ethical strategy and the need for an ethical decision-making process. Why is it important that a venture have both?

EXERCISES

EXERCISE 9-1

Employees of businesses sometimes do unethical acts in order to help the venture make money. Assume you are the owner of a landscaping firm that has grown some but is struggling to make profits. Prepare a memo to your workers (no more than two paragraphs) to explain that ethics are more important than profits.

EXERCISE 9-2

When Donald Burr began People Express Airline in the 1980s, there were only three job classifications, everyone was cross-trained, most employees bought stock in the company, and most worked up to eighty hours a week. And yet, the employees loved it and the airline prospered. (Only after competitors began matching fares and Burr tried to expand via acquisitions did the company get into financial trouble.) Discuss whether Burr's human resource strategy made sense (a) in the beginning and (b) after the venture had grown substantially. You may need to look up the history of People Express to formulate the answer.

EXERCISE 9-3

In Venture Perspective 9-1 Tom Darling and his partners were building their advertising strategy. They figured approximately how much and what kind of advertising they needed. The costs for each medium and campaign were purposely not included. Survey the different media in your community to determine the total cost of the first year's advertising budget.

• •

ENDNOTES

1. Ronni Lundy, "An Education in Ice Cream," *Esquire*, 102, August 1984, 30; Calvin Trillen, "Competitors (Ben & Jerry's Homemade Market Foreclosure Case against Häagen Dazs)," *The New Yorker* 61, July 8, 1985, 31–32.
2. Kathleen J. Kelly and Robert F. Hoel, "The Impact of Size, Color, and Copy Quantity on Yellow Pages Advertising Effectiveness," *Journal of Small Business Management* 29, no. 4 (October 1991): 64–71.
3. Ernest W. Walker and J. William Petty II, *Financial Management of the Small Firm*, 2d ed. (Englewood Cliffs, NJ: Prentice-Hall, 1986), 44.
4. *Dun's Business Month*, published by Dun and Bradstreet, Inc.; *Robert Morris Associates Annual Statement Studies; Standard and Poor's Industrial Surveys; The Almanac of Business and Industrial Financial Ratios; The FTC Quarterly Financial Report*, published by the U.S. government; *Value Line;* and *Business Week*'s "Corporate Scoreboard." Each of these has its advantages and disadvantages and is presented in different ways. See Charles H. Gibson and Patricia A. Frishkoff, *Financial Statement Analysis: Using Financial Accounting Information*, 2d ed. (Boston, MA: Kent Publishing Company, 1983), 100–110.
5. Adapted from *Small Business Reporter: Understanding Financial Statements* (San Francisco, CA: Bank of America, 1987).

◆ Conveniesse, Inc. ◆

Functional Plans

With the development of the Conveniesse site moving along on schedule, Yolanda suggested to Jason and Sarah that the three of them hold their next planning meeting at her apartment in New York. They could work Saturday during the day in her home office, putting together the strategic plan. She would fix dinner for them and then they could take in a play. Then they could work more on Sunday if needed. After they arrived, Yolanda handed each of them a laptop computer she had brought home from the office. Jason's eyes lit up.

"Laptops!" he exclaimed. "Laptop computers!"

"Yes, Jason," Yolanda replied, somewhat annoyed. "Those are indeed laptop computers."

"I know what a laptop computer is," Jason said. "I own one, but I forgot to bring it with me. Now if I had just arrived here for a meeting, on a weekend, away from any home office branches, and if I really needed one. . ."

"You would rent one!" Yolanda exclaimed with her annoyance turning to excitement.

Sarah had not caught on yet. "So?"

"*Where* would you rent one? At night or on a Saturday?" prodded Jason.

Sarah suddenly caught on. "Oh, perhaps at a Conveniesse store!"

They began a lively discussion about computers regarding what kinds, how many different word processors or spreadsheet programs they would need, if chart-making capacities and modems would be appealing, what printers would be good, and what they should charge. This discussion continued until Yolanda reminded them why they were really together today.

Settling down to work on their strategic plan, which they laughingly dubbed "The Conveniesse Way," the three made relatively short work of the overall strategy, their idea of the competition, and what they saw as key strengths, including the fax, the copier, the automated teller machine (ATM), and the rentable laptops. Then Sarah suggested that they needed more detail.

"I'm not talking now about specific detail like who cleans up at night. But bigger things like how much and what kind of advertising are we going to do? What will be our pricing policy? How do *we* operate as a team once the thing gets going? Suppose we want to expand? If we need money again, how much and what kind? Even things like what kind of people are we going to hire to work for us? I don't want an unskilled person renting out those laptops. How about a security policy? What about insurance? Oh, and most important—how are we going to split up all our earnings? And. . ."

"Let me take the lead on this," Yolanda interrupted. "this was my life before my latest promotion. I lived and breathed this stuff. Now I don't mean decisions like who to hire or how much security, but taking an overall product marketing plan and breaking it down into workable parts that nonmanagement people could relate to."

Bringing up the relevant data on her computer, Yolanda continued. "What I have here is a number of formats, complete with checklists and key questions to ask regarding each chosen area. Some of these aren't germane to our specific venture, but a number of them are. We can also do some brainstorming and develop our own set of questions that we can then come back to. See this section on goals? We always insisted that managers, distributors, and anyone else who had anything at all to do with our products have both current and long-range goals. I thought our whole plan for development would be a lot easier if we could use these models."

Using the guides, the three carefully worked through each of the functional strategy areas. The guides did not give them concrete answers, but they did give them suggestions, and they could also check them against industry norms that came with a financial package Yolanda had purchased. They used the financials that the consultant had helped them with earlier and adjusted them as they felt necessary based on industry norms and/or other information they had obtained since the financial plan was done.

The rest of that day and part of the following were spent building the plan based on the formats Yolanda provided. Once they had completed all the entries and had written all the narrative that they thought was needed, they put the whole thing into a format, saved it on a disk, and ran a copy on Yolanda's laser printer. They each read their copies, taking notes on changes they thought should be made. Once this was done, they made the adjustments and printed final copies.

"This definitely will be useful," Sarah said as they put their copies in binders. "It will help keep us on track."

"More than that," added Yolanda, "It will give us a baseline for future reference. And it will be a way to keep us from responding from the hip every time somebody comes up with a new idea."

"The part I liked best was the process," said Jason. "It makes all these functional strategies fit together as a unified whole."

With the task behind them, Jason and Sarah returned to Buffalo to begin the final tasks for the opening. The developer had indicated that they would vacate the premises approximately a week later, giving the Conveniesse group approximately three weeks to remodel the store, bring in the equipment, and stock the shelves. They decided to hire two assistant managers from local area convenience store branches and train them in "the Conveniesse way." They also hired two individuals who would each serve as combination security guard and greeter for two eight-hour shifts that together covered the sixteen hours a day that the store would be open.

Assignment

Using what you wrote from last chapter's assignment, finish your version of the Conveniesse strategic plan. Use the format from Chapter 4, starting with 4–B. Include what you think would be appropriate goals for the next one year and five years. Then add the financials from the financial plan to the strategic plan, making any changes you think are necessary.

10 Franchising

LEARNING OBJECTIVES

After studying this chapter, you should be aware of the following:

1. The significance of franchising in the economy
2. The advantages of franchising from the viewpoint of both the franchisor and the franchisee
3. The disadvantages of franchising from both the franchisor's and franchisee's perspective
4. The need to study a franchise carefully before purchasing one
5. The methods to use in studying a franchise
6. The need to study the franchisee agreement carefully
7. The nature of the franchise triad

KEY TERMS

Franchise   Franchise opportunity
Franchisor   Franchise agreement
Franchisee   Franchise triad

CONSIDER THIS!

- All franchises are not alike.
- Franchises are a blend of small business and big business.
- McDonald's is *not* a typical franchise.
- Some franchises may cost several hundred thousand dollars plus a royalty fee.
- Franchising is not for everyone.
- Some opportunities can be better tapped without a franchise.

Franchising as it is known today, is a unique approach to business that originated in the United States and has spread throughout the world. Approximately 35 percent of all retail sales in the United States are attributed to franchised businesses. Sales of goods and services by all franchise companies reached $716 billion in 1990. There are about 542,000 franchised units in the United States employing more than seven million people full time or part time.[1] Franchising has been such a success for some firms that they have become giants within their respective industries. Companies such as McDonald's, Holiday Inn, and Hertz Rent A Car have become distinct leaders, comparable in scope of operation and sales volume to some traditional giants of American business.

While survival rates among businesses are always questionable due to the difficulty in reaching those who failed, the survival figures for

ENTREPRENEURIAL PROFILE

FRED DELUCA
Subways, Inc.

Being rated the number one franchise by *Entrepreneur* magazine is an honor any company would want to add to its list of achievements, at least **once** in a lifetime. But how many companies can claim to have received this honor *four* times?

In 1965 Fred Deluca began a submarine sandwich shop called Pete's Submarines. He and his partner realized that the name was often confused with a competitor's, "Pizza Marines," so the name was changed to Pete's Subways and then to Subway Sandwiches. The initial move into franchising began in 1974.

Growth of the company has been phenomenal and has surpassed even Deluca's predictions. He had hoped to have five thousand stores open by 1994; he reached that goal in 1990. His new goal is to have eight thousand stores open

by 1995, and he is looking toward matching McDonald's on a store-for-store basis. As of April 1992, Subway had 5,861 stores open in the United States and 296 in Canada. Stores are now open in twelve foreign countries including South Korea, and the most recent one opened in Ireland in May 1992. The total number of stores now exceeds 6,500. This puts Subway thousands of stores ahead of its nearest competitor in the sandwich market, giving it almost 80 percent of the market.

Wanting to expand his interests, Deluca bought a stake in Cajun Joe's in 1989. Cajun Joe's sells premium roasted and spicy or mild fried chicken, gumbo, black-eyed peas, fried okra, and rice pilaf. Many of the Subway franchisees are picking up the Cajun Joe's franchise in addition to the sandwich store. There were thirteen Cajun Joe's when Deluca bought into it. By January 1991 there were ninety-three open in twenty-nine states and 297 in development. This put Cajun Joe's in the top ten chicken franchises and 291st overall in *Entrepreneur*'s top 500. Deluca has also started franchising We Care Hair, a hair salon for inexpensive, standardized hairstyling.

SOURCE: Subway Sandwiches and Salads, Milford, CT. Used with permission. Photo courtesy of Subway Sandwiches.

franchises are impressive. Robert Bond suggests that independent businesses show a first year survival rate of 62 per cent and a five year rate of 23 per cent. Franchises, however, have a first year survival rate of 97 per cent and a five year rate of 92 per cent.[2] Because of these significant statistics, franchising is an appealing method of entering a business.

This chapter covers the nature of franchises and the advantages and disadvantages of franchising from both the franchisee and the franchisor viewpoints. It explains what the entrepreneur needs to consider in planning a venture's strategy and determining whether a franchise is the best strategy for the situation.

This chapter is an adaptation of excerpts from chapters 1 and 2 of Robert Justis and Richard Judd, *Franchising*, (Cincinnati, OH: South-Western Publishing Co., 1989). Used with permission.

FRANCHISING DEFINED

A **franchise** may be defined as a business opportunity whereby the owner (producer or distributor) of a service or a trademarked product grants exclusive rights to an individual for the local distribution and/or sale of the service or product, and in return receives a payment or royalty and conformance to quality standards. The individual or business granting the business rights is called the **franchisor,** and the individual or business granted the right to operate in accordance with the chosen method to produce or sell the product or service is called the **franchisee.**

The United States Department of Commerce provides a broader definition: "Franchising is a method of doing business by which a franchisee is granted the right to engage in offering, selling, or distributing goods or services under a marketing format which is designed by the franchisor. The franchisor permits the franchisee to use the franchisor's trademark, name and advertising."[3]

Franchising can be approached from the perspective of both the franchisor and the franchisee. For a franchisor, franchising allows the expansion of a proven concept and method of operation from a single unit to a large operation with multiple locations and multiple product or service offerings. The franchisee has the opportunity to use proven methods of operation, large-scale, high-impact advertising, recognized brands or trademarks, and continuing management and technical assistance. These advantages are not available to the independent entrepreneur who may be selling the same product or service.

A franchisor uses the franchisee's community goodwill, financial equity, business location, and personal drive and motivation to expand the franchised business. The franchisee uses the franchisor's brand or trademark, proven methods of operation, marketing resources, and technical advice to enter, develop, and maintain consumer demand, and ultimately to succeed as an entrepreneur within the community. The franchisee is often given an opportunity to be part of a turnkey operation (site, building, architecture, equipment, work flow, and customer service plans completely determined and installed by the franchisor), with limited capital and prior experience, while having a very good chance of success.

This business arrangement or **franchise opportunity** has three major components: (1) a trademark and/or logo, (2) the use of a product or service following a marketing plan, and (3) a payment or royalty fee. These components constitute the essence of what is generally referred to as a franchise, whether the arrangement happens to be in auto and truck sales, convenience food stores, restaurants, cleaning services, gasoline retailing, or a host of other products and services.

TYPES OF FRANCHISING

In the United States, there are two major types of franchising: product-and-trade-name franchising and business-format franchising. Product-and-trade-name franchising has evolved from suppliers making sales contracts with dealers to buy or sell certain products or product lines. In this relationship, the dealer acquires the trade name, trademark, and/or product from the supplier. The dealer (franchisee) identifies with the supplier (franchisor) through the product line. Historically, this approach to franchising has consisted of distribution from a single supplier (or manufacturer) to a large number of dealers either directly or through regional supply centers. An objective of the supplier is to have a dealer (or dealership) in each community or area to provide the product to all potential customers within the geographic area. This franchising approach has been used in the auto and truck, soft drink, tire, and gasoline service industries.

Product-and-trade-name franchising accounted for about 71 percent of all franchised sales in 1987, or approximately $420 billion.[4] This approach to franchising appears to be in the late maturity phase of its life cycle. The number of new franchisees entering this type of franchise relationship has decreased over the past ten years. The total number of gasoline stations, for example, has been in steady decline. The number of automobile and truck dealerships, as well as soft drink bottlers and distributors, has also gradually declined. In 1987 there were approximately 146,000 franchised business units under the product-and-trade-name approach, a decrease of about 31 percent from a decade earlier.[5] However, even though the number of units has declined, total sales volume remains impressive.

Business-format franchising is concerned with the format or operations procedures to be used by a franchisee in providing the franchisor's product or service line to the customer. Business-format franchising has been responsible for the tremendous growth in franchising since the 1950s. This approach to franchising has fostered rapid expansion in the restaurant, food service, hotel/motel, printing, retailing, and real estate sectors of our economy (Table 10-1). Most new franchise agreements today are of the

TABLE 10-1

Franchises by Industry
Group

SOURCE: *Franchising in the
Economy, 1988–1990,* IFA
Educational Foundation &
Horwath International, 1990.

Automotive Products & Services	38,561
Auto/Truck/Trailer Rental	10,613
Business Aids & Services	42,734
Convenience Stores	17,467
Construction/Home Improvement	28,270
Educational Products/Services	13,265
Employment Services	7,552
Hotels/Motels/Campgrounds	11,103
Laundry/Drycleaning	2,629
Miscellaneous	8,402
Real Estate	16,995
Recreation/Entertainment/Travel	10,344
Rental Services	3,358
Restaurants	102,135
Retailing—Food	25,374
Total	392,854

business-format type. The number of franchised units in operation that use this approach to franchising increased to more than 352,000 in 1987 and almost 393,000 in 1990.[6]

In general, the types of products or services distributed under the business-format approach are in growing industries. The number of new franchisees entering these types of businesses is increasing and sales volume continues to expand.

FRANCHISING BASICS

Franchising has been a successful means of operating a business for several reasons. Two primary reasons are (1) the tremendous preparation a franchisee undertakes before opening an outlet and (2) the degree of personal involvement brought to the business activities by both the franchisee and the franchisor. The greatest difference between starting a franchised business venture and opening an independent business lies in the extensive training and preparation provided to the franchisee before the opening of an outlet. A franchisee is taught how to plan, start, operate, and control all of the functions of the business.

The franchisor will generally grant the franchisee limited use of the trademark or trade name and the system (business format) in return for a royalty fee. The franchisee receives training, guidance, and preparation to use trade secrets, operational procedures and practices, and system-wide promotions to develop and maintain a profitable franchised business. The initial training of the franchisee and any employees of the franchised unit is essential to the successful continuation of the business.

For example, Orange Julius allowed its franchisees to use its name, trademark, and logo, and to sell special drink products in return for a royalty fee of 5 percent of gross sales, plus an additional advertising fee of 1 percent of gross sales. In addition, most of the leases or outlet locations are controlled by the franchisor—Orange Julius—and subleased back to the franchisee.

Another example is First Interstate Bancorp of California, with franchises that have converted from independent institutions to part of the First Interstate banking network. The local ownership and equity are maintained by the franchised bank, but the name and logo of First Interstate Bancorp, plus the basic services including automatic teller machines and other financial services, are controlled by the franchisor, First Interstate Bancorp. In return for this banking franchise, the local bank pays First Interstate Bancorp a fee based on increased interest income. It is important to note that use of the trade name and the financial services system constitute the "value added" so that both parties achieve success as a franchise system.

The use of the franchise system generally includes the product or service sold by the franchise. In the automotive industry, the trademarked automobile is readily seen as the greatest value that the franchisor provides to the franchisee. Gasoline stations and fast-food restaurants, however, often see advertising as the greatest value added by the franchisor to the franchisee.

ADVANTAGES AND DISADVANTAGES OF FRANCHISING

There are many success stories in franchising. McDonald's, Singer Sewing Machine, General Motors, Coca Cola, Kentucky Fried Chicken, Midas, Century 21, Wendy's, and Holiday Inn provide visible examples of large, successful franchised businesses. Increasingly, other types of businesses such as financial institutions are seeking growth through franchising. First Interstate Bancorp (Los Angeles, California) is franchising banks throughout the United States to build financial strength and expand market share. Doctors, lawyers, dentists, accountants, and opticians are also developing franchise systems, some of which already have multi-state markets. A carefully designed and operated franchise system minimizes risk for the franchisee and the franchisor. The benefits to be gained from a successful franchising chain are enormous.

Advantages to the Franchisee

The franchisee gains a number of potential advantages from being involved in a franchising relationship. Some of these have been mentioned briefly before. The following paragraphs elaborate on these plus others.

Established Product or Service

The major advantage to the franchisee, as previously discussed, is that the franchisee enters a business that has an established, highly marketed product or service name. Consumers are already aware of the name and reputation of the product or service the franchisee will be offering. This advantage is assured to the franchisee by the fact that every year large franchisors spend millions of advertising dollars to keep the public aware of their products or services. Such franchisors will generally spend a large portion of their advertising budget on national campaigns through television commercials and full-page advertisements in popular magazines. If a franchise system deals with a specialty product, as Snap-On Tools does, the most effective advertising may be through trade publications targeted at specific markets such as home repair buffs or auto mechanics.

Technical and Managerial Assistance

A second major advantage to the franchisee is the technical and managerial assistance provided by the franchisor. The franchisee benefits from the accumulated experience and knowledge of the franchising organization. Franchisors provide the instruction necessary to operate a franchised unit, including on-the-job training in a pilot store. Once operating the unit, the franchisee receives assistance in managing day-to-day operations as well as advice for dealing with crisis situations. Therefore, a person can enter business without prior experience in that particular field because the franchisor will supply the pilot training needed to develop experience and will provide follow-up assistance once the franchised unit has begun operations.

Most business consultants would warn a potential entrepreneur not to attempt a business venture in an unfamiliar field. Franchising provides the opportunity to do exactly that and be successful. In fact, some franchisors *prefer* franchisees who have no prior experience in their particular business field. The franchisor can then train the new franchisee in the methods and procedures of the franchising company, and there will be little or nothing to be unlearned and no bad habits to break. Some franchisors are looking not for people who know the industry but for those who are motivated and willing to follow instructions.

In addition to managerial guidance, the franchisee will receive technical assistance from the franchisor. Technical assistance often includes location and site selection, store layout and design, store remodeling (if the franchisee is converting an existing site), inventory control and suggested stock purchases, equipment and fixture purchasing, and the grand opening of the store. It should be noted that although many franchisors provide these specific services, some provide only selected types of assistance. The types of technical assistance provided are usually what the franchisor has found to be absolutely essential for helping the franchisee to be successful. A franchisee should therefore realize that a full range of technical assistance is not always part of the franchising package.

Quality-Control Standards

A third major advantage to the franchisee concerns the quality-control standards imposed by the franchisor upon the franchisee. Properly administered and controlled, such standards help the franchise to achieve constructive, positive results by ensuring product or service uniformity throughout the franchise system. By setting and maintaining high standards, a franchisor does the franchisee a genuine service. Often franchisees appreciate having standard methods of operation and product or service delivery. If the reason for quality standards being maintained is clearly understood, the franchisee will learn what operations and performance are necessary to be a success. Further, standards of quality are vital in presenting a consistent patronage image, ensuring return business, maintaining employee morale and pride in work, and instilling in employees the value of teamwork.

Why would a franchisee want to continually have to meet standards imposed by someone else? As long as the quality standards are assessed and maintained in a benevolent authoritative manner, the standards serve both franchisor and franchisee. For example, in franchised restaurants, if franchisees courteously and efficiently serve an appealing meal in an attractive and comfortable setting, they have a better chance to attract and maintain a large, loyal clientele, which clearly benefits the franchisor as well.

Less Operating Capital

The fourth major advantage is that in many cases an entrepreneur can open a franchised business with less cash than if an independent venture were started. Often, a franchisee can start with considerably less operating capital because the business may not require as much inventory as a comparable non-franchised business. The knowledge and experience of the franchisor concerning how much stock is needed and when to reorder can dramatically reduce the potential for aging of stock, waste or spoilage of perishables, and unprofitable storage of low-demand items. Also, a new franchisee may be able to receive some financial assistance from the franchisor or from the franchisor's financial sources. Other specifics associated with a new venture, such as having access to existing architectural drawings for the store and knowing how best to use floor space for the product or service, can save the franchisee countless hours and dollars.

Other facets of this advantage can be realized once the business is in operation. A franchisee can expect to share in certain collateral benefits, such as business insurance and health insurance that, because of the group buying power of the parent company, are often less expensive than the same coverage sought independently. A franchisee can also expect to have a higher profit margin than a comparable independent business owner because of group purchasing power and other benefits of associating with the franchisor. This, of course, returns cash to the franchisee.

Opportunities for Growth

A fifth advantage to the franchisee concerns growth opportunities for operating the territorial franchises. The growth opportunities may come either from negotiating a territorial franchise or from the availability of additional single-unit franchises. A territorial franchise guarantees that there will be no competition from the same franchisor within the specified geographic boundaries. A territorial franchisee may sub-franchise or license other persons to operate stores within the allotted area. Even in the case of single-unit franchisees, sometimes called operating franchisees, additional units can often be added either within the local geographical area or in other areas. Existing franchisees often have a chance at adding units as other franchisees decide to retire or sell their units. Some franchisees own a number of units in one or more areas and achieve much of their own growth through opening more units.

Accompanying all of these advantages is the advice and assistance available from the franchisor that the franchisee could not have gained without years of experience in the field. This opportunity to benefit from another's experience—to learn from someone else's mistakes—is a primary advantage of entering a franchising relationship.

However, these five advantages have to be tempered with a disclaimer since they may not accrue to every franchisee. What might be a decided advantage to one could be inconsequential to another. Therefore, the advantages and disadvantages for an individual should be considered in relation to the conditions surrounding a particular franchising opportunity.

Advantages for the Franchisor

Just as there are major advantages for the potential franchisee to enter a relationship with a franchisor, there are significant advantages for the franchisor. Even though the franchisor appears to be the major player of the two, the franchisor simply cannot achieve the amount of growth alone that can be gained through the franchise relationship. Thus, it is important to consider the advantages of franchising from the franchisor's viewpoint.

Expansion

Perhaps the single greatest reason for an entrepreneur to create a franchising chain is to allow a business to expand with limited capital, limited risk, and limited equity investment. A franchisor does not have to spend large sums of money or incur major debt to expand the business into new locations. Franchisors can authorize and then place franchised operations in selected areas gradually or they can choose to develop business locations throughout a region or country. A franchised company requires few managers and therefore has a lower staff payroll and fewer staff problems. This provides a greater likelihood of effective monitoring and control of company operations. Also, a franchisor may find potential investors willing to buy into the franchised company if the company is seen to promise continuing profitability. Similarly, persons with little or no experience in the franchisor's business field may be willing to buy a franchise as a potentially profitable investment. Thus, franchising can attract capital through direct investment in the parent company or through the sale of franchises to be used for expansion of the franchise system.

A related advantage is that the franchising approach provides an opportunity for the parent company to expand into geographic areas that otherwise might not be likely locations for expansion. When a franchised company contracts with a franchisee within a particular community, that franchisee may be able to acquire a commercial site that the parent company would be unable to acquire. Communities may be more willing to work with local entrepreneurs than with a remote corporation. Therefore, zoning and other local regulations may be more easily obtained by franchisees than by a large corporation from another city.

Expanding through franchising also simplifies the management structure and reporting requirements associated with expansion. Significant growth by a traditional corporation requires the formation of a sizable management structure to develop, implement, monitor, and control the enhanced level of operations. The capacity of the firm's management to control the business activity may not be sufficient to keep pace with the growth of the corporation itself. In contrast, rapid expansion through a franchising network enables the franchisor to devote more time to operational planning, market analysis and assessment, quality control, and strategies for improving the franchise system itself.

Motivation

A major advantage of franchising as opposed to expanding company-owned outlets is that franchisees are generally more highly motivated than company-employed managers. When a franchised unit is operated by an owner rather than a company-employed manager, that unit will usually benefit from the owner's motivation, self-direction, and personal interest in the success of that operation. In addition, the franchisee is often a respected and influential member of the local community, which may result in greater community support of the venture.

Bulk Purchasing

A further advantage exists for franchisors in businesses that require inventory of parts, completed units for sale, and supplies or packaging associated with the production or sale of the product. Economies of scale in purchasing can be achieved more rapidly by a company choosing franchising compared with a company that expands through company-owned units. This is because the total number of units increases much faster, giving the parent company more purchasing power because of the additional volume.

Shared Advertising

In typical franchise relationships, the franchisee pays an advertising fee of 1 percent or 2 percent of sales to the franchisor in addition to the royalty fee. This is then combined with the franchisor's commitment to advertising in order to provide a greater financial investment in advertising. This combined amount is sufficient in most cases to offer regional or national advertising. This provides economies of scale since a single ad can typically be run in all market areas. If the expansion were through company-owned units only, the parent company would have to underwrite all the cost of advertising for the entire chain. Since more capital would have been spent in the operation of the units, less would be available for advertising purposes.

Disadvantages for the Franchisee

Most franchising agreements work well for both the franchisor and the franchisee. The franchise agreement is meant to develop a strong relationship between these two mutually bound profit seekers. The franchising approach helps both to realize profits and to develop a healthy and prosperous business life. However, there are some disadvantages to the franchisee that can be associated with the franchising relationship.

Failed Expectations

The franchisor's business expertise, experience, selling methods, trademark, and advertising typify what a franchisee implicitly seeks to acquire. Because of such assistance, the franchisee sees value in the franchisee-franchisor relationship. Without such assistance, there would be very little reason for a prospective business owner to enter a franchising agreement. But if a franchisor's sales practices mislead a potential franchisee about what will be received from the franchisor, the franchisee's expectations will not be met. Misleading or fraudulent sales practices can actually victimize some potential franchisees.

Franchises are promoted through newspapers, magazines, trade conventions, telegrams, and even phone calls from franchised companies. Some prospective franchisees fail to carefully read the "fine print" or consult an attorney and as a result have little or no understanding of the legal

Franchise	Franchise Fee	Royalty	Advertising
Tuffy Service Center	$18,500	5%	5%
PIP Printing	40,000	6–8	1
Mr. Donut	25,000	4.9	0.5
T. J. Cinnamons	25,000	5	2
TCBY	20,000	4	3
Kentucky Fried Chicken	20,000	4	4.5
Nutri/System	13,000–60,000	7	0
Century 21	13,500–25,000	6	2

TABLE 10-2

Selected Franchise, Royalty, and Advertising Fees

SOURCE: Robert E. Bond and Christopher E. Bond, *The Source Book of Franchise Opportunities* (Homewood, IL: 1991).

and practical implications of the agreement. What the franchisor will provide is written in the franchising agreement, not in the sales literature associated with the agreement. Since these agreements can be rather lengthy and are often in small print, some prospective franchisees truly do not understand what they are about to agree to legally.

Royalty Fees

A major cost of franchising for the franchisee is the royalty fee. Most franchisors have a royalty fee and an advertising fee. The royalty fee ranges from 3 percent to 6 percent and the advertising fee, if there is one, can go up to 5 percent. Thus, the total fee for royalty and advertising can be as high as 10 percent of sales. This is, of course, in addition to the franchise fee itself.

Overdependence

A second potential disadvantage to the franchisee concerns the franchisor-franchisee relationship. The relationship may prove to be detrimental if a franchisee develops a problem of *overdependence* on the franchisor. A franchisee can become too dependent on the advice of the franchisor to address operations, crises, changing market conditions, pricing strategy, or promotions, and so may fail to apply common sense and knowledge of local customers and market conditions. For example, price discounting can make sense only if the local market conditions warrant such a move.

A situation involving a franchisor of auto parts illustrates this disadvantage. The franchisor has a policy of "no price discounting" if possible to maintain a uniform pricing structure across the franchised organization's outlets. A franchisee in a large city in the Southwest failed to take note of the phrase "if possible" and so lost an opportunity to substantially increase volume by attracting the regular business of an auto repair and service center with seventeen locations. The franchisee could have obtained a contract with the repair center if he had been willing to adjust the bid downward only two-tenths of 1 percent. In this case, the franchisor rightfully scolded the franchisee for not using common sense. A fairly knowledgeable businessperson knows that the guarantee of a large volume of business is a solid reason for price discounting.

Restrictions on Freedom of Ownership

Another potential disadvantage for the franchisee is that the franchising contract may contain restrictions or requirements that an independent businessperson would not have to satisfy. For example, territorial restrictions imposed by the franchisor may limit the number of potential customer contacts a franchisee might seek. Territories may overlap or be inequitably determined by a franchisor. The franchisee might also be required to offer a particular product or service that would not be offered if the venture were independent. Further, a franchisee may believe that some of the franchisor's advertising or promotions are impractical given local market conditions or that inappropriate products are targeted for heavy promotion.

Termination of Agreement

The next major disadvantage concerns a franchisee's decision to terminate the franchising relationship as a result of perceived or real differences with the franchisor. Lack of cooperation from the franchisor can make it difficult to sell the business to a prospective buyer or to simply dissolve the business entirely. Virtually every franchising agreement contains provisions concerning the franchisee's transfer rights, termination and renewal of the agreement, and a covenant not to compete. Any one or all three of these provisions could be invoked by the franchisor if the franchisee fails to heed all the provisions of the franchising agreement.

Performance of Other Franchisees

Perhaps the least-considered potential disadvantage to the franchisee is the effect that lackluster performance by other franchisees can have on one's own business. If the franchisor becomes lax in managing the franchise system or does not enforce the quality standards imposed throughout the network, the poor performance of some in the franchise network can affect the sales of others. Usually, a customer of a multi-unit franchised company will tend to blame the entire franchise and not the single operating unit for poor service or low quality. As a franchising adage goes, a cold cup of coffee at one location will lose customers for the other locations.

In summary, the franchisee must determine whether the advantages of the franchisor's training, operations manuals, blueprints, and products and services outweigh the disadvantages always present in working with a parent company. The franchisee needs to weigh carefully the possible advantages against the disadvantages while, at the same time, analyzing the potential profitability of the business to determine the willingness to enter into a franchise agreement. Even though the franchisee owns the business, certain standards and performance quotas will be established and demanded by the franchisor to ensure that the franchise system will be profitable and successful in the competitive business environment. Ultimately, the decision to enter the franchising field always rests with the prospective franchisee. Even though there are disadvantages, in most cases, the advantages tend to outweigh the disadvantages.

Disadvantages to the Franchisor

Franchising is by no means a miraculous or problem-free solution to a distribution problem. The idea of using money belonging to other individuals to finance the major part of a business expansion is no doubt exciting, but the application of that idea can be fraught with difficulty. The foremost problem or challenge is how to maintain control of the expanding franchise system and oversee the general operations of each business. In addition, a franchisee may in time re-evaluate the franchising relationship and come to the conclusion that the particular business unit would be better off without the franchisor. This particular disadvantage of franchising, as well as others, is discussed below.

Company-Owned versus Franchised Units

Expanding operations by establishing company-owned units has several clear advantages over expanding by franchising. A parent company, or owner, has more control over units the company owns, can institute changes in policy and procedures more readily, can change company mission and market strategy more quickly and perhaps more effectively, and can test out new products or processes with less time and paperwork. Also, since the company controls the outlets by virtue of ownership, the system of reporting—that is, the managerial monitoring and control of the operating units—should be more efficient and effective because the company chain is set up as a hierarchy of managerial authority. The owner not only establishes company strategies and operating policies but is also assured of the implementation of these strategies. Those responsible for carrying out the operations of a company-owned retail outlet are employees of the company, not independent business owners. Further, regardless of whether the parent company chooses to expand through company-owned outlets or through franchising, it will need to offer basically the same services from the home office. These services include sales promotion, marketing research, accounting and information systems, and a field sales department or unit.

Two other significant points tend to favor the company-owned approach over the franchising approach to expansion. First, a franchisee might typically expect to recover the initial investment in perhaps two to three years. That is a 33.3 percent to 50 percent return on investment to the franchisee. This means that the franchisor has effectively lost out on making this profit since the money necessary for expansion could be gained more cheaply by dealing directly with equity investors or obtaining loans from financial institutions. Second, there can be some legal advantages to a company-owned, fully integrated operation. Integrated chains of stores such as Wal-Mart Stores and May Company, which owns Famous Barr and Venture Stores, have become quite successful without franchising. According to Charles Vaughn, "Integrated chains do not so often come under antitrust fire, class actions suits, and other legal attacks."[7] Litigation can drag on for so long and become so costly that a business owner considering franchising could be scared off for the legal reason alone.

Franchisor-Franchisee Problems

Within the franchisor-franchisee relationship, there are three categories of potential disadvantage for the franchisor. These are problems of recruitment, communication, and freedom.

Recruitment   The recruitment problem concerns the difficulty of finding promising franchisees. While there are many who seek franchising as a means to enter business, most lack the experience or motivation and many do not have the proper capital backing they will need to become successful franchisees. In addition, prospective franchisees may not fully realize the amount of time, work, and responsibility required to own and operate an ongoing franchised business.

Communication   As in any business relationship, communication problems can arise. The franchise agreement should be well written in clear language in order to minimize difficulties and misunderstandings. This is particularly true in regard to royalty and other fee payment formulas. Most franchisees pay fees to the franchisor on the basis of the franchised unit's gross income. Some franchisees may have a difference of opinion as to what constitutes "gross income," or may be reluctant to disclose gross income figures to the franchisor. For this reason it is important that the formula for determining any fees or royalties be clearly stated in the written franchising agreement and understood by both franchisor and franchisee. When such understandings exist, the likelihood of resentments based on unclear language or personal intent can be minimized.

Communication problems can also arise between the field office staff and the individual franchisees. The franchisor's staff is available to assist as well as monitor performance of franchisees. Both parties play an important part in the successful delivery of the product or service through the franchised company network. In any organizational arrangement, however, misunderstandings, personality differences, and political maneuverings can blunt the effectiveness of the franchising system to deliver that product or service. This frequently happens after the franchise has been in operation for a while. The franchisee becomes more adept at running the venture and eventually concludes that the franchisor is no longer needed. As a result, the franchisee communicates less frequently with the franchisor's staff and tends to resist disclosing information about the franchised unit's operation. Each party to the franchising agreement should operate within the proper boundaries of the agreement, the laws governing business transactions, and professional codes of ethics. When those involved in continuing business transactions deal with one another openly, honestly, and professionally, communication problems will occur less frequently.

Loss of Freedom   The third potential relationship problem concerns the franchisor's loss of freedom as new franchisees become part of the franchise system. Independent businesspersons can easily make decisions and change policies within their organizations. But once a franchise system is developed, the franchisor or parent company must get permission (often negotiated individually) from franchisees to introduce new products, to add or eliminate services, or to change operating policies. Thus, the franchisor stands to lose a substantial amount of control once a franchise system increases in size to any great degree. It can become extremely difficult for the franchisor to modify a product or process in order to meet the ever-changing needs of customers, particularly if the franchise system is spread across a large geographic area containing varied consumer markets.

In summary, potential franchisors and franchisees should carefully examine the advantages and disadvantages of the franchising approach to business. Franchising can be a positive arrangement for both franchisor and franchisee, but each should also understand the drawbacks of being involved in a franchising relationship.

Careful examination of the franchise-only approach compared with the company-owned-only approach to business growth has brought many successful companies to the following conclusion: The use of a combination of company-owned and franchisee-owned operating units appears to be superior to the use of either approach exclusively.[8] Thus, the two approaches do not have to be considered mutually exclusive. They can supplement each other, stimulating growth for the company and strengthening the firm's ability to meet the challenges and opportunities of the marketplace.

INVESTIGATING A FRANCHISE

Every business investment involves risk. For a potential franchisee, investing in a franchise is somewhat different from buying stocks or bonds or investing in bank certificates. Investing in a franchise generally requires both time and money. For most franchisees, time will be the greatest contribution made to the business venture. Sixty-five to eighty hours of work every week is common during the start-up of a franchised outlet.

The cost of investing in a franchise also varies according to the success of that particular franchised company. Coca Cola bottlers, General Motors dealerships, and McDonald's restaurants are often known as "blue-chip" franchises because of their successful track records. In fields such as electronics and computing, franchised companies are newer and investments in them are perceived as being more risky or speculative, even though these companies may be very successful in the future.

There are several issues a prospective franchisee should consider before investing in a franchise. The *Franchise Opportunities Handbook*, developed and distributed by the United States Department of Commerce, suggests seven areas of protection one should consider before investing in a franchise (Figure 10-1).

When investigating a franchise, the potential franchisee is relying not only on the performance record of the company but also on personal experience, business skills, and aptitude for franchise ownership. It is important that prospective franchisees have a good understanding of their current business strengths and weaknesses in the field being considered, as well as the management skills necessary to run any business.

A person thinking of buying a major appliance, car, or house will almost always do comparison shopping to determine which has the best value for the price. Similarly, it is wise to investigate the franchise being

FIGURE 10-1

Seven Steps for
Protection before
Franchise Investment

Source: *Franchise
Opportunities Handbook*, U.S.
Department of Commerce,
(Washington, DC: U.S.
Government Printing Office,
1984), xxx–xxxii.

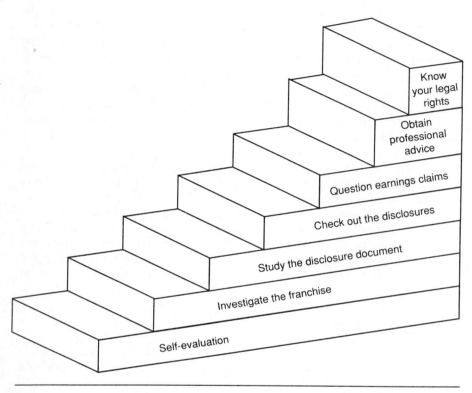

Know your legal rights

Obtain professional advice

Question earnings claims

Check out the disclosures

Study the disclosure document

Investigate the franchise

Self-evaluation

considered by comparison shopping other franchises in the same line of business. A disclosure document (sometimes called an offering circular or prospectus) will help in making the comparison in risks involved, expectations of the franchisor, franchising fees, any continuing payments required after the franchise is open, restrictions on the product or service offered, assistance and training available, statistical information about the franchise, financial statements of the franchisor, and any claims of earnings.

After careful examination of the disclosure documents, a potential franchisee should check the accuracy of the information included in the disclosure document by talking with several franchisees of that company. Talking with other franchisees is critically important since no single opinion can accurately paint a composite picture of the company. If the franchise is worth considering, it is a good idea to talk with three or more franchisees who have been in business at least one year, as well as with a new franchisee and a well-established franchisee with a proven track record. Across this range of franchises, one should be able to get good advice about what to expect in the first year as well as in ensuing years.

It is also important to examine any claims made by the franchisor or the franchised company's representative concerning sales, income, or profits expected from the franchise. Earnings claims are only estimates. There is no assurance that every franchisee will do as well.

Before purchasing a franchise, it is important to obtain independent professional assistance in reviewing and evaluating the franchise. It is especially advisable to have an attorney review the documents. Such assistance and advice is of particular importance in reviewing the disclosure statement, the financial statements provided, and the franchising agreement to be signed. The assumption should not be made that a disclosure document reveals all that needs to be known about the rights, responsibilities, and consequences of signing a franchising agreement with a company. The disclosure document is not designed to serve that purpose. Prospective franchisees should learn precisely what they will be legally bound to do or restricted from doing, any requirements of state or local laws as they apply in the particular business field, and answers to any personal liability or taxation questions that should be considered before signing a binding contract and entering business. There is no way of stating everything that should be considered before signing, but effort should be made to be certain that every important promise made by the franchisor is in writing and clearly stated in the contract.

FINANCIAL REQUIREMENTS

Franchising offers the franchisor the opportunity to obtain wide distribution of products or services at lower costs than would be required if company-owned expansion were the method used. Likewise, the franchisee is able to start a venture that would be more difficult and probably less profitable if started without the franchise. In either case, however, a substantial amount of advance financing must be in place to launch either the total franchise or the individual units. This section discusses the financial requirements that both franchisors and franchisees must consider when developing or entering a franchise system.

Requirements for Franchisors

For the franchisor, there are areas of capital requirement that must be addressed both before the development of a franchise system and on a continuing basis as the system is maintained and further developed. These categories are interrelated, but each is distinct and important to the continuation of the franchise system. The four categories are as follows.

1. Capital requirements for industrial research, prototype development, marketing research, and blueprint development
2. Capital requirements for the franchise package including all disclosure statements, franchisee recruitment, promotions, product/service development costs, and operations development costs
3. Working capital requirements involving the initial advertising and franchisee recruitment expenditures
4. Reserve and legal capital requirements, including money for registering the firm to do business within a state and for meeting the state's licensing or disclosure requirements (in many states, a certain amount of capital is required to be maintained as a reserve in order to do business in that state)

TABLE 10-3
Franchisor Capital
Requirements

Item	Minimum Requirements	Maximum Requirements
Research blueprint	$ 5,000	$ 50,000
Franchise development	25,000	100,000
Working capital	50,000	500,000
Reserve legal capital	30,000	300,000
Total capital required (excluding prototype development)	$110,000	$950,000

In addition to these considerations, there can be hidden costs that must be borne, including unexpected legal, accounting, and research costs. The franchisor should consider each category of expenditure both from a chronological perspective and in terms of the total financial commitment. A chronological perspective means that capital must be available as each phase of the franchise development plan is entered. It is important that capital in all requirement categories be available when payment for these expenditures comes due. This places a formidable burden upon the franchisor in efforts to develop a franchise system.

The capital requirements for a franchise operation can vary according to the particular type of activity and business involved. However, certain key capital requirements seem to be associated with any franchise organization (Table 10-3). Typically a franchisor's initial capital requirements will fall somewhere between $110,000 and $950,000, plus those expenses necessary to build and furnish a company-owned prototype store or outlet. For example, a prototype outlet may be the original restaurant, used as the "design store" for all those that follow. Often a prototype is also used as the showcase or training facility for prospective franchisees. The prototype expenditures will involve the costs of land, building, fixtures, and equipment. The fixed costs of the prototype can run anywhere from $5,000 for leasing space, to more than $1 million for a restaurant, and as much as $7 million to $15 million for a hotel or motel.

Requirements for the Franchisee

Like the franchisor, the franchisee will also have financial requirements to consider before becoming part of a franchise system. Specifically, the capital requirements or concerns of a franchisee can be enumerated in the following six categories.

1. Franchising fee
2. Real estate or rental costs, including building costs
3. Personal living and travel costs
4. Equipment costs
5. Start-up expenses and inventory
6. Working capital

The startup expenses include all legal costs associated with opening any business plus the review by an attorney or other professional of the franchising agreement and any leases or contracts to be signed by the franchisee. In addition, an initial inventory must be purchased and financial commitments made before the business opens. Inventory selection may be guided by the terms of the franchising contract. For example, a drive-up and walk-in restaurant would likely have napkins, cups, plates, food packaging, place mats, and other items carrying the franchise trademark or logo. Auto parts stores and auto repair shops would perhaps have a specified inventory that comes from the parent company. Different franchises vary considerably as to how much trademarked product or packaging is required for an initial inventory level in a startup franchised business.

Other costs can become substantial and must be carefully considered. For example, to be considered seriously as a franchisee of Wendy's Old Fashioned Hamburgers, one should have about $700,000 in credit and $150,000 in liquid assets with which to lease or buy the land, building, and equipment, purchase supplies, and hire employees to operate the restaurant. If, on the other hand, Wendy's locates the restaurant site and arranges to have the restaurant built, the additional cost to the franchisee would be $20,000. Added to the franchising fee of $20,000, this means a new Wendy's franchisee would need $40,000.[9] These figures are not out of the ordinary, while at the same time not all franchising fees or startup expenses and required credit lines are in the same range as those required by Wendy's. Some are higher, such as in hotel or motel franchises, and many are lower. For example, a franchisee may be able to open a carpet cleaning franchise with as little as $5,000 total capital commitment.

Initial costs can be substantial, and working capital requirements to maintain adequate cash flow and keep the business solvent can be heavy. A franchisee should not discount personal living costs either. An owner of a franchised business puts in 60 or more hours per week and should be compensated for that time in salary as well as in profits.

With the financial resources required, personal time and energy committed, and risks associated with entering any business venture, franchising is not really a get-rich-quick opportunity for either the franchisors or the franchisees. Certainly there are some who have "made it rich quick," but many franchisors consider their businesses to be long-term investments and will shun prospective franchisees interested only in a fast buck.[10] In effect, franchisees aren't advised to get into the game unless they are planning to remain for the long haul.

The primary consideration for the franchisee is that the capital required will likely be the same or more for buying into a franchise business as it will be for starting an independent business in the same field. Almost all basic business expenses (real estate, equipment, inventories, personal expenses, and startup costs) remain the same regardless of whether the business is independent or a franchise. There are additional costs for a franchise including franchising fees, royalties, travel costs to and from the training facility, and training fees. It is likely that total costs will be higher because many people would not start their own business with the amount of new equipment, the same size of building, the amount budgeted for advertising, and the costs incurred for training as they would in many franchised businesses.

THE FRANCHISE AGREEMENT

Typical elements included in a franchising agreement are listed in Table 10-4. The list is not meant to contain specific elements included in *all* **franchise agreements**. Rather, it indicates what is *typically* included in an agreement. Each franchise system is unique, having particular requirements or conditions that may not be found in the agreements of other franchise systems. Yet, the listed elements are common, and so should be understood and planned for in considering a franchised business.

It should be kept in mind that the franchise agreement is written by the franchisor. Most elements in the agreement are not subject to negotiation. For example, signage, hours of operation, reporting and bookkeeping, general decor, equipment, and maintenance schedules are expected of all franchisees and are fundamental to the entire franchise mode of operation. Other areas such as products offered, the franchise fee and royalties, location requirements, and the number of personnel may be negotiable in some cases. Potential franchisees can learn much about the negotiability of franchise agreement items by visiting with other franchisees. Legal advice is also recommended to scrutinize both the spirit and letter of the agreement.

FRANCHISOR-FRANCHISEE RELATIONSHIP

Franchisors and franchisees have a relationship somewhat different from relationships in other cooperating business ventures. Being a franchisee is more than just managing an outlet of a company-run distribution system, or carrying a product for retail sale that has been purchased and inventoried from a variety of wholesalers, distributors, or manufacturers. Being a franchisor requires planning, monitoring, and an involvement with the franchisee that differs from the sort of interaction between the head of a

TABLE 10-4
Typical Elements Covered in a Franchising Agreement

Franchising fee	Signs
Quality control	Business hours
Advertising	Decor
Products and/or services available	Reporting
Royalties	Bookkeeping
Equipment	Supplies
Location requirements	Personnel (appearance and training)
Facilities	Franchisor-franchisee relationships
Maintenance	

VENTURE PERSPECTIVE 10-1

· · · · · · · · · · · ·

THE FRANCHISOR-FRANCHISEE RELATIONSHIP

Jim Gaylord, a Kentucky Fried Chicken franchisee in Lincoln, Nebraska, describes the franchisor-franchisee relationship rather clearly:

What is the relationship like? Well, it's like a triangle, or triad. We really have three types of relationships. There is the legal agreement between the franchisor and franchisee which requires certain activities and responsibilities from each party. Then, there is the business relationship which ties the two firms together in day-to-day ac-

tivities of providing service to customers. The legal relationship is static, while the business relationship is dynamic—moving and flowing with the changing conditions of being in business. It is this business relationship that really bonds the franchisor and franchisee together—trying to meet consumers' needs through your franchise business. I call this relationship the "marriage." It has its ups and downs, but the basic understanding exists to meet the public's needs while relying on one another to provide the

best products and services to the customer as possible. The third relationship is the hardest to describe. There are two independent business people, a franchisor and a franchisee, each acting individually for their own best interest. After all, each is a separate business. They don't have a joint tax return!

SOURCE: Interview with E. James Gaylord at Joint Industry/Academy Advisory Council meeting held at the University of Nebraska, Franchise Studies Center, September 1985.

company and the managers of the company-owned outlets or retailers willing to carry the product line.

The author's discussion with other franchisees and several franchisors operating businesses in auto parts, lodging, carpet cleaning, and phone book covers reaffirms Gaylord's idea, though different words are used and different examples given. In effect, the franchisor-franchisee relationship has three distinct elements or parts and may be referred to as the **franchise triad:** the legal agreement or contract, the business relationship to deliver the agreed-upon product or services to the customer, and the independent stature of each party as franchisor or franchisee.

Awareness of the three-part relationship is essential to understanding the franchising approach to business. It is very important to understand the relationship, the perspectives, and the approaches of both parties and the agreement in the relationship. This triad is also useful for describing the reasons franchising has become so successful as an approach to business. Because a franchisee is, in theory, generally more motivated and personally involved than a salaried manager of a business and so works harder, a franchisor needs fewer employees to maintain the same number of operating stores. In addition, the quality controls established by the franchisor, when properly developed and reasonably enforced, help maintain standards of excellence throughout the franchise system and so help to ensure the profitability of an individual franchise unit.

The legal agreement and the operations manual typically describe the role in the franchise system that both the franchisor and franchisee play. The supporting descriptions and guidelines in these documents provide direction for the operating policies and procedures contained in the operations manual.

FIGURE 10-2
Franchisor-Franchisee
Triad Relationship

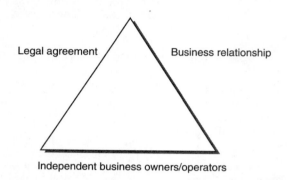

SUMMARY

Tremendous preparation is needed before a franchisee opens a franchised outlet. There is a strong degree of personal involvement brought to the business activities by both franchisor and franchisee. To a franchisor, franchising means potential for growth at a rate that can far exceed the rate typical of growth through wholly owned outlets. To a franchisee, franchising means the opportunity for extensive training and preparation before opening an outlet, plus use of a recognizable name, trademark, or logo associated with the products or services to be offered.

Both franchisor and franchisee face advantages and disadvantages in the franchising relationship. The greatest advantage to the franchisee is the help available from the parent organization. Possibly the franchisee's greatest disadvantages are the restrictions on business practices and the inclination to become overly dependent on help from the franchisor. For the franchisor, perhaps the greatest single advantage is the chance to expand the business with limited capital risk and equity investment. Because of the investment by the franchisee, a franchisor does not have to spend large sums of money or incur major debt to expand the business into new locations. The greatest problem or challenge is maintaining control over an expanding franchise system while overseeing the general operations of each outlet.

The franchisee-franchisor business relationship is a common mission to ensure that both the franchisor and franchisee succeed. A franchisee is vulnerable if another franchisee does not maintain the same quality standards. Similarly, if the franchisor seeks to modify the product line, eliminate a service, or change an operating policy or other facet of the franchise system, it can be extremely difficult to achieve consensus among all franchisees regarding the proposed change.

Investing in a franchise, like any other business investment, involves risk. There are seven steps for protection from the risks of franchising: investigating the franchise, studying the disclosure documents, checking out the disclosures, questioning earnings claims, obtaining professional advice, and knowing your legal rights. A potential franchisee will want to consider these steps before signing a franchising agreement.

The capital requirements of franchising were discussed from the perspective of both franchisor and franchisee. A franchisor will have capital requirements that must be addressed before development of a franchise system as well as on a continuing basis as the system is maintained or further developed. A franchisor's initial investment may range from $100,000 to more than $1 million.

Like the franchisor, the prospective franchisee will also have financial requirements to consider. The capital requirements are divided into six categories: franchising fee, real estate or rental costs, personal living and travel costs, equipment costs, startup expenses and inventory, and working capital requirements. Initial costs, as well as working capital requirements, can be substantial. Depending on the franchise an individual seeks, however, one can enter franchising for as little as $5,000. Entering a franchised business may be more costly than entering the same field of business as an independent entrepreneur. However, the added financial commitment can pay dividends for those seeking a safer way to enter business.

Typical elements included in a franchising agreement identify what a prospective franchisee should consider before buying a franchise. The franchisor-franchisee relationship can be imagined as consisting of three parts. This triad involves the legal agreement between the franchisor and franchisee, the business relationship between the two, and the recognition that each of the players is also an independent businessperson.

- -

1. Who would benefit most from buying a franchise; a person who is already a highly successful entrepreneur or a person just starting a business for the first time? Why?

2. Why is talking with existing franchisees critical before buying a franchise?

3. Why is it important to talk to some new franchisees, some relatively new franchisees, and some who have had the franchise for years?

4. Discuss the relative benefits of a major franchise such as McDonald's compared to an unknown franchise. What are the advantages and disadvantages of each?

5. Can the benefits of a franchise be achieved by an entrepreneur starting an independent venture? Why or why not?

6. What is the primary advantage of franchising for the franchisor?

7. Obtain a copy of a franchise agreement from a local franchisee. Compare it with advertising literature provided by the franchisor. What differences are there?

8. Discuss the capital needs for a franchisee. How are these different than for an independent entrepreneur starting a similar venture?

9. What are the three parts of the franchise triad discussed in this chapter? Why are they so important?

DISCUSSION QUESTIONS

EXERCISES

EXERCISE 10-1

Find and study a franchise advertisement in a popular business magazine such as *Inc.*, *Entrepreneur*, or *Entrepreneurial Woman*. What are the advantages and disadvantages of this franchise for a potential franchisee? What other information would you like to have?

EXERCISE 10-2

Interview the franchisee of one of the Hardees, McDonald's, or Burger King franchises in your community. Focus on the advantages and disadvantages of franchising for them. Then interview the owner of another franchise that is not in the fast-food industry and is less well known (a muffler franchise, a ten-minute oil change store, and a real estate franchise are examples). Do you get the same answers?

ENDNOTES

1. *Franchising in the Economy, 1988–90* and *Franchising in the Economy, 1991* (Washington, D.C.: International Franchising Association with Horwath International).
2. Robert E. Bond and Christopher E. Bond, *The Sourcebook of Franchise Opportunities* (Homewood, IL: Dow Jones-Irwin, 1991), 4.
3. *Franchising in the Economy, 1985–1987*, U.S. Department of Commerce, International Trade Association (Washington, D.C.: U.S. Government Printing Office, 1987), 2.
4. Ibid., 1–3.
5. Ibid., 3.
6. *Franchising in the Economy, 1985–1987*; *Franchising in the Economy, 1988–1990*.
7. Charles L. Vaughn, *Franchising*, 2d ed. (Lexington, MA: Lexington Books, D. C. Heath Company, 1979), 65.
8. Vaughn, 65.
9. "Where's the Beef in Franchising?" *Money* (March 1985), 149.
10. Ibid., 152.

◆ Conveniesse, Inc. ◆

A New Opportunity

Roughly ten months had passed since Conveniesse first opened its doors. In most cases, actual results had exceeded even the optimistically determined business plan results by a factor of about 20 percent. The most important part was that the difference between actual results and planned results seemed to be widening somewhat each month. Sarah and Jason had been able to operate the venture pretty well by themselves with Yolanda coming in from New York on some weekends to give them a break and to get a feel for whether she wanted to join them permanently. Her job in New York was still going well, and she was at a point that she would quit only if they needed her. Since she was not drawing a salary except for the weekend visits, this saved some on the total costs for the venture.

The only place where there seemed to be concern was in the area of labor costs. Sarah and Jason had worked it out where they would generally split the day with a one- or two-hour overlap at about 2:00 P.M. The assistant managers did the same. This gave them two people in the store at all times, not including the security guard. The advantage to this arrangement was that all four of the operating managers would be there at the same time in case they needed to have a meeting. They did find, however, that both people were required to be on the floor most of the time, and this did not leave sufficient time for the book work. Further, an additional person was often needed around the lunch hour, late afternoon, and early evening. They finally decided to hire another person to come in at noon and stay until 8:00 P.M. This would give a total of three on the floor when needed and allow Sarah or Jason to go into their small office and do paperwork when not needed on the floor. This eased the work flow considerably, but added significantly to labor costs.

Then one day they received a call from Mr. Akins, the developer, who wanted to talk with all three of them at their earliest convenience. The soonest they could meet was 8:00 P.M. Friday when Yolanda arrived. Sarah and Jason quickly briefed Yolanda, though they said they had no clue why Akins had called. They went to the meeting with more than a little trepidation, not knowing whether they were going to lose their lease. They imagined a dozen scenarios, most of which were bad.

Mr. Akins asked, "How is Conveniesse doing now? Hasn't it been ten months or so since you opened?"

Sarah, being the president, responded somewhat shakily, "Well, sir, it has been going quite well. It turns out that we have beat our plan every month, and the gap has been increasing. It appears that we may end the first year up about 20 percent from projections."

"Well, that's what I figured was occurring. I've been watching your operation from afar, and you know that I have been in fairly frequently myself for quick purchases. Let me get right to the point. You know, of course, that this isn't the only office building I own in Buffalo. I own one more in the inner loop area, one out near Highway 990 and the SUNY campus, and one near the airport. And I also have property in Syracuse and Montreal. Have you ever considered the possibility of expansion?"

After a moment of total silence from the three, Yolanda said, "Tell us what you have in mind."

"It amounts to this," Akins replied. "Each of the three Buffalo buildings is designed roughly the same way as the one where Conveniesse is now located. Frankly, clients in those buildings have asked for a store similar to yours. I have two or three choices. I could start the stores myself. But I'm in the real estate business, not the convenience store business. I could find someone to put some in. Or," he paused for effect, "or, you people could do it."

Again, there was silence. Then Sarah broke the quiet.

"What kind of timetable do you have in mind? And can you help with the financing?"

"The one downtown is definitely first," the developer said. "The airport area would probably be second since that area is growing. Third and least important would be the SUNY area. I haven't given funding a lot of thought, but we could probably do at least what we originally did for Conveniesse. Well, it is apparent that I caught you off guard, and I apologize for that. Give it some thought and get back to me. But don't wait too long.''

The three shaken entrepreneurs went to Sarah's, called the assistant manager on duty to do the close, and collapsed on Sarah's overstuffed furniture. They had ridden to Sarah's apartment in virtual silence and continued that silence until Sarah suggested, ''Maybe we should return to Yolanda's computer.''

''No,'' said Yolanda, ''There's not a program in my computer that suggests how to raise $2.5 million.''

''Why $2.5 million?'' Jason asked.

''Conveniesse cost almost $500,000. He wants us to add three in Buffalo, one in Syracuse, and maybe one in Montreal,'' answered Yolanda. ''That's $2.5 million, especially if you add a little for inflation. And you never know where he might lead us then. He may have 'friends' all over the United States and Canada. Right now we are a couple of hundred thousand dollars in debt not counting three 'friendly' investors.''

''You know,'' said Sarah, ''on that very first day we met, we were talking about starting Conveniesse. We didn't really say just one store. I think our dreams then were to do a *chain* of upscale convenience stores. Looks like we have a chance here to do just that.''

''If, of course, we ignore the minor problem of $2.5 million,'' Jason added rather sardonically.

''Well,'' said Yolanda, ''It looks to me like we have three choices at least. Regardless of which choice, it looks like I'm going to kiss New York City good-bye. Choice one would be to go back to the developer. Since the buildings are all his, perhaps we could strike up a partnership of sorts with him in which he provides major funding for each site in exchange for a healthy ownership percentage. We could buy out our small potatoes friends and form a new corporation of him and us.

''A second choice,'' Yolanda continued, ''would be to go outside for funding. I suspect that with the ten months' track record, we could probably get some decent venture capital funding if we put together a business plan showing not just his buildings, but stores in buildings across the Midwest and Canada in similar situations. There have to be a number of cities that would be possible. That funding would have to come in stages and we are likely to give up majority ownership, but we could get big-time growth. The third method is to franchise. I don't know how much that would cost, but we might consider duplicating Conveniesse once in his other downtown building and simultaneously work on a franchising plan.''

Assignment

After having studied franchising, does Conveniesse seem to you to be a good candidate for franchising? Given the three methods of funding growth, which of the three seems like the best? Which gives the three partners the largest control? Which offers the greatest returns?

11 International Entrepreneurship

LEARNING OBJECTIVES

After reading this chapter, you should know:

1. The nature of international business
2. The reasons why an entrepreneur will "go international"
3. The factors to consider in deciding how to export
4. How to decide what to export
5. How to decide where to export
6. Sources of information on exporting
7. Other methods of selling in the international market

KEY TERMS

Exporting
Export management company
Export trading company
U.S. and Foreign Commercial
   Service

Freight forwarder
International trade shows
Licensing
Joint venture

CONSIDER THIS!

- Most firms that export have fewer than one hundred employees.
- Even large firms make mistakes in international business decisions.
- Exporting is just one of the ways to sell in the international market.
- Firms should *not* try to take advantage of every opportunity that is presented.
- The U.S. government and many state governments provide significant assistance to companies wishing to export.
- New and emerging companies should *not* use exporting to offset downturns in the domestic market.

THE NATURE OF INTERNATIONAL ENTREPRENEURSHIP

The international arena is a major market area for U.S. firms. In 1991, U.S. firms exported $421.6 billion of products and imported $488.1 billion worth. The United States accounted for 12.0 percent of the world's merchandise exports and 16.5 percent of its imports. U.S. exports in 1991 consisted of 82 percent manufactured goods, 9 percent agricultural goods, and 9 percent minerals and crude materials. Exports accounted for nearly eight million jobs in the United States in 1990, accounting for about one in six U.S. jobs in manufacturing.[1]

RICHARD SPENCER
SLM Instruments, Inc.

"**E**xporting takes patience and dedication. You can ruin your reputation if you are not dedicated. You must be ready to commit." So says Richard Spencer, president of SLM Instruments of Urbana, Illinois. "You can't just say, 'Well, there's a good market,' and think you can sell there without an effort. You have to realize that developing an export business is not one-way traffic. Once you decide to go after a market, you have to go there and get to know your customers. You have to find good people to sell your products. And you have to send people there to service your products."

Richard Spencer began SLM Instruments in 1973 after completing his Ph.D. in biophysics at the University of Illinois. The firm manufactures instruments used in medical, cosmetic, pharmaceutical, cancer, oil, and geological research.

SLM started exporting in a small way. Its first sale was to Mexico City, its second to London, and its third to Canada. After touring Europe in 1978 and 1979, Spencer became serious about exporting. When he had established a base in Europe, he turned his attention to the Far East in the 1980s. Today, SLM sells in Japan, Korea, Taiwan, Hong Kong, and China.

SLM's exports account for almost 40 percent of its total sales. Plans are for exports to make up 50 percent in the near future. Spencer maintains that every country is different and sales techniques and products must be adapted to the target countries. Exporters have to master exporting fundamentals, such as letters of credit and worldwide product liability. Spencer now has two employees that focus strictly on exporting.

SOURCE: "Exporting Pays Off," *Business America* 111, no. 16 (August 27, 1990): 22. Used with permission.

Most involvement in international marketing by new and growing firms is through exporting. **Exporting** is the shipping of products made in one country for sale in another. Like business in general, the number of small businesses that export far exceeds the number of large exporters.

Becoming involved in the international arena is different for small and growing entrepreneurial firms than it is for major corporations. Large corporations have more alternatives for selling in the international marketplace than do smaller ventures. Because of their size, large firms have in-house staffs to direct international operations. Further, many large companies have direct investment abroad—that is, they own complete manufacturing facilities or major operations in foreign countries. Most small companies, on the other hand, are restricted to exporting or licensing.

An international strategy is beneficial for the emerging venture because it provides major opportunities for expansion in sales. It also provides a legitimacy for the venture's domestic operations. Yet, the international decision must be made carefully after considerable discussion and analysis both within and outside the firm.

Market	Amount (in billions)
Total	$421.6
1. Canada	85.1
2. Japan	48.1
3. Mexico	33.3
4. United Kingdom	22.1
5. Germany	21.3
6. South Korea	15.5
7. France	15.4
8. Netherlands	13.5
9. Taiwan	13.2
10. Belgium-Luxembourg	10.8
11. Singapore	8.8
12. Italy	8.6
13. Australia	8.4
14. Hong Kong	8.1
15. Saudi Arabia	6.6
16. China	6.3
17. Brazil	6.2
18. Switzerland	5.6
19. Spain	5.5
20. Venezuela	4.7
21. Malaysia	3.9
22. Israel	3.9
23. Thailand	3.8
24. Former U.S.S.R.	3.6
25. Sweden	3.3

TABLE 11-1

Top Twenty-five Export Markets for U.S. Firms

SOURCE: John Jelacic, "The U.S. Trade Outlook in 1992." *Business America* 113, no. 7 (April 6, 1992): 5

THE INTERNATIONAL DECISION

Aside from the decision to launch or to end the venture, the decision to "go international" is perhaps the most difficult decision to make. This is due largely to the possible *magnitude* of the decision, especially if the owner decides to enter several markets simultaneously. The international decision entails distribution problems that do not exist domestically. Language and cultural differences can dramatically affect the prospects for success. Currency exchange makes dealing with other countries more difficult. Control of operations, product quality, marketing, and service is difficult because of the distance between the headquarters and the ultimate customer. In spite of these concerns, however, thousands of small companies do export. Those that do decide to go international must do so only after careful study.

The Need for Planning

The focus throughout this book has been on planning, which is perhaps most important when considering the international dimension. Figure 11-1 shows the planning model presented in Chapter 4 and adapted to address the international question.

The changes in the model are significant. First, block 2 notes that we must analyze *domestic* opportunities. Domestic opportunities should be compared with the venture's capabilities to see if both a *need* and a *capability* to enter the international market exist. Only after a determination has been made that internationalization should and can be done will international markets be analyzed for opportunities. The strategy development phase entails determining how to enter international markets and identifying target countries. The implementation phase then includes the steps of establishing relationships with intermediaries and government agencies, assembling resources, establishing controls, and beginning the actions. Resources must be assembled for most methods of entering markets abroad because of the extra efforts and players involved in the process.

The Need for Commitment

Entering international markets *for the first time* is a time-consuming task. Substantial analysis and study of international markets must be done. Much of the preliminary research can be done at minimal cost, but the time required to do the research and establish necessary relationships is measured in months. This is time and energy that could be used to further domestic operations. One of the greatest mistakes that can be made is to enter international markets because domestic markets are down and then abandon the international arena when the domestic side picks up again. The international decision must be carefully considered because it must be viewed as a major, long-term strategic commitment. A short-term commitment will surely be doomed to failure.

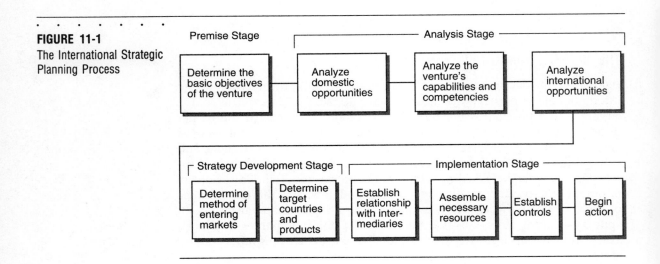

FIGURE 11-1
The International Strategic Planning Process

Related to the commitment is the need for a well-established, stable domestic operation. Given the magnitude of the exporting task and the effect it will have on internal operations, exporting should not be considered until the domestic market is well under control.

The Need for Analysis

Popular writings on international business are replete with examples of firms that have attempted to market products abroad only to find that they have made a faux pas that not only precludes sales but is embarrassing to the company. Notable examples include the attempt by General Motors to sell the Chevrolet Nova in Spanish-speaking countries and Gerber's attempt to market its baby food in some third world countries. *No va* in Spanish means "don't go." In the Gerber case, the tradition in some third world countries is to put a picture of the contents on the jar label. Thus, Gerber's picture of a baby on its baby food jars was not received well.

These examples of mistakes by major corporations underscore the need for careful analysis of foreign markets before making the decision to enter those markets. Entrepreneurs must be knowledgeable about the international market even if the product or service will only be exported or licensed. Mistakes that could be easily corrected domestically will be difficult to rectify abroad.

DECIDING TO EXPORT

There are a number of compelling reasons for moving into international markets.[2] Entering international markets creates major expansion for the company. The increase in sales adds to the total output of the venture. It not only increases revenues, but it also allows for fixed expenses to be spread over a larger base. Thus, the unit costs of producing both the international and domestic products is reduced. It offers outlets for products and therefore uses capacity that is not needed for domestic production. It allows the company to add jobs and thereby contribute to the community. And, if done well, it will improve the overall return on investment.

In addition to increased sales, there are other benefits. By entering international markets, the entrepreneur can offset either seasonal or cyclical product life cycle decreases in domestic sales. For example, selling to countries in the southern hemisphere may offset seasonal fluctuations in sales. Other parts of the world may be in different stages of economic cycles than the United States. Accordingly, selling in those geographical areas can offset recurring declines in domestic sales. Similarly, a product that has reached the maturity stage domestically may be in an earlier stage of the life cycle in other parts of the world.

Other reasons for entering the international market relate to the foreign markets themselves. The entrepreneur may need to consider moving into foreign markets to offset competitors who are making similar moves. International efforts can yield substantial knowledge about both markets and technology abroad. And finally, considering international expansion

TABLE 11-2

Reasons for Exporting

Source: *A Basic Guide to Exporting*, International Trade Administration, U.S. and Foreign Commercial Service, U.S. Department of Commerce (Washington, DC: U.S. Government Printing Office, 1986), vii.

- Increase overall sales volume
- Enlarge sales base to spread out fixed costs
- Use excess production capacity
- Contribute to the company's general expansion
- Create more jobs
- Improve overall return on investment
- Compensate for seasonal fluctuations in domestic sales
- Find new markets for products with declining U.S. sales
- Exploit existing advantages in untapped markets
- Take advantage of high-volume foreign purchases
- Learn about advanced technical methods used abroad
- Follow domestic competitors who are selling overseas
- Acquire knowledge about international competition
- Test opportunities for overseas licensing or production

provides the opportunity to study production processes and costs abroad and to compare them with current domestic operations.

Some smaller firms might *not* want to export. The chief reason is the cost and effort of starting an exporting operation. The cost of exporting will include additional transportation costs, the cost of rewriting labels and instructions in various languages, the cost of intermediaries who will be involved in the process, and the cost of additional packaging or packing to enable the product to be shipped abroad. The extra effort consists of the time and personnel required to analyze the foreign markets, establish relationships with intermediaries, and work with government officials to assure that legal and political issues are adequately handled. However, with proper planning, these costs can be incorporated into the price of the product.

Another issue in the decision to export concerns the capacity of the venture to meet international demand. Estimating international demand is even more difficult than estimating domestic demand because of the number of distinct markets that must be researched. Entering the international market will certainly require substantial capacity to meet the indeterminate demand. Thus, the entrepreneur must consider whether sufficient capacity exists or can be easily acquired to meet the increased demand. The downside risk, of course, is that additional capacity may be acquired and then international demand does not materialize.

A third area of concern is the ability to service the product after the sale. Meeting service or warranty needs becomes far more complex when dealing with major distances, other languages, and a number of different countries. For example, will extensive travel be required to deal with the product's problems? Is shipping the product back to the firm's headquarters for repair uneconomical? The answers to these issues may be a function of the nature of the product or the target countries. Still, answers must be obtained before the decision is made to begin exporting (Table 11-3).

Management Objectives

What are the company's reasons for pursuing export markets?

How committed is top management to the export effort?

What are management's expectations for the export effort?

Experience

With which countries has business already been conducted?

Which product lines are mentioned most often?

Are any domestic companies buying the product for sale or shipment overseas?

Is the trend of sales and inquiries up or down?

Who are the main domestic and foreign competitors?

What is known from past export attempts?

Management and Personnel

What in-house international expertise does the firm have?

Who will be responsible for the export effort?

How much senior management time should and could be allocated?

What organizational structure is required?

Who will follow through once planning is done?

Production Capacity

How is the present capacity being used?

Will filling export orders hurt domestic sales?

What will be the cost of additional production?

Are there fluctuations in annual work load? When? Why?

What minimum order quantity is required?

What would be required to design and package products specifically for export?

Financial Capacity

What amount of capital can be committed to export production and marketing?

What level of export department operating costs can be supported?

How are the initial expenses of export efforts to be allocated?

What other new development plans are in the works that may compete with the export plans?

By what date must an export effort pay for itself?

TABLE 11-3

Management Issues Involved in the Export Decision

Source: Adapted from *A Basic Guide to Exporting*, International Trade Administration, U.S. and Foreign Commercial Service, U.S. Department of Commerce (Washington, DC: U.S. Government Printing Office, 1992), 1-4.

The discussion regarding both the pros and cons of exporting can be summarized in the following question. How well does the export plan fit with the overall strategy of the venture? Once this question can be answered to the entrepreneur's satisfaction, then discussion can move to the next issue: To what countries or markets should the firm export?

DECIDING HOW TO EXPORT

Aside from the decision *whether* to enter the international arena, the most important strategic decision is *how* to enter it.[3] This section discusses

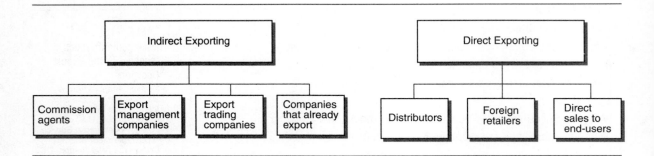

FIGURE 11-2
Methods of Entering
International Markets
SOURCE: *A Basic Guide to
Exporting* (1992), 4-1 to 4-4.

methods of entering international markets, focusing on the advantages and disadvantages of each.

The two broad categories of exporting methods are indirect and direct. The primary difference between the two is whether the entrepreneur deals directly with a foreign buyer or not. If the product is sold to someone domestically who in turn exports the product, the firm is using indirect methods of exporting. If the exporting firm deals with a buyer in the foreign country, then direct exporting is used (Figure 11-2).

Indirect Exporting

The advantage of using indirect exporting is that the producing company does not have to be involved with the actual export or final sales of the product. The product is sold to another domestic company. That company assumes ownership of the product and then exports it using whatever means it wants. Thus, the risks associated with the actual exporting process and the risks of failure in the foreign market are assumed by the exporting company rather than by the producer.

The downside of indirect exporting is that the producer does not maintain control of the process. Thus, the producer cannot control the marketing, the distribution, nor the servicing of the product once it arrives in the target country.

Commission Agents

Many foreign firms or governments want to find products that can be sold in their countries. They commission agents or "finders" in other countries to locate products that are in demand in their home country. These finders purchase products in the producing company and ship them to the government or company that, in turn, sells them in that country. The agents are paid a commission by the purchasing firm or government. Note that in this case the commission is paid by the buyer and not the seller.

Export Management Companies

An **export management company** (EMC) works as the exporting arm for one or more producing companies. It solicits sales for the company abroad. It may or may not actually purchase the goods from the producer, and it may be paid a salary, a commission, or a retainer plus commission. An export management company will work for a number of noncompeting

VENTURE PERSPECTIVE 11-1

. . . .

BARTEX CORPORATION

Bartex Corporation, located in Portland, Oregon, exports irrigation and agriculture equipment for U.S. manufacturers that do not want to be involved in exporting the equipment. Rather than operate under a commission system, Bartex buys the products outright and resells them in the Middle East and Far East, with some sales in Latin America and Europe.

According to Dr. Anthony Francis, president of Bartex, "For the manufacturer, our arrangement is just like a domestic sale. It's clean and simple. We take full responsibility; we handle the shipping, the export financing, and other details."

This saves the manufacturer both the risk and the hassle of getting paid. Once the sale is made to Bartex, the manufacturer gets its money immediately.

SOURCE: Glen Morgan, *Passport to Successful Exporting* (Altamonte Springs, FL: Parkway Publications Inc., 1989), 33–34.

firms simultaneously and typically specializes in a particular set of products or industries. Thus, the company has expertise in its particular area and knows the foreign markets well.

The EMC works essentially as a manufacturer's representative would domestically except that the sales effort is in other countries. Among the approximately two thousand EMCs in the United States, only a few are large enough to be able to finance sales abroad or actually take possession of the product. Most will work on a commission basis and will forward orders to the company for direct shipment. Even without taking possession of products, the export management company provides a valuable service by serving as an internationally oriented manufacturer's representative.

Export Trading Companies

The export management company typically does not take possession of goods and works primarily at obtaining orders for the producer. The **export trading company** (ETC), on the other hand, may take possession of products and provides a number of services to aid in getting the product distributed overseas. Export trading companies may be partially underwritten by bank holding companies or industry groups and they have a close working relationship with government agencies. Thus, they can provide additional services and assistance to the domestic company interested in indirect exporting. Bartex Corporation, described in Venture Perspective 11-1, typifies the ETC that takes possession of products and resells them abroad. Venture Perspective 11-2 discusses Medical International, a combined EMC/ETC that will either work on commission or take possession of products.

Marketing through Other Companies

The EMC and ETC are companies that are specifically created to export products produced by other firms. Potential exporters may find, however, that an additional avenue of exporting is to work with *existing* exporters.

VENTURE PERSPECTIVE 11-2

· · · · · · · · · · · · · ·

MEDICAL INTERNATIONAL, INC.

Medical International of Spring Lake, New Jersey, is both an export management company and an export trading company. It exports hospital and physicians' supplies and equipment, orthopedic appliances, rehabilitation equipment, home health care products, X-ray equipment, dental supplies, and other products. It will either buy products from manufacturers outright or it will act as their export management agent on a commission basis. Most of its business is via purchase of products.

Medical International's management feels that it provides a real service both to the customer and to the producer. For the customer, it provides a single source of several different products within the medical line. It publishes a catalog that shows pictures of the various products of the seventy client manufacturers. For the manufacturer, Medical International either provides assistance in exporting products or buys the products directly and then resells them in the international market. The company also provides market research and consulting services, promotes products, works at international trade shows, helps with financing, and works with documentation, shipping, and consolidation services.

Currently, Medical International has sales in Asia, the Middle East, Latin America, Europe, and Africa. Sales for 1990 exceeded $800,000; the company added ten new countries to its list of markets, and increased its client base by 35 percent.

SOURCE: "Exporting Pays Off," *Business America* 112, no. 4 (February 25, 1991), 35.

Potential exporters may contact companies that already export complementary products. Since the existing exporter already has a distribution system in place, it takes little extra effort to include the new firm's products. The existing exporter is often pleased to add the new products, as it adds to the total product line being sold abroad. Both the new exporter and the existing exporter benefit from the relationship. The new exporter benefits from an entree into the international markets. The existing exporter benefits from an expanded product line and an enhanced image.

In these situations, the existing exporter typically purchases the inventory of the new producer. The two firms agree on arrangements such as packaging, brand names, fees or shares of profits, and the length of the contract.

Direct Exporting

Entering the international arena via direct exporting has one primary difference from indirect exporting. That is, the exporter deals directly with the buyer in the foreign market. This difference is significant because it substantially increases the risk to the producer while simultaneously providing the firm's management with complete control over the product until it reaches its ultimate destination. Direct exporting is much like selling in the domestic market in regard to channels of distribution. Essentially the same channels are used except that the transportation involves shipping abroad.

Selling to Distributors

Selling to distributors domestically consists of selling to wholesalers or brokers who then break the shipment into smaller quantities for further shipment to retailers. The wholesaler takes possession of the product and assumes the risk associated with the product. In the international market, the same thing happens. A wholesaler or other distributor in the foreign market orders a given quantity of product from the producer. The producer then packages the product, makes the necessary shipping arrangements, and ships the product to the foreign wholesaler. Actual ownership typically changes once the product is loaded onto the boat. Once the product arrives at the distributor's warehouse, the distributor breaks the shipment into smaller quantities and ships it to its own customers in that geographical area.

Selling to Retailers

As with domestic sales, selling to foreign retailers involves selling the product directly to the retailer. This gives the owner more control over the distribution and assures that the desired retailers carry the product. The downside of this strategy is the difficulty in locating a sufficient number of retailers to carry the product. But this strategy does eliminate intermediaries that can add to the ultimate cost of the product.

Selling directly to foreign retailers is virtually impossible for small exporters because of lack of knowledge of retail markets abroad and lack of distribution systems. Locating sufficient retailers abroad to make the international market worthwhile is quite difficult. This also assumes that the producer or wholly owned distributor knows the geographical area well enough to understand its customs, culture, and buying patterns.

Selling to End-Users

Selling abroad directly to end-users may be useful depending on the product and customer. This would, of course, not be appropriate for products such as soft drinks, small computers, televisions, or even automobiles since these products go through intermediaries when sold domestically. However, specialized equipment may be a candidate for this type of foreign distribution.

The direct sale may be appropriate if the product is quite complex, requires training to operate, or is purchased by institutional customers. Examples of this include products or services to banks, hospitals, schools, or governments.

DECIDING WHAT TO EXPORT

Many products are not exportable. Products that typically would not be exportable are those that are already produced in the target countries, those that are produced more cheaply abroad, and those that encounter significant trade barriers.

The nature of the products themselves determines the degree to which exporting could be successful. A small toy or a ballpoint pen would require little in the way of instructions, training, or warranties. Little adaptation other than labeling would be required. Small electrical appliances could be readily exported to countries that use the same electrical current that the originating country does. In this case, some mechanism for warranty processing and complete instructions for usage in various languages would be necessary. Computers require software that is readable in a variety of languages, and this would make exporting more difficult. Specialty equipment may require extensive training of operators by the producing firm's personnel. Thus, exporting becomes more complex. Finally, major installations of electrical generating equipment might have to be specifically designed for the customer and would thus require substantial dealings between the customer and the producer's representatives.

Table 11-4 lists some of the concerns that must be addressed in determining whether a product is readily exportable or not. Addressing these concerns requires considerable research and study. For example, determining whether the product really does meet needs in foreign markets may require extensive market research. Both marketing and engineering aspects of the potential export must be carefully researched. Attempting to export a product that will not operate to its fullest capacity in the foreign market is futile. Perhaps even more futile is exporting a product that does in fact work but is so poorly marketed that making sales is difficult or impossible. Both of these issues must be solved within the country targeted. This brings us to the next area for discussion, the countries to which the company should export.

DECIDING WHERE TO EXPORT

The preceding sections have made clear the need to consider the international decision in terms of the overall strategy of the firm. This is especially true in deciding where to export. In the 1986 edition of *A Basic Guide to*

TABLE 11-4
Product Concerns in Exporting
Source: Adapted from *A Basic Guide to Exporting* (1992), 5-1 to 5-3.

1. Does the product meet needs in the foreign market?
2. Will the product require modification to compete in foreign markets?
3. Are specific features needed for the foreign market, or does the product have features that are either distasteful or unnecessary in the foreign market?
4. Does the product require servicing? If so, can we provide it or must we contract with foreign companies to provide the service?
5. Are there competing products in the international market? Are they formidable?
6. What changes in brand names, packaging, or labeling will be required?
7. Are weights or measures appropriate for the market?
8. Will substantial installation by experts be required?
9. What changes will need to be made in warranties?

VENTURE PERSPECTIVE 11-3

. . . .

THE CANADA-U.S. FREE TRADE AGREEMENT

Canada and the United States have always been each other's largest trading partner. In 1989, the United States and Canada did $220 billion of business. In 1988, however, the two countries signed the Canada-U.S. Free Trade Agreement (FTA), which will increase the amount of exporting each country does with the other and make existing business easier to conduct.

The agreement is designed to:

- Facilitate fair competition
- Eliminate all tariffs and

most other restrictions over a ten-year period

- Unravel a tangle of customs formalities that disproportionately burden small businesses
- Establish a set of principles covering trade in several sectors including agriculture, autos, energy, financial services, and government procurement
- Expand investment opportunities
- Establish procedures for the

avoidance and resolution of trade disputes

- Facilitate business travel between the two countries
- Lay the foundation for further bilateral and multilateral cooperation

SOURCE: The Illinois World Trade Center, *An Illinois Business Guide to the Canada-U.S. Free Trade Agreement*, 321 N. Clark Street, Chicago, IL 60610 (undated), 4. The agreement is complex (more than 1,400 pages) and considers problems such as transfer of products that were originally imported from third countries, export subsidies in agriculture, the export of services, and transborder investments.

Exporting, published by the U.S. Department of Commerce, three of the twelve most common mistakes in exporting deal with where the firm exports. Perhaps the most serious mistake, especially for the relatively new exporter, is chasing orders from around the world instead of establishing a basis for profitable operations and orderly growth. This occurs when the new exporter attempts to export to a number of unrelated areas of the world, each of which may have different customs, cultures, languages, and uses for the product. The firm becomes so entangled in attempting to deal with the various customers that none are dealt with well. The better option is to begin exporting to a particular country or region. Once the product is successfully marketed in that region, the firm can then move to the next selected region.[4]

A case can be made that new exporters should start with countries that are as close as possible to the culture and language of the venture's home country. The most obvious first target for U.S.-based companies is Canada. For Canadian ventures, the first target should be either the United States or the United Kingdom. In the U.S./Canada exchange, there is little language difference (except for Quebec), trade restrictions are being eliminated, the currency is easily convertible, the distance between seller and buyer is acceptable, and shipping does not require seaborne transportation. Exporting to Mexico is not quite as easy due to language and culture differences and differences in the economies. Still, Mexico is the United States' third largest trading partner. The European Community (EC) is a high-potential target, especially since 1992. This market is large and has few internal trade barriers.

VENTURE PERSPECTIVE 11-4

· · · · · · · · · · · · ·

THE NATIONAL TRADE DATA BANK

The National Trade Data Bank (NTDB) is a new U.S. Department of Commerce service that selects the best international trade and economic information available and provides it in a consolidated and convenient electronic format. Updated monthly, the NTDB CD-ROM contains more than ninety thousand documents of current information from fifteen U.S. government agencies. The NTDB is an invaluable resource for businesses making decisions about exporting.

Information included on the CD-ROM includes the complete *Industrial Outlook* and *World Fact Book* for the current year, government-sponsored market research by country and product, foreign interest and exchange rates, stock price indexes, foreign labor costs and rates, and import and export statistics by country and commodity. It also contains a list of import-oriented foreign organizations, along with a description of the organization and the products they are interested in importing.

The information is user friendly and is menu driven. Users can look for information about a particular country and industry, for which pricing information is also available. The entire data base can be searched for a particular topic or even a specific word. The information can be viewed on the screen or can be transported to other software such as word processors and spreadsheets.

SOURCE: Melissa Malhame, "The National Trade Data Bank: A Valuable Resource for Exporters," *Business America*, 112, no. 2 (1991): 13–14.

Conducting Market Research

Market research for international operations consists of identifying those countries or regions that are potential markets for the venture's products and then collecting and analyzing information about each. Information should include trends in the usage of the product over the past five years, the number and kind of potential users, the number of competitors, and the nature of the product's distribution channels. Both foreign and U.S. trade barriers should be identified. For example, the country of interest may have tariffs that would be prohibitive. In addition, the United States may have trade restrictions that prohibit the export of a particular product to a given country. Conversely, the United States or the foreign country could have incentives that would encourage exporting the product.

Once information has been obtained and analyzed for a number of potential markets, several markets should then be selected for further study to implement the exporting strategy.

Sources of Market Information

There is a wealth of information available about foreign markets. The primary source of information on exporting in general and on countries in particular is the **U.S. and Foreign Commercial Service** (US & FCS) district offices. These are located in most industrial centers of the United States. In addition to personal counseling and advice, the US&FCS can provide secondary information on most countries and most industries.

Business America, a bi-weekly publication of the U.S. Department of Commerce, contains country-by-country marketing reports, economic analyses, world-wide trade show leads, and success stories of export marketing. The *Economic Bulletin Board* is a modestly priced PC-based on-line source for trade leads. The *U.N. Statistical Yearbook,* one of the most complete statistical resources available, contains annual information for 220 countries on population, agriculture, manufacturing, export-import trade, and many other areas. It has 900 pages and costs $100. A number of other data sources exist that are published by the U.S. Department of Commerce or other government agencies. The single best source, available in many libraries, is the National Trade Data Bank. It is on a CD-ROM and includes most information available about international business (Venture Perspective 11-4).

In addition to the written information available, the U.S. Department of Commerce and most states have offices staffed with experts in international business. These individuals provide information and assistance at no charge to potential exporters.

IMPLEMENTING THE INTERNATIONAL STRATEGY

It has been noted that the international strategic planning process must include a consideration of the firm's domestic strategy. This is followed by an analysis of opportunities and capabilities. Once the analysis is thoroughly done, the entrepreneur is then ready to develop the actual international strategy. This consists of the how, what, and where questions discussed earlier. Finally, the strategies have to be implemented. This consists of steps taken to put the strategies into action. The three most important actions are to establish relationships with intermediaries, obtain the necessary financing, and establish strategy controls.

Establishing Relationships with Intermediaries

Entrepreneurs considering entering the international market for the first time will almost always use exporting, and in many cases will use indirect exporting. If indirect exporting is used, the entrepreneur's task is to identify either an export trading company, an export management company, or a manufacturer that is currently exporting complementary products. Once one of the three firms is identified, negotiations between the entrepreneur and the exporting company will determine the cost to the entrepreneur; necessary adaptations in product, labeling, and packaging; and the expectations resulting from the agreements. The firm actually doing the exporting will handle all arrangements, shipping, and the ultimate sale abroad.

If direct exporting is chosen, the entrepreneur has additional tasks to complete. In this case, arrangements must be made for proper packing, shipping the product to the coast, getting it on board a ship, getting it off the ship in the destination port, and getting it to the ultimate customer. Adding to the difficulty is the plethora of documents that must accompany or precede the shipment, arranging for payment for the goods, insuring the goods against loss, theft, or damage, and financing the entire process. These tasks can be overwhelming.

Part of the process can be eased by using a **freight forwarder.** The freight forwarder is an intermediary whose job it is to move the product from the plant to its overseas destination. These agents are familiar with the import rules and regulations of foreign countries, methods of shipping, U.S. government export regulations, and the documents connected with foreign trade.[5] They can advise the exporter of the freight costs, port charges, consular fees, cost of special documentation, and insurance costs, as well as their handling fees. All these costs go into determining the ultimate price of the product overseas and the net return to the entrepreneur. They see the product through international customs offices and can reserve space on the ship.

Even though the use of a freight forwarder is an added expense, the benefit is well worth the cost to a new exporter. Dealing with other aspects of the total export process is difficult enough without having to handle all the shipping arrangements too. Once the entrepreneur has experience in exporting, the use of a freight forwarder may be reconsidered.

Sources of Financing

A natural conflict exists between exporters and their customers. Given the distance and required time for a product to reach its customer, a considerable financial burden can arise for the exporter, the customer, or both.

FIGURE 11-3
Letter of Credit
Transaction Process
Source: *Letters of Credit,*
Hongkong Bank.

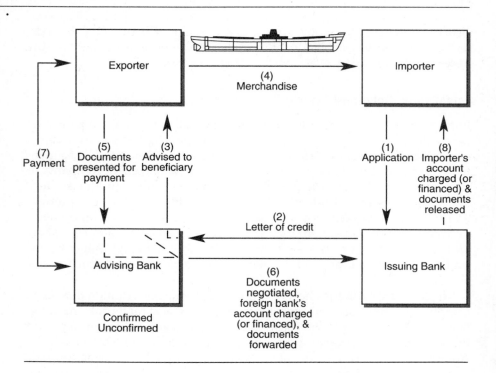

Exporters would like to be paid as soon as the product leaves the manufacturing plant. Customers importing the product, however, want to have the product in hand before paying for it, but this creates a significant time lag for payment from the exporter's point of view.

The more willing an exporter is to provide financing, the more competitive the product will be for the customer. Unfortunately, the exporter may not be able to underwrite the manufacture and shipping of the product and bear the delay in payment. In addition, there is substantial risk in the transaction because of the distance and unfamiliarity between the two parties.

General funding for exporting can be obtained through a local bank that deals in international financing, the U.S. Small Business Administration, or the Export-Import Bank (Eximbank), which specializes in international financing. This financing can be used to offset the delay in payments as well as underwrite the manufacture of the product.

Getting payment from the buyer to the seller for a specific shipment of goods in a timely fashion also requires the services of an international bank. Although many forms of payment exist, the letter of credit has become increasingly popular. The letter of credit is a commitment by the buyer's bank to pay the entrepreneur a sum of money upon compliance with the terms of the shipment. Once shipment has been made, the entrepreneur or the freight forwarder presents the required documents to the local bank, which reviews and forwards them to the foreign bank. If all conditions of the letter of credit are met, the foreign bank transfers monies to the local bank, which deposits the money in the entrepreneur's account. In many cases, this can be completed before the shipment arrives in the foreign country (Figure 11-3).

Typical of international banks is the Hongkong Bank. It is a British-managed bank with 1,300 offices in fifty countries. Among the many services it provides to export-oriented businesses are loans, trade introductions, letters of credit, financing in conjunction with the Eximbank, credit insurance, and foreign exchange information.

Controlling the Strategy

Controlling exporting is more difficult than controlling domestic sales because of the difficulties caused by distance, currency differences, customs and conditions in foreign countries, and the more complex shipping process. Establishing and maintaining controls throughout the process is a difficult but important task.

Many of the control decisions are made when the method of entering the international arena is chosen. For example, the decision to export directly gives more control than indirect exporting. Check Technology Corporation (Venture Perspective 11-5) believes that having its own distributors in each country is the best method to assure control. Licensing gives very little control over either product quality or distribution abroad. Conversely, setting up one's own distribution system in the target countries or selling the product directly to the user adds immeasurably to the amount of control possible.

VENTURE PERSPECTIVE 11-5

. . . .

CHECK TECHNOLOGY CORPORATION

Check Technology Corporation discovered that its computer-controlled electronic printing systems fill a need overseas for producing small orders of personal checks at a low cost. It turned its attention to exporting and found a much larger market than it had at home.

In other countries, checking account customers of banks receive twenty-five to seventy-five checks per order, compared with two hundred to eight hundred per order in the United States. Check Technology's system allows setups for low-volume runs more efficiently and therefore produces cost savings when small orders are printed.

Check Technology increased its international sales staff by more than 50 percent and soon found that its exports represented 60 percent of its total sales. The company sells its equipment through its own subsidiaries in the United Kingdom, France, Spain, and Australia. It has found that a direct presence in each market is necessary to provide the service, support, and maintenance of its equipment.

SOURCE: Glen Morgan, *Passport to Successful Exporting* (Altamonte Springs, FL: Parkway Publications, Inc., 1989), 7–9.

As with domestic sales, control is achieved to a large degree by the effective use of planning and budgeting. With the assistance of expert help from international specialists, the entrepreneur can develop an export budget. This initial budget will likely be far different from actual results, but it becomes a baseline from which to compare later performance.

Another source of control is the careful selection of export management companies, export trading companies, freight forwarders, and foreign distributors or retailers. Checking performance of potential partners in the distribution process can prevent many headaches later. Additional control can be gained by requiring frequent reports from distributors regarding sales, service requirements, complaints, and product returns.

Finally, and most important, control can best be gained in international markets by frequent trips to those markets, talking to distributors face to face, visiting with customers, and assessing opportunities for expansion or threats from competitors. Only through personal visits can an entrepreneur make a totally objective assessment of performance, problems, and opportunities.

TAPPING THE INTERNATIONAL MARKET

The preceding sections have discussed the planning necessary to begin an international strategy. The actual strategy begins by getting out the word about the firm's products. This can be done by attending trade shows or catalog shows. It can also be done by contacting international trade offices for assistance in generating leads.

VENTURE PERSPECTIVE 11-6
. . . .

SANDCO

Sandco is a manufacturer of printing supplies and equipment, located in Tulsa, Oklahoma. When Carolea Wheeler took over the management of Sandco, she thought that there must be international markets for their products. Wheeler started traveling to international trade shows around the world where she met dealers interested in Sandco's products.

Today, attending trade shows remains one of Sandco's most effective ways of expanding foreign sales. The company now sells through dealers in seventy countries and exporting accounts for approximately 40 percent of sales.

SOURCE: Glen Morgan, *Passport to Successful Exporting* (Altamonte Springs, FL: Parkway Publications, Inc., 1989), 29.

International Trade Shows

Industrywide **international trade shows** are held in this country and in foreign locations. Some are annual, some are biannual, and some are only held periodically. Attendance at these trade shows can be beneficial for domestic firms, but it is especially valuable for firms thinking of entering the international market.

The advantage of trade shows is that the company's products can be displayed for many potential customers to view. This is especially important in industrial markets because industrial customers routinely attend the shows. International distributors also attend the trade shows. Thus, the producer and distributor can meet right at the trade show. Export management company representatives also attend trade shows for the industries they represent. The entrepreneur interested in indirect exporting can meet with EMC personnel to discuss possible contracts.

Catalog Shows

Catalog shows differ from trade shows in that the entrepreneur's firm does not have to be personally represented. Instead, the firm produces a catalog of its products that is then displayed at a show. Potential customers can then browse the catalogs for desirable products. This is not as effective as being fully represented at a trade show, but it is far less expensive and may be sufficient for some markets.

Contacts through Government Agencies

A number of information and assistance sources are available to the entrepreneur at little or no cost. The U.S. government provides assistance to internationally oriented companies through several departments and agencies. The most significant of these is the Department of Commerce through the International Trade Administration's U.S. and Foreign Commercial Service (US&FCS). Table 11-5 lists the district offices of the US&FCS. In

ALABAMA
*Birmingham—Rm. 302, Berry Bldg., 2015 2nd Ave. North, 35203, (205) 731-1331

ALASKA
Anchorage—World Trade Center, 4201 Tudor Centre Dr., Suite 319, 99508, (907) 271-6237

ARIZONA
Phoenix—Federal Bldg., 230 North 1st Ave., Rm. 3412, 85025, (602) 379-3285

ARKANSAS
Little Rock—Suite 811, Savers Fed. Bldg., 320 W. Capitol Ave., 72201, (501) 324-5794

CALIFORNIA
Los Angeles—Rm. 9200, 11000 Wilshire Blvd., 90024, (213) 575-7104
Santa Ana—116-A W. 4th St., Suite # 1, 92701, (714) 836-2461
San Diego—6363 Greenwich Dr., Suite 145, 92122, (619) 557-5395
*San Francisco—250 Montgomery St., 14th Floor, 94104, (415) 705-2300

COLORADO
*Denver—Suite 680, 1625 Broadway, 80202, (303) 844-3246

CONNECTICUT
*Hartford—Rm. 610-B, Fed. Office Bldg., 450 Main St., 06103, (203) 240-3530

DELAWARE
Serviced by Philadelphia District Office

FLORIDA
Miami—Suite 224, Fed. Bldg., 51 S.W. First Ave., 33130, (305) 536-5267

•Clearwater—128 North Osceola Ave. 34615, (813) 461-0011
•Orlando—College of Business Administration, CEBA II, Rm. 346, University of Central Florida, 32816, (407) 648-6235
•Tallahassee—Collins Bldg., Rm. 401, 107 W. Gaines St., 32304, (904) 488-6469

GEORGIA
Atlanta—Plaza Square North, 4360 Chamblee Dunwoody Rd., 30341, (404) 452-9101
Savannah—120 Barnard St., A-107, 31401, (912) 944-4204

HAWAII
Honolulu—P.O. Box 50026, 300 Ala Moana Blvd., 96850, (808) 541-1782

IDAHO
•Boise (Portland District)—2nd Flr., Joe R. Williams Bldg., 700 W. State St., 83720, (208) 334-3857

ILLINOIS
Chicago—Rm. 1406, 55 East Monroe St., 60603, (312) 353-4450
•Wheaton—Illinois Institute of Technology, 201 East Loop Rd., 60187, (312) 353-4332
•Rockford—515 North Court St., P.O. Box 1747, 61110-0247, (815) 987-8123

INDIANA
Indianapolis—One North Capitol Ave., Suite 520, 46204, (317) 226-6214

IOWA
Des Moines—817 Fed. Bldg., 210 Walnut St., 50309, (515) 284-4222

KANSAS
•Wichita—(Kansas City, Mo., District) 151 N. Voltusia, 67214-4695 (316) 269-6160

KENTUCKY
Louisville—Rm. 636B, Gene Snyder Courthouse and Customhouse Bldg., 601 W. Broadway, 40202, (502) 582-5066

LOUISIANA
New Orleans—432 World Trade Center, No. 2 Canal St., 70130, (504) 589-6546

MAINE
•Augusta—(Boston District) 77 Sewall St., 04330, (207) 622-8249

MARYLAND
Baltimore—413 U.S. Customhouse, 40 South Gay St., 21202, (301) 962-3560
Gaithersburg—c/o National Institute of Standards & Technology, Bldg. 411, 20899, (301) 962-3560

MASSACHUSETTS
Boston—World Trade Center, Suite 307 Commonwealth Pier Area, 02210, (617) 565-8563

MICHIGAN
Detroit—1140 McNamara Bldg., 477 Michigan Ave., 48226, (313) 226-3650
•Grand Rapids—300 Monroe N.W., 49503, (616) 456-2411

MINNESOTA
Minneapolis—108 Fed. Bldg., 110 S. 4th St., 55401, (612) 348-1638

MISSISSIPPI
Jackson—328 Jackson Mall Office Center, 300 Woodrow Wilson Blvd., 39213, (601) 965-4388

MISSOURI
*St. Louis—7911 Forsyth Blvd., Suite 610, 63105, (314) 425-3302

. . . .

TABLE 11-5
International Trade Administration U.S. and Foreign Commercial Service (US&FCS)

Kansas City—Rm. 635, 601 East 12th St., 64106, (816) 426-3141

MONTANA
Serviced by Portland District Office

NEBRASKA
Omaha—11133 "O" St., 68137, (402) 221-3664

NEVADA
Reno—1755 E. Plumb Ln., # 152, 89502, (702) 784-5203

NEW HAMPSHIRE
•**Concord**—(Boston District) c/o Department of Resources and Economic Development, Division of Economic Development, 172 Pembroke Rd., P.O. Box 856, 03302-0856, (603) 271-2591

NEW JERSEY
Trenton—3131 Princeton Pike Bldg., # 6, Suite 100, 08648 (609) 989-2100

NEW MEXICO
•**Albuquerque** (Dallas District)—625 Silver SW., 3rd Fl., 87102, (505) 766-2070
•**Santa Fe** (Dallas District)—c/o Economic Develop. and Tourism Dept., 1100 St. Francis Drive, 87503, (505) 988-6261

NEW YORK
Buffalo—1312 Fed. Bldg., 111 West Huron St., 14202, (716) 846-4191
•**Rochester**—111 East Ave., Suite 220, 14604, (716) 263-6480
New York—Fed. Office Bldg., 26 Fed. Plaza, Rm. 3718, Foley Sq., 10278, (212) 264-0600

NORTH CAROLINA
*****Greensboro**—400 W. Market St., Suite 400, P.O. Box 1950, 27401, (919) 333-5345

NORTH DAKOTA
Serviced by Omaha District Office

OHIO
*****Cincinnati**—9504 Fed. Office Bldg., 550 Main St., 45202, (513) 684-2944
Cleveland—Rm. 600, 668 Euclid Ave., 44114, (216) 522-4750

OKLAHOMA
Oklahoma City—6601 Broadway Extension, 73116, (405) 231-5302
•**Tulsa**—440 S. Houston St., 74127, (918) 581-7650

OREGON
Portland—Suite 242, One World Trade Center, 121 S.W. Salmon St., 97204, (503) 326-3001

PENNSYLVANIA
Philadelphia—475 Allendale Road, Suite 202, King of Prussia, Pa., 19406, (215) 962-4980
Pittsburgh—2002 Fed. Bldg., 1000 Liberty Ave., 15222, (412) 644-2850

PUERTO RICO
San Juan (Hato Rey)—Rm. G-55 Fed. Bldg., 00918, (809) 766-5555

RHODE ISLAND
•**Providence**—(Boston District) 7 Jackson Walkway, 02903, (401) 528-5104, ext. 22

SOUTH CAROLINA
Columbia—Strom Thurmond Fed. Bldg., Suite 172, 1835 Assembly St., 29201 (803) 765-5345
•**Charleston**—JC Long Bldg., Rm. 128, 9 Liberty St., 29424, (803) 724-4361

SOUTH DAKOTA
Serviced by Omaha District Office

TENNESSEE
Nashville—Suite 1114, Parkway Towers, 404 James Robertson Parkway, 37219-1505, (615) 736-5161
•**Knoxville**—301 E. Church Ave., 37915, (615) 549-9268
•**Memphis**—The Falls Building, Suite 200, 22 North Front St., 38103, (901) 544-4137

TEXAS
*****Dallas**—Rm. 7A5, 1100 Commerce St., 75242-0787, (214) 767-0542
•**Austin**—P.O. Box 12728, 816 Congress Ave., Suite 1200, 78711, (512) 482-5939
Houston—2625 Fed. Courthouse, 515 Rusk St., 77002, (713) 229-2578

UTAH
Salt Lake City—Suite 105, 324 South State St., 84111, (801) 524-5116

VERMONT
Serviced by Boston District Office

VIRGINIA
Richmond—8010 Fed. Bldg., 400 North 8th St., 23240, (804) 771-2246

WASHINGTON
Seattle—3131 Elliott Ave., Suite 290, 98121, (206) 553-5615

WEST VIRGINIA
Charleston—405 Capitol St., Suite 809, 25301, (304) 347-5123

WISCONSIN
Milwaukee—Fed. Bldg., U.S. Courthouse, Rm. 606, 517 E. Wisc. Ave., 53202, (414) 297-3473

WYOMING
Serviced by Denver District Office

SOURCE: *Business America* 113, no. 7 (April 6, 1992): 49.

*Denotes regional office with supervisory regional responsibilities
•Denotes trade specialist at a branch office

addition to providing assistance through its offices, it also publishes *A Basic Guide to Exporting* and *Business America*, a biweekly periodical with articles, features, and success stories. In order to organize information on resources available through the U.S. government, the Interagency Task Force on Trade publishes the *Exporter's Guide to Federal Resources for Small Business*. This book lists the offices and contact persons for dozens of agencies that can be of assistance. It even lists suggested speakers that could address groups interested in international issues.

Many state governments also provide assistance to companies within their states that have an interest in entering the international market. This is particularly evident in states with a large number of exporting or multinational firms. Some universities are also involved with export assistance. This is often in conjunction with state commerce agencies, which provide funding for the establishment of international trade centers on university campuses.

OTHER FORMS OF INTERNATIONAL ENTREPRENEURSHIP

The major part of this chapter has dealt with exporting. There are, however, other forms of international involvement. In regard to selling U.S.-based products outside the United States, avenues include direct investment, licensing, or joint ventures. Entrepreneurial firms may also be interested in importing rather than exporting.

Direct Investment

Direct investment means that the U.S.-based company or individual begins a complete operation in a foreign company. It may be a firm designed to sell U.S.-made products, or it may be a manufacturing company that exports products back to the United States as well as to other countries. In the case of retail or service businesses, direct investment means setting up an entire venture in another country. In most cases, these ventures will be similar to those in the United States. In some cases, however, the venture is started from scratch in the foreign country.

Licensing

Licensing refers to the agreement with a foreign firm to produce and sell the entrepreneurial firm's products. This differs from exporting in that the U.S. firm does not produce the product for export. Rather, it licenses the rights to produce and sell the product to another firm in exchange for a royalty payment. To an extent, then, licensing to overseas manufacturers is similar to franchising. The originating firm prescribes the specifications for the production of the product as well as requirements for distribution, service, and warranties. The advantage of licensing is that the firm does not have to use its own capacity for production or bear the risks associated with overseas distribution. The downside of licensing is that the firm has little control over the production, distribution, and service of the product. Thus, the possibility exists whereby the image of the overall firm could be harmed in the market abroad. This could be especially harmful if the firm should decide to change from licensing to exporting products.

Joint Ventures

A **joint venture,** in domestic as well as international markets, refers to the partial joining of two separate firms for the purpose of developing or marketing products or services. Often, the two firms will form a separate firm that is jointly owned by both. The ownership percentage is determined through negotiation, and it need not be 50-50.

In the international arena, the joint venture often involves one U.S. firm and one foreign firm. The two firms form a joint venture for the purpose of manufacture and distribution of the U.S. firm's products. Since each is a part owner, each will have a vested interest in the quality of production and distribution. In some cases, components for the product will be manufactured in the United States but assembled in the foreign country. The advantage of the joint venture is the shared risks, technology, and access to foreign markets. In some countries, joint ventures are strongly encouraged by the country's government because of the contribution to the area's economy. Joint ventures can, of course, be used conversely for selling products originating in foreign countries in the United States.

Importing

Entrepreneurs in all product-related ventures—manufacturing, wholesaling, and retailing—may choose importing as a major part of their strategy. Importing may be the chosen form of acquiring goods because of perceived differences in quality, cost, or availability of products. Many of the products are finished goods such as automobiles, luggage, or VCRs. Others will be components such as automobile engines, material for apparel manufacturers, or computer parts.

The decision to import should be made with the same care as the decision to export. The international strategic planning model shown in Figure 11-1 should be studied again from the perspective of the potential importer. In particular, the overall strategy of the firm should be considered before determining how the importing strategy fits. The strengths and weaknesses of the venture should be considered in light of their impact on an importing decision. In the strategy development phase, overall plans for importing should be developed. Once the strategy is determined, relationships must be established with foreign country exporters, intermediaries, and banks that operate in international markets. As with any strategy, controls must be determined to ensure that actions go as planned.

The importer has many of the same decisions to make as the exporter, with the difference being the direction of movement of the products and payments. For example, a retailer selling imported goods in Alabama must decide which country and company to buy from and agree on the method of shipment from the producer. The retailer may have the option of dealing directly with a producer in Germany or working with an import broker in New York. The seller of imported goods may search world-wide for producers just as the producer of goods may search world-wide for buyers.

Financing must also be considered from the perspective of the importer. Figure 11-3 can be studied just as well from an importer's viewpoint as from that of an exporter. In this case, the importer works with an

VENTURE PERSPECTIVE 11-7

BEIJING PIZZA

Richard Rosenzweig is not the typical pizza entrepreneur. His first restaurant is in Beijing, China. It is an interesting challenge to open a pizza restaurant. It is even more interesting when the restaurant is in Beijing, China. And it is amazing when considering the fact the Chinese diet does not include cheese.

Rosenzweig's idea is for a New York-style, 600-seat pizzeria complete with New York street signs and American pop music. The Chinese diet does not include cheese, so customers will be able to order cheeseless pizza with tomato sauce, vegetables, and pork, China's staple meat. Pizza is not totally new to China since some western-run hotels serve it to foreigners, but this will be the first restaurant selling pizza mainly to Chinese.

Rosenzweig's New York City Pizza Corporation became part of a joint venture with Beijing Yanhai Development and Trade Corporation, a subsidiary of the Chinese Ministry of Agriculture in 1989. The Chinese put up $1.8 million, including the site in central Beijing and will own 60 percent of the venture. Rosenzweig's side put up $1.2 million and will train the staff in the craft of making thin-crust, New York-style pizzas.

A slice of pizza, an ice cream, and a soft drink sell for seven yuan ($1.90)—more than a day's wages for the average Chinese worker.

SOURCE: "Beijing to Get Slice of Big Apple in Guise of N.Y. Pizza," *Los Angeles Times*, Aug 28, 1989, p. 3.

international bank in the United States to arrange payments to a foreign exporter via a bank in the exporter's country. Letters of credit will be used in the same way as for exporting.

U.S.-based importers have as their main concern the receipt of goods of desired quality at a price that allows them to be competitive. They must receive the goods in a timely manner in order to have the products in inventory at the appropriate time. The products must also be appealing to customers, with clear instructions and labeling. Warranties must also be clear.

Entrepreneurs interested in importing can use the services of the same government agencies as can exporters. Officials in the foreign trade offices can assist in finding products to import and work with the companies or country governments to expedite the shipment of the products. Just as in exporting, the first-time importer is well advised to seek counsel available from government agencies.

SUMMARY

International markets are certainly an exciting arena for entrepreneurial firms that desire additional growth. At the same time, international sales is not for everyone. Entering the international market for the first time can be a time-consuming and frustrating venture. But if sufficient information and assistance can be obtained, the entrepreneur stands ready to achieve major growth compared to that possible in domestic markets.

The international decision should not be made independent of the firm's domestic strategy. In fact, the domestic strategy should be carefully analyzed to determine if an international move is advised. The strategic planning model introduced earlier in the text was adapted in this chapter for use in analyzing the international arena. Decisions that are most important include: should the firm export, how should it export, what should it export, and where should it export. Each of these decisions requires careful study and research.

Firms may want to export directly or indirectly. Direct exporting offers additional control of the process but is more costly and more difficult for first-time exporters. Conversely, indirect exporting is much easier for the producing firm but has the disadvantage of loss of control over the product after it is sold to intermediaries. Intermediaries who either purchase goods or provide assistance include export management companies (EMCs), export trading companies (ETCs), freight forwarders, or other companies that may purchase the firm's products to include with their own.

Significant advice and information are available regarding exporting. Most notable is the United States and Foreign Commercial Service of the U.S. Department of Commerce's International Trade Administration. A number of excellent books and periodicals are available that provide information on exporting.

Entrepreneurial firms may also be interested in other forms of international involvement. For ventures with products to sell outside the United States, either licensing or joint ventures are appealing to some. Other firms may be more interested in importing as part of their strategy.

· ·

1. What are the advantages of exporting? Should an entrepreneur consider exporting before the domestic market is saturated? Why or why not?

2. What should be studied before the decision to export is made?

3. What is the effective difference between the strategic planning model as presented in Chapter 4 and the model presented in this chapter?

4. Why should a firm's overall strategy be analyzed before embarking on an international strategy?

5. Is the decision regarding what to export separate from the decisions regarding whether, how, and where a venture should export?

6. Why is financing an export venture more difficult than financing a domestic venture?

7. What information would an entrepreneur need about a country in deciding whether to export to that country? Which information is most important?

8. Where would you find the information for your answer to question 7?

9. Why should an entrepreneur *not* take advantage of all export opportunities?

10. What control measures should be taken to assure that exports successfully satisfy customers?

11. Using the library, study the Eximbank. What does it really do for potential exporters? For importers?

DISCUSSION QUESTIONS

12. How is a joint venture different from direct exporting? From indirect exporting?

13. Is licensing desirable? What factors should be considered in deciding whether to export or license?

14. What information does an entrepreneur need to determine whether to import a product or component? Where would that information be found?

EXERCISES

EXERCISE 11-1

For the following list of products, determine whether there is an export market, where the market is, and how best to tap the market.

1. Mechanized sweepers (similar to street cleaners except smaller and used in manufacturing plants)
2. Hard drives for computers
3. Golf balls
4. Textbooks for college classes
5. String-type weed trimmers
6. A product of your choice

EXERCISE 11-2

Develop an export plan for a company. Discuss the necessary information with an International Trade Center specialist, other university faculty or staff with expertise in international business, or a state or federal government representative specializing in international business.

ENDNOTES

1. "U.S. Trade Facts," *Business America*, U.S. Department of Commerce, 113, no. 9 (World Trade Week 1992): 34.

2. *A Basic Guide to Exporting*, International Trade Administration, U.S. and Foreign Commercial Service, U.S. Department of Commerce (Washington, DC: U.S. Government Printing Office, 1986), vii.

3. *A Basic Guide to Exporting* (1992), 4-1 to 4-6.

4. *A Basic Guide to Exporting* (1986), 85–86.

5. *A Basic Guide to Exporting* (1992), 12-1 to 12-4.

◆ Conveniesse, Inc. ◆

Going International

Yolanda, Sarah, and Jason worked diligently to prepare expansion plans for the new stores in Buffalo and Syracuse. Using one of the rentable laptops, they worked throughout the night on projections for various scenarios. They did not know how much time Akins would give them to come up with a plan. Yolanda flew back to New York, turned in her resignation effective in two weeks, and began finishing up or turning her projects over to others. She had Jason and Sarah begin looking for an apartment for her in Buffalo. During the evenings, between packing and other activities, she worked on spreadsheets and financial projections and either faxed them to Buffalo or sent them via the modem to the laptop.

A week after Yolanda arrived back in Buffalo, the trio went back to see the developer with a sketched out proposal. They had rejected franchising for now until they saw how the replicated units went. They proposed to the developer that he invest $800,000 into their corporation. Seventy thousand dollars would buy out the three informal investors, giving them a 16.7 percent return in less than a year, and $80,000 would pay off Akins's loan to them. The remaining $650,000 would go toward developing the next two locations. They would go to the bank for another $250,000.

The $800,000 would entitle Akins to a 49 percent share of the corporation. They would retain 51 percent. Their own investment would be the $150,000 they had first invested, the approximately $400,000 in loans, the retained earnings for the first year of operations, and their own time and talent. The new capital would be used to develop the other downtown Conveniesse and the airport store. A further stipulation was that the three could buy out Akins's portion at any time from their retained earnings. They presented a summary of the proposal and had several pages of projections showing that it could work if successive units of Conveniesse were as profitable as this one appeared to be.

Akins listened carefully to their presentation. Then he rubbed his chin and said, "Well, I'll have to run these figures by my financial V.P. to make sure I'm coming out all right," he paused, "but the concept looks good to me. I'll get back to you within forty-eight hours. And then let's get to work. I want those stores in my buildings!"

Jason, Sarah, and Yolanda felt as if a ton of bricks had been lifted from their shoulders, but to an extent another ton was placed on them. They realized they had just entered a whole new era and were beginning what could be a really high growth operation. None of them had enough business experience to fully contemplate where or how far they were headed.

The next two years were spent developing three new stores while continuing the original one. They determined that the location near the SUNY-Buffalo campus was not sufficient to support a Conveniesse store, but the other three and the original Conveniesse were all doing well. A few months later, the developer called them in again.

"What do you know about Canada?"

"I'm Canadian," Sarah replied. "I lived in Montreal my entire life and moved to Buffalo only when we opened Conveniesse."

"Ah, Montreal," he mused. "How would you like to move home?"

"What!"

"Perhaps start a, shall we call it, Conveniesse Canada. In Montreal. Perhaps two or three in Montreal. Then maybe move to Quebec. Or go the other way to Ottawa and Toronto."

"That's interesting," Sarah replied. "Only last week we were discussing the fact that we could expand now that we are essentially out of the store management business and into managing the chain. We are giving some thought to going west toward Detroit, Cleveland, or Indianapolis either through our chain or via franchising."

"However you want to do it. But as before, don't wait too long."

The three went back to their office for another one of their planning sessions, which had become more frequent in recent times as their operations had grown rapidly. In this session, three topics were on the agenda. One, did they want to expand? Two, did they want to expand to Canada? And three, how were they going to do it?

While the three had matured over the past few years, their limitations had also become more apparent. Yolanda continued to be the analytical but cautious member of the team. Sarah's abilities at running her own accounting firm had been sorely stretched as the demands of financing more rapid growth increased. But she turned out to be very good at store management and handled training of new managers, employee handbooks, and payroll. Jason had matured emotionally and became the key person for dealing with outsiders, such as handling supplier problems, working with bankers, and being in charge of customer relations. Yolanda took care of all marketing issues and did most of the financial analysis work. She also took the lead in any planning related to the growth of the venture. She still became impatient when others did not see her conclusions as rapidly as she thought they should have. Still, the three generally got along quite well in spite of a few minor rifts.

Even though Conveniesse had seen great growth in three and a half years, going from one store to four, the stores were all essentially alike and all were either in Buffalo or Syracuse. It seemed like they might be at a crossroads. They could grow relatively slowly, at the pace that the developer wanted. Or they could break loose from the developer and grow at a rate they found more challenging and with greater possible returns. The trio decided they were not quite ready to either enter a very rapid growth phase or enter into franchising. They had no experience in franchising, the cost of a new unit was beyond the capital available to them, and an office building convenience store didn't appear to lend itself as much to the benefits of franchising as some other ventures might. So they decided to stay for now with the developer, but reconsider in two years.

With this in mind, they could now turn their attention to the Canadian market. It appeared at the outset that Conveniesse Canada would go as well as the original. With colder weather in Canada, an office building convenience store seemed plausible. Montreal, however, is primarily French speaking, although most residents know English. Sarah knew Montreal and had owned a small business there. But doing business in Montreal as a U.S. company might be entirely different. Despite Sarah's confidence, Jason and Yolanda were unsure whether customs in Montreal might differ enough to be of concern.

Assignment

What does Conveniesse need to know before moving into the Canadian market? Are there any customs that would be different? Should they expand within the current organizational structure of Conveniesse, Inc., or should they set up a separate corporation? Where should they go to get additional information, and how should they analyze it? Finally, does this seem like a good idea?

IV

PLANNING FOR ENTREPRENEURIAL MANAGEMENT

Structuring the Venture

•

Managing Growth

•

Intrapreneurship

12 Structuring the Venture

LEARNING OBJECTIVES

After reading this chapter, you should be familiar with:

1. The alternative ways to organize a venture's internal structure
2. How to recognize when a given structure is not effective
3. The unique features of a family held venture as they relate to the venture's structure
4. The reasons why a particular structure is appropriate
5. The methods of assimilating new ventures into existing ventures
6. Problems that can arise from inappropriate structure choice
7. The value of a board of directors

KEY TERMS

Basic structure

Functional management structure

Divisional structure

Wholly owned subsidiary

Separate ventures

Holding company

Board of directors

CONSIDER THIS!

- The structure of a venture should be a function of its proposed strategy, but it also may affect what strategy is selected.
- Some long-standing inefficiencies in business organizations are eventually traced to inappropriate structures.
- The method of assimilating a new venture into an existing one may send definite messages to workers in both groups.
- The structure of ventures within a parent company may be a function of financing, politics, legal issues, and egos.
- In an acquisition situation, the new and existing companies have cultures and structures that may be significantly different and may not mesh well.
- A board of directors is as important for new and small ventures as it is for larger corporations.

Previous chapters have dealt with how to analyze a venture, how to launch it, how to finance it, and how to build strategies for it. Attention now turns to planning the structure of the venture. Regardless of its size, each business organization adopts a structure based upon its strategy. In order for the strategy to be successful, the structure must fit the strategy. For the

HOWARD SMITH
Clarity Software, Inc.

Howard Smith was all set to go on a sabbatical leave from Silicon Graphics, Inc. (SGI), a Mountain View, California, maker of computer workstations for three-dimensional graphics. He had been vice-president of engineering at SGI. However, he was plagued by the same problem that plagues many companies that have networked workstations or a combination of DOS-based, Apple, and Unix-based machines. That problem is how to allow users on different operating systems to communicate formatted information.

Instead of taking his sabbatical from SGI, Smith decided to quit the company entirely and start his own software firm, Clarity Software, Inc. The purpose of Clarity was to develop software that would allow users to create and distribute formatted documents. Using $100,000 of his own capital, Smith launched Clarity Software in early 1990 and hired his first employee in March. Fifteen months later, in June 1991, the first version of Rapport was ready to market.

Howard Smith was not born rich. He attended Booker T. Washington High School in Shreveport, Louisiana. He had an interest in chemical engineering but the only school in

Louisiana with that major was Louisiana State University. Unfortunately, in 1957 the school did not allow blacks. He moved to California where he lived with his father and attended Los Angeles City College and later graduated from California State University at Los Angeles and received a master's degree from San Jose State University.

After graduation, Smith worked for Lockheed Missile and Space, IBM, EDS, and Hewlett-Packard before joining SGI. At that time, SGI was a startup company with approximately one hundred employees. When Smith joined SGI, it had sales of $5 million; when he left, it had sales of $400 million.

Financing to develop Rap-

port came from three local venture capital firms that provided a total of $3 million. Later, those three firms and an additional firm provided another $3.5 million. Sales projections, originally calculated to be approximately $10 million by the end of 1992, were revised to approximately $3 million because of the recession in the early 1990s. Because of the predicted growth for the product, sales are projected to be $20 million by 1994. The challenge is to get as many copies of the software in place as quickly as possible. This improves the chances that Rapport will become the industry standard. The need to move quickly is underscored by the possibility that a larger firm could come out with a similar product and capture market share.

Significant possibilities exist for Clarity's Rapport software. The past few years have not seen rapid growth in computer sales. Networked workstations, however, have grown substantially; they increased by 19.7 percent in 1991. This suggests that Rapport may have a ready market in the coming years.

SOURCE: Matt Rothman, "Station to Station," *Inc.* 14, no. 4, April 1992: 82–90; interview with Howard Smith. Used with permission.

entrepreneurial business, the structure is also a function of the entrepreneur's personality and abilities, the size and nature of the business, and the number of family members involved in the venture.

Structuring the firm can take two different forms. The first, which is required of all ventures, is to determine the internal structure of the venture itself. The second is to assimilate a new venture into an existing one. The overall structure is a function of many variables including the number of ventures, their type and culture, control issues, and power and motivation issues. It is important to plan the initial structure of firms before their launch or acquisition in order to maximize both the efficiency and the effectiveness of the organization.

A final structure topic is to design a board of directors or advisors to assist the entrepreneur in managing and controlling the firm.

DETERMINING THE INTERNAL STRUCTURE OF A VENTURE

It is especially important to plan the structure of a new venture well since it is the most malleable when it is new. Like modeling clay, the structure of an organization is harder to change after it has set for some time. This section will discuss the basic structure likely to occur upon the launch of a venture and will then consider the appropriate structures once the venture begins to grow.

Basic Structure

The most **basic structure** of new or small businesses is one in which there is a single manager. All other employees answer to the single manager who is typically the owner or founding entrepreneur. This type of structure is used among most low-growth ventures and initially among many growth ventures. The basic structure has both advantages and disadvantages.

The advantages of the basic structure center on its simplicity. The basic structure is easy to administer, and everyone knows who is in charge. With the basic structure, the single manager is totally in command. All decisions, all resource allocation, all hiring, firing, promotion, and assignments are made by a single person. Regardless of whether the decision is related to marketing, production, finance, personnel, or venture strategy, the authority and responsibility for and control of activities rest with the owner/manager/entrepreneur. There is no problem with conflict among managers since there is only one manager. Employees need not worry about different people telling them different things since only one person has that authority.

The disadvantages of the basic structure also revolve around its simplicity. Since there is only one manager or one authority figure, the venture can encounter severe problems if that manager is unavailable. Small ventures often have problems when the owner/manager is also the chief salesperson and is frequently busy with clients. If the manager spends substantial time on the phone making quotes or dealing with suppliers, then employees or other customers must wait before getting their own questions answered. The need for the entrepreneur's presence also reduces the possibilities for vacations or needed business trips.

The basic structure also demands so much of the manager's time that little *effective* time is left for planning, working with financing, developing new customers, or working in the community. The National Federation of Independent Business (NFIB) surveyed entrepreneurs who had been in business for three to five years. It found that the average entrepreneur spends 45 percent of the time either in direct selling or in production while spending only 5 percent of the time in planning for the venture's growth. Ten percent of the time is spent dealing with employees and 10 percent is spent arranging financial matters.[1]

The time constraints on the entrepreneur in a basic structure organization flow over into typical nonwork hours. A similar NFIB survey reported on the amount of hours worked by entrepreneurs.[2] Only 23 percent reported working *fewer* than fifty hours per week in the venture. Fifty-one percent reported working between fifty and seventy hours a week, and 25 percent worked more than seventy hours per week for the venture. Interestingly, most entrepreneurs surveyed started their ventures when they were between twenty-five and forty years of age, the age when most had small children at home.

The basic structure works well when the venture is small or when it faces a stable environment. As the venture grows or the environment becomes more dynamic, the basic structure causes the venture to suffer significant inefficiencies. The venture may become so *inefficient* that it is no longer *effective* in achieving the objectives set for it. The key to the inefficiencies is the size of the venture and the dynamics of the environment; time is not a factor. As long as the venture remains small, inefficiencies will not be severe regardless of how long the business has existed. Only when growth or turbulence are encountered will problems develop.

Recognizing Inefficiencies

New and small ventures begin to suffer inefficiencies resulting from their basic structure when the owner/manager/entrepreneur becomes increasingly unable to make the necessary decisions to enable the venture to operate smoothly. There are several signs that indicate that structural inefficiencies are becoming excessive. These fall into categories of customer concerns, employee concerns, administrative concerns, and non-business concerns.

Inefficiency-caused *customer concerns* are those problems where a customer is lost or is poorly treated because the manager is unavailable. The unavailability may be because the manager is talking on the telephone. It may be because the manager is closeted in the back room trying to get the accounting records to balance. Perhaps the entrepreneur is out prospecting for new customers and is therefore unavailable for existing customers. Telephone customers who are left on hold for excessive periods of time become irritated. Potential customers who cannot get a quote because the owner is the only one who can make the quote find other sources of the product or service.

Employee concerns resulting from problems with the basic structure typically revolve around inability to get definitive answers from an overworked boss. Training of new employees is often poor. Unwillingness to delegate authority—a frequent problem with entrepreneurs—results in employees not being able to make simple decisions without first checking with the owner. Confusion among employees caused by inadequate communication and guidance often results in frustration among employees and errors in dealing with outsiders or paperwork.

Administrative problems result from diseconomies of scale in the new venture. Bills don't get paid, invoices don't get sent out, bookkeeping doesn't get done, and plans don't get made. Many entrepreneurs do not like paperwork anyway. The additional stress caused by work overload means there is even more reason for *not* doing the paperwork. As a result, the administrative tasks get further and further behind.

The entrepreneur's time schedule can affect *non-business* activities such as family activities. Missed birthday parties, preoccupation with business matters while at home, insufficient time to participate in church or community activities, and a reduction in the entrepreneur's social life are all indications of an overcommitment of time and energy caused by the entrepreneur's trying to do all things for the new venture.

Table 12-1 lists these and other signals of venture inefficiencies caused by an overstressed basic structure. Many of these are easy to recognize, and occur from time to time in most ventures. Their occurrence with excessive frequency gives clear signals that restructuring the venture is needed.

Resolving the Problem

Two solutions can ease the problem without structural changes. However, if the venture continues to grow, there will be no recourse except to restructure the organization. The two solutions are to delegate better and to use time management in order to use the scarce time that is available more efficiently.

Customer Concerns
1. Unanswered phone messages
2. Telephone customers left on hold
3. New customers not being able to reach an authority figure
4. Delays in getting quotes or bids
5. Delays or problems in resolving customer complaints

Employee Concerns
1. Lack of clear instructions
2. Confusion regarding when to act versus when to ask
3. Errors in paperwork because of inadequate communication
4. Frustration among employees because of unavailability of owner/manager

Administrative Concerns
1. Missed deadlines
2. Paperwork ignored or delayed
3. Lack of knowledge regarding how the firm is doing, caused by not keeping records up to date
4. Cash flow problems caused by delayed sending of invoices or billing notices
5. Management by crisis rather than by plan; constant reaction to the latest demand rather than working from an operational plan

Nonbusiness Concerns
1. Family/business conflicts, often caused by insufficient time for the family
2. Insufficient time for community activities, evidenced by dropping out of church, school, and social activities

TABLE 12-1
Signals of Venture
Inefficiencies

Many entrepreneurs, and especially low-growth entrepreneurs, are reluctant to delegate authority to others. This reason perhaps more than any other, causes the inefficiency problems discussed above. This unwillingness is, unfortunately, a character trait of many entrepreneurs and is therefore difficult to change. Entrepreneurs may find, however, that there are tasks that they do not like to do anyway such as billing, recordkeeping, or ordering. These tasks then become prime candidates to be delegated to others. If competent employees can take over those activities, this will reduce the time constraints on the entrepreneur. This, in turn, will allow more time to handle other activities and can possibly reduce other inefficiency problems.

Time management is necessary for all managers regardless of organizational type or size. Time management refers to the arrangement of activities in order to produce more in the same amount of time. Having a secretary screen mail and calls reduces time spent at these tasks. Scheduling blocks of time for specific actions such as ordering, bookkeeping, or planning gives priority to tasks that might otherwise be delayed. Reducing the length or frequency of meetings can eliminate a frequent time waster. These and other time management changes, coupled with better delegation, can provide at least some slack to improve the efficiency of a venture without resorting to restructuring.

Functional Management Structure

As a venture grows, the management of the operation becomes increasingly difficult for a single entrepreneur. Having two general partners in a venture will delay the need for functional management. If the venture continues to grow, however, and signs of inefficiency continue to increase, the need for a functional management structure will become clear.

A **functional management structure** is one in which each or most of the functional aspects of the venture—marketing, accounting, production, personnel—is headed by a manager. The functional management structure evolves over time rather than being created in one bold stroke. For example, as the entrepreneur sees that the bookkeeping is getting further behind and less accurate, he or she may decide to hire a bookkeeper. The bookkeeper may also double as an office manager if none previously existed. Note that in the evolutionary process the person hired is a book-

FIGURE 12-1
Differences between Basic Structure and Functional Management Structure

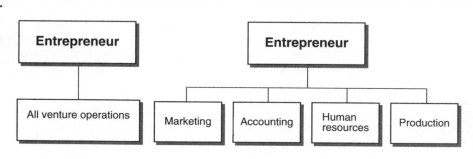

keeper and not an accountant. That position may come much later only after it becomes apparent that the actual accounting should be done in-house rather than being done by an outside accounting firm.

Assuming that the venture continues to grow, either a marketing manager or a production/operations manager might be hired next. If the entrepreneur's strength is in marketing, then an operations manager might be hired to take care of the production aspects of the venture. If the entrepreneur's strength is in operations, then a marketing manager might be hired or promoted. After the company has grown to perhaps one hundred employees or if the employees have joined a union, then a full-time personnel director must be hired. If the company continues to grow, additional staff in all areas will be added. Additional managerial levels may also be added. This is particularly true in growth-oriented ventures.

The key to management-level growth is the increasing size of the venture and/or the dynamic nature of the environment—not simply the passage of time. Some low-growth ventures can keep the basic structure indefinitely. Others grow rapidly and need the functional structure almost immediately after the launch.

Advantages of the Functional Management Structure

The functional management structure has several advantages over the basic structure. The two most significant advantages are the spreading of managerial decision making and the specialization of tasks. Having more managers, regardless of their specialty, is advantageous simply because it dilutes management and increases the number of employees who have decision-making power. Thus, if customers, suppliers, or employees need to talk with someone with decision-making authority, they do not have to wait for the owner/entrepreneur. Similarly, the total number of decisions to be made in the venture is spread among a larger set of managers. Each manager makes a smaller number of decisions and, hence, can give more attention to those that are made. Spreading authority allows more decisions to be made in less time with higher-quality results.

The second advantage of the functional management structure is specialization. Having a manager of marketing, for example, increases the odds that good marketing decisions will be made. Having a trained accountant handle the record keeping improves the quality of both the record keeping and the information provided by the records. The improved quality of decision making in the functional specialties is partially a function of the cumulative attention being given to the area and partially a function of the expertise of the manager. As individuals work more in one specific area they become increasingly adept at decision making related to that area. Hiring managers with education or training in the area gives more expertise and background as a foundation for good managerial decisions.

Disadvantages of the Functional Management Structure

Few disadvantages exist for the functional management structure when compared with the basic structure. The added value of specialized decision making and spreading of authority generally outweighs problems caused by the structure. However, three factors should be considered before moving to a functional management structure. First, adding managers is not necessarily cheap. The cost of the manager must be offset by increased revenues or decreased expenses. Second, the entrepreneur must carefully select the functional managers. If a poorly selected person does not work out in a *large* corporation, other parts of the corporation can absorb the effects of the problem. If a weak manager is selected for a small or new venture, the effect could be disastrous.

The third factor is that the evolving structure can cause confusion about who is in control. Employees are frequently unsure of who is authorized to make which decision, when they can go around the functional manager to the entrepreneur, or how much jurisdiction a manager may have outside the area of expertise. Suppose, for example, that an entrepreneur hires a marketing manager to coordinate sales and develop an advertising program. If the marketing manager then goes to the office manager/bookkeeper requesting a check to a television station to underwrite a major TV ad campaign, should the bookkeeper write the check or ask for authorization by the owner? This problem can be overcome *if* the entrepreneur effectively delegates authority *and* communicates that fact to the employees. Even so, employees may still look to the entrepreneur for the ultimate answer.

Divisional Structure

The basic structure and the functional management structure are the two structure types most often used by new venture entrepreneurs. In the case of high-growth ventures, however, both the basic and the functional management structures eventually become inefficient and must be replaced by a more complex structure: the divisional structure.

The **divisional structure** is an arrangement whereby separate divisions of the venture are developed around either products, processes, customers, or geographical territories. The company is large enough that most divisions have complete administrative facilities. Thus, each division is almost free standing. Any division could be sold, expanded, or closed down without seriously affecting the rest of the venture.

The divisional structure is particularly advantageous if the separate divisions have unrelated products or services or if one division is substantially more risky than the others. This would facilitate making any needed strategic changes in one division without disrupting the others.

The two disadvantages of the divisional arrangement are the duplication of administrative processes for each division and the lack of coordination between divisions. The divisional structure, when fully developed, requires an administrative support structure for each separate division. This requires additional personnel for areas such as marketing and human resources for each division. Thus, the cost can be substantial. The coordination problem comes from the fact that the separate divisions have little need to communicate with each other because of their autonomous arrangement. Thus, one division may make decisions that inadvertently cause problems for another.

The divisional structure will seldom, if ever, be used initially for a new venture unless the new venture is a combination of two or more existing firms. As with the functional arrangement, the divisional structure tends to evolve. A venture with an existing functional management may acquire or develop new product lines that are sufficiently different that they require their own separate structure. In this case, a single unit of the total venture is set up as a separate division with all or most of the administrative support functions duplicated for that division. The remainder of the unit operates under the original functional management structure. As more growth occurs, other sections of the venture may be restructured into divisions until, eventually, the entire firm is under a divisional arrangement.

Developing Line/Staff Relationships

Every management principles textbook has a discussion of line and staff relationships and the problems they cause in organizations. This is a particularly important issue in emerging firms because of the dominant role that the entrepreneur plays in the new venture. Line authority extends directly from the entrepreneur down through the various levels of the venture. In new or small ventures there may be only two or three levels. In growth ventures and larger firms, more levels of management exist.

In most situations, the line authority passes in a relatively straightforward manner. Typically, problems arise only when lower-level managers or nonmanagerial personnel attempt to circumvent the chain of command and go directly to the entrepreneur. Personnel in staff positions, however, may experience far more problems than those in line positions do.

As the venture grows, the necessity of adding staff personnel arises. Staff functions tend to be more advisory, more administration oriented, and tend to require more specialized expertise. Line/staff conflicts exist in all organizations regardless of their size. These conflicts can be serious in the entrepreneurial firm because of the dominant role of the entrepreneur. Line workers, accustomed to dealing directly with the entrepreneur, may resist staff suggestions or demands. Staff personnel who legitimately issue orders in their functional area may find those orders either ignored or appealed unless they are specifically approved by the entrepreneur. It is critical for the entrepreneur to establish the legitimacy of the staff function in order for the staff person to be able to operate effectively. Even with that legitimization, a significant amount of line/staff conflict must be expected.

The problems staff personnel encounter include working with significant customers, suppliers, and other outside contacts. Entrepreneurial firms tend to have a less formal structure, fewer rules, fewer standard operating procedures, and fewer established or contractual relationships than larger, more established firms have. Dealings are much more on a personal, one-to-one basis. The entrepreneur plays such a dominant role in the venture that all parties look to that person as the ultimate source of authority. But establishing rules, procedures, and relationships detracts from the key strength of entrepreneurial firms. The entrepreneur must carefully walk the fence between too much structure and too little structure.

STRUCTURING THE FAMILY VENTURE

There is nothing about a family venture that dictates the structure it must have. Yet, the family venture has unique characteristics that should be considered in the structure decision. Family firms deal with a concept known as institutional overlap.[3] Institutional overlap is the merging of the norms and culture of the family with the norms and culture of an enterprise. When a new venture is launched, the family venture typically benefits from the overlap between the two institutions. During the formative stage, the firm's social dynamics are still highly organic, with all the employees reporting directly to the entrepreneur. The family norms typically carry over into the firm. This increases the loyalty and commitment of all those involved with the venture (Figure 12-2).

As both the family and the business enter new stages in their life cycles, the complexity of relationships increases. First, there are more members of the family who are not direct descendants of the entrepreneur. Thus, a plethora of nieces, nephews, cousins, grandchildren, and so on are in the family. Some of these will have interests in the business. But with the larger group of family members, cohesive values are not as much the norm (Figure 12-3).

At the same time, the business grows and more layers of management and additional employees are needed. Because the needs of the business outstrip the desires of family members to work in the business, an increasing percentage of *nonfamily* members work in the business. This sets the stage for family versus nonfamily conflicts as well as intergenerational conflicts and family versus business conflicts.

As the entrepreneur selects and develops the maturing venture's structure, the complexity of relationships must be considered. Places must be made in the business for additional relatives who can and want to fit in. Yet, other family members as well as nonfamily employees may have concerns over the changes in structure.

A large percentage of family ventures are low-growth or moderate-growth ventures. In these cases, a single entrepreneur or a husband and wife team launches the venture. Children or other relatives may work in the venture. Low-growth family ventures will typically not grow beyond the need for the basic structure. Some will move to a hybrid between the

FIGURE 12-2
Family/Venture Relationships in a New Venture

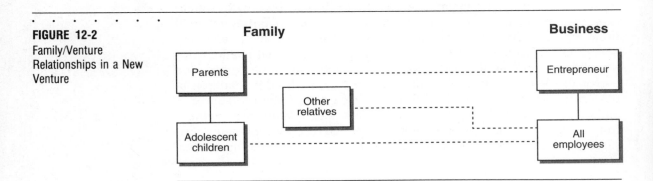

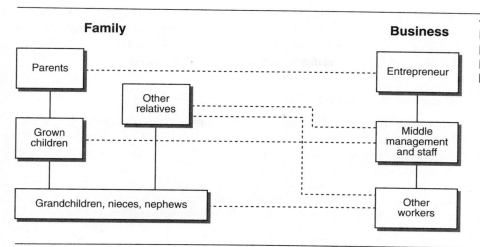

FIGURE 12-3
Family/Venture
Relationships in a Mature
Business

basic and the functional management structure, but most will not grow into a complete functional management structure. Since the owner of a family business must be cognizant of both the needs of the business and the needs of the family, decisions must be made with both institutions in mind. The structure used may not be the most efficient for the venture itself, but may be the best when the venture *and* the entrepreneur's family are considered.

Related to the structure issue is the issue of management succession in the family firm. The succession process is difficult for any firm and even more difficult for the family business.[4] When family business owners were questioned in a study regarding the single most important problem area faced in the transfer process, the most frequent answer related to equal and fair treatment of the children. This topic will be treated in more depth in Chapter 16, Harvesting the Venture.

ASSIMILATING THE NEW VENTURE

This section begins by assuming that the entrepreneur or entrepreneurial team has an existing venture or ventures. The task, then, is to create a home for a new venture that maximizes the efficiency and effectiveness of the total operation while minimizing the costs and risks. Maximizing efficiency and effectiveness, however, is a broad concept and must be treated carefully, for there are many ramifications of any particular structuring scheme that can affect both the efficiency and the effectiveness of the total venture.

Methods of Structuring Ventures

There are four primary methods for assimilating new ventures into existing ones. These are (1) to absorb the new venture totally within the existing venture, (2) to bring in the new venture as a subsidiary of the existing venture, (3) to maintain two separate entities owned by the same entrepreneur, or (4) to create a new corporation as a holding company that owns the stock of both the old and the new ventures.

Absorbing the Venture

If the new venture is small or is related sufficiently to the existing venture, the appropriate structure is to simply absorb the new venture totally into the structure of the existing venture. In this situation, the new venture ceases to exist. All assets and liabilities are transferred to the existing venture, and all staff, production processes, marketing, and services become a part of the existing venture. Although the name of the new venture could conceivably be maintained, that can be cumbersome (Figure 12-4).

Creating a Subsidiary

Rather than absorb the new venture completely into the existing one, the entrepreneur may opt to bring the new venture in as a wholly owned subsidiary of the existing company. A **wholly owned subsidiary** is a business which is totally owned by another business. In this case the entrepreneur buys another venture, and, the acquired firm then legally moves, intact, to the new company (Figure 12-5). Often there is no change in the physical location of the acquired venture. Typically, the acquired venture will retain its identity and, at least initially, most of its structure. In some cases, the previous owner of the acquired venture will join the new venture as a vice-president and possibly maintain the presidency of the acquired firm even though it becomes a subsidiary of the acquiring firm.

The significance of the subsidiary structure is that the acquired venture retains its identity from the perspective of customers or suppliers, but it relies on the parent company for financing and planning. Further, the parent company will ultimately control the operations of the acquired venture. Of course, the degree of control is a function more of the management style of the acquiring entrepreneur than of the particular structure. Still, the subsidiary manager reports to the parent company president.

FIGURE 12-4
Absorbing the New Venture into an Existing One

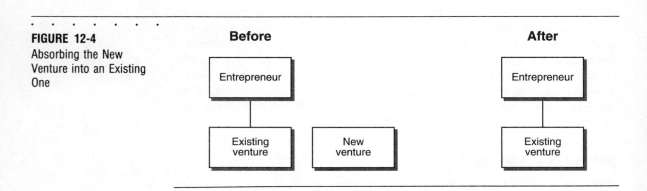

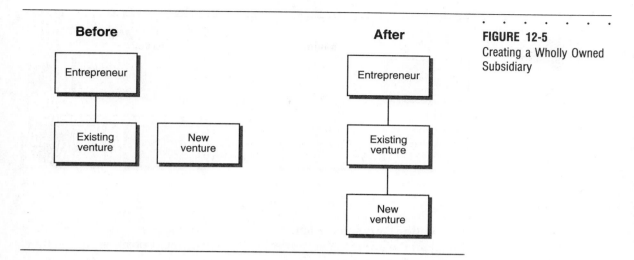

FIGURE 12-5
Creating a Wholly Owned Subsidiary

Maintaining Separate Ventures

Rather than absorb a new venture into the existing venture, the entrepreneur may decide to maintain the two ventures as totally **separate ventures,** related only by their common ownership (Figure 12-6). This gives each not only a separate identity, but also separate control systems, separate accounting systems, separate bank accounts, and separate philosophies. This is often the cleanest way for a low- or moderate-growth entrepreneur to structure an acquisition, because each is kept totally separate from the other. There is little danger of either consciously or unconsciously mixing records, finances, or personnel. Offsetting the cleanliness of the separate structures is the lack of any efficiencies that would be gained by joining the structures.

Creating a Holding Company

The final method of structuring an acquisition is to create an entirely new company that then owns both the existing firm and the acquired firm as subsidiaries. The new company, which owns the stock of both the existing venture and the acquired venture, is called a **holding company.** Or, the two owners can form a new company that then absorbs both the existing firm and the acquired firm. This arrangement is officially called a consolidation. The key to both versions is that both the existing firm and the acquired firm cease to exist as legal entities, although they may retain their separate identities in the eyes of their customers. The new firm absorbs all the assets, debt, personnel, and products of the two ventures. This can be useful if the perception of a larger venture is important or if the entrepreneurs think that a new name and entity would make the venture more competitive. This also sometimes happens when, as part of the deal, the acquired firm's owners insist on a new entity rather than being rolled into

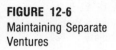

FIGURE 12-6
Maintaining Separate
Ventures

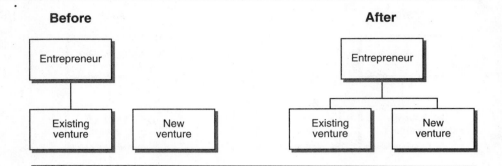

the existing corporate structure. The owners of the previous firm will often then join the acquiring entrepreneur in management positions in the new, larger venture (Figure 12-7).

Factors Affecting Structure

There are a number of factors that influence the way a new venture is assimilated into an existing one. Some of the factors are strategic in nature, some are cost oriented, some could be tax related, some affect the amount and types of personnel required, and some are related to the motivational aspects affecting key managers in both the acquiring and acquired firm.

Strategic Factors

Strategic factors directly influence the ability of ventures to compete in their markets. These may include the name and image of the new and old ventures, the locations of each, or the relationship between the strategies of the two ventures. The *name* of the acquired venture may be significant

FIGURE 12-7
Creating the Holding
Company

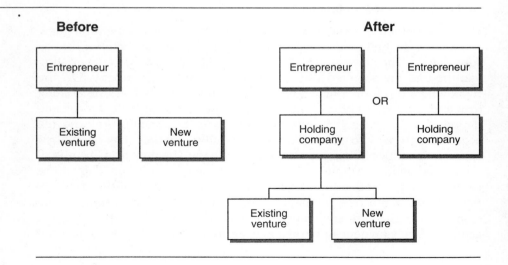

and may need to be maintained in order to give customers a sense of continuity. Maintaining the existing name can be an important issue if the acquired venture is well respected in the area or industry. Maintaining a name, however, is not an absolutely critical issue in the structure because it is the public's view of the name rather than the legal view that is most important.

The *location* of the acquired venture in relation to the acquiring venture may have significant strategic implications for the firm. It may be necessary to adopt a particular structure in order for locational differences to be either minimized if that is the problem or emphasized if separate locations are important. In retail stores, for example, it may be useful to give the perception of competing businesses even though both ventures are owned by the same person or parent company. Thus, two differently named ventures with different locations can offer slightly different merchandise to customers who perceive the stores to be competitors. The two ventures may achieve some synergy by being sister companies while still giving the customer the perception of choice. The opposite conclusion may be reached if there is a strategic reason to combine the two ventures. An example of this reasoning is the need to show a continued growth in sales. As new ventures are acquired, they are absorbed into the existing venture and lose their previous identity. The acquiring company then shows only the combined sales of the units on its income statements, giving the impression that the firm is growing significantly.

A particular structure might better differentiate *similar* ventures. Conversely, strategic and operating issues may suggest different structural forms if the two ventures compete in *unrelated* industries. If two or more significantly different ventures coexist, it may be advisable to keep them separated structurally in order to minimize inadvertent overlap of authority structures, budgets, resource allocation, or personnel. Separating the two ventures clearly makes each exist on its own merits without subsidization by the other. This helps solve one of the worst problems of multiple-venture organizations: the unwarranted mixing of assets, personnel, expenses, and attention between two or more businesses.

Cost Factors

Decisions of structure may be related to costs because of their effect on the current and future profitability of the firm. Costs include the expense of maintaining two separate legal entities, maintaining two separate staffs, duplicative marketing, and redundant production facilities.

Entrepreneurs must consider both the advantages and the disadvantages of each type of structure as they relate to the costs of operating the overall venture. Care must be given that *total* costs are considered rather than costs for one portion only. Further, the cost of a particular structure must be weighed against the other benefits gained from that structure.

In addition to the direct costs associated with a given structure, indirect costs must be considered. Direct costs refer to the cost of staffing, facilities, and transportation. Indirect costs are those costs that are not directly attributable to the structure but are incurred because of the structure. For example, monitoring performance may be easier with one structure than with another. If changes in performance can be corrected more easily with one structure than with another, then that structure is, indirectly, lower in cost.

Tax Issues

The Internal Revenue Service has worked in recent years to reduce the effective differences in tax treatment of the various structure types. Two separate entities are sometimes desirable if one is a corporation and the other has been a sole proprietorship. If the two can be successfully kept separate, then the proprietorship would be taxed on the entrepreneur's personal tax form while the other would be taxed as a corporation. This might be especially important if the proprietorship were losing money. It could then be used to offset earnings from the other ventures. The key to the tax issues related to the various structures is typically not how the entities are structured, but who owns and controls the ventures. There is little difference in tax ramifications between having a holding company and having two freestanding corporations or having one corporation become the subsidiary of another. If they are ultimately owned by the same individual or group, the tax treatment is virtually the same. Even if one of the ventures has substantially higher profits than the other, the graduated tax rates must be prorated between the two ventures rather than being applied separately to each.

Personnel Issues

The amount and type of personnel required for two or more ventures can often be reduced if the ventures are merged into a single entity rather than operated as separate ventures. The savings on personnel may not be as much from efficiencies in the production process as they are from differences in the amount of *administrative* staff required. The overhead costs of two combined ventures may be little more than that of a single venture. For example, accountants need keep only one set of books if there is only one venture, regardless of the size or complexity of the venture. If two ventures are maintained, the accountant must ensure that each venture in the fold has a separate and sufficient set of records.

The opposite argument is also relevant, depending on the nature of the two ventures. If the two ventures are significantly different or are separated geographically, then attempts to merge the administrative functions will often result in significant inefficiencies. This would require staff personnel to commute between the two ventures as well as learn the intricacies of two separate kinds of firms. These inefficiencies can then affect the speed with which administrative decisions can be made, and this in turn may affect morale and productivity.

Motivation Issues

The acquisition of a venture assumes that the personnel will come with the rest of the venture. The acquirer purchases the assets, the liabilities (unless prearranged differently), and the production processes. Implicit is that at

VENTURE PERSPECTIVE 12-1

. . . .

AVERY MFG. AND EKSTRA CO.

"I can't believe he sold us down the river! I updated my resume last night. I've worked for Ekstra for five years, and I'm not about to go to work for some manufacturing outfit!"

"I can do personnel work for anyone. I'm flexible. But I certainly don't like being in an office with ten other people when I'm accustomed to working only with Barb. I'll continue to work with Avery for now because I really don't want to look for a new job. But if Barb Hatcher leaves, I sure don't relish being the only Ekstra person at Avery."

These comments were typical of those heard after Avery Manufacturing agreed to purchase Ekstra from its retiring owner. Avery manufactured a line of water treatment equipment that was sold both to other companies and to home owners. The equipment was good quality and the retail version of the equipment was typically sold through hardware stores bearing the store's house brand. Ekstra, on the other hand, was a manufacturer's

representative company, which represented a number of manufacturers' products throughout the Northeast and Midwest. Avery was one of the companies whose products Ekstra marketed. When the former owner of Ekstra decided to retire, he contacted Avery to see if Avery would be interested in purchasing Ekstra. Gerald Acres, president of Avery, decided that buying Ekstra would be a good way to eliminate the intermediary in marketing their products as well as provide overall growth for his company. He studied Ekstra's books and its operations, liked what he saw, and made an offer, which was accepted.

Gerald Acres then gave considerable thought to what the relationship between Ekstra and Avery would be. Since the CEO of Ekstra was retiring, Acres knew of no one who would be capable of taking over the reins of Ekstra. Further, Ekstra had done reasonably well over the past few years, but Acres thought that more could

be done if he could be closely involved with the operations of the venture. Although Ekstra did have a small support staff, Acres could see no need to maintain it separately from Avery. In fact, some efficiencies could be obtained by having the staff co-located and cross trained so that members of each could do work for the other in slack times.

Acres determined that the most optimal arrangement in his view would be to dissolve Ekstra's corporate structure, maintain the name for a few years, have the manufacturer's representatives report to Avery's vice-president of marketing, and have all the other administrative personnel simply absorbed by the Avery structure. Barb Hatcher, Ekstra's office manager, would become the first full-time human resources manager for Avery Manufacturing and would handle recruiting and training for both Avery's workforce and Ekstra's representatives. It all looked good—in theory.

least some of the workers, management, and staff will also join the new organization. In many cases, the personnel see virtually no differences before and after the acquisition.

It is important, however, to consider the motivational aspects of the structuring schema used. Consider the example in Venture Perspective 12-1. The employees were clearly upset when they found that the company would lose its identity as a freestanding company. The combined firm could have operated nearly as well as a separate company, but the company president opted to absorb Ekstra into the existing structure of Avery Manufacturing. As a result, some of the staff of Ekstra left and the morale of the remaining workers was low for quite some time.

It is difficult to assess the motivational aspects of a particular structure. Having two separate, autonomous units has some positive aspects for the workers since they see themselves as closer to the top-level decision making rather than buried within another's corporate structure. Working in a wholly owned subsidiary of a parent firm may not be of concern to most workers, but it may be distressing to the managers who see their autonomy reduced. Being totally absorbed into the acquiring firm will often have the results alluded to in Venture Perspective 12-1 unless the acquiring firm's management does an excellent job in making the new workers feel at home and important in the new structure.

Employees in the acquiring firm may also be concerned about merging a new entity with the existing organization. If the staff of the new venture is eliminated, this may cause additional work for existing staff. Bringing other workers into the organization may also threaten the security of existing staff competing for promotions or bonuses.

Conversely, meshing two organizations together may have some positive impact because the employees see the new organization as a larger, growing organization. They may realize that opportunities exist in the combined firm that did not exist in the previous, smaller venture.

Power, Ego, and Control

The preceding paragraphs addressed the motivation of workers and managers in the acquired firm. Perhaps even more critical is the impact on the acquired firm's *top management*. Peter Drucker says that, in any acquisition, management of the acquiring firm must be able to replace the key managers of the acquired firm within one year. "The buyer has to be prepared to lose the top incumbents in companies that are bought. Top people are used to being bosses; they don't want to be 'division managers.' "[5] In many cases, the acquisition has made the previous owners wealthy, so they don't really need to work in a subordinate position. Even top managers who were not owners may find positions with other companies that give them more autonomy and prestige than they would have under either an absorbed structure or a subsidiary arrangement.

The impact on the ego of the acquired firm's managers is related closely to the power and control issues. If the acquired firm is absorbed or becomes a subsidiary, the egos of the acquired firm's top managers will most assuredly be bruised. Conversely, if the acquiring entrepreneur believes strongly that the management of the acquiring firm should remain intact, then either the separate entity or the holding company structure should be used. The holding company structure may be best since both the acquiring and acquired firms are subsumed into a new parent corporation whose managers will likely come from both firms.

Although the acquiring firm's management must be concerned about the motivation of the acquired management, an equally important issue is that of management control. Control refers to the issues of who makes the decisions, who allocates the resources, who reports to whom, who ensures that the desired work is completed, and where the acquired firm falls on the overall organization chart.

Concern for control of the corporation often results in a structure for the acquired firm that is roughly opposite of what would be determined if motivation and autonomy were the primary concerns. If the acquiring entrepreneur wants to ensure personal control of the combined venture, then the structure selected will likely be either the subsidiary structure or the absorbed structure. This ensures that the entrepreneur will have full control over both the strategy and the resource allocation. The separate entity structure, on the other hand, allows the acquired venture's management to retain some control over the operation.

CREATING A BOARD OF DIRECTORS

Chapter 3 briefly discussed creating an advisory board as part of the entrepreneurial team. The concept is discussed here from an organizational structure viewpoint. The need for a board of directors, along with its composition and use, is examined.

Sole proprietorships and partnerships are not required to have boards of directors. Corporations are required to have a board of directors, which is technically required to meet. Most meet only perfunctorily to satisfy state charter requirements. Astute entrepreneurs, however, develop boards of directors or informal advisory boards to provide guidance in developing the strategy and operations of the venture.

A **board of directors** is a formally constituted group that meets periodically to advise the entrepreneur. Board members may or may not own stock in the company and may or may not be paid either a retainer or a per meeting fee. The power that a board of directors has is a function of the percentage of ownership its members hold. Some boards have the power to remove the entrepreneur if desired. Usually, they serve as a source of advice and counsel for the entrepreneur.

Informal advisory boards are less structured, meet only when the entrepreneur desires, and are not perceived as a great threat to the entrepreneur's power and ego. Both the formal and the informal board provide significant advantages to the new venture and should be considered as an integral part of the structure of the venture.

The primary advantage of a board of directors is its role as a sounding board for the entrepreneur's ideas. Entrepreneurs tend to be action oriented and can often benefit from the more thoughtful consideration typically provided by a board of directors. If board members have substantial business experience of their own, they may have a feel for whether an idea is viable or not. Further, having to prepare for an "audience" encourages the entrepreneur to think carefully through an idea to avoid being embarrassed in front of the board.

Board members are also often sources of contacts for financing, suppliers, or customers. Board members who also have their own business will often know reputable service firms such as printers or electrical contractors. They will usually have an established relationship with bankers and are willing to set up appointments for the new entrepreneur. Board members may also be willing to refer their own customers to the new venture if applicable.

Board members may be selected from a number of sources. In a *Wall Street Journal* interview, consultant John L. Ward suggests that a board have at least three outsiders, preferably people you *don't* know, who can

HARRINGTON OFFICE SUPPLY

Linda Harrington owned and operated a medium-sized office supply store. It carried the normal assortment of goods found in that type of store plus a selection of good quality office furniture. It did not carry computers but did sell furniture that computer users would buy. The store did quite well for its size and had contracts with some businesses and organizations as their only supplier.

Within a six-month period, all that changed. Sam's Wholesale Club opened a new outlet near Harrington's Store and Office Max followed a few months later. Both sold office supplies and limited furniture at deep discount prices. In the next two months, Harrington's sales dropped by 20 percent. She realized that she could not survive by matching the discount prices dollar for dollar, but she was also concerned that she might not survive if she didn't.

Harrington had been considering putting together some sort of advisory board for a couple of years but simply had not done it. She knew this was not the best of times to do it, but decided that it might be a way to develop a competitive strategy to combat the discounters. Since she had been a member of the chamber of commerce for several years, she contacted it to get suggestions for board members. Through chamber meetings she had met a number of other business owners but had never established a working relationship with any other than her own customers.

With the help of the chamber representatives she identified individuals who would be good board members. James Overhill operated a printing company. He was not a customer of Harrington's, since he ordered paper directly from wholesalers and bought little else. But he had been in the community a number of years. Harold Burkmeyer had just retired as administrator of Methodist Memorial Hospital and had long been active in community affairs. He was also an accountant. Anita Blackwell was the director of public relations for one of the manufacturing

bring you a fresh perspective. Best are active owners from companies larger than yours who have successfully dealt with issues you are going to face. Bankers, accountants, and attorneys need not be included on the board because the entrepreneur already has access to that advice through normal relationships. Further, Ward suggests ruling out friends, customers, competitors, and suppliers since they would have difficulty being totally objective.[6] Some business professors are a good choice as a board member if they have a particular expertise needed by the entrepreneur. Whatever the source, potential board members should have substantial experience in their field and be able to make a quality contribution to the board in advising the entrepreneur. It is wise to select board members based on what they can contribute to the venture rather than because they are friends or are in community leadership positions. Thus, having a board member who has some expertise in retail business might be good for a venture that sells through retailers. Having a board member who has expertise in human resources would be beneficial if the venture's human resource needs were growing.

Paying the board members is at the discretion of the entrepreneur. Some entrepreneurs feel that board members should be paid in order to assure that they give priority to the responsibility. Others believe that the board member will work with an entrepreneur for free for altruistic or firms in the area. The fourth member was Averil Ziller, who owned a number of restaurants in the city. Ziller was a fierce competitor within the restaurant industry and had done well in spite of the influx of national chains. Harrington also added Jane McComb, one of her key managers, making a total of five besides herself. The board members agreed to serve without charge.

She spent the first meeting educating the board members on the operations of Harrington Office Supply and its competitive situation. She showed them the sales figures indicating the precipitous drop when Sam's and Office Max had opened. She then asked the board members to return in two weeks to continue the discussion.

The second meeting was eventful. Burkmeyer had already spent some time going over Harrington's sales figures, pricing policy, and other aspects of the operations. Since he had just retired, he offered to spend some time "nosing around the community to see what was going on." The group returned and spent two hours listening to Harrington, McComb, and Burkmeyer. They then put together a strategy that would focus on lowering prices somewhat and attempting to become the sole supplier for more companies and organizations in the community.

They realized that they could not match Sam's and Office Max dollar for dollar, but if they combined marginally higher prices with service and delivery, they might stem the decline. They also considered the possibility of expanding the geographical market that Harrington reached and focusing on the smaller suburbs and communities that were further from the discounters. It was not yet known whether the strategy would be successful, but the future at least looked less dim.

personal reasons. Some larger firms may be able to put the board members on a retainer while others will pay them only on a per meeting basis. A compromise is to pay a token amount or honorarium as an expression of gratitude, but not to pay so much as to affect the financial condition of the venture.

The frequency of meetings is also discretionary. Since most potential board members who are of high quality are also busy, it is not logical to expect them to meet more often than once every month or so. On the other hand, meeting less often than once per quarter or, at the minimum, semiannually, negates the value of the board.

An active board of directors is an immensely valuable part of a venture's structure. Although a board is not required for most ventures and not used by many, establishing a board of directors is one of the best decisions an entrepreneur can make.

SUMMARY

Choosing the correct structure for a venture can greatly affect the ability of the venture to compete over the long term. The discussion of venture structure includes both determining the organizational structure of a venture and the methods of meshing an acquired venture into an existing one.

The internal structure of a venture affects both the efficiency and the effectiveness of the business. New and small ventures often use the basic structure, which has only one person in a position of authority. This structure works well as long as the venture does not experience rapid growth and does not face a turbulent environment. If the venture does achieve growth, the basic structure becomes inefficient. A functional management structure will evolve to compensate for the entrepreneur's inability to single-handedly manage the venture's growth. If even more growth is achieved or if acquisitions increase the size of the venture, then a divisional structure may evolve.

The structure of a venture is especially important if the business is a family firm. Although no particular structure is best in all situations, the entrepreneur must consider the motivational impact of having family versus nonfamily members in authority positions. In addition, management succession in the family venture must be considered as the structure is determined or adjusted.

New ventures that are purchased or developed must be assimilated into the existing structure. The structure used in assimilating the new venture can either add to or detract from the potential of both the new and old ventures. The choices for the combined structure are to operate both as separate ventures connected only by a joint ownership, absorb the new venture totally into the existing one, create a subsidiary of the existing venture, or create a new company that absorbs both the new and the old ventures. The choice of structures depends on the relative cost of each structural type, the autonomy each allows, and the impact of the structural type on the motivation, power, and egos of the different players in the combined venture.

Boards of directors are not required in most new or small ventures, yet they can be a valuable part of any venture structure. Members of a board of directors that are carefully selected and well used can make a tremendous contribution to the survival of the venture.

DISCUSSION QUESTIONS

1. Why is structure an important issue?
2. The basic structure is used for most new and small ventures. Yet it is well known that the functional management structure is better. Why, then, is the basic structure used?
3. As a venture evolves from the basic structure to a functional management structure, why is the bookkeeping/accounting function frequently the first to develop?
4. Aside from the accounting area, which function will most likely develop next if (a) the entrepreneur is strong in marketing or (b) the entrepreneur is a technical expert in the development or production of the product?
5. In which stage will the family venture cause the most conflict with the family: (a) launch and first year, (b) later growth stages, or (c) stability years and harvest?
6. In which stage will the family venture cause the most conflict with

nonfamily employees: (a) launch and first year, (b) later growth stages, or (c) stability years and harvest stage?

7. Most new and small ventures tend to be flexible and able to react to changing demands. Which methods of assimilating new ventures into existing ones will maximize the flexibility?

8. Why are the power and the egos of the acquired venture's managers important considerations for the structural type selected?

9. What are the disadvantages of the structure in which both firms remain separate except for joint ownership?

10. Boards of directors have been shown to be valuable to new and small ventures. Why are they so seldom used?

11. Will a board of directors be found more frequently in a low-growth venture or in a growth-oriented venture? In which type of venture is the board most valuable?

EXERCISE 12-1　Structuring Businesses　　　　　　　　　　　　　　**EXERCISES**

You are a consultant specializing in small business acquisitions and management. Over the period of a week, the following individuals have come to you for advice regarding how to structure their ventures. For each of the individuals, recommend an organizational structure for the venture. If the case involves an acquisition, recommend a total structure.

1. Joe Machias currently operates an auto repair shop with five mechanics besides himself. He is the best mechanic in the shop, but splits his time between working on cars and dealing with customers. He has one employee who does most of the scheduling and handles the bills. The company currently is operating at near capacity and is quite profitable.

2. Amy Adams operates an accounting firm and tax preparation service in a medium-size city. She has six CPAs and some interns from a nearby university working for her. Two of the CPAs specialize in tax issues. She has an administrative manager who allocates new clients, runs the office, and does other miscellaneous duties. The facilities are large enough to accommodate 20 percent more staff. Adams is in the process of buying out a competitor several blocks away in the same section of the city. The competitor has five CPAs, but it is likely that two of them will not join Adams' firm. The competitor also has a competent administrative manager who is willing to stay.

3. Frank Chou owns a computer software firm that caters to individual medical offices such as doctors and dentists who have their own practices. The software aids in billing and patient scheduling. The company is growing rapidly as more clients see the benefits of computerizing small medical offices. Chou has added new programmers and marketing personnel at the rate of two or three every two months. The advertising budget increases each quarter and seems to be effective, as sales are also steadily increasing.

4. Joe Machias (from case 1) just received a call from the owner of a transmission specialist shop three blocks away. The business is for sale, and Machias sees this as a good way to expand beyond the one transmission mechanic in his current shop. It will also increase his total sales by nearly 50 percent.

5. Theresa Delgado graduated from college with a degree in marketing and a concentration in entrepreneurship. She currently owns four businesses. Three are women's apparel stores catering to different clientele in different parts of the city. The fourth store is a car wash, which she bought from her brother when he moved to another city. Each store has a manager who reports to Delgado. Two of the three apparel stores are doing well, but one is struggling. The car wash is modestly successful.

6. Eric Montgomery has expanded his office equipment manufacturing firm to the point that it competes well throughout the western United States. By now it is fully staffed with managers for each functional area. Two developments are in the works. First, Montgomery's company is considering moving into computer equipment for offices. Second, Montgomery is making plans to expand the equipment sales nationwide.

EXERCISE 12-2

Reread Venture Perspective 12-1 on Avery Manufacturing and Ekstra. How would you organize it? Do you think the choice that Acres made was good?

EXERCISE 12-3

You are part of a team of students that has been asked to analyze a growing company in the community. The president of the company gives you the following information: The company is now four years old. It produces specialty gloves for sale to handlers of hazardous waste. The market is growing. Currently the firm has two vice-presidents and thirty employees working one shift. One vice-president handles sales and the other handles manufacturing. The president handles all administrative, personnel, advertising, accounting, and financial matters. There is only an office manager/receptionist/bookkeeper to help out. As might be expected, the president is stressed out. What advice would you give?

· ·

ENDNOTES

1. Carrie Dolan, "Entrepreneurs Often Fail as Managers," *Wall Street Journal*, May 15, 1989, B1.

2. Mark Robichaux, "Business First, Family Second," *Wall Street Journal*, May 12, 1989, B1.

3. Ivan Lansberg, "Managing Human Resources in Family Firms: The Problem of Institutional Overlap," *Organizational Dynamics* 12, no. 1 (Summer 1983): 39–46.

4. Nancy Bowman-Upton, "Family Business Succession: Issues for the Founder," *Proceedings of the United States Association for Small Business and Entrepreneurship* (October 1987).

5. Peter Drucker, "Five Rules for Successful Acquisition," *Wall Street Journal,* October 15, 1981, 28.
6. Barbara Marsh, "More Small Firms Are Employing Outside Directors," *Wall Street Journal,* June 11, 1991, B1.

◆ Conveniesse, Inc. ◆

Organizing for Growth

Conveniesse is now six years old and consists of ten units. These include three in Buffalo, one each in Syracuse and Cleveland, Ohio, and five in Canada. The Canadian units include two in Montreal, one in Quebec, and two in Toronto. The eleventh and twelfth stores are planned for Detroit and will open within the next four months.

Conveniesse has evolved into an interesting organizational structure. Conveniesse, Inc., became an umbrella organization that consists of Conveniesse, U.S.A., and Conveniesse, Canada. The organizational structure has also evolved. Yolanda took over as president and CEO of Conveniesse, Inc. Sarah moved back to Montreal and is president of Conveniesse, Canada, and an executive vice-president of Conveniesse, Inc. Jason assumed the role of president of Conveniesse, U.S.A., and is also an executive vice-president of Conveniesse, Inc. In addition, Yolanda also heads the marketing activities in each of the subsidiaries. A small managerial staff was added to each of the divisions primarily to supervise the management of the stores within the divisions. Both Jason and Yolanda work out of the Buffalo headquarters and Sarah comes down every other week for management meetings.

Plans are to add the two Detroit stores, move on to Grand Rapids with one, and then expand south to Indianapolis and Cincinnati, and back east to Columbus and Pittsburgh. Indianapolis would have two, Cincinnati might have two, Cleveland would likely get one more, and Pittsburgh could eventually get two. Other cities such as Columbus and Grand Rapids would likely have one. On the Canadian side, Ottawa would get one and Montreal and Toronto would each get one more. The new expansion, from Detroit on, differed from the rest. All the preceding ones had been in office buildings owned by the developer or his friends. Starting with Detroit, none of the units would be in real estate connected to the developer.

The three primary owners were slowly buying out the developer. The earnings from the chain of stores were sufficient to fund most growth and to reduce the percentage that Akins owned. Conveniesse had gotten to the point where it was using relatively little borrowed funds to finance the rate of growth it was achieving.

The organization for Conveniesse had worked well in the past few years but was beginning to be a problem. In the early years with only one store, the organization was simple. Sarah was technically the president with Jason and Yolanda being vice-presidents. In actuality, there were not many differences among the three regarding their responsibilities. Sarah was not treated any differently than the others and did not covet the power or status associated with being the president of a company.

As more units were added, the three partners worked longer hours. The stress of the added work took its toll on their relationship. The opportunity for Sarah to move back to Montreal was fortuitous since she increasingly disagreed with the others' suggestions regarding management of the stores.

With the prospects of the additional growth, the three wondered if the existing structure was sound. Right now, the structure is essentially a Canadian division and a U.S. division. But with the possibility of several more stores, primarily in the United States, would two divisions in the United States be more useful? Someone would have to be hired to manage the third division. Or perhaps a developer-owned division and an independent division would be better. One of them could head the developer-owned division and the other could handle the independent division. Another possibility is to have a "new store development" division. This would allow Jason or someone new to concentrate efforts on growing Conveniesse as quickly as possible while still controlling it. The remaining division or divisions could then run with perhaps a wider span of control.

Assignment

Analyze the organizational structure as it exists now. What are its strengths and weaknesses? What changes should be made in order to accommodate the new growth? Draw an organization chart for Conveniesse, Inc., as it exists now and as you propose it to be in the future.

13 Managing Growth

LEARNING OBJECTIVES

After studying this chapter, you should be familiar with:

1. The need to keep the venture's resources in line with the natural growth of the market
2. Sources of additional resources that can enable continued growth
3. The need to continue growth once the market tapers off
4. Methods of extending venture growth beyond the normal growth cycle
5. The problems of maintaining and encouraging growth while controlling it
6. The nature of stress in a growth venture

KEY TERMS

Growth enabling actions

Growth extending actions

Growth rejuvenating actions

Controlled growth

Entrepreneurial stress

CONSIDER THIS!

- Maintaining growth may be more difficult than achieving it initially.
- Maximizing growth may not be wise.
- The level of growth achieved by a venture is partially a function of the growth in the market and partially a function of the firm's ability to keep up.
- Growth can sometimes be maintained beyond that of the market as a whole.
- Some ventures fail because of too much growth.
- Entrepreneurs in growth ventures may actually exhibit *less* stress than managers in larger organizations.

Chapter 12 discussed the need to plan the structure of the venture in the beginning and as it develops. This chapter continues the discussion of ongoing ventures and focuses on managing a growth-oriented firm. Chapter 14 then discusses entrepreneurship in large, established firms.

At first glance, it would appear that the goal of any growth-oriented venture is to maximize growth in a given time period. A better goal, however, is to maximize *controlled* growth over time. These two goals are quite

MICHAEL DELL
Dell Computer

Some universities retire the uniform number of their superstar players. The University of Texas should retire the *dorm room* that Michael Dell occupied in 1984. Dell didn't occupy the room for very long because his company, Dell Computers, quickly outgrew the room. It has continued its growth since. In 1990, Michael Dell was named *Inc.*'s "Entrepreneur of the Year."[1] Dell went from zero sales in 1984 to $69.5 million three years later. By 1991, revenue was at $546.2 million, and Dell was ranked first in personal computer customer satisfaction by more than ten computer industry customer satisfaction surveys.[2]

Michael Dell grew up in Houston hanging around computer stores. He learned a lot about computers and how to sell them. Most important, he learned that computers could be sold directly to the customer. Dell reasoned that many computer users today do not need the services offered by retailers and that customers would gladly forego them if they could save substantially on the price of the computers. He began with direct response advertising, added telemarketing, and later hired a direct sales force to target corporate clients.

Dell started the company with a $1,000 investment, added a $21 million private offering in the third year, and raised $30 million in an initial public offering (IPO) in July 1988. He also pioneered direct service, a necessity for direct sale computers. Customers can call Dell on an "800" number if they have a problem. If the problem cannot be solved over the phone or with faxed information, a contract technician is dispatched directly to the home or office to solve the problem.

SOURCE: Tom Richaman, "The Entrepreneur of the Year," *Inc.*, January 1990, 43; *Wall Street Journal*, July 18, 1991, B3; Dell Computer documents. Used with permission.

different. Uncontrolled growth maximizes sales revenue, but has little to do with costs or profits. Although revenues may increase rapidly, costs eventually begin to increase even more rapidly. More important, the venture's operations get out of control. Because the growth demands so much attention and so many resources, the scope of the venture exceeds the managers' ability to control it. The next two sections of this chapter will consider opposite sides of growth. The first is to maintain and encourage the growth and momentum of the venture. The second is to control the growth so that the venture can both grow and survive over time. The final section of the chapter discusses stress in the growth-oriented venture.

New ventures that achieve significant growth over the life of the venture go through three stages. The first is the rapid-growth stage in which the firm's products are sold to an increasingly large customer base. In the second stage, the growth for the company begins to taper off. In the last stage, the venture's management either works to rejuvenate growth or its revenues begin to decline. This is referred to as the entrepreneurial life

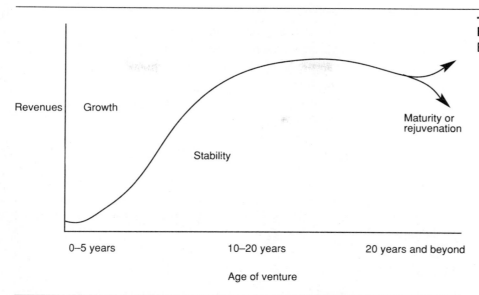

FIGURE 13-1
Entrepreneurial Life Cycle

cycle or business life cycle (Figure 13-1). John Ward suggests that the growth period will typically last up to five years. In this phase, market demand exceeds supply, and the task for the entrepreneur is to keep the entrepreneurial wheels greased in order to *enable* the venture to produce at maximum capacity. The second stage, which could be called the stability phase, may last from ten years to twenty years. As the venture moves into and through this phase, the task is to operate in such a way as to take advantage of remaining growth and to *extend* that growth as long as possible. The maturity/decline phase begins at the end of the stability phase. Here the critical task is to keep the venture from failing by *rejuvenating* its strategy.[3]

GROWTH ENABLING ACTIONS

A number of issues must be considered in managing the venture's growth during the relatively short rapid-growth period. The entrepreneur must attend to a number of **growth enabling actions** that allow the venture to take advantage of the natural growth of the market.

Rapid-growth ventures often grow as fast as they do because they have a product or service that is in increasing demand by the public. Growth in many such ventures tapers off not because of the declining growth in demand for the product, but because of inadequate ability of the firm to continue the growth. The task for entrepreneurs of these firms is to take those actions that will allow the firm to grow at its natural rate. The *natural rate of growth* is defined as that rate of growth that is achieved simply by meeting increasing demand for the product.

The growth-enabling actions revolve around increasing resources for growth and, ultimately, increasing the financing necessary to acquire those

1. Increasing human resources
2. Increasing production capabilities
3. Increasing raw material sources
4. Adding distribution channels
5. Accessing second-stage financing
6. Going public
7. Forming strategic alliances

necessary resources (Table 13-1). Resources must be continually increased to allow the production and distribution of the product (or service) to meet its demand.

Human Resources

Human resources, particularly in the production area, must be increased at a rate just slower than the rate of growth of product sales. This will require frequent additions of staff as well as constant use of temporary help to smooth the growth in permanent staff. In order to assure that growth in personnel expenses does not exceed the dollar inflow from product sales, these personnel additions should lag product growth just slightly. Further, adding additional staff is often done in a stair step fashion rather than a totally smooth growth curve (Figure 13-2). This is because existing employees are often required to work more and more hours until the entrepreneur decides that the only way to regain efficiency is to hire a number of additional workers. Temporary workers can sometimes be hired to smooth the growth without committing the firm to permanent workers prematurely.

Physical Resources

Just as human resources must be increased, physical resources must also be increased. Increasing facilities, however, requires more careful decision making because of the major financial requirements. Facilities cannot be acquired in small incremental amounts. Manufacturing businesses in particular have the problem of increasing facilities to match growth in product sales. The amount of time required to build or purchase facilities may be from perhaps three months to more than a year. Consider the case of Dell Computers discussed at the beginning of this chapter. Even though the company sells computers through the mail, it still has to assemble the product. As Dell experienced its phenomenal growth, it continually had to expand the production facilities necessary to meet the demand.

Hedging the need for additional facilities can be achieved temporarily in three ways. First, additional shifts can be added. Incidentally, this can be done in some service businesses as well as manufacturing firms. Offering after-hours service, for example, may expand sales while using facilities more efficiently. Second, some gains can be achieved by renting additional facilities or rearranging existing facilities. A third method of hedging the

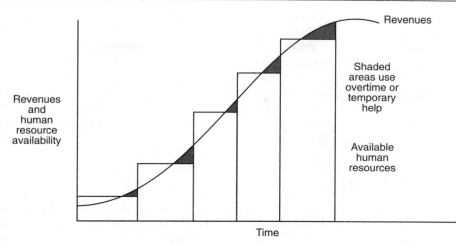

FIGURE 13-2
Human Resource
Availability Compared with
Increasing Revenues

need for additional facilities is through subcontracting production of products or components (Figure 13-3).

Supplier Availability

Restrictions on growth may occur not because of the venture's own capabilities but because of supplier inabilities. This happens when the growth is rapid and especially when the technology is new or there are few suppliers of the components. The critical task for the entrepreneur then becomes finding alternative sources of quality components. Included in the options is to produce the component in-house or to acquire the component producer in order to control production of the supplier's products. If funds are available, acquiring a supplier (vertical integration) is a strategy worth considering. If the end product is part of a growth market, then buying a supplier allows both the control of supplies to the venture as well as a market for any excess the supplier firm produces.

Distribution

In a growth company, production itself may not be the problem. Getting the product to the customer may be the problem. Fortunately, this problem is relatively easy to identify. If customers are back ordering the product or if sales in one geographical area are stagnating for no apparent reason while other areas are still seeing robust growth, evidence of distribution problems exists. Evidence also suggests distribution problems when retail or wholesale levels are out of stock while inventory sits in the production area.

Solving the distribution problem may be more difficult than recognizing it. But a number of solutions do exist. One solution is to use multiple distribution channels. For example, it is possible to use manufacturers' representatives and common carriers to sell and transport products to small retail stores, while using direct sales and venture-owned trucks to deliver to large retail chain distribution centers. Another example is to use multiple delivery methods regardless of the channel used. Venture-owned trucks or contract carriers can be supplemented by using the U.S. Postal Service or United Parcel Service if the product allows. Establishing regional distribution centers can also be useful. One of the keys to Wal-Mart's growth was the use of centrally located distribution centers, each of which serviced a relatively small number of stores. Each of these choices must be considered carefully, and the solution will be based more on the particular product than anything else.

Financial Resources

Obtaining additional financing is the key to maintaining growth. Financing growth is the overall greatest limiting factor in maintaining the natural rate of growth of a venture. Obtaining major growth enabling financing is time consuming and often means giving up part ownership and/or control of the venture. Venture capitalists are frequent sources of growth financing and will often require a significant ownership percentage as well as a seat on the venture's board of directors. Continuing rapid growth will result in taking the company public. Although this often makes the entrepreneur wealthy, it also dilutes ownership in the venture. Adding private or public investors poses the risk of the entrepreneur eventually being forced out of the very venture that she or he had founded a few years earlier. Steve Jobs of Apple Computer is perhaps the best example of this. John Scully, whom Jobs had hired, eventually forced Jobs out of Apple. This would not have been possible had Jobs maintained ownership control of the venture. On the other hand, Apple Computer could not have grown to its current position without additional financing.

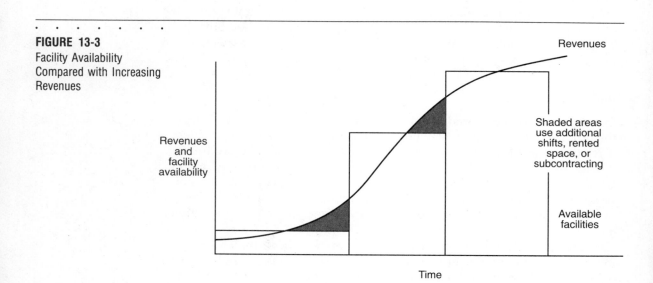

FIGURE 13-3
Facility Availability
Compared with Increasing
Revenues

Another source of later-stage financing is the formation of strategic partnerships or alliances with larger corporations. These partnerships or joint ventures give the venture both a financial boost and possibly an operations or strategic boost by allying with a company that can provide both financing and strategic assistance. These strategic partnerships sometimes result in the outright purchase of the venture by the larger corporation a few years later.

GROWTH EXTENDING ACTIONS

Growth extending actions are those that attempt to continue the growth rate past the natural peak. In other words, these actions will prolong growth when it could be expected to taper off. The three most common types of actions are to expand the venture geographically, introduce additional products, or acquire competitors.

Geographic Expansion

Expanding growth geographically is a viable strategy if the firm does not already sell throughout the entire continent. Even if North America is saturated, the rest of the world awaits. As was discussed in Chapter 11, expanding internationally is a relatively easy task providing it is simply one of distribution. If expansion requires additional plants, the issues change somewhat. If the products must be altered for different domestic or international areas, then the issues change still more.

Geographic expansion can be either to contiguous regions or to high population centers in other regions. Concentric expansion to an ever expanding circle of contiguous regions has the advantage of minimizing total distance from headquarters. It may, however, require that less populated areas be saturated rather than more populated areas in other regions. Wal-Mart's growth illustrates this. Sam Walton chose to start Wal-Marts in small communities in the South. He added stores in similar communities and filled in an entire region. Then he would move to another state or adjoining region and fill it in. Additional distribution centers were built in the center of the target region to simplify distribution.

The opposite strategy is to target high population areas regardless of region. This would give the largest possible markets for the product. Once the population centers were established, the firm would then have the choice of expanding concentrically around each regional center or jumping to the next high population area without filling in. Each strategy has its advantages and disadvantages.

Additional Products

Bringing out variations of existing products can also extend the growth rate of the venture. As growth of the initial product(s) begins to fade, the introduction of ancillary products can achieve overall growth at an increasing rate. This cannot be done indefinitely if market saturation occurs, but it can extend growth significantly over the short run. Depending on the product, bringing out higher-quality or more sophisticated sequels will extend growth. By 1989, for example, Sierra On-Line, Inc., had brought out King's Quest IV, which provided new situations and better graphics for computer game players. Each of the newer versions was timed appropriately so as to give another burst of growth as the preceding King's Quest version's sales slowed. Police Quest and Space Quest games were also added.

Software producers and textbook publishers routinely publish improved versions or later editions of their products. The later versions of the products update and improve the originals. The major impact, however, is that customers are encouraged to purchase new or improved products rather than continue to use the older versions.

Expansion through Acquisition

Acquiring competitors can also extend growth beyond its natural rate. It is logical, of course, that the advent of competitors is a primary cause of declining growth rates, and seldom will a successful venture be unchallenged. Acquiring competitors will not only eliminate competition, but it may open up opportunities for new products and distribution that the competitor possessed. This is perhaps the most common method of expansion among service ventures. Even geographical expansion is frequently obtained via acquisition. Assuming the price is right, this is an excellent way to maintain growth.

The expansion via acquisition need not be exclusively the acquisition of a competitor. The geographical expansion discussed above can be done with acquisitions. Acquisition expansion can also be used to acquire suppliers in a vertical integration strategy or to acquire unrelated ventures. In the vertical integration case, the venture's expansion is extended by becoming more involved in the production of the product. In the case of the unrelated acquisition, the original product may be allowed to continue its natural path while additional growth is obtained in another product line.

REJUVENATING GROWTH

As growth in the demand for the venture's product ends and a decline in sales begins, the entrepreneur has two choices. The first is to ride the decline, making as much money as possible via cost cutting. Eventually, the venture will fail, stagnate, or perhaps grow slowly. The second choice is to rejuvenate the company. The task for the entrepreneur is to find new products to produce or new services to provide.

Growth rejuvenating actions require a return to the strategic planning process discussed in Chapter 4. The strengths and weaknesses of the venture must be analyzed. The environment must be scanned for new and relevant opportunities. The environmental opportunities and the firm's capabilities must be compared in order for new strategies to be developed.

In some cases, the rejuvenation can come from a repackaging or remarketing of the existing product to meet a new set of customer demands. For example, an entrepreneur may find that a particular product no longer is in high demand in the form it is offered. But if a major demographic

VENTURE PERSPECTIVE 13-1

. . . .

NEW HORIZONS BAKERY

The New Horizons Bakery was begun in the early 1970s to take advantage of the relatively small group of health conscious customers, many of whom were carryovers from the 1960s activists. The bakery served a niche in its early days because traditional bakeries were not interested in whole grain breads and other health-related foods. In the 1980s, New Horizons saw rapid growth because the baby boom generation was becoming more aware of the need for healthful foods. Thus, throughout the 1980s, New Horizons flourished.

As would be expected, other companies also noted the trend toward healthful foods and began either producing more healthful breads or, more often,

simply repackaging their breads in such a way as to make them appear to be more healthful. Thus, they began to cut into New Horizons' market niche to the extent that New Horizons became little different than any other bakery.

As the 1990s began, New Horizons realized that something had to be done. The larger, traditional bakeries were taking so much of its share away that New Horizons was almost on the brink of bankruptcy. The owners of New Horizons brought in a consultant to determine whether a new direction could be developed for the venture rather than closing or selling out to competitors. The consultant concluded that by using smaller pans and

bread sacks, New Horizons could tap a market that was being totally ignored by the traditional bakeries. That market was the singles market. Single individuals throw away half of most loaves of bread and sometimes all but one or two hamburger buns. By producing miniloaves of bread and packaging hamburger and hot dog buns in two-packs and four-packs, New Horizons was able to increase its sales dramatically. Further, they found that singles are not as price sensitive regarding breads since they know they will waste half of a full loaf anyway. Thus, New Horizons was able to price the miniloaves at a higher price per ounce than regular loaves and still be competitive.

group can use the product in a different form, a whole new opportunity for the existing product can be generated simply by reformulating the product (Venture Perspective 13-1).

If the demand for a venture's products is declining and there is little hope of rejuvenating that particular product, then the task is to find new products or services. The existing product is usually maintained since it may still be a ready source of cash for the company. That cash can then be redirected toward new products or services that will eventually provide a greater proportion of the venture's total sales and profits.

CONTROLLING GROWTH

Maximizing **controlled growth** suggests that the venture grows as fast as possible given the controls set in place by the entrepreneurial team. This rate of growth will likely be somewhat slower than uncontrolled growth would be, but it will be steady and maintainable. Although much attention will be placed on increasing the growth rate, attention will also be given to controlling costs, personnel actions, equipment, defects, and order processing.

Identifying Control Problems

The key issue regarding how much growth should be allowed is to know when to put on the brakes (or let off the accelerator). Slowing down too soon does not take the maximum advantage of the opportunities. Waiting too long to slow the rate of growth risks losing control of the venture's operations. It is only with great difficulty and questionable accuracy that one can identify when to make changes in the venture's operations. The problem is often akin to giving directions to a friend to turn two blocks before she gets to the red building. Only when she gets to the red building does she know that she has gone too far. The solution is to give clues or landmarks along the way so the friend can anticipate the desired corner.

Table 13-2 lists some of these clues for entrepreneurial ventures. None of the items, by itself, unequivocally identifies problems. The appearance of more than a few items, however, should give cause for concern.

It is easy to see how these clues can result from too much growth. As growth occurs, entrepreneurial managers try to squeeze more and more out of a twenty-four hour day. They work longer hours trying to keep up with orders, production, and distribution. Because of inadequate staff and inadequate controls, problems develop. Beyond some point they can no longer handle all the demands, and the team resorts to crisis management. That is, they frantically move from problem to problem trying to solve the most pressing problem first while others are getting worse. As cash in the bank is used up, the team members begin to rely more and more on "check float"—the time between when a check is written and when it is cashed. They learn quickly which suppliers have stringent credit policies and

---

TABLE 13-2
Indicators of Potential
Control Problems

1. Missed deadlines
2. Backlogged orders
3. Excessive defects, especially if trend is recent
4. Employee discontent or sudden increase in turnover
5. Customers being left "on hold" and phone calls not returned
6. Lengthy phone calls with customers explaining delays or other problems with products or services
7. Monthly and quarterly reports either not done or done haphazardly
8. Discussions regarding which bills to pay and which to let ride until additional notices are received
9. Discussions with a banker regarding additional funding for operating capital when sales are not increasing proportionately
10. Failure to pay taxes
11. Frequent discussions regarding the chain of command and the need for delegation of authority
12. Returned checks (either the company's or from customers)
13. Excessive hours worked by members of the entrepreneurial team, especially to handle frequent crises
14. Financial results that are significantly different than budgeted

VENTURE PERSPECTIVE 13-2

. . . .

OSBORNE COMPUTER CORPORATION

In the early 1980s, before the advent of laptop computers, Adam Osborne revolutionized the personal computer industry. Through careful assessment of consumer needs and astute marketing, Osborne's venture sold a computer that was selling ten thousand a month by 1983. Annual revenues exceeded $100 million.

Osborne's approach was simple. He developed a technologically sound machine, the Osborne I, sold it at a price that was about two-thirds that of competitors, and he offered approximately $1,500 of software at no cost. The best part was that his machine was packaged in a twenty-six pound, easy-to-carry unit. This was, indeed, a breakthrough in the computer industry.

As always happens in entrepreneurship, success in one venture breeds competition from others. The Osborne I soon had competition from other manufacturers who recognized the viability of this particular segment of the market. To address this competition, Adam Osborne developed an even better machine, the Osborne Executive. It was IBM compatible, had more memory than the Osborne I, had a larger screen, was still relatively lightweight, and was still attractively priced.

Because Adam Osborne knew the Osborne Executive was a superior machine, he began touting it in computer-related media publications in order to have a ready market when the machine came off the production lines. Customers were impressed with the prospects of the Osborne Executive. Dealers were also impressed. In fact, the dealers were quite impressed. They were so impressed that they stopped ordering the Osborne I because they knew that selling them would be difficult once the Osborne Executive hit the market.

Unfortunately, production problems delayed the introduction of the Executive. Dealers were anxiously awaiting the arrival of the new machine, but it was not available. Since many dealers had stopped ordering the Osborne I, Osborne Computer Corporation's cash inflow was dwindling rapidly. The lack of cash inflow could not match the outflow of cash used in the development of the Executive.

The eventual death of Osborne Computer Corporation resulted directly from the inability to control production in a high-growth environment.

which are lax. But these problems require more and more of the team members' time, which in turn causes more problems. Customers become irate as they find that they can't get through to management as products are delivered late, incorrectly, or not at all. This will again take management's time, and the problems continue to spiral.

It is ironic, however, that sustaining losses or marginal profit is not, by itself, an indicator of uncontrolled growth. Rapid-growth ventures usually lose money in the early stages because of the massive investment in plant, equipment, marketing, distribution, and personnel. Operating capital is seldom sufficient to maintain rapid growth in a venture. The need for venture capital in high-growth ventures is not to *create* growth but to *underwrite* the growth that is naturally occurring because of the demand for the product.

The unfortunate result of uncontrolled growth is that the venture fails in spite of the rapid growth of the venture and of the industry. Osborne Computer in Venture Perspective 13-2 exemplifies this well. It was achieving growth, and its new computer could have ensured even more rapid growth. But its inability to produce the new model by the time it indicated it would—in addition to the strategic error of telling the world that it was coming—caused its failure.

Controlling through Budgets

Chapter 9 contained a brief discussion of budgets as part of the analysis preceding the development of financial strategies. Budgets are revisited here because of their importance in controlling growth. The creation and use of effective budgets is perhaps the most important aspect of the control process. This is especially true in the case of high-growth ventures since there may be a tendency to assume that additional growth will take care of any problems.

The problem of the early 1980s oil boom alluded to in an earlier chapter illustrates this point well. During the oil boom many entrepreneurial firms entered some facet of the oil industry to capture their share of wealth that was to last forever. Growth was encouraged by bankers who were willing to underwrite virtually anything without requiring budgets or any other control measures from the entrepreneurs. As growth continued, the need for additional money was willingly met by those in the financial community who were also sure the growth would continue forever. The ease of gaining additional money masked the need for control of expenses. But the attitude of "growth forever" was inappropriate, and the end of the boom signalled the end of existence for many entrepreneurs as well as a number of banks.

The careful creation and use of budgets can bring to light myriad problems besetting a growth venture. At the end of each budget cycle, the entrepreneurial team can analyze the performance of the venture compared with that projected at the beginning of the cycle. Differences between projected and actual figures are then studied to determine if the variation is significant enough to warrant concern. Significant variation from budget in either revenues or expenses should send analysts on a mission to find the cause of the variance. Once the cause of the variance is found, action can then be taken to prevent recurrence of the problem.

Care must always be used in analyzing and correcting budget variances. A rapid-growth firm will—and perhaps should—be near the edge most of the time. In order to keep up with or ahead of competitors, entrepreneurs must make quick decisions that can have disastrous consequences if wrong. The margin between acceptable and unacceptable differences may easily be subject to interpretation. Entrepreneurs may choose to ignore *minor* variations from budget since these may well be simply an aberration caused by the rapidity of the growth.

Budgets should be developed for the entire venture and for each of the functional areas. Of particular importance are the cash budget, production budgets, and marketing budgets. Each should be studied carefully in order to determine when or if corrective action is needed.

Implementing Control

The issue of control in entrepreneurial ventures must be addressed with great caution. The reason for this concern is that the venture can suffer from either too little control or too much control. The previous section clearly made the case that too little control could cause the demise of the venture. The converse of this, however, is that too much control can also create grave problems. Too much control can stifle creativity and innovation, key ingredients in entrepreneurship. Hewlett-Packard experienced this a while back.[4] The company was well known for its entrepreneurial climate and the autonomy given to the engineers who worked there. Autonomy problems developed, however, to the extent that some of its products were incompatible with other products that Hewlett-Packard made. John Young was brought in as CEO to bring some control to the firm. As he added structure to the venture, however, many of the engineers who were used to high levels of autonomy left the company to work with other high-tech ventures.

Control in entrepreneurial ventures can be obtained in four ways. The first is in the *establishment of effective policies and procedures*. Indeed, having written procedures can often aid productivity by establishing agreed-upon methods of handling most decisions. This eliminates the need for a member of the entrepreneurial team to decide on routine matters. Written credit policies, for example, eliminate the need for a manager to determine each customer's needs on a case-by-case basis. Standard operating procedures in the manufacturing process reduce the time spent in determining the order of production or length of production runs. Inventory ordering and control models can aid in controlling both the amount invested in raw material inventory and time required to decide when and how much material should be ordered.

The second major method of maintaining control is through the *hiring process*. Team members who find themselves constantly overwhelmed by the demands of the job are well advised to consider hiring additional staff to ease the administrative burden being carried by the team. If key players in the venture spend their time in routine tasks rather than strategic or operational management tasks, then they are being extremely inefficient. Hiring additional intermediate-level staff can rid managers of unnecessary time spent on issues that can be done by others so that they can spend time on the growth and development of the venture.

It is necessary when considering the hiring of staff or additional team members to hire those who will offset the weaknesses of existing team members. For example, an entrepreneur whose venture is out of control in the production area because the entrepreneur is a marketing person should consider hiring an experienced operations management person from an existing firm. If accounting and finance are not the entrepreneur's fortes, then perhaps a controller's position should be created at the vice-president or partner level to provide a balance to the venture.

The third control-oriented suggestion, which incorporates parts of the preceding two, is to *maximize delegation of authority*. It is granted that too much delegation and autonomy can create the problems faced by Hewlett-Packard. This is seldom the problem facing entrepreneurs, especially low- to medium-growth entrepreneurs. It is an inherent characteristic of most entrepreneurs that they want to be completely in charge of every aspect of the venture. One of the most difficult things for an entrepreneur to do is to delegate authority to those lower in the organization. But by delegating to others, they motivate employees better and they get better decisions made while freeing themselves for higher-level decision making.

Making appropriate *strategic decisions* can also influence the control of the venture. A temptation among entrepreneurial ventures is to introduce the founding product or service and then follow up quickly with variations or even completely new products or services. The problem with this is that attention is taken away from the original product before it is stabilized in the operation of the venture. Having a well-focused mission, clear objectives, and appropriate strategies not only gives general guidance for entrepreneurs, but it keeps them from wandering off into areas they should ignore. For example, rather than introduce a variety of products within a given region, it may be easier to control the expansion of the original product to a greater geographical area. In doing so, marketing resources can be concentrated on the single product and efficiencies may be gained by marketing to a wider area. But most important, manufacturing facilities and personnel can concentrate on the single product rather than spreading resources across the development of multiple products. After the original product has stabilized both from the production viewpoint and from the market growth viewpoint, then successive products can be introduced.

Entrepreneurs should always be aware that some strategies are more controllable than others. The high-growth, multiple product strategy is not as controllable as a slower growth, single product strategy. A strategy using known technology will be more easily controlled than one involving newer, recently developed technology.

The combination of developing controllable strategies, developing and using budgets, setting policies and procedures for the routine portions of the venture, hiring appropriately skilled staff or managers, and delegating as much as possible to them can free up an amazing amount of time for the management team to focus on growth and development of the venture. It cannot be overstated, however, that a certain amount of free-wheeling, shoot-from-the-hip, risk-taking action is the essence of entrepreneurship. The entrepreneur must simultaneously guard against too much control and too little control in order to maximize controlled growth.

MANAGING STRESS IN GROWTH VENTURES

The discussion in this chapter has centered on the task of management within the growth-oriented venture. The focus has been on how the entrepreneur can affect the performance of the venture. The reverse of this is that the venture can affect the entrepreneur. It is especially true in the growth venture that the entrepreneur encounters significant amounts of stress while building and growing the venture. This stress, if left unchecked and unmanaged, can take its toll on the entrepreneur and also on the performance of the venture. Thus, it is important in this concluding section to discuss the causes, effects, and techniques for managing stress in the growth venture.

Managing stress is important because of the cost of not managing it. Stress can result in illnesses, reduced productivity while at work, turnover, strained interpersonal relations with co-workers, and a host of indirect problems when the job-related stress is carried home. The effect of stress on managers, employees, and their families is not easily measurable but surely runs into the millions of dollars.

Entrepreneurial stress is defined as stress that arises primarily from the pressure of running one's own venture. All managers—and all employees—encounter stressors on their jobs. Employees encounter stress from the nature of the job itself, role conflicts on the job, ambiguity and uncertainty related to the role they play in the job, as well as stressors outside the workplace.[5] These sources of stress are common and are increasingly being addressed by management in some more progressive large corporations. But entrepreneurs face the usual stressors in addition to substantial stress resulting from owning and operating the venture. Thus, entrepreneurial stress is different from normal work stress.

Entrepreneurs, like others, vary greatly in the amount of stress encountered and in their reaction to it. Some entrepreneurs thrive on stress. They are energized by it. They work long hours, make important decisions daily, risk substantial personal capital, juggle appointments, deal with unhappy customers or difficult employees, and buy or sell assets or companies—and they love every minute of it. In fact, research has found that although self-employed individuals put in longer hours per week and put more effort into the job, they experience significantly higher job satisfaction, life satisfaction, general happiness, and exhibit less psychosomatic symptoms than do those that work for someone else.[6] The primary cause of this lower stress is the substantially greater autonomy they have when they own their own ventures. Thus, even though they work long and hard, they work when they want, where they want, and how they want. Although the Naughton study did not address the sex of the entrepreneur, a more recent study by Stoner, et al., showed that the relationship holds true when the entrepreneurs are women. Their study of women in management found that those women who owned their own ventures reported greater satisfaction with life than did those who worked for someone else.[7]

This is not to say, however, that entrepreneurs do not encounter stressors or have reactions to stress. Significant stressors do exist in entrepreneurship, and inability to handle them can result in ulcers, heart attacks, and other symptoms of stress.

Sources of Entrepreneurial Stress

Stress comes from three sources: from within the venture, from outside the venture but related to it, and from sources unrelated to the venture. The first source consists of stress caused by the demands of the venture. The second is most often family related stress that is related to operating the venture. The third source is miscellaneous causes of stress that occur in everyone's life.

Venture-caused stress is more likely to be felt in high-growth ventures rather than in low-growth enterprises. These growth-oriented businesses require long hours by the entrepreneur or the entrepreneurial team. More important, they require extensive work in keeping the venture going and growing. Growth entrepreneurs must constantly be seeking new financing, developing new products, analyzing markets, adding management or

VENTURE PERSPECTIVE 13-3

. . . .

WASTE CONSULTANTS, INC.

"I've had it! Either you change or it's all over! I don't mind picking the kids up at the day-care center. I don't mind doing the kitchen chores. I don't even mind doing the laundry. But the kids have not seen you in almost a week. And Sunday afternoon was the only time the week before! The children need *two* parents. I can't be father and mother both!" Ellis's voice grew louder with each sentence.

Ever since Jane Scott and a fellow manager had bought out Waste Consultants, Inc., Jane had spent more and more hours with the business. Before the purchase, things had worked rather smoothly for the Scotts. Jane was a vice-president for a small consulting company that worked with municipalities to solve the growing need to recycle urban wastes. Ellis taught at the local community college and was therefore flexible enough that he could deliver and pick up the children from day-care. Over the past couple of years he had become a pretty good cook, a task that he grew to like. Then the purchase occurred. The president of Waste Consultants was enticed by a large city to join its staff permanently as their recycling expert rather than working as a consultant to them. Jane Scott and Ed Drew consulted their spouses and decided to purchase the growing firm.

Waste Consultants had done well under the previous owner, but Jane and Ed made it reach new heights. The two owners spent much time on the road traveling to cities in their state and contiguous states giving lectures and working as consultants to an expanding number of municipalities. With state and federal laws increasingly forcing cities to find alterna-tives to landfills, Jane and Ed found that an amazingly large percentage of city councils and mayors had little knowledge of how to solve the problem. They were more than willing to hire Waste Consultants for one- to three-day consulting stints.

Thus, Jane encountered increasing pressures from Ellis, who took over more and more of the domestic chores. They found themselves spending a greater percentage of their time together arguing over a variety of topics. In addition, the children seemed to be acting more distant around her and went to Ellis for any help or requests. As Jane lay awake that night—as she increasingly did—her thoughts alternated between the need to reconcile the growing rift between her and Ellis and putting the finishing touches on the speech she would give the next afternoon five hundred miles away.

nonmanagerial employees, negotiating deals, and traveling extensively to solicit business or funding. All of these actions can be high-pressure tasks requiring critical decision making and face-to-face interaction with other key people.

Venture-related stress is stress caused by interaction of the entrepreneur with those outside of the venture who have a vested interest in either the entrepreneur or the venture. Most commonly, this stress results from the entrepreneur's family, whose priorities are not the same as the entrepreneur's. Put differently, the entrepreneur's family tires of its family member never being home, being tense at the dinner table, falling asleep in the middle of conversations, not being willing or able to take part in the rearing of children, seldom having time for vacations, and spending evenings doing paperwork for the business. Venture-related stress is magnified if the entrepreneur is a single parent or married to a spouse who does not share parental or household responsibilities. In this case, the entrepreneur must balance the demands of operating the business with all responsibilities on the home front.

Unrelated stress results from those stressors that occur naturally in one's personal life. The death or illness of family members or friends, marriage or divorce, moving, children's problems with schools, dealing with elderly parents, paying for college expenses, or a spouse's work responsibilities are all frequent sources of stress unrelated to the venture. As family life cycles and venture life cycles move somewhat in tandem, the unrelated stressors typically occur while the venture is in its growth phase. When these stressors are added to stresses arising from the other two sources, considerable pressure may build on the entrepreneur.

Managing Entrepreneurial Stress

It must be stated again that the issue of stress is more important to some entrepreneurs than to others. Some entrepreneurs view the hectic and high pressure demands as a desired life-style. Indeed, some entrepreneurs (and some workaholics in large corporations, academe, and government) find anything other than this life-style to be boring and a waste of time. Their work is their life, and life without the stress and its challenges is meaningless. Families of entrepreneurial workaholics suffer, but the entrepreneurs themselves do not.

Stress management is important for those who do experience stress caused by stressors associated with owning and growing a business. The task is to find ways to remove the stressors if possible or, if that is not possible, to find ways to reduce the impact of the stress (Table 13-3).

Some entrepreneurs are hard-driving, competitive people. They need to excel in whatever they do regardless of the cost. Hence, they set objectives for themselves and their companies that are both unrealistic and unnecessary. Maximizing growth is an admirable goal, but not if it results in stress overload.

Entrepreneurs, whether growth oriented or not, convince themselves that they are indispensable. They believe that the venture cannot operate unless they are present. In some cases this may be true. But in even more cases, it can operate at least acceptably well in the temporary absence of the entrepreneur. Further, the astute entrepreneur will always be planning ahead, and those plans should include contingency planning. What if the entrepreneur is ill? What if a vacation is desired by the owner's family? What if a key team member is injured or called away on an emergency? What if the entrepreneur dies? If there are no answers to these questions, major changes need to be made. This leads to the next two items.

Much stress among entrepreneurs is due to their maintaining total control of the venture. By shifting management responsibilities to other team members and by delegating authority to those lower in the organization, the entrepreneur gains in two ways. First, the other team players feel much more a part of the venture. Their own commitment to the well-being of the firm will be enhanced. In addition, however, the entrepreneur will also benefit from the released time. Time not spent on routine tasks can be spent on planning, on acquiring additional financial resources, and on assessing the future.

TABLE 13-3
Stress Management
Techniques

1. Convince yourself that the objectives you are striving for are not as important as you thought. Perhaps 100 percent growth per year is not required.
2. Force yourself to take time off. Most entrepreneurs think that the venture cannot operate without them. It can.
3. Shift responsibilities to other management team members.
4. Delegate. Delegate. Delegate. This is difficult for most entrepreneurs, but is important for many reasons.
5. Use time better. Schedule blocks of time for planning.
6. Eat right and get sufficient rest and exercise.
7. Learn to relax.

Scheduling blocks of time for planning is also important. Planning cannot occur while talking on the phone, answering mail, and working with customers. The entrepreneur must find time to do those things that require significant blocks of time. Once this occurs, concentrated effort and thought will result in a better run operation. Creating the blocks of time, of course, is difficult. By delegating and shifting responsibilities and better use of time management, the growing venture can be less stressful and, simultaneously, better managed.

Finally, taking care of the body helps one endure stress. Eating a healthful diet, getting sufficient exercise and rest, and learning to relax can all help reduce the effects of stress.

SUMMARY

This chapter has dealt with managing a growth-oriented venture. Launching a venture is difficult. It may pale, however, in comparison to the challenge of maintaining and controlling growth once the venture is launched. When a venture's products are in the high-growth phase of the product life cycle, the primary task for the entrepreneur is to keep up with the natural growth in demand. This will require adding resources and taking other actions to better match the firm's capabilities with the rate of growth.

Once growth begins to taper off, the task for the entrepreneur becomes one of extending the venture's growth beyond the natural growth cycle. This can be done through geographic expansion, vertical integration, and acquisitions. As market growth begins to decline, the entrepreneur must then take actions to rejuvenate the growth for the firm. This will require significant planning.

Throughout the growth cycle, the issue of control is paramount. The entrepreneur must determine how much control is necessary and desirable. Control can be gained through the effective use of budgets and management techniques that maximize the entrepreneur's time and ability to plan. The problem with controlling growth is that too little control may result in failure in spite of the growth. Too much control may inhibit the creativity needed for the entrepreneurial venture.

Many entrepreneurs thrive on the excitement and pressure of entrepreneurship, and research tends to support this contention. At the same time, entrepreneurs must be able to identify stress both within themselves and among their subordinates. Failure to manage stress appropriately can cause problems of decreased productivity because of turnover or absenteeism of workers. It can also result in physical and/or emotional wear and tear on the entrepreneur.

- -

1. What is meant by "natural growth rate" of a venture? Why is the concept important for rapid-growth ventures?

2. Will growth-enabling actions and growth-extending actions normally be done together? Could they be? Give examples. What limitations would there be to doing both at the same time?

3. Why do we frequently hear of ventures failing because of too much growth? How can too much of a good thing be deadly?

4. Controlling growth is a double-edged sword. Why?

5. Develop a method for controlling growth of a venture without restricting autonomy of team members.

6. Interview the owner of a growth-oriented venture. What are the most notable problems in managing the venture? Are the answers what you had anticipated?

7. Why are budgets important for high-growth ventures? Won't the figures always be over budget because of the growth?

8. How can you reconcile the need to pay close attention to financial performance with the need to allow maximum freedom within the growth venture?

9. What is it about entrepreneurs that makes them energized by the same demands that would be considered stress producing for others?

10. How can an entrepreneur separate venture-caused stress from other kinds of stress?

DISCUSSION QUESTIONS

- -

EXERCISE 13-1

EXERCISES

Consider the indicators of control problems shown in Table 13-2. For each of the fourteen indicators, recommend a solution. In other words, what can be done to prevent recurrence of the problem?

EXERCISE 13-2

Consider the following scenario. You are the owner of a three-year-old firm that is known as a benefits processing firm or a third-party administrator. That is, it does not provide personnel benefits for companies, but it provides the paperwork processing. Thus, it is a link between a company that offers its employees benefits and the insurance companies and pension plan companies that provide the benefits. More and more companies are finding that using the third-party administrator is beneficial because it provides better service than the insurance companies could. Your company is experiencing rapid demand because of the growth trends in the concept of third-party benefit administration. Unfortunately, you are beginning to get complaints because you cannot keep up with the processing.

1. What can you do to solve immediate problems?
2. What can you do to prevent problems from recurring as growth continues?

ENDNOTES

1. Tom Richaman, "The Entrepreneur of the Year," *Inc.*, January 1990, 43.
2. Advertisement in the *Wall Street Journal*, July 18, 1991, B3.
3. John L. Ward, *Keeping the Family Business Healthy* (San Francisco: Jossey-Bass Publishers, 1987), Chapter 2.
4. "Can John Young Redesign Hewlett-Packard?" *Business Week*, December 6, 1982, 72–74.
5. W. Alan Randolph and Richard S. Blackburn, *Managing Organizational Behavior* (Homewood, IL: R. D. Irwin, Inc., 1989), 268–76.
6. Thomas J. Naughton, "Contrasting Models of Quality of Working Life Among the Self-Employed: An Empirical Test," *Academy of Management Best Papers Proceedings 1987*, edited by Frank Hoy (New Orleans, LA: Academy of Management, August 9–12, 1987), 79–81.
7. Charles Stoner, Richard Hartman, and Rajinder Arora, "The Differences Between Female Entrepreneurs and Female Managers," paper presented at the Midwest Business Administration Association Annual Meeting, Chicago, 1991.

◆ Conveniesse, Inc. ◆

Supporting Growth

Conveniesse continued to grow over the next few years. The three entrepreneurs were pleased with the progress. However, disagreements continually arose regarding the future. One such disagreement was particularly acrimonious.

"Well, do we want to grow or not?" Jason repeated angrily. "We're poised to do something really great here. We can either commit ourselves to real growth or we can be happy at being a small regional chain of twenty or so office building convenience stores. But if we are going to grow, it's going to take resources, lots of resources. We are profitable now and we have been able to fund our limited growth almost entirely internally. Akins doesn't help us any more and we have bought out most of his ownership—on his terms, I might add.

"I think it is time to bust loose here and do a major growth strategy," he continued vehemently. "We have hardly skimmed the market in the Great Lakes region. We could add two or three more units easily in each of the large cities we are in and perhaps another one or two in some of the smaller ones. But what about the rest of the Midwest? What about the rest of the Northeast? So far we have avoided New York and Chicago. What about them? And this doesn't even address the southern part of the United States. Do we have to be content with the status quo?"

"Okay, okay, I see your point," Yolanda responded. "But we can't just grow for the sake of growth. Plus, there are some problems associated with all this growth. First, how are we going to fund it? Second, how are we going to control it? You remember, don't you, that in the last two years our expenses have increased faster than our revenues have. And you also know, if you read the last annual report, that the increase in expenses was almost totally in overhead. I'm not sure we are controlling well what we have now."

"Well, you guys do what you want," Sarah added. But I'm perfectly content running the eight stores in Canada. I'm fifty-five years old now. I'm not planning on retiring any time soon, but I am frankly getting tired of all the travel. I don't even like to come down to Buffalo for management meetings. In fact, if you can find a way to do it equitably, I would be happy to trade my share in Conveniesse, Inc., for your shares of Conveniesse, Canada. That way, I can just go my own way and you guys can grow all over the world if you want."

There was a moment of silence while all three absorbed what Sarah had said.

"Well, we might just do that," Jason retorted. "That would give us a lot more flexibility and we wouldn't have to be constantly battling over every strategic move."

"What do you mean by 'us,' Jason? Did you ask me?" shouted Yolanda. Then calming down somewhat, she suggested that they break for the evening since it was nearing midnight.

The next morning went smoother. Sarah confirmed that she really would like out of Conveniesse, Inc., and was interested in trading her shares for their shares of Conveniesse, Canada. This, of course, had to be approved by Akins, who still owned 20 percent of Conveniesse, Inc., but the idea had merit. The typical Conveniesse, Canada, store wasn't quite as profitable as the average Conveniesse, U.S.A., store and there were only eight of them compared with fifteen now in the United States. On the other hand, Sarah would be trading 40 percent of Conveniesse, Inc., for 60 percent of Conveniesse, Canada. So they decided to take the idea to their attorney who would draw up the change and also determine how much money should change hands.

Once this was done, Conveniesse, Inc., was owned 20 percent by Akins, with the remaining 80 percent being owned on a one-third basis by Jason and a two-thirds basis by Yolanda. They decided to go ahead and buy Akins out so the remaining fifteen stores would be totally theirs. The only relationship with Akins now would be that he owned the buildings in which the Buffalo and Syracuse stores were located. Akins maintained his 20 percent share of Sarah's Conveniesse, Canada.

The entire process of trading with Sarah and buying out Akins had taken a couple of months. But Jason and Yolanda were already beginning to look for growth opportunities. With stores in Buffalo, Syracuse, Grand Rapids, Detroit, Indianapolis, Cincinnati, Columbus, and Pittsburgh, the remaining two partners began to consider where and how they wanted to grow. The trade and buyout had pretty well depleted their capital, at least temporarily.

Approximately a year later, the two were again discussing the possibility of a growth strategy. They had absorbed the departure of Akins and Sarah both financially and emotionally. They decided it was now time to move. One day Yolanda pulled a copy of the original plan from the files. They chuckled at the relative cost now to add a store compared to the cost twelve years ago. However, in looking at it they marveled at how close the operational portion had stayed the same.

Jason and Yolanda took out a road atlas. They had decided still to stay out of New York, Chicago, and other major cities because of the cost of downtown locations. But they looked south and west at cities such as Lexington and Louisville, Kentucky; Nashville, Memphis, and Knoxville, Tennessee; Little Rock, Arkansas; and Charleston, West Virginia. Closer to Buffalo would be Toledo and Akron in Ohio; Rochester and Albany in New York; Hartford, Connecticut; and Portland, Maine. It appeared that Conveniesse, Inc., could easily double its size. And the speed with which it doubled would be strictly a function of how quickly the necessary resources could be assembled.

Assignment

How would you underwrite the growth for Jason and Yolanda? Can they do it without giving up ownership share again? Other than financial resources, what is needed? For example, what additional management personnel are needed? Do they need to lease a private jet to make the rounds among stores easier? Do they need a centralized training program for store managers?

14 Intrapreneurship

LEARNING OBJECTIVES

After reading this chapter, you should be aware of:

1. The nature of intrapreneurship
2. Barriers to intrapreneurship
3. How to encourage entrepreneurship in large corporations
4. How to evaluate intrapreneurial proposals
5. Different ways to structure companies to accommodate intrapreneurial activities
6. The unique challenges of intrapreneurship in not-for-profit organizations

KEY TERMS

Corporate entrepreneurship

Intrapreneurship

Barriers to intrapreneurship

Intrapreneurial champion

Intrapreneurial culture

Throughout this text, the focus has been on new venture creation and the process of growing entrepreneurial ventures. The discussion has ranged from the nature of entrepreneurs to methods of analyzing opportunities, financing ventures, developing strategies, and managing the ventures once they are launched. But throughout the discussion, the emphasis has been upon new or small or rapidly growing ventures. Regardless of whether the venture was started from scratch or purchased, the focus was on the individual entrepreneur and the freestanding entrepreneurial

ALLEN JACOBSON
3M

Allen Jacobson is not a typical entrepreneur. In fact, he has never worked for a small company. He began working for 3M in 1947 in the company's tape laboratory after receiving a degree in chemical engineering from Iowa State University. He progressed through the ranks from tape production superintendent to chairman and chief executive officer of 3M in 1986.

Allen Jacobson and 3M do, however, epitomize *corporate entrepreneurship*. It was under Jacobson's leadership that some of 3M's oldest businesses produced some of its most promising new products, including Post-it brand repositionable notes—one of the world's best-selling office products—and Very High Bond brand tapes that are so strong they replace welds, bolts, and rivets in some applications. 3M produces almost sixty thousand products, using about one hundred identifiable technologies, and operates in nearly sixty countries around the world. Its products range from sandpaper to heart-lung equipment, tape to laser imagers, and roofing granules to systems for delivering precise doses of medication.

Jacobson says that 3M is not a company with an extensive rule book. Rather, he asserts that 3M has a culture with goals and fairly high expectations of people. The two key words that permeate his many speeches are "quality" and "innovation." His emphasis on quality and innovation is legendary within the corporate culture at 3M.

What follow are key quotes from Jacobson's speeches and from interviews with him and with his predecessors. They illustrate well 3M's commitment to corporate entrepreneurship and the role that Jacobson played in fostering that entrepreneurship within the large corporation.

- Each year we want 25 percent of our sales to come from products new in the last five years.

- How do you get people to

venture. Attention now turns to a unique brand of entrepreneurship: entrepreneurship in the large or established organization.

The study of entrepreneurship within established organizations has spawned new terms in the entrepreneurship literature. The most appropriate term is *organizational entrepreneurship*. The concept is one of entrepreneurship within established organizations regardless of whether the organizations are large corporations, the government, not-for-profit organizations, or smaller businesses that have lost their sense of innovation and creativity. Since most of the emphasis among business writers is on large corporations, the term *corporate entrepreneurship* is often used.

A term recently coined by business writer Gifford Pinchot that has become popular is *intrapreneurship*, which is entrepreneurship *within* an organization.[1] These three terms—organizational entrepreneurship, corporate entrepreneurship, and intrapreneurship—will be used interchangeably within this chapter except where a given term is needed for clarification.

be innovative? You ask them.

- Over the years we've *built in* safeguards against getting set in our ways.
- We allow and encourage our technical people to spend up to 15 percent of their time in laboratories on projects of their own choosing.
- We put our money where our mouth is.
- Sometimes unusual projects need more than time. They need money. So we've set up programs to fund unique projects that can't find a home in the company.
- Innovation is no accident. You expect it. You set a goal. Then you organize to make it possible. You give real responsibility to people close to the job. You

provide resources. And you find space for the unique and unusual.

- For all the problems our economy has had in the last fifteen years, we're still the most innovative and entrepreneurial society in the world.
- Outsiders say we are very lenient in rewarding failure.
- Perhaps the resource that an innovator needs most . . . is the backing of management.
- [Some innovators] would rather face mustard gas than a budget forecast. What these people need is a system that rewards them for their innovative abilities without forcing them behind a manager's desk where they will be miserable.
- Mistakes will be made. But

if a person is essentially right, the mistakes he or she makes are not as serious in the long run as the mistakes management will make if it undertakes to tell those under its authority how they must do their jobs.

- Human beings are endowed with the urge to create, to bring into being something that has never existed before. . . . [D]eveloping entrepreneurs simply means *respecting* that dimension of human nature and honoring it within the context of a profit-making enterprise.

SOURCE: Speech to the Society of American Business Editors and Writers, May 3, 1988; Speech to Marquette University President's Executive Senate, April 11, 1986; "Keeping the Fires Lit Under the Innovators," *Fortune*, March 20, 1988; company documents. Used with permission.

Intrapreneurship—or **corporate entrepreneurship**—is defined as the process in which innovative products or processes are developed by creating an entrepreneurial culture within an existing organization. As will be shown in later sections of the chapter, there are a variety of ways in which the intrapreneurship process operates. An appendix to the chapter discusses the case of Art Fry of 3M who invented the Post-it Note. It is a fascinating story of corporate entrepreneurship at its best.

THE NATURE OF INTRAPRENEURSHIP

Corporate entrepreneurship shares many of the key aspects of traditional entrepreneurship. It also has some significant differences. Looking at the similarities first, both focus on innovation. The innovation may be in new products or services, new processes, or new management methods. Both focus on creation of value-added products or services. The idea here is that entrepreneurship isn't just finding ways to make employees happy or developing a new color or model of an existing product. Something new and different must be developed in order for the process to be entrepreneurial. Both require investment in activities that are more risky than normal. Individual entrepreneurship risks the entrepreneur's time and capital. Intrapreneurship risks the capital of the parent company, and takes attention away from its existing products.

The differences between entrepreneurship and intrapreneurship are perhaps more dramatic than the similarities. Intrapreneurship is often *restorative* where individual entrepreneurship is *developmental*. Restorative action is taken to counter stagnation within a large organization. Intrapreneurship can restore growth and innovation to an otherwise traditional or slow-growth company. It is restorative in that it restores an entrepreneurial culture to an organization that perhaps long ago became overly structured and hierarchical. New products or processes may result from the changes brought about by intrapreneurship, but its ultimate goal is the restoration of an entrepreneurial culture. Individual entrepreneurship, on the other hand, creates something out of nothing. It develops a process or product where none existed before. In the case of a new venture, even the entity itself is new.

A second difference between individual and corporate entrepreneurship is the firm's antagonist. In the case of individual entrepreneurship, the "enemy" is the market. The task for the entrepreneur is to overcome obstacles within the market in order to persevere and become a competitive force. But in the case of intrapreneurship, the corporate culture may be the primary foe. Depending on the relationship, the company itself can stifle the very entrepreneurial processes it seeks to encourage. Thus, in addition to overcoming market obstacles, the corporate entrepreneur may also have to overcome organizational obstacles.

A third difference between the two kinds of entrepreneurship is perhaps the antithesis of the second one: in some cases the parent company can be a friend, not a foe. If the relationship between the parent company and the corporate venture is good, the intrapreneur in charge may have access to substantial funding from the deep pockets of the parent company. Although corporate funds are not unlimited and allocation of money requires the approval of executives at various levels, the amount of funds readily available is substantial if the venture opportunity warrants it. The individual entrepreneur, on the other hand, has to use personal wealth or scramble to obtain funding from various outside sources.

BARRIERS TO CORPORATE ENTREPRENEURSHIP

We begin this section by asking somewhat rhetorically, "Why aren't large companies entrepreneurial? Why can't they 'do entrepreneurship' as new and emerging companies do? What are the differences between small and large companies regarding entrepreneurial skills and abilities?" In actuality, these are not rhetorical questions at all. It is ironic that the basic goal of entrepreneurship is to grow ventures as rapidly as possible, although succeeding in that goal inevitably creates a large organization. There are definite reasons why large corporations have trouble staying entrepreneurial and why they have trouble regaining a level of entrepreneurship once it is lost. This section discusses some of the **barriers to intrapreneurship** in the corporation or large organization. Attention will then turn to solutions provided by intrapreneurship.

The Inherent Nature of Large Organizations

Large companies have trouble being entrepreneurial simply because they are too large. Their size requires managers to structure the corporation in order to be able to control it. As the company grows larger, additional layers of management are added in order to keep the operation manageable. But adding the additional layers of management means that the vertical distance between the CEO and the lowest level of workers increases. The inability of the CEO to work directly with the workers or lower management creates an *impersonal relationship*. Once the entrepreneur loses contact with the workers, it is difficult to ensure that the appropriate level of entrepreneurship exists within the organization.

Multiple layers of management also create *too many levels of approval* between the innovator and the person in charge of resources. If a worker develops an innovative idea or product, the authority to pursue that product often must come from someone four to six levels higher in the organization. Each level has the potential to kill the project before it gets funded. Thus, the odds of implementation of an innovative idea are extremely small.

A third problem with large organizations is the *need for control*. As the business grows, the need to control performance also grows. As a result, corporate management is forced to establish fixed, quantifiable performance standards. Thus, paperwork and reports may take precedence over planning, performance reports receive more attention than performance results, and rules and standards become more important than entrepreneurial behavior.

A fourth problem is the nature of the *corporate culture*. According to Hisrich and Peters, the corporate culture has a climate and reward system that favors conservatism in decision making.[2] They assert that:

> The guiding principles in a traditional corporate culture are: follow the instructions given; do not make any mistakes; do not fail; do not take initiative but wait for instructions; stay within your turf; and protect your backside. This restrictive environment is of course not conducive to creativity, flexibility, independence, and risk taking—the jargon of intrapreneurs.

A fifth difference between large organizations and entrepreneurial ventures is the *specificity of the time dimension*. Quarterly and monthly reports lead corporate middle managers to have a myopic view of performance. Budget cycles force managers to think in terms of resource allocation from the corporate "bank" and to plan short-run cost reduction mechanisms in order to stay within the budget. The key to this is that reports and performance have to be completed as of some date. Thus, even though a corporation may have a planning horizon of five to ten years, its actual performance revolves around very specific dates or cycles. It is difficult for an individual to be creative when results are measured in short-run cycles.

Need for Short-Run Profits

Apart from those characteristics inherent to large corporations that make entrepreneurship difficult is the need of most publicly held ventures to show short-run profits. Established corporations thrive on short-run profits; they are the organization's measure of success. Corporations must also secure short-run profits in order to keep stock prices up and attract investors. Thus, there is constant pressure on top managers to devise strategies for short-run performance rather than long-run investment. Entrepreneurial ventures, on the other hand, may lose money for some time; their key to survival is cash flow. They need to attract money into the venture without guaranteeing the investor a sure return.

Lack of Entrepreneurial Talent

There are very few true entrepreneurs in large organizations. Typically, they are *not attracted to large organizations* in the first place. From outside, they see the corporate organization as a gray haze of automatons in pin-stripe suits all marching to a single corporate drummer. They prefer the riskier life of small ventures to the more secure, but stilted, life of a corporate staffer. Those that do find their way into the corporation typically leave after a few years.

A second reason that true entrepreneurs are seldom found in large organizations is that the *organizations do not encourage them.* They see the entrepreneur as a loner rather than as a team player and as an eccentric who is more interested in pet projects than in getting the corporate work done. Entrepreneurs are often viewed as cynics, as rebels, or as free spirits, who are late and do sloppy work that does not conform to standards set by the corporation. One article suggested that, "Creative people are, to be honest, a pain in the neck. They disrupt the established order by asking questions and experimenting with new ways of doing things when well-established procedures are available to provide direction. They come in late and leave early even if they do work three or four hours a night at home and most of the weekend."[3] Management consultant Marsha Sinetar adds that an entrepreneur will have problems working either as a team member or as a subordinate.[4] She suggests that entrepreneurs can alienate others by their intensive drive, their focus on pet projects, and their idiosyncrasies. And their style and even their thinking ability can clash when reporting to more traditional managers. As a result, the entrepreneurial individuals seldom rise through the ranks of the corporation as their more traditional colleagues do. This, in turn, contributes to their job dissatisfaction and, hence, to their departure.

Inappropriate Compensation Methods

Most organizations have few ways to compensate creative employees. Corporations use different pay schema for different levels of employees. Non-managerial workers, often unionized, are paid on an hourly basis regardless of their productivity. Managers and professional staff people are paid on a salary. Raises for these individuals may be based somewhat on productivity, but productivity is defined by input/output measures rather than by innovation in new products or processes. Many managerial and staff jobs have no firm definition of productivity other than getting the work done.

Any wage or salary schedule that is based on an hourly wage or a monthly salary will fail as an incentive for intrapreneurs. Even though monetary rewards may not be especially important to entrepreneurial individuals, some mechanism of rewarding innovation must be evident if innovation is to be continued.

Nonmonetary rewards for innovation are also typically missing from corporate structures. Promotion, a traditional method of rewarding managers, seldom works for intrapreneurs for two reasons.[5] First, the normal progression is that talented individuals are promoted into management. But this takes them out of the arena in which they were innovative and puts them into management. Second, intrapreneurs typically do not make good corporate managers. They do not have the temperament needed for management and they may cause problems that did not exist before.

Thus, neither monetary nor nonmonetary rewards in a traditional organization serve to encourage intrapreneurs. Some solutions to this problem do exist, and these will be discussed in a later section.

PLANNING FOR CORPORATE ENTREPRENEURSHIP

Previous sections of this chapter have clearly indicated the need for intrapreneurship, while discussing the barriers that prevent it. It should be clear that corporate entrepreneurship is *not* self-starting. It must be carefully planned and implemented in order to maximize its possibility for success. There are five distinct but related issues facing the corporate CEO who wishes to instill entrepreneurship within the corporate framework (Table 14-1). Each of these five factors is critical to the intrapreneurship process. Inadequately planning any one of them will doom the process to failure.

Committing the Organization

Innovation in organizations is necessarily a bottom-up process. Corporate entrepreneurship can only work when innovation comes from the lower levels of the organization. But only when shop floor workers, engineers, clerical workers, research and development staff, and others throughout the organization are given both authority and encouragement will intrapreneurship survive. *Commitment to intrapreneurship, can only be a top-down process.* Encouragement for entrepreneurship can come from anywhere

1. Committing the organization to the concept of intrapreneurship
2. Determining the corporate entrepreneurship model
3. Developing an intrapreneurial culture
4. Identifying intrapreneurs
5. Developing an intrapreneurial compensation schema

TABLE 14-1
Intrapreneurship Issues

inside or outside the organization, but the authority that must go hand in hand with that encouragement can only come from the top of the organization.

Top management commitment means that the CEO is a firm believer in the benefits of corporate entrepreneurship. This in itself is unlikely. Many chief executive officers have risen through the ranks of the corporation and may have had thirty or more years of experience in the traditional corporate culture. A traditional CEO who becomes committed to intrapreneurship will either be pushed into it by a turbulent environment or pulled into it by consultants or other executives who espouse its benefits. In some cases, corporate entrepreneurship comes at the same time as a change in CEOs.

Looking back at the barriers to intrapreneurship clearly shows why corporate entrepreneurship can only come from the top. First, the hierarchical structure dictates that any major change in strategy or corporate culture must come from the top. Top management must sanction the change in order for it to work its way *down* through the organization. Managers who have been accustomed to managing a traditional organization in traditional ways must be totally "reprogrammed" to accept the new culture. Even if a given department is unrelated to any of the new corporate ventures or processes that are developed, they must at least be sensitive to the needs of those who are involved.

A second reason for top management direction is that corporate entrepreneurship will require changes in the reward system. Those changes must be endorsed by top management. Depending on the size and structure of the corporation, changes in the reward system may have to have the personal stamp of approval of the CEO in order to carry the weight of the change throughout the organization.

Determining the Corporate Entrepreneurship Model

Once a chief executive officer becomes committed to the concept of entrepreneurship within the corporation, the next step is to determine the form it will take (Table 14-2). Intrapreneurship exists in different forms. The

TABLE 14-2
Structure for
Intrapreneurship

1. Entire organization adopts intrapreneurship. An organic structure is developed throughout the organization.
2. Multi-disciplinary "New Products Division" is formally established at vice-presidential level to shepherd new products and encourage others in the organization.
3. "New Products Subsidiary" is established, with autonomous structure. The unit accepts proposals from individuals, evaluates them, and determines whether proposal is worth funding or not.
4. An autonomous venture capital company is formed to underwrite and assist either internal or external proposals that meet normal venture capital criteria.
5. A section within human resource department is established to train or send managers to intrapreneurship conferences.

form that is appropriate in one organization may not work for another. The ultimate placement of a particular innovative product is not as important as the formalized structure that supports the overall concept.

Developing an *organic organization* requires major commitment to the concept of corporate entrepreneurship. Very few organizations have developed to that stage. 3M Corporation, noted in the entrepreneurial profile is one. The others could be counted on one hand. This requires a new thought process throughout the company. It is extremely difficult, if not impossible, to develop a totally organic organization from a traditional mechanistic or bureaucratic company.

A *new products group* at the vice-presidential level requires both the financial and the moral support of the company. If done correctly, the vice-president of new products will have the authority to restructure parts of the organization as necessary to develop a fully funded division on the same level as other divisions within the company. The vice-president becomes the **intrapreneurial champion,** that is, the corporate person who encourages potential intrapreneurs, cajoles management into funding programs that develop the organization's culture, and works with the human resources department to hire and train people who want to work in an open environment.

A *new products subsidiary* requires less commitment from the CEO than the establishment of a company division does, because the subsidiary is a separate unit, funded by the parent company. The benefit of the separate unit is that the parent company can benefit from the *results* of intrapreneurial activities without those activities disrupting the rest of the parent company. In other words, the traditional part of the company remains traditional. But the subsidiary operates on its own in developing new products or processes. It receives proposals from individuals within the company, evaluates them, and works with those individuals to develop them if they appear profitable. The subsidiary does not have a blank check from the CEO, but does have substantial discretionary funds to use in new product or process development.

Chapter 7 discussed venture capital firms as a financing source for new ventures. The *corporate venture capital firm* solicits proposals by individuals both within and outside the company. Some companies require that proposals relate to the industry in which the parent company operates. Some prefer proposals in industries that are different but are in areas into which the company would like to expand. Others require only that they have potential for significant profits.

The final alternative is to establish a *section within the human resources department* that encourages and trains individuals who show an interest in entrepreneurship. The training may consist of in-house seminars for all managers. It may consist of identifying and underwriting off-site seminars and conferences for selected managers or employees. This structure will have marginal impact on a large firm because of the limited commitment by top management and the lack of structure and incentives throughout the organization.

The model of intrapreneurial structure selected is primarily a function of the commitment of the CEO to the concept (Figure 14-1). It may, however, also be a function of the size and age of the firm, the industry in

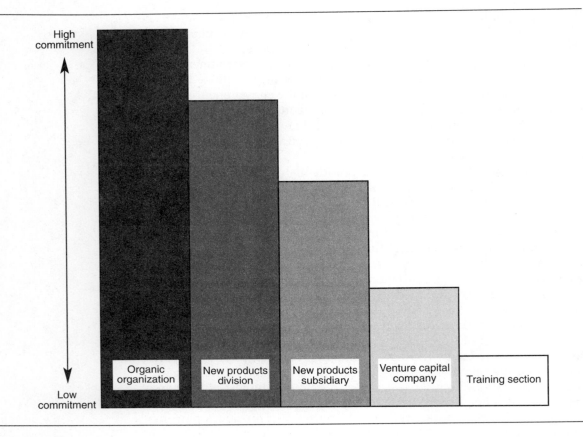

FIGURE 14-1
Intrapreneurial Structure
Compared with
Commitment

which it competes, and the competitive dynamics of the firm. An older firm in a manufacturing industry may not be able to reconstruct its entire corporate culture. Thus, using a venture capital company or new product subsidiary may be the best that can be expected. A company in a service industry that is highly competitive may find that it can well benefit from a total revamping of its method of operations. Because it is in a more dynamic environment, it may also be easier to make necessary changes.

Developing an Intrapreneurial Culture

The previous two sections discussed the need to commit the organization to intrapreneurship and the need to determine an appropriate model for corporate entrepreneurship in a given organization. Included in those discussions was the notion that traditional managers, workers, and departments may resist the change to a more open, innovative structure that fosters the entrepreneurial environment.

If a corporation is to be truly intrapreneurial, the entire corporate culture must be assessed and adjusted to fit the intrapreneurial mode. This cannot be done immediately. Instead, with the full commitment of top management, it can develop over time.

1. Self-selection
2. No handoffs
3. The doer decides
4. Corporate "slack"
5. Ending the home-run philosophy
6. Tolerance of risk, failure, and mistakes
7. Patient money
8. Freedom from turfiness (turf wars)
9. Cross-functional teams
10. Multiple options

TABLE 14-3
Indicators of an
Intrapreneurial Culture

An **intrapreneurial culture** is one in which entrepreneurship is allowed to flourish within the general constraints of the organization. Pinchot suggests several indicators of an intrapreneurial culture (Table 14-3).[6]

Self-selection means that intrapreneurs appoint themselves to a task rather than being appointed to it by the organization. They pursue their own ideas with or without the support of the organization. They are entrepreneurial without regard to their formal position in the company. Sometimes they work at night, sometimes they bootleg time during the day, and sometimes their supervisor gives them time and resources. But the important point is that they are self-starters and don't just carry out an official assignment.

In large traditional organizations, it is not unusual for a project to be routed through many different departments throughout its development. The *no handoffs* rule counters this tendency. In an intrapreneurial environment, the inventor or initiator is involved with the project throughout its development. Other individuals may be brought in from time to time, and another person may ultimately have developmental responsibility, but the originator retains membership on the intrapreneurial team. The logic of this is that including the originator throughout the process gives continuity to the concept and also serves as a real motivator to the originator of the project. A sort of "ownership" exists whenever a person sees a project through from beginning to end.

The typical corporation has several, if not many, layers between top management and the lowest worker level. Approval for resources must come from somewhere in the upper strata of the company. This not only takes time away from the project's development, but in some cases also squelches the project completely if it does not suit the fancy of higher-level managers. The story of Art Fry and his Post-it Notes in the appendix to this chapter illustrates how *the doer decides* concept worked at 3M. If Art Fry had been completely stymied by higher management, a legendary intrapreneurial story never would have happened. The originator of the idea simply *must* be allowed to proceed as long as the project is viable.

Corporate slack refers to an excess of resources beyond those required for the normal output of the company. These are discretionary resources that are not prebudgeted for planned activities. Thus, corporate slack is funding that can be channeled to an intrapreneur for a specialized project that might not be funded otherwise. This is a stumbling block for some corporations. Many companies, in their quest for financial control, attempt to reduce all expenditures to a line item on a printout. This is the antithesis of intrapreneurship. In order for corporate slack to exist, there must be either contingency funds within departmental accounts or separate funds within the corporation that are nonbudgeted and available for quick access.

Ending the home-run philosophy addresses the excessive need in some corporations to score big or not score at all. Many intrapreneurial ventures will fail and many more will be only partially successful. Using baseball terminology, intrapreneurship encourages singles while being pleasantly surprised if some hits turn out to be doubles, triples, or home runs. But the real emphasis is simply to find as many batters as possible who are interested in swinging an entrepreneurial bat.

A basic tenet of entrepreneurship and of intrapreneurship is that there will be mistakes. There will be failures. There will be wasted efforts. In order for intrapreneurship to thrive, a *tolerance of risk, failure, and mistakes* must exist. One of Allen Jacobson's comments in the entrepreneurial profile leading off this chapter addresses this well. He says, "Mistakes will be made. But if a person is essentially right, the mistakes he or she makes are not as serious in the long run as the mistakes management will make if it undertakes to tell those under its authority how they must do their jobs."

Patient money refers to the willingness to invest funds in intrapreneurial projects without an expected immediate return. Projects may take years to complete, especially if they are essentially "bootleg" projects—those that are worked on whenever time permits. Even in the case of 3M, which allows employees to spend up to 15 percent of their time on projects of their own choosing, the time to fruition could still be long.

Departments, divisions, functions, hierarchical levels, and individuals in corporations are prone to protect their own turf when it comes to resources and idea ownership. Intrapreneurship thrives when there is a *freedom from turfiness*. This means that employees, regardless of their position, do *not* engage in turf wars. The corporation is seen as a family of teams, all of whom work toward the same goals. Turfiness is a win/lose situation. What one group gains, the other must give up. Freedom from turfiness is a win/win situation. The intrapreneurial culture creates situations where everyone benefits. Working together as a group is encouraged. Resources are shared. Ideas are exchanged. Moral support is given. Assistance is given without regard to ownership claims. Turf battles do not exist.

An integral part of the freedom from turfiness is the use of *cross-functional teams*. This is difficult for bureaucrats in traditional structures to accept. But in order for intrapreneurship to work at its best, individuals must be allowed to work in teams regardless of their specialties. In fact, individuals with different specialties should be *encouraged* to work together to benefit from the different skills and perspectives of each team member. In its purest sense, formal teams are formed around the projects or, as Pinchot calls them, "intraprises." Each intraprise has its own leader and a

VENTURE PERSPECTIVE 14-1

. . . .

LINN MOLLENAUER
Bell Laboratories

Bell Laboratories physicist Linn Mollenauer had worked for years trying to develop "perfect" light pulses for sending messages by undersea phone cables. But three years ago, Arno Penzias, the head of AT&T's labs, ordered him to give up and work on something else. In spite of the order, Mollenauer continued to tinker at his lab table, which was covered with lasers and loops of fiber-optic cable.

Subsequent progress led Penzias to apologize for his doubts and praise Mollenauer's persistence in a talk to Bell Labs' top researchers. "Occasionally I allow researchers to overrule me when I'm wrong, and people in the organization convinced me my call wasn't right," said Penzias. In this case, Bell Labs was fortunate. Last year Mollenauer sent his special pulses six thousand miles through a glass cable

without generation, ten times the commercial distance record. If he is successful in perfecting the process, it could give AT&T a big edge in what is anticipated to be a $750 billion-a-year global market for optic transmission of data and telephone and television signals.

SOURCE: John J. Keller, "Defying Boss's Orders Pays Off for Physicist and His Firm, AT&T," *Wall Street Journal*, June 25, 1991, A1.

full complement of operative and functional personnel chosen by the team leader. These people then stay with the project throughout its development.

The last item, *multiple options,* refers to the various avenues that a project may take. Some projects will be short lived. Some will need substantial capital. Some will be marketable in-house, and some will be distributed outside. Some projects will require major commitments of time, personnel, and physical resources. What is most important is that the particular tactics that will be used to bring a project to fruition may not be known at all when it starts. Thus, intrapreneurship demands that multiple options be allowed.

Rosabeth Kanter suggests similar actions to achieve an intrapreneurial company.[7] In addition, she notes the need to reduce bureaucracy, restructure the company to be less segmented, do joint ventures within the company and between the company and outsiders such as suppliers or customers, and change accounting and budgeting procedures.

Identifying Intrapreneurial Talent

In a truly intrapreneurial firm, identifying intrapreneurs is unnecessary since many employees in the firm fit the category of the intrapreneur. In a more traditional firm that is moving toward corporate entrepreneurship, there is a need to identify those individuals with entrepreneurial tendencies. Two groups of individuals should be identified. The first group consists of innovators who preferably also have some managerial talent. The second is potential team members to join with the innovator to fully develop the concept.

Identifying Individual Intrapreneurs

It is necessary to first identify innovative individuals who also may have potential project ideas. In some cases, these individuals will surface on their own. They may have projects that they have been working on secretly or at least have been developing in their minds. Once the intent to endorse corporate entrepreneurship is made public, these closet innovators may readily come forth. Others will not. Thus, attempts must be made to identify innovators within the traditional organization. This can be done by organizational newsletters, memos from the CEO, bulletin board postings, memos through departments, and more informal means.

The task for organizational managers is to identify those who have entrepreneurial tendencies, *and* have the managerial skills to manage a project within the confines of a large organization, *and* have a project or idea that could be marketable. Intrapreneurs must have the ability to carry projects through to fruition, working with others to develop, produce, and market the concept.

Not all aspiring entrepreneurs make good venture owners and not all individuals who think they are creative make good intrapreneurs. Some highly creative individuals have little management ability. There are not likely to be many of these free spirits in a large organization. Good results can be achieved, however, by pairing a creative person with an individual who has management skills.

The opposite extreme is perhaps more prevalent in a large organization. In this case, an individual may identify a product or concept but is too much of a traditional corporate worker or bureaucrat to take the necessary risks associated with its development. The employee either does not have the risk-taking propensity, or does not have the drive, or does not have the vision necessary to bring the product to market. Thus, for whatever reason, the originator of the idea may not be an appropriate person to develop or manage the project. In the case of either the highly creative person with no management talent or the innovative but unwilling person, managers must then find intrapreneurs to work as a team to develop the concept.

Most of the entrepreneurial characteristics discussed in Chapter 3 are relevant for intrapreneurs. In particular, those characteristics that relate to growth-oriented entrepreneurs are relevant for corporate entrepreneurs.

The intrapreneur is both an entrepreneurial person and a good corporate manager. The intrapreneur is a results-oriented, ambitious, rational, competitive, and questioning person who dislikes bureaucracy and is challenged by innovation. But in addition, the intrapreneur understands the organization, can resolve conflict, and has a basic faith in other workers (Table 14-4). Thus, the intrapreneur is an individual who combines the best parts of both the entrepreneur and the corporate manager.

Identifying Team Members

In addition to locating individual innovators, management must locate individuals to serve as team members to develop concepts. These individuals are not normally the originators of ideas. More likely, they are team members or support staff. In any case, the need is to identify people who have entrepreneurial tendencies and are able to work through the corpo-

1. Focuses on results
2. Questions the status quo
3. Has faith in other employees
4. Is motivated by problem solving and rational decision making
5. Is ambitious and competitive
6. Believes that reward is in the work as much as in the pay
7. Finds bureaucratic systems frustrating
8. Can resolve conflicts
9. Understands the organization as a system
10. Is motivated by change and innovation for self and employees

TABLE 14-4
Intrapreneurial
Characteristics
SOURCE: Adapted from Joel E. Ross and Darab Unwalla, "Who Is an Intrapreneur?" *Personnel* 63, no. 12 (Dec. 1986): 45–49.

rate system. The identified individuals must be comfortable with the intrapreneurial culture. They must possess a willingness to deal with uncertainty, long lead times, indefinite resources, and new concepts or products. The team members can come from any department or division within the company. The key to the identification process is that these people have entrepreneurial characteristics as well as management skills.

Rewarding Intrapreneurs

Compensation of intrapreneurs poses complex problems in the traditional organization. This is because most personnel in the company are paid a straight monthly salary, an hourly wage, or a commission. Intrapreneurs may not be willing to give up a salaried position in the firm and switch completely to the risk-based reward system that their entrepreneur counterparts face. At the same time, the traditional reward system is insufficient for intrapreneurs. They rightfully think that if they are to work on more risky projects, they should benefit from that risk.

Designing a reward system for intrapreneurs requires that top managers be aware of both the needs of the intrapreneurs and the needs of traditional workers in the firm. The reward system for intrapreneurs must be both monetary and nonmonetary. In fact, the nonsalary aspect of the system may be even more important to the intrapreneur. Nonsalary rewards can be formal recognition of performance, the provision of discretionary funds, the establishment of support groups, or dual promotion systems based on performance in innovative project development.

An example of the dual promotion system is that used by 3M. Employees can be promoted either through a management hierarchy or through a technical structure. On the technical side, employees are given higher rank but are not constrained to purely administrative jobs. This recognizes that many intrapreneurs are technicians. As such they are more valuable in the lab than in administrative management. Others prefer administration. The dual promotion system allows both types of individuals to be rewarded while maintaining the interest of all workers in the intrapreneurial organization.

Providing structural changes that encourage the intrapreneurial culture is also a method of rewarding intrapreneurs. Some companies use technology councils to provide interaction among technicians to generate new product ideas. Other companies provide small work groups that permanently replace assembly lines. The work groups can then structure their own operations in the most effective and innovative fashion.

Monetary rewards may be in the form of bonuses, shares of profits of the newly developed products, or what Pinchot refers to as "intracapital."[8] Intracapital is the freedom to use increasing amounts of corporate resources to fund additional product development. As projects reach fruition and return capital to the parent organization, additional funds are provided to the intrapreneur for discretionary use. These are nonbudgeted funds to be used by the intrapreneur in any application.

Finally, bonuses and profit sharing are forms of reward that transcend normal salary schedules. In the first case, the intrapreneur is given a bonus periodically as a reward for innovation within the company. In the case of profit sharing, the intrapreneur indirectly reaps the benefits of innovation as the newly developed products provide additional profit to the company.

EVALUATING INTRAPRENEURIAL PROJECTS

The remaining task for managers in intrapreneurial companies is to evaluate proposed projects. Virtually everything regarding evaluation in Chapter 5 is equally applicable here. However, several additional factors must be considered. A study done by DeSarbo, MacMillan, and Day suggested eight variables that are significant as managers evaluate proposals (Table 14-5).[9]

The odds of a proposal being funded are higher if the proposal fits nicely with the firm's existing strategy. Also, the lower the initial investment required for a proposal, the greater the probability that it will be accepted. A venture champion can be the innovator or a team member who will be in charge of the development of the concept. If the venture champion has had previous experience with intrapreneurial products, the chances of approval will be higher. If the firm has previous experience with the particular product or service, this will also add to the probability that the proposal will be approved. Market issues affect intrapreneurial ventures just as they do entrepreneurial ventures. Thus, low competitive

---

TABLE 14-5
Criteria for Evaluating
Intrapreneurial Proposals

1. High corporate fit
2. Low initial investment
3. Experienced venture champion
4. Experience with product/service
5. Low competitive threat
6. Proprietary technology
7. High gross margin
8. High rate of return

threats, proprietary technology, high gross margins, and the prospects for high rates of return all affect the approval decision.

The concept of high fit with the company merits further discussion. Of critical importance are the two concepts of strategic fit and cultural fit. The first is the strategic fit with the company. This refers to the closeness of the proposal to the firm's current strategy. Although some companies accept proposals without regard to strategic fit, the odds of acceptance and of success are much higher if there is a strategic tie.

The second aspect of corporate fit is the corporate culture. All organizations, regardless of type or size, have an identifiable corporate culture. This culture, or tone, of the organization permeates the entire company. In all but the most aggressively innovative firms, the corporate culture will enter into the decision process. Thus, proposals relating to certain industries would likely be rejected out of hand. Products or services that violate the firm's philosophy will be rejected before any financial or strategic analysis is made.

An additional issue not discussed above is that of corporate politics. Political issues can affect the acceptance process in a number of ways. Proposals from individuals with a known, positive track record will receive better consideration than those from individuals with less respect in the firm. Sometimes a certain number of proposals will be accepted from each department, rather than accepting only the best proposals. Individuals who are more visible in the organization are more likely to be funded than those who tend to be organizational recluses.

Overriding all the criteria discussed above is the fact that internally developed proposals require *careful thought and judgment* in the approval process. Funding corporate entrepreneurship ventures can never be as objective as funding decisions for traditional new ventures because the firm can never totally divorce itself from the project. The arm's-length negotiation is difficult to maintain when the proposal comes from long-time employees. Corporations moving toward intrapreneurship should develop policies guiding the project approval process such that necessary objectivity can be gained while encouraging individuals to propose innovative projects for consideration.

ADMINISTERING INTRAPRENEURIAL PROJECTS

Once a new product proposal is accepted, it must be assigned to an administrative location. Assignments may be based on the closeness of the concept to the firm's core strategy as well as on the ability of the firm to make valuable input into the development.[10] A given project may be integrated into the normal operations of the firm, assigned to a new products unit or subsidiary, or funded through the venture capital subsidiary. If the proposal has merit but is not of any strategic or operational interest to the firm, the company may work informally with the innovator to find ways in which the proposal could be developed outside the company. The key to intrapreneurial projects, of course, is to support the innovator so that both the innovator and the company benefit. The important factor is that the company establish some policy and communicate that policy to workers who may have innovative concepts to consider.

ENTREPRENEURSHIP IN NOT-FOR-PROFIT ORGANIZATIONS

Entrepreneurship in the public sector is, in its purest sense, a contradiction in terms. Since entrepreneurship is profit oriented, requires risking one's own capital, and assumes the creation of a new business enterprise, the concept of public entrepreneurship is antithetical to most aspects of entrepreneurship.[11] Yet the concept of intrapreneurship can be applicable to a not-for-profit organization almost as well as it can be to a large corporation. This is especially true because not-for-profit does not necessarily mean noncompetitive. For example, any community that is large enough for two or more hospitals is surely aware of the competition between the two organizations even though one or more may be not-for-profit. In addition, moves toward outpatient diagnostics and treatment, more specialized equipment, and more cost-efficient care are indicative of entrepreneurial actions. Years ago, the March of Dimes was nearly put out of business when the cure for polio was found. Completely changing its mission, and instead fighting birth defects, was indeed an entrepreneurial move.[12]

Public and private health maintenance organizations (HMOs) have arisen only in the last decade. Universities in the 1980s began strategic planning in the face of declining numbers of high school graduates. The results for some universities could be considered innovative in the truest sense. For example, some private universities have provided computers in all residence hall rooms, and many universities have used innovative means of attracting nontraditional students. Some have converted unused dormitories to offices or business incubators and technology centers. Young cites a number of examples of entrepreneurship in organizations as diverse as social service agencies, the American Cancer Society, charitable foundations, and museums.[13]

In addition to entrepreneurship in basic mission-related activities, many not-for-profit organizations have auxiliary enterprises that more closely resemble small businesses than they do the parent organization. Some not-for-profit organizations, especially in the community development area, have even established profit-making subsidiaries. In one survey, more than 60 percent of the respondents indicated that at least some of their revenues came from enterprise activities.[14] Even churches, long assumed to be bastions of tradition, have found innovative ways to serve the community. These examples are all evidence of entrepreneurship in action in the public sector. Thus, while entrepreneurship in its truest sense cannot exist in the not-for-profit organization, it can and does flourish in selected organizations in the broader context of the word.

Not-for-profit intrapreneurship must overcome challenges that neither new venture entrepreneurship nor corporate entrepreneurship face. Two problems in particular abound. The first is that the public sector typically does not have an entrepreneurial culture. The government is the clearest example. Organizations of this type tend to be bureaucratic with limited autonomy and little room for risk-taking. Individual employees are not encouraged to be innovative; rather, they are implored to "go by the book" and not stray from established procedures. The second reason why entrepreneurship does not flourish in the not-for-profit organization is that the managers of these organizations tend to be program oriented rather than management oriented. Thus, they often have some difficulty in controlling all aspects of innovative programs or ventures.

Even with the natural bias against entrepreneurship in many not-for-profit organizations, intrapreneurship can be encouraged. The issues raised in this chapter regarding the encouragement of corporate entrepreneurship apply equally well to organizational entrepreneurship. Commitment must be made by top managers, an intrapreneurial culture must be developed, nonmanagerial employees must be identified and encouraged, and projects must be evaluated as objectively as possible. Although the constraints may be greater, the process is similar.

· ·

Intrapreneurship, or corporate entrepreneurship, is in many ways similar to new venture entrepreneurship. It requires innovation, risk-taking, commitment, an objective analysis of opportunities, and sufficient funding. Entrepreneurship in the corporate setting, however, faces a number of obstacles. The large size of a corporation stifles entrepreneurship because of the number of layers in the hierarchy and the necessary controls in place to direct such a large organization. Large corporations do not attract true entrepreneurs because of the limited autonomy within a bureaucratic system. Further, if entrepreneurs do find their way into a large corporation, they typically do not stay. The need for fixed time frames and budgets in large corporations makes investing in entrepreneurial ventures difficult. Finally, compensating intrapreneurs is complex within the framework of a traditional corporation.

SUMMARY

Five steps must be taken in order to develop intrapreneurship in large corporations. First, the corporate management must be fully committed to entrepreneurship. Second, a model or structure for corporate entrepreneurship must be determined. Third, an intrapreneurial culture must be developed throughout the organization. Fourth, intrapreneurs must be identified and encouraged. And fifth, a reward system for intrapreneurs must be developed. Once corporate entrepreneurship is endorsed and implemented, then proposals must be evaluated, and successful proposals must be housed somewhere in the overall corporate structure.

Entrepreneurial proposals within a corporation must be evaluated much as any new venture proposal might be evaluated by venture capitalists. Aside from market factors, strategic fit and the corporate culture are the two most important issues in determining whether a proposal will be funded. Other criteria include the amount of funding needed, the competition, and the probability of high rates of return.

Entrepreneurship in the not-for-profit organization exists in a broad sense even though the concepts of personal capital investment, the profit motive, and new venture creation are not present. Encouraging entrepreneurship in the not-for-profit organization may be even more difficult than in the corporation because of the nature of the organization, its managers, and its culture. Not-for-profit organizations, however, can benefit from entrepreneurial actions that make them more competitive or more cost effective. The appendix to this chapter is a speech by Art Fry, the originator of the Post-it Note at 3M.

DISCUSSION QUESTIONS

1. How does corporate entrepreneurship differ from new venture entrepreneurship? What similarities are there?
2. Is it possible to completely change a traditional corporation into an entrepreneurial corporation? Why or why not?
3. What are the barriers to intrapreneurship? Are they surmountable?
4. Develop a scenario for encouraging intrapreneurship in a traditional corporation. Once you have it developed, show it to a classmate for comments. Then show it to a manager in a corporation. Will the comments be the same?
5. Will corporate entrepreneurship be viewed the same by top level managers and middle managers? Why or why not?
6. Why is developing a compensation plan for intrapreneurs difficult? What factors must be considered?
7. Is it possible to have an organization that is part intrapreneurial and part traditional?
8. How does evaluating intrapreneurial proposals differ from evaluating new venture proposals? Assume that a corporate venture proposal and a new venture proposal are similar. What would be the differences in how they might be evaluated? In which case would we expect the proposal to get the most favorable rating?
9. Why are politics significant in intrapreneurship?
10. Is there anything in particular that would differentiate a not-for-profit organization that is entrepreneurial from one that is not?
11. Why are personnel in many not-for-profit organizations not likely to be intrapreneurs?
12. This chapter did not attempt to predict the future of corporate entrepreneurship. What would be your prediction? Why?

EXERCISES

EXERCISE 14-1

The Situation

You have just been hired as the new president of a relatively large manufacturing subsidiary of a Fortune 1000 company. The president of the parent company tells you that your subsidiary's performance has not been up to the expectations of the parent firm's board of directors. Before bringing you in, they considered selling off the subsidiary but finally decided to bring in a new president to turn the subsidiary around. The final words to you as you left the office were, "I don't care how you do it, but I want better performance. You have three to five years to do it. At the end, you'll either become a vice-president of the parent company or you'll be fired."

You have the choice, of course, of slashing costs, firing workers, and selling off assets. You also have the choice of rejuvenating the company. Upon arrival at your new assignment, you are somewhat amazed that the culture of the subsidiary is dull. People seem relatively happy and the work gets done, but there is no vision and no sense of excitement.

Your Task

Prepare remarks for a speech to be given to an assembly of all managers from first-line supervisors up.

EXERCISE 14-2

Research the mission and mode of operations of a not-for-profit organization in your community. Interview the person in charge and one or more lower-level staff persons. Does the organization seem intrapreneurial? If not, could it be made so?

. . . .

1. Gifford Pinchot III, *Intrapreneuring* (New York: Harper & Row, 1985).
2. Robert D. Hisrich and Michael P. Peters, *Entrepreneurship: Starting, Developing, and Managing a New Enterprise,* 2d ed. (Homewood, IL: Irwin, 1992), 534.
3. W. Jack Duncan et al., "Intrapreneurship and the Reinvention of the Corporation," *Business Horizons* 31, no. 3 (May–June 1988): 17–18.
4. Marsha Sinetar, "Entrepreneurs, Chaos, and Creativity—Can Creative People Really Survive Large Company Structure?" *Sloan Management Review* Vol. 26, no. 2 (Winter 1985): 57–62.
5. Duncan et al., "Intrapreneurship and the Reinvention" 19.
6. Pinchot, *Intrapreneuring,* 198–256.
7. Rosabeth M. Kanter, "Supporting Innovation and Venture Development in Established Companies," *Journal of Business Venturing* 1, no. 1, (Winter 1985): 47–60.
8. Pinchot, *Intrapreneuring,* Chapter 11.
9. Wayne DeSarbo, Ian C. MacMillan, and Diana L. Day, "Criteria for Corporate Venturing: Importance Assigned by Managers," *Journal of Business Venturing* 2, no. 4 (Fall 1987): 329–50.
10. Robert A. Burgelman, "Designs for Corporate Entrepreneurship in Established Firms," *California Management Review* 26, no. 3 (Spring 1984): 154–66.
11. Ravi Ramamurti, "Public Entrepreneurs: Who They Are and How They Operate," *California Management Review* 27, no. 3 (Spring 1986): 142–58.
12. Dennis R. Young, "Entrepreneurship and Organizational Change in the Human Services," in *The Nonprofit Organization: Essential Readings,* edited by David Gies, J. Steven Ott, and Jay M. Shafritz (Pacific Grove, CA: Brooks/Cole Publishing 1990), 301–14.
13. Ibid., 301–14.
14. James C. Crimmins and Mary Kiel, "Enterprise in the Non-Profit Sector," in Gies, Ott, and Shafritz, *The Nonprofit Organization,* 315–27.
15. Material in this appendix excerpted from "The Post-it Note: An Intrapreneurial Success" *SAM Advanced Management Journal* 52, no. 3 (Summer 1987): 4–9. Used with permission.

ENDNOTES

◆ Conveniesse, Inc. ◆

The Need for Innovation

The twenty-five units of Conveniesse, Inc., now spread across eighteen cities in eight states. The oldest of these, the Buffalo unit, is now fourteen years old. The newest, in Charleston, West Virginia, is eight months old. The management of Conveniesse includes Yolanda as president and CEO, Jason as executive vice-president with general oversight of expansion and new store development, and vice-presidents of four areas: marketing, human resources, corporate operations, and finance. The management team has included this full management staff for several years.

Growth has tapered off in the last two years with only one new store, in Charleston, opening in the last eighteen months. At the current time, no new stores are planned. The growth per store is near zero although it is to be expected that growth within individual stores would be low once they become firmly entrenched. Growth in both the hotel and office markets is limited to the growth in the area around them. The size of the market varies among the cities. Advertising is limited to in-hotel brochures and limited advertisement in or around the store itself. Advertising on television or in the newspaper has been of little value.

During a management meeting, Yolanda reported on a phone call from Akins.

"He said he was becoming more and more concerned with the appearance and other problems in the Buffalo stores," Yolanda said. "He said he had already dropped Sarah's lease on two of her stores and was thinking of closing more. The main problem, he said, is just that the stores no longer look upscale, they haven't kept up with the times, and frankly he wasn't pleased with the clientele that seemed to be frequenting the stores in the past year or so. He made it perfectly clear. We have about three months to get our act together or we are history in his buildings."

"That's what I have been trying to tell you for almost a year," said Mike Cassidy, the Conveniesse marketing vice-president. "We have to keep investing in these stores or we're going to lose our business. Two of the three Buffalo stores, the Grand Rapids store, and the Pittsburgh store are actually declining in sales even though they're still profitable. It won't be long before they move into the red if we don't do something."

"Not so fast," countered David Owens, the vice-president of corporate operations. "We don't even know why sales are declining. Maybe the recession hurt us. Maybe downtown demographics are changing. Maybe there are new competitors in the market. Plus, if we go in and invest, say, $150,000 per store in a face-lift, new equipment, new logo, and new advertising, we stand to get very little in return. Plus, all that remodeling really makes a mess. You either have to shut down or make it virtually impossible to shop."

"Dave, I tend to agree with Mike," Cindi Short, the financial vice-president responded. "I bet we haven't changed the product mix in the stores significantly in four years. And I know we haven't changed the decor in all the years I have been here. Face it. Conveniesse is no longer upscale in the minds of the customers. We are in excellent financial shape now. If we invested $150,000 in each store—and the newer ones probably need less—it would still only cost us less than $4 million. We would probably have to take on more debt to do it, but not an exorbitant amount."

Yolanda and Jason remained quiet throughout the discussion, which continued for another thirty minutes. The meeting did not end with a clear decision on the topic. After the meeting, the two owners who had launched the entrepreneurial venture almost fifteen years ago were now facing a new set of problems. With an office building convenience store chain of twenty-five units, problems were different than when the chain was small but growing. Just how much can you rejuvenate sales and profits through reinvestment into the stores? Was Akins serious in his threat to pull their lease? His actions with Sarah in Canada suggested that he indeed was. More important, if the answer is that rejuvenation must occur, the bigger question is how? Dave Owens might be right. It is possible that a big investment will only stem the drain and might even cause more problems.

Assignment

Assume you are a consulting firm called in to give Conveniesse, Inc., advice regarding how to rejuvenate the Conveniesse chain. What innovations would you suggest? Would they be cosmetic or would they hit at the heart of Conveniesse? More important, how would or could you change the thought patterns of the owners and managers in order for them to think more entrepreneurially?

. . . .

THE POST-IT NOTE: AN INTRAPRENEURIAL SUCCESS
Art Fry, Corporate Scientist, 3M Corporation

The entrepreneur, working in a smaller arena, must have many different skills under one hat to direct all phases of a project—management, production, engineering, marketing, economics, materials, packaging, process technology, legal, and so on.[15] Few of us are so well-rounded. But even if we were, many challenges, including the development of Post-it Notes, require so many skills and so much time that they could not be met by one person in one lifetime.

Fortunately, the role of the intrapreneur offers an alternative. We can put a team together, and with those other skills, form a new corporate body—a "super-person" with more time and talent. Some of the people on the team may also be intrapreneurs in the true sense, but are investing a smaller portion of their time and talents than you are in a particular project. In short, there are more ways to be an intrapreneur than an entrepreneur.

Intrapreneurs are a different breed—burrs under the saddle for many managers. They want to change things, spend money, think long term, ask embarrassing questions, challenge authority, and perhaps be disruptive. Truth, and the chance to make something happen, are often more important to them than the conventional motivations of money or power.

Nevertheless, in hiring those innovators and intrapreneurs we give them time and money and freedom and a perspective of the company. We hire them to look without knowing what they will find.

The 3M Approach

Statistics show that small companies develop the greatest number of new products. And yet, at 3M, we have been astonishingly successful in new products. With over 40,000 products, we are the world's most successful new products company. We have a goal: that 25 percent of sales must come from products that did not exist five years before.

How does 3M foster this creative climate? The first part of the answer is that innovators aren't just found in management. As a matter of fact, very few breakthroughs result from top-down decisions.

New-to-the-world things require perspectives, associations, and new information that is not always available to the executive. Top-down decisions are fine if you are going after an established market with existing technology.

New things generally come from the inside-out, from people scattered throughout the entire organization. Also, while innovation starts with the initial idea for a product, a lot more creativity and new ideas are needed to build the idea into a business. Innovation and "intrapreneuring" must be allowed at every level of the corporation. If managers aren't innovative, if they don't provide the climate for creativity, if they can't set aside their carefully laid plans to take advantage of a new opportunity, then intrapreneurs have little encouragement.

3M is intrapreneurial. Our roots are easy to trace. We were blessed with innovative founders, who hired others like themselves. As a result, this particular trait was passed down from the first employee to the most recent; it's in our company's genes.

One of our early innovators was a man by the name of Dick Drew. Back in 1923, Drew saw the need for a tape that would quickly and accurately mask two-tone automobiles for painting. His first tape was too rigid and didn't conform to the curves and angles of the auto body. William McKnight, 3M's chief executive officer at the time, ordered Drew to stop working on the tape because it was giving our quality sandpaper products a bad name.

Drew did stop working on the tape—for exactly one day. During that period, he stumbled across a crepe paper toweling substrate that was being considered for use on sandpaper. It stretched, and it was perfect for Drew's tape.

Drew began working on the tape in his spare time. Shortly thereafter, Mr. McKnight walked through the lab. Even though Drew didn't really have any spare time, and even though Drew's project directly contradicted his order, McKnight didn't stop him.

As a result of that episode, Mr. McKnight instituted 3M's policy of allowing its researchers to spend up to 15 percent of their time on projects of their own choosing. This was a pretty revolutionary policy, particularly for the 1920s, but it's one 3M supports today.

I'd like to say a word about that 15 percent, or "bootleg" rule, as we call it. No one really has extra time. Often, the 15 percent is time that's put in after 5:00 or on weekends. That's where some of my bootleg time came from when I first started working on Post-it Notes, because I was working on a high-priority project, developing a shelf arranger tape for library shelves.

The bootleg rule gives us a chance to shape our own careers. McKnight recognized that people give their best efforts to the projects they're most interested in. The reward for the extra effort is that we are soon officially asked to do what we wanted to do all along. Many of 3M's major new products were developed by people giving extra effort to champion something new.

Dr. Spencer Silver, the 3M researcher who discovered the Post-it Note adhesive, is a good example of modern creativity at 3M. He discovered the Post-it Note adhesive accidentally, while trying to develop the opposite—super strong adhesives.

Although the adhesive wasn't his original target, Silver was convinced of its merits. He took it to others within 3M and asked how they thought it might be used. There was a definite lack of enthusiasm for his discovery.

In other companies, this might have been discouraging and all the reason needed to drop the idea. But Spence didn't feel obliged to. At 3M, we're a bunch of ideas. We never throw ideas away because you never know when someone else may need it.

Obviously a delicate balance must be maintained between skepticism and encouragement. People need the opportunity to make errors, to explore what look like blind alleys, and to do so with some confidence in themselves and the organization. But at the same time, they need to be challenged and tested.

Developing the Post-it

So now let's talk about the story of how Post-it Notes came to be. The idea originally came to me when I sang in the choir at North Presbyterian Church in 1974.

I was a member of my church choir and marked hymnal responses with pieces of scrap paper. Invariably they'd fall out of the book or slip between the pages—a big nuisance. My mind began to wander one day during the sermon, and I thought of Spence's adhesive. If I could coat it on paper, that would be just the ticket for a better book mark.

I went to work the next day, ordered a sample of the adhesive and began coating it on paper. I only coated the edge of the paper so the part protruding from the book wouldn't be sticky.

In using these bookmarks for notes back and forth from my boss, I came across the heart of the idea. It wasn't a bookmark at all, but a note. Spence's adhesive was most useful for making paper adhere to paper, and a whole lot of other surfaces as well. And yet, it wasn't so sticky that it would damage those surfaces when it was pulled off. The notes were a systems approach to communicating because the means of attachment and removal were built in.

This was the insight . . . . it was a whole new concept in pressure sensitive adhesives. It was like moving from the outer ring of the target to the bull's-eye.

Post-it Notes wouldn't have gotten anywhere if I had stopped with submitting the idea and hadn't gone to the work of getting materials and making samples. The old story that invention is 10 percent inspiration and 90 percent perspiration is true, and my perspiration on this project had just begun.

I encountered serious technical problems very early. First there was the problem of getting the adhesive to stay in place on the note instead of transferring to other surfaces. I think some of those church hymnals have pages that are still sticking together.

Have you ever noticed how our pads are no thicker at the adhesive layer than in the rest of the pad? Even though 3M is noted for its coating expertise . . . . we didn't have the coating equipment capable of giving us the necessary precision on an imprecise backing such as paper. And once we had the paper coated, we didn't have a good way of measuring the coating weight.

Some of the early bookmarks wouldn't stick at all and others couldn't be pulled off without ripping the paper. It was difficult to maintain a consistent range of adhesion.

All of these things bothered our production people, but I was delighted by the problems. If there is anything that 3M loves, it is to create a product that is easy for the customer to use, but difficult for competitors to make.

Eventually, we had to develop new ways of coating and measuring, but then these problems became our strengths. Problems are really opportunities in disguise. The tougher they are, the better. If the problems are easy to solve, your competition will soon be making it too.

Now that is the beauty of bootleg projects. They allow you to keep a low profile during the time when the early, tough problems arise that require creative solutions. Sometimes it just takes time to work out those creative solutions or to learn the new skills that you need to accomplish the task.

Throwing a lot of money or people at the task doesn't speed it up, but it does cut down on management's ability to afford to be patient. Things can be killed before they get a chance.

The corporation had provided me with just enough time and money to get started. We were able to get Post-it Notes into pilot scale manufacturing because I had enough latitude to keep working on this project, because of teamwork and help from my boss, because 3M divisions are under constant pressure to create new products, and because the system was leaky enough that a bag of this and a drum of that would magically appear in the lab when needed.

Even though we had a prototype, we still had a long way to go. Each new product must be adopted by one of our business development units. People in those units must be convinced that new products have sufficient market potential.

Through the new business development units [BDUs], we got a little more money and were able to put together teams of lab, engineering, marketing, cost accounting, packaging and production people. Still, we had trouble generating serious enthusiasm for Post-it Notes.

While I continued my selling efforts with the new BDUs, I was getting some important help from my lab director, Geoff Nicholson. He started passing out samples of the product to our senior executives' secretaries. They promptly fell in love with these little yellow notes and began using them. Before long their bosses began borrowing them, and soon a few very highly placed people started showing up in our labs just to see how we were doing.

That brings up another point about 3M's creative climate. No matter how much power you have, no matter how persuasive the arguments for a product, you always need someone in management to be your sponsor or advocate.

If it weren't for Geoff, my immediate supervisor Bob Molenda, and Joe Ramey, who was our division vice-president, Post-it Notes never would have emerged from the lab.

These three were especially supportive when we received disappointing results from an initial market test. Joe Ramey and Geoff jumped on a plan and made unannounced calls to end-users in a test market to gauge customer reaction and determine what to do with the idea. Post-it Notes were more expensive than regular scratch paper. Would customers pay the extra price?

After successfully taking orders for Post-it Notes in Richmond, Virginia, and hearing users pleading for us to continue sales, Ramey was convinced that Post-it Notes were marketable.

The marketing strategy was reformulated to emphasize sampling. We formulated a critical path diagram with a box for each job and step that had to be done, from the prototype stage through national introduction. We had no idea of how we would accomplish all the jobs within a certain time. But we managed to do it, working as a team.

3M's Reward System

In many other companies, a technical person like myself would have to manage people and budgets to receive additional pay and recognition. The 3M dual ladder system allows people to advance on the technical side of the ladder, assuming additional responsibility for technologies instead of people or budgets. That means that people who are happiest working in the lab can remain there without losing pay raises or recognition.

Since I began working on Post-it Notes, I've received three promotions to my present title of corporate scientist, the highest title on the technical side of 3M's dual ladder.

That means I don't have to scrounge for supplies and materials. It means I can choose many of the projects to work on and help to define technical paths for others.

People involved with intrapreneuring identify with the company; there is a sense of community. The usual polarizations do not occur, such as union/company, management/employees, and our department/their department. Intrapreneurship adds excitement and interest to our lives. It makes us givers, not just users. It gives us some control in our lives. It enables us to leave something for someone else; to improve the quality of life for ourselves and others.

V

PLANNING THE ENTREPRENEURIAL FINALE

Valuing the Venture
•
Harvesting the Venture

15 Valuing the Venture

LEARNING OBJECTIVES

After reading this chapter, you should be able to:

1. Differentiate between "price" and "value"
2. Understand when a venture should be valued
3. Identify factors to consider in reaching a value
4. Differentiate between the perspectives of buyers, sellers, and financiers
5. Understand various valuation methods
6. Realize the role of risk in valuation
7. Understand the effect of the "deal" on final price

KEY TERMS

Price	Asset based approach
Value	Market comparables
Negotiating range	Present value approach
Comparable firms method	Deal

CONSIDER THIS!

- Valuing a venture is both an art and a science.
- The correct price may not be the correct value.
- The magnitude of the negotiating range may vary widely as situations change.
- There may be no one "right" method of reaching a value.
- Even if all parties are using the same data and they are all impartial observers, they may still not agree on the appropriate value.
- Even after objectively valuing a firm by more than one method, an analyst may still have to make a qualitative judgment concerning the appropriate value.

One of the most difficult tasks in entrepreneurship is valuing a venture. This is particularly true if the venture is a sole proprietorship, a partnership, or a privately held corporation, since there is no stock price to use as a starting point. It is also difficult when the venture is new, when it is growing rapidly, or when the market in which the venture operates is volatile. This chapter will discuss issues surrounding the valuation process and will then present methods of valuing a venture. Finally, the value of a venture will be calculated using a number of the methods discussed.

ENTREPRENEURIAL PROFILE

JACQUELINE MOORE
Ridgaway Philips

When Jacqueline Moore was considering adding a venture to her home health care business, she needed to know how much her own firm was worth in order to get an idea of how much money she would have to raise externally to make the acquisition. She hired a valuation specialist in her industry to do an appraisal.

Because of Moore's past earnings, the specialist arrived at a value of $6.8 million based on projected future earnings. He also compared the value of the firm with prices that competing firms had sold for and, in the process, considered the potential of the market. And he did a valuation based on the firm's assets, which yielded a lower value of $5.8 million.

Moore graduated from Antioch College with a B.S. in social work. She later received a master's degree in public administration and worked as a utilization review manager for a large health insurer. She had plans to go into health care consulting to work with companies to reduce their health care costs. But at that time, she found that companies were not particularly interested in lowering their health care costs. Moore believed that health care consulting was sure to be a growth industry, but she needed a way to underwrite the business. As a result, she started a home health care and nursing service to generate funds for her original plan.

Ridgaway Philips focuses on the catastrophically ill and injured. Although it serves patients, whose average age is in the 30s, its clients are typically insurance companies. Moore's company is working with insurance companies to hold down health costs and provide better service in the process. The patients receive treatment at home that would otherwise require hospitalization. And the cost of the treatment in high-tech cases can be as low as one-third the cost of in-hospital treatment.

The valuation gave Moore an idea of the worth of her business in order to help her decide what to do with it in the future. She has an interest in working with destitute and orphaned children, and plans may include a method to provide funds to a social service agency through a transfer of ownership of part of her company. The company continues to grow and now has offices in suburban Philadelphia and Bethlehem, Pennsylvania. It has several hundred employees and requires day-to-day management that is delegated to a team of managers, thereby allowing Moore to pursue other entrepreneurial interests. So it is not unreasonable to expect that the venture will someday be used to underwrite additional ventures in either the profit or not-for-profit sectors.

SOURCE: Interview with Jacqueline Moore; Terri Lammers, "Know Your Worth," *Inc.*, August 1991, 90–91. Used with permission.

PRICE VERSUS VALUE

It must be made clear that price and value are not the same thing. **Price** reflects the amount of money that actually changes hands upon a sale. A proposed price may be suggested by either the buyer or seller. An agreed upon price will be determined through negotiation between the buyer and the seller. The final price may be either above or below the value of the venture.

The **value** of a firm is determined by one or more interested parties based upon some acceptable valuation method. The value may vary depending upon the perspectives of the individuals involved. Buyers may value the venture differently than sellers. Different buyers may value the venture differently because they may interpret data differently or have different goals for the proposed purchase. Lenders, underwriters, and venture capitalists may value it still differently from the others based upon their experience and expertise.

There is no one correct value for a venture. In a consummated buy/sell agreement, however, *there is a correct price*. That correct price is simply the price that both the buyer and the seller agree upon. Regardless of what either thought the appropriate value of the venture was, if they agreed upon a fair price, then that price was the correct price. Similarly, if a venture is being taken public, the correct price is the equilibrium price of the venture's stock after the initial trading is complete.

OCCASIONS TO VALUE A VENTURE

Since valuing a venture is such a difficult and time-consuming process, it is not something that an entrepreneur will do routinely. There will usually be a specific occasion that precipitates the valuing process. These occasions include when a venture is being bought or sold, when major debt financing is desired, when a partner is being added or leaving, and when the venture is being taken public.

Before Purchase

Amazing as it may seem, many ventures are bought or sold without a formal evaluation by the buyer. Unfortunately in the case of a purchase, the buyer often accepts the seller's price and conditions, or arbitrarily deducts, say, 20 percent and bargains from that point. In these cases, the buyer has little objective notion of what the true value of the venture is and may find out too late that the picture was not as rosy as was painted by the seller. It has been said that everything has its price. It has also been said that some things are not a bargain even if they are free.

Let us assume for a moment that the prospective buyer has carefully read the previous chapters in this text and determined that the opportunity presented by a for-sale firm is worthy of pursuing. The choice still exists to start the venture from scratch or find a similar firm to purchase. The choice is *not* simply to buy or not to buy. At one price, the proposed purchase may be the optimal choice. At another price or with some constraints, the proposed purchase may be the least optimal choice.

The buyer must spend at least as much effort and use perhaps more objectivity in valuing the venture than was spent in assessing the opportunity. Only with a carefully valued venture can the entrepreneur be assured that the venture has the best chance of successfully capturing the opportunity.

Before Sale

The preceding section suggested that buyers who do not take the time to value a venture are doing what old-time farmers called "buying a pig in a poke." The old farmer wisdom also addresses "selling the barn along with the horses" if insufficient analysis of a venture's true worth is not completed by the seller.

The seller must value the venture carefully in order to establish a bargaining range. If a price is arbitrarily set too high, then it is unlikely that serious buyers will be attracted to the business. Conversely, if the price is set too low, then a less than optimal return on the sale will be realized. By accurately valuing the venture, the seller can set a price that will be attractive to potential buyers while providing sufficient return. This is particularly true in the case of an entrepreneur who starts a business with the intent to grow it as rapidly as possible and then sell out, take the proceeds, and start another venture.

Before Obtaining Debt Capital

Low- and moderate-growth ventures will get much of their funding from banks. Rapid-growth ventures may use some bank financing as well as other forms of debt financing particularly in early stages of the venture. Lenders will rely heavily on their judgment of the proposed use of funds in determining whether to grant the loan request or not. They will also, however, look at the net worth of the venture. In doing so they may determine a value for the venture. Lenders will often use an asset-based valuation method since the venture's assets may be pledged for collateral. It will be helpful for the entrepreneur to value the venture before going to the lending agency in order to provide the lender with a proposed value for the venture and also to illustrate to the lender that the venture has, indeed, been examined carefully.

Before Partners Join or Leave

Many ventures change from sole proprietorships to partnerships, or from partnerships to larger partnerships, or to a corporation. The entrepreneur or entrepreneurial team may determine that the venture needs an infusion of equity capital or human resources. This may be because the business is not successful with the existing structure or because it is quite successful but has reached its limits of growth. When a partner is being added, some mechanism must be used to determine how much the new partner must contribute in order to be considered an even partner. If a new partner chooses to contribute a fixed amount to the partnership, then the existing partners must determine what percentage of the venture will belong to the new partner in exchange for the contribution.

If the venture is changing from a partnership to a corporation, the value of the venture must be determined in order to determine the value of the shares of stock. If the venture is already a corporation, then a value must be placed on existing stock in order to determine how many shares must be given up in exchange for a particular amount of capital.

The venture must also be valued if partners are departing instead of joining the venture. In this case, some value for the total business must be determined in order for one or more of the remaining partners to determine an equitable price to pay departing partners. This is particularly true among low-growth ventures. In many cases, two partners launch a venture. They then find that the venture will not support both partners. In other cases, the venture may be quite profitable, but one or more partners decide to pursue other interests. The decision may have nothing to do with the value of the venture, but the venture's value must still be determined.

Before the Venture Goes Public

Assume for the moment that an enterprise is launched and is doing well exploiting a market opportunity. The team members determine, however, that there is a national market opportunity that can be further exploited. Even though the venture may be quite profitable, additional profits would be possible if the firm competed nationally. The entrepreneurial team members reason that giving up significant portions of ownership in exchange for a major infusion of equity capital will allow everyone involved to reap profits from the venture, so they take the venture public. The underwriters will value the firm, make a projection of future sales, and then reach a price for their initial public offering (IPO). The price for the IPO must be carefully determined in order that the maximum returns can be gained from the offering.

Other Occasions

Numerous other occasions or reasons to value a venture exist beyond these major ones. These include settling estates, divorces, spin-offs from a parent company, tax required valuations, contributions, litigation, corporate reorganizations, going private, acquisitions or mergers, determining adequacy of insurance policies, employee stock option plans and other employee benefit programs, and dissident owner demands.[1]

FACTORS AFFECTING VALUE

Regardless of the method used to either collect the data, manipulate the model, or reach objective conclusions, the results of a valuation will be colored by several factors that may substantially alter the value determined. Similarly, the price asked, offered, and agreed upon will be determined to a large extent by the following factors (Table 15-1).

The Value Analyst's Perspective

In this discussion, any individual who makes an effort to value the venture is referred to as a *value analyst*. Value analysts may be one or more of the principals involved in the venture. They may be lenders, venture capitalists, or stockholders. They may be any other individual who has a financial interest in the venture's value, or they may be professional appraisers or

TABLE 15-1
Factors Affecting Value

1. Analyst's perspective
   - Seller's perspective
   - Buyer's perspective
   - Financier's perspective
2. Nature of assets
3. Value of inventory
4. Nature of the market
5. Goodwill
6. Other intangible assets
7. Venture-specific factors

business brokers. In any case, the value analyst may ask for and receive financial, operating, and market data in order to make an objective assessment of the venture's value. The values they determine, however, may vary widely depending upon the perspective they have regarding the venture. Three particular analysts' perspectives are considered here. These are the seller, the buyer, and the financier.

The Seller's Perspective

The seller must value the venture carefully to determine the best asking price for the business. The seller will probably not be totally objective, however, because of the financial and psychological ties to the venture. Further, the seller knows that no astute buyers will pay the asking price. There will always be at least some negotiating occurring between the seller and prospective buyers. The seller's role is to set the *upper boundary* on the **negotiating range.** Obviously, the final price will never be higher than the top of the bargaining range. Thus, the initial asking *price* will likely be higher than the *value* determined by the seller even though that value itself will likely be higher than that determined by others.

The value reached by the seller will likely be an optimistic assessment of (1) the assets of the business, (2) the return on investment likely to be realized by the buyer, and (3) the market for the venture's product or service. It must be kept in mind that this value will be reached based on essentially the same data that other analysts will use. Yet the value may still be higher. For example, the seller may value equipment at or near replacement cost. Even if depreciation is acknowledged, the seller will be familiar with the equipment, know its quirks, be aware of the real expected life remaining, and what output it is capable of producing. Thus, the seller may value fixed assets substantially higher than other analysts will. Similarly, the seller knows what the true revenues of the venture are, which may or may not be the same as that reflected on tax returns.

The seller's assessment of the market will likewise be optimistic because of the knowledge of the market. The seller will have operated within that market for possibly several years and knows the market well, knows contacts within the market, knows the distribution system, and is familiar with the product lines and other aspects of the product or service.

The Buyer's Perspective

The prospective buyer will determine the value of the proposed firm with, it is hoped, the same level of objectivity as the seller. Much of the information that is available to the seller is also available to the buyer. A serious buyer will usually be able to obtain financial information from the seller. The buyer must determine whether the information is accurate and credible. In some instances little information is available, and this leaves the buyer with the choice of completing the purchase without sufficient information or opting not to purchase the company because of the lack of information.

The buyer's task is to determine the value of the company knowing that, if an agreement is reached on price, substantial investment may be required. Hence, a conservative value will likely be determined. The price offered that results from the valuation will establish the *lower boundary* of the bargaining range. With this in mind, the price offered will likely be somewhat lower than the buyer's determined value. Yet, it cannot be so low as to dissuade the seller from further negotiations.

Factors influencing the buyer's valuation will be the intended use of the assets to be purchased and the buyer's assessment of the quality of those assets. Also included will be an assessment of the opportunity that the purchase is intended to capture. The buyer's assessment may be substantially different from the seller's assessment although it may or may not be lower. The buyer must also determine as part of the valuation process any additions to the venture that must be made to make it more competitive than it is now. The cost of any required additions when added to the capital required to purchase the venture may make the venture noncompetitive after the purchase.

The Financier's Perspective

The term *financier* is used here as a catchall term for the providers of either debt and/or equity capital. These include bankers, venture capitalists, independent investors, state economic development agencies, the Small Business Administration, and stock underwriters. Each of these may have unique valuation methods and perspectives. As a group, however, they should have more objective assessments of value than either a buyer or a seller. This is because they typically will not have a vested interest in the operation of the venture and can restrict their assessment to the monetary value of the venture and its prospects for performing in the marketplace.

The financier's valuation will be based primarily on three factors. These are the projected cash flow, the projected profits, and the asset value of the venture. The value determined by the financier will tend to be conservative—particularly if the analyst is a debt provider. Any loan provider will have a concern for what happens if the entrepreneur should default on the loan. Thus, assets will often be appraised based on salvage value rather than on replacement value. This is particularly true in the case of equipment that could not be easily sold to another party. Equity providers will tend to value the venture on a return on investment or cash flow basis more so than on the venture's asset value. The value determined may also be a function of the type of ventures in which the venture capital firm invests and the strength of the business plan.

The Nature of Assets

It is obvious that the value of the venture is affected by the amount of the venture's assets. It is not so obvious that the *type* of assets may also have a substantial impact. In addition, the *quality* of the assets must be considered.

Some assets are easily appraised. Land and buildings fall into this category. Even though it may be difficult to arrive at a perfectly accurate value of these assets, at least some indication of market value should be obtainable. It is relatively more difficult to assess unique equipment. Equipment in manufacturing facilities is often specially made for that particular venture. Even though the equipment may be old, it may have great value to anyone producing the particular product made by that venture. Conversely, the equipment may be virtually useless for any other type of venture. Valuing equipment is often done by comparing it to other similar equipment in another firm or by discussing its value with either a manufacturer or a re-seller of that type of equipment. If the equipment is unique, however, there may be no similar equipment that may be used for comparative purposes.

Measuring the true value of depreciated assets is difficult if not impossible. Although age and wear and tear certainly reduce the value of an asset, there is no formula that can be used to assess the actual value of the asset.

The Value of Inventory

Inventory poses a different but important problem. Buyers and sellers usually agree that the buyer will purchase the existing inventory. A relatively simple method of valuing inventory in a retail venture is to value it at a given percentage of the *retail* price. This is an easy way to value inventory because the price tags are on the merchandise and valuation is simply a matter of counting the inventory. For example, suppose a hardware store is for sale. A prospective buyer agrees to purchase the inventory at 50 percent of retail giving the buyer a 100 percent markup when the inventory is later sold. The two parties then hire some temporary help or a firm specializing in counting inventory, and spend a day detailing the quantity and price of each item. This gives them a quite accurate assessment of the inventory.

The problem with valuing inventory, however, is with the difference between the actual and the desired *quantity* of the inventory as well as the *quality* of the merchandise. If the seller has planned to sell the venture for some time, the inventory may be artificially low since the seller had not invested in more inventory once the decision to sell was made. The buyer may find after purchasing the venture that 30 percent to 40 percent more inventory is needed to effectively compete. Perhaps more important is the quality of the inventory. Much may be excessively old inventory or what is referred to as dead inventory. This is merchandise that the original owner bought but could not sell. It still sits on the shelf or in the back room but is not really salable merchandise. It not only will not sell, but it also takes up space that might be used for inventory that *will* sell. Similar problems exist with valuing inventory in an industrial company. There may be inventory that is obsolete as far as current customers are concerned. And it may be even more difficult to dispose of industrial goods inventory than retail merchandise.

The Nature of the Market

The discussion of opportunities in Chapter 5 focused on market-related factors in deciding whether or not to launch a venture. Similar factors must be considered in valuing an existing venture. Key issues are the size of the total market, the number of competitors, the recent growth of the industry, and any trends that may affect future earnings. Some of these factors can only be measured subjectively.

Market-related factors do not appear directly in valuation formulas. Hence, they must be used to qualitatively adjust either the variables used in the formulas or the final calculated value of the venture. For example, verifiable market trends may be used to support higher estimates of future revenues. Newly developing technology may suggest a higher value than objective data support. Conversely, historical analysis of a venture's revenue stream may indicate a value that is higher than appropriate if the market is rapidly becoming saturated. Competitive dynamics within a market may also be used to arrive at a final value. It should be kept in mind that these adjustments may not be viewed the same by different analysts. The adjustments may even be key aspects of the negotiation process as both buyer and seller question each other's assumptions.

Goodwill

Perhaps no other issue in valuation involves as much subjectivity as goodwill. Some formulas include some measure of goodwill within the formula itself or in the underlying assumptions. Others ignore it completely. Even various definitions of goodwill exist and—because the concept is vague—all are probably at least partially right. One author defines goodwill as "those elements of a business that cause customers to return to that business and that usually enable a firm to generate profit in excess of that which is required for a reasonable return on all of the other assets of the business."[2] Another author refuses to define goodwill at all and simply considers it one of the most intangible of the intangible assets.[3] Nevertheless, the amount of goodwill that a firm has will affect the value of the venture. Goodwill will certainly enter into the price negotiation process as, indeed, it should. All parties are aware of the subjectivity of the concept. All may also use it (or lack of it) to their advantage.

Other Intangible Assets

Intangible assets refer to the value a venture's managers may place on certain factors that, while not physical assets, do add significantly to the venture. They are aspects of the venture that the owners will readily include in the valuation process even though they do not fit cleanly into a particular category of assets. Examples of intangible assets include significant patents, copyrights, trademarks, covenants not to compete, lease terms, purchase contracts with raw material suppliers, computer software (although laws relating to this are still developing), and proprietary know-how.[4]

Venture-Specific Factors

Adding to the subjectivity of the venture valuation process are a number of factors that are venture specific but do not directly enter the valuation process. Some analysts might contend that these are implicitly included in the valuation process and, indeed, they are. But analysts need also to be aware that some of these factors are of substantial importance and must be considered above and beyond the numerical valuation process.

Among the venture-specific factors to be considered are the quality of employees, the location of the venture, the number of venture team members who will remain with the venture after the valuation, the efficiency of the manufacturing processes, the quality of the product produced, warranties in effect that are transferrable, facility expansion possibilities, local business codes, transferability of clients, the nature of accounts receivable and accounts payable, and the impact of local economic conditions.

It is perhaps because of the preceding factors that the valuation process has been called an art rather than a science. This may be too harsh because it suggests that the whole valuation process is of limited value. A better way to characterize valuation is that it is scientific, but the science is not an exact science. It is for that reason that multiple valuations are recommended and that they are seen as only a starting point for the negotiation process.

VALUATION METHODS

There are several approaches available for estimating the underlying value of the firm. Each is an attempt to objectively reach an unbiased value for the venture. Once an objective value has been determined, appropriate modifications can then be made to arrive at a final value. In general, the approaches that are used to value a firm should reflect open market prices for similar firms in similar industries. That is, the valuation methods should be consistent and should reach similar values for similar firms. As will be seen in the following paragraphs, the different valuation methods each have strengths and weaknesses.

Comparable Firms Approach

One method that is frequently proposed is to locate a similar firm in the area that has changed ownership and use that firm's price as a basis for determining the value of the firm under consideration. This method is called the **comparable firms method.** The analyst valuing Ridgaway Philips in the entrepreneurial profile introducing this chapter did that as one part of the valuation process. This method often cannot be used since new and/or similar ventures are sold only very infrequently and substantial adjustment may be required should one be able to locate a "comparable" sale. But this method does have the advantage of giving a market value to a firm that may otherwise be difficult to value. This is especially true in the case of new or rapidly growing ventures where other forms of estimation are difficult to do accurately. It is seldom wise to use this method exclusively, but it may be used to confirm values determined by other methods.

Asset-Based Methods

Another frequently used method of valuation is the **asset-based approach.** Under this method, the *assets* of the company are individually valued, and the sum of the asset values (sometimes net of associated liabilities) constitutes the value of the firm. Four variations of the asset-based approach are the use of the book value of assets, the market value, the replacement value, and the liquidation value. *Book value* refers to the balance sheet value of the assets net of depreciation. The book value of the firm is the net value of the assets minus any liabilities. The problem with this method is that the book value of assets is seldom a good measure of the true value of the assets. For firms with older assets, the method may be highly inaccurate and may not reflect the amount someone would pay for the assets *now*. The *market value* is better in that each individual asset is valued at some market value for which it could be sold to another similar business. It assumes that an accurate market value can be determined, usually through an appraiser. *Replacement value* of the assets is the value of the assets if they were to be purchased new. This gives an artificially high value for the company. *Liquidation value* is the value of the same assets if they were sold individually at an auction or a distress sale. This typically gives the lowest value of all valuation methods.

The asset-based methods will give different answers depending on which method is used and who is doing the valuation of the designated assets. For example, the easiest method is to consider book value of the assets. But the true value of assets may be either considerably higher or lower than stated book value. Thus, the asset-based valuation methods are better than no method at all, but the final result is subject to interpretation. An additional problem with asset-based methods is that they do not include the earnings potential of the assets. This is particularly true in service businesses that have relatively few assets.

Market Comparables Approach

The **market comparables approach** may be readily implementable for even the smallest of firms. Generally, even though a particular firm may be small or highly specialized, firms exist in the same industry whose stock is actively traded in one or more securities markets (i.e., NYSE, AMEX, OTC). These firms, their earnings, and their price characteristics may be used to establish the value of the firm being valued. The published price/earnings ratios for those firms can be multiplied times earnings of the target firm to determine a value estimate. As in the asset-based approaches, this value will be an estimate only and subject to some interpretation.

Related to this is the use of industry averages. Industry averages can be readily obtained in many libraries. The ratios and other financial figures can be used to gain an approximation by comparing industry figures with the firm's data.

Present Value Approach

The **present value approach** includes the discounted cash flow and discounted earnings methods of valuation. It develops the value of the firm based upon the market's assessment of risk and risk compensation. In this approach, projections of future cash flow or earnings that will be generated by the firm are calculated, and these are then discounted by a factor based on an assessment of the riskiness of the venture. The present value methods assume that the higher the future cash flow, the higher the value of the firm. It also assumes that a dollar earned five years from now is not worth as much as a dollar earned today.

Conceptually, the present value approach provides the most defensible value and is consistent with the reason individuals really buy firms. Additionally, it accounts for risk in a proper manner as well as the time value of money. The present value approach is also a very long-run approach. The approach is particularly suited for service businesses since they have relatively few assets.

The fisCAL financial software that is provided with this book is discussed in the Appendix to the text. Included in fisCAL are methods of valuing firms. It should be noted that fisCAL uses slightly different methods and terminology than this chapter does. This reflects the diversity in valuation methods. An interesting aspect of fisCAL's valuation methods is that it offers a weighted average of each of the methods used, thereby giving a combined estimate. The combined estimate is not necessarily the most accurate, but it does indicate the benefit of using multiple methods of valuation as was suggested in this chapter.

A VALUATION EXAMPLE

Learning how to calculate a firm's value is much easier if actual data are available to use. Venture Perspective 15-1 presents the situation facing Micro-Print, Inc. A value for Micro-Print is then calculated step by step using some of the methods discussed above.

VENTURE PERSPECTIVE 15-1

. . . .

MICRO-PRINT, INC.

Micro-Print, Inc., is a medium-sized printing firm located in the metropolitan area of Phoenix, Arizona. Its clients are broad based, and its operations include general shop work as well as being the primary printer of owner manuals for a producer of computer-related equipment. Its sales are projected to grow at a steady rate over the next several years. The current owners have accumulated the information shown in Tables 15-2 through 15-6 to use in developing a valuation. Some of the information is taken from current records of the firm while other information is externally generated.

Table 15-2 presents the comparative balance sheets of the firm for the periods ending December 31, 1987, through 1991. Table 15-3 provides comparative income statements for those same periods. Table 15-4 shows growth rates and changes for 1988 through 1991. Table 15-5 shows projected cash flows assuming a moderate and stable growth rate for the next ten years. Table 15-6 provides some key external elements for the valuation pro-

cess. Some of these elements will be used for the estimation of the financial position of the firm in the future and others will be used as bases for the various valuation methods, and still others are provided to get a "feel" for the attributes of Micro-Print, Inc.

Table 15-4 indicates that the company's sales growth rate has averaged 16 percent during the 1988 to 1991 period. The compound growth rate (geometric mean) has been 20 percent. The firm's cost of goods sold has had an average growth of 4 percent per year with a compound growth of 32 percent per year. It appears that these values may not reflect "normal" operating results because of the large changes in 1991. Another means of estimating cost of goods might prove more meaningful. Cost of goods as a percentage of sales has averaged a reasonable 34 percent over the five-year period. Operating expenses as a percentage of sales have averaged 53 percent of sales and interest and other income (expense) has an average annual growth rate of 56 percent. The

compound growth rate for interest income is −45 percent because of the decreases in three of the years. This is viewed positively since a growing firm should have smaller amounts of interest income as it uses more of its cash. Net income has grown on the average of 47 percent per year or a compound rate of 41 percent. These figures are indicative of a rather healthy, growing young firm with rather high, but volatile growth in key elements.

The firm's depreciation has averaged $372,000 per year and has increased at a compound rate of 13 percent per year, indicating a continuing increase in scale, or ability to produce. The remaining elements in Table 15-4 are provided for the purposes of identifying values for the estimation of cash flow, which will be required for the present value approach.

SOURCE: Based upon actual data from an existing firm. In order to preserve the firm's anonymity, its name and location and the dates have been changed. Appreciation is expressed to Philip Horvath for providing the information on the firm and the actual evaluation.

	1987	1988	1989	1990	1991
Assets					
Current Assets					
Cash	$ 3	$ 14	$ 34	$ 11	$ 167
Investments	440	585	8	1,033	360
Accounts receivable	917	1,496	1,478	2,766	2,422
Inventories	932	746	833	763	1,071
Prepaid expenses	64	40	78	99	135
Other current assets	118	102	287	147	260
Total current assets	$2,474	$2,983	$2,718	$3,819	$4,415
Fixed Assets					
Gross property, Plant, and Equipment	$3,201	$3,581	$4,422	$4,600	$4,383
Accumulated depreciation	1,379	1,596	2,035	2,588	2,544
Net fixed assets	$1,822	$1,985	$2,387	$2,012	$1,829
Other assets	413	461	538	592	718
Total assets	$4,709	$5,429	$5,643	$6,423	$6,962
Liabilities					
Current Liabilities					
Accounts payable	$ 211	$ 257	$ 553	$ 199	$ 270
Mortgage payable	28	31	34	37	300
Capital lease payable	30	52	46	0	0
Accrued expenses	186	168	339	496	486
Other current liabilities	192	293	80	658	668
Total current liabilities	$ 647	$ 801	$1,052	$1,390	$1,724
Long Term Liabilities					
Long term debt	$ 934	$1,045	$ 700	$ 576	$ 402
Total liabilities	$1,581	$,846	$1,752	$1,966	$2,126
Shareholder's equity	$3,129	$3,582	$3,893	$4,457	$4,836
Total Liabilities and Equity	$4,710	$5,428	$5,645	$6,423	$6,962

• • • • • • • •

TABLE 15-2
Comparative Balance
Sheets as of December 31
(in thousands)

Income	1987	1988	1989	1990	1991
Net sales	$11,302	$13,784	$16,906	$20,293	$19,773
Cost of sales	4,305	5,197	6,660	7,632	4,098
Gross profit	$ 6,998	$ 8,587	$10,246	$12,760	$15,674
Expenses					
Selling expense	$ 2,992	$ 3,615	$ 5,186	$ 5,249	$ 6,727
General & administrative	2,551	2,840	3,514	4,596	6,337
Operating expenses	$ 5,544	$ 6,455	$ 8,700	$ 9,845	$13,064
Note: Depreciation expense included in G & A	249	261	325	364	539
Operating profit	$ 1,454	$ 2,132	$ 1,546	$ 2,915	$ 2,610
Interest expense	$ 38	$ 119	$ 72	$ 74	$ 44
Other expense (income)	377	(68)	185	36	24
Earnings before tax	$ 1,039	$ 2,081	$ 1,289	$ 2,806	$ 2,541
Taxes	$ 367	$ 499	$ 255	$ 779	$ 654
Net income	$ 672	$ 1,582	$ 1,034	$ 2,027	$ 1,888

TABLE 15-3
Income Statement Summary for Years Ended December 31 (in thousands)

Variables	1988	1989	1990	1991	Average	Geometric Mean
Sales (rate)	0.22	0.23	0.20	−0.03	0.16	0.20
Cost of goods sold (rate)	0.21	0.28	0.13	−0.46	0.04	0.32
Cost of goods sold (% sales)	0.38	0.39	0.37	0.21	0.34	
Operating expense (% sales)	0.47	0.51	0.49	0.66	0.53	
Interest & other income (expense)	−0.88	4.06	−0.58	−0.37	0.56	−0.45
Net income (rate)	1.35	−0.35	0.96	−0.07	0.47	0.41
Depreciation (values)	$261	$325	$364	$539	$372	0.13
Investments (% sales)	0.01	−0.03	0.05	−0.03	−0.002	
Accounts receivable (% sales)	0.04	0.00	0.01	0.03	0.022	
Inventories (% sales)	−0.01	0.01	0.00	0.02	0.001	
Prepaid expenses (% sales)	0.00	0.00	0.00	0.00	0.001	
Other current assets (% sales)	0.00	0.01	−0.01	0.01	0.002	
Accounts payable	0.00	0.02	−0.02	0.00	0.002	

. . . .

TABLE 15-4
Growth Rates and
Changes

. . . .

TABLE 15-5
Estimated Cash Flow (in
thousands)

Variables	1992	1993	1994	1995	1996
Sales	$22,841	$26,386	$30,481	$35,211	$40,676
Cost of Goods Sold	7,706	8,902	10,283	11,879	13,722
Operating Expenses	12,156	14,043	16,222	18,739	21,648
Operating Profit	2,979	3,442	3,976	4,593	5,306
Interest & Other	38	21	11	6	3

Variables	1992	1993	1994	1995	1996
Taxes (at 39%)	1,147	1,334	1,546	1,789	2,068
Net Profit	1,794	2,087	2,418	2,798	3,234
Depreciation	607	683	769	865	974
Accounts Receivable	(2,926)	(2,344)	(1,671)	(893)	5
Inventories	(1,093)	(1,068)	(1,039)	(1,006)	(967)
Prepaid Expenses	(154)	(132)	(106)	(77)	(43)
Other Current Assets	(309)	(252)	(187)	(111)	(24)
Accounts Payable	310	356	409	471	542
Accrued Expenses	578	683	700	719	741
Other Current Liabilities	803	960	984	1,012	1,045
Net Cash Flow: Operations	($390)	$973	$2,278	$3,778	$5,507
Net Cash Flow: Investment	($650)	($732)	($824)	($928)	($1,044)
Free Cash Flow	($1,040)	$241	$1,453	$2,851	$4,463
Discount Rate	0.1172	0.1254	0.1240	0.1242	0.1237
Discount Factor	1.1172	1.2573	1.4132	1.5887	1.7852
PV Cash Flow	($931)	$192	$1,028	$1,794	$2,500

Variables	1997	1998	1999	2000	2001
Sales	$46,989	$54,281	$62,705	$72,436	$83,678
Cost of Goods Sold	15,852	18,312	21,154	24,437	28,230
Operating Expenses	25,007	28,888	33,371	38,550	44,533
Operating Profit	6,129	7,080	8,179	9,449	10,915
Interest & Other	2	1	1	0	0
Taxes (at 39%)	2,390	2,761	3,190	3,685	4,247
Net Profit	3,738	4,318	4,989	5,763	6,658
Depreciation	1,096	1,234	1,389	1,564	1,760
Accounts Receivable	1,042	2,240	3,625	5,224	7,071
Inventories	(923)	(871)	(812)	(744)	(665)
Prepaid Expenses	(3)	43	95	156	226
Other Current Assets	77	194	329	484	664
Accounts Payable	624	719	829	955	1,102
Accrued Expenses	766	795	829	868	913
Other Current Liabilities	1,082	1,125	1,175	1,233	1,300
Net Cash Flow: Operations	$7,500	$9,798	$12,448	$15,504	$19,030
Net Cash Flow: Investment	($1,175)	($1,323)	($1,489)	($1,676)	($1,887)
Discount Rate	0.1253	0.1254	0.1252	0.1247	0.1249
Discount Factor	2.0089	2.2609	2.5439	2.8611	3.2185
Free Cash Flow	$6,324	$8,475	$10,958	$13,828	$17,143
PV Cash Flow	$3,148	$3,748	$4,308	$4,833	$5,326
Sum of Present Value	$25,947 × 1.6477 = $42,752 = Value of Firm				

Variables	1987	1988	1989	1990	1991	Average	STD DEV
Market values (NYSE index)	94.92	95.85	119.33	142.12	138.23	117.89	20.30
Return on market (r[m])		−0.0007	0.2581	0.1910	−0.0274	0.11	0.12
Cash flow: operations		1619.17	1320.94	2673.25	1384.87	1749.56	544.73
Cash flow: finance		1147.17	516.95	2630.25	902.86	1299.31	800.60
Industry Averages:							
Five-year average high PE ratios	13.5						
Five-year average low PE ratios	8.7						
Year end PE (high)	27.3						
Year end PE (low)	11.7						
Average Price/book value equity	3.2						

TABLE 15-6
Other Parameters

COMPUTING THE VENTURE'S VALUE

This section will use three of the four methods discussed above to calculate a value for Micro-Print, Inc. The comparable firms approach will not be illustrated since its calculation is self evident and because it requires a detailed knowledge of a similar firm that has been recently sold. Each of the three methods illustrated will make use of the financial statements and other information given in the exhibits in Venture Perspective 15-1. In addition, the information is provided on the fisCAL data disk for use with fisCAL's valuation program. Ideally, these financial statements should be audited by an independent certified public accountant. Individuals considering new or small ventures for valuation seldom have the luxury of working from audited financial statements. Care must therefore be taken in estimating value as the statements may not conform to the strict accounting standards imposed by an independent auditor.

Asset-Based Approach

Although a number of asset-based approaches are available, only the book value approach can effectively be used here given the available information. This is because we do not know the actual market value of the assets nor their liquidation value. Table 15-2 shows assets of $6,962,000 and total liabilities of $2,126,000, giving net assets of $4,836,000, which is, of course, the amount of shareholder's equity. On the other hand, if a conservative banker chose to value Micro-Print, the value might be closer to the liquidation value. Again, it is difficult to get an accurate estimate of the true value of the assets, so an attempt may be made to obtain a value on a percentage of balance sheet figures. In this case, cash and investments would likely be valued at 100 percent, accounts receivable at 80 percent, inventories at no more than 50 percent, and prepaid expenses at 100 percent. Fixed assets valuation would depend upon the nature and condition of the assets, but it is not inconceivable that equipment might be valued at no more than 25 percent of book value. Since there is some land and plant involved for Micro-Print, we might assume for our consideration here that fixed assets are valued at 50 percent of the net fixed assets figure. This gives a total assets calculation of $4,311,000. Subtracting liabilities leaves a value of $2,185,000.

Market Comparables Approaches

These methods use "comparables" in the market that determine relationships between the firm's earnings, equity or other such value, and the market-determined price of the firms traded in active financial markets.

Generally, the industry in which the firm to be valued most closely fits is determined by Standard Industrial Classification (SIC) code. In the case of Micro-Print, the firm is classifiable as a printing firm. Care should be taken here as all firms have some unique attributes that may make classification very difficult. If classification in one industry does not really capture the essence of the firm, two or more industries may be combined by a subjective weighting system. Once the firm's industry is determined, the search continues for several firms (at least five firms in the same SIC code with similar operating characteristics) that may be used as a substitute for the industry. Sources for information may be found in investment service publications such as Moody's, Standard and Poor's, and Value Line. Micro-Print's comparables are a number of printing firms whose securities are more or less traded frequently on the OTC market. Through the examination of the secondary sources we have developed comparables for: (1) five-year average high price earnings ratio; (2) five-year average low price earnings ratio; (3) year-end high price earnings ratio; (4) year-end low price earnings ratio; and (5) year-end average price book value of equity ratio.

The concept is that the value of the firm may be estimated by the historical *average of the highest price earnings ratio* for each of the historical five years. This price earnings relationship would be the approximate market value for a firm with superior operating characteristics and expectations as characterized by the firms in the sample. Table 15-6 provides that the five-year average high price earnings ratio for the industry is 13.5. This multiplier, when applied to the average earnings after taxes of the firm being valued, would yield its high value. Micro-Print's value, using this method, is $19,450,000.

On the other hand, the lowest value of the firms traded in the market relative to earnings would provide a lower boundary on the valued firm's price. In Micro-Print's industry, the *average of the lowest price earnings ratios* for the industry is 8.7 as illustrated in Table 15-6. Again applying the multiplier to the average of the firm's earnings over the preceding five years gives the value $12,534,000 for the firm.

The value of the firm using the market "comparables" method thus far indicates that the value should lie between $19,450,000 and $12,534,000.

The historical relationships reflected in the five-year average approach, however, may not adequately reflect the market investors' *current* expectations about the future of the firms. The current, or *year-end price earnings ratio* should reflect these expectations and provide a different value for the firm. Table 15-6 indicates that the year-end high price earnings ratio in the industry is 27.3. Applying the multiplier 27.3 to Micro-Print's current earnings gives an estimate of its value at $51,539,000. The market is *currently* valuing earnings much higher than the *average* for the "high risk, high performers."

Applying the current market assessment to the comparables method also dictates that we find the current or year-end *low* price earnings ratio. In Table 15-6 the *year-end low price earnings ratio* is seen to be 11.7. Multiplying the firm's current earnings by 11.7 gives the value of the firm to be $22,088,000. Again, the value is estimated *currently* to be above the low for the *average* of the past five years. The market is currently valuing the firms in the industry between $22,088,000 and $51,539,000.

A final comparable to be used is the *average price to book value of equity ratio*. This relationship ostensibly measures the market value of the assets of the firms in the industry less outstanding obligations against those firms. Presumably, the market assesses the value of the assets, the earning power of these assets over some future time period, and the risk of the earning power and discounts it back to reveal some multiplier. Currently, in the market, firms in this industry have traded on the average of 3.2 times total book value of equity (Table 15-6). Applying the multiplier to the book value of equity yields value for the firm of $15,475,000. Evidently the market is valuing equity much more conservatively than earnings.

Net Present Value Approach

The present value approach suggests that the value of the firm is simply the present value of the stream of cash flow generated by the firm and available to the owner. The present value is determined by first estimating future profits and then, from that, estimating the future cash flows. This is shown in Table 15-5, estimated cash flow.

Estimating Future Profits

In this phase of the valuation process, "reasonable" estimates of the rate of growth of sales have been selected as a starting point. In this portion of the process the concept is to capture the nature of the elements determining cash flow that can be expected to be representative of the subsequent, say, 10 years (others may use only five years as they argue that the uncertainty in the sixth to tenth years is very high and the present values are very low and may be ignored). However, ten years is a common holding period for many entrepreneurs. In Table 15-4 sales are estimated to grow at the average of 16 percent. Cost of goods was estimated to be, on average, 34 percent of sales. Cost of goods was estimated in this manner as both the mean and geometric mean historical growth rates were not thought to represent reasonable future activity. As with cost of goods, operating expenses were estimated on a percentage of sales basis. Again, it would probably be preferable to estimate these expenses independently of sales where estimates appear to mirror future operating characteristics. Operating profit, then, is expected to be anticipated sales less anticipated cost of goods and operating expenses. Interest and other income (expense) were estimated using the compound average, which is negative. This value was selected over the average as it is felt that a well-run firm would, in the long run, not sustain a 47 percent rate of growth from a positive base. In order to be conservative, this portion of the cash flow estimate is acknowledged but allowed to deteriorate to zero. Income was estimated to be taxed totally at the marginal tax rate of 39 percent. Summing these up produced a net profit estimate.

Calculating Estimated Future Cash Flows

The net profit estimate now has to be converted into cash flow because the dollar value of expenses reported on the income statement is different than the dollars actually paid out for those purposes. Depreciation was reported on the income statement, but the firm paid no actual cash for that particular expense so that amount is added back to net income. Depreciation is estimated to continue to grow at 13 percent per year as indicated in Table 15-4.

Other adjustments are required to recognize that not all of the revenues reported as sales were transformed into cash during the year and some of the sales reported in the previous year were collected this year. Accounts receivable are estimated to be 2.2 percent of sales, and the adjustment is the negative of the dollar change in accounts receivable from each year. The change is negative as increases in accounts receivable represent values that the firm has essentially "loaned" its customers and is essentially a cash outflow. A similar argument applies to inventories and prepaid expenses. These elements represent increases in inventory and prepaid expenses that were paid in cash but not yet reflected in cost of goods on the income statement. In the same way, current liabilities represent cash that is essentially "loaned" to the firm by its suppliers. Accounts payable represents goods purchased from suppliers for which Micro-Print has been billed but for which it has not yet paid. This represents cash inflow to the firm. Accrued expenses represent wages and other expenses that the firm has borrowed from its employees and suppliers of rented space, insurance, and other expenses: the firm has yet to pay cash for them. Accounts payable, accrued expenses, and other current liabilities are estimated using the average values indicated in Table 15-4.

Summing the above for each year provides a reasonable estimate of the cash flow from operations. This cash flow is sometimes used as the basis for the valuation of the firm. While cash flow from operations is most important as it provides the cash basis for the funding of the firm's capital investment and its ability to continue financing activities (borrowing and selling more stock), cash flow for financing seems more appropriate as a value measure. Cash flow from operations requires that some investment be made in the firm to maintain the scale of the firm (production capacity). If, on the average, the firm's cash flow in investment equals the negative of its depreciation, the firm is just replacing its capital as it is used. If the firm's cash flow from investment is a larger negative value than depreciation, then the firm is growing: its productive capacity is increasing. If, on the other hand, the cash flow from investment is a smaller negative value than depreciation is positive, the firm is decreasing its scale and may be in the process of using itself up. Micro-Print has historically had a larger negative value of net cash flow from investment at 107 percent of depreciation. It seems reasonable that during the subsequent ten years the firm could maintain this pattern. This assumption is reflected in Table 15-5, under "net cash flow: investment." The difference between net cash flow from operations and net cash flow from investment represents "free cash flow" to be used to return to the providers of debt and equity capital. The free cash flow is what individuals receive in return for investing in the firm.

Applying the Discount Rate

Because of the riskiness of future cash flows, along with the normal riskiness of a particular industry, a discount rate must be calculated to use in determining the net present value of the estimated cash flows. The calculation and use of the appropriate discount rates is complex and assumes a knowledge of both statistics and finance. The discount rates for Micro-Print are shown in Table 15-6.[5]

These discount factors are then divided into each year's free cash flow and represent the present value of that year's cash flow. Summing up those values for Micro-Print gives the first approximation of the value of the firm. It is $25,947,000, which represents the present value of the stream of estimated cash flow for financing.

While $25,947,000 represents a reasonable value for Micro-Print, at the end of the tenth year some action will be taken with the firm. While some analysts assume no enduring value beyond ten years, others assume that either the current purchaser will sell Micro-Print or the operation will be continued at assumably the same scale. In that case, an infinite replication factor is applied to the present value of the initial ten-year period.[6] Applying the infinite replication factor of 1.6477 to Micro-Print yields a value of $42,752,000.

Comparing the Results

Micro-Print has estimated values, using market comparables and present value approaches, ranging from $12,534,000 to $51,539,000 (Table 15-7). This is quite a broad range reflecting the differences in the valuation methods. There is, however, one more adjustment to be made. The value of Micro-Print derived by each of these methods relies upon market values of some sort. A new or small firm, however, is not likely to have had its securities traded on organized exchanges. Frequently there is no market even envisioned for the firm's ownership securities. The claim on the firm lacks the marketability and liquidity that is reflected in the market "comparables" approaches and the present value approaches. Typically one would then expect to discount the values obtained in these methods. A common discount to the current price would be about 20 percent. Further, the securities prices used in the above methods are very likely to represent

Method	Value	Adjusted Value	TABLE 15-7
Asset-Based Approaches			Summary of Values for
Book value	$ 4,836,000	$ 4,836,000	Micro-Print, Inc.
Liquidation value	2,185,000	2,185,000	
Comparable Firm Approach	N/A	N/A	
Market Comparables Approaches			
Average 5-year high P/E*	19,450,000	16,532,000	
Average 5-year low P/E	12,534,000	10,654,000	
Current high P/E	51,539,000	43,808,000	
Current low P/E	22,088,000	18,775,000	
Average price book value	15,475,000	13,154,000	
Present Value Approach	42,752,000	36,340,000	

*P/E = price/earnings ratio.

very small portions of the ownership of the firms traded in the markets. The firm being considered for purchase is likely to be a majority or complete ownership transaction. Thus, a premium should be applied as complete ownership reduces certain costs and enhances certain kinds of benefits the owners may receive. A typical premium would likely be in the neighborhood of 5 percent. The adjusted values, representing 85 percent of the calculated values of the firm, are now estimated in Table 15-7 to lie between $10,654 and $43,808. These premiums would not apply, however, in the asset-based approach or the comparable firm approach since actual assets are being evaluated in the first case, and the discount would have already been taken into account in the latter.

Table 15-7 shows several different values for Micro-Print. The final single estimate may be any one of the values or a combination of the values. Different values may be used depending on the use of the valuation and the reason for the valuation. And as stated at the outset, the *price* negotiated will likely be different from all of the values.

Analysts may want to combine the results of the various methods in order to determine a final value. Determining an average or a weighted average can result in a value that recognizes the strengths and weaknesses of each method. As noted earlier, the fisCAL financial software provided with the book uses valuation methods that are similar to the ones presented here. They are weighted based upon the perceived accuracy of the methods.

THE EFFECT OF THE "DEAL" ON PRICE

The preceding section illustrated the calculation of value for a firm, while realizing that the agreed upon price will fall somewhere within the boundaries of the price quoted by the seller and that offered by the buyer. The price agreed upon will reflect one more factor: the nature of the "deal."

The **deal** refers to the agreements between buyer and seller regarding how the purchase will be financed, how the payment will be made, the role of the former owner in the new operations, and any noncompete agreements necessary to consummate the sale. For example, a buyer may be willing to pay a substantially higher price for the firm if the owner will make more desirable credit terms available than could be obtained on the open market. The price may also be higher or lower depending upon the nature of payment to the previous owner. The owner may desire a lower price in order to reduce capital gains taxes with an agreement to be retained as a "consultant" for a given number of years at some agreed-upon salary. Likewise, the new owner may be willing to pay more to the previous owner if a noncompete agreement can be signed preventing the previous owner from starting a new venture in the same industry. There may be other factors that may be desirable as part of the deal and these should be carefully considered in negotiating a final price for the firm.

SUMMARY

This chapter has discussed one of the more difficult aspects of entrepreneurship, that of valuing a venture. It is easy to see after reading the section on factors influencing value and, especially, the section on methods of calculating value, why many entrepreneurs do a poor job in this area.

It is important to differentiate between value and price. The most appropriate value is estimated by one of the methods discussed in this chapter. The most correct price is ultimately the price on which all interested parties agree, and this may be adjusted by factors included in the deal.

There are many occasions in which a venture may need to be valued. These include the purchase or sale of a venture, obtaining financing for the venture, bringing in or buying out partners, taking the venture public, harvesting the venture, settling estates, and others.

A number of factors exist that will affect the value of the firm. These include, among others, the nature of the assets, the industry, the intended use of the purchased venture, and the perspective of the individual doing the valuation.

There are four basic approaches to valuing a firm. The first is the comparable firm approach. It is simple to use providing that a similar firm is available and can be accurately compared with the firm under consideration. The lack of availability of adequately comparable firms causes this approach to have limited usefulness. The asset-based approaches value the actual assets of the venture. Four asset-based methods were discussed. These include book value, market value, replacement value, and liquidation value. The market comparables approach assumes the similarity of publicly traded firms in the same industry as the one being valued. Publicly available ratios from the industry or similar firms are combined with the target firm's data to determine a value. The net present value approach is the most accurate of the approaches but requires a knowledge of statistics and finance to do the valuation accurately. Whatever method is used, the final value determined must be discounted by a factor to account for uncertainties associated with a new or small firm. The actual price agreed upon will usually be affected by the "deal" between the buyer and seller.

1. Are price and value closely related? How?

2. Why is it important to value a venture before bringing in a new partner? Is this important regardless of whether the venture is a partnership or a corporation?

3. Rank the factors influencing the value of a firm for the following types of ventures. What accounts for the differences?

   A small manufacturing venture

   A rapidly growing, but money losing, software venture

   A dentist's office

   A service business such as an insurance agency

   A ten-year-old firm that has grown rapidly into a national competitive force

4. Why are asset-based methods of valuation inherently inaccurate?

5. Why do many analysts resist the present value approach even though it is the most accurate approach?

6. At what points can the estimation process go wrong?

7. Will the most appropriate valuation method differ for low-growth firms compared with high-growth firms?

8. What methods are appropriate for service firms?

9. In using the price/earnings ratio multiples, why is it important to consider both a five-year average and the most recent year-end figures?

10. What problems are there in using the market comparables method?

11. How do items such as inventories, accounts payables, and prepaid expenses enter into the cash flow calculations?

12. Why do some analysts include the infinite replication factor as part of the present value calculation and some do not?

13. Why is the final value for smaller firms discounted by 20 percent or so to arrive at a more appropriate figure? Why is there a 5 percent premium for one-person control?

EXERCISE 15-1

Suppose I have a consulting firm called University Consultants. The company has been modestly profitable but with wide swings between high profitability and moderate losses. A competitor has offered either to buy me out or to merge the two firms. She would serve as CEO and I would be the company president. We would each own 50 percent of the merged firm. In order to get an idea of what I should do, I need to value my firm. First, which methods should or could I use and which should or could not be used? Second, would either the value or the valuation method chosen differ depending on whether I sold out or merged?

EXERCISE 15-2

In the Micro-Print, Inc., case, the value was determined to be somewhere between $10 million and $44 million. Using teams of three to five people, determine a single value for the firm under the following conditions.

Team 1 You are passing the venture on to one of your children and need to calculate how much cash to give your other two children in order to be equitable to all.

Team 2 You are about to retire and want to sell the firm to three of your key managers.

Team 3 You have been offered $32.5 million for the firm by a competitor who has been slowly buying other printing firms in Phoenix.

Team 4 You are considering soliciting private investors in order to expand into additional cities.

Team 5 You are considering changing insurance policies and need a value for the company in order to know how much insurance to buy.

Team 6 Your partner, who owns 25 percent of Micro-Print, wants to sell his interest and start a printing supply company. He has agreed to a noncompete agreement.

Team 7 The IRS is about to foreclose on another of your ventures for nonpayment of taxes and may well draw this business into the deal.

ENDNOTES

1. Gordon V. Smith, *Corporate Valuation: A Business and Professional Guide* (New York: John Wiley & Sons, 1988), Chapter 3; Shannon P. Pratt, *Valuing a Business*, (Homewood, IL: Dow Jones-Irwin, 1981), Chapter 1.

2. Glenn Desmond and John Marcello, *Handbook of Small Business Valuation Formulas*, (Los Angeles: Valuation Press, Inc., 1987), 11.

3. Smith, *Corporate Valuation*, 144.

4. Ibid., Chapter 7.

5. A discussion of the calculation of the most appropriate discount rate can be found in finance or valuation textbooks.

6. Calculation of the infinite replication factor can be found in finance textbooks.

◆ Conveniesse, Inc. ◆

Valuation of the Firm

Two years after the remodeling program had ended, it appeared that both the pessimistic Dave Owens and the optimistic Cindi Short had been right. The cost to Conveniesse had come in at slightly over $2 million, considerably less than projected. The units that were remodeled saw a modest jump in sales. Mr. Akins seemed pleased with the units in Buffalo and Syracuse. Jason opened three more units in the Midwest, and so the overall revenues for Conveniesse increased significantly. However, Jason and Yolanda had been with Conveniesse for seventeen years. They had seen it grow from an idea to the reality of the first Conveniesse, to four units, to fifteen, and eventually to twenty-eight units. They had enjoyed the returns from the growth of Conveniesse. They saw that growth taper off substantially as growth in new units slowed and per-unit sales stabilized. They saw a resurge in sales and profits with a major facelift. Yet, they could see that they were at another crossroads now. They had made good money over the years and were both living comfortably. Yolanda had married several years ago and had bought a pleasantly elegant house. Jason had remained single and had bought a condominium. He had also dabbled in real estate and was beginning to spend increasing amounts of time on real estate development instead of Conveniesse.

At one of their meetings, they spent some time with the other managers discussing possible options. The options included the one extreme of taking the company public and going national with it. At the opposite extreme was selling out completely. In between was the possibility that Yolanda might buy out Jason's interest and thereby own 100 percent of the stock. There was also the possibility that one or more of the vice-presidents might want to buy in.

"Regardless of what we do, it is obvious that we are going to have to value this organization," Yolanda mused. "Cindi, pull together the relevant figures. Value the company using a number of different methods and with a variety of different assumptions. Bring us back some figures at our next session. We still won't know what we are going to do with Conveniesse, but at least we will have a feel for what we are worth."

Assignment

What advice would you give Cindi Short? In particular, what assumptions would you make regarding future sales and profits? Will the valuation method you choose be affected by the assumptions you make or vice versa?

16 Harvesting the Venture

LEARNING OBJECTIVES

After studying this chapter, you should be aware of the following:

1. The nature of harvesting a venture
2. Reasons for harvesting a venture
3. Why both healthy and ill businesses may be harvested
4. Various methods of harvesting a venture
5. Why some methods of harvesting are better than others for specific situations
6. The types of harvesting that are most appropriate for ventures with different levels of growth
7. The types of bankruptcy and their significance
8. The need to plan a harvest strategy

KEY TERMS

Harvesting

Employee stock option plan

Management buyout

Initial public offering

Liquidation

Bankruptcy

CONSIDER THIS!

- Many businesses that close are not failures.
- Harvesting a venture does not necessarily mean that the business ceases to exist.
- Sometimes harvesting a business makes the owner quite wealthy; sometimes it leaves the owner broke.
- An employee stock option plan is a way to harvest the venture while leaving it in the hands of those who helped grow it.
- A very small percentage of businesses are taken public.
- Leveraged buyouts have both significant advantages and significant disadvantages for everyone concerned.
- Many bankrupt firms continue to operate.
- Harvesting a venture by passing it on to heirs can be either a very easy task or a very complex one depending on the situation.
- A harvest plan is almost as important as a strategic plan.

This chapter brings us to the end of the entrepreneurship cycle. Earlier chapters have discussed analyzing opportunities, launching a venture, acquiring financing, developing strategies, and managing the growing venture. In the end, all ventures will *eventually* either (1) close, (2) change

BERNARD GOLDHIRSH
Inc.

In this final chapter on entrepreneurship, it is appropriate to profile an individual whose story is an intriguing example of entrepreneurship and whose current venture should also be of interest to other entrepreneurs. Bernard Goldhirsh has experienced many of the facets of entrepreneurship discussed in this text—having a dream of a venture but not sufficient capital, starting a venture on a shoestring, growing it into a successful company, and later selling it in order to finance an even more compelling opportunity. *Inc.* is the premiere entrepreneurship magazine today.

Bernard Goldhirsh received his B.S. degree from Massachusetts Institute of Technology (MIT) in 1961. He did not start out planning to publish an entrepreneurship magazine. He did not plan to start any magazine. Goldhirsh stated that his goal was "to own and operate a schoolship, and sail around the world with students and faculty to promote the cross-fertilization of ideas between the world's diverse cultures and have the students develop a global sensibility." He was

working at the time on a schoolship in the Caribbean, teaching academic subjects to students taking courses on the ship.

Since Goldhirsh had no money to buy the ship, he considered ways to generate some cash. There were no sailing schools at the time as only the children of the wealthy went sailing and they were taught in yacht club junior programs. However, fiberglass sailboats were just beginning to replace wooden boats. This brought the cost of sailing down to where the general population

could afford it. The only magazine related to sailing was *Yachting,* which catered only to the wealthy and had little educational value. Goldhirsh thought there was a need for a sailing magazine that would include "how-to" articles and "what to do if this occurs" pieces. He sailed back to Boston from the Caribbean in May 1966 with $65 in his pocket and an idea to publish an annual on sailing. Using a printer's downtime he produced his first annual at minimal cost and sold it through newsstand dealers, who took copies on consignment. He included an offer for subscriptions to booklets he entitled *Sail.* By January 1970, the booklets had become quite popular, businesses were contacting him wanting to run advertisements in *Sail,* and the booklets were turned into a magazine.

By 1972, *Sail* was generating enough money to keep it going, and Goldhirsh joined another sailing schoolship heading for the Galapagos. Soon after he returned he met the woman he was to marry, and he also realized that his dream of owning a

owners, (3) go public, or (4) be passed on to succeeding generations. Hence, it is necessary to discuss the concept of ending the venture or, as it is commonly called, harvesting the venture.

Those readers who have had experience in agricultural settings may think of harvesting as reaping the crop at the end of the growing season. In fact, the analogy between growing crops and growing businesses is close. A significant difference, however, is that when a crop is harvested, it ceases to exist. It is dead, and only the stubble remains. When a business is harvested, the venture will, in most cases, continue to exist. It may be in ship to sail around the world would not become reality in at least the forseeable future. But by this time he also realized that he enjoyed publishing. With *Sail* well underway, he tried to start a motorboat magazine. Unfortunately, this was just at the time of the oil embargos, and that venture failed.

While working on *Sail* and experiencing the difficulties of gaining financing and other problems of operating a new venture, he realized that there was not a magazine that would help those who wanted to start new businesses. Just as there was a void a few years earlier in how-to magazines for sailing, there was also a void in how-to magazines for those wanting to start businesses. He realized that he could have benefitted from just such a magazine when he was launching *Sail*.

To confirm his belief, he returned to MIT and asked a marketing class to do research on the market for the magazine as a class project. They concluded that there was indeed a market for a magazine that targeted individuals who either owned or were interested in owning their

own business. Still, Goldhirsh was not convinced that he wanted to start a new magazine that would take time away from *Sail*. He had three choices. He could sell *Sail* and start a new magazine, he could keep *Sail* and not start the new magazine, or he could do both. He pondered the decision. In June 1978, while he was navigation coach for the Naval Academy entry in the Newport to Bermuda race, he considered his alternatives and made his decision.

Goldhirsh decided to sell *Sail* if he could find a buyer who would keep it in Boston. He did not want to sell it to a company that would close it down or move it away from the people he had worked with for several years. He started gearing up for his next magazine, *Inc.*, while looking for a buyer for *Sail*. In 1980, Goldhirsh located a Des Moines, Iowa, company, the Meredith Corporation, which agreed to buy *Sail* and leave it in Boston. The purchase price was approximately $12.5 million—not bad for an entrepreneur who started with $65 in 1966.

The first issue of *Inc.* was published in April 1979. It included a feature on two young computer entrepreneurs, Steve Jobs and Stephen Wozniak, who had developed a new computer in their garage. The launch of *Inc.* in the late 1970s was timed well. It was the beginning of the move into personal computers, software development, and the general surge in entrepreneurship. The times yielded great subjects to write about—entrepreneurial ventures and the entrepreneurial process. Goldhirsh attributed *Inc.*'s rapid growth to readers and advertisers and a terrific staff.

Inc. now has circulation of 650,000 and annual revenues of $50 million. In addition to the magazine itself, Goldhirsh's company also sells books, video tapes, and financial plan software oriented toward helping entrepreneurs launch, finance, and grow their ventures successfully.

SOURCE: Interview with Bernard Goldhirsh; "The *Inc.* Roundtable: After the Sale," *Inc.*, August 1990, 38–50. Used with permission.

a different form. It may have different owners. It may have changed from a few owners to many owners. But except in the case of a liquidation, the business itself continues.

Harvesting a business is changing the ownership form of the venture in such a way that the previous owner receives tangible or intangible value for the venture. This definition requires additional explanation. "Changing ownership" means that the business was either sold, merged, liquidated, given away, or in some way transferred to new owners. Only in the case of liquidation does the business cease to exist. "Tangible or intangible value," in the vast majority of cases, is money or stock. In the case of a bankruptcy, the tangible value is a reduction of debt. In the case of a family business being passed on to other family members, the previous owner may receive a tangible value if the venture is sold to family members or if it is part of the owner's estate planning. It can, however, be intangible if the parent simply passes the business on to children without reaping any significant monetary value.

THE NEED FOR A HARVEST STRATEGY

Most businesses are not launched with the intent of soon harvesting them. Only in a small minority of cases does the entrepreneur intend to launch the venture, grow it quickly, and then sell it. Thus, one would think that there is little need to discuss the concept and methods of harvesting a venture. That is not true at all. All business owners need to be continually aware of the value of their venture and to be cognizant of strategies to harvest the venture. Entrepreneurs should constantly run the venture in such a way that it could be harvested if needed even though there are no plans to do so. Though most entrepreneurs will not be as intent on harvesting the business, they should still keep one eye open toward the possibility of a harvest.

In addition to the general caveat that ventures should always be run as if they were to be harvested soon, there is also a value in a *planned harvest*. A venture harvest strategy should be developed well in advance of an intended exit from the venture. This negates the potential disadvantages of a quick sale. Further, it puts the harvest firmly under the control of the entrepreneur rather than the buyer. It allows the entrepreneur to craft a harvest in a way that either maximizes personal wealth or leaves the venture in an excellent condition for new owners. Even if the venture is an intrapreneurial venture as discussed in Chapter 14, it will likely be harvested by the parent company in the form of a spin-off, an outright sale, or a management buyout. The intrapreneurial venture needs a harvest strategy as much as the entrepreneurial venture does.

As will be discussed near the end of this chapter, the harvest strategy should be planned carefully. The strategy may take several months to develop and several more months or years to implement.

REASONS FOR HARVESTING A VENTURE

Some may think that the only reason to harvest a venture is upon the owner's retirement, when the venture goes broke, or when some opportunity to sell it arises. However, there are a number of other reasons why a venture might be harvested (Table 16-1).

Harvesting because of Changes in Personal Situations

Although there are few statistics to support this speculation, it is hypothesized here that more businesses are sold because of changes in personal situations than any other reason. When we consider that most businesses

Changes in personal situation
- Retirement
- Relocation
- Life cycle changes
- Stress

Unmet expectations

Pursuit of other opportunities

Personal wealth

Passing on the family venture

Estate planning

Facilitate growth

are low-growth ventures it becomes easier to understand the variety of reasons under the "personal situations" heading. The gift shop illustrated in Venture Perspective 16-1 shows how this can happen. Over a ten-year period The Heights Delights was sold because one owner found a better opportunity, one had failing health, one's husband was transferred, and one wanted more freedom to travel.

Retirement

A frequent reason to harvest a venture is the retirement of the entrepreneur. As the owner nears retirement age, the desire to reduce stress and enjoy retirement may exceed the desire to operate the venture.

From the 1970s to the early 1990s, three phenomena were occurring somewhat simultaneously. First, many low-growth entrepreneurs who had started businesses back in the 1950s and 1960s were nearing retirement age. If, as was often the case, the business had not been passed on to family, there was no one to continue the business. Second, the period of the late 1970s and early 1980s and the early 1990s were recessionary periods when sales and profits were suppressed. The third phenomenon is the growth in chain stores and planned shopping centers. Chain stores were sometimes in direct competition with the smaller stores. In other situations, either the chains or the developers simply needed real estate on which to build their larger stores. Many of the entrepreneurs who were nearing retirement during this period decided that the time was ripe to retire.

Even if the entrepreneurs are not quite to retirement age, the opportunity to harvest the venture may be too good to pass up. They then find jobs working with others—sometimes the very people they sold to—until they retire. In one example, a former oil company executive decided to start his own gas station, keying on what was the new concept of self service. He expanded from one station to eleven, and his company became the premiere self-service chain in the area. As he neared retirement, he was approached by a similar chain that had previously operated in a nearby

VENTURE PERSPECTIVE 16-1

. . . .

The Heights Delights

The Heights Delights was begun in the early 1980s as a high-quality gift store in a quaint suburb known as The Heights. The entire shopping area housed gift shops, antique shops, a bath decor store, tearooms, quilting and stitchery shops, a craft supplies store, and an ecology store. The area catered to the middle- to upper-class customers who would come to the area specifically to shop for unique gifts or for decorative items for their homes.

The original owners of The Heights Delights were Trudy Young and Yvonne Mitchell. They were middle-aged women whose children were grown. It seemed to be a perfect opportunity. The two women were friends and both had an interest in upscale gifts. The store made a modest profit. After two years, Young and Mitchell were considering whether the store was profitable enough for two owners, when Young decided to leave and start an upscale toy store. So she sold her interest in The Heights Delights to Mitchell.

The sole proprietorship was perfect for Mitchell. It made enough profit to be comfortable and she had benefitted from Young's help in starting the business. After two more years, Mitchell's health began to deteriorate. Although her health

problems were unrelated to running the venture, she decided to sell it in order to reduce stress.

Mitchell found Louise Appleton, who had been wanting to start a retail business. Appleton's husband worked for a major corporation in the city and had recently been transferred from Canada. Through her many travels with her husband, Appleton had seen a number of different types of gift shops and had seen sources of gifts in many cities and countries. Thus, The Heights Delights was the store for her—a perfect choice. Unfortunately, eighteen months after buying the store, Appleton's husband was transferred back to Canada, and she reluctantly sold The Heights Delights to Marcella Anthony.

Anthony was married and had two children, and The Heights Delights served her needs well. Using part-time help, she could structure her hours to be home when needed while still giving time to the store. It was a perfect situation. Anthony kept the store for six years. During this time it was still modestly profitable. It provided additional income for the family, and she enjoyed both the challenge of running the venture and the association with customers, many of whom

were repeat customers who had grown to know the quality of The Heights Delights merchandise. After five years, however, Anthony's two children were in college at different schools in neighboring states. Although the venture had underwritten the college expenses, operating the retail store left no time for vacations and travel. In particular, Saturdays were the busiest days and this prevented Anthony from attending football games and other social events at either of the two colleges. Further, when the children were home from college on some weekends, she had to be at the store. Thus, selling the store became more and more desirable.

Through an intermediary, Anthony contacted Charlotte Alexander. She was an aggressive, well-educated woman who had re-entered the workforce after her boys started school. She had been in marketing and sales but freely admitted she did not like working for other people. Her current job was in selling insurance, benefits programs, and estate planning to business owners. She enjoyed the challenge but did not like the hours, most of which were in the evenings. The Heights Delights was a perfect choice.

city. A deal was struck whereby he would sell his entire operation to the neighboring chain and stay on with the new company as a consultant focusing on growth. The stations retained the old name, and even new stations were given that name if they were in the trade area. The original owner stayed on for awhile before completely retiring while maintaining stock in the new company.

Relocation

Louise Appleton in The Heights Delights case illustrates a second personal reason for harvesting a venture. In some cases, it is the entrepreneur who decides to relocate. Sometimes it is a spouse. As with retirement, the relocation decision usually has a significant lead time. This allows the owner to build a harvest strategy. If, as in the case of the sudden transfer of a spouse, the owner does not have time to develop a preharvest strategy, then the business must be valued based on how it is at the time. This is one reason why businesses should always be operated as if a harvest were being considered.

Change in Life Cycle Stage

Marcella Anthony in The Heights Delights illustrates the effects of life cycle changes. She bought the business when her children were in grade school and sold it when they were in college. Some ventures may be started by a single person or couple and sold when children demand time and a constant cash flow. Divorce is the cause of some venture sales. If the divorce requires a splitting of family assets, selling the venture may be either the only way to accurately split the assets or the only way to get the necessary cash to settle the divorce. Another cause may be the aging of parents. As the entrepreneur's parents require additional care and concern, the stress of the venture added to the stress of caring for parents may be too much. In this case, the venture may be sold to allow the entrepreneur the time and cash necessary to care for the aging parents.

Stress

Owning a business is desirable, rewarding, and challenging, but it is not easy. Some ventures are harvested because the entrepreneur is tired. Or because the entrepreneur's family is tired of being lonely. Or because the entrepreneur is suffering from stress. This is especially true when the venture demands long hours—hours away from the family, hours at home doing the day's reports. Ultimately, eliminating the fatigue and the stress become more important than operating one's own business. Hence, the venture is harvested, and the entrepreneur either starts a less-demanding venture or goes to work for someone else.

Closely related to the stress issue is that of physical health. In some cases, of course, health problems have nothing to do with the venture. This was the situation for Yvonne Mitchell in The Heights Delights. In others, however, the health problems are at least partially a function of the stress of the job. Regardless of the cause, the health of the entrepreneur may cause the harvest of the venture.

Harvesting Because of Unmet Expectations

The previous section dealt with harvesting the venture for personal reasons that are unrelated to the performance of the venture itself. Many ventures, however, are harvested simply because they do not perform up to the standards set by the entrepreneur. Caution must be used here, however. Not performing up to standards says nothing about the standards. One entrepreneur may sell a venture that is making significant profits. But if the returns, while significant, are not as great as desired, then the venture will be harvested. Conversely, another venture may be making only a marginal profit or possibly may be losing money. Yet the owner retains the business.

It is for this reason that little has been said in this text about business failures. Business failure is *not* a synonym for bankruptcy. Statistics in newspapers, journal articles, or textbooks frequently attempt to determine the reasons for business failure. The problem with this research is the difficulty in defining failure. Certainly bankruptcy would be an indication of failure. Yet, Chapter 11 bankruptcies are designed to allow the business to continue operating while debts are restructured. Many businesses go through a bankruptcy and become highly profitable later. Conversely, a profitable venture may be terminated because it was a failure *in the eyes of the entrepreneur.*

Two caveats are relevant for the entrepreneur harvesting because of unmet expectations. The first is that the standards or expectations themselves should be addressed. Perhaps the expectations are too high. Maybe the venture will take ten years instead of five to reach a highly profitable level. Maybe an "adequate" standard of living rather than an excellent life-style should be acceptable for the low-growth entrepreneur. Second, the entrepreneur must consider to what degree and for how long the standards have not been met. Many ventures take a while to reach desired levels of profitability or cash flow. Most are also subject to the whims of the economy. Thus, if a venture is not meeting expectations, but there are signs that the economy is rebounding after a recession, then perhaps the harvest is not appropriate.

Harvesting in Order to Pursue Other Interests

Harvesting a venture to pursue other interests may be indicative of emerging opportunities or it may indicate a simple loss of interest in the venture. A significant characteristic of entrepreneurs is that they are opportunity oriented. Although low-growth entrepreneurs typically do not *seek* new opportunities, they may occasionally be presented an opportunity that is desirable. If it is sufficiently attractive, the current venture may be harvested in order to raise the capital to purchase or start the second one. Growth-oriented entrepreneurs may encounter opportunities as they relate to the primary business. If this happens, the entrepreneur may then harvest weaker units of the existing venture in order to add stronger units. Related to this, it is not atypical for growth-oriented ventures to grow through acquisitions. If this happens, some of the acquired ventures may either not perform as well as expected or not relate to the primary venture as well as first thought. Thus, it is not unusual for an entrepreneur to buy and sell ventures periodically as the primary venture's mission is refined over time.

Rapid-growth entrepreneurs are especially focused toward studying the environment for new opportunities. These entrepreneurs, because of their very nature, are constantly analyzing both existing ventures and potential ventures to determine what can be added or eliminated. Harvesting an existing venture is a prime method of acquiring capital to start new ventures.

Entrepreneurs are an opportunity-seeking group. Some entrepreneurs can also be characterized as restless. They are action oriented. They have little interest in shuffling papers, so they often get bored with a venture after it has been launched and stabilized. They prefer the challenge of the launch and financing phases to the more mundane day-to-day operations. This restlessness and boredom with the mundane may result in the entrepreneur harvesting a business simply in order to take on a new challenge.

Harvesting for Personal Wealth

Entrepreneurship at its best occurs when an entrepreneur harvests a venture and becomes wealthy. The profitable harvest was defined in Chapter 3 as the definition of success for some entrepreneurs. Even though most entrepreneurs typically do not plan to sell their businesses before retirement, the opportunity to harvest the venture profitably signifies the ultimate in the successful end to the venture.

Once the venture is harvested, the now wealthy individual can use the profits to invest in new ventures or just to live comfortably.

Passing on the Family Venture

A reason to harvest a family venture is to pass it on to the next generation of family members. Some readers may not consider this a harvest since the venture will continue and will still be owned by members of the same family. Yet, the venture is still being harvested since it is changing ownership. Another difference in this harvest is that it may be a gradual harvest rather than a specific event. The venture may be slowly passed on to a family member.

In a family business, the actual date of transferring the venture is less critical than when the operational control is changed. And this change in operational control may occur over a long period of time. In fact, the actual relinquishing of control may be over a period of five years or longer while the preparation of successors may take even longer.

The importance of an official harvest of the family business is to formally establish both the new ownership and the new operational control. At some time, the previous entrepreneur should cut ties with the venture and have the successors take over. In actuality, many ventures are never really transferred until the death of the original owner. The entrepreneur may stay either totally in control or at least be involved in policy decisions far beyond normal retirement age. Although there is a benefit if the original entrepreneur stays with the company as long as possible, it can also have a downside impact. It will almost certainly cause conflict between the parent and child as the parent ages. The parent cannot be pushed out since he or she is the official owner of the firm. At the same time, the new generation cannot effectively implement new ideas as long as the parent is in control.

Harvesting and Estate Planning

While the previous section addressed harvesting the venture by passing it on to successive generations, ventures may be harvested in order to ease the *estate planning process* for the entrepreneur. This is useful in general, but is especially useful in the case of the family held business. Consider the situation facing Leonard Jaroszewski in Venture Perspective 16-2. The venture was harvested because Jaroszewski was moving toward retirement and wanted his estate to be clean upon his death even though that might not be for twenty more years.

Facilitate Growth

It may seem ironic that one would harvest a venture in order to grow it. Yet this happens with some frequency. A venture may have substantial growth opportunities. But the structure and financing of the venture do not permit it. If the venture is privately held, for example, the entrepreneur may not be able to obtain sufficient funding for it. Inadequate facilities or equipment may convince the entrepreneur that the only way to grow the business is to merge it with another venture that is larger and has more resources.

If growth is the primary motivating factor for the harvest, the entrepreneur will choose one of the methods discussed below that does not require exiting from the venture. In staying with the venture, the entrepreneur can then direct the growth, subject of course to the parameters set by the new structure and/or owners. This can be risky in that the entrepreneur must give up some or all of the control of the venture in order to gain the desired growth. If conflict should arise between the entrepreneur and the new owner(s), a forced exit could occur.

METHODS OF HARVESTING A VENTURE

Just as there are numerous reasons why a venture may be harvested, there are several methods of harvesting a venture (Table 16-2). Some are glamorous such as taking the venture public or using a leveraged buyout to sell the venture to managers of the company. Others, such as liquidation or bankruptcy, are heartrending. This section will discuss the most logical methods of harvesting ventures along with the advantages and disadvantages of each.

Direct Sale

The direct sale or outright sale of a venture is the most common method of harvesting. In the direct sale, the entrepreneur sells the business to an unrelated person. In exchange for the tangible and intangible assets of the firm, the entrepreneur receives cash or a combination of cash, notes, or

Jaroszewski Furniture

Leonard Jaroszewski began his career in the furniture business as part of the delivery crew of the only furniture store he would ever work in. He worked his way up through the ranks from a high school student working summers in the delivery crew to assisting on the sales floor, doing actual selling, being the top salesperson, being appointed sales manager, and moving into the ordering side of the business. He eventually bought the business from his previous boss.

Over the years Jaroszewski developed the business from a small one-store venture to a small chain of four stores within a fifty-mile radius. Of his four children, only one had shown any interest in working in the company. His second child, Andrea, had virtually grown up in the store. Like her father, she had done a variety of jobs in the store. At age thirty-seven, she had been made a vice-president in the company with specific duties in the areas of ordering and in store layout. By the time she was forty-three, she was essentially running the company, with Leonard doing more in the strategic planning area as well

as being more involved in community activities.

Leonard was by this time in his late sixties. Major heart surgery made him realize that he was not immortal and would not be able to run the company forever. Plus, Andrea was doing an excellent job and had developed significant growth in all the stores. Even more, Leonard reflected back that some of his more enjoyable times had been the travels to the furniture shows each year. He and his wife decided that it was time to formally turn the company over to Andrea so that they could do more travelling on their own.

The issue was what to do with the company as it related to Andrea and to the other three children, all of whom had careers of their own outside the furniture business. Since virtually his entire wealth was tied up with the expanding company, giving the store to Andrea would neither be fair to the other children nor give him the funds for retirement. On the other hand, Andrea did not have the capital to purchase the company outright.

With the help of an estate planning advisor, Leonard came up with the following

plan. Twenty-five percent of the value of the company was deeded to Andrea at no cost. A note to Leonard was then drawn for the remaining three fourths of the company at an interest rate that approximated the inflation rate. A payment schedule was worked out such that Andrea could make payments from the profits of the company while allowing funds for normal expansion. These payments were sufficient to allow Leonard and his wife to live comfortably and accumulate savings.

The estate plan was then written in such a way that if Leonard and his wife died before the note was completely paid off, it would be transferred to the three remaining children. If the note was fully paid at the time of both parents' death, Andrea would receive only that portion of the estate that was equal to one-fourth of the accumulation since the note was paid. Andrea received, in essence, her share of the estate immediately. The other three would not receive their share until the death of Leonard and his wife, but the estate would be increasing because of the interest Andrea paid.

perhaps stock in the buyer's existing company. The deal is written in any form desired. That is, the seller may sell physical assets only, may or may not sell the name, may include an agreement to work for the buyer for a specified time, and may or may not include a noncompete clause.

The advantage of the direct sale is that it is clean and makes a clear break in ownership and operational control. The selling entrepreneur leaves the business unless otherwise stipulated in the sell agreement. The

. . . .

TABLE 16-2
Methods of Harvesting a
Venture

Direct sale

Employee stock option plan

Management buyout

Leveraged buyout

Merger

Going public

Liquidation

Bankruptcy

Passing venture to family members

business will typically continue to operate although that is subject to the desires of the buyer. Employees of the venture may be retained if the buyer desires. In other words, unless something is stipulated in the sell agreement, the seller is completely disassociated from the venture and relinquishes all rights to it. This gives the buyer total control over the operation of the venture. The seller is free to do whatever is desired with the proceeds of the sale.

Employee Stock Option Plan

A method of harvesting that is appealing to many people and especially to the employees of a venture is the **employee stock option plan** or ESOP. Under an ESOP, the venture is gradually sold to the employees. The process may take several years, or it can be done in as little as two or three years. The original entrepreneur may or may not stay with the firm, but often does. In fact, many companies that are large enough to have a pension plan are finding that ESOPs are excellent alternatives to the pension plan.

Under an ESOP, the value of the company is transferred to the employees under a carefully written arrangement. In some cases, the entrepreneur sells the firm to a trust company, which then administers the employee stock option plan. In other situations, especially those in which the entrepreneur is in no particular hurry to exit the business, the employees buy the firm directly from the entrepreneur.

The employee stock option plan has three particular advantages for the entrepreneur. First, it provides a ready market for the venture without going through the effort and expense of finding a buyer. Second, it allows the entrepreneur to transfer the company to the loyal employees who helped bring the company to its current stature. It is seen as somewhat of a payback for the commitment the employees have shown over the years. Third, the ESOP can be a powerful motivating device. Once the workers realize that they are, in essence, working for themselves, they become even more committed to making the company succeed. Every dollar they can either make or save for the venture is that much more to be distributed among the employees.

The employee stock option plan is not an easy method of harvesting a venture even though it has valuable characteristics. The primary problem is simply the time it takes to work through the establishment of the ESOP. The company must be carefully valued in order to determine the total ESOP package. Once the valuation is finished, the plan administrator must then determine the payout ratios, the amount the workers must invest annually, and how taxes will impact both the entrepreneur and the employees. The percentage of the firm's value that is transferred to employees each year is determined by the agreement and may range from 1 percent or 2 percent a year up to 10 percent or more each year. Each employee will receive a portion of that amount. The ESOP agreement will also specify if and when employees can buy or sell more stock and whether they have voting rights. The entrepreneur can either receive full value for the venture at the time of the adoption of the plan or will receive small amounts of the proceeds each year depending on how the agreement is worded.

Management Buyout

Rather than selling the venture to all of the employees, an entrepreneur may opt to sell it to key managers in the firm through a **management buyout.** This is not an uncommon method of harvesting the venture, especially when the entrepreneur decides to retire and when there has been a good working relationship between the owner and the firm's active managers.

Various ways of financing the management buyout exist. The first is simply a cash transaction in which the managers use personal funds to buy the venture. Seldom, however, do the managers have the necessary cash to consummate the sale unaided. A more likely approach is that the managers will borrow the additional funds necessary to pay off the entrepreneur. Depending on the price of the venture, the funds may be borrowed from a bank or a combination of banks. Another option is that the entrepreneur may carry the note. This is often desirable if the entrepreneur is retiring. In this case, a certain percentage of the price is paid in cash. The remainder is then paid to the entrepreneur over time, providing a steady flow of cash throughout the retirement years. If substantial capital is needed to purchase the venture, the managers may sell portions of the stock to friendly investors. In this case, the new venture would be partially owned by the managers and partially owned by the outside investors. Still another method of financing the purchase of the venture is the leveraged buyout, which will be discussed in the next section.

There are many advantages to the management buyout as a method of harvesting. First, the venture continues in virtually the same manner that it had been operating. One of the managers will be designated the president or CEO of the venture. Depending on how the transfer is done, and the previous roles each party played, customers may not even know the venture has been sold. This gives continuity to the venture that is critical during transition. Second, the founding entrepreneur feels comfortable that the company is left in good hands. Most entrepreneurs have strong emotional ties to their ventures, especially if they have owned them for a number of years. If so, a feeling of passing the venture on to "family" may exist even though the managers are not related to the entrepreneur. This makes for easy and friendly transition of the venture from the original entrepreneur to the new owners. A third advantage for the founding entrepreneur is that the buyers are at hand. There need not be a search for qualified buyers along with the sometimes acrimonious negotiations before a final price is agreed upon. Since the managers have experience in the venture, they have a feel for the true value of the venture. The negotiation is a smoother process since both the buyer and seller have the interest of the venture itself at heart. This is not to say that there will be no negotiation. Rather, the negotiation will be in a manner in which each party has at least some concern for the welfare of the other.

Leveraged Buyout

The leveraged buyout has received substantial publicity over the last decade as larger and larger companies have been purchased via this financing method. Kraft, Beatrice, and RJR/Nabisco are three well-known companies that were purchased by investment firms specializing in leveraged buyouts. In these particular instances, typical of large firm buyouts, the companies were previously publicly held firms. And in some situations, large companies are taken private by managers of the firm via a leveraged buyout in order to escape the hostile takeover by other companies.

At the entrepreneurial level, the leveraged buyout is a method in which individuals, often the managers, can buy the venture from the original entrepreneur. The managers, short of necessary funds and unwilling or unable to take on sufficient debt personally to buy the venture, use the leveraged buyout to purchase the venture.

The leveraged buyout works in the following way. The buyers of the venture go to an investment house or lending institution for funding. The buyers put up relatively small amounts of capital themselves. The remainder of the capital is provided by the lending institution, often either a large bank or other source of debt capital amenable to leveraged buyouts. The debt is not taken out in the name of the new owners. Rather it is in the name of the venture itself. The venture changes hands and is owned by the new owners, but the venture's balance sheet is now heavily loaded with the debt liability from the purchase. In other words, the company is now heavily leveraged, hence the name leveraged buyout.

The leveraged buyout has some advantages and some very severe risks. The advantage, of course, is that it is a viable financing method for the purchase of the venture. The new owners are not personally liable for the debt of the company since the debt belongs to the company and not them. The obvious disadvantage is that the venture is now heavily leveraged. This will pose two major risks.

The first risk is that the venture will have trouble expanding significantly since it is already heavily leveraged. The possibility of additional debt funding is slim. The only way to get additional capital would be either to sell part of the stock or to sell off part of the assets. The even more significant risk is that, with the heavy debt load, the venture must do well simply to service the debt. If the venture does well over the next few years, it can eventually overcome the burden. But if the economy should happen to deteriorate as happened in the early 1990s, or if competition or other external forces should cause bad times, the firm very quickly gets in a financial straitjacket. If action cannot be taken quickly to overcome the problem, the owners may have no choice but to sell the venture or to declare bankruptcy.

Merger

The merger is often an opportunistic move rather than a planned event. It entails the merging of stock and/or assets of one company with that of another. The entrepreneur harvests the original venture by combining it with another venture. Several different scenarios may occur in the merger harvest. The venture may be merged with another on a zero cash basis. That is, the stock or assets of the entrepreneur's venture are traded for stock in the second venture. The amount of stock exchanged is a function of the relative valuations of the two companies. If desired, the merger can be on a stock plus cash basis in which the payment is in stock of the second venture plus an agreed-upon amount of cash. The merger may result in one or both ventures losing their identity. The two owners may agree that one will be absorbed into the other, that one will become a subsidiary of the other, or that both will be absorbed into the new jointly owned venture.

The significance of the merger as opposed to the outright sale is that the entrepreneur retains partial ownership in the merged company. This may be desirable when there is a synergistic relationship between the two companies. That is, the two companies are worth more together than they are separately. One or both owners will remain active in the merged venture, often with one of them serving as CEO and the other as president and with each of them having equal shares of ownership. If the entrepreneur's venture is merged into a larger company, it will most likely be absorbed into the larger company with the entrepreneur possibly becoming a vice-president in the larger company, with a minority ownership position. Again, the logic of this is that the entrepreneur becomes part of a larger venture that can become a more competitive force than the original venture could.

Going Public

A final method of harvesting a growing or profitable business is to take it public. Here the entrepreneur is truly rewarded for the investment of time, talent, and resources in the venture. The venture is valued by underwriters who then take the necessary action to sell the stock on the open market. If the **initial public offering** (IPO) is successful, the venture has a major infusion of cash, and the entrepreneur becomes wealthy simultaneously.

Going public is not without its costs. Particularly since the stock market decline in 1987 and the recession in 1990–1992, both the number and success of IPOs has diminished dramatically. The time required to do an initial public offering is enough to discourage all but the most ardent entrepreneurs. Once the decision has been made to go public, more than six months will pass before most ventures' stock is actually offered. The costs associated with going public are also surprisingly high. The cost of the offering will generally be between $300,000 and $600,000 and can be up to 30 percent of the total proceeds of the offering.[1]

The harvest via going public has advantages beyond the simple wealth of the entrepreneur. Most important, the significant addition of equity funding provides the resources for quantum leaps in growth of the venture. It can be the difference between a regional company and a national company. In addition, it gives a market value to the firm. Stockholders wanting to buy or sell stock in the firm have an automatic valuing mechanism in order to determine whether they should buy or sell shares. Further, the equity funding of the publicly held company provides a basis for additional debt funding if needed. Thus, harvesting via the public offering makes a compelling case even though it is not without costs.

Liquidation

The previous methods of harvesting a venture—the direct sale, management buyout, leveraged buyout, ESOP, merger, and public stock offering—are all methods of harvesting a growing or at least stable venture. There are two methods of harvesting a venture that may be appropriate when the venture is not doing well. These are the liquidation and bankruptcy.

Liquidation is the selling off of the venture's assets as individual assets such that the venture ceases to exist as an operating company. The assets may be sold to other similar ventures or they may be sold via brokers or an auction. The key to the liquidation harvest, however, is that a buyer purchases the assets as nonoperating assets. That is, the facilities, equipment, raw materials, inventory, customer lists, patents, and possibly even accounts receivable are purchased because of the buyer's need for them rather than for the contribution they made to the previous owner's operations.

Although the liquidation of assets is often the sign of a venture's failure, it is not always the case. If an entrepreneur decides to retire or pursue other interests and a buyer for the entire venture cannot be found, the entrepreneur may decide to simply liquidate the venture. In some rare instances, an entrepreneur may have acquired some very specialized equipment that is difficult to duplicate. If the entrepreneur is approached by someone with an offer to buy the equipment at a premium price, the decision may be made to liquidate the entire venture for the price of the individual assets. Although it could technically be true for any liquidation, in this case it is especially true that the venture is worth more dead than alive.

The liquidation can be handled in different ways. If the venture's assets are few and are easily salable, the easiest way to liquidate may be to contact possible buyers personally. This may be the case when the venture is a small retail store in leased quarters with the assets consisting only of inventory and a few fixtures. A similar situation could exist in the case of manufacturing ventures where the equipment is standard for the industry. If substantial equipment or inventory must be liquidated, then a broker or liquidation specialist may be hired to handle the actual liquidation process. Again, this may be typical in the case of retail stores where significant inventory exists. The liquidation specialists come in and handle the complete liquidation including advertising, discounting the inventory successively over a period of days or weeks, and disposing of fixtures. In other situations—a used car dealer, for example—an auction of the inventory might be the best method of liquidating the inventory. Few assets aside from the inventory would require liquidating.

The proceeds of the liquidation can be used for whatever is deemed appropriate by the entrepreneur. In the case of bankruptcy, the court may dictate how the funds will be spent. If bankruptcy is not involved, then the entrepreneur will likely pay off any debts and use remaining proceeds, if any, for future investment or personal use.

Bankruptcy

The liquidation may or may not be for bankruptcy reasons. Conversely, bankruptcy may or may not include a liquidation and, hence, may not be considered by some to be a harvest. Yet, **bankruptcy** can be a harvest of sorts. Since bankruptcy offers protection from creditors, the entrepreneur benefits from a bankruptcy by either temporary or permanent avoidance of the debt.

There are two commonly used bankruptcy methods. The first is the reorganization method commonly referred to as a Chapter 11 bankruptcy. The second is the liquidating bankruptcy known as the Chapter 7 bankruptcy. Other methods exist for specialized situations, such as farm businesses.

The reorganization bankruptcy is voluntary and is chosen whenever the entrepreneur feels that the business can be turned around if time and better management will permit. The concept of the Chapter 11 bankruptcy is that, with restructuring, the creditors may eventually get more funds out of the venture than they would otherwise. They therefore have a vested interest in seeing the company survive. In some cases, the creditors exchange their debt for equity positions with the company. In others, they write off part of the debt for the venture or will accept extended terms. If successful, the reorganized capital structure for the venture, coupled with a closely monitored strategy, may allow the venture to return to profitability.

The liquidating bankruptcy, Chapter 7, may be either voluntary by the entrepreneur or involuntarily forced on the entrepreneurs by creditors. In the liquidation bankruptcy, trustees are elected by the creditors with the approval of the bankruptcy court. The assets are then sold with the proceeds going to the creditors.

Since either form of bankruptcy is difficult, time consuming, and rarely allows creditors or the entrepreneur to emerge with full value of assets or loans, the entrepreneur may be well advised to negotiate with the creditors on possible extended terms rather than going through the painful harvest via the bankruptcy proceedings.

Passing the Venture to Family

It was noted earlier that one *reason* to harvest the venture is to pass it on to other family members. Passing the venture to other family members is also

Methods	Reasons						
	Change in personal situation	Unmet expecta-tions	Pursue other interests	Personal wealth	Pass on to heirs	Estate planning	Facilitate growth
Direct sale	X	X	X	X		X	
Employee stock option plan	X			X			
Management buyout	X		X	X	X	X	
Leveraged buyout	X		X	X		X	
Merger							X
Public offering				X			X
Liquidation	X	X	X			X	
Bankruptcy		X					
Pass to family	X		X		X	X	

FIGURE 16-1
Methods and Reasons for Harvesting

a *method* of harvesting the venture. Some would hesitate to call this a harvest since the venture will stay the same and will stay in the family. Yet, from the viewpoint of the founding entrepreneur, it is indeed a harvest since the founder will no longer own the venture. The venture can be passed on via either a sale or a transfer. The difference can have tax ramifications, but more important it can have impacts on the family if there are family members who are not actively involved in the management of the venture.

MATCHING HARVEST METHODS WITH REASONS FOR THE HARVEST

The two major sections of this chapter have discussed reasons for harvesting the venture and methods of harvesting it. It is now time to put the two together to discuss which methods are appropriate for which situations. In the paragraphs that follow it must be kept in mind that these are the most common matches. There will be exceptions.

Figure 16-1 shows the various reasons for harvesting and the different methods of harvesting. Each of the methods will be discussed in turn.

A change in one's personal situation can be accommodated in at least six primary ways. The entrepreneur can sell the venture to an unrelated person or company, set up an employee stock option plan if time permits, sell the venture to management, sell it to anyone including management via a leveraged buyout, liquidate it, or pass it on to family members. Most of these options will include exiting the venture. If the change in personal situation is retirement, the entrepreneur may wish to exit slowly. Any of these methods can be done in such a way as to give the entrepreneur that option with the exception of liquidation. In liquidating the venture, the business will be closed. Reducing stress, relocation, and changes in family structure can all be accommodated via one of the six methods.

Harvesting the venture because it no longer meets expectations has far more limited choices. Only one positive choice exists. That, of course, is to sell the venture. Depending on how well the new owner examines the business, it may not be sold for a desirable price, but it can generally be sold at some price. If it cannot be sold, then the entrepreneur has only the two negative options available. These are to close the business and liquidate the assets or to declare bankruptcy. In the bankruptcy option, the two suboptions of Chapter 7 or Chapter 11 give the entrepreneur the choice of closing the venture or restructuring the debt in order to attempt to turn the venture around. Neither of these may be desirable and the Chapter 11 may not be possible for some. In fact, in some cases the venture goes into involuntary bankruptcy. That is, the creditors force the entrepreneur to enter bankruptcy.

Harvesting because of lack of interest or the decision to pursue other projects can be handled in any of the ways that do *not* require the entrepreneur to stay on with the venture. Thus, selling the venture is an option. Management buyouts and leveraged buyouts are options. Liquidating the venture is an option. Passing the venture on to family members is an option although it would be used less often for this reason than for others. The employee stock option plan could be used although it is not likely that an entrepreneur who wants to pursue other interests would invest the time and energy to set up an ESOP for the venture. The negative option of bankruptcy would not be necessary. The options of a merger or a public offering assume that the entrepreneur would want to stay on with the venture at least in the short run.

Harvesting for personal wealth does not assume that the entrepreneur either will or will not stay with the venture. Hence, selling it either to unrelated individuals, managers, or employees in general all allow the entrepreneur to reap cash from the venture. Taking the venture public, of course, provides the most cash to the founding entrepreneur if the initial public offering works successfully. The difference among the methods for wealth generation is one of timing and the amount of wealth accumulated. The public offering gives significant cash immediately after the offering although the IPO may take months to prepare. The direct sale, ESOP, or buyouts could provide either the full current value immediately or they could stretch the proceeds into a future stream of revenue for the selling entrepreneur.

The only logical harvest method for the entrepreneur who wants to pass the venture on to heirs is to pass it on to those heirs. Management buyout is also shown here to indicate that the transfer to the next generation may well be to children who are currently involved in managing the venture. In this case they may "buy" the venture for an agreed-upon sum. This is especially true if there are family members who are not part of the venture's management and who must receive a share of the venture's worth.

Before discussing methods appropriate for estate planning purposes, it is important to note that any of the methods can have an impact on the entrepreneur's estate. Taking the company public, for example, will have a dramatic positive impact on one's estate. For the purposes of the discussion here, we consider those methods that are most appropriate if the entrepreneur simply wants to ease the administration of the estate.

The primary key to estate planning is that the estate be turned into cash or into investments that can be readily valued or sold. Thus, the direct sale, the buyouts, liquidation, or passing the venture on to family members all are methods of making estate execution easier. Turning the ownership of a venture into easily divisible cash or investments alleviates later decision making in settling one's estate. If the entrepreneur is assured that no family members have an interest in the venture, then selling the venture is an obvious answer. If one or more family members have an interest in remaining in the venture, then some valuation method may be needed in order to assure that the venture is passed on in an equitable fashion.

The final reason to harvest is to facilitate growth. As was mentioned earlier, sometimes harvesting the venture is the only way to see the venture grow. Here, any of the methods involving the sale or liquidation of the venture would *not* be desirable since the entrepreneur has an assumed interest in the growth of the venture. Selling the venture would separate the entrepreneur from the venture.

The two most obvious methods of harvesting for growth are the merger and the public offering. Each offers the opportunity to give the venture an added boost toward sustainable growth. The merger can be a viable method of assuring growth if there are significant synergies between the two ventures. The synergies may be in terms of complementary products, a better distribution system, or simply the strength of the combined firms in the marketplace.

Even if there are no apparent synergies, the merger could still be a desirable harvest strategy for the entrepreneur personally. Rather than simply selling the venture outright, the entrepreneur may wish to merge with another rapidly growing company. As such, the entrepreneur then becomes part of a growth-oriented company and rides the growth of the combined venture.

Taking a venture public is the sine qua non of entrepreneurship. Harvesting via the public offering provides the real boost for dramatic growth of the venture as well as the potential to make the entrepreneur wealthy. Most firms now studied as companies epitomizing growth could not have achieved that growth without going public.

DEVELOPING THE HARVEST PLAN

Just as many entrepreneurs do not plan a launch well, many do not plan a harvest well. Thus, the venture is not prepared when an opportunity arises. A harvest opportunity window exists just as much as an opportunity window exists for a product launch. Missing the harvest window—by being either too early or too late—may mean a lower return on investment from the harvest or, in some cases, may mean that an opportunistic harvest is missed completely.

Ten steps should be followed in developing a harvest plan (Table 16-3). The first step is to determine the type of harvest desired. The first question to ask is, Why do I want to harvest the venture? This will reduce the pool

1. Determine the type of harvest desired
2. Determine an approximate date of harvest
3. Create a reverse timetable
4. Determine the players involved in the harvest
5. Acquire the necessary expertise
6. Establish rapport with key outsiders
7. Value the company
8. Make changes in operational strategies necessary to put the venture in desired shape by the harvest date
9. Announce the harvest to key employees
10. Begin final approach

TABLE 16-3
Steps to a Harvest Plan

of harvest methods to ones that make sense given the particular reason. From the list of logical methods, the method that seems most appropriate should be selected. It should be kept in mind here that more than one method is appropriate for most reasons. Thus, multiple options may be developed either sequentially or simultaneously.

Once a harvest method is identified, the next important step is to set an approximate date for the harvest. This is critical. It is important to establish a harvest window in order to plan the necessary actions to develop the strategy. This forces the entrepreneur to focus on the harvest as a goal or target. Entrepreneurs are action-oriented people and often are not good planners. They tend not to do well at reaching closure on a task unless there is a specific beginning and end to the task. Establishing the harvest date provides that end goal. Only with a general date in mind can the entrepreneur begin to muster the necessary forces involved in the harvest.

The third step in the harvest plan is to create a reverse timetable. This timetable will be tentative at first and will likely be revised a number of times. The value of the reverse timetable is to give an idea of when specific actions should occur. For example, if the harvest strategy is to pass the venture on to family members, then the timetable must include the date of the transition—perhaps the entrepreneur's seventieth birthday—and then work backwards through the necessary actions so that the entrepreneur is comfortable with passing the venture on at that time. Actions may include promoting one or more children into successively responsible positions, providing training in all facets of the business rather than just a specialty area, working with attorneys or accountants in order to consider family members not involved with the venture, and making strategic changes in the venture to assist the different family members that will stay in the venture. These do not all begin at the same time. In this case the harvest strategy may require up to five years to complete. But the reverse timetable does give rough estimates as to when a particular part of the strategy should begin and when it should be completed.

Step four is to identify the players in the harvest. In what is probably the most simple case, the direct sale, the players are simply possible buyers. At the opposite extreme, taking the company public will require identification of investment bankers or underwriters, attorneys, accountants, and partners or other management team members to be involved in the strategy. In some cases, as in the family transition, the players will be known. In other cases, the players will be unknown at the beginning of the planning process.

Acquiring the necessary expertise can mean one of two things. First, it can be simply an educational process for the entrepreneur. Thus, the entrepreneur needs to learn valuation methods or a general knowledge of estate planning or a knowledge of the merger process. The other part of acquiring expertise is the hiring of necessary consultants or specialists to assist in the process. The easier methods may require little more than an attorney and an accountant who may already be available. If a sale is envisioned, the consultant may be a valuation expert or a business broker. This specialist will then work with the entrepreneur throughout the process to give guidance, provide possible buyers, or establish contacts with others necessary to complete the process.

Establishing rapport with key outsiders is important for the more complicated methods such as taking the company public. Hisrich and Peters suggest that rapport be established with a number of possible underwriters as much as a year in advance.[2] These underwriters or investment bankers may have been identified during earlier funding stages or they may be recommended by mutual contacts. Establishing the rapport gives the entrepreneur a view of how the underwriter operates as well as giving the underwriter a feel for the venture. Even if the venture will be harvested only with a direct sale, establishing rapport with bankers, brokers, and others in the region may ease the buyer identification process later.

The next step, although it can be done at any time before the beginning of the harvest strategy, is to value the company. Using one or more of the valuation methods discussed in Chapter 15, the entrepreneur should get at least a rough idea of the value of the firm. The valuation process will likely be repeated later, but at least the initial valuation should be done in order to have a ballpark estimate of the probable proceeds and to determine actions necessary to change the value if desired.

By this time, the entrepreneur should have a clear idea of how the venture will be harvested, approximately when it will occur, and the actions necessary to complete the harvest. The valuation process will likely give a good feel for the strategic and operational changes desired to fine tune the venture before the harvest. A change may be as mundane as a sale to reduce obsolete inventory. It may, however, be the acquisition of second- or third-tier financing as a prelude to taking the company public later. It might include the acquisition of another firm to round out a product line or, conversely, to sell off a portion of the venture's operations to make the remaining assets more productive.

Announcing the harvest plans to key employees is debatable from a number of viewpoints. Some would suggest that the entire harvest strategy should be discussed with key employees and managers from the outset. There is logic to this in that all employees will be aware of the impending harvest and can help mold the harvest strategy. If the harvest involves either a management buyout, an ESOP, a public offering, or passing the venture on to family, it is well advised to communicate the plans early. On the other hand, if the harvest is in the form of a sale, a liquidation, or a merger, communicating the strategy too early could adversely affect morale to the extent that the venture could become less salable by the time the entrepreneur is ready. Key managers could quit, employee productivity could drop dramatically, and even actions such as increased employee theft could hamper the preparation for the harvest.

The entrepreneur must weigh the communications issue carefully. Certainly a responsibility to employees exists, and the entrepreneur must consider the impact of the harvest on both management and nonmanagement employees. The reason that the announcement is suggested for this step rather than earlier is that many of the actions in the earlier steps do not commit the venture to a harvest. Nor do they commit the entrepreneur to a specific type of harvest. Many of the actions necessary can be done either by the entrepreneur alone or in a more or less routine manner in the interest of making the venture more productive. Thus, it is easily justifiable that many of the actions that move the company toward a possible harvest will help the firm even if no harvest occurs.

The final step is to begin the final approach. It occurs once the harvest is announced internally to employees and externally, especially beyond the players involved in the harvest. Certainly, some of the external players will be aware and involved long before this time either in an advisory capacity or in active behind-the-scenes negotiations. The actions involved for a family venture may consist of preparing for legal transfer of the venture to family members and promoting selected family members to higher managerial positions. The ESOP actions at this time would be to work with the plan administrator, management, and employees to work out the details of the plan. In the IPO, the actions would be the agreement with the prime underwriter regarding the amount and types of stock to be offered. In the management buyout, the actions could be the development of funding mechanisms that would allow the selected managers to purchase the firm.

With the harvest strategy underway, the entrepreneur will likely be totally enmeshed in the actions necessary to complete the process. At the same time, the day-to-day operations of the firm must be maintained in such a way that the venture's momentum is not lost during the transition period. The key to the entire process, like the key to successful entrepreneurship in general, is the development of a plan that is well thought out, carefully formulated, and well executed.

· ·

SUMMARY

Harvesting the venture is the natural ending of the entrepreneurship cycle. Like the rest of entrepreneurship, the harvest must be well planned in order to succeed. Careful thought and thorough analysis will aid in successfully preparing for and executing the harvest.

Numerous reasons exist for harvesting a venture. Perhaps the most frequent is simply changes in the entrepreneur's personal situation. These may be retirement, relocation, a change in the health of the entrepreneur, or a change in the life cycle stage of the entrepreneur. The venture may be harvested because it no longer meets the expectations of the entrepreneur. This does not mean that it is a failure, but rather that the venture did not meet goals envisioned by the entrepreneur. If, indeed, the venture was doing extremely poorly, harvesting the venture may be the only way to protect any part of the entrepreneur's original investment. The desire for personal wealth is a stereotypical goal of entrepreneurs, and harvesting a highly profitable venture is the epitome of entrepreneurship. Some harvests provide the entrepreneur with substantial capital to use either for future investments or for underwriting a comfortable life-style. Passing the venture on to family members or caring for one's estate planning are also reasons to harvest a venture even though some may not feel that passing the venture on is truly harvesting it. Finally, in some cases, harvesting the venture is the only way to allow for the venture to grow.

Just as there are many reasons to harvest a venture, there are many methods of harvesting it. A direct sale to an unrelated person is perhaps the most common and easiest to do. Once a buyer is found, the process is only to value the company and agree on a price and terms. Establishing an employee stock option plan has many advantages. It provides a ready buyer for the venture, rewards loyal employees, and can be a powerful motivating tool. It is somewhat time consuming to develop the plan, which can take a number of different forms. Selling the company to key managers is another frequent harvest method. This may be done with or without a leveraged buyout. The leveraged buyout, often in conjunction with the management buyout, provides a means to purchase the venture when cash is not available. But it leaves the venture highly leveraged and may prevent future expansion. The merger is desirable when the entrepreneur wants to stay with the firm at least temporarily but wants to reap the benefits of possible synergies with the acquiring firm. Taking the company public via an initial public offering is a complex, expensive process. If successful, however, it can make the entrepreneur quite wealthy while providing funds for significant expansion. Not all harvest methods are of a positive nature. Liquidation may be appropriate when the firm is not doing well or when the entrepreneur simply decides to close the business. Sometimes the liquidation involves the bankruptcy of the venture, although some do not. Conversely, the Chapter 11 bankruptcy does not require the closing of the venture.

It is important that the entrepreneur develop a harvest plan. The plan should include the type of harvest selected, cultivating outsiders that may be involved in the process, acquiring the expertise needed to process the harvest, valuing the company, and making strategic changes necessary to position the venture for harvest. The plans for the harvest should be communicated to employees in the venture, but the timing of the communication must be carefully considered. In order to harvest the venture at a desired date, reverse planning should be done in order that all the necessary actions come together at the appropriate time.

DISCUSSION QUESTIONS

1. Explain the importance of developing a harvest plan. What are likely pitfalls if a harvest strategy is not developed?
2. Why do most low- to moderate-growth entrepreneurs fail to plan for an eventual harvest?

3. Will either the reasons for a harvest or the methods of harvesting change with changes in the environment? How would changes in the following affect the decision?
   • the inflation rate
   • new competitors
   • a recession
   • a sudden debilitating illness of the entrepreneur
4. Which reasons for a harvest are most likely for a low-growth entrepreneur? A rapid-growth entrepreneur?
5. Can any of the harvest methods be used simultaneously?
6. In looking at the matches between harvest reasons and harvest methods in Figure 16-1, are there any *other* matches that seem reasonable to you? Why?
7. Why is the reverse timetable important for the harvest strategy?
8. Who should be key players in a harvest involving an employee stock option plan? a liquidation? a family transfer?
9. When would be an appropriate time to communicate the harvest plan to others in the firm if the harvest method is to take the company public? How would this be different if the firm were to be merged with another?
10. Is the communication plan an ethical issue? Why or why not?

EXERCISE 16-1

EXERCISES

Consider the case of Micro-Print, Inc., in Venture Perspective 15-1. What methods of harvesting that venture are appropriate? What additional information would be needed in order to make a decision regarding which method to use?

EXERCISE 16-2

If your school has a Small Business Development Center, Small Business Institute, or similar assistance organization, develop a manual for its staff to use with clients who indicate an interest in selling their businesses. Make it general enough that it could be used for passing on family businesses, but be specific in actions necessary to create a good harvest plan.

ENDNOTES

1. Robert D. Hisrich and Michael P. Peters, *Entrepreneurship: Starting, Developing, and Managing a New Enterprise* (Homewood, IL: BPI/Irwin, 1989), 311.
2. Ibid., 315.

◆ Conveniesse, Inc. ◆

Selling Out

Yolanda had asked Cindi Short to present figures regarding the value of Conveniesse, Inc. Both Jason and Yolanda were interested in the results that Cindi provided at the next meeting. In particular, they were surprised that the value was as high as it was. Neither had individually done any calculations, but Cindi's results were at least 20 percent higher than they had anticipated. They were especially surprised at the discounted cash flow result. It was almost 40 percent higher than what Jason and Yolanda had anticipated.

They quizzed Cindi.

"How accurate are your calculations? Did you make assumptions that gave it an artificially high value?"

"No," Cindi replied. "I used a 20 percent discount rate. Our business is relatively stable and is growing slowly. The 20 percent discount rate is somewhat of a middle-of-the-road rate. Naturally the value would be higher or lower if we used a 30 percent or 10 percent rate. I think I did a pretty good job of estimating cash flow to the two of you, also. For example, I considered the net income for the business for the year. Then I added back in your salaries, plus depreciation, plus interest income on the investments, plus some of the perks that are above and beyond the norm. There were some other items that I included to get to the net cash flow for the two of you. Anytime someone does a valuation, there will be a range of values, and that is what you have in front of you. Note that the adjusted book values are low because Conveniesse, Inc., really has very few assets. Since we do not own any of the real estate we occupy, our fixed assets amount to the equipment. And most of that has been depreciated out."

"Well, thanks, Cindi," Yolanda said after Cindi finished. "This will certainly give us something to think about."

Later, Jason and Yolanda continued their discussion.

"Jason," said Yolanda, "I don't know whether this makes me want to stay or get out. The higher than expected value on the one hand makes me want to stay and continue to operate the corporation. On the other, it makes me want to take the money and run."

"Well, I have been doing a lot of thinking ever since you gave Cindi the assignment in the first place. We both know that our growth has tapered off during the last few years. I know that part of the reason is that I haven't beat the bushes as hard as I did earlier. I feel a little like Sarah did several years ago. I have been spending most of my time on the road, and I am really ready to do something else. Frankly, the fun has gone out of this. Do you realize that if we include the eight units that Sarah had at one time, that we have really replicated the original Conveniesse thirty-five times? Maybe we should have franchised this after all. I guess we will never know that. Anyway, I am really ready for some other challenge. I know we aren't old yet. Hey, we aren't much older now than Sarah was when we started. So I could go either way now. If we keep Conveniesse, I think I will continue to expand my real estate businesses on the side. If we sell out, I will dedicate more time to the real estate and maybe do some other things."

"I, too, have done some thinking," Yolanda responded. I have really enjoyed the last fifteen years. I know we haven't achieved the growth in the last few years that we probably could have, but hey, we've had fun doing what we have been doing. It is so much better doing something for yourself than working sixty hours a week for someone else. And I haven't missed New York City once. I am in a position that some people would envy. I am president of a twenty-eight unit chain of stores that we developed our way. I am financially secure and am not even fifty yet. I have a husband who would really like for me to join him in his business. But he isn't pressing me. So I really can do about whatever I like. I wouldn't mind selling out to someone and then staying on as a consultant. Or if some other chain of retail stores would offer to merge and would offer the right deal, that might be a new set of challenges, too."

"Do you think Dave or Mike or Cindi or Pete would want to buy us out?" asked Jason.

"Oh, I doubt that any one of them could. We haven't had the profit-sharing plan long enough for them to accumulate that much. Now perhaps if they did it as a team, and if we financed it for them, they might. Should we ask them?"

"Guess it wouldn't hurt to feel them out. They already know that we are getting restless. Asking them might ease their minds if nothing else. Plus, let them struggle together to put together a proposal. We did our share of that over the years."

"Now, I'm not ready to give away the corporation just because they decide they want it," Yolanda mused. "I think we should spend a little time seeing if we can rustle up some interest among outsiders. I suspect that one of the major chains like Southland's 7-Eleven or Convenient Mart or one of the others might see this as an interesting diversification. Let's spend a couple of weeks looking around to see what's out there and then see what the inside group has to offer. You know, Cindi's no dummy. It's always possible that she valued Conveniesse too low just in case we might decide to include them in some future negotiation."

"Good thinking, Yolanda. But that would make it even more valuable than she calculated."

"Sure, and if some existing chain wanted to add us as a diversification move, they might be willing to pay a premium to get us. Adding an upscale convenience chain to a standard chain could certainly look good to stockholders of a publicly traded firm. Let me make a few phone calls tomorrow before I come in. I would prefer that the rest of the group doesn't know what we are doing."

Later the next day, Yolanda called Jason and suggested that he come over to her house for some "interesting" discussion. When he arrived Yolanda showed him what she had.

"I ran down the names of every convenience store chain in the country on my CD-ROM. Then I looked for ones that seemed about our size or were similar in other ways. Obviously, there are more than we knew about and there are more than we would ever care to contact. Two seemed appealing, however. One is a California-based chain of stores that reads like it is quite similar to ours. They have eighty-eight stores across the South. Many of them are in downtown malls rather than either office buildings or suburban areas. Another was a standard-type convenience store chain out of Nashville that seems to be growing rather rapidly. We might be of interest to them."

"Have you called them?" asked Jason.

"I'm waiting for them to return my call."

Assignment

What would you recommend for Yolanda and Jason? Are there alternatives that they have not considered? Is it possible that Cindi valued Conveniesse, Inc., low on purpose? What value is there in selling it to their current managers? Are they morally bound to sell to their managers, even if they have a better offer from someone else?

VI

BUSINESS PLANS

Conveniesse, Inc.

AN UPSCALE CONVENIENCE STORE

EXECUTIVE SUMMARY

Conveniesse, Inc., will be an upscale convenience store located in an office building near the Buffalo Convention Center and hotels. It will feature relatively high-priced products including over-the-counter drugs, cosmetics, hosiery, high-quality soft drinks, beer, wine, and imported liquors. It will include a high-quality deli and offer freshly baked pastries during the morning hours. Limited grocery goods will be available to those who wish to purchase items on the way home at the end of the day. Attractive features of Conveniesse include an ATM machine, a copier, a fax machine, and a floral referral service.

There are two target markets for Conveniesse. The first is workers in and around the office building in which Conveniesse is located. The second target market consists of hotel guests in the area. The two target markets are generally distinct and nonoverlapping.

Conveniesse, Inc., is a New York corporation owned by Sarah Tondeur (40 percent), Yolanda Williams (40 percent), and Jason Stone (20 percent). The three owners will invest $60,000, $60,000, and $30,000 respectively for a total of $150,000. This business plan seeks the infusion of $310,000 of debt and/or equity capital to underwrite startup costs of Conveniesse.

NATURE OF THE VENTURE

Background

There is currently not a convenient place in the convention center area of Buffalo for office workers to buy deli sandwiches, over-the-counter drugs, and other necessities during the day. Similarly, hotel guests in the con-

458

vention center area do not have a place to buy necessities or to purchase high-quality alcoholic beverages. Some hotel gift shops carry a limited assortment of items, but these are primarily gifts and magazines rather than food and drink items. There is a need for an upscale convenience store that is easily accessible by office workers and by hotel guests.

Nature of the Product/Service

Conveniesse will provide a wide variety of products and services in an upscale environment. Products will include bakery goods during the morning hours, deli salads and sandwiches for lunch or for carryout in the evening, a variety of grocery goods, cosmetics, hosiery, and over-the-counter drug items, and a variety of soft drinks, beer, wine, and imported liquors. Soft drinks will include the more exotic juice-based drinks, mineral waters, and seltzers. Services will include an ATM cash machine, fax machine, floral referral service, and the provision of local area information and directions. All workers in the store will wear distinctive uniforms that will include the Conveniesse logo. The floral service will consist of a catalog of bouquets and other flowers that may be delivered. Conveniesse has an agreement with a local florist who gives Conveniesse a 20 percent commission for all orders called in. A small inventory of popular flowers is maintained on site for immediate purchase. Hours for Conveniesse are 7 A.M. to midnight.

Location of the Venture

Conveniesse will be located in an office complex approximately two blocks from the Buffalo Convention Center. There are two hotels within two blocks of the building. The ground floor of the office building is open twenty-four hours a day.

DESCRIPTION OF THE MARKET

Market Trends

There are two distinct target markets for Conveniesse. The first is office workers in and around the building in which Conveniesse is located. The building itself is twelve stories high and houses nearly eight hundred workers. These are almost evenly divided between male and female. Two office buildings within one block are somewhat smaller, but they do not have a convenience store. Thus, at least some of those workers would come to Conveniesse during their lunch hour or on the way to or from work. Customers from this target market will typically come to Conveniesse early in the morning, during the lunch hour, or at the end of the workday.

The second target market is hotel guests at the two hotels within two blocks of the store. This target market would come to Conveniesse for those items not available in the hotel gift shops. This market will primarily patronize Conveniesse in the late afternoon and evening. The two hotels together house up to twelve hundred guests per night.

A third, and obviously secondary, market is those individuals attending convention center activities. Those customers may stop by either before or after events to pick up needed merchandise or use the ATM machine.

The first target market, office workers, is stable. Conveniesse will reap significant sales from this market, and it will grow until all those in the building and surrounding area are familiar with the store. Once Conveniesse has fully tapped that market, the customers should be stable, but loyal. The hotel market will obviously be a function of the hotel business. As convention center activities increase, this will have some impact on hotel guest listings. The growth in this market is expected to be low to moderate. Overall, the growth is expected to rise significantly during the first few months and then grow at approximately 5 percent per year.

Demographic and Economic Trends

Changes in demographic trends are not likely to be significant within any foreseeable time period. Since the two markets are either business or hotel related, demographic changes within the area will have little direct impact. Economic trends on the other hand can have an impact to the extent that companies choose to send employees to Buffalo for meetings or individuals choose to come to Buffalo hotels in order to see convention center events. The office worker market would be affected by the economy only to the extent that vacancies occur in the office suites.

Current Competitors

There are currently no direct competitors. A liquor store exists three blocks from the Conveniesse location. However, it tends to serve a much different target market than Conveniesse does. Hotel gift shops provide some of the same products, but they tend to have a much more limited selection. Further, they carry none of the food products that Conveniesse carries and they provide few services.

UNIQUENESS OF PRODUCT AND SERVICES

The unique aspect of Conveniesse is the selection of products and services that it will offer. Fresh-baked goods will be offered in the mornings, deli salads and sandwiches will be sold around lunch, and either deli or other food products may be purchased by office workers on their way home at the end of the day. The real uniqueness of Conveniesse lies in the services to be provided. The ATM machine will draw significant numbers of customers into Conveniesse. A fax machine will be useful for some office workers, and will appeal to hotel guests away from their home offices. A floral referral service will be offered. It should be appealing to both the office workers and the hotel guests who want to send flowers either within Buffalo or elsewhere in the nation. A small inventory of fresh flowers will be maintained for immediate purchase. The advantage of the referral service is that customers can choose flower arrangements from a catalog rather than either calling a florist to send flowers sight unseen or going to a florist.

The employees will enhance the upscale image of Conveniesse as they will be highly knowledgeable about Conveniesse products and services as well as about locations and happenings in Buffalo. For example, the combination greeter/security guard will also be the source for information regarding the area. All employees will be impeccably dressed in uniforms with the Conveniesse logo prominently displayed.

MANAGEMENT TEAM AND OWNERSHIP

Conveniesse, Inc., is owned jointly by three individuals. Sarah Tondeur will serve as president and will also be responsible for the accounting tasks for the corporation. She owned her own accounting and tax service in Montreal for ten years. She merged it with another firm and later sold out to her partner. She owns 40 percent of the stock of Conveniesse.

Yolanda Williams is a vice-president and is currently responsible for marketing activities for Conveniesse. She is a product manager for a major pharmaceuticals firm in New York. Williams has a B.S. in marketing from State University of New York at Buffalo with a minor in French. She has been with her current employer for eight years. She will continue in her present job for now and will commute to Buffalo on weekends for Conveniesse planning meetings. She will also work in the store on weekends as time permits.

Jason Stone is a vice-president and is responsible for public relations and customer relations and interaction with members of the financial community. He has a B.S. in English with a minor in business from the University of Texas at Arlington. He is currently employed by a public relations firm in Detroit, but will leave that job once funding for Conveniesse is approved.

OBJECTIVES AND GOALS
Short-Term Goals

The major short-term goal of Conveniesse is to gain funding for the upscale convenience store, launch the venture, stabilize the operations, and manage its growth. Financially, Conveniesse has the goal of breaking even within the first three months and increasing profitability each month until sales growth stabilizes during the second year. Profits will be sufficient to pay off debt within ten years while returning 20 percent to owners' investments.

Long-Term Goals

The long-term goal of Conveniesse is to make the Conveniesse store increasingly profitable and to consider adding additional stores in the future.

STRATEGIES

The overall strategy of Conveniesse is to maintain and enhance the upscale image of the store through decor, products, services, pricing, and highly trained employees.

Marketing Strategy

Conveniesse will use constant but limited advertising. The office target market will initially be attracted through flyers and other information provided to offices in the building and surrounding area. The specific products and services, such as the ATM machine, will be highlighted and are expected to draw office workers to the store. Advertising to the hotel and convention market will consist of advertisements in hotel brochures, convention and tourism booklets, the Buffalo airport, and at the Buffalo Convention Center. These methods should reach the majority of visitors to the downtown part of Buffalo.

Other marketing activities will include the distinctive logo of Conveniesse, which will appear outside and inside the store and on all cups, bags, and other carry-out products. Conveniesse will also be a participant in downtown activities such as parades, trade shows, and other visual events.

Pricing at Conveniesse will be high but bearable. Prices will be significantly higher than grocery or drug stores and somewhat higher than suburban convenience stores. This is justified by the relatively captive market

CONVENIESSE, INC.
Estimated Startup Costs
and Six Months Operating Costs

Desired Minimum Cash Balance		$ 30,000
Initial Inventory plus Net Additions		150,000
Rent (6-month lease)		50,000
Prepaid Insurance		1,500
Salaries and Wages (First six months)		
Salaries (Stone, Tondeur)	$37,500	
Salaries (Asst. Managers)	24,000	
Wages	17,500	
Total Salaries and Wages		$ 79,000
Miscellaneous Prepaid Expenses		
Supplies	$ 1,000	
Advertising	2,500	
Legal Fees	1,500	
Licenses	2,000	
Total Miscellaneous Expenses		$ 7,000
Building and Equipment		
Leasehold Improvements	$30,000	
Equipment	97,500	
Fixtures	15,000	
Total Building and Equipment		$142,500
Total Startup Costs		$460,000
Owner Equity		150,000
Additional funding requested		$310,000

and because many of the products are not price sensitive. Customers will expect to pay higher prices due to the convenience and the upscale ambience of the store. This pricing strategy will allow Conveniesse to have an excellent return.

Conveniesse will offer a wide breadth of products rather than a depth of selection. It will carry only one brand of any given product, which typically will be a well-known brand. The exception to this is in the imported and specialty alcoholic beverages and soft drinks where a wide choice of brands and flavors will be available.

Human Resource Strategy

A key to the success of Conveniesse is the highly trained and knowledgeable employees. As a result, it is imperative that employees be motivated, conversant, and possess a wealth of information regarding both Conveniesse and Buffalo. Therefore, Conveniesse will hire only experienced employees who already have knowledge of the convenience store business. Floor managers will be hired from among managers or assistant managers of local convenience stores. Employees must be local and have positive and outgoing personalities. Conveniesse will pay higher than the prevailing rates in order to attract and retain excellent employees.

CONVENIESSE, INC.
Opening Day Balance Sheet
(projected)

Assets			
Current Assets			
Cash	$134,000		
Inventory	125,000		
Prepaid Rent	50,000		
Prepaid Insurance	1,500		
Prepaid Expenses	7,000		
Total Current Assets		$317,500	
Long-term Assets			
Furnishings and Equipment		112,500	
Leasehold Improvements		30,000	
Total Long-term Assets		$142,500	
Total Assets			$460,000
Liabilities and Owners' Equity			
Liabilities			
Notes Payable—Bank	$310,000		
Stockholders' Equity			
Common Stock	$150,000		
Total Liabilities and Owners' Equity			$460,000

CONVENIESSE, INC.
Proforma Income Statement
End of Year 1

	Jan	Feb	Mar	Apr	May	Jun
Sales	$ 50,000	$75,000	$95,000	$110,000	$125,000	$125,000
Cost of Goods	32,500	48,750	61,750	71,500	81,250	81,250
Gross Profit	$ 17,500	$26,250	$33,250	$ 38,500	$ 43,750	$ 43,750
Operating Expenses						
Salaries (owners)	$ 6,250	$ 6,250	$ 6,250	$ 6,250	$ 6,250	$ 6,250
Salaries (managers)	4,000	4,000	4,000	4,000	4,000	4,000
Wages	2,916	2,916	2,916	2,916	2,916	2,916
Rent	8,333	8,333	8,333	8,333	8,333	8,333
Telephone and Utilities	200	200	200	200	200	200
Insurance	300	300	300	300	300	300
Advertising	750	750	750	750	750	750
Maintenance	200	200	200	200	200	200
Legal Fees	200	200	200	200	200	200
Licenses	150	150	150	150	150	150
Depreciation	2,375	2,375	2,375	2,375	2,375	2,375
Net Operating Profit (Loss)	$ (8,174)	$ 576	$ 7,576	$ 12,826	$ 18,076	$ 18,076
Interest Expense	2,583	2,566	2,547	2,530	2,512	2,493
Net Profit (Loss)	$(10,757)	$ (1,990)	$ 5,029	$ 10,296	$ 15,564	$ 15,583
Taxes						
Net Profit After Taxes						

Financial Strategy

Conveniesse is currently totally owned by three individuals, Yolanda Williams (40 percent), Sarah Tondeur (40 percent), and Jason Stone (20 percent). They would prefer to maintain complete ownership control of Conveniesse. If possible, they prefer that initial outside funding be totally debt financing. If equity funding is required, it will be limited in such a way that the three primary owners retain financial and managerial control of Conveniesse. Future funding should be available primarily through the retained earnings of the corporation.

	Jul	Aug	Sep	Oct	Nov	Dec	Totals
	$115,000	$115,000	$125,000	$125,000	$120,000	$95,000	$1,275,000
	74,750	74,750	81,250	81,250	78,000	61,750	828,750
	$ 40,250	$ 40,250	$ 43,750	$ 43,750	$ 42,000	$33,250	$ 446,250
	$ 6,250	$ 6,250	$ 6,250	$ 6,250	$ 6,250	$ 6,250	$ 75,000
	4,000	4,000	4,000	4,000	4,000	4,000	48,000
	2,916	2,916	2,916	2,916	2,916	2,924	35,000
	8,333	8,333	8,333	8,333	8,333	8,337	100,000
	200	200	200	200	200	200	2,400
	300	300	300	300	300	300	3,600
	750	750	750	750	750	750	9,000
	200	200	200	200	200	200	2,400
	200	200	200	200	200	200	2,400
	150	150	150	150	150	150	1,800
	2,375	2,375	2,375	2,375	2,375	2,375	28,500
	$ 14,576	$ 14,576	$ 18,076	$ 18,076	$ 16,326	$ 7,564	$ 138,150
	2,475	2,456	2,438	2,419	2,400	2,381	29,800
	$ 12,101	$ 12,120	$ 15,638	$ 15,657	$ 13,926	$ 5,183	$ 108,350
							30,338
							$ 78,012

Assumptions

Assume that sales will increase during first several months and then stabilize. Sales will be lower in December, January, August, and September.
Cost of goods sold is 65 percent of sales. Salaries and wages will increase
by 5 percent in second year, and all operating expenses will increase by 5
percent in succeeding years. Equipment is depreciated over five years with
a straight line depreciation. The loan request assumes a 10 percent interest
rate for $310,000 to be paid off in eight years. Salaries are for two owners
(Stone and Tondeur) and for two assistant managers.

CONVENIESSE, INC.
Proforma Income Statement
End of Year 2

	Jan	Feb	Mar	Apr	May	Jun
Sales	$95,000	$105,00	$110,000	$120,000	$132,000	$132,000
Cost of Goods	61,750	68,250	71,500	78,000	85,800	85,800
Gross Profit	$33,250	$36,750	$ 38,500	$ 42,000	$ 46,200	$ 46,200
Operating Expenses						
Salaries (owners)	$ 6,560	$ 6,560	$ 6,560	$ 6,560	$ 6,560	$ 6,560
Salaries (managers)	4,200	4,200	4,200	4,200	4,200	4,200
Wages	3,062	2,062	3,062	3,062	3,062	3,062
Rent	8,333	8,333	8,333	8,333	8,333	8,333
Telephone and Utilities	200	200	200	200	200	200
Insurance	300	300	300	300	300	300
Advertising	780	780	780	780	780	780
Maintenance	200	200	200	200	200	200
Legal Fees	200	200	200	200	200	200
Licenses	150	150	150	150	150	150
Depreciation	2,375	2,375	2,375	2,375	2,375	2,375
Net Operating Profit (Loss)	$ 6,890	$10,390	$ 12,140	$ 15,640	$ 19,840	$ 19,840
Interest Expense	2,361	2,342	2,322	2,302	2,282	2,262
Net Profit (Loss)	$ 4,529	$ 8,048	$ 9,818	$ 13,338	$ 17,558	$ 17,578
Taxes						
Net Profit After Taxes						

Jul	Aug	Sep	Oct	Nov	Dec	Totals
$122,000	$122,000	$132,000	$132,000	$128,000	$102,000	$1,432,000
79,300	79,300	85,800	85,800	83,200	66,300	930,800
$ 42,700	$ 42,700	$ 46,200	$ 46,200	$ 44,800	$ 35,700	$ 501,200
$ 6,560	$ 6,560	$ 6,560	$ 6,560	$ 6,560	$ 6,560	$ 78,720
4,200	4,200	4,200	4,200	4,200	4,200	50,400
3,062	3,062	3,062	3,062	3,062	3,062	36,744
8,333	8,333	8,333	8,333	8,333	8,337	100,000
200	200	200	200	200	200	2,400
300	300	300	300	300	300	3,600
780	780	780	780	780	780	9,360
200	200	200	200	200	200	2,400
200	200	200	200	200	200	2,400
150	150	150	150	150	150	1,800
2,375	2,375	2,375	2,375	2,375	2,375	28,500
$ 16,340	$ 16,340	$ 19,840	$ 19,840	$ 18,440	$ 9,336	$ 184,876
2,242	2,221	2,200	2,180	2,160	2,137	27,010
$ 14,098	$ 14,119	$ 17,640	$ 17,660	$ 16,280	$ 7,199	$ 157,866
						44,202
						$ 113,664

CONVENIESSE, INC.
Proforma Income Statement
End of Year 3

	Qtr 1	Qtr 2	Qtr 3	Qtr 4	Totals
Sales	$325,500	$403,200	$394,800	$380,100	$1,503,600
Cost of Goods	211,575	262,080	256,620	247,065	977,340
Gross Profit	$113,925	$141,120	$138,180	$133,035	$ 526,260
Operating Expenses	83,034	83,034	83,034	83,034	332,136
Net Operating Profit	$ 30,891	$ 58,086	$ 55,146	$ 50,001	$ 194,124
Interest Expense	6,283	6,086	5,883	5,676	23,928
Net Profit	$ 27,296	$ 55,536	$ 53,641	$ 47,541	$ 170,196
Taxes					47,655
Net Profit After Taxes					$ 122,541

CONVENIESSE, INC.
Proforma Income Statement
End of Year 4

	Qtr 1	Qtr 2	Qtr 3	Qtr 4	Totals
Sales	$341,775	$423,360	$414,540	$399,105	$1,578,780
Cost of Goods	222,154	275,184	269,451	259,418	1,026,207
Gross Profit	$119,621	$148,176	$145,089	$139,687	$ 552,573
Operating Expenses	87,186	87,186	87,186	87,186	348,744
Net Operating Profit	$ 32,435	$ 60,990	$ 57,903	$ 52,501	$ 203,829
Interest Expense	5,463	5,245	5,022	4,793	20,522
Net Profit	$ 26,972	$ 55,745	$ 52,881	$ 47,708	$ 183,307
Taxes					51,326
Net Profit After Taxes					$ 131,981

CONVENIESSE, INC.
Proforma Income Statement
End of Year 5

	Qtr 1	Qtr 2	Qtr 3	Qtr 4	Totals
Sales	$358,863	$444,528	$435,267	$419,061	$1,657,719
Cost of Goods	233,261	288,943	282,924	272,389	1,077,517
Gross Profit	$125,602	$155,585	$152,343	$146,672	$ 580,202
Operating Expenses	91,545	91,545	91,545	91,545	366,180
Net Operating Profit	$ 34,057	$ 64,040	$ 60,798	$ 55,127	$ 214,022
Interest Expense	4,558	4,317	4,070	3,817	16,760
Net Profit	$ 29,499	$ 59,723	$ 56,728	$ 51,310	$ 197,262
Taxes					55,233
Net Profit After Taxes					$ 142,029

CONVENIESSE, INC.
Balance Sheet
End of Year 1
(projected)

Assets
Current Assets
Cash and Investments	$256,281	
Inventory	131,250	
Prepaid Rent	8,333	
Prepaid Insurance	1,500	
Total Current Assets		$397,364

Long-term Assets
Building and Equipment		$114,000
Total Assets		$511,364

Liabilities and Owners' Equity
Liabilities
Notes Payable—Bank	$283,352	

Stockholders' Equity
Common Stock	$150,000	
Retained Earnings	78,012	
Total Liabilities and Owners' Equity		$511,364

CONVENIESSE, INC.
Balance Sheet
End of Year 2
(projected)

Assets
Current Assets
Cash and Investments	$392,748	
Inventory	137,812	
Prepaid Rent	8,750	
Prepaid Insurance	1,575	
Total Current Assets		$540,885

Long-term Assets
Building and Equipment		$ 85,500
Total Assets		$626,385

Liabilities and Owners' Equity
Liabilities
Notes Payable—Bank	$253,914	

Stockholders' Equity
Common Stock	$150,000	
Retained Earnings	222,471	
Total Liabilities and Owners' Equity		$626,385

CONVENIESSE, INC.
Balance Sheet
End of Year 3
(projected)

Assets
Current Assets
    Cash and Investments $503,861
    Inventory   144,703
    Prepaid Rent   9,188
    Prepaid Insurance   1,653

    Total Current Assets $659,405
Long-term Assets
    Building and Equipment $ 57,000

Total Assets $716,405

Liabilities and Owners' Equity
Liabilities
    Notes Payable—Bank $221,393
Stockholders' Equity
    Common Stock $150,000
    Retained Earnings   345,012

Total Liabilities and Owners' Equity $716,405

CONVENIESSE, INC.
Balance Sheet
End of Year 4
(projected)

Assets
Current Assets
    Cash and Investments $620,639
    Inventory   151,938
    Prepaid Rent   9,647
    Prepaid Insurance   1,736

    Total Current Assets $783,960
Long-term Assets
    Building and Equipment $ 28,500

Total Assets $812,460

Liabilities and Owners' Equity
Liabilities
    Notes Payable—Bank $185,467
Stockholders' Equity
    Common Stock $150,000
    Retained Earnings   476,993

Total Liabiliites and Owners' Equity $812,460

CONVENIESSE, INC.
Balance Sheet
End of Year 5
(projected)

Assets
Current Assets
    Cash and Investments $743,296
    Inventory   159,535
    Prepaid Rent   10,129
    Prepaid Insurance   1,823

    Total Current Assets $914,783
Long-term Assets
    Building and Equipment   0

Total Assets $914,783

Liabilities and Owners' Equity
Liabilities
    Notes Payable—Bank $145,761
Stockholders' Equity
    Common Stock $150,000
    Retained Earnings   619,022

Total Liabiliites and Owners' Equity $914,783

Kryos, Inc.

The World Leader
in Applying Vitrification Technology
to Organs for Transplant

Bringing preserved organs to recipients in need

February, 1989

Copy No. _____

TABLE OF CONTENTS

*These sections of the Kryos, Inc., business plan, as well as notes to financial statements, have been omitted. The full text is available from the author.

 X. Financial Data 496

XI. Financing Plan 498

    Exhibit 1: Schedule and key milestones 501

    Exhibit 2: Market survey notes . . . . .omitted

    Appendix . . . . .omitted

       Résumés: Greg Fahy, Ph.D.
                Clyde R. Goodheart, M.D., M.B.A.

I. EXECUTIVE SUMMARY

Kryos, Inc., was incorporated in Illinois on November 23, 1988, to apply a unique new technology in cryobiology, called vitrification, to organs for transplant. Vitrification permits organs to be preserved in a viable condition for an indefinite period, so that banks of organs will be available when needed for scheduled surgery. Transplant procedures for major organs (kidneys, livers, hearts, pancreases) will be elective rather than emergency, as now. The storage period will also permit better testing methods for matching, which will improve the chance of success and reduce the need for expensive, and toxic, anti-rejection drugs. It will also be possible to remove one or both kidneys from a patient needing treatment with a chemotherapeutic agent that is strongly toxic for the kidneys, and to replace the kidneys after the course of chemotherapy.

Although estimates place the number of suitable organ donors at about twenty thousand yearly, organs are actually used from less than five thousand. At the same time, many people who need a new organ are unable to obtain one. The current system, with altruism as its driving force, does not and cannot meet current needs. Demand is unsatisfied, yet 80 percent of suitable organs are wasted.

In 1987, more than ninety-eight thousand patients were on dialysis. Of those, nine thousand received a kidney transplant and another nine thousand were on the approved waiting list. Patients can be maintained by dialysis, but at a high cost. The federal government, which pays for the dialysis, *would save over $400 million yearly* if sufficient transplant kidneys were available. Recipients would return to a productive life instead of being a drain on the economy. The improvement in their quality of life cannot be measured. About eleven hundred livers and fourteen hundred hearts were transplanted in 1987. The waiting list for these organs is much smaller than for kidneys, because patients with liver or heart failure cannot be sustained as easily as patients with failed kidneys.

Kryos will obtain organs for which no recipient is available: organs that would otherwise be wasted. The organs will be transported to a central processing facility for preservation and storage until a suitable matching recipient is found. They will then be prepared for implantation and transported to the recipient's hospital. For this service, Kryos will charge its fee to the donor's hospital, the custodian of the organ. The hospital will pass on the charges to the recipient's hospital and ultimately to the patient or third-party payer. At no time will Kryos own or have title to any organs.

Kryos plans to begin by furnishing pancreatic islets to insulin-dependent diabetics. Islets can be vitrified with a minimum of special equipment, and with no further development of technology. Kryos will finish the development of the technology for vitrifying kidneys, so they will be available for transplant by the end of year two. Livers will be available in the third year, and hearts in the fourth. Neither the Food and Drug Administration (FDA) nor any other governmental agency regulates organ transplantation or any of the peripheral equipment or solutions, as long as Kryos maintains control of the solutions and uses them only "in house." *There will therefore be no delays or uncertainties due to regulatory problems.*

Kryos will market its preserved organs with the help of renowned transplant surgeons. By consulting in the developmental stage, they will be adept at using the technology and will be eager to use preserved organs in their own patients. When their successes become known, other surgeons will be anxious to follow suit.

Kryos's goals of over $80 million in gross revenues with after-tax profit of about $14 million in five years are achievable because:

- Most of the required technology is already available
- The market for vitrified organs and tissues exceeds several billion dollars
- Kryos will seek the world's scientific leader in this complex technology as its scientific director
- Kryos will raise insurmountable barriers to entry of potential competitors
  - through patent applications
  - through trade secrets
  - by establishing solid relationships with donors' hospitals so as to maintain an adequate supply of organs
- Kryos will be known as the *expert* in vitrification; anyone in research, business, or the government—foreign or domestic—who wants to know about this technology will contact the company
- To help maintain its forefront position, Kryos will establish a board of medical and scientific advisors to:
  - assist in technical aspects and consult with Kryos
  - plan and host annual scientific and clinical meetings in cryobiology and transplantation for all interested scientists and physicians
  - help recruit leading scientists for Kryos's research staff

To implement Kryos's plans will require an initial round of financing of $1.5 million to be obtained from private investors or venture (seed) capital funds. The second round of $2 million, at the beginning of the second year, will be from a venture capital fund. The third round ($9 million) is planned as a public offering early in the third year, permitting initial investors to cash out if they desire. Other alternatives, such as selling equity to large corporations, will be considered as opportunities occur.

People to Contact Regarding This Business Plan

Clyde R. Goodheart, M.D., M.B.A., President and CEO
Accountants: To be selected from a Big Eight firm
Legal counsel: To be selected

II. THE MARKET

- Kryos, Inc., has identified a new technology for long-term (months or years) preservation of organs for transplant. This key breakthrough will allow the company to supply the currently unmet and rapidly increasing market for well-matched organs.

- The new technology can be applied immediately to preserving islets of the pancreas, and to treating insulin-dependent diabetes, providing a market of at least $2.4 billion.
- About 9,000 kidney transplants were performed in the U.S. in 1987, at an estimated total cost of about $428 million; the annual compounded growth rate for the past five years is 12 percent.
- More than 98,000 patients are currently on dialysis, at an annual taxpayer cost of $25,000 each. If sufficient matched kidneys were available, at least one-third of these patients would receive a transplant.
- Through the company's technology, transplants to eligible dialysis patients will save taxpayers a forecasted $450 million in the first five years and potentially over $2 billion per year.
- About 1,100 livers were transplanted in 1987, for an estimated total cost of $232 million; the growth rate for the past five years has been 65 percent per year.
- About 1,400 hearts were transplanted in 1987, for an estimated total cost of $180 million; the growth rate for the past five years has been 75 percent per year.
- Demand for organs far exceeds the number available, because it has not been possible to preserve organs.

Background

Modern medical technology has made it commonplace for surgeons today to use tissues, organs, and artificial devices as substitutes for damaged or diseased parts of patients' bodies. Human heart valves, at the border between tissues and organs, are available frozen. For at least twenty years, kidneys and some other major organs have been transplanted with constantly improving success. Hearts, livers, and heart/lungs are being transplanted more and more frequently. As will be described in the section on technology, *the company has identified a new technology that is almost completely developed, to preserve living tissues and organs for an indefinite period* so that many more can be used as transplants with much better matching than is possible today.

The company will provide the service of:

- acquiring donated organs that otherwise would not be used
- preserving the organs
- supplying the organs to transplant surgeons to implant when needed

Demand for Pancreatic Islets

About 600,000 to 2 million Americans are insulin-dependent diabetics, and each year another fifty thousand new cases of diabetes are diagnosed. These people must receive insulin by injection to control their diabetes, because a portion of the pancreas has become inactive. This inactive portion consists of about a million small groups of cells, called islets, that normally make insulin and secrete it into the bloodstream in response to changing blood sugar levels. As will be discussed in later sections of this business development plan, the company's technology can be applied to preserving islets from donors for injection into tissue-matched recipients. This replacement of lost islets will provide better control of blood sugar levels than can be achieved with injected insulin.

Demand for Major Organs

Livers, Hearts, and Pancreases

The need for these organs far exceeds the supply, but estimates vary considerably:

- *Transplantation Proceedings* places the current U.S. demand for livers, hearts, and pancreases at about 2,300 to 3,500 organs of each kind. Yet the actual need is far higher, for the journal grossly underestimated the need for kidneys. For example, the number of new dialysis patients in the United States is twice as high as the journal's estimated total current need for kidneys.
- U.S. transplant centers working with organs other than the kidney project an annual need for about 10,000 hearts, and for 5,000 to 10,000 each for livers and pancreases. In contrast, the American Council on Transplantation projects an annual need for 30,000 hearts; while Robert Jarvik, inventor of the artificial heart, places the figure at 50,000 hearts each year.

The potential transplant population must be far higher than these estimates suggest. For example:

- According to the National Institutes of Health, in 1985 alcoholic cirrhosis was listed as the cause of death for 26,767 people in the United States. Contrary to expectation, alcoholics who receive a new liver usually stop abusing alcohol; this group at risk of liver failure has not previously been included in estimates of the total need for liver transplants.
- Because of the lack of transplant organs and the unavailability of organ banking, current criteria for accepting a patient into a transplantation program are highly restrictive. Those restrictions will surely be relaxed when more organs become available.
- Organ transplants are not feasible now for patients who suffer a sudden heart attack or lethal trauma to one or two organs. If local organ banks were available, many patients could be kept alive by artificial means for the few hours needed to obtain a suitable organ.

Kidneys

Kidney disease, among the five leading causes of death, currently afflicts more than ten million Americans, and end-stage renal disease is diagnosed in fifty thousand people each year. The mortality rate for patients on long-term dialysis is about 20 percent each year. The number of kidney transplants performed is so inadequate that in 1987, the number of new dialysis

	1982	1983	1984	1985	1986	1987
Patients on dialysis	65,765	71,987	78,483	84,797	90,886	98,432
Transplant	5,343	6,098	6,933	7,676	8,948	8,949

TABLE 1

Demand for Kidney Transplants

SOURCE: Health Care Financing Administration, End Stage Renal Disease Program, January, 1989

patients was approximately equal to the number of kidney transplants performed. *In other words, twice as many transplants would have been needed just to stop the increase in the number of dialysis patients.* Table 1 summarizes the grim statistics.

Patient Pools

There is no question that transplantation is superior to dialysis. It provides a longer, more productive life, costs much less, and reduces the amount of time and effort needed for therapy. Transplant surgeons believe that at least one-third to one-half of dialysis patients would benefit from transplantation. This figure may increase to three-fourths as immunological problems are overcome by better tissue matching and by even better techniques to prevent rejection. But because of the shortage of well-matched organs, very few patients are even placed on the list for a kidney transplant. More than half who do reach the list are difficult to match. Thus, the demand is not for kidneys of random tissue type, but for kidneys that are matched closely enough to prevent organ rejection—or at least to reduce the need for expensive and potentially toxic immunosuppressive drugs. *The only way to satisfy this demand is to accumulate large numbers of organs and to store them until exactly the right recipient comes along.*

A similar pool of patients needing livers or hearts does not exist. These patients simply die. Patients with heart disease—the leading cause of death in the United States—who need a heart replacement cannot be maintained until a human heart becomes available. Artificial hearts have served on rare occasions as "bridges," but their use has been suspended.

Clearly, a tremendous, unmet need for transplantable kidneys, livers, hearts, pancreases, and other organs exists across the world, and will continue to increase as populations mature and as the success rate of transplants continues to improve. Until recently the worldwide demand was about twice that of the United States, but changes in Japanese law have added that large and wealthy country to the international "market" for organs, greatly escalating the worldwide demand. The population of Japan is about half that of the United States.

Supply of Major Organs

Problems and Solutions

As is the demand for organs, the potential supply of organs is uncertain. The vast majority of decedents are not eligible donors because of their terminal disease or age. But there is general agreement that at least twenty thousand organ donors are available each year in the United States. A 1981 study by the Centers for Disease Control (CDC) estimated that there were

TABLE 2
Transplants Performed in the U.S.
SOURCES: United Network for Organ Sharing, January 1989, and American Council on Transplantation.

Transplant	Year 1983	1984	1985	1986	1987
Kidney:					
cadaver	4,328	5,264	5,819	7,082	7,532
living relative	1,784	1,704	1,876	1,878	1,980
total kidneys	6,112	6,968	7,695	8,960	9,512*
Heart	172	346	719	1,368	1,438
Liver	164	308	602	924	1,159
Pancreas	61	52	130	140	162
Bone marrow	990	1,000	1,200	1,160	—
Heart/lung	20	22	30	45	—

*Note: Because of different sources, these totals do not completely agree with those in Table 1.

2.3 eligible donors for every hundred hospital deaths, or about twenty-seven thousand donors in all. An earlier survey suggested that, depending upon the strictness of criteria for donation, 177 to 231 kidneys are potentially available out of every 1 million people, or 20,350 to 26,600 donors.

As Table 2 indicates, the number of organs used is far short of the potential—and far short of the demand. Between 1984 and 1987, five major meetings and task force studies delved into the urgent need for increasing the supply of organs for transplantation—yet the problem persists today.

Increasing the use of kidneys from living related donors is not the answer. The use of living donors is considered ethical only because of the shortage of cadaver donors. In any case, 80 percent of potential kidney recipients do not have such potential donors.

Why the shortfall of cadaver organs? Given current technology, it is not possible to transplant all potentially available organs. Their short shelf life (the time from donor death to organ implantation in the recipient) does not permit finding a matched recipient. Knowing this, health professionals lack motivation to try to obtain organs. Another reason cited is failure to obtain donor consent from the next of kin, but it has been shown that obtaining consent is usually possible, given sufficient motivation.

Extending the viability of organs for only a few hours greatly increases the usable supply. Current shelf lives are about 48 to 72 hours for kidneys (this may increase by 48 hours in the near future), 24 hours for livers, 12 to 24 hours for pancreases, and 4 to 8 hours for hearts. With such short shelf lives, it is easy to see why so few organs are transplanted. In fact it is amazing that so many transplants take place. *Preserving organs as viable implants for weeks to years, through cryopreservation, will increase the supply dramatically.*

Comparing the organ transplants listed in Table 2 reveals that only a few available organs other than kidneys are used. According to Cardio-Metrics, Inc., about three thousand hearts were procured in 1986, but less than half were implanted. Most could not be preserved long enough to reach recipients. And according to CryoLife, Inc., about 85 percent of recently procured hearts were discarded because of improper short-term preservation.

In June 1988, the *Wall Street Journal* discussed a study in which medically acceptable donor organs were obtained with consent of the next of kin. All 63 kidneys obtained were transplanted, but only 20 of 40 livers, and 23 of 42 hearts. Hospital workers made 411 phone calls to try to place the 39 unused hearts and livers, which were never removed from the donors' bodies. (How much simpler to have notified an organ bank of the imminent arrival of these organs.) Some transplant centers preferred to wait for a local donor; others did not have a retrieval team available, or a room in intensive care. All such problems will be solved when organs can be preserved as long as it takes to find an appropriate recipient.

Long-term preservation will also allow the use of many extra-renal organs (organs other than kidneys) from "unsuitable" donors. When someone dies soon after an accident or a stroke, before an adequate medical history and disease-risk determination can be obtained, the organs cannot be used within their shelf lives without the risk of transmitting disease. When additional time would reveal these donors to be medically suitable, organ banking will mean the difference between transplantation and waste.

About 20 percent of the kidneys collected in the United States between 1981 and 1987 were discarded. More than half of these were discarded because the limits of safe hypothermic preservation time were exceeded before a suitable recipient could be found. Included were pediatric kidneys, which rarely become available when children need them; and kidneys from donors with rare blood types. In Europe, where far fewer organs are procured per capita, only about 6 percent of kidneys are wasted. A procurement increase in the United States would require a huge increase in personnel to seek matches in the time available. *Without the technology to bank unmatched and unplaced organs, an increased supply will result only in greater wastage.*

A 1984 study indicated that some physicians and hospital administrators are not motivated toward organ transplantation. To quote, "In general, physicians and surgeons responsible for the care of patients with lethal head injuries and strokes *would rather not be bothered with the whole issue of organ retrieval.* The resistance . . . is rarely direct." Similarly, the CDC found that 58 percent of potential donors were never referred to the transplant program by physicians.

Establishment of a true organ bank will markedly improve physician motivation, since every organ collected will eventually be used. The Kryos transplant coordinators will ensure that organ donations are requested, and that all necessary consents are in order, greatly decreasing demands on physicians. Established mechanisms for organ retrieval, storage, and placement will inspire physicians, administrators, potential donors, and donors' families to help make organs available.

Table 2 also indicates that very few pancreases are used. Yet almost all of the approximately four thousand cadaver donors of kidneys could also have donated their pancreases. This pool of unwanted pancreases will yield islets for Kryos to vitrify as its entry into preserving and placing vitrified organs, as outlined below.

Organ Transplanted	Cost per Transplant	Annual Total U.S. Cost (Current $million)					
		1982	1983	1984	1985	1986	1987
Kidney	$ 45,000	$241	$275	$314	$346	$403	$428
Heart	125,000	13	22	43	90	171	180
Liver	200,000	12	33	62	120	185	232
Total annual cost		$266	$330	$419	$556	$759	$840

TABLE 3
Costs of Major Transplantation Operations

Economics of Transplants

Transplanting a liver costs about $200,000; a heart, $100,000 to $150,000; and a kidney, about $45,000. Obtaining the organ accounts for only a part of the cost. For example, a hospital typically is paid $1,000 or $2,000 for removing a kidney from a cadaver and shipping it to the recipient's hospital. If the donor is living, the operation and hospital stay cost an additional $8,000 to $10,000. In both cases, tissue typing tests may add a few hundred dollars. The total estimated cost of transplanting major organs is shown in Table 3.

Liver and heart transplants cost more than kidney transplants. This is due to greater surgical complexity, and to the high cost of obtaining surgeons, operating theaters, and private jets on the emergency, nonelective basis needed. Given the very short preservation time, it is amazing that so many hearts are used. When hearts and livers can be transplanted electively, the lowered costs will more than pay for making preserved organs available.

In 1972 and 1973, legislation amending Medicare and Social Security regulations made chronic dialysis and kidney tranplantation financially feasible for almost anyone. The federal government now pays for dialysis of more than ninety-eight thousand patients, and for about eighty-three hundred kidney transplants, at a cost in 1987 of $2.8 billion (Table 4). One-third to three-fourths of the dialysis population would be eligible for a kidney transplant if well-matched organs were available.

TABLE 4
Cost to the Taxpayer (Medicare/Medicaid) of ESRD* Program
SOURCE: The End Stage Renal Disease Program, January, 1989.

	1982	1983	1984	1985	1986	1987
Number of patients on dialysis	65,765	71,987	78,483	84,797	90,886	98,432
Taxpayer cost of dialysis[†]	1,644	1,800	1,962	2,120	2,272	2,461
Number of taxpayer-paid transplants	4,917	5,591	6,304	7,073	8,258	8,299
Taxpayer cost for transplants[‡]	221	252	284	318	372	373
Total cost to taxpayer of ESRD program	1,865	2,052	2,246	2,438	2,644	2,834

*End Stage Renal Disease
[†]ESRD fund (Medicare/Medicaid) pays up to $25,000 for all costs of dialysis; all costs in table are in $million
[‡]ESRD funds pay up to $5,000 per patient for all costs of a kidney transplant.

	Actual 1987	Additional Placements Forecasted by Kryos			Potential (16,000 Donors)
		Year 3	Year 4	Year 5	
Dialysis patients	98,432				
Annual cost/patient	$25,000				
Total dialysis cost*	2,461				
5-year total cost*	12,304				
Kidneys transplanted	4,917	63	912	5,100	32,000
Cost of procedure	$45,000	45,000	45,000	45,000	45,000
Cost of kidney	$ —	6,000	6,000	6,000	6,000
Yearly maintenance cost					
First year	$15,000	15,000	15,000	15,000	15,000
Years 2 through 5	$ 8,000	8,000	8,000	8,000	8,000
5-year total cost*	221	3	47	260	1,632
5-year cost for same patients by dialysis*	615	8	114	638	4,000
Savings to taxpayers by transplanting kidneys*	394	5	67	378	2,368

*in $million

TABLE 5
Cost Savings of Kidney Transplants for Dialysis Patients in 1987, and Additional Expected Savings Based on Kryos's Forecasts

Transplanting one-third of the current dialysis patients would require 16,405 kidney donors. As previously shown, this can be done. Even with the $8,000 yearly cost of maintaining each posttransplant patient, the annual savings would be $475 million. Also, increased productivity of these patients would increase tax revenues. Three consecutive years of transplantation at this level would dramatically decrease the dialysis population, reducing the financial burden of the End Stage Renal Disease Program. Total revenue to Kryos for sixteen thousand donors (thirty-two thousand kidneys) would be $192 million. Savings to taxpayers, through savings in the Medicare/Medicaid program, are shown in Table 5.

Who will pay for organ tranplants? The U.S. government, which pays for dialysis and kidney transplants, would save money by transplanting as many kidneys as can be supplied. Home insulin maintenance for each diabetic patient costs about $2,000 per year; a curative injection of islets would pay for itself in three years. Elective scheduling of heart and liver transplants and cost reduction through improved tissue matching would substantially reduce costs, perhaps allowing a doubling of transplants with no net increase in outlays from insurance companies or private funds.

The increase in transplantation will emphasize the need for catastrophic health insurance, broadening the base of support. The twenty thousand estimated potential donors represent less than 0.01 percent of the U.S. population, limiting the liability of insurance companies and premium payers. Also, the vast savings from the End Stage Renal Disease Program could very well be applied to the coverage of these other organs.

Lawmakers and agency officials have repeatedly recommended that the government pay for heart transplants for Medicare patients, as it now does for liver transplants for some children. The Task Force on Organ Transplantation believes that all proven-effective transplants should be covered by existing public and private health insurance, and a new publicly financed program should be set up for the needy. A fifty-state survey showed that most state Medicaid programs have already financed more than one type of organ transplant for the needy. Insurance companies often refuse to pay, claiming that transplants are experimental, but the routine success of today's transplants makes this position increasingly difficult to maintain.

As will be discussed later, the company will begin operations by marketing pancreatic islets. This is a key element in Kryos's strategy for establishing a dominant position in placement of preserved organs. Islets can be readily vitrified, using minimal equipment and currently available techniques. Also, the economics for supplying vitrified islets are quite favorable. Other companies looking at replacement islets have used a price of $5,000 to $6,000 per patient as economically feasible, since it represents the amount that the typical patient will save in two to three years by not buying insulin. Also, hospital costs will be reduced, since patients with functioning islets experience fewer complications of diabetes. Since there are 600,000 to 2 million patients using insulin, the potential market amounts to between $3 billion and $10 billion dollars. The fifty thousand new cases diagnosed yearly represent an additional $250 million market.

Market Survey

Kryos commissioned a market research firm to survey the attitudes of transplant surgeons toward long-term organ preservation. Ten surgeons were contacted, in person or by telephone, from different parts of the country. The survey verified that extended preservation of organs would virtually eliminate organ wastage, greatly improve matching of donors and recipients, expand the base of organ recipients, increase the success rate of transplantation, and, in short, revolutionize the transplant field. A few highlights:

- Making transplant surgery elective rather than emergency will be a great improvement.
- Because of the tremendous demand for transplant organs, inventory buildup is hard to imagine—even if organs can be stored for long periods.
- New forms of cancer therapy will be made possible.
- Storage will allow development of better tissue-matching tests; some of these may take several weeks to perform, but will provide information permitting far better tissue matching than is now possible. Their development is not even considered now because of the short shelf lives of organs.
- The ability to preserve organs for long periods at reasonable cost will "blow the field open."

III. THE INDUSTRY

- Two companies supply synthetic or chemically treated blood vessels for use as grafts, and one company supplies frozen blood vessels and heart valves.

- Medical personnel use several interrelated computer networks to match patients with donor organs.

- Buying and selling organs is illegal under federal law, but providing preservation and placement services is not.

- The present voluntary system, based on altruism, cannot meet current and especially future demand.

The "industry" supplying tissues and organs for human transplantation consists primarily of individuals working for hospitals and for non-profit organizations. These people are responsible for acquiring and placing tissues and organs for thousands of procedures. About forty companies provide living cells or tissues for transplantation in humans or animals, or for research. Many companies in the livestock industry maintain sperm banks and perform *in vitro* fertilizations and embryo transplants. There are also blood banks, bone banks, connective tissue banks, and banks for corneas and skin.

Tissues

Tissue banks store tissues that have been preserved by freezing; for example, bone and membranes that normally surround the heart or brain. Unlike organs, tissues are generally not viable when implanted. They act as dressings or as scaffolds to support the growth of recipients' tissues. Banked tissues do not require careful tissue typing, since the graft is not viable and may not be permanent. Tissue banks are operated by hospitals, private practitioners, industry, and the American Red Cross. Tissue banks coordinate to some extent with each other, informally or through the American Association of Tissue Banks, which has established industry standards.

Organs

Since organs cannot presently be stored indefinitely, true organ banks do not exist. Finding suitable organs for transplant depends upon chance and volunteer help. If a hospital with a dying accident victim finds a matching recipient listed in the computer system, the hospital notifies the recipient's hospital, and the organs are removed, packed, and shipped. If no match is found within the time of viability of the organs, the organs may not even be removed from the donor.

Of several organizations involved in the computer system, the principal one is the United Network for Organ Sharing (UNOS), headquartered in Richmond, Virginia. Its databases contain information for selecting an appropriate recipient when a donor organ becomes available.

Because the "industry" for organ procurement, preservation, and placement is so diffuse, standards vary, and technique varies greatly from region to region. For example, when an accident occurs in a remote area, the attending physician may lack training in specialized organ removal techniques, so the organs removed may not be usable. A centralized organ procurement and processing center will set standards and educational requirements. Eventually, it may have its own aircraft and trained teams to retrieve organs, so that organ processing can begin on the way back to the processing center.

Kryos will use the new technology to supply organs to the markets served by this relatively disorganized industry. The organs targeted have been chosen based on the relative market size and on the ease of tailoring the technology. Instead of encroaching on the existing industry or interfering with transplants arranged by current means, the company will begin by procuring organs that would otherwise be wasted.

Organs cannot be ordered to meet certain specifications. CryoLife, Inc., is the only company supplying frozen parts of organs. Its main business is supplying heart valves, at $3,200 each. It is actively developing methods to freeze arteries, pancreatic islets, glandular tissue, ligaments, and knee joints. CryoLife, to be discussed in the section on competition, currently has annual sales of about $7 million, with profits of about $2.5 million, according to published reports.

A New Industry

Applying the company's new technology to the preservation of organs will create a new industry. The ultimate consumers—the recipients of organs—will benefit in many ways. More organs will be available for transplant, so that fewer people will die while waiting. Better matches of tissue compatibility and organ size will raise the success rates. Standardized organ procurement, testing, and processing procedures will improve quality control. The cost of the new acquisition, preservation, and distribution systems will be more than offset by decreasing the wastage of organs, reducing the need for more expensive hemodialysis, and restoring to productive lives the people who would otherwise need continuous care or would die.

Regulations Affecting the Industry

At last count, forty-five states have enacted laws requiring doctors and hospitals to request permission of the next of kin of a potential organ donor. The new requirements address one of the problems in the supply of organs, but do not improve the timely matching of donor and recipient.

In 1984, Congress enacted the National Organ and Transplant Act (PL-98-507; also known as the Gore bill) to enhance and coordinate private initiatives. This act includes provisions for the temporary creation of a special advisory task force; for the creation of a national organ procurement and transplant network (OPTN) to match donor organs and prospective recipients; for the distribution of grants to establish new organ procurement organizations (OPOs) and to expand existing organizations; and for prohibition of the sale of organs and tissues. The task force rendered its final reports, including seventy-eight recommendations, in April 1986. The national OPTN was contracted to UNOS, a previously existing private network. OPOs were not funded until 1986, despite great efforts by Senator Albert Gore.

Based on the task force report, in 1986 Congress passed the Omnibus Budget Reconciliation Act, which amended the Social Security Act so that state Medicare and Medicaid funds would be spent only on hospitals within the national OPTN (UNOS). These hospitals must establish written protocols that inform families of their option to donate, encourage discretion with respect to family views, and notify a specified organ procurement agency of potential donors. Memberships in UNOS entails adherence to its rules, and thus becomes a significant regulatory factor. Similarly, the Joint Commission on the Accreditation of Health Organizations adopted standards, effective January 1, 1988, requiring each accredited hospital to establish procedures to identify and refer potential organ and tissue donors to appropriate procurement agencies.

The provision making it illegal to buy or sell organs was established in response to a perception that poor people in the United States or in foreign countries might be tempted to sell a kidney to raise money. There is also a general feeling that it is wrong for a company to profit by buying and selling organs, especially an organ donated by the deceased (or next of kin). For this reason Kryos will provide only the service of obtaining, processing, storing, and placing organs. It will never actually own the organs.

The FDA does not regulate organs for transplant. In a recent article, Dr. Frank E. Young, Commissioner of the FDA, said, "It should be reemphasized that the FDA does not regulate organs for transplant, nor does it have any immediate plans to do so." Later, in the same article, he stated, ". . . transplantation as it is currently practiced is adequately regulated on a voluntary basis by the parties involved; there has been no need for the FDA to do what is already effectively accomplished in the private sector." And, again, he commented on quality control as follows: "Nothing in the Act deals directly with aspects of quality assurance, that is, with regulating the way in which organs are treated from the time of harvesting to the time of transplantation."

In early September 1988, we consulted an FDA official by telephone to obtain feedback on the company's plans and to find out about any change in the FDA's stance on organ transplants. The official stated that the FDA does not regulate organs, nor does it plan to do so. Solutions prepared by the company for its own use in transporting or perfusing organs (cryoprotectant solutions, for example), would not be regulated as long as the solutions were not allowed to be used by others. He stated further that the company would not even need to register with the FDA.

When organs can actually be vitrified and stored, however, the FDA may decide to regulate them after all. If so, the company will help set the standards, playing its natural role as the leader in vitrification. Again, the company will help set standards that it can easily meet but others cannot.

IV. THE TECHNOLOGY

- Organs preserved by freezing do not function after thawing because ice crystals disrupt the tissues.

- Vitrification—cooling to low temperatures without freezing —can preserve organs indefinitely.
- The company's scientific director will be the world leader in organ vitrification; he has the world's only patent in this field, and is developing several additional patent applications.

Many people die because they need an organ that is not available. This is especially true for livers and hearts. Yet many suitable organs are wasted because they are available at an inopportune time or place. Teams of scientists and physicians have worked for decades, at a staggering cost, to extend organ preservation to the relatively modest extent possible today. Freezing a complex organ does not work. Ice crystals grow in the organ and disrupt its structure so that it does not function when thawed. Clearly, a new technology is urgently needed to preserve organs for extended periods and increase the supply.

We will recruit Dr. Gregory Fahy as scientific director. He is the originator of the alternative technology for cryopreserving organs, and the world leader in developing this technology. For the past eight years, he has worked under the auspices of the American Red Cross with funds from the federal government through the National Institutes of Health (NIH). He has patented a major aspect of the technology and has additional patents in various stages of application. Our informal contacts with Dr. Fahy have indicated that he is willing in principle to serve as scientific director of Kryos once funding for the company has been obtained.

His alternative to freezing is a process called vitrification. The word "vitrification" indicates that an organ is converted to a glassy state rather than a crystalline state. A glass is a solid that has the disorganized structure of a liquid. In contrast, when ice forms, major structural changes occur in the liquid component of an organ, causing damage and cell death. Vitrification is thus an ideal method of long-term preservation, for the transition from the liquid state to the glassy state (solid state) preserves tissue without causing damage.

Vitrifying individual cells, such as sperm, eggs, and embryos, is being done with relative ease. Islets are small masses of cells, and they, too, have been vitrified with nearly 100 percent survival. They can be vitrified and warmed again at normal pressures; Dr. Fahy's patent, assigned to the Red Cross, does not apply to vitrification of islets. But using Kryos's proprietary method for packing, islets can be shipped in the vitrified state to the recipient's hospital, warmed in the operating room, and implanted in the patient's liver, spleen, or kidney by methods already available (it is not necessary that islets be in the pancreas to function). Further, methods are already developed to removed islets from the pancreas. The larger an "inventory" of islets, the better will Kryos be able to tissue-match the recipient. Better matching will prevent rejection problems that have plagued previous attempts to implant islets. Even partial success will enable patients to use less insulin.

With today's methods for removing islets from the pancreas, one pancreas yields enough islets to treat one patient, although recovery is still low. Experience will increase the recovery so that up to four patients can be treated with the islets from one donor. Because the technology is already developed, if Kryos successfully recruits Dr. Fahy, Kryos will have islets available early in its second year of operation. This will give an early positive cash flow, allowing Kryos to establish itself with donors' and recipients' hospitals, and with transplant surgeons. It will also demonstrate the practicality of vitrification, so that natural skepticism will wane before Kryos begins providing other organs.

In contrast to islets, organ vitrification is technologically complex. It involves perfusing the organ with a specially formulated, nontoxic mixture of various chemicals, called cryoprotective agents or cryoprotectants, that inhibit crystallization (perfusion means pumping the solution through the organ's blood vessels). Then the organ is cooled as the surrounding pressure is increased to about one thousand times atmospheric pressure. The high pressure boosts the effectiveness of the cryoprotectants, preventing ice formation. Once the organ is chilled sufficiently, its liquid content spontaneously transforms (vitrifies) to the solid state and the pressure can be returned to normal. The liquid containing the organ remains vitrified for indefinite periods at atmospheric pressure as long as it is held somewhat below the glass transition temperature (below about −125°C, depending on the cryoprotectant solution used).

To return to ordinary temperatures, the organ must again be placed under high pressure. It is warmed in a few seconds, and the pressure can then be released. If it is warmed too slowly, or under insufficient pressure, ice crystals form and the organ is destroyed. After the organ is warmed, the vitrifying solution is washed out and the organ is ready for transplantation. In an emergency, a vitrified organ can be ready for transplantation in approximately two to three hours, the time required to wash out the vitrification solution. This is why no competitor will be able to supply organs as rapidly as Kryos.

Vitrification has permitted excellent survival of mouse embryos, human and monkey pancreatic islets, human monocytes (white blood cells), and human red blood cells. In some experiments, kidney slices vitrified at one atmosphere and warmed quickly enough to avoid devitrification have appeared virtually unchanged. Rabbit kidneys perfused with vitrifiable cryoprotectant solutions, but not vitrified, have supported life over a long term as the sole kidney after transplantation. Organ vitrification with subsequent life support function has not been attempted yet; a device to cool and warm large organs under high-pressure conditions so as to avoid crystallization during warming has been designed and is being built. Although more developmental work is necessary, the results described above provide ample reason for our enthusiasm for having the remaining developmental work completed by Kryos, so that Kryos will be the owner of the technology.

Licensing of Technology

Dr. Fahy's work in developing the technology for vitrification to its current state has been done during his employment at the American Red Cross in Rockville, Maryland. He is the inventor on a patent assigned by him to the Red Cross, and is the applicant on several more patents.

General inquiry of the legal staff at the Red Cross indicates that the association is generally willing to enter into licensing agreements, and to permit its employees to consult with the licensee to assist in transferring the technology. Our company was not identified and the Red Cross was not told which patents we wished to license, so that specifics of terms were not discussed.

We feel the best motive for the Red Cross to license its technology to us is that we know how to use it to maximum advantage in the marketplace, and that we have the drive and talent to do this far better than the Red Cross—far better even than the most logical competitor, CryoLife. The Red Cross makes very conservative decisions and does so extremely slowly. The Red Cross will earn much more revenue by licensing its technology to Kryos than by refusing to do so. In addition, from a humanitarian standpoint, if Kryos completes the technology, the Red Cross is ethically obligated to permit this technology to be applied for the benefit of mankind.

Negotiations with the Red Cross will begin when the initial round of financing is complete and the Red Cross can see clearly that our intentions are serious and that our capabilities are equal to the task. Ideally, it is better to obtain licensing rights before the technology is fully perfected rather than afterwards, when the value of the technology becomes more obvious.

VIII. MARKETING PLAN

- The company will be marketing a service; providing efficient, dependable service will be the number one priority.
- Marketing of vitrified transplant organs will phase in over several years:
  - islets of pancreas twelve months after start-up
  - kidneys twenty-one months after start-up
  - livers thirty-two months after start-up
  - hearts forty months after start-up

Overview of the Marketing Plan

Marketing the service of providing vitrified organs will include increasingly difficult organs as we perfect and extend our technology.

Kryos plans first to market islets. A significant market exists, and the technology for vitrifying islets is available. Failures of grafted islets are not life threatening, since at worst the diabetic would continue insulin injections. Marketing islets will give Kryos an early start on establishing procurement and placement networks and visibility to the transplant community. The decision makers, procurement and placement people, and other health professionals involved with islets will be the same ones involved with major organs. While establishing its channels for islets, Kryos will finish developing the technology for major organs. No negotiations with the Red Cross will be necessary for islets, nor are any regulatory bodies involved.

Successful marketing of vitrified organs will depend initially on providing the decision makers—transplant surgeons—with credible evidence that the organs will function as expected. Such evidence will come from experimental data presented in seminars, videotapes, and published reports. Marketing will also depend on presenting information on the underlying technology. Understanding the vitrification process, and how it differs from freezing, will help convince surgeons that vitrified organs will be viable after implantation.

Our service will extend beyond providing viable organs on demand. Quality control of the organs will be rigorous and extensive, far exceeding current standards. With ample time for testing while the organs are stored, we will provide tissue matching far better than anything currently available.

With many organs "on the shelf," we will have great flexibility in choosing one that most closely matches the recipient's needs. This will help increase the transplant success rate. Our service will include delivery of the organ to the recipient's operating room "just in time" to be implanted, maximizing organ viability. Our marketing efforts will emphasize these and other advantages of cryopreserved organs, among them a potential savings of $400 million or more per year in the government's End Stage Renal Disease Program.

Board of Medical and Scientific Advisors

Kryos will establish a board of medical and scientific advisors, consisting of experts in transplantation and cryobiology. These experts will be paid a monthly retainer and a per diem to attend meetings. Travel expenses will be reimbursed. Their duties will include the following:

- Attend two meetings annually with company scientists and provide technical input to the research and development effort.
- Organize an annual scientific/clinical meeting as described below.
- Be on call for consultation with company scientists to help solve technical problems.
- Help the company find key technical personnel.
- Help the company find additional contacts and business.

The board of medical and scientific advisors will plan and host a scientific/clinical meeting each year on cryobiology and transplantation, open to all interested scientists and clinicians. Invited speakers will include scientists involved in cryobiology as well as cardiovascular and transplant surgeons. Topics will rotate in successive years through kidneys, livers, hearts, and other organs, in keeping with changing technology. The proceedings will be published as a book. Holding such meetings will help establish the company's leadership position in vitrification. Such meetings generally are held on a break-even or slightly profitable basis. For that reason, no budget is shown in this business plan for the meetings.

Publication of Research Results

To ensure that the image of Kryos as the leader in the new technology is maintained and enhanced, Kryos will encourage company scientists to publish medical and research findings so long as publication does not impair patentability or divulge proprietary data. Scientists will be encouraged to take part in national workshops, seminars, and similar activities.

Building Awareness

Kryos will station transplant coordinators in major medical centers as constant reminders of the need to save all potentially available organs. During the final stages of development for each of the organs and during the introduction stage, an active, aggressive public relations campaign will increase awareness of the company and its services, and will keep the physician community informed about the technology behind the organs.

Islets

Kryos will begin its activities with pancreatic islets. These are small clusters of cells that secrete insulin to maintain a constant blood sugar level. The islets are lost or malfunction in some kinds of diabetics; replacement of the islets restores this normal function and eliminates the need for insulin injections. It is a good beginning for Kryos for a number of reasons:

- There are at least 600,000 insulin-dependent diabetics. At Kryos's planned fee of $5,500 for a curative number of tissue-matched islets, the market is worth at least $3 billion. The limit is on the number of donor pancreases available, not the number of recipients.

- Islets are obtained from pancreases, which now are rarely recovered from donors since only a few pancreas transplants are performed. Further, pancreases can be obtained from donors not eligible for donating other organs.

- Vitrification of islets requires relatively simple equipment, since the high pressure needed for organs is not necessary for islets.

- Islets have been vitrified and rewarmed with virtually 100 percent survival and function.

- Any early failures of the islets to function will not result in death of the recipient; at worst, the patient will have to continue insulin injections.

- Islets can be shipped to the recipient's hospital in the vitrified state, and warmed after the patient has been prepared to receive them, using Kryos's proprietary system.

- Collecting pancreases for islet preparations will allow Kryos to establish its network and contacts for obtaining organs.

- Successes with vitrified islets will alert transplant surgeons to this new technology, helping pave the way for more complex organs later.

Kidneys

The technology will be completed and vitrified kidneys will be available about twenty-one months after start-up. By then, the company will be fully functional with acquisition and distribution systems in place.

Most patients with kidney failure are maintained by dialysis, and transplantation usually is not an emergency procedure. Nevertheless, a considerable backlog of approved patients registered with the End Stage

Renal Disease Program awaits suitable kidneys. The federal government pays for most dialysis procedures, and has already determined the economic benefit of transplants in place of dialysis.

Two or three nationally known transplant surgeons near the company's research facility will work with the company as consultants, especially during finalization of the research and development work on kidneys. Because of their familiarity with the company's vitrified kidneys, and their help in development, we expect these surgeons to be the first practitioners to use the kidneys in their own patients when marketing begins. During the first quarter that kidneys are available, we expect to place nine kidneys for implant.

During the first quarter of marketing, promotional efforts will be directed at transplant surgeons in about two hundred medical centers in the United States. Studies show that the best way to procure organs is to link transplant services to trauma centers with neurosurgical services. Linking Kryos coordinators with neurosurgeons and neurologists will be the most effective way to increase the donor pool. More than one-third of the fewer than six thousand neurosurgeons or neurologists in the United States can be reached through identified professional journals and associations.

For transplant surgeons, the primary means of communication will be direct mail, using commercial lists. Initially, a brochure will describe the kidneys and our service. Technical literature will be sent in response to a mail-back card included with the first mailing. Telephone follow-up and personal sales calls will be included. By then, the company sales force will consist of six salespeople. The goal of this marketing effort will be to make transplant surgeons aware that our vitrified kidneys are available, that leading surgeons are using them successfully, and that we offer technical expertise and rapid, efficient service to supply kidneys at the time of need.

Toward the end of the second quarter of marketing, and through the third quarter, when the awareness level has been established, we will hold seminars in major medical centers, with notices sent to transplant surgeons nationwide. The seminars will answer any questions and technical doubts surgeons may have about using the kidneys. "How-to" presentations by our three consultants will describe surgical details of the procedure. Other topics will include the acquisition of the kidneys, a description of the vitrification process and the quality control procedures performed, and an outline of the "just in time" delivery. Videotapes will be sent to surgeons unable to attend the seminars, and will provide credit toward continuing medical education requirements.

Beginning with the first major national meeting of surgeons, the company will have a booth where technical questions can be answered. Several times each year, mailings will be sent to all transplant surgeons with reprints of medical papers and reports of other technical developments related to the company's vitrified kidneys.

In calling on transplant surgeons, salespeople will emphasize the advantages of vitrified kidneys over random cadaver kidneys or kidneys from related living donors:

- Functional, viable kidneys are delivered to the operating room when desired rather than unpredictably.

- Surgery can be scheduled at any site, whenever the recipient is in optimum condition for the procedure, and whenever the surgical team and operating theater are conveniently available.
- The large inventory and long holding times possible for available kidneys provide better tissue matching and size matching.
- New surgical interventions are now possible, such as a temporary removal of kidneys for a course of radiation and chemotherapy or administration of large does of nephrotoxic drugs; afterwards, the kidneys can be reimplanted.
- It is not necessary to take a kidney from a healthy donor, risking that person's health and life, and adding significantly to the cost of the transplantation.
- The repository will not only have kidneys available when needed, but will accept all otherwise unplaceable organs for immediate and guaranteed reimbursement.

After the initial introductory period, placements of vitrified kidneys will increase at a rapid rate because of the demand backlog, the clear advantages to using vitrified kidneys, and the shortage of alternative kidneys. As surgeons see that implanted kidneys remain functional and viable, transplants will increase even more rapidly. Kidneys are the organ of choice for initial trials in humans because any early failures will not cause death of the patient.

Because of the costs involved, we will charge a fee of $6,000 for preservation of each kidney. This cost is small compared with the overall cost of the transplant procedure itself as well as the cost of dialysis for the balance of a patient's life. It is also small compared with the cost of obtaining a kidney donated by a relative. The cost is higher than the cost of a cadaver kidney, but the lack of alternatives and the superiority of matching (which may save more than $5,000 annually for immunosuppression) will make it worthwhile. The current costs of obtaining a cadaver kidney range from $2,000 to $10,000, so an extra charge of $6,000 to preserve that kidney seems highly appropriate. Even simple heart valves cost $3,200 from Cryo-Life. And if no other kidney is available, cost is immaterial.

Livers

We will complete the development work on vitrification of livers and will have livers available for transplant in the third quarter of the third year after start-up. By that time, the company will have well-established mechanisms for acquiring, processing, and delivering organs. It will also have an experienced sales force and will have an excellent reputation among transplant surgeons.

The market for livers is similar to that for kidneys, but some differences exist. There is no significant backlog of patients waiting for livers, since patients die when a liver does not become available in time. Also, the federal government has no payment program for liver transplants. Many insurance companies consider liver transplantation to be experimental, so their policies do not cover the procedure. Lacking significant third-party payers, patients must pay the cost themselves or raise funds through a public appeal.

Recent studies have shown that most alcoholics whose failed liver has been replaced actually stop drinking and do not destroy their new liver transplant. Replacing livers of patients who have alcoholic cirrhosis will add a considerable market opportunity.

Liver transplants differ in another important way. With many patients, the choice will be to try a vitrified liver or die. With an attitude of "what can I lose except some money (which I can't take with me anyhow)?" and with the strong possibility that a nonvitrified liver will be unavailable when needed, many patients will opt to try a vitrified liver.

As with kidneys, we plan to sign up transplant surgeons as consultants when we finalize the development work for vitrified livers. These surgeons will be the first to implant vitrified livers when marketing begins. During the third quarter of the third year (the first quarter for marketing livers), the company expects to place six livers. During the second quarter of marketing, the company expects to place ninety livers, for the reasons described above. Placements are expected to increase rapidly from that level since there really is no good alternative.

The technology for vitrifying livers is more complex and more expensive than that for kidneys. We therefore plan to charge a fee of $16,000 for preservation of each liver. That is roughly 5 percent to 10 percent of the total cost of the procedure, and many people will be willing to pay that amount in order to live. Under these conditions, if a vitrified liver is available and no alternative exists, cost becomes important.

Hearts

Preserving hearts presents technical problems not present with kidneys or livers: Even with twenty-four hour machine preservation of hearts, after shipping to the processing center, there will be very little time for vitrification; the inner lining of the heart will require specialized techniques to permeate with vitrification solution; the contractile apparatus of the heart requires special attention; and so forth. Kryos will finish developing the technology for preserving hearts, and will have hearts available for implantation, in the fortieth month after start-up.

The overall plan for introducing hearts is similar to that outlined for other organs, except that by then, Kryos will have established its reputation, and decision makers will have accepted the technology. We will charge a fee of $16,000 for each heart.

IX. MANAGEMENT AND KEY MILESTONES

- Management for the initial start-up phase is in place.
- Additional management people will be added soon thereafter:
  - vice-president, research and development
  - vice-president, marketing
  - chief executive officer

The founders of the company will provide its initial management. Dr. Clyde R. Goodheart will be the president and CEO because of his prior experience in starting companies in pharmaceuticals and biopharmaceuticals. For instance, he recently sold a company that he started and had operated since 1969. The company's business was performing cancer research for the federal government, performing contract research for corporations (Armour Pharmaceuticals, for example), and developing and marketing tissue culture products for the research market. He recently has helped organize another company to produce a biopharmaceutical and has raised the seed capital for its start. In addition to his background in research and business starts, Dr. Goodheart has his M.B.A. degree from Northwestern University's Kellogg Graduate School of Management (finance, marketing, and management policy).

It is planned to recruit Dr. Greg Fahy to be chairman of the board, and initially to serve as director of research. Dr. Fahy is the worldwide leader in cryobiology and has led the development of vitrification with its biological applications. Not only is he active in many organizations related to cryobiology, but he knows other leaders in the field. Dr. Fahy's patent and patent applications, assigned to the American Red Cross, are the only ones in the field of biological vitrification. He will make additional applications based on the development required to complete the work to vitrify organs.

The founders recognize the need for additional management. They plan to select as associates people with the highest credentials and experience in their respective fields. Although Dr. Fahy will supply the technical knowledge for perfecting vitrification, there is a need also for a vice-president for research and development who has had experience in the pharmaceutical industry and who has brought products from the scientific concept stage to the market. Two such individuals have been interviewed and have expressed interest in joining the company.

Early in the development process, the company will add a vice-president of marketing. This person will have had considerable experience in pharmaceuticals or in transplantation, especially in marketing fast-growth, new products. He or she will help in the development stage, so that the services provided by Kryos in getting organs to recipients on time will be certain to meet needs of the market.

When vitrified organs are ready to be marketed, a president/CEO will join the company. This person will have carried a young company or division through fast growth to the $25 million sales range.

The founders will collectively hold one million shares, with Dr. Fahy receiving 50 percent for inducement to join Kryos.

Key milestones related to operations are depicted in Exhibit 1.

X. FINANCIAL DATA

Placements of the islets and three major organs selected by Kryos as its initial targets will exceed $83 million in five years, yielding an after-tax profit of more than $14 million.

The following financial statements present the founders' forecasted outcome of the investments and operations of Kryos, Inc., based on their estimates of the events most likely to occur, as described in the preceding pages of this business plan.

The forecasts were prepared on a quarterly basis for the five-year planning horizon. Annual summaries are included in this document; detailed quarterly statements are available on request for further review. The accompanying notes describing the accounting policies and assumptions used in preparing the forecasts are an integral part of the forecasts and should be read in conjunction with the statements.

The following forecasts indicate in detail the expected use of the proceeds from the staged financings. The use of the proceeds during the first year from the first round is summarized briefly below:

Use	Amount
Fixed asset purchases	$ 603,000
Production	138,000
R&D	338,000
Working capital	421,000
Total	$1,500,000

KRYOS, INC.
Forecasted Balance Sheets

	End of				
Assets	Year 1	Year 2	Year 3	Year 4	Year 5
Current assets					
Cash and equivalents	$ 134,813	$ 605,319	$ 8,851,480	$ 6,158,224	$ 3,696,120
Accounts receivable, net	—	825,000	2,493,500	5,487,000	13,763,750
Inventory	138,323	1,129,314	2,662,058	6,381,615	16,402,343
Total current assets	$ 273,136	$ 2,559,633	$14,007,038	$18,026,839	$33,862,213
Fixed assets, net	486,130	397,599	628,349	1,458,364	4,534,591
Total assets	$ 759,266	$ 2,957,232	$14,635,387	$19,485,203	$38,396,804
Liabilities and Stockholders' Equity					
Current liabilities					
Accounts payable and accrued liabilities	$ 125,810	$ 466,724	$ 1,296,251	$ 2,781,495	$ 5,862,520
Income taxes payable	—	—	50,426	252,611	1,203,909
Total current liabilites	$ 125,810	$ 466,724	$ 1,346,676	$ 3,034,106	$ 7,066,429
Stockholders' equity					
Common stock	1,500,000	3,500,000	12,500,000	12,500,000	12,500,000
Retained earnings (deficit)	(866,544)	(1,009,491)	788,711	3,951,096	18,830,376
Total stockholders' equity	$ 633,456	$ 2,490,509	$13,288,711	$16,451,096	$31,330,376
Total liabilities and stockholders' equity	$ 759,266	$ 2,957,232	$14,635,387	$19,485,203	$38,396,804

KRYOS, INC.
Statement of Forecasted Operations and Retained Earnings

	Year 1	Year 2	Year 3	Year 4	Year 5
Revenues from Operations					
Islets	$ —	$ 3,289,000	$14,575,000	$24,530,000	$32,395,000
Kidneys	—	—	378,000	5,472,000	30,600,000
Livers	—	—	96,000	2,848,000	19,040,000
Hearts	—	—	—	112,000	1,088,000
Total Revenues	$ —	$ 3,289,000	$15,049,000	$32,962,000	$83,123,000
Cost of Goods Sold	—	1,620,862	6,777,764	14,994,035	39,010,922
Gross Margin	$ —	$ 1,668,138	$ 8,271,236	$17,967,965	$44,112,078
Operating Expenses					
Depreciation	$ 116,970	$ 196,531	$ 199,350	$ 384,985	$ 1,236,873
General and Administrative	302,573	405,404	2,400,309	3,750,134	5,067,525
Selling Expenses	161,700	736,700	1,723,000	3,102,600	5,821,800
R&D	337,600	544,160	2,275,680	5,998,320	7,665,840
Total Operating Expenses	$ 918,843	$ 1,882,795	$ 6,598,339	$13,236,039	$19,792,038
Income (Loss) Before Interest and Income Taxes	$(918,843)	$ (214,657)	$ 1,672,897	$ 4,731,926	$24,320,041
Interest Income	52,299	71,710	629,562	452,313	72,220
Income (Loss) Before Income Taxes	(866,544)	(142,948)	2,302,460	5,184,239	24,392,261
Income Tax Expense	—	—	504,258	2,021,853	9,512,982
Net Income (Loss)	$(866,544)	$ (142,948)	$ 1,798,202	$ 3,162,386	$14,879,279
Retained Earnings (Deficit) at Beginning of Period	—	(866,544)	(1,009,491)	788,711	3,951,096
Retained Earnings (Deficit) at End of Period	$(866,544)	$(1,009,491)	$ 788,711	$ 3,951,096	$18,830,376

XI. FINANCING PLAN

1. $1.5 million in equity financing is required to start Kryos as described herein, with the investor(s) receiving 42 percent of the equity.

2. A second round of financing, for $2 million, will be needed in the beginning of the second year. Investors in that round will receive 25 percent of the equity.

3. A third round of financing, for $9 million, will be needed in the second half of the third year. A public offering of 20 percent of the stock is planned.

The forecasts indicate that $1.5 million is required to start Kryos, Inc. That and later additional capital will provide the means for Kryos to develop the full potential of the market it will own. It will also permit establishing and maintaining a strong competitive position, by substantial fund-

KRYOS, INC.
Statement of Forecasted Cash Flows

	Year 1	Year 2	Year 3	Year 4	Year 5
Cash Flows from (Used by) Operating Activities					
Net Income	$ (866,544)	$ (142,948)	$ 1,798,202	$ 3,162,386	$ 14,879,279
Non-Cash Item: Depreciation	116,970	196,530	199,350	384,985	1,236,873
Cash from (Used by) Changes in					
Accrued Income Taxes	$ —	$ —	$ 50,426	$ 202,185	$ 951,298
Accounts Payable	125,810	340,914	829,527	1,485,245	3,081,024
Accounts Receivable	—	(825,00)	(1,668,500)	(2,993,500)	(8,276,750)
Inventory	(138,323)	(990,991)	(1,532,744)	(3,719,557)	(10,020,728)
Net Cash Flow from (Used by) Operating Activities	$ (762,087)	$(1,421,495)	$ (323,740)	$(1,478,256)	$ 1,850,997
Cash Flow from (Used by) Investing Activities					
Fixed Asset Purchases	(603,100)	(108,000)	(430,100)	(1,215,000)	(4,313,100)
Net Cash Flow from (Used by) Investing Activities	$ (603,100)	$ (108,000)	$ (430,100)	$(1,215,000)	$ (4,313,100)
Cash Flows from Financing Activities					
Proceeds from Sale of Common Stock	1,500,000	2,000,000	9,000,000	—	—
Net Cash Flow from Financing Activities	1,500,000	2,000,000	9,000,000	—	—
Net Increase (Decrease) in Cash	134,813	470,505	8,246,160	(2,693,256)	(2,462,103)
Cash—Beginning of Period	—	134,813	605,318	8,851,479	6,158,223
Cash—End of Period	$ 134,813	$ 605,318	$ 8,851,479	$ 6,158,223	$ 3,696,119

ing for research and development, which will help in image building and will protect against technological obsolescence, and by providing funds for an aggressive marketing effort. These, and other strategies described in this business development plan, are designed to decrease the risk of starting Kryos.

As indicated in the statement of cash flows, the capital, all equity, will be required as follows: round one of $1,500,000 to start, round two of $2,000,000 at the beginning of year two, and round three, of $9,000,000 (net of 10 percent underwriting fees) early in the third year. Rounds one and two most appropriately will come from private investors or venture capital funds, while round three will be most appropriate from an initial public offering. The public offering will also afford the investors of rounds one and two a chance to exit their investment if they so desire.

After reserving 500,000 shares of common stock for options for key employees, it is proposed that the investors will receive the following amounts of common stock (or other securities convertible to common) for their investment, which would have the following values:

	Prior	Round 1	Round 2	Round 3
Proceeds of offering	$ 1,000	1,500,000	2,000,000	9,000,000
Number of shares sold	1,000,000	1,086,207	862,069	862,069
Reserved for options	—	500,000	—	—
Cumulative outstanding	1,000,000	2,586,207	3,448,276	4,310,345
Percentage sold	—	42%	25%	20%
Market value/share	$ —	1.38	2.32	11.48

By the end of the fifth year, at ten times earnings, the market value of the company will be $140 million. Although the plan is for an initial public offering in the third year, the owners of the company at that time may prefer to sell Kryos to a major company. Which method is best for liquidation and exit will be decided at that time depending on circumstances.

	YEAR 1				YEAR 2				YEAR 3				YEAR 4				YEAR 5			
	Q1	Q2	Q3	Q4	Q1	Q2	Q3	Q4	Q1	Q2	Q3	Q4	Q1	Q2	Q3	Q4	Q1	Q2	Q3	Q4
Complete round 1 financing	X																			
Lease research facility	X																			
Order equipment	X																			
Prepare facility	X																			
Receive first equipment		X																		
Developmental work on islets		X	X	X																
Hire VP marketing		X																		
First placement of islets				X																
Developmental work on kidneys																				
Rabbit			X	X	X															
Pig				X	X	X														
Human					X	X	X													
Complete round 2 financing					X															
Recruit board of advisors					X	X	X	X												
Finish development on kidneys							X													
First placement of kidneys							X													
Development work on livers																				
Rabbit					X	X	X	X	X											
Pig							X	X	X											
Human								X	X	X										
Complete round 3 financing								X												
Finish development on livers										X										
First placements of livers											X									
Developmental work on hearts																				
Rabbit									X	X	X									
Pig											X	X								
Human											X	X								
Annual general scientific meetings									X				X				X			
Finish development on hearts													X							
First placements of hearts													X							

EXHIBIT 1 SCHEDULE AND KEY MILESTONES

VII

CASES

A

The Artisan's Haven

Neil H. Snyder and Brooke Garrett

THE DECISION TO GO INTO BUSINESS

John and Katie Owen were confronted with a serious problem in 1973. John was fired from his job with a large chemical company in Trenton, New Jersey, for which he had worked for thirty-three years. The Arab oil embargo had caused a recession in the U.S. economy, and the nation was bracing itself for anticipated high inflation. After working for one company for so long and giving the firm his best years, John was emotionally upset over his dismissal. It was not as though he had made a big mistake or that he had done anything wrong. He was simply one of the older employees whom the company wanted to replace with younger, more energetic people. The recession gave the firm the opportunity it needed to make wholesale changes in personnel.

Finding a job during a recession is not easy, and for a fifty-five-year-old man whose experience is limited to one industry, it is almost impossible. John felt helpless. He did not know what to do and his frustration turned into anger as he realized for the first time in his working life that he was just a pawn in a great game of corporation chess. After several weeks of fear, anxiety, and doubt, John reached a major turning point in his life. He knew that he never wanted to work for anyone or for any firm again.

The decision not to work for others was a major one, but John still did not know what to do. Should he retire? If he did, it would not be a comfortable retirement. Should he start his own business? If so, what kind of business should it be? He knew that he did not want to be involved with chemicals. Even before he was fired, John had begun to have reservations about producing dangerous chemicals and dumping harmful waste into rivers. But his pay was good, and he did not have the time or the inclination to think about these deep questions too seriously. It was more important to John to pay his bills, to take nice vacations, and, in general, to have fun.

Although John likes to take credit for the idea, Katie is the one who suggested that he consider opening a store to sell arts and crafts. John's hobby for many years had been making gold jewelry, and he had become a very good goldsmith. Katie was an amateur interior designer, and she also enjoyed doing cross-stitch and making dried floral arrangements. Starting a business to sell something they enjoyed making and knew something about seemed like a very good idea. In addition, John and Katie could work together in this kind of business, and Katie had always wanted to spend more time with John.

In 1974, they opened their first store in Trenton, and it was very successful. Their location was excellent, and their merchandise was high quality. Everything they did just seemed to work, and by 1980, the Owens owned six stores in New Jersey and Pennsylvania.

In 1980, John and Katie were both sixty-two years old, and they were more secure financially than they had ever been. When John lost his job with the chemical company, his net worth had been about $150,000, and almost all of it was tied up in his house and furnishings. His income at the time was comfortable, but not great. Now, his net worth was in excess of $1 million, and John and Katie could do many of the things they had always dreamed of doing. One thing they had dreamed of doing was retiring to a nice southern town and enjoying life.

So, at age sixty-two, John and Katie decided to sell their stores in New Jersey and Pennsylvania and move to Athens, Georgia. A couple with whom they were very close had moved to Athens several years before, and John and Katie had visited them several times. They liked the town, they liked the University of Georgia, they liked the people, and they liked the climate. The move just seemed like the right thing to do.

MOVING TO ATHENS, GEORGIA

John and Katie settled into their new way of life in Athens very quickly. They joined a local church that consumed a fair amount of their time. Katie got actively involved in the Christian Women's Club. John joined the Lion's Club and was able to contribute a great deal of time to many of its projects.

However, one thing was missing. While they were in business, John and Katie had enjoyed making decisions and watching the bottom line of their income statement change to reflect the quality of their judgment. None of their activities in Athens provided the same sense of excitement and satisfaction that owning and operating a business had provided. After a year, John asked Katie about opening a business in Athens, and Katie agreed.

STARTING OVER AGAIN

In the fall of 1981, the Owens opened The Artisan's Haven in downtown Athens directly across the street from the University of Georgia, and the community responded enthusiastically. The store sold handmade gold and silver jewelry, pottery, dried floral arrangements, woodcrafts, and various other handmade objects. Upon entering the store, customers were over-whelmed by the quality of the merchandise. It looked like it could have come out of a magazine like *Country Living* or *Southern Living.* All of the merchandise was made with great care and attention to detail.

Part of the immediate success of the new store was due to the popu-larity of arts and crafts at the time. But the Owens themselves were the main attraction. John and Katie seemed to be more relaxed about life and the rapport they developed with their customers was nothing short of amazing. They offered classes to teach their customers how to make many of the items sold in the store. Katie became an interior decorator whose advice was sought by many prominent and influential people in the com-munity. John organized the artists and crafts people in the northeast Geor-gia area into a guild. As a result of their work, the Owens developed a large, wealthy customer base and an excellent supply of high-quality goods to sell.

DEMOGRAPHICS OF ATHENS

The population of Athens and Clarke County, the county surrounding Athens, is approximately eighty-three thousand people. Twenty-one per-cent of the residents are professionals, and almost a third of them are students at the University of Georgia. A recent study of household incomes in Athens revealed the following (see Table 1).

COMPETITION

The Artisan's Haven has no direct competition in Athens. Traditionally, few residents in the community have shown much interest in high-quality goods and services. Cultural events, such as plays and musical shows, are occasional attractions. Until very recently, the best restaurants in town were steak houses and catered primarily to students, and there were fast-food chains and small locally owned operations. Big events in Athens that set it apart from other communities in the area are University of Georgia football games and fraternity and sorority parties.

However, things in Athens are changing, and the wealthier residents in the community are beginning to pay attention to their quality of life. The only stores selling products that compete with The Artisan's Haven include jewelry stores, department store chains, and a few lower-end specialty shops. These stores are not considered direct competitors, because the quality of their merchandise is inferior to the quality of the merchandise

TABLE 1

Household Income*	Number of Households*
Greater than $50,000	4,719
$35,000 to $49,999	6,426
$25,000 to $34,999	7,691

*An average household in Athens is composed of 2.5 people.

sold in The Artisan's Haven. The store's closest direct competitors are in Atlanta, the state's capital about seventy miles away, and many of Athens's wealthier residents go there routinely to shop.

MANAGEMENT AND PERSONNEL

John and Katie own and operate their store. In addition, they make many of the products they sell. The Owens have been very fortunate to get to know two retired, upper-middle-income women who are looking for opportunities to stay busy doing things they enjoy. These two women work part-time for the Owens for nominal wages. Besides being excellent employees, their friends visit them in the store, and many of them have become regular customers.

The Owens' most important employee is Rachel Thompson, who is fifty-seven years old. They first met her when she was a customer in the store. After they got to know her, they discovered that Rachel's hobby was interior decorating and that most of what she bought was for friends' homes. She was not paid for any of this work. When she was approached by the Owens, Rachel was more than delighted to accept their offer of employment. Rachel's primary responsibility is to work with Katie on interior decorating jobs and to wait on customers in the store. She works about twenty hours a week.

Madeline Murray lives next door to the Owens. She is fifty-three years old and a very skillful craftswoman, who developed her talent by doing needlework in her home and the homes of her children, relatives, and many friends. The Owens first bought needlework from her by the piece, because it was impossible for Katie to do all of the cross-stitching and to wait on customers all day. After it became obvious to the Owens that Madeline enjoyed working with them and that they enjoyed her, they invited her to join them at the store. Her job was to do needlework for sale in the store and to work with customers who wanted custom-designed needlework made for their homes. Madeline also works about twenty hours a week.

Rachel and Madeline are like part of the family. Customers frequenting The Artisan's Haven sense the warmth and friendliness of everyone in the store, and they tell John and Katie regularly how enjoyable it is to shop there.

MARKETING

When the Owens first opened the store in Athens, their marketing efforts targeted local residents, tourists, and students. They used radio and newspaper advertising primarily. After several months of operation, they surveyed their customers to evaluate the effectiveness of their promotion effort. Not surprisingly, they learned that word of mouth and the Owens themselves were by far the most effective forms of advertising. Additionally, they learned that students were not attracted to their store in large numbers, because of the prices of the goods sold and because they were not furnishing homes in which they intended to live for lengthy periods.

Tourists did not flock to the store, either, because Athens is not known as a tourist attraction.

The Owens decided early on that The Artisan's Haven did not need extensive print or broadcast media support. However, they did continue to run an occasional radio spot or ad in the local newspaper.

ORGANIZATION

The Owens incorporated The Artisan's Haven in the beginning, because they wanted to limit their liability. They were not certain about how to incorporate. They learned that there are major differences between a Sub-chapter C corporation and a Sub-chapter S corporation. Both offer several important features, such as continuity of life, centralization of management, limited liability, and easy transferability of interests. The S corporation is usually preferred by small business owners, because it is treated like a partnership for tax purposes.

Although the Owens could have incorporated The Artisan's Haven as an S corporation, they chose the C corporation. The C corporation allowed the Owens to deduct certain fringe benefits, like medical and health insurance, and to shelter earnings for later use. Because of their age, these were important issues to the Owens.

The major disadvantage of a C corporation is double taxation. The Owens were not as concerned about this issue as the others, because they were able to pay themselves attractive salaries that were tax-deductible expenditures.

FINANCE

Exhibits 1, 2, and 3 contain pertinent financial information for The Artisan's Haven. The income statement shown in Exhibit 1 indicates that the largest expenses for the Owens are wages, travel, and rent. The 1981 data are a little misleading, because the store was in operation for only half the year. Travel is a major budget item, because the Owens travel a great deal to visit crafts people and art shows. Advertising in 1981 was a large expense item, because the Owens were establishing their name and reputation.

A MAJOR DECISION

In July 1987, John Owen suffered a massive heart attack, and he was told by his doctors to restrict his activities significantly. Before the heart attack, John and Katie had discussed the possibility of selling the business. Now Katie was certain that she wanted to sell it.

Four months before the heart attack, a local entrepreneur named Don Lassiter, who was in the business of buying and selling businesses, had approached the Owens about buying The Artisan's Haven for his wife. They had told him no. At the time, the Owens were in no hurry to sell; but

EXHIBIT 1
Income Statement

THE ARTISAN'S HAVEN
Consolidated Income Statements for the
Period Ending January 31, 1986

	1981	1982	1983	1984	1985	1986
Sales	$ 16,610	$55,673	$78,736	$105,928	$123,683	$153,186
Cost of Sales	8,305	27,827	35,968	43,441	60,201	75,806
Gross Profit	$ 8,305	$27,836	$42,768	$ 62,487	$ 63,482	$ 77,380
Expenses						
Rent	$ 3,900	$ 7,800	$ 7,800	$ 7,800	$ 7,800	$ 7,800
Wages to Officers	10,000	11,000	15,500	20,000	25,000	50,000
Other Salaries	0	0	0	4,526	9,688	10,803
Utilities	434	612	712	862	1,002	1,165
Advertising	35,000	2,000	2,000	2,000	2,000	2,000
Travel	391	774	933	1,171	1,394	1,654
Supplies	649	835	971	1,175	1,366	1,589
Insurance	145	560	560	560	560	560
Depreciation	168	535	535	535	535	535
Interest	0	278	278	278	409	409
Total Expenses	$ 50,687	$24,394	$29,289	$ 38,907	$ 49,754	$ 76,515
Profit before Tax	(42,382)	3,442	13,479	23,580	13,728	865
Tax	0	0	0	0	5,805	423
Net Income	$(42,382)	$ 3,442	$13,479	$ 23,580	$ 7,923	$ 442

John's physical condition had caused Katie to become very anxious. She was concerned that John would want to keep the business and literally work himself to death. She was also worried that she could not take the pressure of running the business and taking care of John. Katie wanted to sell the business, and the sooner the better. When she raised the issue with John, he agreed.

Once they decided to sell The Artisan's Haven, John and Katie needed to determine how much the business was worth and if Don Lassiter still wanted to buy it. There were other issues to be considered, too. For example, Lassiter might not be the only potential buyer. How would they contact other people who might be interested in their business?

Although they had gone through the process of selling a business several years before, neither John nor Katie knew much about the intricacies of calculating the value of a firm. They had relied heavily on their accountant, who was a close friend, to help them in that deal. The Owens were very knowledgeable about arts and crafts and people, but not finance.

The more they thought about it, the more they realized that a multitude of decisions had to be made. John told Katie that any buyer would

THE ARTISAN'S HAVEN
Consolidated Balance Sheets
as of January 31, 1986

Assets	1981	1982	1983	1984	1985	1986
Current Assets						
Cash	$ 0	$ 68	$ 5,823	$16,532	$22,018	$20,996
Inventory	$ 18,000	26,262	30,651	35,398	40,782	62,168
Prepaid Expenses	2,089	1,973	1,862	2,239	2,355	2,451
Total Current Assets	$ 20,089	$ 28,303	$ 38,336	$54,169	$65,155	$85,615
Long-Term Assets						
Equipment	$ 4,675	$ 4,675	$ 4,675	$ 5,752	$ 5,752	$ 7,860
Furniture	3,897	3,897	3,897	3,897	3,897	4,623
Less: Accrued Depreciation	168	703	1,238	1,773	2,308	2,843
Total Fixed Assets	8,404	7,869	7,334	7,876	7,341	9,640
Total Assets	$ 28,493	$ 36,172	$ 45,670	$62,045	$72,496	$95,255
Liabilities & Stockholders' Equity						
Current Liabilities						
Current Maturities	$ 278	$ 278	$ 278	$ 278	$ 278	$ 597
Accounts Payable	2,122	7,899	10,211	14,447	17,901	21,870
Accrued Expenses	1,093	1,240	1,829	1,942	2,068	2,189
Total Current Liabilities	$ 3,493	$ 9,417	$ 12,318	$16,667	$20,247	$24,656
Long-Term Debt	47,382	45,695	38,813	27,259	26,207	34,115
Total Liabilities	$ 50,875	$ 55,112	$ 51,131	$43,926	$46,454	$58,771
Stockholders' Equity						
Common Stock	$ 20,000	$ 20,000	$ 20,000	$20,000	$20,000	$30,000
Retained Earnings	(42,382)	(38,940)	(25,461)	(1,881)	6,042	6,484
Total Equity	$(22,382)	$(18,940)	$ (5,461)	$18,119	$26,042	$36,484
Total Liabilities & Equity	$ 28,493	$ 36,172	$ 45,670	$62,045	$72,496	$95,255

• • • • • • •

EXHIBIT 2
Balance Sheet

require them to sign an agreement not to compete. Neither of them objected to that stipulation. Also, there was a question about how much time John and Katie were willing to work with the new owner(s), and in what capacity, after the business was sold. Both of them were uncertain about how to approach this question, and this was not the kind of question they could rely on a financial advisor to answer.

How many more questions would they need to answer? John and Katie did not know.

Year	Quarter	Sales by Quarter	Total Sales	EXHIBIT 3
1981	3	$ 3,246	$ 16,610	Sales by Quarter
	4	13,364		
1982	1	3,080	55,673	
	2	10,397		
	3	4,512		
	4	37,684		
1983	1	5,511	78,736	
	2	17,321		
	3	8,663		
	4	47,241		
1984	1	9,533	105,928	
	2	25,422		
	3	10,595		
	4	60,378		
1985	1	10,021	123,683	
	2	32,033		
	3	14,841		
	4	66,788		
1986	1	12,195	153,186	
	2	44,906		
	3	17,961		
	4	78,124		

QUESTIONS

1. Using the fisCAL software provided, calculate a value for The Artisan's Haven. What weights would you put on each method?
2. Using fisCAL, prepare proformas for the next three years.
3. How will the value of The Artisan's Haven be affected by not having John and Katie involved in the business?
4. Suppose you were representing John and Katie Owen. What price would you ask for The Artisan's Haven? What price would you accept?

B International Learning Corporation

Catherine Ward and Marilyn Taylor

Robert Owen, president of International Learning Corporation, hung up the phone following a conversation with his financial advisor. It was January 1985. His two-year-old company was out of money and he was out of time. A decision regarding the future of ILC had to be made. Owen reviewed the three proposals on his desk from venture capital investors. He was concerned about a number of issues. Which investor/management, if any, would guarantee ILC's future? Which was the best fit with ILC? How much control could he sacrifice and still guide ILC to its full potential? How much was that potential worth? He knew the time had come for him to decide to which group he would entrust his company.

THE ORIGIN OF THE COMPANY

The idea for International Learning Corporation originated while Robert Owen was a doctoral student at Midwestern University in St. Louis. Owen entered Midwestern in 1977 drawn by its reputation in learning theory. He developed an instructional theory that Owen recalled ". . . was a real breakthrough. Members of the faculty, who were leaders in the field, referred to my theory as a 'revolutionary philosophy of education.' "

Owen noted the superior results in his remedial math course sections. Dropout ratios were 5 percent compared to the average of 50 percent across all sections. Owen's students attained A- averages on department wide tests compared to the overall average of 70 percent.

Owen noted that his students did "about three times better on novel items," i.e., sets of questions they had not previously been exposed to, as contrasted to students in other sections. Owen concluded:

This case was prepared by Marilyn Taylor of the University of Kansas and Catherine Ward of Burns and McDonnell Engineering, as the basis for class discussion rather than to illustrate either effective or ineffective handling of a managerial situation. Distributed by the North American Case Research Association. Used with permission. All rights reserved to the authors and the North American Case Research Association. Permission to use the case should be obtained from the authors and the North American Case Research Association.

This ability to migrate or transport learning is important. Some people are able to undertake this generalization process better than others. Thus, the better schools, like Harvard, have a strategy of picking the brighter kids and expecting them to make the generalization or migration of their learning. That's okay if you're a Harvard and can be very selective. But you can't use selection as a general strategy for education because there are only so many people sitting out on that tail end of the distribution. My work in the Remedial Math Department demonstrated that the training process could get the generalization result from run-of-the-mill students. Really, everybody can be educated.

Owen started a consulting firm that would allow him to work with corporate departments of training. His objective was to teach management how to evaluate and measure existing training programs and improve performance and results by applying his learning theory.

In the fall of 1982 Owen sent letters of inquiry to 150 major corporations in the New York area. In the direct mailing, Owen noted that ILC's concepts were based on "more than a dozen field tests conducted with more than ten thousand people throughout the country (in which) the ILC learning system produced:

- seven times faster learning
- three times more retention
- more than two times better transfer of training than all other learning methods."

Furthermore, the piece noted, "ILC can train seven employees in the same time and for the same money you spend on one." Response was very high, with more than one-third of the companies expressing interest in ILC's services. Owen visited twenty of the most promising prospects and began work immediately with one client. He incorporated International Learning Corporation in February 1983.

THE CORPORATE MARKET

ILC's consulting services were based on procedures from Owen's basic research. ILC (1) analyzed corporate training procedures, (2) critiqued data base usage, and (3) edited existing computer-based training (CBT) courses. Based on this analysis, Owen recommended and helped implement reorganization to improve the overall existing training program. ILC was competing against in-house training departments in large corporations, large training companies, and small highly specialized training companies, as well as general consultants.

Owen explained the concept underlying ILC's theory for training:

What we did at ILC was help students/employees develop *fluency* in a subject area through speed and accuracy in response. Fluent knowledge is knowledge that is easily applied. It is essential for greater retention and transfer of training. Fluent knowledge lasts. In fact, it's the only knowledge you'll see people applying long after the training period is ended. It can be compared to the flashcard system used to teach children at early ages. We monitor and record the speed of individual responses, producing fluent knowledge for *every* trainee, *every* course, *every* time.

The positive results from Owen's approach were very clear. For example, Owen noted results with a COBOL programming course for one major company and a telephone operator course for another "reduced learning time by 50 percent and increased mastery by 50 percent." However, Owen encountered opposition to his methodology in the corporate world. Companies were unwilling to enforce the required structured drills on their employees. Owen explained:

> What we were doing was viewed as too revolutionary. It was different from any kind of corporate training that had been used in the past. The executives we dealt with at our client companies felt that it was unacceptable practice for adults. I was very frustrated by this lack of acceptance and forced to consider the alternatives for ILC.

Owen discussed the possibility of merger with several larger consulting firms, to no avail. He felt that the reputation and client base of a large firm would have been advantageous in establishing ILC's methodology in the corporate marketplace. However, large firms found ILC too small and inexperienced to be of interest.

CHANGING MARKETS

By the summer of 1983, Owen concluded that his current noncomputer-based approach had much less opportunity than he anticipated. He continued his current consulting activities, some of which focused on revising existing company courses and others on helping companies evaluate the results from various kinds of training. However, all excess operating revenues were dedicated to developing a software program that would deliver his method of training in a computer-based format. Owen began developing an "authoring system," a sophisticated software package that enabled the user to write, edit, and produce CBT courses. There were a number of authoring systems available for use on most mainframe systems. Some were available for microcomputer systems.

The unique aspect of the CBT courses Owen's authoring system would offer was artificial intelligence (AI) capability. The introduction of AI was a tremendous improvement in CBT technology. No other authoring system yet incorporated artificial intelligence algorithms. AI drastically reduced the decisions made by the author by automatically branching the user to the appropriate lesson. It also reduced the time involved in authoring by creating a set of answers for the author. AI allowed the CBT training programs to adapt to each individual's performance. The CBT program drilled the user repeatedly on important information until mastery was obtained, i.e., the desired level of accuracy and speed in response was achieved. It adjusted the speed at which material was presented to the user to the user's level of performance. Questions to which the user responded correctly and at the designated level of speed were dropped and reintroduced randomly for reinforcement.

The CBT program broke concepts into basic facts. Questions were asked to guarantee that the user learned the basic relationships that comprised the concept. For example, to understand the relationship between

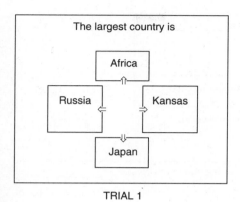

The largest country is

Africa
Russia   Kansas
Japan

TRIAL 1

The largest country is

Russia
Canada   North America
China

TRIAL 2

EXHIBIT 1
Incorrect Answers
Become Closer to Correct
Answer

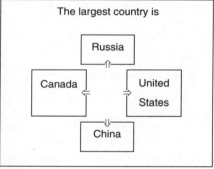

The largest country is

Russia
Canada   United States
China

TRIAL 3

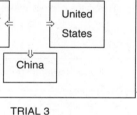

The largest country is
You are correct!
the answer is
RUSSIA

FEEDBACK SCREEN FOR
CORRECT ANSWER

"Ronald Reagan," the "United States," and "president," a series of questions such as the following would be presented:

    Ronald Reagan is president of _____

    The chief executive of the United States is _____

    The president of the United States is _____

The user filled in the answer on the line.

    The program began with multiple-choice questions, where the user only needed to recognize the answer. The multiple-choice questions were presented in a logical order for three runs and then randomized. The position of the multiple-choice answers was randomized each time a question was repeated. The incorrect options became more and more similar to the correct answer as the user's performance improved. (See Exhibit I: Incorrect Answers Become Closer to Correct Answers.) To select an answer, the user pressed the arrow keys.

    Once the trainee answered correctly each multiple-choice question for two consecutive times at the required speed and accuracy level, the trainee proceeded to the highest level of difficulty, fill-in-the-blank questions. To

EXHIBIT II
A Second Chance for
Misspelled Words

> The author of Ulysses is _____
>
>
> James Jiyce _____
>
> (fill in your answer on the line above.)

The answer is misspelled

> The author of Ulysses is _____
>
>
> Your answer wasn't spelled correctly
> please retype
>
>
> James Joyce _____
>
>
> (fill in your answer on the line above.)
>
> CORRECT

If you answer correctly

> The author of Ulysses is _____
>
>
> Jomes Joyce _____
>
> (fill in your answer on the line above.)
>
>
>
> JAMES JOYCE _____
>
> This is the correct answer

If you answer incorrectly again

avoid inappropriate instruction due to misspelled words, the program asked the user to retype the answer when it appeared to be misspelled. (See Exhibit II: A Second Chance For Misspelled Words.)

Users received immediate feedback for correct and incorrect answers. If the response was correct, the question and answer appeared on the screen along with the statement "You are correct!" If the response was incorrect, the question and the user's answer, marked over by a large X, appeared on the screen. On the same screen, the feedback statement read "The correct answer is _____" The correct answer was displayed in large, bold letters. If the question was not answered within the time limit, then the correct answer was shown along with the message, "Out of Time". If the correct answer slightly exceeded the time limit, the user received the feedback, "Your answer is correct but out of time."

Owen called his authoring system that produced these CBT courses *Learn!* He described the program:

> It was really a data base program. The data base contained questions and information relating to those questions such as graphical materials. The data base had a set of eight correct and incorrect answers that had a hierarchy of incorrectness. Different combinations of these answers were presented to the student depending on his or her current level of mastery. For example, early

on when the student was not very fluent with the material, the set of answers would have greater spread of incorrectness. Later, the set of wrong answers presented would be less distinguishable from the right one.

The program kept a tremendous data base on student performance. Based on this data the program made the decision regarding what to present to the student, in what order, how, and at what speed. Thus, each course diskette became personalized. The longer a person used the disk the more the system knew about that person's ability and thus, it adjusted the system to produce better learning. In addition, the instructor established criteria such as the targeted level of mastery. *Learn!* offered more results from its system with less human input than anything on the market at the time. The system took over a great deal of responsibility for the presentation and delivery. And its decisions were based on good measurement.

In some ways *Learn!* was like a word processor that was so sophisticated it could help you put a whole course together. In fact, the system was like a programming language where the person designing a course could uniquely program for each student.

As a result, our system *Learn!* produced much better learning. It also cut course development costs by as much as 80 percent. I'm not sure any of the venture capital companies fully comprehend this key factor.

I'm not sure it's even wise to call it an authoring system. I mean, it's really unique. If we list it in the annual evaluation of authoring systems, its strengths will not really be demonstrated because the criteria are either unnecessary or automatically handled by *Learn!*

CBT was relatively new in the area of management training. With the continuing trend toward a service-oriented economy, the size of the corporate training industry had grown to approximately $100 billion and was continuing to grow steadily at a 14 percent rate. Of this total, 80 percent was spent on seminars and other traditional training methods compared to 2 percent on computer-based training. The remainder was spent on miscellaneous training methods and tools. (See Exhibit III: Corporate Market Penetration.)

Owen explained his strategy for ILC:

We plan to create generic computer-based training courses to get into the market. The customer base is very large—small and medium-sized companies that don't have the money to spend on custom training. We look at this market segment as a "cash cow" for ILC. Once we establish a position and bring in sales revenue, we will be able to offer custom programming to major corporations and sell ILC's authoring system too. Our biggest potential profits are in the custom market.

	1984	1985*	1986*	1987*	1988*	EXHIBIT III
Total business training	100	114	130	150	169	Corporate Market Penetration (Billions $)
CBT component	1.75	2	3.3	4.6	7	
Micro CBT	.87	1	2	3.1	5	SOURCE: Future Computing, Talmis, International Data Corporation, McGraw Hill, Predicasts, Yankee Group

*Estimates

The "courseware" market for CBT was extremely fragmented. There were no standard pricing levels and no acknowledged leader in the industry. Owen analyzed the competition in the market on the basis of industry position, product offering, and financial strength. Competitors ranged from small courseware-only companies to industry giants that offered both authoring system and customer services. (See Exhibit IV: Competitor Profile Data.)

. . . .

EXHIBIT IV
CBT Training Competition Groups

	Year Established	1984 Revenues (Millions $)	System Type	Training Products	International	Pricing
Companies That Produce Generic Courseware						
ATI	1981	3.5	micro	45 CBT courses	no	$40–$80/course
ASI	1968	40.7	micro, mini, mainframe	75 CBT courses	yes	Rent, license or buy; $80–$90/course
THOUGHTWARE	1983	NA	micro	11 CBT courses	no	$3,495 library; $350–$450/course
HUMAN EDGE	1983	2.3	pc	3 CBT courses	no	$50–$695/course
Companies That Do Not Have Their Own Authoring System But Produce Custom Courseware for Other Companies Using Customer's Authoring System						
DELTAK	1970	88.2	micro, mainframe	26 CBT courses	yes	$70/course
CDEX	1982	10	pc, mini	50 CBT courses	no	$40–$350/course
Companies That Sell Their Own Authoring System and Produce Custom Courseware for Other Companies						
GOAL	1975	10	mainframe, micro	Phoenix** generic course-ware	no	System $15,000–$38,500; $1,370–$9,086/course
ADR	NA	89	mainframe	ADROIT** CBT courseware	yes	Permanent license $20,000
LEARNCOM	1974	NA		SAM**	yes	Annual license $3,500–$6,500/year
SPECTRUM	1979	5	micro	The Educator** 11 CBT courses	no	System $3,500/year, $99/course, Series $870
GRWTH	1981	NA	mainframe	16 CBT courses	no	Annual license $2,000–$4,500/year perpetual licenses $5,000–$13,500
IBM	1911	51,500	pc, mini, mainframe	11S, PCIS**	yes	Perpetual license $1,100
Apple	1976	1,516	pc	Pilot, Super Pilot**	yes	$250/course
AT&T	1885	33,188	pc	Unix**	yes	System $5,000–$7,000
McGraw Hill	1925	1,400	micro, mainframe	4 generic CBT courses	yes	System $1,500; $30–$350/course

**Indicates proprietary authoring system.

Purchase of courseware was strongly influenced by the hardware base of the customer. Although computer-based training courses were originally developed for the mainframe market, Owen's goal for ILC was to produce the highest quality courseware available for microcomputers. His research indicated that the microcomputer market was growing more rapidly than the mainframe market. Indeed, in 1983 there were $19.6 billion in sales for micros as opposed to $16 billion for mainframes. The proposed product line from ILC would be the Mercedes of the micro market—it would set a new standard for high performance and high quality.

THE DEVELOPMENT OF ILC COURSEWARE AND LEARN!

Owen targeted a number of vertical markets for further in-depth analysis including telecommunications, financial services, insurance, health care, and publishing. Industries with high potential for ILC's products exhibited certain characteristics. Companies within these high-potential industries allocated large training budgets and targeted human resource development as a key success factor. Technologies were changing rapidly, producing fast-growing and highly volatile markets with high employee turnover. In addition, the companies were microcomputer users and familiar with applications of computer-based training within the industry.

Owen described the situation at ILC: "We had spent months on research and market development. It was fall of 1983 and we were getting desperate. We had wasted a lot of time. The competition and the market had nearly doubled. ILC had to establish its position as the premier product line on the market as soon as possible." Although the development of the authoring system was underway, the time required for completion put the company at a definite disadvantage. There were a number of competing authoring systems that he could use, but none produced the level of results Owen desired. The degree of modification required to upgrade an existing system would also be time consuming and expensive. As a result of the effort required to build the authoring system, Owen's consulting activities slipped to a minimal level.

Owen's decision for an all-out effort to develop *Learn!* required ILC to add personnel and accelerate development of the prototype. The first employee Owen hired for ILC was Madelaine Caillard. Madelaine described ILC at this stage:

I was a graduate student in Owen's department at the university. In the fall of 1982 I helped him implement the first direct mail effort for ILC. There was no money available to pay me any kind of salary until May of 1983. ILC had received payment on a consulting contract and obtained a small amount of local financing. Even then, compensation was meager. I have worked for $500 a month for the past two years.

In August of 1983 Owen hired Ruth. She was a doctoral student in his graduate department at the university. I think Ruth received $700 a month. She worked with Owen to produce client work and develop new business. About the same time he hired our first programmer to work on the authoring system prototype. Ralph was paid on some kind of contingency schedule—when consulting fees came in, he received a check. I know sometimes he has gone three to four months without being paid.

Two other staff members have been added since to help with office administration and market research. We have all been paid very low salaries, but
money hasn't been our motivation. We're just out of school. We believe in
Owen's vision for the company and share his desire to revolutionize the educational process across the country. We saw Steven Jobs' huge success at
Apple and have been very optimistic about ILC's prospects. People our age
have become millionaires. We are getting in on the ground level and there will
be equity for our commitment to the company during its developmental stages.
This ownership is very important to all of us. We have worked very hard to
develop specifications for the authoring system. It is our future.

By the end of 1983 the company was seriously undercapitalized. It was
clear that ILC could not complete the *Learn!* prototype and necessary testing without raising investment capital. In fall 1984 Owen reflected:

From the very beginnings of my research and the inception of my theory, I
have always considered ILC "mine." Now, I have to raise investment capital
without the prototype. This situation almost certainly means giving up a large
percentage of equity in my company. Otherwise ILC will be dead.

I'm just not prepared for that to happen. I am determined that ILC survive. I was able to borrow enough working capital from my family and friends
to keep ILC going through the summer of 1984. During this period I've spent
most of my time writing a business plan for ILC and learning more about the
market and pricing structures. Revenues from consulting slipped to almost
nothing and our expenditures on product development keep increasing. I have
to find a more permanent source of investment capital for ILC soon.

THE VENTURE CAPITAL COMPANIES

In August 1984 Owen completed a business plan and sent letters to forty
venture capital firms. (See Exhibit V: Excerpts from Business Plan.) Ten
companies originally expressed interest in funding ILC. Owen screened
the companies based on the amount of funding offered, amount of equity
demanded, expertise in startup companies and the microcomputer industry in particular, and compatibility in management style and philosophy.
Owen commented on the results, "Three of the companies appeared to
meet our expectations and presented offers to ILC. I had to decide which
source of capital was the best for ILC, and at the same time offered the best
deal for me."

The following paragraphs briefly summarize the three venture capital
proposals.

National Securities, Inc., approached ILC with an offer of $500,000 to
$700,000 for 40 percent equity. NSI was a one-hundred-year-old West
Coast brokerage firm, well known for its experience and successful support
of startup companies. They had extensive expertise in software and knowledge of ILC's product/market. NSI had no regional preference with regard
to the location of companies it funded. NSI proposed a "hands off" management situation, leaving Owen to manage ILC and bring the product to
the market. Under the NSI proposal a public stock offering would be made
as soon as possible, which would raise the desired capital but would require detailed disclosure of the technology and increase the burden on

A. The Company's Financial Status

Assets	$52,000
Cash in bank	20,000
Accounts receivable	10,500
TOTAL ASSETS	**$82,500**
Accounts payable	$ 2,500
Notes payable	12,500
Bank loans and leases	8,000
TOTAL LIABILITIES	**$23,000**
SHAREHOLDERS' EQUITY	**$59,000**

B. Expected Use of Funds

The company is seeking $400,000 for 10 percent of the company's equity. Organizations and individuals providing funds in Phase 1 would have the right of first refusal in the next fund-raising round and an option to sell their stock in a public underwriting (planned for 1987–88). The company will apply the funds as follows:

Back wages owed to key personnel	$100,000
Computer programming and software development	100,000
Salaries	100,000
Marketing and direct-mail advertising	75,000
Equipment leasing	15,000
Overhead and office expenses	10,000

C. Expected Revenues, January to June 1985

Authoring system licensing fees	$125,000
General consultation	50,000
Custom program development	50,000
Advanced from publishers	75,000
	$300,000

D. Financial Projections

Revenue in Millions of Dollars

	1985	1986	1987	1988	1989
Generic courses	0.2	2.5	9.3	16.9	21.7
Authoring systems	0.3	1.8	4.2	5.5	7.8
Custom contracts	0.1	1.4	3.3	4.1	5.0
Disk usage/royalty	0.0	2.2	14.7	42.0	84.6
Total revenue	0.6	7.9	31.5	68.5	119.1
Pretax profit	(1.1)	1.6	12.6	32.7	60.8
Percentage of revenues	N/A	20.2	40.0	47.7	50.3

EXHIBIT V
Excerpts From ILC's
Business Plan

E. The Company's Objectives

The company's primary objectives are:

1. To be recognized by 1986 as one of the five most knowledgeable and influential companies providing microcomputer-based training and education.
2. To be recognized by 1988 as the absolute leader in learning technology and the producer of the most effective learning programs in the industry.
3. To achieve by 1990 $200 million in sales volume and a minimum 25 percent profit before tax.
4. To maintain more than 30 percent return on equity.

The company's management is confident the company can achieve the above objectives because:

1. Microcomputer use is expected to expand throughout society.
2. The worldwide market for goods and services that develop human resources will continue to grow rapidly.
3. The company has the advantage of a proprietary technology, and the personnel and skills needed to strengthen and maintain this advantage for six to ten years.

Marketing Plan, 1985–86

1. Publicize products by conducting workshops and demonstrations at regional conventions and by publishing articles.
2. Convince customers in the computer-based training and education fields of the company's product advantages through published articles and research findings and conference presentations.
3. Establish relations with leaders in several major industries.
4. Direct-mail campaign targeting Fortune 500 companies in the San Francisco and New York metropolitan areas.
5. By 1986 develop sufficiently strong client bases in New York and San Francisco to open marketing offices. In 1986 target Dallas/Houston and Chicago areas for intense direct mail advertising; open offices there in 1987. Target three cities per year until fifteen U.S. sales offices are established by 1990.
6. Support direct-mail advertising with advertising in *Training and Development Journal* and vertical industry (i.e., banking, real estate) magazines.
7. Establish six Fortune 500 sites for the company's products by 1985; thirty by 1986.
8. Develop popular generic training programs; e.g., planning, supervision, leadership, sales training, decision making, time management and Japanese management.
9. Develop HRD support training programs; e.g., scheduling, accounting, training program evaluation, and decision making.

Marketing Plan, 1987 and Beyond

1. To major companies, sell a library of generic computer-based training (CBT) products packaged with a license for the authoring system. In this way, clients who employ in-house course designers can convert their existing training programs to CBT and customize the generic products to meet their specific needs. As part of the package, the company's instructional design experts will train the client to use the authoring system and provide consultation.
2. To smaller companies, sell only generic CBT with the minimum required support services.

Leading companies will buy from the company because:

1. Industry leaders look for state-of-the-art products for all aspects of their business.
2. Their well-trained HRD staffs are most likely to recognize the shortcomings of other CBT products.

. . . .

EXHIBIT V
(continued)

3. Most CBT vendors do not offer customized CBT or support services, such as training and consultation in the use of their authoring systems. Yet market research indicates that leading corporations are shopping for both these advantages.

4. The company's authoring system embodies an instructional design that has proved itself superior to all the most tested instructional methods and the fastest and easiest to use.

5. In a recent survey, trainers expressed their reasons for not implementing CBT. Their strongest objections were to the time it took to create courseware using currently available authoring systems and the lack of instructional expertise possessed by authoring system programmers. Our program directly addresses these difficulties.

Second-tier companies will buy the company's generic CBT because:

1. The company's generic CBT will outshine all others in quality.
2. It will be reasonably priced.
3. It will be easy to use.
4. Employees will like using it.
5. For a small charge, the company will customize it for the client.
6. The second tier will follow the industry leaders, who will be using the company products.
7. Second-tier companies will be targeted for intensive direct-mail and public campaigns.

EXHIBIT V
(concluded)

Owen's management to handle investor relations and lengthy reporting procedures.

Howard Farrell was a well-connected independent venture capitalist who proposed putting together a syndicate of investors that would back a $500,000 to $1,000,000 research and development contract in exchange for 20 percent equity plus a portion of royalties resulting from product sale (up to five times the original investment amount) with provision to convert to warrants and options. Farrell had no direct knowledge of the training and software markets, but was highly respected in the Silicon Valley community in Southern California and would relocate Owen and ILC to that area. Under Farrell's proposal the company would remain private with Farrell assuming an active role in management. The terms of the loan required a short payback period that could be a burden to ILC financially and a disincentive to other investors during that time.

Taylor Consulting Associates offered ILC the largest contract: $2 million to $2.5 million for 80 percent equity. Located in Denver, TCA was a mid-size company that provided technical consulting and training in engineering and the semiconductor market. TCA had little or no experience in software start-ups, but would provide strong management expertise and resources in other areas where required. This arrangement would allow Owen to concentrate his time almost entirely on the development of the product. TCA expressed no regional preference; ILC would be located wherever conditions were most favorable for its development and growth. TCA also offered a valuable network of connections across the United States and Europe, including key people within the trade and senior management of major prospect companies. TCA proposed a public stock issue to help fund ILC after three to five years of growth and development.

QUESTIONS

1. Which of the three venture capitalists' proposals should Owen accept? What are the significant differences between the proposals?
2. How much equity should Owen be willing to give up?
3. How should Owen structure the deal in order to maintain operation control?
4. What is your assessment of *Learn!?* Does it have the potential Owen thinks it does?

Doorstep Video, Inc.

John Dunkelberg and Robert Anderson

BACKGROUND

The growth of the video and electronic industry had always interested twenty-one-year-old Clay Lindsay. Clay was more than one year away from finishing his education, and he planned to start and run his own business after graduation. He constantly thought about different business ventures that he felt could be profitable. He also wanted to start a business that had never been tried before. While on winter break, Clay came up with an idea for what he thought could be a very successful business venture—a video rental store that delivered movies, similar to the established pizza delivery service.

Clay discussed this idea with his parents and close friends. They criticized the concept and doubted that such a business could be profitable. Clay's father, who had owned and operated a drugstore in downtown Salisbury, North Carolina, for over thirty years, was one of those who doubted its profitability. He thought that Clay should finish his education before becoming involved in a new, time-consuming business venture. Clay, however, did find support from a couple of friends. One, Brent Snipes, whom Clay had known for about eight years, was very interested and recommended that they pursue the idea as a team. Brent would graduate from college that May, although Clay would not finish for another year.

Brent and Clay planned to start the business in June, with Brent controlling the everyday operations; Clay could come home when necessary since there was only a forty-five minute drive between college and home.

NAME AND LOGO

The two budding entrepreneurs immediately began to brainstorm for ideas on what to name the business, and Clay came up with the name Doorstep

This case was prepared by John Dunkelberg, Wake Forest University, and Robert Anderson, College of Charleston. It is intended as a basis for classroom discussion rather than to illustrate effective or ineffective handling of a business situation. Used with permission.

Video. After discussing other possibilities, they adopted Doorstep Video as a name that was easy to remember and one that conveyed the concept of what the business would be.

The next step, the design of a logo, took the two planners a little longer. They wanted a logo that would stick in the minds of their customers and one they would be proud to display. They decided that red and white would be the store colors, as they felt these very dominant colors would demand attention. Brent and Clay felt details like this were necessary to project a professional image. In particular, Clay wanted this store to be an independent store that operated with the efficiency of a chain store.

LOCATION

The next order of business was to determine where to locate the business. Brent and Clay had lived in Salisbury, North Carolina, all of their lives and felt that the contacts they had established in the area would be a major factor in the success of their planned business. Clay's father owned the building in the downtown shopping district that housed his drugstore. Clay was able to convince his father to rent them a small vacant space in the back of the building that was completely separate from the drugstore.

Brent and Clay knew that they must establish a basic plan of operation, including name, location, and a business plan, in order to gain the support of their parents. This would be a key to the success of their new business. After evaluating the preliminary steps the two had taken, Clay's parents seemed a little more positive about the idea than they had been at first. Brent's parents, however, remained very skeptical, and Brent decided not to pursue the business venture.

Clay, who strongly believed in the idea, continued to develop a business plan by learning more about the video industry. He conducted an extensive search of the existing literature using a computer data-based search program located at the college library. Although the number of existing articles on the videotape rental industry were few in number, Clay found several articles that gave him some ideas about the industry, the competition, and what the future might be like. A capsule summary and his findings indicated that the industry was passing from the pioneering stage into the fast-growth stage, and the future seemed to belong to the large, well-funded chain stores that would contain thousands of titles. In addition, he spent many hours visiting existing video stores to see what features they had that he liked.

About two months later, during his spring semester, Clay mentioned his idea to a fraternity brother, Garret Barnes, whom he had known for about two years. Garret thought the idea was worthwhile and something with which he would like to become associated. Like Brent, Garret would graduate in May and would be able to begin work on a full-time basis. Clay had already developed a preliminary business plan that included an estimate of the startup costs. These figures indicated that an investment of approximately $14,000 was required to open the doors. After talking with their parents, Garret and Clay decided to explore the business venture further.

THE ENTREPRENEURS

Clay Lindsay, from Salisbury, was a business major at a nearby private university. He was active in his fraternity and had always been interested in assuming leadership positions. His goals were to be self-employed and to start a business that offered a better product or service than its competitors. He also wanted to establish a business that was interesting and that had the potential for rapid growth. Clay's business experience involved working at his father's retail drugstore and gift shop. He began janitorial work there when he was twelve. He was soon handling everyday functions, such as personnel management, special promotions, the purchasing of imported goods, and advertising. Clay later managed the gift shop for his father during the holiday season.

Garret Barnes, a twenty-two year old native of Florida, was active in the student legislature and intramurals, and he served in leadership positions within his fraternity. Garret's interests included competitive sports and other extracurricular activities. His goal was to start his own company, which he could develop and nurture to a point that it would yield healthy returns for this future.

Before his involvement with Clay, Garret had no business experience; however, he was completing his bachelor of science degree in business. Garret thought this opportunity suited his needs perfectly and that it had the potential for a good career. He made friends easily and worked hard to make a good first impression on the people he met. In his fraternity, Garret was known as a hard worker and one who handled public relations very well.

VIDEO INDUSTRY

During the latter part of the 1970s, videocassette recorders (VCRs) became popular. By the end of 1980, approximately two million homes had VCRs. At that time, the national sales rate of videocassette recorders was only seventeen thousand units per month; but, by 1981, VCR sales rose to more than 140,000 units per month. In 1984, nearly seventy and a half million VCRs were sold, and by the end of the year VCRs were in 20 percent of the homes in America. By the end of 1987, 52 percent of American homes had at least one VCR.[1]

The rise in VCR sales was enhanced by an increase in the availability of prerecorded cassettes. In the late 1970s, the thought of selling prerecorded cassettes to consumers frightened the major movie and television studios in the United States. Many were afraid revenues from both television and movie theaters would be greatly decreased as viewers turned from movies and television to cassette tapes. However, a small number of studios decided to gamble on the idea of selling prerecorded cassettes to the home viewer. In the spring of 1978, there were only about one hundred prerecorded cassettes available through studio distributors.

After some thorough market research, several other studios decided to enter the market. The market research indicated that consumers preferred renting prerecorded cassette tapes to buying by a margin of seven to one. At that time, cassette tapes sold for about $50 and rented for about $5 per day. Since then the cost of renting videotapes has dropped from $5 per day to as low as $1 per day. This, of course, was caused by the increased competition within the industry. On the other hand, the price of prerecorded cassettes has risen to as much as $70 and sometimes even higher for the biggest hits.

The home video market changed rapidly. Rental and sales outlets seemed to pop up in every shopping area. The industry enjoyed incredible growth over the next five years, but with growth came change. When home video first started, there were two formats available, Beta and VHS. Beta and VHS competed with each other in software and hardware and neither was interchangeable with the other—if you bought a Beta VCR then you could only show Beta tapes and vice versa. However, over the past several years, the VHS format became the dominant choice of consumers, and Beta now accounts for only a small percentage of the market. At first, many video stores handled both the VHS and Beta software; however, today it is almost impossible to find a Beta rental store.

In 1983, eleven million prerecorded videocassettes were sold to retailers. By 1984 that number rose 100 percent to twenty-two million cassette tapes. As a result, rental stores can offer a large selection of titles. The smaller stores carry as few as five hundred titles, while the superstores may have ten thousand or more titles for the consumer to select from. Today, the average video specialty store carries about two thousand six hundred different titles.[2]

The prerecorded cassettes are divided into two categories, "A" and "B" titles. The "A" titles are the "hit" videos and the most costly to produce. The "B" titles are those that are lesser known and are considered budget films. Examples of "A" titles would be *Top Gun* or *Fatal Attraction*; "B" titles would include *Creepozoids* or *The Curse*. Since the "B" titles were less expensive than the "A" titles, video rental stores did not have to rent them as often as the "A" titles to earn a profit. In the United States, the average number of rentals (per tape) for an "A" title was 108 and for a "B" title was sixty-two.

The videotape rental industry was one of the nation's fastest growing and one of the most fragmented. Nationwide, there were more than twenty-five thousand video rental stores, mostly small entrepreneurial-type operations. In addition, there were about thirty-two thousand rental outlets, such as convenience stores, that rented videotapes as a sidelight to their major business. These rental outlets usually carried only the newer movies, which they received three to four weeks after the release date, and stocked less than 250 titles.

As often happens in fast-growth industries, a shakeout seemed inevitable. Chain stores had started to exert pressure on the smaller and undercapitalized stores, and the growth of the superstore chains, carrying more than six thousand five hundred titles, seemed to be just around the corner.[3]

BUSINESS PLAN

Clay and Garret planned to operate their business in the back of a warehouse owned by Clay's father. Since they planned to take telephone orders for rental tape deliveries, the only space requirement was space for the storage of tapes and enough room for the order taker and the driver. The existing warehouse area would require the construction of some walls to create a separate area for Doorstep Video's operations. (For store layout see Exhibit 1.) The rental business would operate much like a pizza delivery service, with customers calling and placing orders for videotapes, which would be delivered in thirty minutes or less. The planned hours of operation were Monday through Friday from 4 P.M. until midnight and Saturday and Sunday from noon until midnight.

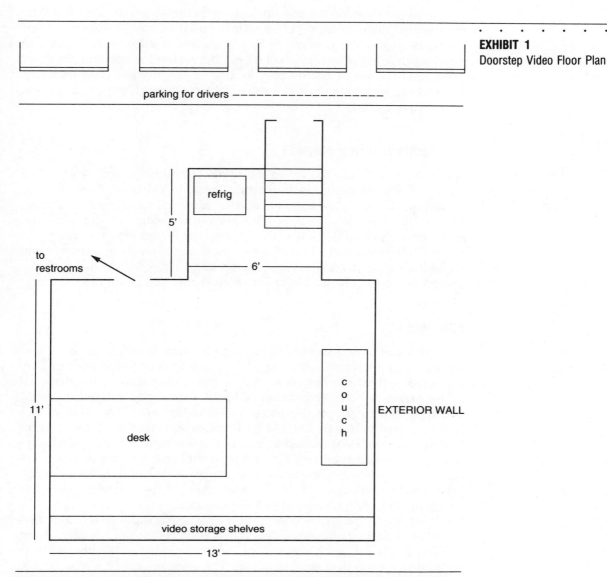

EXHIBIT 1
Doorstep Video Floor Plan

Note: All interior walls will be added by Clay and Garret to minimize cost. Total cost of the project will be $400.

Clay and Garret also planned to deliver popcorn and soft drinks along with the videos to allow customers to receive some of the full effect of a movie theater without leaving their homes. Videos would be returned by the customer to one of four return boxes positioned strategically throughout the town. The videos would be delivered by part-time drivers, who could make approximately seven deliveries per hour. Drivers (students from a local small private college) would be paid the minimum wage of $4.25 per hour plus an incentive rate of 40 cents per delivery. Clay and Garret thought that, by delivering the videos, the possibility for theft should decrease since they would actually know the customer's correct address.

Although they did not attempt any marketing research, Clay and Garret saw the potential for rapid growth in rental videotape delivery. Their goal was to test the concept in Salisbury, and if successful, expand to locations in other relatively small cities. The reason for operating in small cities was that major chains only located in larger cities, and Doorstep Video could gain strength in the video industry through growth in the less competitive markets.

SALISBURY'S VIDEO MARKET

Salisbury, a small city located in the center of North Carolina, had a population of about twenty-five thousand. Doorstep Video's delivery area included the city and a few areas outside the city, with a total market of about twenty-eight thousand people. The per capita income in this area was approximately $10,000, while the average total household income was $28,000. Currently there were fourteen video rental stores in Salisbury and an additional fourteen convenience stores and other outlets that rented a small selection of videos. No major video chains had located in Salisbury.

PURCHASING

A major factor to consider in any business is where to obtain merchandise. Since he was interested in buying used as well as new videocassettes, Clay contacted several sources across the country. One source, International Movie Merchants (IMM) in Dallas, Oregon, was a used video distributor, and it agreed to supply Doorstep Video. IMM sent Clay a list of five hundred used videos that would be available and suitable to the needs of Doorstep Video. IMM quoted a price of $13,000 for the five hundred videos, for an average cost of $26. After several changes, the list was approved. According to Clay, never settle for paying what the seller is asking; therefore, the bargaining process began. After a short time the cost was finally agreed upon and set at $20.30 per video.

Doorstep Video also needed a source for new releases. Baker and Taylor Video, a major nationwide distributor, soon became that source. Baker and Taylor provided weekly catalogs, which included all the new releases scheduled for the next several weeks. The average cost of a new release was $65 plus shipping, which usually added another $3. Garret later found another source, Schwartz Brothers, which offered savings of $1 to $2 per video, but shipping costs remained approximately $3. Schwartz Brothers also offered weekly catalogs, which included all the new releases and some special deals.

A key to buying new releases is knowing how many of each title to purchase. Garret took on this task, which included a lot of guesswork. The only thing he could do was base purchases on how similar titles had sold in the past and on how popular the title had been in the theater. Interestingly, Garret's research indicated that what was popular in the theater was not always a popular rental. On the other hand, some titles that were sleepers in the theater were in high demand in the rental stores. There seemed to be no real formula to use when buying new releases. However, there is a lot of gut feeling involved in the selection process. Doorstep Video set its new release budget at $1,500 per month. Since there are not returns on opened merchandise, if Doorstep Video bought too many of a new release it could only sell the used video to a used video distributor like IMM. Unfortunately, these distributors purchase the video for about one-third of its original cost.

Doorstep Video also needed a source for the purchase of VCRs suitable for renting and for the plastic cases, which were needed as protective carrying cases for the videos. Commtron, a major distributor in Atlanta, was contacted, and it offered to sell Doorstep Videos the rental-type VCRs for $239 each. The plastic cases could be purchased at prices that ranged from $0.49 to $0.55 each, depending on the quantity ordered.

INVENTORY SYSTEM

The inventory system used by Doorstep Video would be an index card system. Each video would have a card, which would be placed in the out file when the movie was rented. The customer's number would be written on the card as well as the date rented. This was not the most advanced or efficient system; however, due to lack of funds, a computer system seemed out of the question.

As should be expected in a new technology-oriented industry, several very complete computer software inventory programs were available for video rental stores. Interestingly, one of the best in the nation was produced and sold by a firm located in Salisbury. These systems are capable of handling forty thousand members and 100,000 videos. All transactions are handled by a bar code reader, which makes the system efficient and accurate. The systems created statistics, such as customers with debit balances; rentals per day, month, and year; rentals by customer; rentals per title; and many other management features. The cost for a system, including the computer and printer, was about $5,500.

FINANCING, LEGAL, AND INSURANCE

The total startup cost for Doorstep Video was estimated to be about $15,500 (see Exhibit 2). Based on an estimate of daily rentals, Clay and Garret estimated weekly rentals of 513 titles over the first three months (see Exhibit 3). Rental price was $2.99 for one title and $2.50 each for two or more

EXHIBIT 2
Startup Costs

Inventory	
500 used videos	$10,150
New videos	1,500
Rental VCRs, 2 at $239	478
Opening advertising	
Flyer insert	450
Printing	416
Newspaper ads	198
Furniture and equipment	900
Leasehold improvements	400
Return boxes: 4 at $50	200
Insurance	300
Shirts for employees	170
Telephone installation	95
Office supplies	60
Plastic cases for videotapes	73
Licenses	60
Legal and professional costs	49
Total startup costs	$15,499

EXHIBIT 3
Distribution of Sales by Day

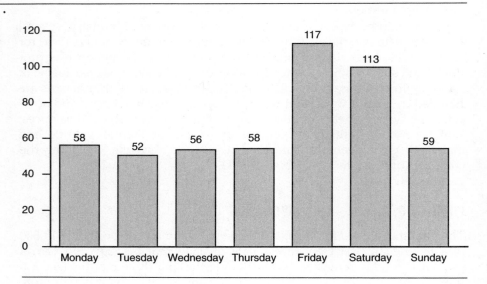

Monday 58, Tuesday 52, Wednesday 56, Thursday 58, Friday 117, Saturday 113, Sunday 59

Videos	$1,500	
Gross payroll	1,100	
Advertising	300	
Taxes	370	
Telephone	115	
Rent and utilities	100	
Miscellaneous expenses	120	
Insurance	30	
Total projected monthly expenses	$3,635	

EXHIBIT 4
Projected Monthly Expenses

titles. Based on what they had observed in other stores and from what they had read in *Video Store*, a trade magazine, Clay estimated that the revenue from the average rental would be $2.63. In addition, they estimated that they could rent the VCRs on an average of seven times per week, at $5 per day. Monthly expenses were estimated to be $3,635 (see Exhibit 4). During the first year of operation, Garret, who would be managing the store, would receive $700 a month salary, and Clay, who would be working only part-time, would not receive any compensation. Any profits would be used to purchase additional inventory. To finance the start-up and leave funds available to cover any possible cash flow problems over the startup period, Clay and Garret each agreed to put up $10,400 from their personal savings.

Due to the potential liability problem, Clay and Garret thought they should organize Doorstep Video as an S corporation. This form of business allows small businesses to enjoy the limited liability benefits of the corporate form of organization yet obtain the benefits of being taxed as a partnership. They talked to an attorney, who agreed to handle the necessary incorporation paperwork for only $49. In addition, a membership application form was designed to provide a measure of protection for Doorstep Video and serve as a contract between Doorstep and its customers (see Exhibit 5).

Clay talked to a local insurance agent about the coverage that would be needed by Doorstep Video. The agent recommended a comprehensive policy that would cover the contents of the store in the amount of $30,000 in case of fire or water damage. Theft insurance was not included. In addition, the drivers were covered by a rider, which provided Doorstep Video with liability insurance for any claim that was in excess of the liability coverage from the driver's own insurance—since the drivers would use their own cars for deliveries.

DECISION TIME

During the last week in April, with the spring semester almost complete, Clay and Garret must make a decision on whether to go ahead with the start-up of Doorstep Video or abandon their plans. They have contacted

EXHIBIT 5
Membership Application

(for office use only)
APPROVAL#______/________
TYPED________________
VERIFIED________________
MEMBERSHIP #____________

APPLICATION FOR MEMBERSHIP

DATE:

(PLEASE PRINT)
NAME____
(LAST) **(FIRST)** **(MIDDLE INITIAL)**

STREET ADDRESS____

____

CITY____________________**STATE**_______**ZIP CODE**____________

TELEPHONE: HOME______________OFFICE________________

DRIVER'S LICENSE: STATE______NUMBER__________EXP. DATE________

SOCIAL SECURITY #________________________________

EMPLOYER____________________**DEPT.**________________

RELATIVE NAME______________**TELEPHONE**______________
(NOT LIVING AT SAME ADDRESS AS ABOVE)

ADDITIONAL FAMILY MEMBERS ALLOWED TO RENT VIDEO TAPES AND/OR EQUIPMENT ON THIS MEMBERSHIP:
(MEMBER IS RESPONSIBLE FOR ACTIVITY OF ADDITIONAL RENTERS)

ADULTS

____

____

CHILDREN **AGE**

____

____

____

ARE CHILDREN ALLOWED TO RENT "R" (OR NR) MOVIES? YES NO

TOTAL NUMBER OF CARDS REQUESTED __________(MAXIMUM 4)

APPLICANT'S SIGNATURE:________________________________
BEFORE SIGNING THIS APPLICATION SEE REVERSE SIDE FOR TERMS AND CONDITIONS.

ACCEPTED FOR DOORSTEP VIDEO:________________

AGREEMENT & CONDITIONS OF MEMBERSHIP

EXHIBIT 5 (concluded)

AFTER DOORSTEP VIDEO, INC., ACCEPTS APPLICATION FOR MEMBERSHIP THIS APPLICATION CONSTITUTES AN AGREEMENT BETWEEN DOORSTEP VIDEO, INC., AND MEMBER REGARDING MEMBER'S ACCOUNT.

MEMBER AGREES:

TO PAY ALL PROPERLY AUTHORIZED CHARGES ON MEMBER'S ACCOUNT WHEN THEY BECOME DUE.

TO RETURN ALL RENTED TAPES AND/OR EQUIPMENT TO THE DOORSTEP VIDEO FROM WHICH THEY WERE RENTED, ON TIME, OR PAY THE APPROPRIATE LATE CHARGES.

TO REWIND ALL RENTED TAPES OR PAY THE APPROPRIATE REWIND FEE—OUR NORMAL POLICY IS TO PERMIT ONE OR TWO UNREWOUND TAPES AT NO CHARGE—AFTER THAT WE ASSESS REWIND CHARGES ON THE MEMBER'S ACCOUNT.

TO RETURN VIDEOCASSETTES IN THE SAME CONDITION AS WHEN THEY WERE OBTAINED. IF, WHEN RETURNED, THE CARTRIDGE OF A "SALE OR RENT" VIDEOCASSETTE, IN WHCH THE TAPE IS ENCLOSED, IS BROKEN OR SMASHED, THE MEMBER WILL BE REQUIRED TO PAY THE RENTAL FEE AND THEN BUY THE VIDEOCASSETTE BY PAYING THE PRICE SHOWN ON THE INVENTORY. IN THE CASE OF A RENTAL-ONLY VIDEOCASSETTE RETURNED WITH A BROKEN CARTRIDGE, THE MEMBER WILL PAY THE COST OF THE CASSETTE AS DAMAGES, PAY THE RENTAL FEES, AND RETURN THE VIDEOCASSETTE TO THE STORE.

IF A VIDEOCASSETTE HAS BEEN TAMPERED WITH, I.E., CARTRIDGE CASE OPENED, MANUFACTURER'S TAPE REMOVED AND/OR REPLACED, MANUFACTURER'S MARKINGS, LABELS OR IDENTIFICATION IS EITHER MISSING OR ASKEW, THE MEMBER IS RESPONSIBLE FOR THE FULL PAYMENT OF THE CASSETTE. IF THE VIDEOCASSETTE IS LOST, STOLEN OR DESTROYED—IF THE MEMBER IS UNABLE TO RETURN A VIDEOCASSETTE BECAUSE IT HAS BEEN LOST, STOLEN OR DESTROYED, THE MEMBER WILL BE RESPONSIBLE FOR PURCHASING THE VIDEOCASSETTE BY PAYING THE RENTAL FEE AND THEN BUYING THE VIDEOCASSETTE BY PAYING THE PRICE SHOWN IN THE INVENTORY.

THE VIDEOCASSETTE MAY BE SHOWN ONLY IN A PRIVATE HOME, WITHOUT ADMISSION OR OTHER CHARGES, IN THE PRESENCE OF THE MEMBER, HIS FAMILY, AND HIS PERSONAL GUESTS. THE MEMBER MAY NOT LOAN THE VIDEOCASSETTE TO ANYONE ELSE FOR ANY REASON WHATSOEVER.

VIDEOCASSETTE PLAYER/RECORDER AND CAMERA AND ACCESSORY RENTAL—MEMBER MUST RETURN VIDEO PLAYER AND CAMERA IN THE SAME CONDITION AS IT WAS RECEIVED AND TO THE SAME LOCATION FROM WHICH IT WAS RENTED. IF THE RENTED ITEMS ARE RETURNED IN A DAMAGED CONDITION, MEMBER SHALL PAY THE RENTAL FEE AND THE COST OF REPAIRING THE DAMAGE. DAMAGE REFERS TO NEGLIGENCE OR MISUSE OF THE RENTED ITEMS. SUCH NEGLIGENCE OR MISUSE SHALL INCLUDE DROPPING OR THROWING THE RENTED ITEMS, OR INSERTING OBJECTS OR OTHER MATERIALS (OTHER THAN VIDEO TAPES) INTO THE WORKING PARTS OF THE PLAYER.

THE MEMBER IS RESPONSIBLE FOR ANY VISIBLE DAMAGE WHILE THE PLAYER IS IN HIS POSSESSION. VISIBLE DAMAGE REFERS TO CRACKED OR DENTED CASE, BROKEN OR LOST KNOBS, ANY MISSING OR BROKEN EXTERNAL PARTS, MISSING CONNECTOR CORDS, WIRES OR ADAPTERS. IN THE CASE OF A PLAYER/RECORDER RETURNED IN A DAMAGED CONDITION, THE STORE WILL ADVISE MEMBER OF THE REPAIR COSTS.

FAILURE OF THE MEMBER TO RETURN A RENTED ITEM SHALL SUBJECT THE MEMBER TO ADDITIONAL RENTAL FEES AT THE BASIC RENTAL CHARGE AS PROVIDED IN THIS AGREEMENT UNTIL THE RENTAL ITEMS ARE RETURNED. AT NO TIME DOES THE MEMBER OBTAIN OWNERSHIP OF THE RENTAL PROPERTY.

IN ADDITION MEMBER UNDERSTANDS THAT DOORSTEP VIDEO, INC., HAS THE RIGHT TO CANCEL MEMBER'S MEMBERSHIP PRIVILEGES AND/OR PURSUE OTHER CIVIL AND CRIMINAL LEGAL REMEDIES PROVIDED BY THE STATE OF NORTH CAROLINA UNDER ITS GENERAL STATUTES IF, IN DOORSTEP'S SOLE OPINION, THE NEED ARISES—ALL WITHOUT ADDITIONAL NOTICE TO MEMBER, EXCEPT AS MAY BE REQUIRED BY NORTH CAROLINA LAW.

students at a local college and found several who are willing to work on a part-time basis. In addition, the local telephone company agreed to give them a local number that helped describe the purpose of their business—636-FAST.

They both feel that the idea of home delivery of rental videos is a good one and one that they can build into a profitable business. Clay, however, does have one more year of college before he can devote full time to the business. To further complicate the decision, Garret received a job offer in sales with a nationally known firm. They agree that they must make a decision no later than the first week in May.

QUESTIONS

1. Describe the environment in which Doorstep Video would operate. Does the idea make sense given the size of town and other characteristics of the market?
2. Consider the startup expenses. Are they reasonable? What changes would you make?
3. Should Clay be expected to go without a salary? What would be the effect of including his salary?
4. Suppose the two entrepreneurs could only provide half the capital needed. If you were a banker, would you loan them money?
5. Calculate a break-even point in terms of the number of rentals per day.

ENDNOTES

1. Subrata Chakravarty, "Give 'em Variety," *Forbes*, May 2, 1988, 54–57.
2. "Video Marketing" published by *Video Store*, Hollywood, Calif., 1987.
3. Ron Stodghill, "Will Video Chains Push Small Stores Out of the Picture?" *The Charlotte Observer*, February 15, 1988, 1 and 13C.

Wisconsin Sealcoating

D

Jeff Totten and Jeff Cornwall

Dr. Chris Wall hung up the phone, leaned back, and thought reflectively about the conversation she had just had with one of her small business clients, Peter Radtke. It was time to update the strategic business plan for Radtke's business, Wisconsin Sealcoating. Since Dr. Wall will soon be leaving the Small Business Development Center, she thinks that this would be an excellent opportunity to train her replacement—you. So she calls you to her office, hands you the file on Wisconsin Sealcoating, and tells you to prepare a preliminary strategic business plan for the upcoming year. The two of you will get together in a week and go over the plan that you have prepared. Here is the information you have pulled together from the file.

HISTORY OF WISCONSIN SEALCOATING

Wisconsin Sealcoating is eleven years old, with nine years servicing the present market of Appleton and northeast Wisconsin, including the Door County peninsula. Peter Radtke started the business in Minnesota, selling heavy equipment. Two years later, he moved the business to Appleton, Wisconsin, and changed to the services of sealcoating and tennis court resurfacing.

Before the sealcoating material is applied to the surface, any cracks are filled with petroleum-based materials. The sealcoating is then applied to the surface and allowed to harden. Most sealcoating is used for the maintenance of parking lots. Initially, the company used oil-based sealer equipment. However, seven years ago, Radtke made a major financial commitment and switched to coal tar sealer equipment. He switched because coal tar sealer is a better quality product than is the oil-based sealer. The

---

This case was prepared by Dr. Jeff Totten of the University of Wisconsin at Oshkosh and Dr. Jeff Cornwall of Carolina Psychiatry and Psychology Clinics as a basis for class discussion rather than to illustrate either effective or ineffective handling of an administrative situation. The names of firms and key personnel and dates have been disguised to preserve the firm's desire for anonymity.

Presented to the Midwest Society for Case Research Workshop, 1988. All rights reserved to the authors and to the Midwest Society for Case Research. Copyright © 1988 by Jeff Totten and Jeff Cornwall. Used with permission.

business is seasonal in nature, due to the severity and length of Wisconsin winters. Normally, the company's productive work season is mid-May to mid-October of each year.

PERSONNEL

The company is owned by Peter Radtke, who has fifteen years of sales experience and no formal business education. He has a B.S. in fisheries management (natural resources). His wife, Beth, is a full-time accounting instructor at the local technical college and takes care of the company's administration. Peter is responsible for all facets of the business except accounting. The company has benefited from both his lengthy sales experience and his belief in providing customer service.

Recently, Wisconsin Sealcoating lost three experienced workers. While Peter hated to see two of them leave, one had caused problems and he was glad to see him go. He hired three replacement workers, who have worked out pretty well, although they need supervision to keep them motivated on the job.

Additional help is usually hired to maintain a staff of six. Peter generally hires a college student and a high school student during the peak time of the business. Recently, he hired another college student to help the company with quotation preparation, appraisals, and sales. The student has also helped develop a new mailing program.

The following people work for Wisconsin Sealcoating:

- Mike, the foreman. Seven years of experience with the company; he's the primary group leader, of even temperament, fair with others, fussy in workmanship, and cooperative; reliable, honest, likable, and cautious in taking action; twenty-six years old, single, and financially motivated. He serves as both trainer and supervisor, handles the "tougher" installations, is responsible for all of the tennis court work, tracks inventory needs, and delegates most work assignments.

- John, Mike's brother. One year of experience; a careful worker, though a slow learner; interested in learning; likes the work; thirty-five years old, married, four children, and financially motivated.

- Bill. One year of experience; hard worker; works all hours that are available; follows instructions poorly; likes the work and wants to advance; married, five children, and also financially motivated.

- Todd. One year of experience; does acceptable work, but doesn't like long hours and isn't a self-starter; does okay in following instructions if they are specific, but he will not do more than he is told to do (may come from his conditioning as a factory worker for ten years); thirty-seven years old, divorced, no children, and is motivated by financial and working conditions.

- Jack, office/sales worker. One year of experience; excellent worker; quick learner, self-starter, willing to try new things, pleasant personality; married, no children.

The morale of the crew is good. Wisconsin Sealcoating has been able to hire enough help so that it could reduce overtime and create better working conditions for all. All employees plan on returning to the company in April of the coming year. Mike was given a nice salary increase last year to keep him around, since Peter needed his experience. Mike is especially valuable as the foreman to Peter, since his strict supervision of the men and his monitoring of all field work allows Peter to concentrate more on sales. One problem with Mike is the limited amount of time he has to spend with the workers, since his responsibility for tennis court work often takes him out of town for several days at a time.

Turnover has been a continual problem for Peter. The valuable employees that he wants to keep around leave primarily because of the seasonal nature of the business and its limiting effect on annual income. Often he is told that they enjoy working for him and doing the sort of outside physical work the company does, but that it just doesn't pay enough. They can find jobs that are not seasonal in nature and pay more than Wisconsin Sealcoating can ever pay.

CURRENT SERVICES

Wisconsin Sealcoating provides the following services in-house to its clients: sealcoating, asphalt repairs, tennis court coatings, tennis court supplies, cold-pour crackfilling, line removal, and consulting. Wisconsin subcontracts the following services: large asphalt repairs, paving, paving fabrics, car stops, striping, and hot-pour crackfilling.

MATERIAL RESOURCES

Current equipment is old but serviceable. The four trucks range in age from fourteen years to twenty years, and require high upkeep costs. The sealcoating truck is an effective unit that was "upgraded" last year at an expense of $3,000 to $4,000. The upgrade allows for more effective spraying applications. However, the sealcoating equipment is not being used to its maximum. It could be in the field more frequently and more spray applications could be sold than have been in the past. The balance of the equipment is in relatively good operating condition. The appearance of the equipment is generally acceptable to clients. At the end of this past season, most of the equipment was repainted. The company has no storage building to protect the equipment or to facilitate repairs. Vandalism and theft have been a problem in the past, though not as much this past year.

The company purchased an IBM personal computer two years ago. Since then, it has been used extensively for word processing, estimating, and mailing list development. To date, no attempt has been made to computerize the accounting of the company.

FINANCIAL CONDITION

The operating statements for the past three years are provided in Exhibits 1, 2, and 3. The statements also include financial ratios for the same three-year period of time. Financially, the company has a very good relationship with all its suppliers. Wisconsin Sealcoating is wholly owned by Peter and

Wisconsin Sealcoating
Income Statement

	2nd year prior	1st year prior	Last year
Sales			
Sealing	$180,801.83	$134,426.13	$ 82,226.14
Tennis Courts	78,850.51	104,475.40	146,851.88
Consulting	——	——	8,192.53
Total Sales	$259,652.34	$238,901.53	$237,270.55
Cost of Sales			
Materials Purchases	$ 67,223.71	$ 59,973.50	$ 48,620.34
Direct Labor	35,925.71	38,307.24	36,119.74
Contract Services	52,183.72	68,520.47	65,567.10
Wage Reimbursements	(2,359.23)	(703.50)	(678.06)
Total Cost of Sales	$152,973.91	$166,097.71	$149,629.12
Gross Profit	$106,678.43	$ 72,803.82	$ 87,641.43
Operating Expenses			
Operating Supplies	$ 6,764.48	$ 4,777.46	$ 7,226.70
Freight & Postage	3,679.23	2,538.16	614.14
Gross Wages	105.88	302.38	——
Pension/Profit Sharing	1,980.00	——	——
Rent—Building	900.00	1,030.60	1,135.05
Rent—Equipment	572.60	712.78	867.54
Utilities	138.00	138.00	138.00
Telephone	2,076.34	2,838.42	3,248.93
Repairs & Maintenance	1,841.29	1,509.25	1,059.00
Vehicle Repairs/Maintenance	5,101.90	3,046.70	2,974.30
Advertising/Promotion	2,539.37	2,087.83	3,593.98
Insurance	3,623.00	5,131.63	10,116.80
Conventions/Seminars	308.06	520.62	33.05
Travel/Entertainment	2,175.13	3,681.88	2,627.98
Property Taxes	104.37	117.46	133.98
FICA Tax	2,540.22	2,761.09	2,582.53
Unemployment Tax	3,256.00	4,167.51	3,704.46
Permits & Licenses	559.75	618.00	743.60
Interest	3,105.62	2,483.70	1,708.96
Vehicle Expense	5,692.16	5,015.49	5,448.91
Bad Debts	800.00	2,772.25	——
Legal & Accounting	1,350.00	1,376.00	1,275.00
Office Expense	3,885.67	4,677.54	1,489.64
Depreciation	8,317.85	9,902.33	6,696.00
Dues & Subscriptions	355.12	586.80	571.00
Laundry & Uniforms	420.00	420.00	420.00
Miscellaneous	——	——	235.20
Total Operating Expenses	$ 62,192.04	$ 63,213.88	$ 58,645.45
Operating Profit	$ 44,486.39	$ 9,589.94	$ 28,995.98
Other Income	——	2,040.00	——
Profit	$ 44,486.39	$ 11,629.94	$ 28,995.98

EXHIBIT 1
Income Statement

Wisconsin Sealcoating
Comparative Balance Sheets (abbreviated)

	2nd year prior	1st year prior	Last year
Accounts Receivable	$18,925.05	$ 3,651.53	$ 2,138.50
Current Assets	21,641.86	5,613.59	9,226.19
Current Inventory	1,532.00	774.00	1,637.00
Total Assets	$46,617.44	$28,704.09	$30,864.64
Current Liabilities	$ 6,813.59	$ 5,128.53	$ 3,429.63
Total Liabilities	$38,362.16	$30,218.79	$11,991.80
Total Equity	$21,755.00	$ (1,514.70)	$18,872.84

EXHIBIT 2
Balance Sheet

	2nd year prior	1st year prior	Last year
Current Ratio	3.18	1.09	2.69
Quick Ratio	2.95	0.94	2.21
Debt to Equity	1.76	−19.95	0.64
Times Interest Earned	15.32	4.86	17.97
Receivables Turnover	——	65.43	110.95
Daily Sales	711.38	654.52	650.06
Collection Period	——	5.58	3.29
Inventory Turnover	99.85	214.60	91.40
Total Asset Turnover	5.57	8.32	7.69
Gross Margin	0.41	0.30	0.37
Net Margin	0.17	0.04	0.12
Return on Assets	0.95	0.33	0.94
Return on Equity	2.04	−6.33	1.54

EXHIBIT 3
Financial Ratios

Beth Radtke. The company has received a line of credit from its bank, and has enjoyed the bank's cooperation with previous financial plans. A critical problem for Wisconsin Sealcoating is cash flow, due to the seasonal nature of the business. The Radtkes hope to retire the long-term debt this coming year.

COMPETITION

Wisconsin Sealcoating's competition tends to be locally based, within a fifty-mile radius of Appleton. There are four major competitors in this market area.

Vande Hey Sealcoating is located in Green Bay, thirty miles to the east. The company is seven years old, and is run by three partners, one of whom is a previously bankrupt paving contractor. The partners apparently desire to establish an "empire" in northeast Wisconsin. Vande Hey specializes in hot-pour crackfilling and spray sealcoating. The sales force is comprised of three salespeople who target large contracts available in the area. Pricing is historically very cheap, and has tended to depress Wisconsin's pricing at times. The company apparently does not hesitate to purchase new or additional equipment when needed. Vande Hey also has a poor reputation among clients. Marketing efforts include extensive yellow page advertising, telephone cold calling, and direct mail campaigns. They tend to go after airports, school districts, and other large public projects.

Rucunski's Asphalt Maintenance is located in Appleton. This competitor moved to this area seven years ago from northern Michigan. Rucunski's tends to emphasize large asphalt repairs, since it has the equipment needed to do larger repairs. The company also provides tennis court colorings and small asphalt paving services. The sole owner is a likable and capable person who has good selling skills. His equipment tends to be older, yet well maintained. Image is not a concern of the owner, who often submits quotations and makes presentations in his work clothes. The owner is involved not only in selling, but also in the actual work itself. The company has been successful in obtaining larger crackfilling contracts, like Fox River Mall, primarily through competitive pricing. Workmanship is generally good; however, Peter feels that their installation is often sloppily done. State-of-the-art crackfilling equipment and proper preparation techniques are not used.

Behring Oil Company entered the business six years ago. It is a well-known gasoline and oil products distributor in the Fox Valley area. However, it operates generally poor equipment, which was purchased new at the time of start-up. The company is very large and quite diverse. It does use the equipment to service its own operations, so outside business may no longer be a major factor. However, should it decide to enter this market, with its name, identity, and financial wherewithal, it could severely dent Wisconsin's sales in this area. Currently its work is extremely poor and installed by low-quality help.

Keilberg Asphalt Sealing has been around for a while. Apparently, the son purchased the business from his wealthy father about five years ago. Since then, the company has shown an interest in expanding into all markets and with all products. It is diversified into sealing, crackfilling (hot), and tennis courts, and services most of the state. Pricing has tended to be quite low and very competitive. Keilberg tends to have large airport contracts. It seems to have a decent reputation for on-time completion and customer satisfaction, and it operates relatively new equipment. Recently, it has moved into the Door County (northeast of Green Bay—heavy tourist/vacationer trade) area doing tennis courts.

Peter believes that his company must maintain a close relationship with Kossel Blacktop, a small paving contractor servicing primarily the Door County area, due to the recent entry of Keilberg into that market. Kossel is well respected and builds a number of tennis courts each year for resort owners. Years ago it had some tennis court failures and decided at that time to discontinue installing the coatings. Kossel appreciates Wisconsin's service and consultation on the tennis construction details with which it is not familiar (i.e., fencing, court accessories). In the past three years, it has had Wisconsin subcontract all the work other than the paving, which they do. Kossel has been a good source of profitable business that has not required an unreasonable amount of selling time for Peter. Kossel's sub-contracted business has assumed a greater percentage of Wisconsin's total sales over the past four years, growing from 7 percent three years ago to a projected 13 percent for this year. Thus, Peter considers Kossel to be an ally, and wants to strengthen his ties with it in order to maintain his presence in Door County.

With regard to the Appleton-Oshkosh market, Peter's biggest competitor is Rucunski's. He recently lost a big contract with a major hospital in the market to Rucunski's, probably due in part to the low price offered by that company. As noted above, should Behring Oil decide to pursue the market more than it is doing now, it would prove to be a big threat to Wisconsin's sales.

TECHNOLOGY

The standard sealer product used in this industry is coal tar sealing. There have been some environmental and health concerns about the carcinogenic nature of these sealants. New generation, environmentally safer sealers are being developed; however, they are not available in the marketplace yet, nor have they been mandated by OSHA and other federal agencies. Newer epoxy-based sealers have appeared on the market. These cost more and are almost as expensive as asphalt overlays, so the adoption rate for these products will likely be slow. These sealers do show improved wear characteristics, which implies better long-term value for the money. Another product has reappeared on the market. Originally developed by the Air Force in the 1930s, rejuvenator sealers are slowly making a comeback. These are easier to apply; however, they are 30 percent more expensive for the customer. Installers must be *very* careful with the application rates, or drying can become a problem and tracking may result. This product does offer the advantage of pavement rejuvenation in addition to the feature of conventional sealers. Wisconsin Sealcoating has been contemplating adding this product to its line. In Peter's mind, the key question is whether or not his company can handle it economically. They do have the equipment that would be needed in order to use the rejuvenation sealer.

In terms of equipment technology, there has been a trend toward sealcoating machines that use spray systems to apply the sealant. However, there are some problems associated with the use of spraying. There is the possibility of greater health hazards for employees with spraying. Also, spraying requires care to avoid damaging buildings and cars due to splattering. On the plus side, there are labor cost savings with spraying and, for some types of work, superior applications can be realized. There is a tendency, though, for companies to use spray systems as a means of shortchanging customers.

OTHER TRENDS

The industry is seeing a trend toward increased usage of private sweepers. In Wisconsin, the privatization of public works service in these areas is historically slow. There is a significant consciousness on the part of customers with respect to the external appearance of buildings and grounds in this state.

Customers are, in general, buying better paving products. Contractors are developing greater acceptance of paving fabrics and grinding products. Wisconsin Sealcoating has been promoting these products and subcontracting the work. Peter is uncertain as to his company's role in this market in the future.

The trend is definitely toward hot rubberized crackfilling, though the equipment is more expensive (approximately $6,000 to $10,000) and there are some health and environmental hazards associated with its use. "Cold pour" crackfillers have challenged the hot process, but have not been able to gain large government contracts. There are some applications for cold pouring in the private market due to cost savings. Hot pouring has one advantage for contractors, in that it can be installed just before sealcoating, thereby saving an extra trip. Recently, Wisconsin began subcontracting hot crackfilling work to another sealcoat company. This is more costly, but it has allowed Wisconsin to offer the service without having the training and equipment responsibilities. However, the needs of customers who have small crackfilling jobs remain unsatisfied. Wisconsin has been using the time provided by the subcontracting to evaluate this competitive service and to wait for the availability of used equipment.

MARKET CONDITIONS

There are basically four customer markets that sealcoating companies target: private commercial business, private homeowner, contractor, and public works. The commercial business market is quite distinct from the private homeowner market. The contractor market is composed of paving contractors who may subcontract some of their tasks. The public works market is made up of city, county, school board, and other governmental bodies that seek bids for a variety of public works projects.

There has been growth in the acceptance of and interest in pavement maintenance in the private market. With this service, Wisconsin Sealcoating provides sealcoating, crackfilling, line painting, and cleaning on an ongoing, scheduled basis for one set fee. Owners are more accepting due to greater awareness of the costs of replacement if the pavement is not properly maintained, and a slowly improving image of installers (Peter characterizes some in his business as being rather sleazy). Contractors have also lent credibility by accepting pavement maintenance themselves. Though prices have declined, the current level of work that is available tends to keep profits in an acceptable range. The business is somewhat recession free since owners will turn to processes like Wisconsin's in lieu of more expensive work during rough times. Activity in the tennis court resurfacing market tends to be related to good economic times and availability of discretionary income.

There is growth potential present in the contractor market. The ability to work as a subcontractor for established paving contractors looks very promising to Wisconsin. Contractors have been accepting the processes that are used by companies like Wisconsin, and this has helped to create customer acceptance. The key to tapping this market lies with the proper nurturing of the relationship between the contractor and the subcontractor.

There is some potential in the public market arena. Airport work in sealcoating still exists, though it seems to have slowed down. This is a very competitive area where high production and low pricing are the keys. Wisconsin has not had much success nor profit in this area. Cities occasionally contract crackfilling work and routinely bid tennis court resurfacing. Wisconsin has not been able to go after the crackfilling jobs since at present it does not offer the service. It has often been underbid by Keilberg on the tennis court jobs. Much more promising areas for Wisconsin are with the negotiated school board bids and the subcontracted public work of paving contractors. In general, public bodies (i.e., cities, counties) have been reluctant to go to private contractors for other services such as repairs and sweeping.

In terms of geographical markets, the local area is becoming better serviced due to more competition. Potential growth areas are rural markets, small towns (north, west, and south of Appleton), and the city of Oshkosh. The Fond du Lac market (south of Oshkosh) is pretty much saturated. Wisconsin Sealcoating has done a lot of work in northeast Wisconsin (north toward the Upper Peninsula of Michigan and northeast, including the Door County peninsula) in tennis court resurfacing and some pavement sealing work.

Lately, Peter has started some consulting work with a large retail company. He inspects its lots and recommends needed treatments for each. The consulting has not generated much work for his employees, and has required some of his time that would normally be spent selling conventional services. Peter sees the consulting market as an area that is currently underserviced and thus it may have some possibilities to be pursued. This is a gut feeling; Peter really hasn't collected any data to prove or disprove the viability of this market.

CURRENT MARKETING EFFORTS

Peter Radtke is currently the only salesperson for Wisconsin Sealcoating. Attempts to get additional assistance have not been successful, though Peter has not persistently worked on this. There has been a reluctance to invest funds in the development of a sales force due to a fear that it won't produce. However, Jack has been helping out with sales, and has been doing a fine job.

Sales come from the following sources:

- Contractors and contractor referrals—an important source of annual sales.
- Cold calling—minimum sales. Potential exists for expansion via contacting prospects identified by visual observation of apparent needs (e.g., asphalt patching).
- Past customers—good source from larger accounts. However, the company has underutilized the extensive past customer file bank that exists. Peter hopes to use the file better with his new computer. The very effective technique of following up outstanding quotes with phone calls has not been implemented effectively.
- Yellow page listings—a productive source of unqualified leads. The size of the listing has recently been cut back since there are now two phone books in the area. Peter did hire some professional help to design a more effective ad.

- Personal contacts and referrals—tend to be slightly less productive than yellow pages-generated leads in terms of volume; however, referrals tend to be of higher quality.
- Direct mail/telemarketing—direct mail has been tried with some success but not in an organized system. Peter plans to send out mailings to selected tennis court prospects at the start of the upcoming season (in April and May). He may also try direct mail on some sealcoating candidates. There are no plans for telemarketing at this time.

There is really no budget for sales and advertising. The company responds to needs as they arise. There has not been any formal campaign to solicit business. During the construction season, they are kept busy replying to call-in inquiries. Peter wants to stress closing the larger important quotations by providing faster turnaround times on the quotes and making personal presentations of proposals.

MANAGEMENT PHILOSOPHY

Peter Radtke wants to provide a service that customers will appreciate, create employment and gain for the company members, operate in an open and honest environment, and provide a comfortable income and retirement future for his family. He describes his company's mission as follows:

> To provide quality maintenance coatings and services to tennis court owners and owners of midsize to large parking pavements.

He would like to accomplish the following in the next year or two:

- Attain a profit goal of $60,000 this year, which reflects an increase in sales of 37 percent over last year.
- Establish a cash reserve system.
- Develop a sales program that can financially support an assistant.
- Delegate administrative and field supervision duties.
- Expand the consulting service.
- Establish a base of repeat business and pavement maintenance.
- Improve employee benefits and pay system to involve them more in the company's growth.

QUESTIONS

1. Develop a preliminary strategic plan for Wisconsin Sealcoating.
2. Consider possible strategic changes for the company. What areas look promising?
3. Should Wisconsin Sealcoating consider merging with another firm in the area? If so, which one?
4. Is selling out a viable possibility?
5. Should Wisconsin Sealcoating attempt to grow via acquisition?

Southern Cabinet Company

Timothy Singleton, Robert McGlashan, and Mike Harris

E

Mike Norris leaned back in his chair and stared alternately between the computer screen spreadsheet and the view through the front window of his suburban home. The view out the window was only a blur, however, as Mike's attention and energy were focused on the information in front of him on the screen. The numbers represented a profit-cost-volume analysis of Southern Cabinet Company (SCC), a manufacturer of kitchen and bathroom cabinets located in a large metropolitan area in the Sunbelt. The president and chairman of the board of the small firm was Mike's father-in-law, Bill Martin. Mike and Bill had often discussed the business over the years when convenience and time permitted. Mike's interest was now more serious, however, as he was considering an offer by Bill to go to work in the business. Mike was a recent MBA graduate while Bill's formal education did not extend beyond high school. But they were both impressed that they often came to the same conclusions regarding various aspects of the business despite different analytical approaches and perspectives.

Southern Cabinet Company was founded in 1954 by Bill Martin, the current president and chairman of the board. In the early days, there were times when Bill was literally the only employee of the company. By 1984 there were thirty-two people in the shop and six full-time office personnel, including Bill's wife Laura. SCC builds kitchen and bathroom cabinets for new residential construction only, including townhouses and condominiums. There are several characteristics of SCC that Bill Martin believed made it unique with respect to the competition:

1. The product, although not strictly a custom cabinet, is of better quality than that built by its major competitors.
2. The price of SCC's products is slightly higher than the competition.

The research and written case information were presented at the Case Research Symposium and were evaluated by the Case Research Association's editorial board. The case was prepared by Timothy M. Singleton of North Georgia College and Robert McGlashan and Mike Harris of the University of Houston-Clear Lake as a basis for class discussion. Distributed by the Case Research Association. Used with permission. All rights reserved to the authors and the Case Research Association. Permission to use the case should be obtained from the Case Research Association and the senior author.

3. SCC is smaller (sales volume) than its competitors.
4. SCC builds a wider variety of cabinet sizes and types than its competitors, with more than eight hundred unique pieces.
5. SCC does not carry a finished goods inventory, i.e., cabinets are manufactured after they are ordered by the customer.

RECENT BUSINESS HISTORY

The nature of SCC's operations in the past four years changed rather dramatically (see Exhibits 1 and 2). Even with relatively good economic fortune in many areas of the Sunbelt, many builders and SCC's competitors were hurt badly due to a combination of high interest rates and heavy debt.

In contrast, SCC had its best years ever during the early 1980s recession. Operations provided the cash flow to support an increase in sales, and the computer acquired in 1980 made it possible to handle the additional administrative and management burden necessary to support increased volume.

KEY PEOPLE AT SCC

If entrepreneurs tend to "march to their own drummer," Bill Martin is no exception. He was born in a small southern town in 1920. Despite being brought up in what some call a "Bible Belt" region, Bill did not care much for the local religion. He developed an interest in other religious philosophies through the years, as well as an interest in movies and film making. Bill still has color film of Hawaii that he took during the second World War when he was stationed at Hickam Field. He was learning to fly B-17s when the Japanese attacked in 1941, and later piloted a B-17 with the 8th Air Force over Germany. In the past ten years, he has produced two full-length homemade films. If not for the demands of the business, which he also continues to enjoy, Bill would gladly spend more time with the movie equipment and other hobbies.

Bill had acquired experience in the construction industry while he was growing up, and decided to start his own business, motivated primarily by a desire to be his own boss rather than to make a lot of money. Bill runs SCC in what his employees consider a very relaxed manner, and with an "open door" policy. If he ever gets very excited about anything, he disguises it well. People at SCC describe Bill as patient, deliberate, and not at all impulsive. He likes to mull things over carefully before making decisions—a habit that for the most part seems to have served him well.

Laura Martin, Bill's wife of forty-three years, handles the accounting and office administration. Laura seems to enjoy the work as much as Bill, and often serves as a sounding board for office and plant employees who discuss business as well as personal matters. Laura is from Bill's home town, and had left home after high school to marry Bill in Hawaii in 1941.

Harry Wood, forty-two, holds the title of vice-president of sales, and has been with the company for more than ten years. He has an assistant, but Harry does all the direct selling to the customer. Harry has a knack for satisfying the customer before and after the sale, and an excellent ability to

Southern Cabinet Company
Comparative Balance Sheets*

	1979	1980	1981	1982	1983	Year-to-Date April 30 1984
Assets						
Current Assets:						
Cash	$ 53,314	$152,524	$236,391	$277,507	$264,094	$ 308,489
Accounts Receivable	221,582	160,568	213,671	175,917	248,592	238,887
Merchandise Inventory (doors and hardware)	121,419	116,902	180,070	180,886	195,020	214,635
Prepaid Expenses	12,789	22,341	20,040	19,044	22,333	23,440
Total Current Assets	$409,104	$452,335	$650,172	$653,354	$730,039	$ 785,451
Fixed Assets (net)						
Land and Building	$ 0	$ 0	$ 0	$ 0	$ 90,941	$ 153,508
Office Furniture	3,359	16,915	13,126	25,088	32,695	28,646
Plant Equipment	18,662	17,360	22,386	22,490	16,926	15,528
Auto Equipment	7,406	47,709	39,215	32,063	21,477	14,766
Other	467	1,582	500	5,000	0	0
Total Fixed Assets	$ 29,894	$ 83,566	$ 75,227	$ 84,641	$162,039	$ 212,448
Other Assets (including prepaid tax)	1,710	54,027	10,321	24,331	563	45,055
Total Assets	$440,708	$589,928	$735,720	$762,326	$892,641	$1,042,954
Liabilities						
Current Liabilities:						
Accounts Payable	$ 76,718	$ 34,282	$ 36,993	$ 30,759	$ 31,824	$ 34,898
Notes Payable	35,164	15,281	13,677	13,229	6,745	6,196
Accrued Wages, Sales Commissions, and Salary Bonuses	46,879	77,995	113,800	74,720	92,935	9,705
Other	6,859	57,523	29,472	12,859	18,768	11,182
Total Current Liabilities	$165,620	$185,081	$193,942	$131,567	$150,272	$ 61,981
Long-Term Liabilities	594	28,518	15,235	2,804	0	0
Net Worth						
Capital Stock	$ 14,590	$ 14,590	$ 14,590	$ 15,000	$ 15,000	$ 15,000
Treasury Stock	0	0	0	410	410	410
Capital Surplus	28	28	28	28	28	28
Retained Earnings	162,448	256,183	358,096	460,449	548,926	724,404
Net Profit Year-to-Date	97,428	105,528	153,829	152,068	178,005	241,131
Total Net Worth	$274,494	$376,329	$526,543	$627,955	$742,369	$ 980,973
Total Liabilities and Net Worth	$440,708	$589,928	$735,720	$762,326	$892,641	$1,042,954

*Fiscal year beginning October 1.

EXHIBIT 1
Balance Sheets

Southern Cabinet Company
Comparative Income Statements

	1979	1980	1981	1982	1983	Year-to-Date April 30, 1984
Sales	$1,541,133	$1,414,931	$1,913,990	$1,914,553	$1,967,429	$1,514,975
Cost of Sales	1,195,531	998,568	1,304,707	1,414,781	1,393,861	1,059,338
Gross Profit	$ 345,602	$416,363	$ 609,283	$ 499,772	$ 573,568	$ 455,637
Operating Expenses						
Office and Administration	$ 143,262	$116,075	$ 138,489	$ 181,542	$ 208,178	$ 134,016
Selling and Advertising	48,551	48,092	60,935	62,306	76,023	59,214
Delivery Expense	55,585	42,907	63,082	60,101	47,651	36,321
Total Operating Expense	$ 247,398	$207,074	$ 262,506	$ 303,949	$ 331,852	$ 229,551
Net Profit from Operations	98,204	209,289	346,777	195,823	241,716	226,086
Installation Income (Expense)	(776)	415	2,344	1,455	1,371	3,669
Other Administrative Income	8,341	7,017	8,819	24,153	19,128	11,377
Net Operating Profit	$ 105,769	$216,721	$ 357,940	$ 221,431	$ 262,215	$ 241,132
Incentive Bonuses*	16,694	68,090	112,111	69,362	84,210	0
Net Profit for Federal Taxes	$ 89,075	$148,631	$ 245,829	$ 152,069	$ 178,005	$ 241,132
Provision for Federal Taxes	15,911	43,101	91,998	47,871	59,986	0
Net Profit after Taxes	$ 73,164	$105,530	$ 153,831	$ 104,198	$ 118,019	$ 241,132

*Office personnel bonuses based on net operating profit.

. . . .

EXHIBIT 2
Income Statements

qualify potential customers. Bad debts were less than one-half of 1 percent of sales in 1983.

Linda Sharp, thirty-two, serves as an administrative assistant to Bill and Laura. Linda does a little of everything, and through the years has gradually assumed more and more administrative responsibility around the office. She has consistently done a good job and demonstrated talent in many areas, including public relations. Harry has even mentioned that he would like to have her in sales. Linda has an assistant, Bud Melman, but she still often handles the front desk and other general office duties such as answering the phone. Linda has been with the company for eight years, and she and Harry are considered to be loyal and invaluable employees.

The key people in the plant have been with the company more than twenty-five years. Jim Mayo, seventy, manages the materials flow and performs maintenance on most of the plant equipment. Despite his age, Jim seems to have more energy than almost anyone in the plant. Oscar Wyatt, fifty-eight, is general shop foreman, and supervises the lead people in the plant who oversee the six departments.

Mike Norris, thirty-four, worked for six years as a senior systems engineer for an aircraft simulator manufacturer and has a Master's degree in mathematics as well as an MBA. Mike's previous experience around construction has been limited to part-time work for a painting contractor during summers when he was an undergraduate student. His recent experience is primarily in software design of various aircraft systems, and he has approximately three years' experience as a department supervisor with fifteen people. In this capacity, his duties included customer contact, report generation, planning, hiring new employees, and employee evaluation. He began the MBA program at a local university primarily as a diversion from the normal day-to-day activities, and because he felt it was a good use of his extra time. As he began to accumulate hours in the business program, he began to think more seriously about changing careers. In fact, he took a six-month leave of absence to complete his MBA. His wife, Melanie (Bill and Laura's only child), continued her career as a nurse at a local hospital.

PLANT OPERATIONS

SCC manufactures cabinets with three different wood finishes, although all contain certain common wood products for the shelves and back. The manufacturing process begins after an order has been received, the dimensions of the kitchen at the construction site have been carefully measured, and the order placed on a schedule. A list of individual pieces (cabinets) that make up an order is produced by the sales department using a detailed hand drawing of the installation site. This list is entered into a computer program, and "cutting lists" are printed and given to various departments in the plant. These lists describe the parts that must be cut to satisfy a particular job order that may contain several work orders. For example, a job may entail building cabinets for several kitchens.

Although there are many steps in the manufacturing procedure, there are a few key steps that give one a feel for the process. There are six major departments. One cuts the parts for the face frame, the frame that fits to the front of the body of the cabinet. A second department, the Cutting Department, cuts parts for the body of the cabinet. Some of the cut parts require more finishing in the Sanding Department before they are gathered in one location so that an audit can be made to verify that all the parts necessary for completion of the work order have been produced. The collection of parts is then moved to the Assembly Department. The cabinets are assembled with staple guns and glue, and the Hardware Department installs the drawer guides and doors. The assembled cabinets are then placed on a dolly and moved to the Paint Department. After staining and finishing, cabinets are stacked until the customer can take delivery.

All the manufacturing processes are relatively simple tasks, and with the exception of painting, require no special skills. Most of the labor when hired is unskilled, and from time to time workers are able to be shifted from one job to another if a worker quits or is ill. Many of the workers in the plant have been with the company more than ten years, and a few for more than twenty years. The average pay is about $6.50 an hour, and all workers in the plant participate in a piece count bonus program on a weekly basis. Starting at five hundred pieces, the entire crew receives extra pay for each piece produced. The incremental pay for each piece increases gradually for each hundred pieces up to a thousand. For a thousand pieces and up, the incremental pay per piece is constant. Mike has noted in looking over the past few months' production and pay statistics that the unit labor cost decreases despite the bonus pay until production reaches around eight hundred to nine hundred pieces per week. At that point, overtime pay expense begins to be incurred, which offsets the benefits of increased volume, and unit labor costs begin to increase. The increase in pay at one thousand pieces, not counting overtime, is $100 per week per employee if the employee has perfect attendance for the week.

CAN'T LIVE WITH 'EM, BUT CAN'T LIVE WITHOUT 'EM

Like most small companies that have been initiated to the uses of micro- and minicomputers, SCC has had its share of problems. Overall, however, SCC has benefited significantly from the use of first a micro, and now its Texas Instruments minicomputer. The primary use continues to be the creation of "cutting lists" for use in the plants as mentioned previously. The accounting system has gradually been placed on the computer over the past year with limited success. The accounting package was built from scratch by Linda Sharp's assistant, Bud Melman, who happens to have extensive programming experience but little actual accounting experience. In fact, Bud took a course in accounting to facilitate the program development. Most of the "bugs" seem to be out of the system at this point, though occasional problems still occur that lead Laura to have little confidence in the system.

A further potential problem with the software is that it is written in TPL language, which is unique to Texas Instruments systems. Consequently the average programmer who has developed business software has never heard of TPL. This makes it much more difficult to modify the software when necessary than if it were written in a more common language. In addition, TPL is not an easy language to use in database development, a feature that usually makes business software development much easier. Mike has also noticed that the current software is not documented. There is no explanation within the code the programmer had developed to facilitate a subsequent programmer's attempts to modify the current software. SCC's latest system, however, does have a new operating system with the ability to run COBOL, a common computer language used in business. SCC has currently invested about $50,000 in computer hardware and software in the past four years. The question now is what to do about the current software, particularly the accounting software.

RECENT DEVELOPMENTS

Sales have been growing steadily over the years, with the last five years' sales history shown in the operating statements in Exhibit 2. Though sales leveled off in 1983, projected sales for the current fiscal year are around $2.5 million. The average price per piece in 1983 was around $63, with a volume of 31,000 pieces. With a lack of space to store the finished product a recurring problem, Bill sees this as a hindrance to increasing sales much beyond current levels. Though the customer takes delivery fairly soon after the order is completed, more sales mean more product to store at one time, and this can be particularly troublesome during winter if the weather is bad and the customer cannot take delivery readily. Bill leases space on a monthly basis to help alleviate this problem. This leads to increases in fixed as well as variable costs that need to be carefully analyzed. Recent cost of the leased storage space was $1,000 per month. This high level of business is a new experience for SCC, and it has not been necessary until recently to give these problems close attention.

The lease on the current building has increased dramatically over the past two years (from $3,500 to $5,600 per month), and the current lease runs out within six months. Seeing these problems coming on, Bill bought three acres of land near the present building a little over a year ago for $90,000 with the intention of eventually building his own facility. Architectural and engineering plans have been completed, bringing the total current investment to $150,000. The cost of the new building is estimated at around $800,000, down from about $1 million in the original estimate. In addition to solving the problems with space, the new building plans show an increase of 40 percent in floor space. Bill has plans for a conveyer in the new building that will more efficiently transfer the assembled products to the paint department, and greatly simplify the paint department operations. Materials handling and storage, scheduling, and myriad other problems would also be alleviated with the extra space in the shop. A 40 percent increase in floor space will also satisfy a need for increased office space. The computer, which is housed in a six-foot-tall cabinet, and a printer currently occupy a space of less than seventy-five square feet that also serves as a coffee room and lunchtime gathering place for plant employees who use a microwave oven in the same room. In addition, all employees also share two restrooms that are located in the office portion of the building. Bill will have to borrow heavily to finance the new building, and feels he ought to hold on to as much cash as possible to provide a safe level of working capital necessary to support current or increased sales levels. The monthly payment on the new building with a thirty year loan is expected to be around $10,000. Bill has not borrowed any money for about three years, and has not aggressively sought a loan, but he foresees no serious problem in getting the money. His major concern is whether to go ahead with the building at the present time. Business for the current year could produce an increase in profit from operations of around 100 percent with an increase in sales volume of 25 percent. Prospects for the next fiscal year are considerably more uncertain, with many economists predicting a downturn in housing starts. Complicating the decision are strong indications that the land Bill purchased for the building may have tripled in value due to rapid development of surrounding property. The land may be worth more in the long run without a building on the property.

In past years, Bill has often wished the company had the financial and physical capacity to carry some finished inventory. He has always considered this a very risky business, however, because it would require more debt than he wanted or could carry, and because of the space limitations mentioned previously. The average material cost in a piece in 1983 was about $24 out of a total variable cost per piece of around $32. The $32 includes variable selling and administrative costs as well as manufacturing costs. Bill's workforce is rather stable throughout the year despite rather wide fluctuations in production, and Mike compiled these cost figures assuming direct labor as a fixed cost. Clearly, it would not be possible to carry inventory on every cabinet. A decision would have to be made about which cabinets to build for the finished goods inventory. Complicating this decision is the fact that SCC uses several types of paint finishes on the cabinets, which would seem to make it impractical to actually store the cabinets in a completely finished condition. Moreover, about 20 percent of the assembled cabinets are shipped without paint finishing.

Several factors intrigued Mike about leasing extra space as a temporary measure rather than building a new facility, as well as possibly carrying some finished goods inventory:

1. Harry Wood has indicated that if the price of the product was a little more in line with the competition, sales could increase significantly.

2. The current workforce, which in 1984 has shown the capacity to produce 60 percent over the average 1983 monthly production, might be more efficiently utilized by spreading the work more evenly over the year, decreasing the level at peak activity with the potential of increasing overall production.

3. It appears that profit from operations could increase substantially with only a moderate increase in sales volume from current levels.

4. Customer uncertainty concerning SCC's ability to provide the product quickly and reliably would be reduced.

Mike is uncertain about the desirability of financing extra inventory for other reasons:

1. A more sophisticated inventory control system would have to be implemented, possibly affecting current computer software needs.

2. Sales volume across the industry is highly dependent on swings in the economy, and it might be difficult to avoid getting stuck with unwanted inventory.

3. The sudden growth in the level of operations is beginning to strain the administrative capacity of management.

The current successful profit picture may indicate SCC should only seek to maintain current sales level while the entire organization adjusts to the growth in the level of operations—adopt a temporary philosophy of "if it ain't broke, don't fix it." If operations continue to produce similar results over the next year or two, the financial flexibility of the company will be greatly enhanced.

TO SELL OR NOT TO SELL

On a recent visit to the plant, Mike was asked by Bill to sit in on a meeting between Bill and Charlie White, a local business broker. Charlie had in the past discussed with Bill the possibility of selling the business. Though Bill was not considering the idea seriously, he liked Charlie, and was interested in what he had to say about the value of the business. In particular, on this day, Charlie was bringing some figures that he had analyzed with the help of a "young man" with a degree in finance. Mike had done his own analysis, and was interested that Charlie had valued the business from the point of view of projected cash flow as well as current asset value. Mike's figures closely matched Charlie's in measuring the estimated present value of cash flow. There was apparently an interested buyer who had seen the last five years' operating statements and had ideas about continuing the cabinet operation as well as using the equipment for other purposes. Though the tax consequences for Bill of a sale had not been analyzed, the amount mentioned was sufficient enough to provide Bill and Laura with a comfortable retirement. The figure mentioned did not include the current cash in the business, which Bill would keep, nor did it allow for the appreciation of the land Bill had purchased the year before. Bill and Laura, however, feel they would have a hard time being comfortable with the retired life. Laura has often said the business "keeps us young." Furthermore, they are naturally concerned about the fate of some of the people in the plant who have been loyal to them for almost three decades.

WHAT'S NEXT?

Bill Martin wants to continue operating SCC for several years. He currently sees SCC as being on the threshold of becoming a much larger company if some of the opportunities and obstacles described above are handled skillfully. Though there seem to be strong indications that SCC may have found a niche in the market with builders who seek to put extra quality in their homes, the size and stability of this market are uncertain. Meanwhile, Bill and Laura have the feeling that a company must change and grow to remain viable.

QUESTIONS

1. Calculate the value of SCC in 1983 using fisCAL or other valuation methods. What is the range of values? For a company like SCC, what are the significant differences between the valuation methods?
2. Discuss whether Mike should formally join SCC. If so, in what role? Should he insist on some ownership or be content with a salary?
3. Should SCC's computer software be scrapped? Why or why not? If so, what should replace it?
4. If you were Bill Martin, would you sell out?
5. Devise a plan for Bill Martin to transfer SCC to Mike over a period of several years, instead of selling it.

F

Gal-Tech and Melanin: A Case of Technology Transfer

John P. McCray and Juan J. Gonzalez

It had been a rough day. Jim Gallas leaned back in his office chair and tried to relax, but thoughts of his current research problems kept plaguing him. For more than five years now, he had been trying to develop an efficient solar energy heat exchanger. To do this he needed a near-perfect solar energy absorber. His efforts had met with frustration. Then he had decided to try melanin.

Melanin is a natural substance found in the skin and eyes of most animals. In humans, melanin darkens the skin when exposed to the sun, thus protecting us from the sun's radiation. In the back of the eye, melanin forms a "black box" that absorbs much of the harmful radiation coming into the eye.

Gallas hoped that melanin would prove to be the perfect energy absorber so he began to research melanin extensively. After several experiments, he found that while melanin absorbed light, it did not generate enough heat for practical energy production. These experiments revealed, however, that melanin had some interesting properties; it absorbed the sun's rays that were most damaging to the human eye. Melanin absorbed virtually all of the ultraviolet light, much of the blue light, and some of the blue-green light. As a result of these experiments, melanin's solar energy prospects did not look good, but Gallas wondered if melanin could be useful in another way.

As Gallas tried unsuccessfully to push out of his mind the frustration of not finding a good energy absorber, he glanced down at his desk at some glass slips with melanin on them. The thought struck him that melanin might make a good sunglass coating. The glass, if covered with melanin, would protect the human eye by absorbing the harmful radiation of the sun. The phone rang, and he was jarred back to more pressing problems. The following week he continued his search for a perfect solar absorber. The thought of coating sunglasses with melanin surfaced again. Where had this idea come from? Oh, yes, he remembered, he had thought of it the prior week! The thought dwelled with him; melanin did have exactly the right properties to block the harmful rays of the sun. Maybe melanin could be a commercial product. But how could melanin be coated onto something like glass or plastic?

Gallas's interest in melanin increased. It seemed to have more potential as a filter against harmful sunlight than as a heat absorber within solar heaters. Although there are substances other than melanin that will block some of the harmful effects of the sun, none are natural, and none will do the job as efficiently or effectively as melanin does. Other substances block the ultraviolet or blue or green or red light, but none block the harmful effects of the sun in the optimum proportion and over the entire light spectrum, as melanin does.

Wherever it was important to block the harmful effects of the sun, melanin could be useful. Some of the products that might use melanin came immediately to mind: sunglasses, eyeglasses, contact lenses, and protective coatings for auto, home, and office windows, and even paint. Also, Gallas hypothesized that adding melanin to plastics would help protect the plastic from the sun's damage and keep it from decomposing. He believed in melanin's great potential, so he continued his research.

Gallas set about the task of mixing melanin, a water-soluble substance, with plastic. First he tried to melt the plastic and mix it with melanin, but this only resulted in a messy glob. Using various techniques, he tried for six months to mix melanin and plastic, but was unsuccessful. As a result of these experiments, Gallas realized that melanin and plastic would have to be mixed at the molecular level.

Mel Eisner, a fellow physicist, became interested in the problem and began to work with Gallas. Mel suggested that a melanin precursor might mix with a plastic monomer. Gallas conducted several more experiments with the advice and help of a chemist, Frank Feldman, and eventually the process worked. He had invented a melanin concentrate that would mix with plastic or could be formed into a film and applied to glass. For their help in developing the process, and with the understanding that they would continue to be active in the development of melanin concentrate into a commercial product, Gallas promised Eisner and Feldman each 15 percent of the future business income from the invention.

GOING FOR A PATENT

Gallas prepared a detailed description of his process and applied for a U.S. patent. The patent authorities rejected his application, because they did not believe that the process he described constituted a true discovery. Gallas rewrote his request and resubmitted, again with no success.

Gallas now wondered what to do. He had a process that he had discovered, and he was convinced the process was unique and therefore patentable. Also, he knew that a patent was absolutely necessary for his invention to become a successful product.

Determined to get a patent, Gallas decided to use a patent attorney. He wanted a law firm with an experienced patent attorney, an excellent reputation, and offices in both Houston and Washington, D.C. He also wanted a firm that believed he could obtain the patent and would fight to get it. He decided to use a well-known patent law firm in Houston, Texas, that met all of his requirements. He was impressed that several attorneys on the staff of the firm were former attorneys at the U.S. patent office.

Since Gallas could not afford to pay the fees that the patent attorneys required in order to file the patent request, he convinced them to accept as payment 15 percent of the final benefits that would be derived from the patent. The patent attorneys accepted his offer and a staff attorney from the firm was assigned to file the patent request. The application was filed for the third time, but the request was again rejected by the U.S. patent office, this time on the basis of "obviousness" because another patent had recently been awarded for putting melanin into a skin cream.

Another year passed but Gallas did not give up. He decided that if he gave a senior attorney at the law firm, Mr. Barnes, a 5 percent interest in the patent, Barnes would be more motivated to get the application accepted. The patent application was rewritten again. A clear description of the Gallas process showed that melanin-treated lenses designed to protect the human eye were significantly different from melanin-treated skin cream, and that no one had a patent to incorporate melanin onto transparent plastic or glass. This argument convinced the examiner, and the patent was granted October 6, 1987.

The patent abstract reads: "Optical lens system incorporating melanin as an absorbing pigment for protection against electromagnetic radiation." The patent protects from duplication the process of applying melanin to surfaces such as plastic and glass. Gallas retained the patent attorneys to protect and defend his new patent. Knowing how important the patent was, he estimated an expense of $10,000 per year for attorney fees to protect the patent once the product was commercialized.

BECOMING AN ENTREPRENEUR

Once he had a patent that would protect his invention, Gallas went about developing his new technology into a business. The patent was owned by a "partnership" of Gallas, 50 percent; Eisner, 15 percent; the law firm, 15 percent; Mr. Barnes, 5 percent; and Feldman, 15 percent.

The patent attorneys helped Gallas to incorporate under the name of Gal-Tech Corporation, which was chartered in December 1987 as a C Corporation. Two thousand shares of stock were authorized, and one thousand were issued. Stock was to be divided using the same percentages as the patent ownership, with each of the final stockholders receiving their stock at $1.00 par value. However, Gallas recognized that rights to the patent did not necessarily carry over to the corporation.

The attorneys had talked of giving their top partner, Mr. Sliplock, 5 percent, which Gallas assumed would come out of the firm's 15 percent. Only later, when negotiations were under way to develop the actual production company, Gal-Tech, did he discover that the attorneys had meant an additional 5 percent. Gallas argued that since Mr. Barnes would receive 5 percent of the company, Mr. Sliplock's percentage should be included with the law firm's 15 percent; they agreed. Because Frank Feldman could no longer give time to the project, Gallas felt that his percentage should be lowered. Feldman agreed to trade his 15 percent of the patent for 2 percent ownership in Gal-Tech. Another chemist was brought in, Robert Williams, who was given 3 percent of the stock, and Feldman's remaining 10 percent was given to Gallas. Gallas was uncomfortable with the Houston law firm owning such a large percentage (10 percent) of the company, and offered to pay them $65,000 for their remaining ownership, payable as soon as the corporation was capitalized. This stock was then divided between Gallas (7 percent) and Eisner (3 percent). In addition, Gallas had promised Mel Eisner $25,000 and Frank Feldman $10,000 for their past work. Eisner and Feldman were willing to take notes with interest-only annual payments at 10 percent, and the principal due at the end of five years. Gallas, who had invested several years and a great deal of his own money, was willing to take a similar note for $100,000. In this way, the patent became the property of Gal-Tech Corporation, and could be amortized over its remaining life. The final stock ownership was Gallas, 67 percent; Eisner, 18 percent; Barnes, 5 percent; Sliplock, 5 percent; Feldman, 2 percent; and Williams, 3 percent.

Gallas knew that before anyone would invest in Gal-Tech, he would have to develop a market for melanin concentrate. While he was applying for the patent, he had been contacted by the television network CNN. Not wanting to discuss his discovery before receiving the patent, he had put them off. Once the patent was issued, he contacted them and arranged for a television interview. After the interview aired, several other media representatives contacted him for interviews and/or articles. While visiting Monterrey, Mexico, Gallas read an article about himself and his process in a local newspaper and realized that his discovery was beginning to gain widespread press coverage. Prompted by the publicity about melanin and its potential, several large companies contacted Gallas about the process, but because he did not have a marketing strategy nor a definite commercialization plan, few maintained their interest.

Gallas began to research possible markets for his discovery. He quickly learned that the ophthalmic industry includes eyeglasses, sunglasses, contact lenses, and surgically implanted intraocular lenses. However, FDA approval would be needed before contact lenses and intraocular lenses could use melanin. The most obvious potential user of the melanin concentrate seemed to be the sunglass industry. He manufactured a few pairs of melanin-treated sunglasses as prototypes. With their amber-colored lenses, the glasses made eye-catching samples to show to prospective investors.

Gallas learned that the sunglass industry already offered lenses that block a specific portion of the light spectrum. Ultraviolet absorbers block a significant percentage of the UV range. Nationwide, optical labs report coating 13 percent of eyeglasses with UV protection, which is the state of current technology for eye protection. Blue-blockers blocked out all of the blue light, but sacrificed color vision. Gallas felt that melanin would be the logical next step because melanin would block the harmful effects of UV, blue, and blue-green light.

Convinced more and more of the commercial significance of his discovery, Gallas began contacting firms that he thought would be interested in melanin. As a physicist, he would ask to speak to the person in charge of technical development, and proudly explain his discovery and its uses to this person. Time after time, he was surprised to hear negative comments about incorporating melanin into their products using his process. Perhaps the greatest turning point in the development of his product was when he realized that the real value of the melanin process was not its technical attributes, but the perception of value by the consumer. This led Gallas to talk to the marketing departments of the companies that he was contacting. He was surprised when he received a much stronger response from the marketing managers than he had from the scientists.

Also, instead of contacting only manufacturers, he began to contact distributors and those companies that manufacture and market their own sunglasses. The marketing managers in these firms brought much more positive responses, and a few firms began to show genuine interest in using melanin.

After many interesting inquiries, two large sunglass manufacturer/distributors began serious talks with Gallas. One represented the high end of the market, the other represented the low end. Gallas believed that the high end might offer a contract before the end of the first year, paying a licensing fee of $200,000 and a 50 cent royalty per pair sold. Because the low-end company's sales were more seasonal, they would probably not produce melanin sunglasses until the second year. Gallas estimated that they would then pay a licensing fee of $100,000, and also pay a 50 cent royalty per pair sold. The high-end distributors estimated that they could sell 1.1 million pairs of melanin-treated sunglasses the first year. Between the two distributors, sales would double the second year, and increase by 50 percent the third year. Sales would be recorded at the time the concentrate was shipped; receivables could be expected to equal six weeks' sales.

The sunglass firms that had contacted Gallas had excellent name recognition, well-established distribution channels, and promotional and advertising capabilities that Gal-Tech could not possibly match. Because of this, Gallas decided that he should negotiate an agreement to let the sunglass firms advertise his product along with their own, instead of attempting to reach the consumer himself. Still, Gallas knew that advertising, promotion, travel, and entertainment would consume $100,000 of Gal-Tech's first-year budget and at least 10 percent of gross income thereafter.

The closer Gallas got to commercializing his product, the more questions he had concerning the structure of his company and the manufacture of melanin concentrate. He had initially planned to license the manufacture of the melanin concentrate, but he realized that allowing others to produce the concentrate might endanger his control of the process and weaken his patent. Gallas decided that Gal-Tech would have to produce the melanin concentrate itself. He reviewed the manufacturing operations of his company. The sunglass lenses would be coated with ten microns of the melanin concentrate. Assuming the average diameter of a lens is about six centimeters, each pair of sunglasses would require 0.85 grams of melanin concentrate. It would therefore require about eighty-five kilograms of melanin to produce the tint for one million pairs of sunglasses. Actual production of concentrate should include an additional 20 percent to be used for internal research and development. Therefore, it would take about 115 kilograms of melanin concentrate to support the sales of one million pairs of melanin-coated sunglasses.

The melanin concentrate could initially be produced in twenty-liter containers in a batch process that takes place over a twenty-four-hour period and yields about seventy-five grams of melanin per container. Assuming 250 days of production per year, each twenty-liter vessel would yield about nineteen kilograms of melanin per year. Because of this short production cycle, only a two-weeks' supply of chemicals will be kept on hand; also, a finished inventory of two weeks' sales will be kept.

The raw materials used in the production of melanin concentrate are peroxides such as benzol peroxide, solvents such as chloroform and methanol, and the melanin precursors such as catechol and L-Dopa. These raw materials are readily available from several suppliers in quantities necessary to produce all projected requirements. Substitute raw materials are available. The raw materials cost approximately $1 per gram of melanin concentrate produced, a cost that is not expected to change within the next three years.

There are no physical properties of melanin concentrate that limit transportation or distribution. Shipping expenses will be about $4,000 the first year.

Personnel would be divided into three important functions at Gal-Tech: production, sales and marketing, and administration and finance. Each function needs a director; production also requires two technicians and a shipping clerk, and administration requires a secretary/bookkeeper. The production chief will be in charge not only of production but also research and development, and will need to have a Ph.D. in physics or chemistry. His or her salary will be included in the cost of sales. Gallas estimates that the kind of people necessary to make Gal-Tech a success would require annual salaries as follows: chairman of the board $20,000; president $55,000; production manager $40,000; sales and marketing manager $30,000; administrator $25,000; shipping clerk $15,000. Individual salaries are not expected to change over the following three years, but Gallas estimates that at the beginning of the third year, they will have to hire two more technicians, one more shipping clerk, and one more secretary to help the marketing chief. Gallas budgets an additional 9 percent for payroll taxes, up to the legal limits. Health and worker's compensation insurance should be about $8,000 per employee for the first year of operations and increase 5 percent each year.

Gallas thinks that the firm will need room to grow. Five thousand square feet of office/warehouse space is available at 50 cents per square foot per month, which includes common area maintenance and property taxes. Finish out will be accomplished by the landlord, including inside walls and HVAC. One month's rent is required as a deposit. Annual insurance should be about $1 per square foot of space. Furniture and fixtures required and their costs are: lab furniture and fixtures $12,000; vent hoods (2) $18,000; scale $10,000; microscope $10,000; ovens $10,000; chemicals $10,000; glassware $5,000; lab computers $5,000; office furniture and equipment $20,000; office computer, software $6,000; and office supplies $2,000.

These costs will be depreciated over five years, using straight-line depreciation. If sales increase according to plan, $100,000 will have to be borrowed at the beginning of the third year to purchase additional equipment. Gallas hopes then to negotiate a note to be payable over five years, at an interest rate of 12 percent. He knows that any investors will require audited financial statements, and is prepared to pay $5,000 per year for this and other accounting services.

In order to remain a viable company, Gal-Tech will have to invest in itself through research and development. The first year of operation, $200,000 will be spent, and 20 percent of gross revenue thereafter for R & D.

BECOMING A GOING CONCERN

Gallas has made an appointment with a venture capitalist, and plans to ask for $250,000 to capitalize Gal-Tech. James Gallas has the vision needed to use his discovery to create a profitable company. He has a patent and a solid knowledge of how his business will operate. What he doesn't have is the formal structure and financial projections required to attract the capital necessary to bring his vision to life. He needs a formal plan, incorporating all that he knows about his target markets, proposed operations, and financial commitments, including pro forma financial statements for three years.

A NOTE ON THE SUNGLASS INDUSTRY

The sunglass industry is composed of three basic components: prescription sunglasses, high-end sunglasses (over $20 per pair), and low-end sunglasses (under $20 per pair). The nonprescription sunglass market is growing steadily. In 1985, 160 million pairs were sold, and 175 million pairs were sold in 1986. Bausch & Lomb's Consumer Products Division estimates that total sales for the industry were $1.3 billion in 1987, a 16 percent increase over 1986. From 1986 to 1987 the under-$20 market segment increased 9 percent, and the over-$20 market segment, which accounts for 40 percent to 45 percent of the total sunglass market, increased 22 percent. There are more than 250,000 locations that sell sunglasses in the United States, according to Bausch & Lomb, with nearly 55,000 locations selling sunglasses that retail at $20 or over. Many traditional optical retailers are now displaying sunglasses separately and setting up kiosks from which to sell sunglasses.

Brand awareness and glamour are important factors in the sunglass business, and sales are often influenced by celebrities' use of a particular brand. The perception of value by the consumer is also important in the marketing of sunglasses. Vuarnet claims its sunglasses "not only protect your eyes and make a fashion statement, they also help your visual performance and through that your physical performance." This perception of quality is apparently well received by consumers, who purchased $50 million in sunglasses from Vuarnet in 1987.

. . . .

The business plan shown below was developed by John P. McCray and Juan J. Gonzalez from information provided in the case. The title page and table of contents have been omitted for convenience. Only three years, by year, are shown on the pro forma statements to conserve space on the spreadsheets.

. . . .

EXECUTIVE SUMMARY

Gal-Tech Corporation, chartered in Texas in 1987, has developed melanin as its principal product, which it plans to manufacture and market to manufacturers of glass and plastic products, specifically sunglasses. A patent is held on the process.

Melanin is a natural product found in the skin and human eye. It is the means for protecting the human eye from light radiation as it absorbs harmful light rays in proportion to their damaging effects. Competitors' methods of blocking the harmful effects of the sun are not only less effective, but sacrifice color vision.

Gal-Tech is now actively pursuing product manufacturers to incorporate melanin concentrate into their products. Firms in the sunglass industry have already shown an interest in melanin. This industry had sales in 1987 of $1.3 billion so the potential is great. The projected revenue from royalties and fees from sunglass manufacturers over the next three years is estimated to be $3,720,000. Sales beyond this initial three-year period are expected to grow rapidly as the public becomes more aware of the product and more uses are discovered for it.

Gal-Tech has a distinctive competence in developing and manufacturing melanin concentrate. Dr. James Gallas and Dr. Melvin Eisner, who are both physicists, developed the concept and process over a five-year period and possess more knowledge and experience than anyone else at this point in time. Therefore, Gal-Tech is in an ideal position to market this unique process.

The pro forma financial statements in Section G of this plan show that, over the three-year period, Gal-Tech will earn revenues of $3,720,000 and earn a net profit of $390,000 for a return on equity of about 30 percent per year. The cash flow, although negative in the startup year, is very positive in subsequent years. The company expects to break even partway through the second year.

Funds required to begin commercial production and marketing of melanin are $250,000. These can be obtained either from debt or equity sources. In the third year of operation, another $100,000 will be required to fund further expansion.

THE COMPANY

Gal-Tech Corporation is a new venture firm whose mission is to develop, manufacture, and market melanin concentrates to other manufacturers for incorporation into plastic or glass commercial products. The company continues to develop new formulations and applications for melanin. The original development of melanin and the patent that was subsequently secured were done by Dr. James Gallas and Dr. Melvin Eisner.

The current key goal of Gal-Tech is to secure initial financing either through debt or equity sources to purchase the patent and required capital equipment and to provide working capital. A second key goal is to sell melanin to sunglass manufacturers. The third key goal is to further develop other formulations and uses for melanin.

PRODUCT

Melanin is a natural substance found in the skin and eyes of most animals. In humans, melanin darkens the skin when exposed to the sun, thus protecting them from the sun's radiation. In the back of the eye, melanin absorbs much of the harmful radiation coming into the eye. It absorbs virtually all of the ultraviolet light, much of the blue light, and some of the blue-green light. Potential uses for melanin are to coat sunglasses, eyeglasses, and various kinds of windows. A patent has been obtained.

The amount of melanin concentrate used to coat the lenses of sunglasses would be enough to provide a ten-micron coating over the entire surface of the lens. Assuming the average diameter of a lens is about six centimeters, each pair would require .085 grams of melanin concentrate. Thus, it will require about eighty-five kilograms of melanin concentrate to produce the tint for one million pairs of sunglasses.

MARKETING

The potential commercial market for melanin includes the ophthalmic, plastics, tinted glass, and paint industries. As a result of receiving national recognition and publicity, Dr. Gallas has had inquiries from several manufacturers in the contact lens, paint, and window film industries.

Potential Market

For the present, the ophthalmic industry, which includes sunglasses, contact lenses, and intraocular lenses, is the most likely user of melanin. Firms in the sunglass industry are interested in melanin as a filter against the harmful effects of the sun's rays. Firms that sell contact lenses and intraocular lenses are also interested, but Federal Drug Administration (FDA) approval is required before melanin may be used in these products and takes considerable time and testing to secure. Therefore, the principal focus of immediate marketing and research is on the sunglass industry.

The sunglass industry is composed of three basic components: prescription sunglasses, high-end sunglasses (over $20 per pair), and low-end sunglasses (under $20 per pair). Nationwide, optical labs report coating 13 percent of eyeglasses with UV protection, which is the state of current technology for eye protection.[1] The nonprescription sunglass market is growing steadily. In 1985, 160 million pairs were sold and in 1986, 175 million pairs were sold. Bausch & Lomb's Consumer Products Division estimates that total sales for the industry were $1.3 billion in 1987, a 16 percent increase over 1986. From 1986 to 1987, the under-$20 market segment increased 9 percent and the over-$20 market, which accounts for 40 percent to 50 percent of the total sunglass market, increased 22 percent.[2]

There are more than 250,000 locations that sell sunglasses in the United States, according to Bausch & Lomb, with nearly 55,000 locations selling sunglasses that retail at $20 or over. Many traditional optical retailers are now displaying sunglasses separately and setting up kiosks from which to sell them.[3]

Brand awareness and glamour are important factors in the sunglass business, and sales are often influenced by celebrities' use of a particular brand. The perception of value by the consumer is also important in the marketing of sunglasses. Vuarnet claims its sunglasses "not only protect your eyes and make a fashion statement, they also help your visual performance and through that your physical performance.[4] This perception of quality is apparently well received by consumers, who purchased $50 million in sunglasses from Vuarnet in 1987.[5] As a natural substance, melanin should be well received by buyers of sunglasses.[6]

Competition

While there is no direct competition for melanin coated sunglasses at the present time, when melanin enters the market through one or more manufacturers, other major manufacturers can be expected to offer substitute coatings. Melanin's blocking power can be somewhat resembled by tintings, films, and dyes. Overlapping films and tints will provide a crude look-alike, but they cannot duplicate the melanin protection and may decompose over time. Other manufacturers could only claim to have a "melanin-like" product due to the patent held by Gal-Tech, which reads in part: "Optical lens system incorporating melanin as an absorbing pigment for protection against electromagnetic radiation."

User Benefits

Melanin is a natural substance found in the skin and eyes of most animals. It absorbs virtually all of the ultraviolet light, much of the blue light, and some of the blue-green present in light from the sun. It will provide to the users of sunglasses that are coated with melanin protection from virtually all of the harmful effects of sunlight on the eyes. This can be accomplished without diminishing the ability of the wearer to see true colors.

Target Market

Gal-Tech will initially target the sunglass industry. It is relatively easy to incorporate melanin into sunglasses, and there is an immediate demand for such a product. Active negotiations are currently underway with two major sunglass manufacturers who represent the high-end and low-end of the market. These firms have expressed an interest in using melanin concentrate in their products. Gal-Tech will manufacture melanin concentrate and supply it to firms upon their signing a licensing contract. It is proposed that the sunglass firms pay an initial licensing fee plus a royalty percentage of 50 cents per pair sold.

Marketing Strategy

Because of consumer brand loyalty, Gal-Tech will market directly to manufacturers. The manufacturer or distributor of melanin products will be expected to advertise the natural benefits of melanin to the general public. Advertising by manufacturers that use melanin will be encouraged through price breaks.

Initial penetration into the sunglass coating market will be achieved by securing a license agreement with one or more of the large manufacturers of sunglasses. With this license agreement in hand, cash flow will be generated to develop other markets. Gal-Tech will maintain control through on-site support. The advantages of this strategy are outlined below:

1. Low initial capital cost.
2. Name recognition within the industry of the manufacturer or distributor.
3. Already established distribution channels will be open to the product.
4. Promotional and advertising capabilities of the manufacturer or distributor exceed those of Gal-Tech.

Projected Sales

Production requirements for melanin concentrate are eighty-five kilograms for each one million sunglasses to be coated plus 20 percent overage to cover the additional material needed by manufacturers for losses and defects in their production process. An additional 10 percent is to be provided for internal research and development. Thus, about 115 kilograms of melanin concentrate will be required to support annual sales of tint for one million pairs of sunglasses. The high-end distributors estimate sales of 1,140,000 pairs of melanin-treated sunglasses the first year. With the advent of the second distributor in the second year, sales are expected to double and continue to increase by 50 percent in the third year. Thus, melanin sales by Gal-Tech are expected to be 115 kilograms, 230 kilograms, and 345 kilograms, respectively, over the three-year period.

PRODUCT DEVELOPMENT

Product development will be an ongoing effort by Dr. Gallas, Dr. Eisner, and the production manager. The direction of future activities, in addition to further developments for the sunglass industry, will include applications for eyeglasses, windows, and paints.

OPERATIONS
Facilities

The production process for melanin will consist of using twenty-liter containers in a batch process that takes place over a twenty-hour period and yields about seventy-five grams of melanin per container. Therefore, it will require twelve twenty-liter containers to produce 230 kilograms of melanin annually, which is the initial production capacity.

Gal-Tech plans to lease five thousand square feet in an office/warehouse development area. Interior finishing to Gal-Tech's specifications will be accomplished by the landlord, including such things as inside walls and air conditioning. Initial equipment that will be purchased includes the following:

Rent deposit	$ 2,500
Lab furniture & fixtures	12,000
Vent hoods (2)	18,000
Scale	10,000
Microscope	10,000
Ovens	10,000
Chemicals	10,000
Glassware	5,000
Lab computers	5,000
Office furniture & equipment	20,000
Office computer & software	6,000
Office supplies	2,000
TOTAL	$105,500

Materials

Raw materials used in the production concentrate are peroxides such as benzol peroxide, solvents such as chloroform and methanol, and the melanin precursors such as catechol and L-Dopa. These materials are readily available from several suppliers in quantities necessary to produce all projected melanin requirements. Substitute raw materials are also available. Pricing is competitive and quite stable.

Distribution

The melanin concentrate will be shipped to buyers by the most cost-efficient means. There are no physical properties of melanin that limit transportation or distribution methods. A large inventory of melanin concentrate will not need to be maintained due to the short production cycle.

Staffing

Because of the simple production process only two technicians with a background in chemistry will be needed initially at a salary of $20,000 each. In addition, a shipping clerk at a salary of $15,000 and a secretary/bookkeeper at a salary of $15,000 will be required initially. At the beginning of the third year the number of employees will be doubled to accommodate growth.

Quality

The quality level achieved in melanin production is very high. Because of time spent in the initial development of melanin and its production, the "bugs" have been worked out.

MANAGEMENT TEAM

The founders and principals of Gal-Tech are Dr. James Gallas and Dr. Melvin Eisner, both physicists who worked together on developing the melanin process since 1982. They will serve respectively as chief executive officer at a salary of $20,000 and president at a salary of $55,000.

The production manager will have a Ph.D. in chemistry or physics and will be responsible for the production activity as well as continue to research and develop new uses for melanin or methods for its production at an annual salary of $40,000.

The sales/marketing manager will have previous experience in marketing of chemical products and an appropriate degree in business administration. This person will be responsible for contacting prospective custom-

EXHIBIT 1
Gal-Tech Organization Chart

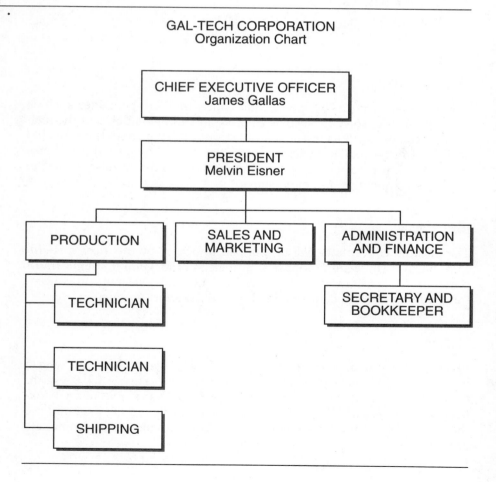

GAL-TECH CORPORATION
Organization Chart

ers and developing an advertising program as needed at a salary of
$30,000.

The fifth management team member will be the administrator at a
salary of $25,000. This person will be responsible for supervising office
personnel and providing financial budgets, data, and reports.

The proposed organization chart for Gal-Tech appears in Exhibit 1.

FINANCIAL ANALYSIS

Following are the pro forma income statement, cash flow statement, and
balance sheet for Gal-Tech for a projected three-year period. The statements represent the expected sales levels and are thought to be conservative. The break-even point occurs at a royalty level of $920,000 (1,840,000

GAL-TECH CORPORATION
Pro Forma Income Statement
Three Years
(In thousands of dollars)

	Year 1	Percentage	Year 2	Percentage	Year 3	Percentage
Revenue						
Royalties	$570.0	74.0%	$1,140.0	91.9%	$1,710.0	100.0%
License Fees	200.0	26.0	100.0	8.1		
Total	$770.0	100.0	$1,240.0	100.0	$1,710.0	100.0
Cost of Sales						
Chemicals	$106.3	13.8	$ 212.6	17.1	$ 318.9	18.6
Labor	95.0	12.3	95.0	7.7	150.0	8.8
Shipping	4.0	0.5	8.0	0.6	12.0	0.7
Total	$205.3	26.7	$ 315.6	25.5	$ 480.9	28.1
Gross Profit	$564.7	73.3	$ 924.4	74.5	$1,229.1	71.9
Operating Expenses						
Accounting and Legal	$15.0	1.9	$ 15.0	1.2	$ 15.0	0.9
Advertising and Promotion	100.0	13.0	124.0	10.0	171.0	10.0
Amortization	13.0	1.7	13.0	1.0	13.0	0.8
Depreciation	21.1	2.7	21.1	1.7	41.4	2.4
Insurance—Property	5.0	0.6	5.0	0.4	7.5	0.4
Insurance—Workers' Compensation	8.0	1.0	8.0	0.6	12.0	0.7
Insurance—Health	8.0	1.0	8.0	0.6	12.0	0.7
Freight out	2.4	0.3	4.0	0.3	6.0	0.4
Rent	30.0	3.9	30.0	2.4	45.0	2.6
Research & Development	200.0	26.0	250.0	20.2	340.0	19.9
Salaries	40.0	5.2	40.0	3.2	55.0	3.2
Officer Salary	75.0	9.7	75.0	6.0	75.0	4.4
Taxes—General	2.0	0.3	2.0	0.2	3.0	0.2
Taxes—Payroll	18.0	2.3	18.0	1.5	24.3	1.4
Other	38.0	4.9	43.0	3.5	59.0	3.5
Total	$575.5	74.7	$ 656.1	52.9	$ 878.9	51.4
Operating Income	(10.8)	−1.4	268.3	21.6	350.2	20.5
Interest Expense	13.5	1.8	13.5	1.1	25.5	1.5
Income before Tax	(24.3)	−3.2	254.8	20.5	324.7	19.0
Income Taxes			66.6	5.4	98.6	5.8
Net Income	$(24.3)	−3.2	$ 188.2	15.2	$ 226.1	13.2

GAL-TECH CORPORATION
Pro Forma Cash Flow Statement
Three Years
(In thousands of dollars)

	Year 1	Year 2	Year 3
Beginning Cash Balance	$ 184.1	$ 27.0	$ 176.1
Receipts:			
Royalties	570.0	1,140.0	1,710.0
License Fees	200.0	100.0	
Less A/R Increase	71.2	71.3	
Total Receipts	$ 698.8	$1,168.7	$1,638.7
Cash Disbursements			
Direct Materials	$ 114.5	$ 281.9	$ 326.1
Direct Labor	98.7	96.9	152.8
Shipping	4.0	8.0	12.0
Operating Expenses	541.4	622.0	824.8
Capital Expenditures	105.5		100.0
Long-Term Debt			(80.0)
Interest Expense	13.5	13.5	25.5
Income Tax Expense		66.6	98.6
Total Disbursements	$ 877.6	$1,025.8	$1,459.8
Net Cash Flow	$(178.8)	$ 142.9	$ 178.9
Cash before Short-Term Loans	5.3	169.9	355.0
Short-Term Borrowing	19.8	6.2	29.5
Short-Term Repayments			
Ending Cash Balance	$ 27.0	$ 176.1	$ 384.5

pairs of sunglasses) or 212 kilograms of melanin. This calculation does not include the initial licensing fees, which make it possible for the firm to generate a profit the second year. A small loss of $24,300 is anticipated the first year of operations.

Once the initial financing is accomplished, cash flow for the first year of operations is negative. However, subsequent years' cash flow is strongly positive.

FINANCIAL STRUCTURE

Gal-Tech is organized as a C-type corporation registered in Texas. Two thousand shares of common stock at $1 par value have been authorized and one thousand shares issued and held as shown below.

Gallas	670 shares
Eisner	180
Barnes	50
Sliplock	50
Williams	30
Feldman	20

GAL-TECH CORPORATION
Pro Forma Balance Sheet
Year Ending
(In thousands of dollars)

	Year 1	Year 2	Year 3
Current Assets			
Cash	$ 27.0	$176.1	$384.5
Accounts Receivable	71.2	142.5	213.7
Inventory:			
Chemicals	4.0	8.0	12.0
Finished	7.9	12.0	18.0
Total Current Assets	$110.1	$338.6	$628.2
Fixed Assets			
Plant & Equipment	$105.5	$105.5	$205.5
Less Depreciation	21.1	42.2	83.3
Net	$ 84.4	$ 63.3	$122.2
Other Assets			
Patents	$200.0	$200.0	$200.0
Less Amortization	13.0	26.0	39.0
Net	$187.0	$174.0	$161.0
Total Assets	$381.5	$575.9	$911.4
Current Liabilities			
Accounts Payable	$ 14.3	$ 18.0	$ 25.0
Accrued Payable Taxes	3.0	3.0	3.0
Accrued Expenses	2.5	5.0	7.5
Current Long-Term Debt			20.0
Total Current Liabilities	$ 19.8	$ 26.0	$ 55.5
Long-Term Debt	$135.0	$135.0	$215.0
Total Liabilities	$154.8	$161.0	$250.5
Equity			
Common Stock	$ 1.0	$ 1.0	$ 1.0
Paid-in Capital	250.0	250.0	250.0
Retained Earnings	(24.3)	163.9	389.9
Total Equity	$226.7	$414.9	$640.9
Liabilities and Equity	$381.5	$575.9	$911.4

The patent upon which the melanin process is based is valued at $200,000 and is owned by James Gallas, 50 percent; Melvin Eisner, 15 percent; Barnes & Sliplock law firm, 15 percent; Frank Feldman, 15 percent; and Barnes, 5 percent. The proposed purchase of the patent by Gal-Tech would be accomplished by issuing notes payable in five years with interest only at 10 percent payable annually. These notes would be issued as follows: James Gallas, $100,000; Melvin Eisner, $25,000; and Frank Feldman, $10,000. The law firm would receive an immediate $65,000 payment for its interest in the patent once Gal-Tech is fully capitalized.

Gal-Tech will require initial funds of $250,000 to begin operations. Dr. Gallas is prepared to negotiate either debt or equity in exchange for the sun needed. The payback terms are also negotiable. The pro forma balance sheet assumes that equity is used and that the one thousand shares are reapportioned rather than issued.

The funds received will be used to buy out the law firm's ownership in the patent, to provide capital equipment and provide working capital. No additional external funding is planned until the third year, when $100,000 would be borrowed for expansion.

QUESTIONS

1. Is the Gal-Tech business plan well done? What changes would you make, if any?
2. If you were a venture capitalist, would you invest in Gal-Tech?
3. Are there any fatal flaws that would keep Gal-Tech from succeeding?
4. Consider the ownership percentages. Would you do them differently? If so, how?
5. How would you value the patent?

ENDNOTES

1. Irving Bennett, *1988 State of the Ophthalmic Industry* (New York: Advisory Enterprises, 1988).
2. Ibid., 16.
3. Ibid.
4. *Consumer Reports*, August 1988, 504.
5. Bennett, *1988 State*, 16.
6. Standard & Poors, October 13, 1988.

G

Movies R Us

JoAnn C. Carland, James W. Carland, and Kirk E. Stephens

Janice was reading a great novel and she was loath to put it down when Donald came striding into the library. "Janice, you just have to go to Shelby tomorrow and get the month-end receipts from Movies R Us to give to the accountant. He's getting pushy again. He said that if we didn't have the data in by Friday, he wouldn't be able to work us in for another six weeks and we have to do closeouts."

Janice was quite resentful at the interruption and Donald's tone of voice. After all, what had started out to be fun was now a nightmare. She didn't even like going to Shelby anymore. She never had time to visit with her friends because they never came into the store anymore, and Carol and Lorna were always complaining about something. She hated it. It had been so much fun getting the video store ready to open and there was even some excitement when the store was computerized, because that was going to make her so much money. But then Donald had forced them to move to Charlotte to be closer to his work. She hadn't even gotten to use that state-of-the-art system she'd installed.

Riding for an hour to check up on your business once a month was no fun at all. She had tried selling the business to a friend, but that hadn't worked either. Thank goodness Donald had had his attorney draw up the paperwork, so that when James had defaulted on his payments, she got the business back, but what to do now?

Noting Janice's lack of interest, Donald sighed, "Okay, I know you're tired of this and I know the business isn't making much money now, but we've tried to sell it! I don't know what to do; maybe we ought to hire a consultant. If we could get someone to come in with a fresh viewpoint, maybe he or she could suggest some alternatives or help us decide what to do."

Janice thought that was the best idea she'd heard lately. She had a contact at a university and she thought that might be a source worth

Case prepared by JoAnn C. Carland and James W. Carland of the School of Business at Western Carolina University and Kirk E. Stephens of Southwestern Community College in Sylva, North Carolina. Used with permission.

exploring. She even thought that she could get this consulting done for free. That was a comforting thought.

BACKGROUND OF THE COMPANY

Movies R Us was founded in June 1982 by Janice and Donald Peters in Shelby, North Carolina, a town of ten thousand people with a college population of six thousand. Janice was to be the principal owner and the manager and it would be her venture. Donald would keep his job, which was the primary source of income for the family, and help Janice in the evenings and on weekends. The firm would engage in the sale and rental of prerecorded video tapes.

The company was highly successful initially since it was the first video rental store of its type to locate in this small town. An advantage that drove their success was the fact that since the town was not densely populated, cable television was not yet a reality here. A few of the more wealthy citizens had satellite dishes, but most people in the area did not even receive television clearly, and even then the maximum reception was only three stations.

Janice and Donald recognized the opportunity and were delighted with the reaction of their customers. Desperate viewers paid $50 to $100 for memberships and might pay as much as $5 for a rental. Quickly, the Peterses realized that there was a market for VCR rentals as well since not many families owned their own equipment. So to cover all the bases, they rented both Beta and VHS tapes. For a while, they even had a room set up for X-rated movies until it became illegal to rent them.

Janice had hired a bookkeeper, a secretary, and two sales clerks for the Movies R Us store in Shelby. Janice worked in the business as manager. The Peterses were so successful that Donald quit his job and they opened four more stores in nearby small towns. The two of them rotated through the stores spending several days each week in each store using the Shelby store as home base. Janice and Don hired local managers for each of their other cities, but maintained an active involvement with these other businesses.

In January 1987, Donald had an opportunity he could not deny. A large company in Charlotte, North Carolina, had recognized his expertise and literally made him an offer that he could not refuse. He would be doing little travel and would be making a six-figure income doing the type of job for which he had trained. He was ecstatic and could not understand why Janice was not delighted for him. Oh, she said all the right things, but you could tell that her heart wasn't in it. Donald thought the new job was a blessing in disguise. After all, the video business had been steadily declining. Where once theirs was the only video store in town, now there were six others, not counting the rental of videos through grocery stores, department stores, and even convenience marts. Everyone was getting into the act.

In 1987 the Peterses began liquidating their holdings. They found ready buyers for their four stores and decided to keep the first store for

Janice, since the whole concept had been hers anyway. It was the strongest store in that it had the largest video collection and the Peterses were extremely well known in Shelby. But the year had taken its toll. The move to Charlotte to be closer to Donald's new job, the renovation of their new home and sale of their old, the children going away to college, and the new duties expected of the wife of a senior officer in a large corporation meant that Janice spent less and less time at Movies R Us. Carol and Lorna, the bookkeeper and secretary, were unhappy. They were alone most of the time and neither had been trained as a manager. They found themselves forced into making decisions because Janice was not available even by phone. They were uncomfortable as unofficial managers and Janice always seemed to second-guess their decisions, even when she ultimately agreed with them. Sales were slipping and Janice was becoming increasingly frustrated.

In December 1988, James Cuthbert came to see Janice while she was working at the store and asked to buy it from her. He made an attractive offer, but he wanted to allow the business to support his purchase because he asked to buy the business on an installment basis. After discussing the proposal with her husband, Janice agreed to sell the store to James. That lasted exactly twelve months, when James defaulted on his installments.

The Peterses took legal action to reacquire the store and Janice assumed the role of manager once again. Even though no financial loss occurred, Janice was extremely concerned because she had a long talk with Carol and Lorna who had stayed on under the new management. Her old friends told her that the store was not doing well at all. In fact, Carol and Lorna thought that James and his sour disposition had managed to run off even their most loyal customers. Now what was Janice to do?

THE VIDEO RENTAL INDUSTRY

Lower-priced videocassettes, under $30, are aimed at consumer purchase rather than rental. Higher-priced tapes, in the $80 to $90 range, are targeted for the rental market. Rental revenue is determined by the number of transactions (rentals) the tape achieves exceeding the cost of the tape and other expenses. The general rule of thumb for rentals is that a movie should pay for itself the first month.

Video Marketing, an industry research firm based in Hollywood, California, estimated that consumers spent $7.46 billion on prerecorded tapes in 1987, including $4.68 billion for rentals and $2.78 billion for purchases. Tape sales were up an estimated 61 percent over 1986, while rental expenditures grew an estimated 16 percent.[1]

According to the *Leisure Time* Industry Survey in 1988, about thirteen million VCRs were sold to dealers in 1987—slightly more than the previous year. This has enhanced the rental figures and negatively affected the equipment rental segment of the industry.[2]

Paul Kagan Associates, a research firm in New York City, claims that home video was the fastest growing component of film revenues for the five years from 1982 to 1987. During that period, Kagan estimates that domestic home video revenues grew at a 53 percent compound annual rate, while foreign home video and foreign television revenues increased at a 37 percent compound rate. Kagan also reports that revenues from television syndication increased at an 11 percent rate, followed by pay television with an 8 percent increase, domestic theatre up 4 percent, foreign theatre up 2 percent, and network television down 6 percent.[3]

Prerecorded videos make money for the distributor as well. Sales for video purchases in the under-$30 market have been led by Paramount. Paramount placed six films among the top ten all-time best-selling movie videos including: *Top Gun*, 2.9 million copies; *Crocodile Dundee*, 2 million; *Star Trek IV*, 1.7 million; *Indiana Jones and the Temple of Doom* and *Beverly Hills Cop*, each 1.4 million; and *Raiders of the Lost Ark*, 1.3 million. Disney has been successful with *Lady and the Tramp* at about 3 million copies and *Sleeping Beauty* at 1.3 million. MCA is expected to break the million dollar mark with *An American Tale* and *E.T.*[4]

Those movies that were priced for rental in the $80 to $90 price range accounted for roughly 300,000 to 500,000 units. These include Paramount's *Beverly Hills Cop II*, HBO/Cannon's *Rambo, First Blood*, CBS/Fox's *Return of the Jedi*, HBO's *Platoon*, MCA's *Back to the Future*, RCA/Columbia's *Karate Kid, Part II*, VESTRON's *Dirty Dancing*, ORION's *Robocop*, and Warner's *Lethal Weapon*.[5]

In 1988, *Forbes* magazine showcased an entrepreneur in the video rental business. Video rental at this time was one of the country's fastest-growing and most fragmented industries. More than half of the U.S. television households had at least one VCR. As mentioned earlier, it is estimated that the rental market accounts for about $5 billion a year, but so far, no single company has claimed the majority of that revenue. According to the *Forbes* article, there are now more than twenty-five thousand video rental stores, mostly small storefront ventures. However, when combined with the rental departments in grocery stores and in record and convenience stores and mass merchants, there are more than fifty-seven thousand rental outlets. Most of these stores stock only a few hundred tapes each.[6]

Wayne Huizenga, the owner of Blockbuster Video, intends to create the first nationwide chain offering huge selections. In 1988, Blockbuster had two hundred stores (129 of them company-owned) in thirty states. Each store stocks a minimum of sixty-five hundred different titles with multiple copies accounting for about ten thousand tapes in all. The video stores stay open from 10 A.M. to midnight, seven days per week. Revenues have been blockbusters as well, growing from $7.4 million in 1986 to $43.2 million in 1987, with expectations of $135 million that were projected for 1988.[7]

THE CONSULTATION

Kirk Simmons and Jane Rector were the consultants who responded to Janice Peters's call for assistance. Assigned to the case by a university professor, they were told only that a video rental store owner had asked for some advice about how she could increase her market. They phoned Janice and set up a meeting.

The consultants found Movies R Us in a strip shopping center on the outskirts of Shelby. The location was not bad. There was plenty of parking. The center was accessible and it was well maintained. Upon entering the store, Kirk and Jane were pleasantly surprised. There was a great deal of room and the shelves were spread for easy viewing by groups of people. There was a large screen television playing a current video selection and the movies were arranged by type. Only tapes on hand were displayed. The boxes for those out on rental were inserted in the tape rack behind the counter, a common practice in video stores.

Jane noticed that there was no special section set aside for the new releases, but found them intermingled with the old. There was, however, a chalkboard indicating which new releases were available. Kirk noticed that there were multiple copies of many of the newer movies. He had just recently watched *Platoon* and knew that it was quite popular, but the store had seven copies of that movie on the shelf. Kirk wondered whether any additional copies were out on rental.

After browsing for a few minutes and allowing the one client to finish his transactions, Kirk and Jane introduced themselves to the person behind the counter.

Cindy Lance was a young college student who worked part-time in the video store as a sales clerk. She was really perplexed when Kirk explained that he and Jane had an appointment with Janice Peters at the store at 11 o'clock. Cindy was alone in the store and had been all morning. Janice was not there and was not expected. Cindy tried to reach Janice by phone after explaining that if Janice were still at home, it would take her an hour to get to the shop.

There was no answer at Janice's home. Cindy tried to reach the bookkeeper and secretary who perhaps could help Cindy track Janice down. No luck. They were not available either. Hoping not to lose a client nor waste time, Kirk asked Cindy a few questions. He discovered that Movies R Us had a state-of-the-art computer system that tracked sales by tape, handled customer accounts, and printed out receipts. They had the typical policy of a free rental after ten rentals and the computer tracked those counts as well.

Further questions indicated that rates varied by newness of the movie. Old tapes might rent for $1 a night while the newest releases might rent for $3. There were also specials such as a three-for-one deal on Wednesdays, or movies rented on Saturday could be returned Monday without penalty. Movies were considered late if returned after 6 P.M. the following day with the late fee often equaling the rental fee. Hours posted on the door indicated that the store was open 10 A.M. to 8 P.M. on Monday through Friday and 10 A.M. to 6 P.M. on Saturday. Jane observed that there was no night deposit box for movies coming in after hours.

Jane had been dying to see *Black Widow*. So after looking at the titles and not finding it, she asked Cindy if it was available yet. Cindy looked on the computer and discovered that it was out on rental. Jane asked if she could reserve the copy when it came in and was told no. Jane was a bit

EXHIBIT 1

Examples of Movies R Us
Inventory

Name of Tape	Number of copies on shelf	Number of copies owned
Rentals priced at or below $30		
Top Gun	1	10
Crocodile Dundee	4	10
Star Trek IV	1	1
Beverly Hills Cop	2	5
Indiana Jones and the Temple of Doom	0	1
Raiders of the Lost Ark	0	1
Lady and the Tramp	2	3
Sleeping Beauty	3	3
Rentals priced in $80-90 range		
Beverly Hills Cop II	8	9
Rambo	3	5
Return of the Jedi	0	1
Platoon	7	10
Back to the Future	0	1
Karate Kid Part II	2	5
Dirty Dancing	4	8
Robocop	3	3
Lethal Weapon	2	3

surprised and asked whether the computer system could keep a running list of reservations for new releases. Cindy looked confused and said that she had never been told how to do that if it were possible.

An hour later, Janice had not appeared and Kirk and Jane decided to leave. Jane had spent her time doing a selected count of tapes on hand and on rental (see Inventory Example in Exhibit 1). During the detailed analysis of the few tapes, Jane was struck by the concentration of Westerns and war movies. Fully a third of the collection seemed to be concentrated in these two areas. Cindy had told Kirk a little about the other employees and given him some financial averages from the computer system (see Exhibit 2 and Exhibit 3). She suggested that they make another appointment to see Janice.

Kirk and Jane called and set up another appointment the following week. Janice was apologetic; she had been occupied at a social function and was unable to escape. Meanwhile, Kirk visited the library and gleaned some industry information while Jane searched for financial averages for the video industry.

On the second scheduled visit, Janice again did not make it. But she had instructed the employees to answer all questions related to the business, although they were not to give out any financial information about the company. Being frustrated again, Kirk asked just a few questions.

- Janice Peters, owner of the firm. Founded Movies R Us with husband, Donald, in 1982. Opened four additional stores in next year. Took active role in management of chain, now manager of only one remaining store. Not dependent on firm for primary source of family income. Has college education in English literature. Has two children, one is in college and the other will enter this year.
- Carol Lance, bookkeeper. Employee since firm's inception. Active bookkeeper for five-store chain, now has duties "on the floor" of the existing store. Deals directly with customers. Holds high school diploma with previous experience in bookkeeping. Has two children, one of whom works in the store.
- Lorna Dorman, secretary to Janice Peters. Now virtually no duties except as clerk in store. Has high school education. Is long-time friend of the Peterses. Employed with firm since inception.
- Cindy Lance, sales clerk. Has two years with the firm. Is enrolled in interior design program at the local college.
- Judy Dorman, sales clerk for six months. Enrolled in local college in management program.

EXHIBIT 2
Personnel, as reported by Cindy Lance

	Industry Averages per Video Store	Movies R Us (as supplied by Cindy)
Store size	2,089 sq ft*	1,200 sq. ft.
Tapes stocked	3,478*	1,853
Individual titles	2,417*	750
Tapes rented daily	185**	45
Percentage of stock rented daily	5.3%**	2.4%
Rental price	$1.89**	$2.00
Wholesale tape cost (new releases)	$50**	$60
Resale price of used tapes	$16**	$20
Full-time employees	3*	3
Part-time employees	4*	2

*Video Software Dealers Association
**The Fairfield Group, Inc.

EXHIBIT 3
Competitive Analysis
SOURCE: *Inc.*, February 1988, 43.

"Does your computer track the return on investment of each of the movies?" Jane was disturbed about the financials. How was one to analyze anything without data?

Cindy did not understand what he meant so Kirk gave her an example. "You have nine copies of *Beverly Hills Cop II* on the shelves; can you show me the revenue generated by that movie?"

Cindy turned to the computer and started looking at the reports menu. Much to her surprise, the system was indeed able to provide detailed return on investment data by tape. She typed in the ID number of *Beverly Hills Cop II* and the following was produced:

Beverly Hills Cop II	Cost $89.95
Tape Number	**Revenue per tape**
902	$56.50
904	58.00
905	51.50
906	58.50
910	41.00
911	59.49
912	58.00
915	59.00
917	57.50

"You mentioned the last time we were here that Movies R Us had been owned by Ms. Peters, then sold to Mr. Cuthbert, and is now owned again by Ms. Peters. Were you here the whole while?" asked Kirk. Jane was studying the printout.

"Oh, no!" exclaimed Cindy. "But my mother was. She's the bookkeeper, you know."

"Well, then how long have you worked here?"

"For two years," replied Cindy.

"Then you were here while Mr. Cuthbert was, is that right?" Kirk was wondering what Jane had found in that printout.

"Well, yes!" replied Cindy.

"Then perhaps you can tell us what changes have been made since the old owner has come back," said Kirk.

"Oh, there haven't really been any changes," responded Cindy. "Just the name of the store."

"What do you mean?" asked Jane, who had now turned her attention to the conversation.

"Well, Mr. Cuthbert called the store Cuthbert's Video Express while he was the owner, but he didn't change anything else," Cindy claimed.

"Did you notice any changes in the number of customers when Mr. Cuthbert owned the store?" inquired Kirk.

"Oh, yes!" Cindy exclaimed. "People quit coming because Mr. Cuthbert wasn't very friendly and he was here all the time. I wanted to quit but I needed the money and my mom persuaded me to stay. Mr. Cuthbert was very abrupt and didn't like people to spend too much time looking around."

"When Ms. Peters took the store back, did she institute any changes?" Jane was getting a bad feeling about this business.

"Well, not really. She changed the name of the store back to Movies R Us and, let's see, she cut down the number of hours and she said that we were in charge. That's all," continued Cindy.

Deciding that Cindy's summation was appropriate, Kirk and Jane left. "What do you think we have here?" mused Kirk as he and Jane drove back to the office. He was reading the printout on *Beverly Hills Cop II* while Jane was driving.

"A clear-cut case," Jane responded.

Kirk wasn't so sure about that, but he was convinced that there would be no further visits to this client. He was ready to close the case. Jane suggested one more attempt. They compromised and decided to try for a telephone interview.

Three days later, Kirk reached Janice by telephone and asked the following questions.

Kirk: Why did you decide to go into business?

Janice: The circumstances were right. My husband and I wanted to be our own bosses for a while. The industry was new, so we took a chance.

K: What are your goals for the business?

J: To double our sales in one year and to build the selections available.

K: What about long-term goals?

J: We haven't really thought that far ahead.

K: What about your personal goals as they might relate to the business?

J: Oh, we just wanted to have a good income and be able to put our kids through college. We didn't really start this business as something they might want to take over some day.

K: How much time is devoted to planning for your business?

J: We evaluate the operations monthly.

K: Do you have a written plan to serve as a benchmark?

J: No, we just do all our planning mentally. We don't need to write anything down because since I'm the owner/manager, I don't need to tell myself anything.

K: What is your distinctive competency?

J: I don't know what you mean.

K: I mean how do you differentiate your business from that of your competition?

J: Oh, we aren't different at all. We do try to have better service than they. But video stores are video stores, aren't they?

K: Do you foresee any threats to your business? Or opportunities not yet realized?

J: There are no threats. As for opportunities, we'll just have to wait and see what the industry brings.

K: Do you see any strengths or weaknesses in your company?

J: Our real strength is our stability.

K: What do you feel are the real bases for competition with other video stores in the area?

J: Well, we supply good service. The sales clerks are very personable. Our prices are good and we have a large number of copies of all the new releases.

K: Who is your target market?

J: Why, the locals, of course.

K: What about the students from the local colleges?

J: We try not to rent to them if we can help it. You know we like to keep steady customers and build up a stable clientele. Students are not always dependable.

K: What kind of advertising do you do?

J: We don't do any formal advertising. After all, we have been at this same location for eight years. People know we're here.

K: Who makes the decisions about the business such as purchases, etc.?

J: Oh, as owner, I make all the decisions about the policies and inventory.

K: Before you started your business, did you calculate any breakevens for your business?

J: No, but obviously, we have been successful.

At this point in the conversation, Janice had to end the call because she was late for an appointment. Kirk and Jane never met with her again nor gained any further information. The consultants prepared their report on the basis of the data they had gathered and the insights they had gained, forwarded the report to the client, and closed the case.

QUESTIONS

1. What are the options available to Janice?
2. Given the changes in the competitive situation since Movies R Us was first started, what can be done to increase sales?
3. Would Movies R Us be a viable business if an owner took a real interest in it?
4. What changes could be made in their inventory policy or operation procedure to make the store more profitable?
5. If you were writing the consulting report for Kirk Simmons and Jane Rector, what would you recommend?

ENDNOTES

1. "Industry Surveys: Home Video is Big Business," *Leisure Time*, March 10, 1988, 23–24.
2. Ibid.
3. Ibid.
4. Ibid.
5. Ibid.
6. S. N. Chakravarty, "Give 'em Variety," *Forbes*, May 2, 1988, 54–56.
7. Ibid.

Campground for Sale!— Sold!

James W. Carland and JoAnn C. Carland

"OK, now tell us about this business you want to buy." Ann James and Jim Randall were meeting with Jack and Linda Calvin. The Calvins had made an appointment to solicit advice about an investment in a business venture. They were in their mid-fifties and were about to sink their life savings into the purchase of a campground.

"Linda and I have always wanted to own our own business. I have been in insurance for thirty years and we've always saved our money. The kids are all grown now and this opportunity has fallen into our laps. We have a chance to retire, start a business that we love, work together, and achieve our dreams." Jack was clearly excited.

"The business is a campground," Linda said excitedly. "We've always loved camping and the out-of-doors! It's located in the mountains of northern Georgia, about twenty-five miles from a small town called Helen. It's absolutely beautiful!"

"Tell us something about the business," said Ann. "What you are getting, how much it is, how it has been doing, and so forth."

Jack referred to some notes that he had brought. "Well, the site has six and a half acres of land with sixty-four campsites. Thirty of those are next to the creek and two join the trout pond. All of those are set for full RV hookup. The rest of the sites can handle campers but don't have full hookup. That just means that they can't handle RVs with air conditioners. There is a primitive tent area that can handle twenty or so campers. There are two bath houses, a playground and ball field, and a swimming pond and a trout pond. The creek is quite large, too, and it has trout in it as well. Both of the ponds are fed by the creek.

"There is a store and office and, best of all," Jack continued, "a lease on a hundred acres of land around the campground. That land is full of hiking trails and has some of the best views in the mountains! We've already talked to the people who own the land and they're willing to let us

This case was prepared by James W. Carland and JoAnn C. Carland of the School of Business at Western Carolina University. Used with permission.

take over the lease. It's a year-to-year lease but the owners don't think they'll be doing anything with it for years to come."

"Everything is run down a bit right now because the present owner hasn't been running the place for the last two years, but Jack is good at fix-up work and we can have it all up and running before this year's season. There's even room above the store for an apartment so we can live there while we're fixing it up and during the season!" Linda wasn't afraid of hard work.

"Why has it been closed? What happened? Was it in operation before?" Jim didn't like the sound of this.

"The guy that owns it lives in Florida," Jack replied. "He had a manager run the place for several years, but two years ago the manager quit and he had to shut the place down. He gave us the figures from when it was operating and they look good, but he's really not interested in running it himself and is busy with some other business that he owns." Jack slid a handwritten sheet across the desk (see Exhibit 1).

"As you can see, the sales were going down that last year, but that's because of the problems he was having with the manager. The important thing is that these figures show a great potential for anyone who is willing to work. These sales occurred with very little advertising and the manager didn't know what he was doing. Think what some effective promotion and hard work would do!"

"Where did these records come from?" Ann had noticed that the sheet was handwritten.

"I copied them from a ledger that the real estate agent had. He got it from the owner. I'm sure they're correct. After all, the owner wouldn't give you numbers that showed a decline unless it were true, would he?" Jack slid another sheet across the desk (see Exhibit 2). "Here's a list of all of the assets and what we figure the stuff is worth. These values are what we

EXHIBIT 1 Historic Income Statements		**1984**	**1985**	**1986**	**1987**
	Gross Income	$ 22,903	$ 19,436	$ 17,810	$14,965
	Cost of Goods Sold	$ 1,767	$ 2,416	$ 964	$ 432
	Labor	5,588	3,425	6,063	498
	Advertising	3,342	1,207	2,759	1,105
	Insurance	3,244	1,240	1,200	1,750
	Interest	8,474	7,539	6,733	
	Repairs	3,547	1,231	1,564	
	Supplies	2,021	1,360	1,132	
	Utilities & Telephone	3,576	2,995	2,158	
	Camp Entertainment	2,109	583	93	25
	Depreciation	11,947	6,336	6,336	6,336
	Miscellaneous	1,330	2,345	1,029	
	Total expenses	$ 46,945	$ 30,677	$ 30,031	$10,146
	Net gain (loss)	$(24,042)	$(11,241)	$(12,221)	$ (4,819)

Asset	Value
6.5 acres of land	$ 35,000
Store and resident building (1,200 sq. ft.)	48,000
Bathhouses and laundry (800 sq. ft.)	32,000
Storage building (200 sq. ft.)	4,000
Equipment (washer, dryer, store fixtures, ice maker, refrigerator, freezer, coke machine, bathroom fixtures)	12,000
Picnic tables (concrete) and grills (70 units)	7,000
Water system (pump, pipes, hook-ups)	4,000
Sewage system (sewage treatment plant, septic tank, sewer lines, hook-ups)	30,000
Electrical system (main switch boxes, lines, hook-ups)	8,000
Satellite antenna system	2,000
Total value	$182,000

EXHIBIT 2
Assets Being Acquired

Sales

Year	May*	June	July*	August*	September	October	Total
1989	2,976	5,760	6,448	4,960	2,880	1,920	$24,944
1990	2,976	6,240	7,936	6,944	4,800	2,880	31,776
1991	3,274	7,392	9,275	8,184	6,336	4,364	38,825

Occupancy

Year	May	June	July	August	September	October	Average
1989	15%	30 %	32.5%	25 %	15%	10%	21.25%
1990	15	32.5	40	35	25	15	27.08
1991	15	35	42.5	37.5	30	20	30

EXHIBIT 3
Forecasts for 64 Sites

*31-day months
Average rates for 1989 and 1990 are $10 per night; $11 for 1991

came up with. We talked to the real estate agent and to a couple other people." Jack handed over yet another handwritten sheet (see Exhibit 3).

"These are the projections we have made for sales in the first three years," Jack continued. "We think they're conservative and we've taken the seasonality into consideration. We haven't even put anything in for sales from the store. We've been very careful with the prices too. These forecasts use $10 and $11 average rates. We camp a lot and we know that the going rate is frequently $12 or $13."

"How much do they want for this place and are you going to have to borrow any money?" asked an uneasy Jim.

"They're asking $125,000," Jack answered, "but there's a mortgage on the property with a balance of $39,000, which we will take over. We'll give them $20,000 down and the owner will take a second mortgage for the rest.

We've got the down payment in savings. The payments on the first mortgage are $460. Payments on the second will be $875, but it will balloon in five years."

"What about money for repairs, fix-up, operations?" asked Ann. "How will you live while the business develops? Won't you need some money to get started?"

"Well, Jack will continue working in Atlanta, where he's making $40,000, and I'll run the place until we get it to the point that it can support us," Linda said. "Then Jack will retire. He'll come up on weekends to help with the place and do the repairs and maintenance. We have a little more money left in savings that we can use for advertising, but there won't be a lot of other expenses because we'll do everything ourselves. We've got everything planned out!"

"Yeah," Jack added, "but we wanted to ask you whether you thought the price was right before we went ahead. What do you think?"

Jim wanted to ask a lot more questions — Have you done a break-even? Where did you get the occupancy figures for the sales forecast? Has the shutdown hurt the business's reputation? Have you seen the tax returns on the business? — but he didn't think there would be much point to it. The Calvins were just not going to hear anything negative about their dream business. At least not today. Ann apparently agreed, because she just said, "We'll go over these figures you've given us, and get back to you."

QUESTIONS

1. Would you purchase the campground? Why or why not?
2. If you answered no to question 1, under what condition would you purchase it? Are there other options that are viable?
3. Are the projections through 1991 reasonable?
4. What method of advertising would you use to increase sales? How would you reach your target market?
5. What will be the impact of Jack maintaining his job in Atlanta?

Christian's

Thomas L. Wheelen, Moustafa H. Abdelsamad, Jeff Curry, Dean
Salpini, Art Scibelli, and Gordon Shanks

BACKGROUND

In the spring semester of 1984 four seniors at the University of Virginia
were trying to decide whether they should invest in Christian's Restaurant,
a small eating establishment located several miles from the university's
campus in Charlottesville, Virginia.

The four students—Jeff Curry, Dean Salpini, Art Scibelli, and Gordon
Shanks—were all business majors who had become involved with Christian's as the result of a management course entitled "Entrepreneurship" in
which they were enrolled. The objective of this course was for the students
to "set up a new company that is completely researched in all phases of the
business (location, services, finance, and so on) and submit the written
business plan for evaluation." The four students had decided to work
together on the project at the beginning of the semester and had quickly
begun investigating potential business ventures in the Charlottesville area.

The group's first idea centered on the opening of a seafood restaurant.
Art believed that a restaurant offering the same product as a local chain of
seafood houses near his home in northern Virginia could prove highly
successful in Charlottesville. These restaurants offered fresh seafood for
relatively moderate prices in a family type atmosphere and additionally
featured several "all-you-can-eat" items on their menu. Art had gotten in
touch with one of the owner-founders of the chain, Mr. Easby-Smyth, and
the group had gone to northern Virginia to meet with him and discuss their
idea.

The meeting with Mr. Easby-Smyth had produced two conclusions:
Charlottesville was probably too small a market to support the size of

This case was prepared by Jeff Curry, Dean Salpini, Art Scibelli, and Gordon Shanks,
under the supervision of Professor Thomas L. Wheelen, University of South Florida, and
Dean Moustafa H. Abdelsamad, Corpus Christi State University. This case was presented
at the North American Case Research Association Meeting, 1984. Copyright © 1985 by
Thomas L. Wheelen and Moustafa H. Abdelsamad. Distributed by the North American
Case Research Association. All rights reserved to the authors and the North American
Case Research Association. Revised 1992. Reprinted with permission.

restaurant the group had originally considered, and the amount of money involved would make the project infeasible for the group. Mr. Easby-Smyth had informed them that the cost of building and outfitting a seafood house of six thousand square feet would be approximately $300,000. The group had no desire to enter into an investment of this magnitude and was also aware of the great deal of difficulty they were sure to encounter in trying to raise the capital for such a venture.

The students still thought a smaller seafood restaurant might be successful in Charlottesville, and began searching for an existing building that would be suitable for their restaurant. Ideally, they would find a restaurant that was selling out and could easily be converted for their purposes. Then news of the Happy Clam reached them.

The Happy Clam was a new seafood restaurant opening up on Route 29 North, the main highway leading from Charlottesville. One visit to the new restaurant confirmed that not only was it located in the general area the group had hoped to locate in, but it was also offering the same basic product mix as they had hoped to offer. In addition, the restaurant's owner had already successfully opened an identical seafood house in nearby Fredericksburg, Virginia.

Up to this point, the area had no restaurant similar to the one that the students conceived. Now, however, they were faced with a direct competitor who had proven he could be successful in the seafood business. It was at this point, as the students reconsidered their strategy, that Art visited a local realtor and found out about Christian's.

Christian's was a small restaurant specializing in sandwiches for lunch, and specialty dishes for dinner (see dinner menu, Exhibit 1). It was being sold as on ongoing business to include the name Christian's. The students met with the realtor handling the sale, William Page, who arranged a meeting with the owners of Christian's.

Peter and Mary Tarpey, a young couple from the New York area, along with a University of Virginia professor who acted as a silent partner, were the owners of Christian's. The students met with Page and the Tarpeys as arranged on a Wednesday afternoon, and the group sat down at a table in Christian's to answer each other's questions and discuss the possible purchase.

Mary Tarpey first showed the group a handwritten profit and loss statement for the period from June 13, 1983, to October 31, 1983 (see Exhibit 2). She explained how some of the expenses were direct payments to the banks and were being written off as business expenses, such as car payments and a life insurance policy, and need not be incurred by a new owner. She also showed the students monthly sales figures for the period of January 1983 to October 1983, as verified by a local CPA firm (see Exhibit 3), as well as a list of assets owned by Christian's (see Exhibit 4).

The Tarpeys defined their target market as "young professional." By this, they meant persons in the eighteen- to thirty-five-year age group who worked in the area and came to Christian's for the menu's variety and the quality of food. They stated that these people eat out about twenty-two times per month for lunch and dinner, and their strategy was to try to get them at Christian's five days a month. The Tarpeys also quoted the average lunch check as being $3.76 and the average dinner check amounting to $5.92.

EXHIBIT 1
Dinner Menu

Soups

French Onion $1.50
Cream of Asparagus $1.25
Vegetable $1.00
Split Pea or Lentil $1.00

Wines

By the glass $1.25
½ Litre $3.25
Full Litre $5.75
Champagne Cocktail $1.25

Entrées

Beef Bazaar $4.25
Marinated beef, onions & green peppers broiled & served on rice
Broccoli Casserole $3.25
Broccoli, tomatoes, onions & eggs topped with cheese
Lobster Scampi $4.25
Langostinos broiled in herb butter & served on rice
Syrian Chicken $3.85
Marinated chicken in pita bread with lettuce, tomatoes
Sausage Lasagne $4.25
An Italian dish that speaks for itself!
Omelet special $3.95
Large dinner omelet filled with pepperoni and provolone cheese
Crêpes $3.75
Chicken Divan or Sauteed Mushrooms

Desserts

Ginger Sherbet	$ .75
Homemade Pecan Pie	$1.00
Cheesecake	$1.25
Carrot Cake	$1.25
Coffee or Tea	$ .35
Soft Drinks	$ .50
Beer	$ .75

The Tarpeys also answered questions concerning Christian's daily operations and suppliers. One of the important issues raised was that of a transition period. The group hoped to hire an experienced, full-time manager for the restaurant, and the Tarpeys agreed that they would stay on for a period of two weeks or so to help train the manager and show him or her the cost-control and portion-control procedures they had used. In addition, the Tarpeys stated that the whole employee staff had expressed their willingness to stay with the restaurant after an ownership change. The group viewed these two factors as distinct assets.

Another important issue was the future plans of the Tarpeys. As it turned out, the Tarpeys would be opening a new restaurant in a shopping center being built three-quarters of a mile from Christian's. Peter Tarpey explained that the restaurant was to be more dinner-oriented than Christian's. He described it as an "Irish cafe with French food," which would

. . . .

EXHIBIT 2
Christian's Profit and
Loss Statement
(June 13, 1983–
October 31, 1983)

Sales		$100,000.00
Cost of Sales		
Beer and wine	$ 2,688.30	
Food	29,189.60	
		$ 31,877.90
Gross Profit		$ 68,122.10
Operating Expenses		
Paper	$ 1,079.88	
Insurance		
Store	600.00	
Car	150.00	
Health	460.00	
Worker's Compensation	950.00	
Employment Commission	360.00	
Laundry, Linen	483.25	
Licenses	250.00	
Sales Tax (State)	4,000.00	
Repairs and Maintenance	250.00	
Rent	2,500.00	
Rubbish Removal—City	448.50	
Salaries and Wages	20,000.00	
Payroll Taxes	6,000.00	
Utilities	4,000.00	
Loan Payment	1,150.00	
Equipment Payments	1,150.00	
Life Insurance	625.00	
Car Payment	1,095.00	
Maintenance	950.00	
Lease Dishwasher	448.50	
Advertising	2,750.00	
Business Association Dues and Expenses	450.00	
Administrative Salaries	5,000.00	
Total Expenses		$ 55,150.13
Income Before Taxes		$ 12,971.97

NOTE: This was a handwritten statement provided by the owners.

EXHIBIT 3
Sales Information

BROWN AND JONES COMPANY
CERTIFIED PUBLIC ACCOUNTANTS
CHARLOTTESVILLE, VIRGINIA 22906

January 9, 1984

Peter Tarpey
Christian's, Inc.
1703 Allied Lane
Charlottesville, Virginia 22901

Dear Peter:

As per your request, enclosed are sales figures for Christian's, Inc., for the ten months ending October 1983 as filed on your monthly Virginia sales tax returns.

January 1983	$18,543.30
February 1983	19,085.43
March 1983	18,097.54
April 1983	19,984.20
May 1983	20,422.71
June 1983	21,836.37
July 1983	19,304.76
August 1983	22,231.69
September 1983	20,002.19
October 1983	20,588.86

If you need sales figures for November 1983 and December 1983, you will have to get these amounts from worksheets in your files. Let me know if I can be of further assistance.

Yours truly,

Thomas L. Brown
Certified Public Accountant

TLB/d

P.S.: The sales figures for November 1983 are: $19,300.00

TLB

serve more expensive meals than Christian's and would also serve liquor, which Christian's did not feature. Tarpey estimated that by his moving and opening a new restaurant, Christian's might lose at most 5 percent of its customers.

A second meeting was held with the Tarpeys at a later date, during which more of the group's questions were answered. A new lease would have to be renegotiated by any new owner in August 1984, which would

EXHIBIT 4
Additional Information
Provided by Thomas L.
Brown
(September 27, 1983)

Attached is a schedule of fixed assets owned by Christian's, Inc., and the estimated market value of each. Since a purchaser of these would have a cost basis for depreciation and useful life different from that of Christian's, Inc., this information is not provided.

21 tables	$ 525
43 chairs	430
2 banquettes	100
6 church pew benches	120
Small refrigerator	300
Walk-in box	1,500
Ice machine	100
NCR cash register	150
3 toasters	225
Jordan box	250
Fogle refrigerator	1,200
Hobart slicer	1,000
Hobart microwave	1,000
Sandwich box	200
Stainless prep table	100
Deep fat fryer	75
Steam table	75
Stainless prep table	125
3 butcher block chef tables	300
Small Hobart slicer	200
3 basin sinks	75
Universal freezer	100
Sears freezer	75
Stereo system	150
Curtains	100
Pots, pans, flatware, china, glassware	600
Placemats, salt and pepper mills	100
New sign	2,000
TOTAL FIXED ASSETS	$11,175

Should you desire additional information in this matter, please contact Peter Tarpey and the data will be forthcoming.

be substantially higher than the current one. The students had questions about Christian's specific suppliers and asked to see the restaurant's books, but the Tarpeys wanted some sort of firm commitment on the group's part before more information about Christian's would be given out.

The price being asked for Christian's was $57,750 and the students estimated that they could put up about $17,500 of their own capital. Because the rest would have to be financed by a loan of some sort, Jeff visited several banks to discuss terms. One of the banks he visited told him that they loaned money for a restaurant only if it was going to be family owned and operated. At Sovran Bank, Jeff got a more positive response. The loan officer there stated that the bank would loan up to 70 percent of the purchase price, fully collateralized. The interest rate would be 14 percent or 15 percent.

At this point, the group decided to evaluate its objectives and "take stock" of the situation. They hoped to run the restaurant as absentee owners and have the full-time manager handle daily operations. Art's immediate plans included law school in September, although he was still unsure which law school he would be attending. Dean planned on going to work in northern Virginia after graduation, and Jeff and Gordon would be returning to the University of Virginia in the fall to complete their degrees.

The students' families, from whom they hoped to borrow some of the initial equity capital, all had reservations about the venture. Most of the doubt centered on the policy of running the restaurant as absentee owners. The families also wondered if it was wise for the students to make such an investment at this time in their careers when their futures were so undecided.

By now it was March 24, and the students knew a decision would have to be made very soon. A call to William Page had confirmed the rumor that another party had entered the scene and was seriously considering buying Christian's. A meeting was called at which the group planned to decide their next move.

At the meeting, the students decided that some sort of comprehensive analysis of the information they had gathered was necessary. Then, with the analysis in front of them, they felt they would be able to reach the best conclusion.

The group decided to break up the information into sections, with Jeff concentrating on the finance, Dean on the marketing, and Gordon and Art on the operations. When they got back together on March 31 (one week away) to put all the results together, the decision would have to be made.

MARKET ANALYSIS

Although Mr. Tarpey assured the group of the existence and loyalty of a definite market for Christian's, it was felt that a marketing survey would strengthen the group's understanding of this market. Using the survey form shown (see Exhibit 5), the survey was conducted among eighty-eight people who were customers at competitive restaurants. The competition was determined from an assessment based on a number of factors, including location, clientele, product offering, and Mr. Tarpey's estimates. Christian's, however, was not included because the group felt that their regular clientele might bias the results in favor of the restaurant.

From the results of the survey, it was discovered that most people were aware of Christian's, but were not being drawn down there to eat. In addition, only seven percent of those who had eaten at Christian's did so at least five times per month, so their repeat business seemed to be lacking. Of those who ate there regularly, most people seemed to prefer the lunch period (60 percent), as opposed to the dinner period, as Mr. Tarpey had claimed would occur. Analysis of the various factors involved with Christian's showed that location was the most significant problem, with 64 percent of the respondents rating it below average. However, a study of

Hello, we are students doing a research study on Christian's restaurant. Could you *please* take a little time to help us complete our survey and help make Christian's a better place to eat? Thank you for your cooperation. (The key results of the survey are summarized below.)

1. Have you ever eaten at Christian's?   YES 50%   NO 50%
   If NO, have you heard of it?   YES 59%   If NO, no further questions. 41%
   If YES, how often do you eat there?
   Less than 5 times a month   93%
   5 times a month   5%
   More than 5 times a month   2%
2. Which meal do you usually eat at Christian's?
   Lunch 59%   Dinner 32%   Both 9%
3. How would you rate Christian's on these factors:

	POOR	FAIR	AVERAGE	ABOVE AVERAGE	EXCELLENT
Location	29.5%	34%	32%	4.5%	
Food Quality			23.3	53.5	23.3%
Price	4.5	11	61.5	16	7
Service		14	48	33	5
Atmosphere	9	11.4	41	34	4.6
Menu Variety		5	33	45	17
Cleanliness	9.5	9.5	36	33	12

4. What is the main reason(s) you eat at Christian's? Answers varied; most were complimentary.
5. How did you hear about Christian's?
   TV 2%   Radio 12%   Newspaper Ads 10.6%   Friends 58%
   Drove By 5.8%   Other (please specify) 11.6%
6. Would you like to see the following at Christian's?

	YES	NO
More Vegetarian Dishes	44%	56%
More Seafood	81	19
More Take-out Variety	48	52
Live Entertainment	19	81

7. An informal survey of age was conducted.

EXHIBIT 5
Marketing Survey

traffic-flow patterns in Charlottesville around the McIntyre Road area, where Christian's is located, revealed that 20 percent of the whole day's traffic passed Christian's between 11:00 A.M. and 2:00 P.M. Price and service seemed to be average and comparable to other restaurants in most respondents' minds.

The most significant factors in a person's decision to eat at Christian's were the menu's variety and the food's quality. Most of those who had eaten at the restaurant named specific food items as their main reason for coming. This also accounts for the major form of advertising that Christian's used, which seemed to be "word-of-mouth" advertising from satisfied customers. As far as changes in Christian's were concerned, most respondents favored the introduction of seafood into the menu (81 percent), whereas the same percentage felt that having live entertainment would be a mistake.

One of the problems that might confront the group was the introduction of Mr. Tarpey's new restaurant down the street from Christian's. Because Tarpey had already developed a loyal clientele, the group was afraid of losing them to his new restaurant, although Mr. Tarpey assured the group that only 5 percent of the market would be affected. According to the survey, the figure to determine those customers that would be lost through a change in management was approximately 6.8 percent, a little higher than Mr. Tarpey's estimate.

Although there were no direct questions addressing demographics on the survey, respondents were asked to place themselves in one of the three age brackets: eighteen to thirty-five, thirty-five to fifty, and over fifty. Age of the customer was thought to be important in the students' decision to purchase Christian's, so that the target market could be firmly established. Overall, it was found that 60 percent of those interviewed were between eighteen and thirty-five years of age, while 31 percent fell into the thirty-five to fifty bracket. Further analysis showed that 98 percent of those who presently eat at Christian's were within the eighteen- to fifty-year age range. Those customers who were over fifty, therefore, figured to be an insignificant number of Christian's target market. Therefore, Mr. Tarpey's claim of "young professionals" as being his primary customers seems to have been supported through this age-group data.

As can be seen from Exhibit 6, sales for eating and drinking establishments in 1982 were 10.5 percent above those of 1981, while total retail sales increased only 6.8 percent for the same period. Households also seemed to be forming at a faster rate than the total population was growing. In addition, the Virginia State Planning Office projections show that the twenty- to thirty-four-year-old segment has shown disproportionate increases, which could explain the faster formation of households. These same figures also show that the twenty-five to thirty-nine-year-old age group will

EXHIBIT 6
The Charlottesville Market[1] (In Thousands)

Year	Retail Sales	Eating & Drinking[2]	Population	Households[3]
1978	$153,995	$ N.A.[4]	38.8	13.8
1979	176,731	N.A.	38.7	14.0
1980	224,588	N.A.	39.0	14.2
1981	235,679	17,882	39.1	14.7
1982	251,766	19,753	38.9	14.7

[1]Data provided by Virginia State Planning Service. [2]*Eating and Drinking Places:* This is a broad classification which includes any establishment selling prepared food or drink. Caterers, lunch counters, and concession stands are included as well as restaurants. [3]*Households:* All people occupying a single housing unit whether related or not. Includes single persons living alone. [4]N.A.: not available.

increase 17 percent between 1980 and 1985. In Albemarle County, in which Charlottesville is located, this increase will be almost 32 percent.

These growth figures were considered important because of the number of people who drive into Charlottesville's central business district (CBD) from the county who use McIntyre Road as a major artery. The CBD itself was also considered to be important, because a large part of Christian's clientele came from there. Over $2 million had been privately invested in downtown since 1982; thus the CBD appeared to be booming. Another important development was the county's move of its executive offices into the old Lane High School building, located down the street from Christian's. This decision would increase Christian's target market, because these people seemed to fit the characteristics of its clientele.

ADVERTISING AND PROMOTION

Christian's present advertising program was very sporadic, with a yearly expenditure of only $2,750. Mr. Tarpey spoke of occasional spots on television that he had used, along with local radio stations and the major newspaper in Charlottesville. However, Dean and the other members of the group felt that the effectiveness of this program was lacking.

OPERATIONS

The students were aware of their lack of experience in the restaurant business, and because the daily operations of Christian's had gone smoothly in the past, they did not plan any significant changes upon their taking over.

The entire employee staff had said they would be willing to remain at Christian's after the ownership change, and Peter and Mary Tarpey agreed they would stay on for a transition period to "show the ropes" to the new manager.

The students had realized early in their involvement with Christian's that they would need to hire a full-time manager for the restaurant. They wanted someone with experience in restaurant management from the Charlottesville area. Their Realtor told them he knew of a man who fit this description and had expressed interest in the opportunity, but the group was unable to get in contact with him before the week ended.

The group planned on putting the manager in charge of general daily operations, to include ordering, cost control, hiring, firing, scheduling, and any other operations-related duty. The students planned on doing the bookkeeping themselves. They planned to pay the manager a salary of approximately $12,000, plus a commission based on the bottom-line figure. This commission would be approximately 11 percent.

It was determined that the following employees would be needed to operate Christian's:

1 manager @ $12,000 salary plus commission
3 cooks @ $5.00/hour
1 grillcook @ $4.75/hour
2 counterpersons @ $4.25/hour

2 prep persons @ $4.25/hour
2 dishwashers @ $4.25/hour
2 cashiers @ $4.25/hour
12 servers @ $1.50/hour plus tips

Employees were to be allowed free drinks and half-price meals while working.

Under the students' ownership, Christian's would continue to buy its food supplies from institutional food distributors from Richmond, Virginia, who delivered to Charlottesville. In addition, they would obtain their beer from local distributors and their soft drinks from local bottling companies.

In the past, inventory had turned over approximately once a week. Normal credit terms of suppliers had been net thirty days.

The marketing survey had indicated that Christian's menu was one of its strongest points, so the group planned few changes. The lunch menu featured more than forty sandwiches along with omelets, salads, and chili. The dinner menu featured specialty dishes such as beef bazaar and Syrian chicken (see Exhibit 1).

In the past, Christian's had varied its dinner menu daily. The students would vary it weekly, and if one combination proved particularly popular, it would be used again at a different time.

Approximately 15 percent of Christian's gross sales came from beer sales. The restaurant carried mainly premium and foreign beers, in keeping with its target market of young professionals.

INVESTMENT

Benefiting from knowledge they had obtained in a business law course the previous semester, the group decided to establish Christian's as a Subchapter S corporation. This business form was chosen because of the tax advantages and flexibility it would allow the group; the business would be taxed as a partnership, but would retain the limited liability of a corporation, to protect the shareholders. Because income tax rates for individuals in this case are substantially lower than for a corporation, the group thought that this form would offer them the best return on their investment.

LEASE

At the time of negotiations, Christian's was paying Allied Realty, the owner of the shopping plaza in which the restaurant was located, a base rent of $350 per month plus an additional percentage of gross sales (4 percent) not exceeding a total monthly rental of $500 per month. However, this lease would expire on August 1, 1984, and a new lease would have to be renegotiated by the new purchaser.

The new rent terms would be considerably higher than those experienced by previous owners and would consist of a minimum payment of $600 per month or 4 percent of sales (whichever is higher), not to exceed $750 per month. Because Christian's historical monthly sales have averaged approximately $20,000, this would mean payments of $750 per month. In addition, there would be an additional requirement that if gross sales exceeded $60,000 in any quarter, the restaurant would pay 3 percent of sales exceeding this amount.

Fortunately, the group was informed by its Realtor, Henry Brasswell, that it might be possible to negotiate a less-expensive lease, so that average monthly payments would be between $650 and $700 per month. Because the outcome of such negotiations was uncertain at the time, however, the group used a figure of $750 per month in developing pro forma statements for the business.

INCOME STATEMENTS

An examination of the 1983 sales uncovered two major factors that had to be considered in the development of pro forma income statements. First, the monthly sales figures supplied by the CPA firm indicated a seasonal fluctuation in sales (see Exhibit 7). The effect of this fluctuation on the cash flows of the restaurant and its ability to meet its debts had to be determined. Secondly, the revenue growth of this restaurant would be limited by its capacity. Jeff needed to establish how close to capacity the restaurant was operating currently. Lunch and dinner sales should be considered separately. Lunch projections would be based on 260 days per year (52 weeks × 5 days) while dinner should be based on the full 312 days during which the restaurant was open. The current owners had already estimated the average check at each meal. The restaurant seated fifty-six people.

In order to get an idea of the expense that the new management could face, Jeff then took the handwritten income statement provided by Mrs.

EXHIBIT 7
Seasonality Index—1983
Sales
(100 = 19,945)

Month	Sales	Actual Seasonality
Jan.	$18,543	93
Feb.	19,085	96
Mar.	18,097	91
Apr.	19,984	100
May	20,423	102
Jun.	21,836	109
Jul.	19,304	97
Aug.	22,231	111
Sep.	20,002	100
Oct.	20,589	103
Nov.	19,300	97
Dec.	18,948*	95*

*Assumed

Tarpey and attempted to adjust it. Several of the perquisites the Tarpeys enjoyed had been discussed during the meeting at Christian's. Excessive long-distance calls and the car payments could be eliminated. The new management would have to add the manager's salary and bonus. A 10 percent annual bonus on pre-tax profits would be offered to motivate the manager to run a tight ship. These expenses had to be separated into variable and fixed expense categories to determine a break-even point. The new estimates were in line with those found in a book entitled *Restaurant Finance*.

Jeff was certain sales in the first year could be maintained at the current level if there was effective advertising. Forecasted sales for the second year are based on expanding lunch sales to capacity. Projections for years three through five assume that the restaurant will operate at capacity for both lunch and dinner. Increased sales will be achieved through advertising.

THE BANK LOAN

With the income statements prepared, Jeff approached the Sovran Bank to discuss the terms of a loan (see Exhibit 8 and 9). The bank was willing to set the monthly payments at a level that would be met by the cash flows of the restaurant, as long as the maturity of the loan did not exceed ten years. It appeared that five years would be an acceptable maturity. This loan would entail monthly payments of approximately $1,000.

The bank would accept 50 percent of the book value (approximately the $11,175 listed as market value by the CPA firm) of the assets as collateral but demanded that the balance be fully collateralized also.

EXHIBIT 8
Pro Forma Income Statement (In Thousands of Dollars)

For the Year Ended July 31	Year			
	Two	Three	Four	Five
Net sales				
Lunch	$120.0	$120.0	$120.0	$120.0
Dinner	144.0	152.0	152.0	152.0
Total	$264.0	$272.0	$272.0	$272.0
Variable expenses (68%)	(180.0)	(185.0)	(185.0)	(185.0)
Operating margin (32%)	$ 84.0	$ 87.0	$ 87.0	$ 87.0
Fixed expenses	(40.8)	(40.9)	(42.4)	(42.4)
Earnings before interest	$ 43.2	$ 46.1	$ 44.6	$ 44.6
Interest	(3.9)	(2.9)	(1.9)	(1.0)
Earnings before bonus (EBB)	$ 39.3	$ 43.2	$ 42.7	$ 43.6
Bonus (.10 × EBB)	3.9	4.3	4.3	4.4
Taxable earnings	$ 35.4	$ 38.9	$ 38.4	$ 39.2

For the Year Ended July 31	Initial	Year 1	Year 2	Year 3	Year 4	Year 5
Assets						
Current assets						
Cash and securities	$ .30	$10.70	$20.70	$20.70	$34.60	$27.70
Inventory						
Beer and wine (.04/month)	$ .80	$ .80	$ .90	$ .90	$ .90	$ .90
Food (.36/month)	7.20	7.20	7.90	8.20	8.20	8.20
Total current assets	$ 8.30	$18.70	$29.50	$29.80	$43.70	$36.80
Fixed assets	$22.30	$22.30	$22.30	$27.30	$27.30	$32.30
Accumulated depreciation	0.00	4.40	8.80	13.20	17.60	22.00
Net fixed assets	$22.30	$17.90	$13.50	$14.10	$ 9.70	$10.30
Intangibles						
Goodwill	$35.20	$35.20	$35.20	$35.20	$35.20	$35.20
Accumulated amortization	0.00	3.52	7.04	10.56	14.08	17.60
Net goodwill	$35.20	$31.68	$28.16	$24.64	$21.12	$17.60
Organization costs	.50	.40	.30	.20	.10	0.00
Total assets	$66.30	$68.68	$71.46	$68.74	$74.62	$64.70
Liabilities						
Current liabilities						
Accounts payable	$ 7.60	$ 7.60	$ 7.90	$ 8.20	$ 8.20	$ 8.20
Note payable	1.00	0.00	0.00	0.00	0.00	0.00
Total current liabilities	$ 8.60	$ 7.60	$ 7.90	$ 8.20	$ 8.20	$ 8.20
Long-term note	40.25	32.20	24.10	16.10	8.00	0.00
Total liabilities	$48.85	$39.80	$32.00	$24.30	$16.20	$ 8.20
Equity						
Stock	$17.50	$17.50	$17.50	$17.50	$17.50	$17.50
Retained earnings	0.00	11.38	21.96	26.94	40.92	39.00
Total equity	$17.50	$28.88	$39.46	$44.44	$58.42	$56.50
Total liabilities and equity	$66.35	$68.68	$71.46	$68.74	$74.62	$64.70

EXHIBIT 9
Pro Forma Balance Sheet
(In Thousands of Dollars)

The loan officer was concerned that the purchase price was too high and that an excessive amount of goodwill would be involved in the new business. He was also concerned that none of the new owners had any experience with operating a restaurant. With this in mind, he wanted to know more about the manager and cook.

EVALUATING THE PURCHASE PRICE

Because several people had expressed concern over the price that the owners were asking, the partners wanted to decide the proper value of the restaurant. They agreed that this should be based on the present value of the income stream that the restaurant could generate. In light of the fact that eight out of ten restaurants fail, the partners selected 25 percent as the hurdle rate that would be used to discount future earnings. The set-up costs should not exceed the present value of the income stream. The partners wanted to include the eventual sales price or liquidation value of the restaurant at the end of five years in the computation of the present value. Assuming various levels of sales would establish a proper price range. The set-up costs included the $57,750 asking price and $500 organizational expense for legal and accounting fees. Because this was an ongoing concern, they would not have to invest significant additional working capital.

CONCLUDING REMARKS

On March 31, at the final meeting to discuss the prospects of purchasing Christian's, the group members were fully aware of the implications such a decision would have. It was generally agreed that such an endeavor provided potential for developing managerial skill and experience in the business world, though none of the group members was certain that this was the route he wanted to take. Faced with exams in the coming weeks, time pressure from the Realtor, and the knowledge that at least one other party was interested in purchasing Christian's, the group set out to make its decision, which for better or worse would affect their immediate futures.

The students were informed by the present owners that they must reach a decision quickly because other purchasers were interested in the same business opportunity.

QUESTIONS

1. Carefully analyze the market survey and other external data. What is your conclusion about the viability of the restaurant?
2. Is the lack of managerial expertise a serious detriment?
3. Do you agree with the banker's judgment? Was he being overly cautious?
4. What other information do you need to know?
5. Using fisCAL, calculate a value for Christian's.

J

Martin Enterprises: "What Are We Worth?"

Jon Ozmun

Board of Directors Meeting
April 20, 1987
(The meeting is in progress.)

And so, ladies and gentlemen, we conclude that the breakup value of Martin Enterprises is $15,638,947, making the breakup value of each share of common stock $59.48. The present value of the proceeds from a "breakup"—discounted at 13.5 percent, assuming 50 percent is received in year one and the balance is received over ten years with 10 percent interest—totals $14,330,775, or $54.50 per share. Therefore, if Martin Enterprises (ME) were to entertain a cash offer for the entire company, the benchmark price should be $54.50 per share. I will now entertain your questions.

The speaker was Doug Cochran, a consultant for the investment banking firm Armstrong and Cochran (A&C). Cochran had just concluded his formal presentation to the nine members of the board of directors of Martin Enterprises. The report, which is shown in Exhibit 1, was essentially a valuation of the eight operating divisions of Martin Enterprises. Cochran acknowledged the board members' questions:

Tish Martin: My question relates to how you calculated the estimated market value for each division of the company shown at the top of Exhibit 1 in your report. Could you explain again how you arrived at those numbers?

Cochran: If everyone would turn to Exhibit 1, I'll go through that analysis again. I'll use the Home Centers Division as an example. We are trying to calculate the market value of this division using the highest of three different accepted methodologies: (1) price to earnings value, (2) required

---

This case was prepared by Jon Ozmun, Northern Arizona University, Flagstaff, Arizona, and is intended for class discussion rather than to illustrate either effective or ineffective handling of the situation. The case has been disguised to preserve the firm's desire for anonymity.

	return on investment value, and (3) estimated tangible asset value. Do you understand each of the methodologies?
Tish Martin:	I'm not sure about the price to earnings value. Would you go over that again?
Cochran:	We use the average pre-tax price/earnings ratio for the home center industry as a basis for estimating the division's value. The calculation is simple. The pre-tax earnings of the ME Home Center Division are multiplied by the adjusted industry average pre-tax price/earnings ratio to estimate the price or value:

Price to earnings value = earnings before interest and taxes × pre-tax price/earnings
Price to earnings value = $72,251 × 7.62
Price to earnings value = $550,553

Tish Martin:	But why didn't you use that amount ($550,553) as the estimated market value for the Home Center Division?
Cochran:	Because the price to earnings value is not the highest value for the Home Center Division. Of the three methodologies we used, the estimated tangible asset value was $6,201,958 and this was the highest for the Home Center Division.
Jack Martin:	And you used $6,150,000 (instead of $6,201,958) as the estimated market value based on your company's experience?
Cochran:	That is correct. If you look carefully at Exhibit 1, you will see that the highest value from the three methodologies was used as the starting point for each division, but in each case, A&C made a downward adjustment to these values.

The questions, answers, and discussion came to a close after about one hour. Joe Walka, CEO and chairman of the board, then thanked Cochran, who excused himself from the meeting room.

Walka then addressed the board members:

> Now that we know what our company is worth, our next step is to find out if any of our "suitors" are in agreement. Our next board meeting is scheduled for 9 A.M., May 12. At that time, purchase offers from Westcor Holdings, B. J. Jennar, and Joe F. Conn will be presented. Each of these groups has requested a copy of the A&C report and at the board's direction, I am sending this to them. I know that you are as excited as I am to see what they will offer.

A few minutes later, the meeting was adjourned and the nine members of the Martin Enterprises board of directors left for lunch, eager to reconvene on May 12.

BACKGROUND INFORMATION

Martin Enterprises (ME) was founded in and around Grand Junction, Colorado, in the late 1800s by John Martin. The company grew quickly from its initial business of cattle ranching on the Bookcliffs Ranch to lumber and hardware retailing as well as trading post operations. In its first forty years, the company grew from its original ventures to several operating businesses with vast land holdings. However, the 1920s and 1930s proved to be a near fatal period for the company due to the economic and financial storms of the times.

The company emerged from this period, under the direction of bank managers, with a reconsolidated, streamlined operation. The second generation of ME management was conservative but still oriented toward moderate expansion.

The current third generation of management recognized the need once again to restructure, modernize, and streamline the company. For the first time in its history, ME brought in a nonfamily member, Joe Walka, a professional manager, to accomplish these tasks.

The ownership base of ME expanded over time as the family grew. Today the company is owned by twenty-two shareholders, almost all of whom are Martin family members. This shareholder base is dispersed across the United States, but a majority of the company's stock is held by family members residing in Colorado.

DESCRIPTION OF THE BUSINESS LINES

The organizational structure of operations for Martin Enterprises is best described as a conglomerate. The company's current lines of business are grouped into six divisions:

1. *Building Materials Group.* The Building Materials Group consists of three segments: Home Centers, Wholesale Materials, and M & J Supply, Inc. The company operates six home centers in southwestern Colorado and southeastern Utah. Each location sells lumber, building materials, and home improvement merchandise to contractor, commercial/industrial, and retail do-it-yourself clientele. The Wholesale Materials Division operates from one location in Grand Junction. The division sells hardware, electrical supplies, plumbing supplies, doors, moldings, and soft goods to contractors, dealers, and, to a limited extent, trading posts. M & J Supply is a door manufacturing plant located in Grand Junction. The company is involved in the manufacture and sale of pre-hung doors, millwork, and related items to the contractor and dealer market in southwestern Colorado.

2. *Department Store Operations.* The company operates six department stores with locations in Grand Junction, Delta, Cortez, and Durango, Colorado, and Monticello and Moab, Utah. These are full-line stores selling upscale merchandise to the retail customer.

3. *Bryce Canyon Operations.* The company operates two retail facilities at the Bryce Canyon National Park, near Moab. These facilities offer groceries and tourist merchandise to Bryce Canyon visitors.

4. *Real Estate.* The Real Estate Division is comprised of two land holding corporations and various other parcels of real estate accumulated since the inception of ME.

5. *Trading Post Division.* ME has established four trading posts on the Ute Indian reservation, at Bluff, Aneth, Monticello, and Moab. In addition,

the Monticello location includes a trading post, motel, restaurant, and trailer park. These opeartions serve the people of the Ute reservation and tourists visiting these locations.

6.   *Cattle Ranch.* The Bookcliff Cattle Ranch encompasses forty thousand deeded acres producing an annual calf crop of approximately 750 head. The Bookcliff Ranch is located northwest of Grand Junction.

STOCKHOLDER DISSATISFACTION

The events that led to the three purchase offers began when Robert Martin, the CEO who hired Walka as the chief operations officer, was forced to resign by the board of directors. Soon after, the board of directors promoted Walka to the CEO position.

Robert Martin made it clear that he wanted to withdraw his equity from the company and he was joined in this position by another large shareholder. Together, the two held approximately 25 percent of the outstanding ME common stock.

Because ME stock was not publicly traded and was held only by members of the Martin family, there were limited options for accomplishing the stock repurchase. The corporation or some of its individual stockholders would have to purchase the shares of those who wished to withdraw their equity. Since the book value of the dissatisfied stockholders' equity was in excess of $2 million, Walka believed that the only alternatives were for the corporation to liquidate assets or to borrow the funds necessary to purchase the stock. With board approval, Walka employed the investment banking firm of Armstrong and Cochran to furnish analysis and recommendations. In order to proceed, the share value of the stock had to be determined. Following this, financing had to be obtained. Thus it was necessary to calculate the fair value of the assets of ME and to develop a strategy to raise the money necessary to purchase the stock of the dissatisfied stockholders. A&C's specific task was to provide an analysis of ME's situation and make recommendations for the following:

> To effect a partial redemption of the outstanding common stock of the company that would allow certain shareholders to liquidate their interests in the company.

A&C's report was presented to the ME board of directors on April 20, 1987.

Before and during the time that A&C's work was in process, rumors circulated that ME was for sale. Although this was not the case, it created some very uncomfortable situations for Walka, ME employees, and the Martin family members.

At a meeting in late March 1987, the board decided that there was no risk involved in considering offers and decided that any serious offer to buy the company would be reviewed. By April 20, 1987, Westcor Holdings, B. J. Jennar, and Joe F. Conn had asked to make presentations of their purchase offers to the ME board of directors. These presentations were made on the morning of May 12, 1987.

Board of Directors Meeting
May 12, 1987

The door to the conference room had barely closed before it seemed that each of the nine people seated around the table began to speak at the same time. Walka acknowledged Gregg Martin's hand in the air and gave him the floor. Walka, Gregg Martin, and seven others who comprised the board of directors of ME had just sat through more than three hours of presentations and discussions by representatives of three different investment groups interested in purchasing ME.

Gregg Martin: I was very surprised at how far apart in dollar amount the offers were. But most of all, I was surprised and confused by the last part of Don Choice's presentation.

Don Choice was the representative of Westcor Holdings, one of the three groups that had made an offer to purchase ME. Like the representative of each of the other two prospective buyers, B. J. Jennar and Joe F. Conn Corporation, Choice had made a formal presentation to the ME board of directors explaining the purchase offer. But unlike the other two representatives, Choice had concluded by painstakingly ripping apart the report of A&C, the investment banking consulting firm employed by ME. It was this critique that had surprised and confused Gregg Martin.

Gregg Martin: If Choice is correct in his criticisms of the report by A&C, then our company is worth a whole lot less than we have been counting on. Gregg went to the chalkboard and wrote the following:

	Value of Martin Enterprises
Armstrong and Cochran	$15,638,947
Westcor Holdings	11,175,375
B. J. Jennar	19,201,000
Joe F. Conn	11,400,000

Gregg Martin: These numbers are taken from the A&C report and the three presentations we just heard. Our consultants (A&C) have calculated the company's breakup value at just over $15.6 million. The other amounts vary considerably. The Westcor Holdings and Joe F. Conn offers are almost identical in amount, while B. J. Jennar's offer is $8 million higher than either of these and over $3 million more than our consultants say we're worth. I have to admit to all of you that what I have heard and read this morning has left me in a state of confusion.

At the other end of the table, Jim Martin spoke.

Jim Martin: Several things presented this morning bother me. First, there are the offers by Westcor Holdings and Joe F. Conn. They are both far below what we had expected. Then, B. J. Jennar offers us substantially more, but the payments are strung out over the next nine years. Furthermore, Choice's criticism of the valuation has left me wondering if we really know what the company is worth. Finally, I don't know where to turn for help in clearing up these concerns. What do you think, Joe?

Walka: First, Choice's criticism of the A&C's valuation must be dealt with. Second, the three offers must be placed in a common framework for evaluation. After this is done, the third issue is "What should we do?" I see it as my responsibility to provide the board with clarification on the first two issues and give you my recommendation on the third. Then it's up to the board to decide. If everyone's calendar is clear, let's plan to meet one week from today.

The members of the ME board of directors agreed to the suggested meeting time and adjourned.

SUMMARY OF ARMSTRONG AND COCHRAN REPORT
Valuation Conclusions

Breakup value	$15,638,947 or $59.48 per share
Present value proceeds	14,330,775 or 54.50 per share

Exhibit 1 outlines the breakup value of Martin Enterprises assuming an orderly divestiture of assets over a twenty-four month period. Following is a list of assumptions that should be read in conjunction with a review of this chart:

Breakup Value Calculation Assumptions

1.   *Estimated Market Value.* The market value of each division, except the Department Store, Real Estate, and Ranch divisions, is assumed to be the highest of estimated tangible asset value, multiple of earnings value, or required return on investment value. This value was then adjusted based upon the experience of Armstrong and Cochran in valuations and mergers and acquisitions.

The Department Store Division is very unprofitable and consequently is assumed to sell at 70 percent of tangible asset value. The ranch is assumed to sell for its appraised value of $3,750,000 plus $400 per head of cattle on December 31, 1986.

2.   *Transaction Costs.* The sales transaction costs for each division, except Ranch and Real Estate, are computed at 1.8 percent to 4.8 percent of the estimated market value depending on the size of the transaction. The larger the size of the transaction, the smaller the percentage used to compute the transaction. Transaction costs for Ranch and Real Estate are computed at 7 percent. Legal fees of $20,000 were then added to arrive at the transaction costs shown in Exhibit 1.

3.   *EBIT.* The 1986 earnings before interest and taxes (EBIT) for each division is provided in Exhibit 2.

4.   *Value Line Industry Pre-Tax P/E Ratio.* The pre-tax ratio applied to 1986 EBIT was derived from *Value Line Industry Surveys.* This ratio was

	Home Centers	Wholesale	M & J Supply
EXHIBIT 1 Martin Enterprises Breakup Value Calculation as of March 30, 1987			
Estimated Market Value (1)	$6,150,000	$2,875,000	$650,000
Less Transaction Costs (2)	121,500	88,750	41,000
Pre-tax Proceeds	$6,028,500	$2,786,250	$609,000
1986 EBIT (3)	$ 72,251	$ 117,456	$ 87,498
1986 After-Tax (assumes 34% rate)	47,686	77,521	57,749
Value Line Industry Pre-Tax P/E Ratio (4)	7.62	7.62	7.62
Price to Earnings Value	$ 550,549	$ 895,011	$666,731
Required Return on Investment (5)	13.75%	13.75%	13.75%
Required Return on Investment Value	$ 346,803	$ 563,787	$419,988
Receivables	$2,000,000	$ 850,000	$ 50,000
Inventories	1,043,143	1,519,641	122,791
Property & Plant	1,594,100	604,250	350,000
Estimated Tangible Asset Value (6)	$6,201,958	$2,973,891	$522,791
Estimated Tax Basis (7)			
Receivables	2,000,000	850,000	50,000
Inventories	2,607,858	1,519,641	122,791
Property & Plant	956,119	165,804	345,942
Total Tax Basis	5,563,977	2,535,445	518,707
Gain from Assumed Sale (8)	464,524	250,806	92,293
Tax on Gain (@34%)	157,938	85,274	30,700
After-Tax Proceeds (9)	$5,870,562	$2,700,976	$578,301

Retail Stores	Bryce Canyon	Real Estate	Trading Posts	Ranch	Total
$ 2,685,305	$2,250,000	$8,978,500	$2,000,000	$4,600,000	$30,188,804
86,000	83,750	628,000	80,000	345,000	1,474,495
$ 2,599,305	$2,166,250	$8,350,051	$1,920,000	$4,255,000	$28,714,309
$(1,195,601)	$ 403,516	$ 608,056	$ 320,520	$ 105,967	
(789,097)	266,321	401,317	211,543	69,938	
N/A	4.99	N/A	6.65	N/A	
0	$2,013,545	0	$2,131,458	0	
N/A	11.50%	N/A	11.50%	N/A	
0	$2,315,831	0	$1,839,506	0	
$ 1,300,000	$ 10,000	0	$ 228,700	0	
1,311,150	404,777	0	454,694	863,000	
1,225,000	836,000	8,978,500	1,244,950	3,750,000	
$ 3,836,150	$1,250,777	$8,978,500	$1,928,344	$4,613,000	
1,300,000	10,000	0	228,700	0	
1,311,150	404,777	0	454,694	47,066	
837,831	792,086	2,427,447	732,720	210,198	
3,448,980	1,206,863	2,427,447	1,416,112	257,263	
(849,676)	959,388	5,922,558	503,888	3,997,737	
(288,890)	326,192	2,013,670	162,322	1,359,231	
$ 2,599,305	$1,840,059	$6,336,336	$1,748,678	$2,895,770	

Martin Enterprises Book Value Dec. 31, 1986	$16,606,714
Total Gain on Sale of Assets	12,107,595
Tax on Gain (@34%)	4,116,583
After-Tax Proceeds	24,597,727
Plus:	
Cash and Notes Receivable	408,208
Less:	
Dec. 31, 1986 Liabilities	(8,984,386)
Preferred Stock	(382,600)
Total Breakup Value	$15,638,947
Per Share (131,475)	59.48

applied only to divisions that have regular earnings bases and whose industry features a number of public companies. Retail Stores, Real Estate, and Ranch were excluded from this exercise. Since these P/E ratios are of large public companies, a 30 percent discount was applied to them due to the comparable difference in the company's size, market presence, and overall strength. Data from the building supplies industry were applied to Home Centers, Wholesale, and M & J Supply. Grocery industry data were applied to Bryce Canyon, and retail industry (special lines) data were applied to Trading Posts.

One of the most widely used determinates of value for common stock is the price to earnings (P/E) ratio. This is simply a matter of applying an appropriate multiplier to the earnings of a company to arrive at a market value. Since different industries have historically had different multipliers, the P/E ratio used should be that of stocks of companies in the same or similar industries as the subject.

5. *Required Return on Investment.* This risk-adjusted rate reflects the rate of return that is required for a sophisticated purchaser. The base rate used is a nonrated, long-term, tax-exempt bond yield of 8.75 percent. This rate was adjusted by adding a 2.75 percent to 5 percent premium for risk. The risk premium required was gauged by 1984-1986 operating performance and the division's outlook for future years.

The after-tax 1986 income was then divided by the required investment rate in order to arrive at a price that would provide the required return.

6. *Estimated Tangible Asset Value.* Estimated tangible asset value includes the December 31, 1986, accounts receivable balance, the December 31, 1986, inventories balance and, except for Ranch and Real Estate, the 1984 depreciated cost of properties listed in the Hanny Insurance Appraisal. The estimated tangible asset value for Real Estate and Ranches equals estimated market value.

7. *Estimated Tax Basis.* Estimated tax basis is the sum of December 31, 1986, accounts receivable and inventories balances plus the book value of property, plant, and equipment provided by the December 31, 1986, fixed asset depreciation schedule.

8. *Gain on Assumed Sale.* The gain on the assumed sale is the difference between estimated market value and estimated tax basis.

9. *After-Tax Proceeds.* After-tax proceeds is equal to estimated market value less transaction costs and any applicable tax on the gain. The assumed tax rate was 34 percent. The total after-tax proceeds is greater than the sum of each division because of tax differences caused by selling the Retail Division at a loss.

A summary of the breakup value calculation is as follows:

Total estimated market value	$30,188,805
Less:	
Transaction costs	(1,474,495)
Tax on gain	(4,116,583)
Dec. 31, 1986, liabilities	(8,984,396)
Preferred stock	(382,600)
	$15,230,741

Add:

Cash and notes receivable	$ 408,206
Total breakup value	$15,638,947
Breakup value per share	$ 59.48

The present value of proceeds from a breakup, discounted at 13.50 percent, assuming 50 percent is received in year one and the balance is received over ten years with 10 percent interest, totals $14,330,775 or $54.50 per share.

Therefore, if ME were to entertain a cash offer for the entire company, the benchmark price should be $54.50 per share.

However, if a less-than-majority interest were to be sold, the shareholders should expect a per-share price in the $39 to $42 range due to marketability/minority interest discount.

All other things being equal, an interest in a business is worth more if the business is readily marketable. Minority interests in privately held businesses lack marketability and are relatively illiquid compared with a controlling or majority business interest. Empirical studies have shown that "lettered stock," defined as similar in every way to normal stock except possessing stringent marketability restrictions, typically sells at a 30 percent to 40 percent discount from its nonletter counterparts. This discount is for its lack of marketability.

In summary, an appropriate discount for lack of marketability for use in applying to ME stock is from 30 percent to 35 percent.

Adjustments to 1986 Statement of Operations

Adjustments were made to the preliminary 1986 Statement of Operations (see Exhibit 2) in order to attempt to properly allocate overhead. These allocations were made as follows:

General and administrative expenses were allocated according to corporate management's estimate of time spent in each division. Personnel expenses were allocated among the eight operating segments according to the number of employees in each segment. One-half of the finance and accounting expenses were allocated equally to the eight divisions on the assumption that if the divisions were individual companies, they would all have accounting expenses. The remaining one-half was allocated according to the employee ratio. Data processing expenses were allocated according to the data processing manager's estimate of resource allocation. This expense included an equal amount for general ledger and payable costs to each division. Credit department expenses were allocated according to a company-provided analysis of costs. The maintenance credit was spread evenly across seven divisions; the assumption was made that the Ranch Division would have no involvement with the maintenance department.

The figures in the eliminations column would be a reduction of the Wholesale Division's sales and costs due to intercompany sales to Home Centers. However, these data remain in the individual division financial review because the intercompany sales are made on an arm's-length basis and sales and costs would remain at the higher figure if the division was owned by an unrelated party.

	Home Centers	Whole-sale	M & J Supply	Retail Stores	Bryce Canyon	Real Estate	Trading Posts	Ranch	Elimina-tions	Total
Sales	$15,946,993	$7,474,724	$1,080,270	$5,376,602	$4,232,870		$2,942,583	$341,088	($1,173,049)	$36,222,079
Costs of Goods Sold	12,539,809	6,169,570	747,282	3,468,512	2,690,983		1,911,562	998	(1,209,806)	26,318,910
Gross Margin	3,407,184	1,305,155	332,988	1,908,090	1,541,887		1,031,021	340,090	36,757	9,903,170
Gross Margin percentages	21.4%	17.5%	30.8%	35.5%	36.4%		35.0%	99.7%		27.3%
Other Operations Income (Expense)	156,605	(20,019)	(3,771)	225,765	18,874	$1,040,772	270,545	25,648	36,757	1,714,419
Total Income	$3,563,789	$1,285,136	$329,217	$2,133,854	$1,560,761	$1,040,772	$1,301,566	$365,738	$36,757	$11,617,588
Controllable Expenses	2,291,426	819,367	158,919	2,358,386	813,731	124,248	605,216	111,191		7,282,483
Partially Controllable Expenses	453,965	121,993	29,635	251,918	109,681	146,302	143,525	64,733		1,321,750
Non-Controllable Expenses	270,148	87,999	4,768	225,321	134,641	106,141	119,463	24,026		976,505
Income from Operations	544,252	255,778	135,896	(701,771)	502,709	664,081	433,362	165,789	36,757	2,036,851
General and Administrative Expenses	91,296	42,793	6,185	140,273	40,078	20,039	40,078	20,039		400,780
Personnel	22,024	8,014	2,634	32,896	8,574	1,738	12,609	2,186		90,674
Finance and Accounting	79,488	46,104	33,284	105,394	47,339	31,148	57,054	32,216		432,124
Data Processing	148,903	19,732	5,382	91,495	5,382	5,382	5,382	5,382		287,041
Credit	132,572	23,958	3,195	126,055	0	0	0	0		285,780
Maintenance	(2,281)	(2,281)	(2,281)	(2,281)	(2,281)	(2,281)	(2,281)	0		(15,964)
	472,001	138,322	48,399	493,831	99,193	56,025	112,842	59,822		1,480,434
	72,251	117,456	87,498	(1,195,601)	403,516	608,056	320,520	105,967	36,757	556,418
Other Income/(Deductions)										63,258
Interest Income										15,124
Interest Expense										(475,694)
Gain/Loss on Sales										48,396
Other (Net)										
Total Other (Net)										(348,917)
Income before Taxes										$ 207,501

EXHIBIT 2
Adjusted 1986 Internal
Financial Statement

WESTCOR REPLY TO ARMSTRONG AND COCHRAN REPORT

Summary of Our General Comments

The scope of the A&C report is limited. A&C was told to find a way to satisfy *only* the objective of buying out the selling shareholders. The stated objective was not to maximize value for all shareholders today. Therefore, a sale of the whole company is not fully considered and is quickly dismissed in the conclusion of its report.

A&C did not highlight the cyclicity of the whole portfolio of businesses. Most of ME's building material sales are to contractors and industrial/commercial customers rather than to the less cyclical do-it-yourself market. Similarly, the Bryce Canyon stores, the department stores, and real estate are also hurt by recessions. This vulnerabiity to recessions should be an important part of any valuation or strategic study.

Summary of Our Comments on the Valuation

The A&C valuation methodology is incomplete. A full valuation includes comparative multiples of earnings, cash flow and book value, liquidation value (net tangible asset value), and a discounted cash flow. Reliance is normally placed on going-concern valuation methods such as multiple of earnings analysis and discounted cash flow; the liquidation value method is a secondary technique to establish the valuation range. Liquidation values only become significant when they substantially exceed the going-concern value and the company would actually be liquidated. As we shall show below, estimating the true net proceeds of liquidation is much more complicated than A&C has shown.

The discount rate used in the study is too low. If the discount rates used in this study, ranging from 11.5 percent to 13.75 percent, are meant to be after-tax returns on equity, they are far too low. Equity investments in liquid public stock would normally command a return in the 15 percent to 20 percent range. Investments in illiquid private companies will be much higher. Venture capital and leveraged buyout returns on equity will exceed 25 percent. Would the board of directors want only a 13.5 percent return on their equity if they were buying ME, assuming a break-up liquidation of several businesses was a key part of the business plan? The discount rate *you* would use is the appropriate one here.

In its report, A&C discounted proceeds from the breakup at only 13.5 percent. Had it used the same assumptions at 20 percent discount rate, the value today would be approximately $48/share and at a 25 percent discount rate, approximately $44/share. If taxes were paid on the 10 percent interest income, the value per share drops below $38 per share.

The valuation of the building material division is excessive. The division is being valued as a whole at $9.7 million before tax and transaction costs. This amounts to over fifty times after-tax earnings as calculated by A&C. Clearly A&C is relying primarily on liquidation value. Even if the building materials earned a more normal 1.5 percent to 2.5 percent on sales ($375,000 to $625,000 on $25 million in sales), it would be difficult to justify going-concern values in excess of $5.5 million to $6.5 million. If the liquidation value method is to be used as the primary method, then the additional cost discussed below should be included.

The liquidation value of the department stores fails to properly estimate the actual liquidation proceeds. Without any significant analysis, A&C assumes that the Department Store Division will sell at 70 percent of tangible asset value, or $2.7 million. This type of "haircut" on asset values is a typical method used by investment bankers to determine a range of value, but is inappropriate when trying to determine actual liquidation proceeds—particularly a retail business. One of the main costs of liquidation, on top of the losses on asset value, is the overhead incurred while selling the inventory. Since the Department Store Division operates with an annual overhead of $2.5 million, a one- to two-month liquidation would cost $200,000 to $400,000. Severance and legal costs would add to those costs. Moreover, the company is still obligated under the terms of its Durango, Delta, and Grand Junction leases. The present value of these lease costs (estimated to be $150,000 per year) or the buyout cost could be as high as $250,000 to $375,000.

The ranch is overvalued because the A&C report underestimates the impact of the time value of money and the terms of sale. A substantial discount on the value of an asset is required for the time it takes to make a sale. A ranch that takes 2 to 3 years to sell would have a *cash value today* of 30 percent to 40 percent less than its nominal value. Furthermore, a ranch would require an additional discount of 30 percent to 40 percent for the noncash portion of the sale in that year. We would expect that a ranch like the Bookcliff would typically sell with a 20 percent down payment.

A&C states that selling shareholders should take a 30 percent to 40 percent discount on their stock for lack of marketability. The block of stock should be valued as a control block. Because the block of stock being sold could be 50 percent or more of ME and because the sale effectively consolidates control of the company with the nonselling shareholders, the stock should be valued as a control block. Therefore no discount to the acquisition value is warranted.

EXHIBIT 3
Summary Valuation
(in thousands)

Realistic cash	A&C Report	Value Today
Building materials	$ 9,150	$5,550–6,000
Retail	2,600	1,000–1,500
Bryce Canyon	1,840	1,500
Trading posts	1,749	1,750
Real estate	6,336	5,000–5,500
Miscellaneous	28	—
Net liabilities	(8,959)	(9,000)
Non-ranch division	12,744	5,750–7,250
Ranch	2,896	1,500–2,000
Valuation	15,639	7,250–9,250
Cash value today	$14,331	$7,250–9,250

Conclusion

In conclusion, we believe the A&C report greatly underestimates the cash needs to take out the selling shareholders. In order to take out the selling shareholders, the real choices the company faces are to shrink the company dramatically (e.g. by selling off the home centers as a whole and reducing overhead substantially), in effect beginning the liquidation of the company, or selling the company to a third party. The liquidation process involves very substantial risks, particularly if shareholder disputes continue or if the liquidation is not handled swiftly and effectively with good management in place. If a partial liquidation process fails to generate sufficient cash, a vicious cycle of selling assets to generate more cash is set in motion. In effect, the company would be "tearing the house down to pay the mortgage," accelerating the decline in equity value and morale.

A lower-risk way to operate is to sell the company to a reputable buyer on terms that would be acceptable to the family. This approach has the added benefit of keeping the company intact.

PURCHASE OFFER—WESTCOR HOLDINGS, INC.

Binding Purchase Agreement

1. *Purchase Price.* The common stock will be acquired by Westcor for purchase price of $42.50 per share ($11,175,375) payable as described below. The preferred stock will be purchased for $382,600 in cash.
2. *Payment Terms.* The purchase price for the common stock to be paid by Westcor on the closing date of the sale and purchase agreement shall be payable as follows:
   a. $6,675,375 in cash at closing.
   b. $1,750,000 in cash upon the sale of the Bookcliff Ranch or at the end of the first year, whichever occurs first.
   c. $2,750,000 in five (5) year secured notes. Such notes shall bear interest at ten percent (10%) per annum payable in arrears. Principle shall be payable at the term of the note (end of year five).
3. *Purchase Agreement.* Upon execution of this letter by all parties, the parties shall work to prepare and execute the purchase agreement containing provisions in accordance with this letter of intent together with such other terms and conditions as the parties may mutually determine. The purchase agreement shall be subject in all respects to the written approval of the parties. The parties consider time is of the essence in consummating the purchase transaction contemplated by this letter.
4. *Closing Date.* The execution of the purchase agreement shall be as early as possible and closing of the purchase transaction shall be no later than June 30, 1987.
5. *Terms of Offer.* This offer is valid until the close of business on May 31, 1987.

PURCHASE OFFER—JOE F. CONN CORPORATION

In accordance with our previous discussions, Joe F. Conn Corporation (Conn) is pleased to present the following offer:

We hereby offer to purchase (1) the interests of Martin Enterprises (ME) and (2) all assets, including without limitation accounts receivable, inventory, and operating assets such as furniture, fixtures, equipment, vehicles, materials, and supplies, currently held by the Bryce Canyon Division of ME, all for an aggregate purchase price of $11,400,000. The offer is structured as follows:

$ 9,650,000	in Joe F. Conn stock at close
1,750,000	estimated net proceeds from the sale of department store inventory, receivables and fixtures, payable at the time of the sale or at the end of the first year, whichever is sooner
$11,400,000	Total

If you find the foregoing offer acceptable, please so indicate by executing the enclosed copy of this letter in the space designated below and returning same to Joe F. Conn Corporation, upon receipt of which all parties shall commence to proceed diligently to closing.

PURCHASE OFFER BY B. J. JENNAR

Descriptive Summary of Agreement of Intent

I. Sale of all stock and all assets of Martin Enterprises (ME)
II. ME sale accomplished by means of a statutory merger
   Procedure:
   A. Board of directors approves plan and recommends it to ME shareholders.
   B. Shareholders vote on plan as approved by the board of directors.
   Discussion:
   A. A majority vote of the board of directors and a majority vote of the shareholders will implement the transaction.
   B. The effect is an acquisition of 100 percent of the stock of ME, all at the same price and terms.
   C. The sale of all interests is complete. There are no residual sales or involvements.
III. Terms:
   A. Holders of ME preferred stock are cashed out at close at $100 per share.
   B. Individual holders of ME common stock each receive cash at the closing plus a specified stream of monthly cash payments over a term. An individualized letter of credit from a national bank acceptable to the parties guarantees the monthly cash payments.
IV. Price:
   A. $19,201,000 total payments
      1. $18,818,400 for ME common stock
      2.   382,600 for ME preferred stock (at close)
         $19,201,000   Total

B. Payment:

Timing	Total
At close	$4,000,000
End of year 1	$ 960,000
End of years 2–8	$1,080,000
End of year 9	$6,681,000

QUESTIONS

1. What does Walka mean by placing the three offers "in a common framework"?
2. Do you agree with the Westcor criticism of the Armstrong and Cochran report? Why or why not?
3. Discuss the differences in purchase mechanisms. Are they substantially different or are the differences cosmetic?
4. What is the significance of payment in cash versus stock?
5. Calculate the Net Present Value of Jennar's offer. What capitalization rate should you use?
6. Which of the offers would you accept? Defend your answer.

K Mail-Order Pharmacy

Herbert E. Brown, Paula M. Saunders, and Rich Gulling

Richard Grabarth had dreamed of owning his own company ever since he had had his own paper route. Now thirty, he had a B.S. in business, an M.B.A. in marketing, and had worked for eight years in pharmacy sales and sales management with a major drug company that sold pharmaceuticals, over-the-counter drugs, vitamins, and home health care devices. He had also recently completed a direct response marketing course at a local university.

Grabarth had considered a number of venture possibilities over the years. Unfortunately, most were outside his area of expertise in the pharmaceutical industry or would require extensive travel and time away from his family. Some required far more capital than he could raise.

CONTEMPORARY PHARMACEUTICAL SYSTEMS

His most recent idea was a firm that would sell pharmaceuticals, over-the-counter drugs, vitamins, and home health care devices both directly to consumers and through a third-party insurance company umbrella. The name he chose for his venture was Contemporary Pharmaceutical Systems. The advantage of this opportunity for him was that it would allow him to stay in the industry he knew, would require limited capital, and would let him in on the ground floor of a rapid growth distribution channel—mail order. He also sensed an opportunity to increase his income without taking too much time away from his family. He was optimistic as he began to develop plans for his venture.

His new firm, Contemporary Pharmaceutical Systems, would sell competitively priced mail-order pharmaceutical products to health insurance company clients and to regular retail customers. Generic drugs would be emphasized. Contemporary operational management techniques would enhance the service to customers. For example, Grabarth planned to set up

This case was prepared by Herbert E. Brown, Paula M. Saunders, and Rich Gulling of Wright State University, Dayton, Ohio. Used with permission.

a patient consultation data base, permitting individualized patient consultation sheets to be included with each prescription.

Contemporary Pharmaceutical Systems's customers and prospects could place orders by calling a toll-free number. Their orders would be delivered to their doorsteps. Each customer would receive a patient consultation printout detailing the important information about the drugs they had ordered. If customers had questions about their medication, private consultation with a pharmacist would be available over the phone. The new company would also offer, for a fee to either the insurer or the insured, analysis of the patient's medication interactions and other services associated with managed health care. Mailings to individuals on insurance company lists and purchased lists and a lead-generation program based on space ads would be used to establish a customer base.

Rich Grabarth felt ready to go. His next step was to seek financing through consultation with a banker. The banker's reaction substantially cooled his venture fever. Grabarth later revealed to a friend that his effort to get financing really opened his eyes to some realities of business. The bank wanted data that defined the business opportunity more clearly and also a business plan. The bank wanted information on trends in the drug industry and the relationship between the direct response marketing channel and the pharmaceutical industry. Surprised by the bank's request, he turned to other investors and discovered they asked the same questions as the bankers, and even more forcefully. Humbled, but undeterred and still very optimistic, Grabarth set about compiling the requested information and putting it down on paper. His findings on the pharmaceutical industry and direct marketing activity within it are summarized in the following sections.

BACKGROUND ON THE PHARMACEUTICAL MARKET

According to the American Pharmaceutical Association, 1.52 billion prescriptions, with an average cost of $16.62, are filled each year. The mail-order share of the prescription drug market, which is growing at a 25 percent annual rate, is expected to reach $6 billion to $9 billion by 1995. Sales of over-the-counter (OTC) drugs, vitamins, and home health-monitoring devices are also growing.

This growth can be seen in retail drug store performance data reported in the May 9, 1989, *Chain Drug Review* state-of-the-industry report. According to *Chain Drug Review*, 1988 total drug store sales were $61.1 billion, a 10.1 percent increase over 1987; 1988 chain drug store sales were $38.2 billion, 10.9 percent over 1987; 1988 independent drug store sales were $22.9 billion, 8.7 percent over 1987; and the 1988 chain drug share of total drug store sales was 62.7 percent.

PHARMACEUTICAL INDUSTRY FRAGMENTATION

The *Chain Drug Review* report also revealed that the pharmaceutical industry is highly fragmented, with the largest drug chain by dollar volume controlling only 8.4 percent of the total market. Twelve drug store chains

TABLE 1
Drug Store Chains with
Over $1 Billion in Sales in
1988
(in billions of dollars)

Chain	Sales
1. Walgreen*	$5.10
2. Osco Drug	3.19
3. Jack Eckerd*	2.95
4. Rite Aid*	2.87
5. Revco*	2.47
6. Thrifty	2.40
7. Shoppers Drug Mart	1.98
8. Long's Drug Stores	1.93
9. CVS	1.82
10. Peoples Drug Stores	1.50
11. Hook-SupeRx	1.30
12. Pay Less NW	1.22

*Denotes chain with existing mail-order operations

had over $1 billion in sales in 1988, accounting for 47 percent of the retail drug store dollar volume (see Table 1). Four of these were known to have mail order operations in place.

BASIC PHARMACEUTICAL MARKETS

Major pharmaceutical product lines include prescription drugs, over-the-counter drugs, vitamins, and home health-monitoring devices. Table 2 contains a matrix that describes the products, benefits, and primary target markets for the vast majority of pharmaceutical products.

Trends in the Retail Pharmaceutical Market

Nine major trends appear to be affecting the retail pharmacy market. These are: (1) one-stop shopping, (2) deep discounting, (3) retail drug industry consolidation, (4) increased use of self-medication and illness-prevention strategies, (5) favorable social and demographic changes, (6) vigorous governmental and private insurer pressures to decrease health care costs, (7) increased use of generic drugs, (8) managed care services, and (9) increased use of mail-order marketing.

One-stop shopping offers consumers the convenience of purchasing many kinds of merchandise at one store. Women in two-income households make up a major part of this market. This group contains more than twenty-seven million families, up from twenty-two million in 1973. Women in this market typically make larger purchases and spend more on high-ticket items than other consumers. For them, convenience is more important than price when making a purchasing decision.

Deep discounting is usually associated with drug chains. Profit is made using a "low margin, high turnover" financial model. Deep discounting is

Product	Benefits	Target Market
Prescriptions	Prolong life, improve health	Patients requiring maintenance therapy
OTC drugs	Mostly improve the symptoms of an ailment	People suffering from illnesses or perceived illnesses
Home health devices	Give patients more knowledge and control over their health	Diabetics, hypertensives, and others
Vitamins	Improve health, prevent disease, help circumvent negative health factors	Almost everyone with an interest in maintaining or improving his/her health

TABLE 2
Product Benefit Matrix

Buyer	Seller	Price (in millions of $)	Stores Added
Pacific Enterprises	Pay 'n Save	$234.0	147
Fleming Cos.	Malone & Hyde	225.0	101
Hook-SupeRx	Brooks	81.5	360
Rite Aid	Imasco	70.0	114
Big B	Imasco	50.0	85
Rite Aid	Begley	18.5	189
SupeRx of AGA	Medicare-Glaser	18.2	84

TABLE 3
Major 1988 Drug Store Chain Acquisitions

still a small part of the total industry, but consumers have been receptive to it. In 1988, the top twenty-five deep discounting chains had a total of 618 stores (about 3 percent of the drug industry's total outlets), 8 percent of total drug store drug sales, and about $3 billion in sales.

A major consequence of deep discounting and one-stop shopping is inconvenience and poor customer service. For example, in a busy major chain pharmacy, the wait for a prescription is frequently thirty minutes to forty-five minutes and even more during peak periods.

Consolidation is another clear trend in the retail drug store chain industry. This is evidenced by several major acquisitions (see Table 3). Acquisition appears to be popular because it offers existing large retailers an easy and low-cost method of expansion into established store locations and markets.

Self-medication and illness prevention is also a significant factor in the retail drug business. Adults suffering from illness or injury do not always seek health care from a physician. In fact, about two-thirds of the U.S. population self-diagnose and use nonprescription remedies. This trend appears to have been reinforced recently by a large number of analgesics and cold remedies being converted from prescription to OTC status.

Favorable demographics also exist for increased home health care and, therefore, for increased mail-order drug marketing. For the population as a whole, prescription use nearly doubles between the ages of thirty and sixty years, from 5.4 prescriptions a year to nearly 10.5. Roughly 13 percent of the U.S. population will be at least sixty-five years old by the year 2000. Home health care costs are now one-third to one-half of the costs of hospital care for a recuperating patient. One by-product of this is that about 40 percent of the surgery patients now return home within one day of operations versus 40 percent within five days only a decade ago.

Health care cost containment movements by the government, employers, and insurers are now being vigorously pursued. The "government" prescription market will soon approach approximately 700 million prescriptions per year, making the government the largest buyer of prescription drugs. This is fueling a variety of government cost containment measures that, if implemented, could have a dramatic impact on the drug industry.

The private sector is also confronted with the prospect of steadily rising medical costs. Insurance plans are now experiencing prescription drug plan costs of $275 to $300 per employee. As a result, an increasing number of both public and private employers are including a mail-order drug option as part of their employee benefit package.

Increased use of generic drugs is being spurred by expiration of patents. It is estimated that 75 percent of the top one hundred U.S. drug patents will have expired by 1995. Generics usually carry a bigger profit margin for drug store operators than branded products do.

Managed care services are also making dramatic inroads into the health care industry. These are made possible by data bases that permit tracking of myriad details of the behavior and practices of individuals, doctors, and other participants in the health care system. For example, doctors can be detected who consistently prescribe drugs for which there is a lower-priced, equally useful alternative, as can drug abusers who use multiple physicians in order to obtain more drugs (and to get insurers to pay for them). Firms that sell drugs are ideally placed to manage these data bases.

Mail-order channel acceptance is growing. Health insurance policies often contain provisions requiring that maintenance medicines be purchased from specified mail-order houses. And, even when they don't require it, policy provisions often contain attractive incentives for policy holders to purchase from insurer-specified direct mail suppliers. For the most part, consumer response to these provisions has been favorable. Consumers have also demonstrated a willingness to use mail order for prescription and other drug purchases without being offered either encouragement or incentives from insurance companies.

According to *American Druggist*, mail-order pharmacies had revenues of $725 million in 1988. The forecasted mail-order channel share of the retail prescription market for 1995 is projected to be a 15.6 percent share or $6.2 billion in sales. Mail-order prescriptions usually cost about 25 percent less than those from drug stores. Most are for maintenance drugs used to treat such diseases as high blood pressure, arthritis, and diabetes.

Growth in the mail-order channel has stirred debate among people in the medical community who are concerned that people buying drugs via mail order will suffer from lack of supervision. This and other concerns are shared by the government, which is particularly interested in marketing practices within the mail-order channel. Senate hearings were held in 1988 to determine the ethical and legal ramifications of drug mail order. To date, however, no significant legislation has been passed.

The largest pharmaceutical mail-order operation is run by an alliance of the Veterans Administration and the American Association of Retired Persons (AARP). In 1988, this organization accounted for almost two-thirds of all mail-order drug prescriptions. Another major player is Medco Containment Services, the largest public mail-order pharmaceutical company, serving about fifteen million persons. Medco had total sales of $450 million in 1988. Home Shopping Network and Cable Value Network entered this lucrative market in 1988 and are just beginning to find their niche.

There are three types of mail-order pharmaceutical companies. One type develops its own customer base and sells directly to retail customers. Another concentrates on working with large health insurers and servicing the drug requirements of the clients on their data bases. Still another type of firm emphasizes third-party marketing through organizations that provide mail-order pharmacy services as a benefit of membership.

Third-Party Mail-Order Pharmaceutical Organizations

AARP is the largest third-party mail-order operation in the United States. The AARP Pharmacy Prescription Service, founded in 1959, presently operates ten regional pharmacies. Each of these has a toll-free number for customer use, making access to the system very easy for the customer. AARP offers a 100 percent satisfaction guarantee on all merchandise except prescriptions, which by law can't be returned.

AARP mails out a forty-eight page, four-color catalog on a biannual basis. The catalog is mailed in a four-page overwrap that describes AARP's prescription service and features some of its products. These materials position AARP as the low-cost provider of prescription and OTC medicines, and emphasize generic brands. The primary thrust of the catalog presentation of AARP's product lines is on the equivalence of generics and brand-name products and the favorable price differential offered by generics.

The AARP catalog is devoted largely to OTC drugs, but also contains a limited number of HBAs (health and beauty aids), diabetic supplies, and a few home health care aids. Prescription drugs are included in a twelve-page, free-standing insert. In all, almost four hundred product and size combinations, or stock keeping units (SKUs), are represented in the catalog. Product categories represented in the index section of this catalog are listed in Table 4.

The top ten product categories in the AARP catalog, based on number of pages devoted to the product category, are shown in Table 5.

Insurance Company–Mail-Order Company Relationships

Insurance companies don't actually buy drugs, but nonetheless are the largest users of mail-order pharmacies. They like the savings mail order provides their insured clients, and thus the contribution they make to

TABLE 4
Product Categories in the
AARP Catalog

Aloe vera	Hosiery
Antacids	Incontinence products
Colds & allergies	Laxatives
Comfort aids	Liniments & rubs
Cosmetics/skin care	Neutrogena products
Dental products	Pain pills
Diabetic supplies & insulins	Prescriptions
Externals	Skin care
Eye products	Vitamins
First aid	
Foot care	
Hair care	
Health & beauty aids	
Hearing aid batteries	
Hemorrhoidals	

TABLE 5
Top 10 AARP Catalog
Product Categories by
Number of Pages of
Listings

Product Category	Number of Pages
Prescriptions*	12
Vitamins	9
Analgesics	4
Dental/denture	3
Allergy/cold	3
Laxatives	3
Antacids	2
Foot care	2
Diabetic supplies	2
Hearing aid batteries†	1

*Included in a free-standing insert
†Included due to its back cover position

cutting insurance costs. The key areas where savings can be achieved are: (1) decreased ingredient costs, (2) reduction of dispensing fees, and (3) a higher generic drug dispensing rate. Some experts feel that the mail-order option could reduce an insurance company's prescription reimbursement costs as much as 40 percent.

Most insurance executives now view the mail-order option as a cornerstone of future health benefit plans. This attractiveness derives from a variety of very tangible benefits that can be provided by mail-order company data bases. These include the ability to develop proactive drug interaction detection programs to resolve potentially health-threatening therapeutic drug interactions. By proactively monitoring these interactions, iatrogenic (physician induced) illness resulting from harmful drug interactions, which accounts for a significant percentage of new hospital admissions, can be reduced. Drug-use monitoring is easier to accomplish if the patient is restricted to purchasing prescriptions at a central location where a complete patient profile is available. This decreases the fraudulent use of prescription benefits, allows for more efficient drug abuse monitoring, and permits detection and exclusion of physicians with patterns of extraordinarily high treatment costs.

MAIL-ORDER MARKETING

Grabarth also investigated the general field of direct marketing to make sure he understood the core issues of the field before proceeding further. The following is the essence of his findings on the direct-response marketing field.

THE MAIL-ORDER CONSUMER

Grabarth found that two major consumer groups have been especially receptive to purchasing prescription drugs and other pharmaceutical items by mail: mature consumers, defined as the fifty-five-plus age group, and consumers who live in rural areas where health care providers are sparse and higher prices are typical.

The mature consumer segment of the market is mobile, affluent, and health conscious. This segment can be further divided into four groups: healthy hermits, healthy indulgers, frail recluses, and ailing outgoers. This is a heterogeneous market and cannot be targeted as though everyone over fifty-five is considered to be old.

In a recent *Drug Topics* survey, mature consumers picked convenience as the most important reason for choosing a pharmacy. Also included as primary choice factors were: past satisfaction with services, the store's reputation, and money-saving incentives.

Rural customers have been receptive to mail order since the advent of the Sears catalog. Since these consumers live in sparsely populated areas, they are limited in choice and must often pay a premium on any type of health care they consume. Thus, mail-order pharmacies allow rural customers to receive quality pharmacy services at prices comparable to the prices charged in a large urban market. Mail-order pharmacies also provide rural consumers with increased convenience. Rural consumers often must travel great distances to get their prescriptions and OTC drugs, but mail order brings these items to the customer's door.

CRITICAL ASSUMPTIONS UNDERLYING DIRECT-MAIL MARKETING SUCCESS

From his direct-response marketing course notes and other sources, Grabarth found that for a direct-marketing program to be successful, the markets that are selected, the means of distribution that are chosen, the offer or offers that are constructed, and the positioning concepts that are used must be the right ones. Assumptions in all of these areas will drive marketing strategy and component decisions. Thus, the strategy that a direct-marketing firm decides to implement, i.e., sending direct-mail packages, soliciting sales by phone, or generating leads by mass advertising, by direct-mail advertising, or by phone, should rest on the "direct-response tripod." The direct-response tripod is comprised of the lists, offers, and positionings, or copy platforms, that are used. Each of these represents areas where mismanagement can lead to failure.

Direct-Mail Lists

A list is likely to be a good one if everyone on it can reasonably be assumed to have an affinity for the product or service being offered. In direct marketing, the list is the "market." For purposes of program development, all buyers other than those on the list being targeted can be disregarded. Conversely, whatever program is put together should be faithful to the needs and aspirations of list members, or segments within the list membership. Grabarth felt this element of his strategy was strong since the insurance companies had offered him their lists at virtually the cost of printing them.

Direct-Mail Offers

A good offer is one that melts away prospect resistance and obtains the desired response now: an order, a lead, etc. The offer involves the product or service, time limits for buyer acceptance, guarantees, payment terms, delivery terms, the price, return privileges, and premiums for ordering now or for ordering at all. In sum, the offer is everything the buyer gives, or commits to give, to the seller and everything the sellers give, or commit to give, to the buyer.

Positioning the Direct-Mail Offer

Positioning is what the basic benefit bundle is all about as seen by the prospect for a direct-response marketing offer. Whether the strategy being used employs direct mail, magazine ads, the telephone, or whatever, experienced direct marketers have found that the strategy works best when it is driven by one, *and only one*, major concept of what the principal benefit bundle is. For example, by accepting the offer, is the buyer going to save money, make money, be relieved of hassle, or have his or her bad dreams about something or another stopped? One such concept must be chosen as the copy platform around which the sales literature will be written. The term *literature* here includes sales letters, brochures, order forms, and even telephone sales scripts.

Direct-Mail Formats

Once the list, offer, and positioning issues have been thoroughly resolved, the strategy has a solid foundation, and the seller is ready to develop the program. This involves selecting between three basic formats: the classic package, self-mailers, and catalogs.

The classic package is a mailing that includes an outside envelope, a cover letter, a brochure, an order form or response device, and a lift device or premium of some sort.

The function of the *outside envelope* is to "get itself opened." That's why there is often a teaser on the mail package envelope. The function of the *cover letter* is to "explain and sell" (motivate the prospect to buy) the offer (of product, at current price, with current premium, etc.) that is being made. The function of the *brochure* is to "show and tell" or explain the product or service. The order form is the *response device*. The function of the *lift device or premium* (which can be a discount, an additional product, etc.) is to induce a decision now, and overcome procrastination—the death knell of direct marketers.

All direct-response mailings must have all of the functions described above performed, but different marketing situations require different degrees of emphasis. For example, if the product is very simple to explain, a one-page self-mailer might be designed to perform all of the functions, and perform them very well. These functions must also be performed when using the catalog format.

CONCLUSIONS

After collecting and summarizing the above data for his potential investors, Rich Grabarth felt more optimistic than ever that his idea would work. After some additional research and analysis, he concluded that he would need to start with a minimum mailing of seventy-five thousand catalogs. These he estimated would cost him about $30,000 in creative and production costs and about $30,000, or forty cents each, to mail. Grabarth decided to base his plans on what he assumed was a conservative response rate estimate of 4 percent, or three thousand orders, from his initial mailing of seventy-five thousand small catalogs. (He felt this was conservative because he would have the endorsement of an insurance company, and therefore increased credibility with his mail-order prospects.) He also assumed an average order of $50, and given his product costs, a 60 percent average gross margin that included consideration of variable order fulfillment costs.

Grabarth's assumptions led him to forecast first-year sales of $225,000, and first-year gross direct profit (sales minus variable costs) of $135,000. In the second and third years, he assumed sales increases of 50 percent and 35 percent respectively. After that, he expected sales to grow at a rate of 20 percent per annum for at least five years.

Grabarth has $50,000 in accumulated savings. He has convinced one investment group to invest approximately $50,000 in the venture—assuming they have a place on his board and an equal partnership, and voice, in decision making. Banks have offered to loan him $50,000 at approximately 18 percent per annum interest. The banks will require him to pledge his equity in a $175,000 home as collateral for this loan. This is worth $65,000.

QUESTIONS

1. Given the facts that Richard Grabarth has assembled, what are his overall marketing strategy options?
2. How viable does the mail-order option Grabarth has selected appear to be?

3. What appear to be the direct-response marketing strategy options available to Grabarth?

4. Delineate an offer or set of offers that Contemporary Pharmaceutical Systems might make to the general consumer market for prescription drugs (as opposed to the insurance company client market).

5. What, if any, are some of the major legal issues that must be dealt with if Grabarth is to use the direct-response marketing channel for medical products marketing?

6. Sketch out a direct-response "classic package" suggesting content of cover letters, brochures, lift devices, envelopes, and premiums.

TeleSell

Jerome Katz

TeleSell[sm] will be America's first fee-for-service, telephone-based motivational program targeted to salespeople in the field. TeleSell reflects the need to maintain high levels of motivation among salespeople in the field. Sales experts repeatedly stress that the state of mind of the salesperson is the key ingredient to securing sales. A motivated salesperson is more likely to be a successful salesperson.

Generating this motivation is the purpose of expert sales and motivational speakers such as Zig Ziglar, Spencer Johnson, or Harvey McKay. Today more than a dozen continually high-selling sales technique books filled with advice and inspiration dominate the business book market. These book sales support active presentation and cassette programs by the speakers. The ideas of these accomplished, well-known experts will be the major product of TeleSell.

USING TELESELL

For the salesperson in the field who has just faced a letdown after a failed presentation, the help and inspiration of speakers, books, and cassettes may seem too far away to be of use. TeleSell is designed to fill the need for immediate advice and inspiration.

As we envision TeleSell in its startup form, the salesperson dialing TeleSell would receive a sixty-second to ninety-second quotation from the books of the sales experts. The excerpts would be read by the sales experts themselves or by professional actors in order to make the message as powerful as possible. Initially, ten to twelve quotes (on the average of one per top-selling sales book) would be used per day, five days a week. This approach makes viable multiple calls per day from a likely group of intensive users of the service.

The thirty-second trailer for the message gives the quote's author and book title, and a mention of the other experts whose ideas are available

---

This case was prepared by Jerome A. Katz of Saint Louis University. Used with permission.

through TeleSell. Users of the "900" number service would require approximately three minutes of phone time (including time to enter a charge card number), while users of an "800" service (where calls are billed to the salesperson's employer) would average two minutes.

TELESELL'S MARKET

The market for TeleSell is national in scope and easily targeted through mailing lists. Of the thirteen million salespeople identified by the Census Bureau in 1988, roughly half are outside salespeople who sell using visits to their customers in the field.[1] Of this group, about half are involved in direct sales through Amway and similar firms, representing a secondary market for TeleSell. TeleSell's primary market consists of the remaining approximately 3.6 million outside salespeople. Estimates indicate that one-third of this target group have purchased books, cassettes, or training from sales experts such as those used in TeleSell. As "the converted," they represent a ready-made core market aware of the need for and quality of the TeleSell product, and are most likely to use it. The other 2.4 million represent potential customers for the sales experts.

Initial marketing efforts would be through a major mail effort among sales managers for "800" number services (the estimated size of the key group based on mailing lists is twenty-two thousand). This effort permits the greatest return on investment and the greatest concentration of users. A trial use program may be used if needed to help potential users become familiarized with TeleSell. Initial funding for the marketing effort is estimated at $325,000.

Once the "800" number service is established and cash flow supports further sales, a second marketing effort will be launched for the "900" number service. Using testimonials from users of the "800" service, the "900" service will be advertised in magazines oriented toward salespeople. Along with this effort, opportunities to use the mailing lists of the sales experts showcased in TeleSell will be sought, as well as cooperative advertising in their sales brochures, should the opportunities be available.

While TeleSell may be useful to salespeople working from fixed locations, the ready availability of colleagues and sales managers would decrease the value of the service. However, for companies that purchase the "800" number service, it would be possible to make it easily available to in-house salespeople.

USAGE COSTS

The cost of the service for the "900" number telephone version would need to be at least $1.50 a minute to cover the costs of the long distance charge, the billing costs, and royalties. At $1.75 a minute, the service would return 16 percent and be priced extremely competitively with other reputable "900" phone services. For the "800" line service, breakeven can occur at approximately $1.20 a call, since billing services are much less complex and expensive. Even adding fee computations for calls above a contracted minimum or threshold number would not add substantially to the above costs.

The telephone technology, voice reproduction technology, and billing technology already exist in accessible and stable form. The sales texts exist. The project can be put into place quickly and requires no new inventions.

COMPETITIVE ADVANTAGE AND GROWTH

To make TeleSell viable, the key element is to obtain access to the works of the top-selling sales experts. What is sought from these individuals or their licensing agents is preferably an exclusive license to excerpt their written works for use over telephone service networks.

Insofar as TeleSell serves to introduce salespeople to sales experts they may not have heard or read before, TeleSell offers the experts another medium for reaching their target market. Because TeleSell offers the ideas of several experts, it is likely to draw not only those salespeople already sold on a particular sales expert, but also new prospects for book, cassette, and training program sales. We see this as an incentive in negotiating low licensing fees for the materials. As far as preliminary research has been able to ascertain, the major authors in this field have not yet established telephone services or sold licenses for telephone use of their materials.

If successful, TeleSell will inspire competition. To make this as unattractive as possible for potential entrants to the market, TeleSell will strive to (1) lock in the top-selling authors, and will aggressively pursue new authors whose works hold promise, (2) defend the exclusivity of the licensing for telephone use of the current authors, and (3) have ready for immediate launch improved versions of TeleSell to leave potential competitors at an economic disadvantage. Among extensions of TeleSell are:

1. TeleSell Select through which users with a touch-tone phone can choose tips for particular classes of sales problems, or advice from particular authors.
2. Customized TeleSell versions keyed to the particular authors or methods favored by a particular company.
3. Customized versions to be marketed for the particular sales experts that preach their approach to their "true believers"—people who consistently use their books and training materials, or to potential customers in cities where they will be running training programs.

START-UP COSTS

With $325,000 allocated for startup marketing efforts, $150,000 allocated for initial licensing fees (with additional royalties based on use, and costed out per call), and $125,000 to be spent in excerpt production and administrative overhead, the total startup cost is projected to be $600,000 for the first year.

Assuming the service starts with the "800" number, a typical call would last two minutes and be billed at $3.50. Using 250 selling days a year, TeleSell would need to average approximately 690 calls a day to break even in year one. In terms of its primary market—outside salespeople who have bought one or more books, cassettes, or training programs from the sales experts—690 calls represents a usage rate of .05 percent per day.

Looked at another way, if one in ten of the more than 1.2 million previous purchasers of expert sales materials try TeleSell even once during the year, the service will break even. When repeat sales to "the converted" and potential sales to field salespeople new to the sales experts are combined, the likelihood of achieving substantial first-year sales increases dramatically.

Based on sales of similarly marketed telephone-based professional services, conservatively TeleSell should be able to generate at least one thousand calls per day by midyear. This would assure breakeven in year one and generate an estimated profit of nearly $70,000 in year two. This profit will permit establishing the "900" service with a $250,000 initial marketing budget and break even for the year on both services. In year three, profits from the two services are projected in the $350,000 range.

START-UP TEAM

Jerome Katz is an entrepreneur and an entrepreneurship scholar. His consulting firm, J. A. Katz and Associates, specializes in helping big business understand small business, and boasts clients such as the Trane Company and Southwestern Bell. Jerry brings to TeleSell more than twenty years' experience in all phases of small business, as an entrepreneur, as a member of his family's firm, and as a professor of entrepreneurship with more than two dozen articles and two edited volumes published in the field of entrepreneurship. His entrepreneurial expertise has resulted in numerous quotes in the *New York Times*, the *Philadelphia Inquirer*, the *Wall Street Journal*, and the *St. Louis Sun*.

His startup team includes a nationally recognized expert in intellectual property law to consult on securing the rights to the sales and motivational experts as well as general startup legal issues; a former computer entrepreneur, now turned MIS professor, who is advising on telecommunications technology issues; and a principal of one of America's leading franchising firms who is a former top national salesperson and sales manager for Xerox to advise on marketing issues.

CONCLUSION

TeleSell represents a unique new service that is a natural extension of existing sales expert training efforts to a different medium—the telephone network. Using established experts with sizable followings, established technologies with known costs, competitive pricing and targeted, aggressive marketing, TeleSell represents a service likely to pay for itself in year one and pay for its own expansion in year two. Given well-designed licensing agreements and cogent plans for growth of the product line, the competitive advantage of TeleSell should be sustainable over the long term. TeleSell represents a potential profitmaker that will also provide its investors with national exposure and an affiliation with high-profile business experts.

QUESTIONS

1. What are the strengths and weaknesses of TeleSell?
2. What intellectual property issues have a major impact on the case?
3. What technology issues play a major role in the case?
4. Overall, how would you rate the opportunity presented in this case? Would you recommend investing $600,000 in the start-up? Why or why not?

ENDNOTE

1. Allan Reid, *Modern Applied Selling* (New York: Prentice Hall, 1990).

M Comic Relief

Carol M. Jessup

"All right, Marie, I'll talk with Patrick again. Stop worrying about him. You've always acted like your two brothers can't do anything for themselves." As Joe hung up the phone, he silently agreed with his sister's concerns—Patrick needed to get out of the house and become involved in some activities.

After dinner that evening he discussed the situation with his wife Linda. Linda, as always, was supportive. She understood that his job with the state Department of Revenue left him wanting more challenge, in spite of the good salary that he brought home after fifteen years of civil service seniority. "Joe, Marie is right, you've got to help Patrick. He's all alone in that house now that Mary's gone. If the tables were turned, I'd want someone to help you if I died. Anyway, it could turn out to be the best thing for the both of you. You've considered starting a comic book collectors business since before I met you, but the timing was never quite right before. Maybe now that you're in your mid-thirties and Patrick's in his forties, the timing could be right. You're both responsible and experienced adults. Between the two of you, it could work."

Joe thought his wife had a good point, but there were other factors to consider before he brought up the subject of a comic book business venture with Patrick. He needed to consider whether to deal with comic books only, or to include original comic art, a market that seemed to be growing more lucrative every year. There was also the mail-order or retail facet to consider. He'd think about it before the weekend, as the Chicago Comic Convention was this weekend, and Patrick had agreed to accompany him this year.

Joe and Patrick had a great Friday night at the convention. The turnout was higher than Joe had expected. The brothers brought several boxes of duplicate comics to trade and sell to the dealers. Both brothers had taken

This case was prepared by Carol M. Jessup of Illinois College. Used with permission.

care over the years to keep their books in mint condition. They sold most of what they had brought due to the large demand for the 1960s superhero issues. Most of what they brought sold in the $15 to $30 per issue price range. However, Patrick sold one of his Spiderman #5 issues for $850 and Joe sold a Fantastic Four #10 for $385 and the Flash #106 issue for $500. What was interesting to Joe was the number of individuals his age and older who were buying comics and original art. Ten years ago, the buyers had primarily been teenagers and younger. Was it his imagination, or was he just now noticing the number of fellow baby boomers interested in what had been for him a lifelong hobby?

Saturday morning at breakfast with Patrick in the hotel, Joe brought up the subject of starting a mail-order business dealing in comic books and original comic art. Patrick was initially more receptive than Joe had imagined. "Well Joey, I've got to do something, that's for sure. I never knew Mary's death would take so much out of me. It was three months ago yesterday, you know. If it wasn't for the guys at work and you two, I couldn't take it. But why a mail-order business? Why don't we just open a shop in my spare garage? That's what we'd always talked about when we were kids. They seem to be doing fine at the shop on the west side, and they don't carry nearly the inventory that we have between us. They looked at me like I was crazy when I asked for Kung Fu Kittens #3 the other day."

Joe responded excitedly, "That's just it. Summerfield already has enough competition in retail stores. Look at it this way. With mail order, we could be a distribution center for the Midwest—close to Chicago, St. Louis, and a number of college towns."

Patrick sighed and raised his voice. "Oh, here you go again, with all your big plans. What do you need me for? Why don't you just do this yourself? What is this—be nice to your big dumb brother?" Joe was patient but firm. "Patrick, stop feeling sorry for yourself. You're as stubborn as ever. Come on, let's get back to the dealer's room. The panel starts at nine, and I wanted to get a chance to talk to that guy drawing the new Ninja series that 's so popular. Networking could be important if we decide to go through with this." The rest of Saturday's business was so good that before the brothers left on Sunday, they replenished their stock with a few key issues. They packed up early so they could get back to Summerfield and unload before it got dark.

Once they got out of the traffic, Patrick spoke. "Joey, I've been thinking about what you said. I think we could work together and I do have a lot of time on my hands, but has Marie put you up to this? I swore the other day I thought she was going to try to fix me up with one of her friends. I don't want to be a charity case."

Joe interrupted, "It wouldn't be that way. Even Linda thought that between us, we could make this work. I can't do something like this by myself and keep my job with the state and take time for Linda and the kids. I have the business sense, you have some extra time and the advantage of having developed your contacts with a lot of the artists over the years. Between our existing collections and contacts, we have the inventory to meet anyone's needs for comics and original art."

Patrick agreed and brought up the recent auction of original comic art that was held at Sotheby's. "I believe the market in original comic art is ready to take off again. I got a letter from that Wisconsin artist who was there. He said his art went for phenomenal prices. There were a number of art collectors present in addition to those interested in comics. Even with the artists retaining the copyright, the art sells because of its decorative and collectible features."

Joe could tell that Patrick was interested. What Patrick lacked in schooling, he made up for in enthusiasm and a depth of knowledge in the matters that interested him. "Patrick, the art can be your area. I'll handle writing contracts, putting together a mailing list, and business details like the proper amount of insurance, and keeping of records of the inventory and the clients. The advantage of a mail-order business is that capital is not an issue. We don't need a fancy space—just some work space. I've already cataloged my inventory on the computer system in my spare time at work and you have kept a manual inventory. I'm flexible as to the form of how we get started. You don't have to be a full partner if you don't want. You would not have to be a partner at all."

Patrick looked wary, "You mean like a real partnership—formal and all? What's at stake here? I changed my mind about using the garage as a shop because I don't feel like dealing with a bunch of strangers—I get enough of that at work. Also, I'm not sure I want anything long term. Nothing is permanent, you know."

Joe responded, "Maybe you could be my employee, or sell your stuff on consignment, or whatever. I just know I need some help and support from my big brother. Besides, my collection is piling up so much that Linda says if I don't start getting rid of it soon, she's going househunting for a bigger place."

Once they were home, there were books and art to unpack. Linda and the kids helped them make the runs up and down the stairs to the spare bedroom where Joe kept his collection. It was a huge collection stacked to the ceiling, but it was organized. Linda tried to get Patrick to stay for dinner, but he said he wanted to get home. As Joe drove Patrick the three blocks home, he tested his brother's feelings on the business venture. Patrick expressed concern, citing two brothers he knew who, as a result of a failed partnership in establishing a neighborhood pizzeria, still weren't talking to one another. Joe acknowledged there were issues to be worked out and that he would put some plans together outlining the advantages and disadvantages of various scenarios. Joe spoke with enthusiasm about what could result over time—possibly a full-time job for the both of them. Patrick said, "I trust you, Joe. You've got a good head on your shoulders and you went to college and all. Let me know what you think is fair. As for me, I can't even imagine what my future holds, other than working eight to four at the post office. See ya later."

Joe watched his brother walk up the stairs to the front door and noticed the sag in his brother's shoulders. Joe thought about how it had been a good getaway weekend, but also that it looked like Patrick still had a long way to go before he would be back to his former self. This idea could be just what the both of them needed.

QUESTIONS

1. Is this business being started for the wrong reason?
2. Discuss the opportunity being considered. Is it a viable opportunity?
3. Will Joe and Patrick make good partners? Why or why not?
4. What are the relevant choices of legal forms of business organization available to Joe and Patrick? What are the relevant issues for Joe to consider in this case regarding the formation of the described business venture?
5. What liabilities and strengths are each of the brothers bringing to a start-up?
6. Determine whether Joe should propose the business be established as retail or mail order. What are the issues?

N Environmental Systems

Alexis Downs

When Ann was invited to the neighborhood Christmas party, she never anticipated the turn of events that would occur. At that party, Ann noticed a familiar face, but she couldn't imagine why he looked so familiar.

"Ann Mitchell!" he exclaimed as he elbowed his way over to her. "Well, it's good to see you. In fact, I have a problem and could use your help."

As the man spoke, Ann finally began to place him. Two years ago, during her last year of the Master of Business Administration program at the University of Oklahoma, Ann had interned in the human resources department of a manufacturing company. This man, Ed Cook, had been manager of that firm's accounting department, which was located in the same building. Now retired from the company, he was working part-time as the accountant for his son-in-law's business. Ann agreed to meet Ed at the business, which was located at the home of his son-in-law, Terry Dobbs. Ed had mentioned that Terry had a personnel problem for which he needed assistance.

HISTORY OF ENVIRONMENTAL SYSTEMS

Terry Dobbs was a chemist with a degree from the University of Georgia. After graduation, he had worked for United Chemicals, a large chemical company with burgeoning waste disposal problems. Terry recognized a need for waste disposal experts. These experts would contract with the larger manufacturers and government units for cleaning up targeted sites where waste had become a problem. Terry left United Chemicals in the early 1980s and founded Environmental Systems. Initially, Terry intended to operate the company as a sole proprietorship and to expand very cautiously.

Terry decided to base the company near Oklahoma City, largely because his wife had relatives in Oklahoma. They bought a home situated on

---

This case was prepared by Alexis Downs of Saint Louis University. Used with permission.

a few acres about twenty miles north of downtown Oklahoma City. The home, which was the headquarters for Environmental Systems, was located in a remote area so Terry could park assorted trucks and equipment without neighbors' complaints and because more land was available for storage, warehousing, and general expansion. Also, the land was far removed from an underground aquifer that served much of Oklahoma. His choice was good; Ann never even noticed the equipment around the Dobbs's home nor the two-story addition to the garage that housed Environmental Systems.

As Ann talked to Terry, she began to understand why Ed had solicited her advice. Two years ago, Environmental Systems's profit was $360,000. Last year, the company lost $50,000. Terry blamed his partner for the loss.

Terry had taken on a partner three years ago. The partner, Alan Archer, was a big spender. Initially, Terry had been impressed with Alan's contacts. Alan knew executives in every company whose business Terry coveted. Alan knew the local politicians, as well as those in surrounding states. Alan had great contacts in Texas, and those connections had been primarily responsible for the large profit two years ago. Unfortunately, Alan wanted to expand too rapidly and wanted Environmental Systems to look great. He wanted offices in downtown Oklahoma City. He had purchased numerous large and expensive vehicles, including a "company" Porsche for himself. Alan committed to every project that came his way, without necessarily considering the ability of Environmental Systems to meet the contract requirements. Consequently, the company was now bearing his debt service costs, losing work due to disgruntled customers, and forfeiting some fee income because of delays in completing the work.

Terry's complaints about Alan's debt service were legitimate. When the partnership was organized, the debt, together with the underlying state-of-the-art equipment, had been contributed to the partnership. Terry had contributed $20,000 and some unencumbered equipment that was older but functionally similar to Alan's equipment. The partnership had agreed to lease Terry's garage/office. In Terry's opinion, he had contributed more than Alan. Nevertheless, the written partnership agreement stipulated equal shares of capital and profits and losses. And, furthermore, both parties had guaranteed any new partnership debt. Unfortunately, Environmental had borrowed $170,000 for equipment purchases that had been authorized by Alan. In the event of a partnership dissolution, the partnership agreement provided for an equal distribution of assets, but Terry feared that he would have the debt and Alan would have the assets.

THE ENTREPRENEUR

Terry Dobbs was angry with Alan. As he said to Ann, "I just want to get rid of the guy. Ed tells me to think about lost business, noncompete agreements, debt guarantees, and tax consequences of a partnership dissolution, so I'll think. But geez, the guy is driving me crazy."

Unlike Alan, Terry was a conservative risk-taker. As an undergraduate at the University of Georgia, he'd owned, operated, and lived in a trailer park. He and Ed's daughter, Laura, married when they were sophomores at Georgia. They worked well together. They had managed the trailer park together and had obtained owner financing on the purchase, so had avoided the need to qualify for a bank loan. In general, Terry looked for owner financing. He looked for deals in which the owner had to dump property quickly in a bad market, but could finance the sale. The Dobbs's home had been such a deal. After the oil bust in the early eighties, Oklahoma real estate prices plummeted. People like the prior owner of the Dobbs's home were moving out of the state when Terry was moving in. Terry could buy with very little down and with relatively little risk. If his business failed in its early years and he lost the home, he wouldn't lose much.

Terry bought used equipment and used vehicles. He paid cash whenever he could, but he had a line of credit at a local bank. Working hard for long hours, he built a business.

If Terry had a fault, Ann decided, it was his determination to have his own way. He said, "I can't stand Alan's wheeling and dealing without my okay. Losing money is one thing, but this guy won't even listen to me. I don't know where he is half the time. He says that he can't find me to talk to me, but I still think that this is my show. If I wanted to report my whereabouts to someone, I'd still be working for United Chemicals."

Ed laughed. "Ann, you've got to remember that Terry is accustomed to working with his wife, his father-in-law, and his own children, plus a few young men who idolize him."

PERSONNEL

"So tell me about the personnel at Environmental," Ann said.

"Terry and I have a mutually acceptable deal," said Ed. "I like to keep busy, but I don't want to earn more than is allowed by the Social Security people. I'm an experienced, inexpensive accounting department. My daughter runs the office and schedules the jobs————"

"When she knows what they are," interrupted Terry. "Alan doesn't always clarify."

Ed continued, "My grandchildren have been brought up to help around here. They file, photocopy, vacuum, whatever. Recently, my daughter hired one of the neighbors to help her while all the kids are at school. And sometimes, when there's a lot of typing, one of the local teenagers comes in after school. Terry has a crew of young men who work on the sites. Because Terry makes a point of buying lunches, having them over to the house, giving them University of Oklahoma football tickets, and such, they think he's wonderful. If he calls them at midnight for an emergency cleanup after some tractor-trailer accident, they jump into their clothes and here they are."

"However," added Terry, "Alan has been creating a few labor disputes. Now, Ann, tell me. Can't I just get rid of the guy?"

QUESTIONS

1. What characteristics of an entrepreneur does Terry possess? How does Alan differ? Does he have entrepreneurial characteristics?

2. What events triggered Terry's venture? What opportunities were captured by Terry?

3. Should Terry dissolve the partnership?

4. In selecting a partner, what should Terry have looked for?

5. If Terry dissolves the partnership, how should he do it?

O

The Fab Lab

Phil Carpenter

John Schroeder was the plant manager of ABC Machining. He had worked his way up through the ranks, starting off as a general machinist after high school. He had fifteen years of machine shop experience. He was ambitious and had high personal goals.

John was dedicated and conscientious in his role as plant manager. Customers would often drop by the shop with questions about various products they wanted made. John was usually able to answer their questions and to give the customers ideas on how to improve their product. He built up a good rapport with numerous customers. On occasion, John would talk with the customers about his desire to run his own machine shop. They encouraged him, and several said that they would give John their business.

John wasn't satisfied with just earning a hefty paycheck; he longed to have the financial benefits and the challenge of successfully starting and operating his own business. Several times he discussed becoming part owner of ABC Machining with the owner, Gene Jackson. Gene agreed that John was valuable to the company and said he would give John some ownership interest. Time went by but the owner never followed through on his promises. Recognizing this, John became increasingly dissatisfied with the owner and his job.

John and Lisa, his wife, discussed their situation and agreed it was time to look into starting their own machine shop. John would run the shop while Lisa, who had previous experience as a bookkeeper, would manage the office. They would need additional financing, so they sought the help of a small business consultant. He assisted John and Lisa in putting together a business plan. Originally they requested $80,000, but since they lacked sufficient collateral, the bank agreed to lend them only $50,000 for seven years.

This case was prepared by Philip R. Carpenter of the Small Business Development Center at Saint Louis University. Used with permission.

The loan was an SBA guaranteed loan, which they planned to use to purchase equipment and to provide them with six to eight months' working capital. They officially started the Fab Lab in September.

John gave his boss two weeks' notice. At the end of the first week, he told Mr. Jackson that he was starting his own business. Fab Lab was similar to ABC Machining in that the company specialized in unusual, one-of-a-kind jobs such as manufactured tooling and hard-to-find replacement parts for aircraft. Fab Lab was willing to take small jobs that were not profitable for ABC Machining.

John aggressively contacted customers from his previous employer, telling them that he was open for business and looking for work. Many of those who said they would give John their business did so. The amount of these sales was near expectations. Even his former employer subcontracted work to John. In addition, because of the goodwill John had built up with customers, they referred him to other companies that were able to use his services. In one instance, John was directed to the referring company's competitor. Several of the referrals gave the Fab Lab a significant amount of sales.

John was continually on the lookout for good used equipment that would expand his capabilities. John found several good used machines, which he had not originally planned to purchase, at reasonable prices. He purchased them using the loan proceeds, which were gone after four months. Fortunately for the business, John received a significant order from a large defense contractor, who prepaid John for the work. This prepayment eased their immediate cash flow situation since a downturn in the economy was delaying payments by other Fab Lab customers.

After about five months, business began to level off. Business was steady and just above breakeven, but was not increasing. John was forced to lay off one of two full-time employees for a short period. He wasn't satisfied with the current sales level, and wanted to grow. Due to time constraints, he thought he was at his limit in developing new sales. Any new sales would probably be the result of cold calls. John was not effective in making unsolicited sales calls. John and Lisa were considering three options.

First, the sales representative for John's former employer operated a small electronics firm, in addition to selling ABC Machining's services. He approached John about forming a joint venture, combining his electronics expertise with John's mechanical knowledge. An electromechanical company would be somewhat unique and could expand Fab Lab's business. The company would primarily manufacture test stations for aircraft avionics and flight simulation gear. These test stations are used to check components of the flight simulator for accuracy. This combination would have a large market potential. He believed this niche was open for competition. It could be risky and if it weren't successful, it would drain scarce resources from Fab Lab.

Second, John could consider government contracting. He realized that he would have to install new procedures and possibly purchase new equipment in order to meet government quality standards. In addition, John was concerned about the paperwork involved in government procurement. An

TABLE 1
The Fab Lab Decision Matrix

	Electromechanical	Government Procurement	New Salesperson
Market size for Fab Lab (annually)	$700,000–$1,000,000	$150,000–$300,000	$250,000–$400,000
Competition analysis	Usually large firms making their own specialized products	Some large businesses and many small businesses with varying capabilities	N/A
Market entry time to establish the business	1–2 years	6–12 months	3–6 months
Estimated cost	$70,000–$100,000 (primarily equipment and personnel)	$5,000–$10,000	$15,000–$20,000 (primarily for equipment)
Estimated market growth	Expanding	Maintaining current level	Dependent on quality of salesperson

extensive amount of technical paperwork would decrease the amount of time John could devote to developing new sales and time on the shop floor providing needed supervision. The small business consultant told John he should be able to meet government quality standards if he were able to meet defense contractor standards.

Third, John also thought he should hire a salesperson. He was concerned that if the salesperson were to generate strong sales, he wouldn't have the machinery or personnel to fill the orders in a timely fashion. The business was not established enough to consider borrowing additional funds for new equipment and personnel. He only had enough capacity for a part-time salesperson. It would be difficult to find a person with the capability and knowledge of the industry to do part-time sales. He wondered if there were any alternatives he was not considering. John constructed a table to assist in making his decision.

QUESTIONS

1. How should John go about building additional sales?
2. What are the constraints John faces and what growth strategy best fits the constraints of his business?
3. What factors should John consider regarding the potential joint venture?

The Creative Mind: A Self-Improvement Supermarket

P

David Tipton and Janet Gillespie

Creativity, vision, and passionate loyalty to his idea were the hallmarks of John Reilly's success as a therapist and as a capital-raiser for his self-improvement supermarket, The Creative Mind. With a degree in clinical psychology from the University of Kansas and having completed his clinical internship (a prerequisite for licensing as a psychologist) in Dallas, John R. Reilly, Ph.D., returned to his hometown of Kansas City, Missouri, in 1979 to establish his practice.

During his years of study and building his practice, Reilly was irreversibly convinced of the power of human beings to create happiness and success in their lives through a quest for self-improvement and personal empowerment. If people could conquer their fears and could see themselves as having the ability to have an effect on their own lives—to take charge of themselves—the potential was unlimited.

THE CONCEPT

Knowing that people who believed as he did were often thwarted in their self-improvement programs by a lack of ready availability of new and exciting support materials, Reilly in 1983 began development of his business idea. The Creative Mind was a self-improvement supermarket that would offer a broad range of products and services to individuals, families, mental-health professionals, and businesses. Much of Reilly's own practice was geared toward helping his patients tap into their own psychological powers and to see themselves as in charge, continually learning, evolving people for whom nothing was impossible. He knew firsthand that it was difficult for them to find the books, tapes, videos, and other inspirational and "how-to" materials that they wanted to buy. In addition to being able

This case was prepared by David Tipton and Janet Gillespie of Saint Louis University. Used with permission.

to refer patients to his store, he saw it as a rich source of referrals to his practice. He viewed the store as an attractive base from which to develop and market a consulting and seminar business.

At the same time, after four years of tediously building his practice through personal referrals, Reilly could foresee a potential threat to the financial status of his practice if he continued to rely on the traditional practice setting: it was clear to him that insurance reimbursements were going to decline. And his enthusiasm for spending six to eight hours daily in the confines of an office were beginning to wane.

These forces led to the concept of The Creative Mind. The range of products available would represent the full gamut of materials available on the market. They would extend from the very personal and intimate to the more practical. Products would include such diverse topics as dealing creatively and positively with death, mastering the art of dating, overcoming a weak backhand, and reducing anxiety over public speaking. The target market would range from students to executives. In Reilly's mind, every businessperson, every parent, every confused teenager, and every person with any problem or with a desire to improve any aspect of his or her life was a potential customer.

FROM CONCEPT TO REALITY

Reilly set about developing a business plan. He consulted with experts: financial people, lawyers, and accountants. He talked with his wife and with his father—himself an unsuccessful entrepreneur. Reilly saw this endeavor as more than a single-unit operation; he envisioned this as a franchise gold mine, with locations sold around the country. Ray Kroc's biography appeared on his nightstand. He immersed himself in his vision. The result of this careful process was a sophisticated, professional business plan. With this business plan in hand, supported by his passionate enthusiasm for the concept and his natural persuasive ability, he had little difficulty attracting investors.

The initial site was in a new strip mall located on the major thoroughfare of Johnson County, Kansas, in an affluent suburb of Kansas City. His store frontage, however, did not face the street. He signed a three-year lease for fifteen hundred square feet, roughly the size of a small three-bedroom house. The store opened in the fall of 1987. By 1990, annual sales were about $350,000, close to breakeven. However, no dividends had been paid to investors and Reilly received no salary for his work. His wife, Nancy, who was trained as a nurse, became more and more involved in running the daily operations in order to take a salary for the family out of the business. Reilly focused on financial issues and promoting potential franchises. Both operating the store and developing a franchise network was new for the Reillys—neither had any experience in either aspect of the business. Hovering just under breakeven at the store left no development funds, however. The business, therefore, continued to require regular infusions of funds from new investors. With his upbeat, optimistic selling style and his passion for the concept, Reilly had little difficulty in finding additional investment capital and exchanged part of his ownership shares for capital. The new funds were used to promote the sale of franchises through mailings, advertisements, and trade shows. Two franchises were eventually sold—in the affluent and trendy St. Louis suburb of Clayton, Missouri, and in Albany, New York. Neither franchise turned out to be profitable, resulting in little return on the franchising effort.

Meanwhile, back in Kansas City, Reilly continued to be bothered by the lack of store frontage on a major thoroughfare. He felt that this was a serious roadblock to getting this store into the black, thus handicapping his vision of growth and franchising. He located an attractive site one-half mile from the original location, next door to an upscale Chinese restaurant likely to attract affluent diners. The rent at the new location was almost doubled but the site had the additional advantage of three thousand more feet of selling space. Outfitting the new store was an expensive proposition, requiring the recruitment of new investors. Again, Reilly exchanged part of his ownership interest for ready capital. Sales at the new location, though, did not expand as expected. The business was perilously close to missing payments on several occasions, but a savior investor was always found at the last minute. Pressures were building as competition from major chain bookstores increased and drained much of his sales volume. By 1990, what had started as a unique store dedicated to creativity and innovative ways of coping with a wide range of self-improvement issues had become a small specialty niche bookstore, making it vulnerable to such incursions on its market.

Reilly thought that much of this vulnerability came from its suburban location and decided that a prestige location in The Plaza, Kansas City's premier dining and shopping area, would attract the kind of customer he was seeking. Financed by a $200,000 bank loan that was guaranteed by investors, the new store opened in the spring of 1991. The business had yet to pay any return to investors and continued having trouble meeting its current obligations. The 1991 holiday season was the crucial period. If extensive sales increases weren't realized, the business could not survive.

QUESTIONS

1. Assuming that The Creative Mind survives the new year, what options are available to make this a *profitable* venture? Explain.
2. Was The Creative Mind a good name for the venture? Why or why not?
3. When would you recommend selling franchises?
4. What should Reilly do before trying to expand?
5. How could The Creative Mind's product or image be changed to decrease its susceptibility to competition from general purpose and discount bookstores?
6. Consider key decision points: opening the store, changing locations, undertaking the franchising effort, expanding to The Plaza. What other options might have been feasible at those times? Explain.
7. What problems can you identify from the case that might have lead to the crisis described at the end?

fisCAL
Financial Analysis Software

Included with *Entrepreneurship: A Planning Approach* is a disk for the fisCAL financial analysis software. The disk is called a *key disk* and is your access to fisCAL. The main program for fisCAL should have been installed on your computer lab network or individual hard drives. The key disk also has data for the Conveniesse, Inc., business plan and for several of the cases considered in Part VII.

fisCAL is a stand-alone financial software program designed to help analyze the status of a business and to do the calculations necessary to develop a business plan. It does not require a knowledge of spreadsheet or database programs. fisCAL does assume that the user is familiar with financial statements. Thus, knowledge of balance sheets and income statements is important. A working knowledge of ratio analysis is also helpful. Since fisCAL allows the user to add variables to the income statement beyond the categories provided, users should know the difference between fixed and variable expenses.

fisCAL has far more capabilities than most users in an entrepreneurship class will need. However, several of its features stand out. Once the balance sheet and income statement information is entered, users can then make comparisons to industry norms, evaluate ratios, and make proforma projections. The program allows the user to make a number of different strategic decisions in creating the proformas. Those interested in valuations can use fisCAL to make four different valuations and

then calculate a weighted average for the firm. The valuation methods are similar to those used in Chapter 15. The software also allows the calculation of a bankruptcy prediction score for a venture.

In order to reduce the amount of data input time, data for the Conveniesse, Inc., business plan is included on the key disk. In addition, data is included for each of the relevant cases in Part VII. It is recommended that the demonstration case and some of the cases in Part VII be considered before attempting to develop a business plan for a new company. This will familiarize the user with the strengths of fisCAL before starting the business plan.

The following material is taken from Chapter 8 of the fisCAL manual, the documentation provided when fisCAL is purchased by banks, entrepreneurs, and other users. The remaining chapters of the fisCAL manual address financial analysis techniques which most students should already know. The information provided in the following sections gives instructions for installing and using fisCAL's capabilities.

USING FISCAL

fisCAL is a completely menu driven system that provides a means to automatically calculate all major financial ratios of a study firm and compare the results to the Industry Standard. fisCAL also calculates the operating capital required, degree of operating leverage, trading cash cycles, breakeven point, common size statements, and Z-score bankruptcy predictor and estimates the cash market value of the firm.

fisCAL produces multiperiod trended analyses, including cash flow and operating ratios, if desired. It also produces committee-ready summaries, both numerical and narrative, to aid in diagnosis.

Through the Strategic Analysis Module, samSON, fisCAL brings advanced diagnostic techniques to the user: the strategic profit model, gross margin return on inventory investment, and index of sustainable growth.

The Proforma Generator, proFOR, offers an expert system for developing multiperiod proforma projections based on a statistical analysis of past trends.

fisCAL is easy to use. We will step through the system, menu by menu, explaining the various options available. The disk included with this package is a "key disk." The user can enter data from financial statements from any IBM compatible computer and produce limited reports. To access all fisCAL reporting functions, the user must use this disk in conjunction with the fisCAL software installed on the main computer station or computer lab.

Booting Up

There are two ways to use the accompanying disk: (1) as a stand-alone program for data entry on any IBM compatible computer with 512K of memory, or (2) in conjunction with the Master fisCAL installation, which will be found on the main computer station or the computer lab at your facility. In this case, only the data files from this disk will be used. Option (1) will not allow the use of multiperiod trends, samSON or proFOR. These programs may be accessed only through Option (2).

Option (1). When using this disk as a stand-alone, use the following procedure to boot up:

Access the A drive and, at the A> prompt, insert this disk in the A drive and type:

FISCALK   <ENTER>

Under this option, you will only be able to enter data, produce financial statements, and

report financial ratios from the single period report menu. Some of the screens described in this manual may be formatted somewhat differently on your key disk. To do advanced diagnostics or proforma projections, you must proceed to Option (2).

Option (2). When using this disk in conjunction with the Master fisCAL installation, use the following procedure to boot up:

At your main computer station or computer lab where the Master fisCAL program is installed, access the directory that contains fisCAL. Typically, this is a directory called FISCAL and is accessed from any C drive directory by typing:

CD FISCAL   <ENTER>

When you have accessed the proper directory, type:

FISCALM   <ENTER>

When prompted to do so, insert your key disk in the A drive and press "ENTER". Data you create in this mode will be saved to your student disk. fisCAL is backward compatible with all key disk versions.

The instructions contained in this appendix include all necessary instructions to operate the full fisCAL installation on the campus computer.

```
            fisCAL
          VERSION 4.31

          a product of
         theHALCYONgroup
          447 Fleming Road
       Charleston, S.C. - 29412
       PHONE  (803) 795-7336

 TODAY IS Monday, February 4, 1991

 PRESS ANY KEY TO DISPLAY MAIN MENU
```

This is the startup screen for fisCAL and provides the address and telephone number for the Halcyon group. When you have finished reading this screen simply press any key to display the Main Menu.

Main Menu

The next screen is the Main Menu.

```
                fisCAL - MAIN MENU
                Select Desired Option


   1  EDIT/ADD STUDY CASE OR STANDARD

   2  SINGLE PERIOD REPORTS

   3  TRENDS ANALYSIS AND REPORTS
   4  samSON
   5  PROFORMA

   6  BREAKEVEN GRAPH

   7  UTILITIES
   8  USING ON SCREEN CALCULATOR
   9  QUIT
```

The options accessed from the Main Menu are described in detail in this appendix. The following Documentation Guide references the appropriate page number for each option:

fisCAL MAIN MENU
DOCUMENTATION GUIDE

Edit/Add Study Case or Standard

Selecting (1), Edit/Add Study Case or Standard from the Main Menu accesses the following Update Menu:

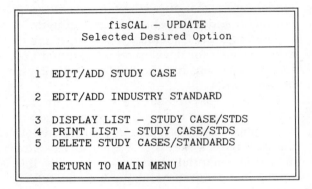

```
                 fisCAL - UPDATE
               Selected Desired Option


   1  EDIT/ADD STUDY CASE

   2  EDIT/ADD INDUSTRY STANDARD

   3  DISPLAY LIST - STUDY CASE/STDS
   4  PRINT LIST - STUDY CASE/STDS
   5  DELETE STUDY CASES/STANDARDS

      RETURN TO MAIN MENU
```

Update Option (1)—Edit/Add Study Case

Option (1) provides a means to add new study cases, to edit existing study cases, to correct the data, or to do "what-if" studies. Selecting this option will display the following screen:

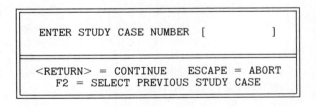

```
   ENTER STUDY CASE NUMBER  [          ]

   <RETURN> = CONTINUE    ESCAPE = ABORT
      F2 = SELECT PREVIOUS STUDY CASE
```

ENTER A NEW STUDY CASE NUMBER OR A NUMBER FROM A PREVIOUSLY SAVED STUDY CASE.

Simply fill in the blanks.

The Study Case Number is an identification that you assign to the current study case. This identification should be unique for each new study case for future reference. Any combination of letters and numbers, up to ten, may be used.

If you are recalling a previously entered Study Case, press <F2> to select from a list of available cases on file. Highlight the chosen study case, press <ENTER> and it will be "pasted" into the study case number field.

Contractors require slightly different information for the Balance Sheet. Enter "Y", if the study case is a contractor.

The study firm input screens are divided into two parts: The income statement and the balance sheet. These are "fill in the blank" type screens.

On the first income statement screen, you are asked to fill in the SIC number of the study firm. SIC is the Standard Industrial Classification, unique for each type of business. Industry Standards are automatically accessed by reference to this number for comparisons by fisCAL. (See discussion of SIC number in Update Option (2)—Edit/Add Industry Standard.) There are three options:

1. If you are using one of Halcyon's optional Industry Standard Data Disks, refer to the Industry Standards Catalog in this Manual or the on-screen catalog described in Option 7—Utilities. This catalog may be accessed at this point by pressing <F2>. Choose the appropriate five-digit code number and enter it at this point. If the selection is made from the on-screen catalog, highlight the chosen number and return to the income statement Data Entry Screen. The chosen number will be pasted into the SIC# field.

2. If you are not using the optional Industry Standards Data Disk, you must enter a number here which corresponds to the code number of a standard you have manually entered on the System Disk. (See Update Option (2)—Edit/Add Industry Standard). A list of available custom standards is accessible at this point by pressing <F2>. If you have entered a number that is the same as one that exists on the Industry Standard Data Disk, fisCAL will default to this manually entered entry.

3. If you do not wish to compare to an Industry Standard, you may enter 00000 for the SIC number. The fisCAL analysis will be run with zeros in all Industry Standard data points.

During Income Statement data entry, there are four unnamed fields. These are useful for combining data into specially named fields. Two of these fields are treated as fixed expenses in the breakeven analysis and two are treated as variable. Be careful to consider the fixed/variable nature of your created fields and enter them in one of the appropriate fields.

fisCAL will handle data entry for numbers up to 999,999,999.99. Standard practice for larger firms, with accounts in the billions of dollars, is to enter data as thousands of dollars. This is done by simply ignoring or rounding off the hundreds and cents places when entering data.

You may use the up or down arrow or page down key to scan through these input screens, correcting and/or amending as necessary. When the last item has been entered on the income statement, fisCAL calculates the net profit or loss and displays the message:

NET PROFIT FOR THIS CASE IS 999,999,999.99

DOES THIS MATCH NET PROFIT ON INCOME STATEMENT (Y/N)?

If they do not agree, there is a mistake in a data entry or the income statement contains an error. Answering "N" to this question will let you correct the data entry. Verify your data before going to the next step.

"Annualizing" Income Statement Data Income statement data must be "annualized" for proper computation in the program. There are three ways to annualize interim period data:

1. Last Twelve Months: This is the preferred method. From the last Annual Statement, subtract the year-to-date data that corresponds to the current statement. Add back the current year-to-date data. This yields a new "Last Twelve Months" Income Statement. Enter this in the program as annualized data.

2. Current Month Times Twelve: Multiply the current month by 12, on the

assumption that sales and cost factors are even throughout the year.

3. Year-to-date Divided by X: Divide the year-to-date statement by X, where X is the fraction of a full year represented by the year-to-date statement.

Methods 2 and 3 may be computed on the computer as follows: Enter interim period year-to-date Income Statement data. After verifying Net Profit, the following question will appear:

% OF ANNUAL DATA INCOME STATEMENT REPRESENTS? [100.00]

You may enter the appropriate number (For example, one month = 8.33% of annual). The program will compute an annualized statement and utilize this in further computations. Data input will be reported both as interim period input and as annualized.

Once you have verified the data and chosen your annualization factor, the computer will display the input screens for the balance sheet.

The first screen allows you to input assets and the second screen allows you to input liabilities. You may use the up or down arrows or the page down key to scan through the balance sheet input screens, verifying and/or amending as necessary.

Upon entering the last item on the balance sheet, fisCAL computes the net worth and displays the message:

TOTAL ASSETS   999,999,999.99
LESS:
TOTAL LIABILITIES   999,999,999.99
EQUALS NET WORTH   999,999,999.00
DOES THIS MATCH NET WORTH ON
BALANCE SHEET? (Y/N) [Y]

If they do not agree, you have made a mistake in entering the data or the balance sheet contains an error. Answering "N" to this question will let you amend the balance sheet information. Verify your data before going to the next step.

Upon verification of the data and answering "Y", fisCAL will check that the sum of Capital Stock and Retained Earnings as entered equals its computation of Net Worth.

If this computation does not clear, the following message will appear:

```
          *** CAUTION ***
AN ERROR EXISTS IN CAPITAL STOCK, RETAINED
EARNINGS OR NETWORTH. OWNERS' EQUITY
(CAPITAL STOCK + RETAINED EARNINGS)
SHOULD = NETWORTH

  CAPITAL STOCK =          499999999.99
  RETAINED EARNINGS =      499999999.99
                          -------------
  OWNERS' EQUITY =         999999999.98
  NETWORTH =               999999999.99
                          -------------
  DIFFERENCE                      -0.01
```

```
(A)  RETURN TO BALANCE SHEET INPUT
(B)  CONTINUE (REPORTS MAY BE CORRUPTED)

ENTER SELECTION (A/B) [ ]
```

Find and correct the erroneous entry now. Exiting this routine and returning to the Main Menu without correcting the discrepancy will retain the error. The accuracy of future reports will be affected.

Update Option (2)—Edit/Add Industry Standard

Option (2) from the Update Menu provides a means to enter Industry Standard Data, which may be used as a standard of comparison in computations.

This option also allows you to correct Industry Standard data. Selection of this option will display the following screen:

```
        ENTER STANDARD NUMBER  [      ]

  <RETURN> = CONTINUE ESCAPE = ABORT
    F2 = SELECT PREVIOUS STANDARD
```

ENTER A NEW STANDARD NUMBER OR A NUMBER FROM A PREVIOUSLY SAVED STANDARD.

Simply fill in the blanks.

The Standard Number is the Standard Industrial Classification (SIC) number for your business consisting of four digits, e.g., 5943. This number should be unique for each standard. It is recommended that a five digit number be used with the last digit representing the asset size of your company. For example you may use 59431 for standard 5943 with asset size under 1MM and 59432 for standard 5943 with asset size between 1MM and 10MM, etc.

Actually, any five digit alpha-numeric combination may be used here. However, in order to utilize this data in reports, you must reference the same code in the Edit/Add Study Case data input (see Option (1)—Edit/Add Study Case).

Construction contractors require slightly different information for the Financial Ratios, so you must enter "Y", if the study case is a contractor.

Line items of the Income Statement are entered as a percent of Net Sales. Net Sales is entered as 100.0%. Line items of the Balance Sheet are entered as a percent of Total Liabilities & Net Worth. Total Liabilities & Net Worth is entered as 100.0%

Note: Income Statement and Financial Ratios data must be in annual figures. (See Update Option (1)—Edit/Add Study Case.)

Update Option (3)—Display List of Study Cases Standards

Selecting Option (3) from the Update Menu will display a complete listing of the Study Cases and Industry Standards entries currently on file on the system disk.

Update Option (4)—Print List of Study Cases/Standards

Selecting Option (4) from the Update Menu will print a complete list of the Study Cases and Industry Standards currently on file on the system disk.

Update Option (5)—Delete Study Cases/Standards

Selecting Option (5) from the Update Menu displays a screen allowing you to delete up to ten (10) Study Cases or System Disk Industry Standards at one time. Simply enter the appropriate

Study Case or Industry Standard numbers at the prompt and press "Page Down".

The following statement will be displayed:

```
IF YOU CONTINUE, THE ABOVE STUDY CASES WILL
BE DELETED.
DO YOU WISH TO CONTINUE ? (Y/N) [    ]
```

Entering "N" will return you to the Main Menu without completing the DELETE routine. Entering "Y" will delete the Study Cases (or Industry Standards) and return you to the Main Menu.

Do not delete the Industry Standard numbered "00000". This has been included on the system disk so a comparison may be made to a "0" standard.

Single Period Reports

Selecting Option (2)—Single Period Reports from the Main Menu will display a print menu that allows you to view or print a complete analysis or select only that portion of the analysis that you want. At the completion of printing all the desired reports, pressing "R" will return you to the Main Menu.

When using the Key Disk as a stand alone, the only selections available from the Print Menu are (1), (3), and (7). All other selections are available by using the fisCAL software installed at the main computer station or computer lab.

```
           ''fis-CAL'' - PRINT MENU
              Select Desired Option

(1) - PRINT COMPLETE ANALYSIS
(2) - PRINT SUMMARY REPORT
(3) - PRINT INCOME STATEMENT/BALANCE SHEET
(4) - PRINT BREAKEVEN ANALYSIS
(5) - PRINT INDUSTRY COMPARISONS
(6) - PRINT OPERATING CAPITAL
(7) - PRINT FINANCIAL RATIOS
(8) - PRINT MARKET VALUE ANALYSIS
(9) - PRINT TITLE PAGE

(R) - RETURN TO MAIN MENU
```

If you select to print the Cash Market Value Analysis (Selection 8) or the Complete Analysis (Selection 1), the value of certain variables must be set. These are the Market Interest Rate, the Capitalization Rate and the Valuation Weight Factors for the Cash Market Valuation. Selecting either of these reports will display the following screen:

```
PRESET DEFAULT VALUES FOR CASH MARKET VALUE
COMPUTATION ARE:

    MARKET INTEREST RATE:        8.0%

    CAPITALIZATION RATE:        15.0%

    VALUATION WEIGHT FACTORS:

      BOOK METHOD:               0.5

      CAP. OF EARNINGS METHOD:   2.5

      STR. CAP. METHOD:          1.0

      YEARS PURCH. METHOD:       1.0

    PREVIOUS VALUATION

    METHOD:                      0.0

DO YOU WISH TO CHANGE THESE VALUES?

(Y/N)  [N]
```

Pressing "N" will default to the preset conditions and start the PRINT routine. Pressing Y will start a two-worksheet routine that will allow you to change any or all of the preset conditions. These Worksheets are menu-driven. Each screen provides guidance for selection of appropriate levels of each of the variables.

Note: When printing the Summary Report for a Study Case, the program will utilize whatever preset conditions have previously been established for that Study Case. The newly set conditions will remain in the database for future computations on that particular Study Case until they are changed by going through the Cash Market Value Worksheet routine. The user is cautioned that if the preset conditions are changed, it could distort a trends analysis of Cash Market Value. However, changes that reflect variations in the cost of money should be made, because these changes will impact on the market value of the firm.

Notes on the Summary Report

Choosing (2) from the PRINT MENU will print the Summary Report. This is a two page report that includes a Narrative Summary and a Numerical Summary with coded flags to identify variances from the norm. The significance of these reports and the code conventions used are discussed below:

A. Narrative Summary

The Narrative Summary feature provides a one-page narrative overview of the full fisCAL report. It extracts the more important variances, highlights them, and directs the analyst to the proper detailed report for further study and correction. When appropriate, it suggests corrective action that might be taken.

The Narrative Summary is intended to direct the analyst quickly to the operating elements that seem to require the most immediate attention. As with any automated routine, this does not mean that other factors should be ignored. fisCAL presents an in-depth analysis, the whole content of which should be studied in order to draw the most valid conclusions. This Narrative Summary is intended as a guide only and does not replace a studied evaluation of the entire output.

B. Numerical Summary

The Numerical Summary abstracts the important results from each of the six detailed reports and presents them on one page. Variances from standard are easily identified and the analyst is quickly led to more detailed study of the appropriate report(s).

C. Sign Convention

For ease in identifying the areas of major interest, a system of identifying signs has been programmed into fisCAL. These signs are in the form of +, -, or *. The + indicates a healthy variance from standard. The - and * alert the analyst that undesirable conditions may exist. Both the Summary Report and The Narrative Summary carry these signs.

The marking concept highlights areas of business performance that may **already be** in trouble and, equally important, those **approaching** trouble. For example, the Z-Score Bankruptcy Predictor indicates serious problems when it falls below 3.0. However, fisCAL provides warnings well ahead of that level, starting when the Z-Score reaches 4.0. Thus, strategies can be developed to relieve problems before bankruptcy factors get out of control.

The sign convention by line item on the Summary Report is as follows:

Line Item	Sign
Balance Sheet	
Cash and Equivalents	*
Accounts Receivable	*
Inventory	*
Accounts Payable	*
Net Worth	+ or -
Income Statement	
Gross Profit	+ or -
Operating Expenses	+ or -
All Other Expenses	+ or -
Profit Before Taxes	+ or -
Breakeven Point	*
Operating Capital Required	+ or -
Ratios	*
Z-Score Bankruptcy Predictor	*

The degree of the variance from standard or the degree by which the computed line item deserves attention is denoted by the number of signs (up to three) accompanying the item. For example, a line item with a *** designation would generally, but not always, be a more important variance than a line item with a * designation. An exception to this is the ratios, which carry only a single * designation regardless of their relative importance or degree of variance from the standard.

The marking code is as follows:

I. Balance Sheet and Income Statement Line Items, Cash Market Value and Operating Capital Requirements:

Mark	Variance
*, +, or -	>10% up to 20%
**, ++, or --	>20% up to 50%
***, +++, ---	>50%

II. Breakeven Point:
 * if Breakeven Point is greater than 85% up to 100% of current annual sales level.
 ** if Breakeven Point is greater than 100% of current annual sales level.

III. Ratios:
 * for any Ratio displaying a negative variance.

IV. Z-Score Bankruptcy Predictor:
 * if Z-Score is greater than 3.5 but less than 4.0.
 ** if Z-Score is between 3.0 and 3.5
 *** if Z-Score is 3.0 or less.

Trends Analysis and Reports

Selecting Option (3)—Trends Analysis and Reports from the Main Menu will display the Trends Menu. This accesses the Trends and Cash Flow Module. Utilizing any two or three Study Cases from the fisCAL data base, it prints any of three reports, at the operator's option. These are Trends Analysis Report, Cash Flow Analysis, and Operating Ratios Analysis. Each of these reports is discussed in detail in the Technical Support Section.

Trends Option (1)—Enter Study Case Numbers

Selecting this option will access the screen shown in Figure A.1.

Insert Study Case numbers that are in your fisCAL System data base. A list of available Study Case numbers from which to choose will be displayed by pressing the <F2> key. Use the light bar to highlight the chosen Study Case. Press <ENTER>. The chosen Study Case number will be pasted into the data entry field.

For analytical purity, the Study Cases chosen must represent financial statements that are annual, consecutive and coordinated. Typically,

FIGURE A.1

```
┌────────────────────────────────────────────────────────────┐
│                                                              │
│  INPUT STUDY CASE NUMBERS FOR TRENDS AND CASH FLOW ANALYSIS  │
│ ┌──────────────────────────────────────────────────────────┐│
│ │     PERIOD 1 (BASE YEAR MINUS 2 YRS) [DEM001    ]          ││
│ │     PERIOD 2 (BASE YEAR MINUS 1 YR ) [DEM002    ]          ││
│ │     PERIOD 3 (BASE YEAR ) [DEM003    ]                     ││
│ └──────────────────────────────────────────────────────────┘│
│        <RETURN> = CONTINUE     ESCAPE = ABORT                │
│              F2 = LIST STUDY CASES ON FILE                   │
└────────────────────────────────────────────────────────────┘
```

IN ORDER TO GENERATE ACCURATE TRENDS AND CASH FLOW COMPUTATIONS,
THE STUDY CASES USED IN THE TRENDS AND CASH FLOW ANALYSIS MUST
BE CONSECUTIVE, COORDINATED, ANNUAL FINANCIAL STATEMENTS.

```
┌──────────────────────────────────┐
│  CHANGE STUDY CASE NUMBERS        │
│  RETURN TO PREVIOUS MENU          │
│  CONTINUE                         │
└──────────────────────────────────┘
```

you will enter the latest Study Case in Period 3 (Base Year). The next latest Study Case will be centered in Period 2. The next latest Study Case will be entered in Period 1.

When all Study Case numbers have been entered, answer the ensuing prompted questions to view or print reports. The following screen will appear:

```
┌──────────────────────────────────────────┐
│       TRENDS ANALYSIS PRINT MENU          │
│ ┌──────────────────────────────────────┐ │
│ │ (1)  PRINT TRENDS ANALYSIS            │ │
│ │                                        │ │
│ │ (2)  PRINT CASH FLOW ANALYSIS         │ │
│ │                                        │ │
│ │ (3)  PRINT OPERATING RATIO ANALYSIS   │ │
│ │                                        │ │
│ │ (4)  PRINT 1, 2, & 3                   │ │
│ │                                        │ │
│ │ (E)  RETURN TO PREVIOUS MENU          │ │
│ └──────────────────────────────────────┘ │
│ ENTER SELECTION (1, 2, 3, 4, E) [    ]    │
└──────────────────────────────────────────┘
```

YOU MAY PRINT ANY COMBINATION OF ABOVE
REPORTS. TO PRINT REPORTS 1 & 2 ENTER 12,
TO PRINT REPORTS 1, 3, & 4 ENTER 134

Choose the reports you wish to print. Press "ENTER."

fisCAL will search for the Industry Standard that has been entered in the Period 3 Study Case data.

There are two sources of Industry Standards to choose from:

1. Industry Standards inserted on the System Disk from your sources.
2. Industry Standards contained on the optional Industry Standards Data Disk.

If the Period 3 Study Case data references an SIC number and standards that have been installed on the System Disk, (see Main Menu Option (2)—Edit/Add Industry Standard), fisCAL will use this data in reports.

If the Period 3 Study Case data references an SIC number that is contained on the fisCAL Industry Standards Data Disk (see Industry Standards Catalog), fisCAL will use this data in reports.

If the same SIC number exists on both the System Disk and the Industry Standards Data Disk, fisCAL will default to the data contained on the System Disk.

Proforma

Selecting Option (5)—Proforma from the Main Menu accesses the optional proFOR, Proforma Generator Module. Using proFOR is discussed at the end of this appendix.

Breakeven Graph

Selecting Option (6)—Breakeven Graph from the Main Menu accesses the Breakeven Graph.

Follow the prompts and key in the appropriate study case number to produce the graph.

Most hardware arrangements will accept the printing of this graph. Options are available to select the type of printer and the size and orientation of the graph. Experiment with these options to find an acceptable one. Some computer/printer combinations are not supported for the "print graph" function.

Utilities

Selecting Option (7)—Utilities from the Main Menu will display the Utilities Menu:

```
                    UTILITIES

 (1)  BACKUP/RESTORE

 (2)  COPY STUDY CASE/STANDARD

 (3)  COMBINE STUDY CASES

 (4)  IMPORT/EXPORT

 (5)  RUN DOS COMMANDS

 (6)  INDUSTRY STANDARD DATA CATALOG

 (7)  PRINT INDUSTRY STANDARD DATA

 (R)  RETURN TO MAIN MENU

          ENTER YOUR SELECTION    [R]
```

Menu-driven utilities are available to copy the data in a Study Case or System Disk Industry Standard to a new Study Case Number or Industry Standard Number, Import or Export Study Case data to or from fisCAL and another compatible software program, reference the Industry Standard Data Catalog, or Print Industry Standard data from the data base.

It is not necessary to have the functions Backup/Restore or Run DOS Commands, Options (6) and (7) on the Utilities Menu so these are not available to the student.

Selecting Option (1) from the Utilities Menu will access the Industry Standards Data Catalog. The following screen will appear:

```
    INDUSTRY STANDARD CATALOG
       Select Desired Option

 CUSTOM STANDARDS

 SMALL BUSINESS STANDARDS

 INDUSTRY STANDARDS

 RETURN TO PREVIOUS MENU
```

Choose the database of your choice, using the light bar to access the desired selection and pressing <ENTER> to make your selection.

A series of screens allows the operator to choose an appropriate 5 digit SIC number from the Industry Standard Data Base supplied by Halcyon. This SIC number will be keyed in where prompted in Study Case data entry.

Selecting Option (2) from the Utilities Menu will allow you to print industry standard data. This permits printing of any SIC Industry Standard available from the Industry Standard Data Disk supplied by Halcyon.

Selecting Option (3) from the Utilities Menu will display the Copy Study Case/Standard Menu:

```
 COPY STUDY CASE
 COPY STANDARD
 RETURN TO MENU
```

This option allows you to copy the data from an existing Study Case or System Disk Industry Standard into a new Study Case Number or Industry Standard Number of your choice. For example, if you wish to change the data in a Study Case in order to do some "what-if" activity but don't want to lose the original Study Case data, then use this option. Use the light bar to highlight the desired option and press <ENTER> to display, correspondingly, one of the following screens:

```
COPY FROM STUDY CASE  [          ]
COPY TO STUDY CASE      [           ]


COPY FROM STANDARD   [     ]
COPY TO STANDARD        [      ]
```

At the prompt insert, first, the number of the Study Case or System Disk Standard being copied. Then, the new number of the Study Case or Standard you wish to create. The new Study Case or Standard will be created, duplicating the original Study Case or Standard but identified by the new number.

This option allows you to copy an Industry Standard resident on the fisCAL System disk. It will not allow you to copy or modify data on the Industry Standard Data disk.

Selecting Option (4) from the Utilities Menu will display the Combine Study Cases screen:

```
                COMBINE STUDY CASE
This utility will combine data from two
study cases. All income statement and
balance sheet data will be algebraically
added to form a new study case. You must
provide a unique study case number, study
case name, and desired data date. During
the combine operation all factors for the
Cash Market Value analysis will be returned
to the default condition. Items entered
under Other Expense Variable and Other
Expense Fixed will be combined and the
description will be blanked out.
CONTRACTORS CANNOT BE COMBINED WITH
NON-CONTRACTORS!

STUDY CASE NUMBER 1  [          ] STUDY CASE
NUMBER 2  [          ]

NEW STUDY CASE NUMBER  [          ]

NEW STUDY CASE NAME     [          ]

NEW STUDY CASE DATE     [ / / ]

CONTINUE/REENTER/ABORT  (C/R/A) [  ]
```

Enter the Study Case numbers that you wish to combine, give the new Study Case a name, and fill in the other fields, as appropriate. fisCAL will algebraically add the two Study Cases, field by field, producing a new Study Case from the combined data. The new Study Case is accessed using the Study Case name assigned.

Selecting Option (5) from the Utilities Menu will display the Import/Export Data screen:

```
This program will allow you to import data
from other programs and to export data to
other programs.
```

```
                IMPORT
                EXPORT
                RETURN
```

Import Data

Use the light bar to highlight the desired option. Press <ENTER> to make the selection. You may import data into fisCAL from any one of three types of data files:

1. System Data Format ASCII file. This file contains records of fixed length separated by carriage return and line feed. Each field is a fixed length with no separators. The end-of-line mark is Ctrl-Z. Unless otherwise specified, the file extension will be assumed to be .txt.

2. Delimited ASCII file. This file contains records of variable length separated by carriage return and line feed. Each field is a variable length separated by a comma. Character fields are separated by double quotes. Date fields must be written in the YYYYMMDD format. The end-of-file mark is Ctrl-Z. Unless otherwise specified, the file extension will be assumed to be .txt.

3. Data Base file. This is a standard dBase III format. Data can be directly entered into fisCAL using this format. Unless otherwise specified, the file extension will be assumed to be .dbf.

Data will be entered into fisCAL field by field in the order listed in the field list at the end of this Section. Data in the source file must be in this order and must be of the same type or errors will exist in the fisCAL data. If the fisCAL field is larger than the source field, the fisCAL field will be filled with blanks (0's for numeric fields). If the source field is larger than the fisCAL field, the data will be truncated.

Export Data

You may export data to any one of three types of data files:

1. System Data Format ASCII file. This file will contain records of fixed length

USING THE ON SCREEN CALCULATOR

```
THE CALCULATOR          ┌──────────────────┐     CAN GRAM EXECUTION.
PRESSING THE F9         │       0.0000     │     PRESSING THE <ESC>
KEY RETURNS TO          │                  │     NORM ESS F9 NOW.
                        │  ┌─┐┌─┐┌─┐┌─┐     │
TO USE THE              │  │7││8││9││*│=MULT│     IF THE CALCULATOR IS
CALCULATOR <ENTER>      │  └─┘└─┘└─┘└─┘     │     INVOKED WHILE THE
MUST BE PRESSED         │  ┌─┐┌─┐┌─┐┌─┐     │     CURSOR IS AT A NUMERIC
AFTER ENTERING EACH     │  │4││5││6││/│=DIV │     ENTRY POINT THE RESULT
NUMBER. FOR EXAMPLE:    │  └─┘└─┘└─┘└─┘     │     MAY BE ''PASTED'' INTO
TO ADD TWO NUMBERS      │  ┌─┐┌─┐┌─┐┌─┐┌─┐  │     THE ENTRY POINT. EXIT
AND MULTIPLY THE        │  │1││2││3││+││C│  │     THE CALCULATOR BY
RESULT TIMES 5 THE      │  └─┘└─┘└─┘└─┘└─┘  │     PRESSING THE <ESC>
SEQUENCE WOULD BE -     │  ┌───┐ ┌─┐┌─┐┌─┐  │     KEY. PASTE BY PRESSING
6 <ENTER> + 8           │  │ 0 │ │.││-││E│  │     THE F10 FUNCTION KEY.
<ENTER> * 5             │  └───┘ └─┘└─┘└─┘  │     USE THIS SCREEN FOR
<ENTER>.                └──────────────────┘     PRACTICE. TO EXIT THIS
                                                 SCREEN ENTER 0.0 AND
                                                 PRESS <ENTER>
```

PRACTICE PASTING A NUMBER HERE [9999.9]

separated by carriage return and line feed. Each field will be a fixed length with no separators. The end-of-file mark will be a Ctrl-Z. Unless otherwise specified, the file extension will be .txt.

2. Delimited ASCII file. This file will contain records of variable length separated by carriage return and line feed. Each field will be a variable length separated by a comma. Character fields will be separated by double quotes. Date fields will be written in the YYYYMMDD format. The end-of-file mark will be Ctrl-Z. Unless otherwise specified, the file extension will be .txt.

3. Data Base file. This file will be in a standard dBase III format. Unless otherwise specified, the file extension will be assumed to be .dbf.

Data will be entered into the produced file field by field in the order listed in the field list at the end of this Section.

On Screen Calculator

Selecting Option (8)—Using On Screen Calculator accesses a practice program for fisCAL's On Screen Calculator.

This is an efficient tool accessed from any field by pressing F9. A description of the operation of the calculator is available by choosing option (8) on the Main Menu.

Pressing F9 accesses the screen shown in Figure A.2.

Practice calculations and "pasting" procedure on this screen.

Option (E)—Exit to MS-DOS Operating System

Selecting option (E) will return you to the DOS operating system. This is the only proper way to exit fisCAL.

INDUSTRY STANDARDS DATA

NAME – OFFICE SUPPLIES AND EQUIPMENT

SIC # – 59431

ASSETS

Cash and Equivalents	7.2
Accounts Receivable – Trade (net)	31.0
A/R Progress Billing	0.0
A/R Current Retention	0.0
Inventory	37.5
Cost & Est Earnings in Excess of Billings	0.0
All Other Current	1.3
TOTAL CURRENT	77.1
Fixed Assets (Net)	16.8
Joint Ventures & Invest	0.0
Intangibles (net)	1.7
All Other Non–Current	4.5
TOTAL ASSETS	100.0

LIABILITIES

Notes Payable – Short Term	9.7
Current Matured Long Term Debt	4.5
Accounts Payable – Trade	23.9
Accounts Payable – Retention	0.0
Billings in Excess of Costs & Est Earnings	0.0
Income Taxes Payable	0.0
All Other Current	7.7
TOTAL CURRENT	46.5
Long Term Debt	18.2
Deferred Taxes	0.1
All Other Non–Current	2.7
Net Worth	32.5
TOTAL LIABILITIES & NET WORTH	100.0

INCOME DATA

Net Sales	100.0
Gross Profit	37.1
Operating Expenses	34.3
Operating Profit	2.8
All Other Expenses (net)	0.7
Profit Before Taxes	2.1

RATIOS	L	M	U
Current	1.3	1.7	2.4
Quick	0.6	0.8	1.1
Receivables/Payables	0.0	0.0	0.0
Sales/Receivables	8.3	10.8	15.2
Cost of Sales/Inventory	3.3	5.1	9.0
Cost of Sales/Payables	6.0	9.0	13.5
Sales/Working Capital	22.1	10.1	6.0
EBIT/Interest	1.1	2.4	5.2
Cash Flow/Cur Mat LTD	0.5	1.3	3.7
Fixed/Worth	1.4	0.5	0.2
Debt/Worth	5.7	2.1	1.1
% Profit Bef Taxes/Net worth	3.5	16.4	44.3
% Profit Bef Taxes/Total Assets	0.7	6.1	13.6
Sales/Net Fixed Assets	13.7	26.1	48.1
Sales/Total Assets	2.1	3.2	4.1

fisCAL FIELD LIST

ITEM	FIELD NAME	TYPE	WIDTH	DEC	
(1)	STUDY CASE NUMBER	CHAR.	10		(1)
(2)	RMASIC NUMBER	CHAR.	5		
(3)	NET SALES	NUMERIC	14	2	(1)
(4)	COST OF GOODS SOLD	NUMERIC	14	2	
(5)	SALARIES-OFFICERS	NUMERIC	14	2	
(6)	PAYROLL	NUMERIC	14	2	
(7)	COMMISSIONS	NUMERIC	14	2	
(8)	OUTSIDE LABOR	NUMERIC	14	2	
(9)	PAYROLL TAX	NUMERIC	14	2	
(10)	ADVERTISING & PROMOTION	NUMERIC	14	2	
(11)	CAR & DELIVERY	NUMERIC	14	2	
(12)	TRAVEL & ENTERTAINMENT	NUMERIC	14	2	
(13)	LEGAL & ACCOUNTING	NUMERIC	14	2	
(14)	OPERATING SUPPLIES	NUMERIC	14	2	
(15)	BAD DEBTS	NUMERIC	14	2	
(16)	RENT	NUMERIC	14	2	
(17)	REPAIRS & MAINTENANCE	NUMERIC	14	2	
(18)	UTILITIES	NUMERIC	14	2	
(19)	INSURANCE	NUMERIC	14	2	
(20)	TAXES & LICENSES	NUMERIC	14	2	
(21)	AMORTIZATION	NUMERIC	14	2	
(22)	INTEREST	NUMERIC	14	2	
(23)	LEASED EQUIPMENT	NUMERIC	14	2	
(24)	FREIGHT	NUMERIC	14	2	
(25)	OTHER FIXED EXPENSES #1	NUMERIC	14	2	(4)
(26)	**TOTAL OPERATING EXPENSES**	**NUMERIC**	**14**	**2**	
(27)	TAXES	NUMERIC	14	2	
(28)	CASH & EQUIVALENTS	NUMERIC	14	2	
(29)	ACCOUNTS RECEIVABLE	NUMERIC	14	2	
(30)	INVENTORY	NUMERIC	14	2	
(31)	OTHER CURRENT ASSETS	NUMERIC	14	2	
(32)	FIXTURES	NUMERIC	14	2	
(33)	VEHICLES	NUMERIC	14	2	
(34)	EQUIPMENT	NUMERIC	14	2	
(35)	LEASEHOLD IMPROVEMENTS	NUMERIC	14	2	
(36)	BUILDINGS	NUMERIC	14	2	
(37)	LAND	NUMERIC	14	2	
(38)	ACCUMULATED DEPRECIATION	NUMERIC	14	2	
(39)	INTANGIBLES	NUMERIC	14	2	
(40)	OTHER NON-CURRENT ASSETS	NUMERIC	14	2	
(41)	ACCOUNTS PAYABLE	NUMERIC	14	2	
(42)	CURRENT PORTION LTD	NUMERIC	14	2	
(43)	NOTES PAYABLE SHORT TERM	NUMERIC	14	2	
(44)	ACCRUED EXPENSES	NUMERIC	14	2	
(45)	OTHER CURRENT LIABILITIES	NUMERIC	14	2	

fisCAL FIELD LIST

ITEM	FIELD NAME	TYPE	WIDTH	DEC	
(46)	NOTES PAYABLE LONG TERM	NUMERIC	14	2	
(47)	BANK LOANS PAYABLE	NUMERIC	14	2	
(48)	OTHER LOANS PAYABLE	NUMERIC	14	2	
(49)	OTHER LONG TERM LIABILITIES	NUMERIC	14	2	
(50)	DATA DATE	DATE	8		
(51)	GROSS SALES	NUMERIC	14	2	
(52)	DISCOUNTS & RETURNS	NUMERIC	14	2	
(53)	STUDY CASE NAME	CHAR.	24		
(54)	A/R PROGRESS BILLING	NUMERIC	14	2	
(55)	A/R CURRENT RETENTION	NUMERIC	14	2	
(56)	COST OF EARNINGS IN EXCESS OF BILLINGS	NUMERIC	14	2	
(57)	JOINT VENTURES & INVESTMENTS	NUMERIC	14	2	
(58)	ACCTS PAYABLE RETENTION	NUMERIC	14	2	
(59)	BILLINGS IN EXCESS OF ESTIMATED EARNINGS	NUMERIC	14	2	
(60)	CAPITAL STOCK	NUMERIC	14	2	
(61)	INCOME TAX PAYABLE	NUMERIC	14	2	
(62)	RETAINED EARNINGS	NUMERIC	14	2	
(63)	DEFERRED TAXES	NUMERIC	14	2	
(64)	PREVIOUS VALUATION	NUMERIC	14	2	(2)
(65)	BOOK METHOD VALUATION FACTOR	NUMERIC	3	1	(2)
(66)	CAPITALIZATION OF EARN-INGS METHOD VALUATION FACTOR	NUMERIC	3	1	(2)
(67)	STRAIGHT CAPITALIZATION METHOD VALUATION FACTOR	NUMERIC	3	1	(2)
(68)	YEARS OF INCOME PUR-CHASED METHOD VALUATION FACTOR	NUMERIC	3	1	(2)
(69)	PREVIOUS VALUATION METHOD VALUATION FACTOR	NUMERIC	3	1	(2)
(70)	**GROSS PROFIT**	**NUMERIC**	**14**	**2**	
(71)	**PRE-TAX PROFIT**	**NUMERIC**	**14**	**2**	
(72)	**TOTAL CURRENT ASSETS**	**NUMERIC**	**14**	**2**	
(73)	**TOTAL FIXED ASSETS**	**NUMERIC**	**14**	**2**	
(74)	**TOTAL ASSETS**	**NUMERIC**	**14**	**2**	
(75)	**TOTAL CURRENT LIABILITIES**	**NUMERIC**	**14**	**2**	
(76)	**TOTAL LONG TERM LIABILITIES**	**NUMERIC**	**14**	**2**	
(77)	**TOTAL LIABILITIES**	**NUMERIC**	**14**	**2**	
(78)	**STOCKHOLDERS EQUITY**	**NUMERIC**	**14**	**2**	
(79)	CAPITALIZATION RATE	NUMERIC	5	2	(2)

fisCAL FIELD LIST

ITEM	FIELD NAME	TYPE	WIDTH	DEC	
(80)	DISCOUNT RATE	NUMERIC	5	2	(2)
(81)	ANNUALIZATION FACTOR	NUMERIC	6	2	(3)
(82)	OTHER INCOME	NUMERIC	14	2	
(83)	BANK SERVICE CHARGE	NUMERIC	14	2	
(84)	DEPRECIATION & DEPLETION	NUMERIC	14	2	
(85)	DUES AND PUBLICATIONS	NUMERIC	14	2	
(86)	EMPLOYEE BENEFIT PROGRAMS	NUMERIC	14	2	
(87)	OFFICE EXPENSE	NUMERIC	14	2	
(88)	OTHER FIXED EXPENSE #2	NUMERIC	14	2	(4)
(89)	OTHER VARIABLE EXPENSE #1	NUMERIC	14	2	(4)
(90)	OTHER VARIABLE EXPENSE #2	NUMERIC	14	2	(4)
(91)	MISCELLANEOUS EXPENSES	NUMERIC	14	2	
(92)	OTHER FIXED EXPENSE #1 NAME	CHAR.	26		(4)
(93)	OTHER FIXED EXPENSE #2 NAME	CHAR.	26		(4)
(94)	OTHER VARIABLE EXPENSE #1 NAME	CHAR.	26		(4)
(95)	OTHER VARIABLE EXPENSE #2 NAME	CHAR.	26		(4)
(96)	LAUNDRY	NUMERIC	14	2	
(97)	**TOTAL EXPENSES**	**NUMERIC**	**14**	**2**	
(98)	CONTRACTOR INDICATOR FIELD	CHAR.	1		(1)(5)
(99)	DIVIDENDS	NUMERIC	14	2	
(100)	OTHER CURRENT ASSETS	NUMERIC	14	2	
(101)	PRE-PAID EXPENSES	NUMERIC	14	2	

TOTAL RECORD LENGTH = 1360

LEGEND:

(1) Compulsory Field. Data must be entered.

(2) Parameters for Cash Market Value Algorithm

(3) Annualization Factor. Enter the percentage of annual activity that the Income Statement data represents. An annualized statement will be calculated from this factor. If no data is entered into this field, it will default to 100.00 during the data transfer routine.

(4) For Operator-labeled Expenses

(5) For distinction of CONTRACTOR vs NON-CONTRACTOR
CONTRACTOR = Y
NON-CONTRACTOR = N

Bold Titles: Calculated Fields. It is not necessary to enter data in these fields. Totals will be computed automatically from the appropriate data fields and entered into these fields during the data transfer routine.

INCOME STATEMENT PROJECTION

STUDY CASE	DATE	STATISTICAL ANALYSIS BASED ON STUDY CASES STY CS +02 STY CS +01 STUDY CASE
STY CS +02	12/31/02	PROJECT OUTYEAR INCOME DATA BY:
NET SALES	120.0	CHANGE 9.4 % PER YEAR
COST OF GOODS	60.0	0.50 * SALES CHANGING BY −1.0 % PER YEAR
GROSS PROFIT	60.0	CALCULATED BY SALES−COST OF GOODS
OTHER INCOME	0.0 (UNDEF)	CHANGE 0.0 % PER YEAR
TOTAL RCPTS	60.0	CALCULATED BY GROSS PROFIT+OTHER INCOME
VAR COSTS	9.8	0.08 * SALES CHANGING BY 14.4 % PER YEAR
CONTRIB (GP−VC)	50.2	CALCULATED BY GROSS PROFIT−VARIABLE COSTS
FIXED COSTS	42.5	42.5 CARRY FORWARD BASE YEAR FIXED COSTS
TOTAL EXP	52.3	CALCULATED BY VARIABLE + FIXED COSTS
BEF TAX PROF	7.7	CALCULATED BY TOTAL RECEIPTS − TOTAL EXPENSES
INCOME TAXES	0.0 (UNDEF)	0.00 * PRETAX PROFIT
AFT TAX PROF	7.7	CALCULATED BY PRETAX PROFIT − TAX
DIVIDENDS	0.5	ASSUMES $000.0
RET EARNINGS	7.2	CALCULATED BY PROFIT AFTER TAX − DIVIDENDS

. . . .

FIGURE A.3

Using proFOR, the Proforma Generator

proFOR, the Proforma Generator Module, is an interactive software program designed to develop proforma financial projections. It interfaces with fisCAL Business Analysis Software.

proFOR generates proforma projections using the same line of reasoning as that of a good analyst. First, a business strategy is developed. Next, a 5 year projection is computed from the strategy. Finally, the projection is modified as desired based on period-to-period policy decisions.

Helpful hint: With proFOR, the analyst makes many decisions during the process of generating a final proforma projection. These decisions can be saved as a hard copy audit trail for reconstructing the proforma. It is a good idea to "PRINT SCREEN" at various places in the procedure to document your progress.

proFOR statistically analyzes an historical spread of financial statements, if they are available, and reports the results on screen. The analyst may accept this computer-developed strategy or modify it. When the desired strat-

egy has been accepted, a 5 year projection is computed and reported on-screen. This projection may also be modified as desired.

For the historical analysis, proFOR uses Study Cases that are available in the fisCAL data base. It will use from one to five years of history in the projection, at the user's option.

As would an analyst, proFOR first concentrates on the Income Statement, then moves to the Balance Sheet.

Income Statement Projection

The first step in generating the Income Statement projection is to develop a projection strategy. To aid in developing the strategy, proFOR statistically analyzes historical data from fisCAL study cases and offers it as the projection strategy.

The format for projecting the Income Statement spread is shown in Figure A.3.

The Income Statements in the historical Study Cases are automatically reformatted into Variable and Fixed Costs according to the standard fisCAL protocol. Each line item account is statistically analyzed and results reported according to the following table:

Item	Method	Variable
Net Sales	Linear regression	Percent change per year
CGS	Latest year	Fraction of net sales
CGS	Linear regression	Percent change per year
Other Income	Linear regression	Percent change per year
Variable Costs	Latest year	Fraction of net sales
Variable Costs	Linear regression	Percent change per year
Fixed Costs	Latest year	Carried forward
Income Taxes	Latest year	Fraction of pretax profit
Dividends		Assumes $0

Other line items in the Income Statement are calculated. The above results may be utilized as the projection strategy or the strategy may be modified. Following the prompts, the analyst may override any of the following variables:

Net Sales	percent change per year
CGS	percent change per year
Other Income	percent change per year
Variable Costs	percent change per year
Income Taxes	percent of Pretax Profit

When the strategy is accepted, proFOR will generate a 5 year spread with the format shown in Figure A.4.

proFOR uses the accepted strategy to generate this spread. For example, Net Sales will increase each year at the rate of change accepted in the final strategy. Likewise, Cost of Goods as a fraction of Sales will change each year according to the rate of change expressed in the final strategy. This adjusted fraction will be used to calculate the Cost of Goods each year.

The second step in generating an appropriate 5 year Income Statement projection is to modify the computer generated projection. Following the prompts, the analyst may change

. . . .

FIGURE A.4

STY CS PRO INCOME STATEMENT PROJECTION
PROJECTION BASED ON STATISTICAL ANALYSIS
STUDY CASE #   DATE
STY CS +02   12/31/02

		YEAR +1	YEAR +2	YEAR +3	YEAR +4	YEAR +5
NET SALES	120.0	131.3	143.6	157.1	171.9	188.1
COST OF GOODS	60.0	65.0	70.4	76.3	82.7	89.6
GROSS PROFIT	60.0	66.3	73.2	80.8	89.2	98.5
OTHER INCOME	0.0	0.0	0.0	0.0	0.0	0.0
TOTAL RCPTS	60.0	66.3	73.2	80.8	89.2	98.5
VAR COSTS	9.2	11.3	13.8	16.9	20.7	25.4
CONTRIB (GP-VC)	50.8	55.0	59.4	63.9	68.5	73.1
DEPL/AMRT/DEPR	1.2	0.7	0.0	0.0	0.0	0.0
OTH FIXED CSTS	41.9	41.9	41.9	41.9	41.9	41.9
TOTAL EXP	51.1	53.9	55.7	58.8	62.6	67.3
BEF TAX PROF	7.7	12.4	17.5	22.0	26.6	31.2
INCOME TAXES	1.5	2.4	3.4	4.3	5.2	6.1
AFT TAX PROF	6.2	10.0	14.1	17.7	21.4	25.2
DIVIDENDS	0.5	0.0	0.0	0.0	0.0	0.0
RET EARNINGS	5.7	10.0	14.1	17.7	21.4	25.2

the projection by overriding any field in the following accounts:

Net Sales
CGS
Other Income
Variable Costs
Fixed Costs
Income Taxes
Dividends

After changes are made, the projection may be recalculated by responding to the prompted question. Changes may be remade as desired until the analyst is satisfied with the projection. When no further changes are required, responding to the prompts will move to the Balance Sheet projection protocol.

Balance Sheet Projection

When the Income Statement projection is accepted, proFOR proceeds to the Balance Sheet projection protocol. Conceptually, the process is exactly the same as development of the Income Statement projection: First, a strategy of projection is developed based on a statistical

analysis of historical data. The resultant Balance Sheet projection is then modified by the analyst to reflect issues not addressed in the strategy. When the Balance Sheet projection has been recalculated and accepted, the analyst is ready to print reports.

The first step in the Balance Sheet projection is to develop a projection strategy. proFOR statistically analyzes historical data from fisCAL Study Cases and offers the analysis as a projection strategy. The format for projecting the Balance Sheet spread is shown in Figure A.5.

The Balance Sheets in the historical Study Cases are automatically reformatted as required. Each line item account is statistically analyzed and the result reported according to Figure A.6.

Other line items in the Balance Sheet are calculated. In calculating the Balance Sheet, excess cash is added into the Cash account and cash shortages are entered into the Notes Payable Short Term account.

The strategy thus developed by proFOR may be utilized as the projection strategy or the strategy may be modified. Following the

. . . .
FIGURE A.5

```
                                    BALANCE SHEET PROJECTION
STUDY CASE #          DATE          STATISTICAL ANALYSIS BASED ON STUDY CASES STY CS +02
STY CS +02           12/31/02       STY CS +01 STUDY CASE
                                             PROJECT OUTYEAR BALANCE SHEET DATA BY:
A CASH               10.9                    0.0572 * SALES + EXCESS CASH
S ACCTS RCVBL         6.5                    0.0750 * SALES
S INVENTORY          11.0                    0.0992 * SALES
E PREPAID EXP         0.0        (UNDEF)     0.0000 * TOTAL EXPENSES
T OTHER CURR          0.9                    MAINTAINED CONSTANT AT CURRENT YEAR
S FIX ASSET NET       0.7                    REDUCED BY DEPRECIATION TO 0
    OTH N-CURR        0.0                    MAINTAINED CONSTANT AT CURRENT YEAR

L ACCTS PAY           3.1                    0.0419 * (CGS)
I CURR PORT LTD       0.0                    MAINTAINED CONSTANT UNTIL LTD=$00.00
A ACCRUED EXP         1.3                    0.0195 * (TOTAL EXPENSES)
B INC TAX PAY         0.0        (UNDEF)     0.0000 * TAX
I N/P SHRT TERM       0.5                    $00.00 + CASH SHORTAGE
L OTH CURR            0.0                    MAINTAINED CONSTANT AT CURRENT YEAR
+ N/P LONG TERM       0.0                    REDUCE @ CURRENT RATE TO $00.00
N OTH LONG TERM       0.0                    MAINTAINED CONSTANT AT CURRENT YEAR
W RET EARNINGS       23.1                    CALCULATED
  CAPITAL STOCK       2.0                    MAINTAINED CONSTANT AT CURRENT YEAR
```

Item	Method	Variable
Cash (Minimum)	Average	Fraction of net sales plus accumulated excess cash
Accounts Receivable	Average	Fraction of net sales
Inventory	Average	Fraction of sales
Prepaid Expenses	Average	Fraction of total expenses
Other Current Assets	Latest year	Carried forward
Fixed Assets Net	Latest year	Carried forward
Other Non-Current Assets	Latest year	Carried forward
Accounts Payable	Average	Fraction of CGS
Current Portion LTD	Latest year	Carried forward until Notes Payable Long Term = $0.00
Accrued Expenses	Average	Fraction of Total Expenses
Income Taxes Payable	Average	Fraction of Income Taxes
Notes Payable Short Term		$0.00 plus accumulated cash shortages
Other Current Liabilities	Latest year	Carried forward
Notes Payable Long Term		Reduce at rate of current portion LTD until LTD = $0.00
Other long Term Liabilities	Latest year	Carried forward
Capital Stock	Latest year	Carried forward

. . . .

FIGURE A.6

prompts, the analyst may override any of the following variables:

Cash (Minimum)	Fraction of Net Sales
Accounts Receivable	Fraction of Net Sales
Inventory	Fraction of Net Sales
Prepaid Expenses	Fraction of Total Expenses
Accounts Payable	Fraction of Cost of Goods Sold
Accrued Expenses	Fraction of Total Expenses
Income Taxes Payable	Fraction of Income Taxes

When the strategy is accepted by responding to the prompts, proFOR will generate a 5 year spread with the format shown in Figure A.7.

In computing the Balance Sheet Projection, any excess cash generated is added to the Cash account. Cash shortages are accumulated in the N/P Short Term account. The Balance Sheet is automatically balanced through these accounts.

The second step in generating an appropriate 5 year Balance Sheet projection is to modify the computer-generated projection. The analyst may change the projection by overriding any of the non-calculated fields. In modifying the cash account, the analyst is actually modifying the *minimum* cash level. Any excess cash will be added to this minimum in the Balance Sheet calculation. Notes Payable Short Term may not be directly modified by the analyst. It is purely a balancing account, accumulating cash shortages. After all changes are made, the projection may be recalculated.

```
STY CS PRO                              BALANCE SHEET PROJECTION
STUDY CASE #        DATE        PROJECTION BASED ON STATISTICAL ANALYSIS
STY CS +02          12/31/02
                                YEAR +1   YEAR +2   YEAR +3   YEAR +4   YEAR +5
A   CASH              10.9        15.1      27.3      43.0      62.2      84.9
S   ACCTS RCVBL        6.5         9.8      10.8      11.8      12.9      14.1
S   INVENTORY         11.0        13.0      14.3      15.6      17.1      18.7
E   PREPAID EXP        0.0         0.0       0.0       0.0       0.0       0.0
T   OTHER CURR         0.9         0.9       0.9       0.9       0.9       0.9
S   FIX ASSET NET      0.7         0.0       0.0       0.0       0.0       0.0
    OTH N-CURR         0.0         0.0       0.0       0.0       0.0       0.0

L   ACCTS PAY          3.1         2.7       3.0       3.2       3.5       3.8
I   CURR PORT LTD      0.0         0.0       0.0       0.0       0.0       0.0
A   ACCRUED EXP        1.3         1.1       1.1       1.1       1.2       1.3
B   INC TAX PAY        0.0         0.0       0.0       0.0       0.0       0.0
I   N/P SHRT TERM      0.5         0.0       0.0       0.0       0.0       0.0
L   OTH CURR           0.0         0.0       0.0       0.0       0.0       0.0
+   N/P LONG TERM      0.0         0.0       0.0       0.0       0.0       0.0
N   OTH LONG TERM      0.0         0.0       0.0       0.0       0.0       0.0
W   RET EARNINGS      23.1        33.1      47.2      64.9      86.3     111.5
    CAPITAL STOCK      2.0         2.0       2.0       2.0       2.0       2.0
```

FIGURE A.7

Accounts receivable turnover A measure of the rate at which a firm collects on its credit sales that is measured by dividing net credit sales by average accounts receivable.

Acid test ratio A measure of the ability of a firm to pay its current bills that is measured by subtracting inventories and prepaid expenses from current assets and dividing the result by current liabilities.

Acquisition The purchase of a new venture, usually made in order to add to an existing venture. A first-time launch by acquisition is usually referred to as a buyout.

Advertising plan A portion of the overall marketing plan that includes the mix of advertising media, the relative allocation of resources to each medium, the message to be communicated, and the scheduling of the advertising.

Angels Informal investors willing to provide capital for high-risk ventures.

Antecedent factor The combination of variables in an individual's background that influences the decision to start a venture.

Asset-based valuation A method of determining the value of a venture by assessing the value of individual assets owned by the firm. See also Book value method of valuation.

Background variable See Antecedent factor.

Balance sheet The financial statement listing assets, liabilities, and owner's equity. It shows the condition of the firm at a particular time.

Bankruptcy The situation in which a firm's liabilities exceed its assets. Bankruptcy may be Chapter 7, liquidation, or Chapter 11, reorganization.

Basic structure The simplest structure of a venture, consisting of only the entrepreneur as a key manager.

Book value The net worth of a company, determined by subtracting total liabilities from total assets.

Book value method of valuation A method of determining the value of a firm by determining the actual net value of the venture's assets.

Break-even The point at which sales equals the sum of fixed and variable costs.

Budget A plan that lays out expected revenues and expenditures and is used as a control for the operation of the venture.

Business plan (1) An overall plan for the venture. (2) A written document designed to guide the strategy of the venture or to gain financing for the venture.

Buyout The purchase of an existing venture as a method of launching a new venture.

Captive supplier A venture that produces a product or provides a service for a single customer.

Cash flow The movement of cash into and out of a venture. For new ventures this may be more important than net income.

Cash flow budget A plan that guides and controls a venture's sources and usage of cash.

Cash flow statement A financial statement that delineates the movement of cash into and out of the firm.

Chapter 7 bankruptcy A bankruptcy filing in which the entrepreneur liquidates the assets of the venture in an effort to pay off the liabilities owed by the firm.

Chapter 11 bankruptcy A bankruptcy filing in which the entrepreneur is provided protection from creditors while reorganizing the venture and developing a strategy to recover from the debt condition.

Co-entrepreneurs Married entrepreneurs, both of whom play an active role in the management of the venture.

Comparable firms approach to valuation A method of valuation in which the selling prices of similar firms become the basis for the valuation of a venture.

Corporate entrepreneurship Entrepreneurship within an established business, usually a large corporation.

Corporation A business organized as a separate legal entity with ownership held by stockholders.

Creativity The ability to develop new ideas, which may result in new products or services.

Current ratio A measure of a firm's debt-paying ability, determined by dividing the firm's current assets by its current liabilities.

Deal (1) The agreement between a seller and buyer of a venture that delineates separate requirements such as noncompete agreements, methods of payment, or consulting arrangements. (2) The arrangement between an entrepreneur and venture capitalists to finance high-growth ventures.

Debt financing Financing in exchange for interest payments, usually granted by banks.

Debt ratio The percentage of assets financed with debt, measured by dividing total liabilities by total assets.

Direct exporting A method of exporting in which the entrepreneur deals directly with buyers in another country.

Direct marketing Selling via direct contact with the customer without the use of intermediaries, usually by using mail or television to reach customers.

Discounted cash flow method of valuation The valuation method that determines a firm's value based on the net present value of future cash flow.

Discounted earnings valuation The valuation method that determines value based on the net present value of future earnings.

Distinctive competency A significant strength of a venture that differentiates it from other ventures. This strength can be exploited in the firm's strategy.

Divisional structure The most advanced structure for entrepreneurial ventures, in which nearly free-standing units each have a full complement of functional management.

Due diligence The careful and objective analysis of a potentially high-growth venture prior to providing venture capital investment.

Employee stock option plan (ESOP) A harvesting plan in which employees of the firm purchase increasing numbers of shares of the company. In small ventures, this may result in the total ownership of the venture by the employees.

Enabling factor The set of variables that makes the launch of a venture possible, including sufficient resources and a viable opportunity.

Entrepreneur An individual who launches a venture and/or significantly improves it through innovative means.

Entrepreneurial equation A conceptual equation that involves combining antecedent, precipitating, and enabling variables in order to assess the likelihood that an individual will launch a venture.

Entrepreneurial personality The set of personality characteristics shared by most entrepreneurs. These include an internal locus of control, a need for autonomy, a need for achievement, and a moderate risk-taking propensity.

Entrepreneurial society A society characterized by a high number of energetic and innovative individuals willing to start or grow their own ventures.

Entrepreneurial stress Pressures encountered by an entrepreneur either because of the direct demands of the venture or because the time required to grow the venture takes away from family needs.

Entrepreneurial team The management of an entrepreneurial firm, especially at the time of launch. The team may include a lead entrepreneur and others with specialty skills.

Entrepreneurial window The range of ages at which individuals are most likely to start their first venture. Most entrepreneurs launch their first venture when they are between 20 and 50; approximately two-thirds of them do so between the ages of 25 and 40.

Entrepreneurship The launch and/or growth of a venture using innovative, risk-assuming management.

Equity financing Funding for a venture that includes at least partial ownership in the venture. Equity financing may come from individuals, informal investors, venture capitalists, or public offerings.

Ethics strategy The development of venture strategies and day-to-day actions based on some ethical creed, model, or philosophy.

Export (1) A product produced in one country for sale in another. (2) The strategy of selling products in other countries through direct or indirect contact with foreign buyers.

Export-Import Bank A government-funded bank designed to provide financing to those firms desiring to import or export products.

Export management company A firm that works as the exporting arm of a domestic company, typically working on a commission basis.

Export trading company An intermediary firm that buys products from a domestic producer and then sells them in other countries.

Factoring Selling accounts receivable at a discount to a financing firm in order to receive funds immediately and not have to deal with collecting the accounts.

Family business A business in which two or more members of a family play an active role.

Financial plan (1) Also known as a business plan. A written plan used to solicit funding for a venture. It includes detailed information including proforma income statements, balance sheets, and cash flow statements as well as marketing and other information. (2) The financial portion of a business plan.

Financial strategy The portion of the overall venture strategy that delineates the kinds and amounts of capital that will be used in the growth and operation of the business.

Franchise A business system in which replicated units of a business are owned by individuals who pay a franchise fee and royalty in exchange for the benefits of the known name and standard operation plan.

Franchise agreement The document that delineates the rights and obligations of a franchisor and a franchisee.

Franchisee An individual who purchases the right to start a franchised business.

Franchise triad The three parts of the relationship between a franchisor and a franchisee, consisting of the legal agreement, the business relationship, and the two independent individuals.

Franchisor A manufacturer or service provider who sells the right to market a product or service using established operating procedures in exchange for a franchise fee and royalty.

Freight forwarder A company that handles the shipping arrangements for an exporter.

Functional structure A venture structure in which there are key managers for each of the functional areas, such as marketing, operations, and human resources.

Going public Selling substantial shares of a company on the open market for the first time. See also Initial public offering.

Growth enabling actions Actions taken by the entrepreneur that allow the venture to grow in concert with market demand. These may include obtaining additional financing, adding facilities, or hiring more employees.

Growth entrepreneur An entrepreneur who launches a venture with the intention of continually growing it.

Growth extending actions Actions taken by the entrepreneur that continue the growth of the venture beyond the normal life cycle. These may include introducing new products, acquisition of other firms, or restructuring.

Growth-oriented venture A venture that is operated in such a way as to experience substantial growth over its life.

Growth rejuvenating actions Actions taken by an entrepreneur to turn around a company whose sales are either declining or have very low growth. May include new product development or restructuring.

Harvest Ending the original venture. Harvesting may take the form of selling, merging, liquidating, or passing the venture on to family members.

Harvest strategy The plan developed by the entrepreneur to guide the ending of the venture. The strategy may include a valuation of the firm, as well as other actions that prepare the venture for the harvest.

High-growth venture A venture that will likely sustain quite rapid growth over a period of time.

Holding company A company that serves no other purpose except to own the stock of other companies.

Incubator An organization or building that houses a number of new or small businesses and provides common services to its tenants.

Indirect exporting Exporting through an intermediary. The producer sells the product to a firm that in turn sells the product abroad.

Informal analysis A fairly quick, unscientific analysis of an opportunity to see if it merits a more in-depth, formal analysis.

Informal investor A person who invests in growth-oriented ventures as an individual rather than as part of a venture capital firm.

Initial public offering (IPO) The first offering of a venture's stock to the general public. An IPO is an expensive, time-consuming process that can yield several million dollars of equity capital.

Innovation The development of new products, processes, services, or strategies that have not previously existed. Also, the transfer of creativity into marketable products.

Internal locus of control The belief that individuals are in control of their own destinies, rather than at the hand of fate.

Intrapreneur A person with entrepreneurial characteristics who works within an existing organization to develop innovative products or processes.

Intrapreneurial culture A corporate culture that makes full use of the entrepreneurial spirit within an established organization.

Intrapreneurship Entrepreneurship within a large corporation. See also corporate entrepreneurship.

Intrapreneurship champion A person within an intrapreneurial corporation who encourages innovation; often a team leader for a specific project or a mentor for other intrapreneurs.

Invention The creation of an entirely new product that did not previously exist.

Inventory turnover ratio A measure of the quantity of inventory on hand compared with the amount of inventory sold, measured by dividing the cost of goods sold by the average inventory.

Investment banker A representative of a large bank that focuses on providing substantial capital to high-growth ventures, often as a prelude to taking the company public.

Joint venture A partnership between two companies for the purpose of developing or marketing a single product.

Leveraged buyout A method of funding the purchase of a business with debt which is then transferred to the acquired company's balance sheet.

Launch The establishment of a new venture; may be either a start-up or a buyout.

Liabilities The debts of a venture; what it owes.

Licensing Authorizing another company to produce and/or market a venture's product. The licensee pays the licensor a royalty for the right to produce and sell the product.

Limited liability A situation in a corporation or limited partnership in which investors are liable for the firm's debts only up to the amount they have invested; a key advantage of corporations.

Liquidation The selling of the venture's individual assets. Liquidation is used most often in a Chapter 7 bankruptcy, but it may also be used when a business is closed for other reasons.

Liquidation value The value of a firm based strictly on the value of its individual assets.

Low-growth entrepreneur An entrepreneur who starts a business but has no intention of growing the business much beyond its original size.

Low-growth venture A venture that, because of competitive factors, the market for the product, or the entrepreneur's desires, is not likely to grow at a rapid rate.

Management buyout The purchase of an existing venture from the current owner by a group of managers within the business.

Management team The key managers of a venture.

Market comparables method of valuation The method of valuing a venture that compares its financial data, such as price/earnings ratios, to that of publicly-traded firms in the industry.

Market segmentation Dividing the total market into specific segments in order to market a product more effectively to its primary customers. Each segment has specific characteristics unique to that group.

Market value The current value of a firm's assets on the open market, as opposed to their replacement value or book value.

Marketing mix The combination of all aspects of marketing a venture's product, such as price, promotion, distribution, and the product itself.

Marketing research The gathering of information about the industry, the customer, the competition, and the product to help analyze the potential for a product and develop a marketing strategy.

Marketing strategy The plan of action that attempts to maximize the sales of the venture's product by appropriate allocation of the marketing mix.

Motivation to start a venture The effect of influences on a person to launch a venture; includes the impact of antecedent variables and triggering variables.

Need for achievement The personality characteristic of having a high need to achieve personal goals.

Need for autonomy The personality characteristic of having a high need for independence.

Negotiating range The price range set by the highest value calculated by the seller and the lowest value calculated by the buyer.

Net income/equity ratio A measure of the profitability of a venture that is calculated by dividing the net income of the firm by its total equity.

Net present value method of valuation The valuation method that takes into consideration the time-value of money; specific methods include discounted cash flow and discounted earnings.

Niche strategy A strategy in which the firm targets a small segment of the total market. This is a common strategy for entrepreneurial firms, but it can be risky.

Not-for-profit organization An organization that provides products or services but does not have profit as a goal; also known as non-profit organizations. Examples include churches, United Way, and the American Red Cross.

Opportunity The possibility of making a profit by marketing a product or service.

Opportunity analysis The careful study of an opportunity to determine if it is feasible. This analysis includes the opportunity's marketing, technological, and financial feasibility.

Opportunity window The period of time during which an opportunity has the greatest possibility of success.

Partnership The legal form of a venture in which two or more individuals share the ownership of and responsibility for the business.

Plan [n] The document that lays out the strategy and/or financial projections for the firm.

Plan [v] The careful study of opportunities and the venture's capabilities and the development of strategies to capture those opportunities.

Planning model The schematic that details the nine steps of the planning process.

Precipitating variable See Triggering variable.

Price (of a venture) In a negotiation, the final determination of the amount of money or stock that will be exchanged for a venture. The price is seldom the same as the value of the venture.

Price/earnings method of valuation A market comparables method in which the price of a venture is based on the price/earnings ratio of a similar publicly-traded firm.

Private offering An offering of stock to informal investors rather than to the general public.

Proforma Projected, as in proforma balance sheets, income statements, or cash flow statements.

Public offering An offering of stock to the general public that is usually handled by investment bankers. See also Initial public offering.

Push/pull hypothesis The theory that entrepreneurs are either pulled, or enticed, into starting a venture, or pushed, or forced, into starting it. The pull is a positive reason; the push is a negative reason.

Quick ratio See Acid test ratio.

Replacement value of assets The valuation of assets based on the cost of replacing them with new assets at today's prices.

Risk assumption The willingness to endure the risk that exists in any venture.

Risk avoidance The overt attempt to minimize the amount of risk one assumes.

Risk capital Capital that is provided to high-risk, high-potential ventures, typically by informal investors or venture capitalists.

Risk-taking propensity The willingness of an individual to accept risky situations. Most entrepreneurs have a moderate risk-taking propensity.

Role model A person that significantly influences another's life. Most entrepreneurs had an entrepreneurial role model.

Sales forecast A carefully determined projection of future sales; may be based on a number of factors.

Small Business Administration (SBA) The government agency that provides financing and management assistance to small businesses.

Small business entrepreneur See Low-growth entrepreneur.

Small Business Investment Company (SBIC) A venture capital company that combines government money with private capital to provide funding for growth ventures.

Sole proprietorship The legal form of a business owned by only one person.

Start-up A new venture that never existed before, as opposed to a buyout.

Strategic plan A document that delineates an overall venture strategy and its supporting strategies.

Strategic planning The task of setting goals, analyzing opportunities, and developing strategies to achieve those goals.

Strategic planning model See Planning model.

Strategy The combination of actions that will lead to the achievement of a venture's objectives.

Sub-chapter S corporation A special form of corporation that has the advantages of a corporation but is taxed as a partnership.

Support strategy A portion of the overall venture strategy that usually relates to one of the functional areas of the firm.

Trade credit Debt capital provided by suppliers who allow buyers to delay payment of their bills.

Triggering factor The combination of influences that directly causes a person to want to start a business.

Value (of a venture) The carefully determined worth of a venture based on one or more valuation methods; a key element in determining the price of the venture.

Venture capital High-risk capital provided to growth ventures in exchange for significant ownership in the venture.

Venture capitalist A representative of a firm providing high-risk capital to growth ventures.

Wholly owned subsidiary A venture that is totally owned by another venture rather than by an individual.

Window of opportunity The period of time in which there is a significant market for a particular product or service.

INDEX

Name and Organization Index

INDEX

Subject Index

IMPORTANT: PLEASE READ BEFORE OPENING THIS PACKAGE
THIS PACKAGE IS NOT RETURNABLE IF SEAL IS BROKEN.

West Services, Inc.
610 Opperman Drive
Eagan, MN 55123

Entrepreneurship Student Key Disk

LIMITED USE LICENSE

Read the following terms and conditions carefully before opening this diskette package. Opening the diskette package indicates your agreement to the license terms. If you do not agree, promptly return this package unopened to West Services for a full refund.

By accepting this license, you have the right to use this Software and the accompanying documentation, but you do not become the owner of these materials.

This copy of the Software is licensed to you for use only under the following conditions:

1.   PERMITTED USES
You are granted a non-exclusive limited license to use the Software under the terms and conditions stated in this license. You may:

    a.   Use the Software on a single computer.
    b.   Make a single copy of the Software in machine-readable form solely for backup purposes in support of your use of the Software on a single machine. You must reproduce and include the copyright notice on any copy you make.
    c.   Transfer this copy of the Software and the license to another user if the other user agrees to accept the terms and conditions of this license. If you transfer this copy of the Software, you must also transfer or destroy the backup copy you made. Transfer of this copy of the Software, and the license automatically terminates this license as to you.

2.   PROHIBITED USES
You may not use, copy, modify, distribute or transfer the Software or any copy, in whole or in part, except as expressly permitted in this license.

3.   TERM
This license is effective when you open the diskette package and remains in effect until terminated. You may terminate this license at any time by ceasing all use of the Software and destroying this copy and any copy you have made. It will also terminate automatically if you fail to comply with the terms of this license. Upon termination, you agree to cease all use of the Software and destroy all copies.

4.   DISCLAIMER OF WARRANTY
Except as stated herein, the Software is licensed "as is" without warranty of any kind, express or implied, including warranties of merchantability or fitness for a particular purpose. You assume the entire risk as to the quality and performance of the Software. You are responsible for the selection of the Software to achieve your intended results and for the installation, use and results obtained from it. West Publishing and West Services do not warrant the performance of nor results that may be obtained with the Software. West Services does warrant that the diskette(s) upon which the Software is provided will be free from defects in materials and workmanship under normal use for a period of 30 days from the date of delivery to you as evidenced by a receipt.

Some states do not allow the exclusion of implied warranties so the above exclusion may not apply to you. This warranty gives you specific legal rights. You may also have other rights which vary from state to state.

5.   LIMITATION OF LIABILITY
Your exclusive remedy for breach by West Services of its limited warranty shall be replacement of any defective diskette upon its return to West at the above address, together with a copy of the receipt, within the warranty period. If West Services is unable to provide you with a replacement diskette which is free of defects in material and workmanship, you may terminate this license by returning the Software, and the license fee paid hereunder will be refunded to you. In no event will West be liable for any lost profits or other damages including direct, indirect, incidental, special, consequential or any other type of damages arising out of the use or inability to use the Software even if West Services has been advised of the possibility of such damages.

6.   GOVERNING LAW
This agreement will be governed by the laws of the State of Minnesota.

You acknowledge that you have read this license and agree to its terms and conditions. You also agree that this license is the entire and exclusive agreement between you and West and supersedes any prior understanding or agreement, oral or written, relating to the subject matter of this agreement.

West Services, Inc.

THIS PACKAGE IS NOT RETURNABLE IF SEAL IS BROKEN